HORSES AND HORSEMANSHIP
THROUGH
THE
AGES

HORSES
AND
HORSEMANSHIP
THROUGH THE AGES

LUIGI GIANOLI

&

MARIO MONTI · TIZIANO M. BARBIERI · MARIA GRAZIA FONTANA · LEO VERGANI

MASSIMO ALBERINI · ENRICO CANTI · PRIMO CASTELVETRO

MAX DAVID · VITTORIO DI CAPUA · NINO GIANOLI

TRANSLATED BY
IRIS BROOKS

CROWN PUBLISHERS, INC., NEW YORK

The author wishes to thank the following for their generous loan of illustrations from their private collections: Gianni Clerici, Gianfranco Gnecchi Ruscone, Daphne Machin Goodall, Mario Monti, John Nestle. Other illustrations were supplied by Agence Recoupé, Agenzia di Stampa Novosti, Massimo Alberini, F. Alinari, ANSA, Federico Arborio Mella, The Associated Press, Josip Ciganovic, Enrico Cinti, Derby, ENCAT, Farabola, FISE, *Gazzetta dello Sport,* Giancolombo News Photos, Olympia, Perrucci, Machatschek-Paris, Publifoto, Roger-Viollet, Oscar Savio, Studio Fotografico Tavera, Harry Weber.

First published in Italian as IL CAVALLO E L'UOMO, © *1967 by Longanesi & C.*
First published in the United States by Crown Publishers, Inc., 1969.
Library of Congress Catalog Card Number: 68-9102.

Printed in Switzerland by Conzett & Huber, Zurich
Published simultaneously in Canada by General Publishing Company Limited.

FOR

HPD, the R's, and HCM,

who put me on a horse of a different color;

with a nod to RJP, at the post

CONTENTS

PART ONE
HISTORY

Origins	9	Etruria	36
Domestication	11	Rome	36
Sumerians	12	The Wheel	49
Hittites	13	Harness and Carts	49
Assyrians	14	Sledges	50
Egyptians	17	Touring	50
Jews	17	The Post	53
Chinese	17	Bits	54
Hiung-nu	18	Stirrups and Saddles	54
Sarmatians	18	Byzantium	57
Persians	18	Persia	63
Auxiliary Aids	21	The Arabs	64
Greeks	22	Veterinary Medicine	65
Xenophon	26	The Goths	66
Gaul	35	The Huns	67

PART TWO
MIDDLE AGES, RENAISSANCE, AND SCHOOLS

The Dark Ages	68	Haute Ecole	132
Marco Polo	68	Airs	135
The Hungarians	71	Versailles and Saumur	137
Nomads and the Barbarian Kingdoms	72	The Spanish Riding School of Vienna	143
The Normans	72	The Hanover School	144
Transport and Communication	75	The Spanish School	144
Chivalry	75	Women in the Saddle	147
The Dawn of European Chivalry	76	The French and the "Filer"	148
The Education of a Knight	87	Nineteenth-Century Italian Equitation	154
The Crusaders	88	Caprilli	157
Tournaments	88	Caprilli's Writings	158
Chivalric Customs	93	Development and Diffusion of the Caprilli System	170
Pas d'Armes	94	Variations on a Theme	171
Developments in Equitation	94	The D'Inzeo Brothers	172
The Renaissance	95	Graziano Mancinelli	176
Origins of the Thoroughbred	96	The French	177
Saddles and Bits	97	The English	178
Armor	98	The Irish	182
School Equitation	103	The Germans	182
Federico Grisone	104	The Spanish	187
Salamon de La Broue	107	The Hungarians	187
Pluvinel and Newcastle	108	The Poles	187
La Guérinière	117	The Argentinians	188
Evolution and Developments in Military Equitation	118	The Soviets	188
Antoine d'Aure	121	The Brazilians	188
François Baucher	123	The Americans	189
General L'Hotte	127	The Mexicans	189
Dressage	127	Competition	190

PART THREE
EQUESTRIAN OLYMPIC GAMES

Development	191	Schools	199

PART FOUR
THEORY

The Rider's Aids	205	Defenses	209
Natural Aids	205	The Jump	209
Artificial Aids	206	Gymnastics on Horseback	210
The Horse Well in Hand	207	Tack	214

PART FIVE

THOROUGHBRED RACING

Introduction	216	Australia	250
England	217	Great Pedigrees	250
France	229	Genetic Curiosities	254
Ireland	234	Stallion Lines	254
Italy	235	Great Champions	260
Breeding in Germany	240	The Owner and Breeder	284
Racing in Russia	243	Horse Breeding	288
United States	244	The Trainer	289
South America	249	The Jockey	289
Japan	249	The Track	290
South Africa	250	Pari-Mutuel Betting and the Totalisator	293

PART SIX

HARNESS RACING

History	295	Italy	317
The Orlov	305	West Germany	319
Gallopers and Trotters	305	United Kingdom	319
United States	306	Scandinavia	320
France	314	Training Trotters and Pacers	320
USSR	317		

PART SEVEN

HORSE-DRAWN VEHICLES

History	326	Harnesses	342
Coach Horses	342		

PART EIGHT

SPORT ON HORSEBACK

Polo	343	Hunting	350

PART NINE

EQUESTRIAN AMUSEMENTS

The Circus	363	Gymkhana Events	377
The Rodeo	369		

PART TEN

ECOLOGY OF THE HORSE

Heredity	385	Finnish Breeds	410
Work	385	Greek Breeds	410
Climate	386	Arabian Breeds	410
Italian Breeds	386	African Breeds	411
British Breeds	392	Turkish Breeds	411
French Breeds	396	Persian Breeds	412
German Breeds	399	Mongolian Breeds	412
Dutch Breeds	400	Southeast Asian Breeds	412
Danish Breeds	400	Australian Breeds	412
Belgian Breeds	400	North American Breeds	412
Swiss Breeds	400	South American Breeds	416
Spanish Breeds	400	Vices and Defects	421
Portuguese Breeds	403	Intelligence	421
Czechoslovakian Breeds	403	Morphology	422
Austrian and Hungarian Breeds	403	Teeth	427
Polish Breeds	403	Coats, Colors, Patterns, and Markings	427
Icelandic Breeds	404	The Feet	428
Russian Breeds	404	Nutrition	439
Norwegian Breeds	410		
Swedish Breeds	410	BIBLIOGRAPHY	441

HORSES AND HORSEMANSHIP
THROUGH
THE
AGES

PART ONE

HISTORY

FOR HUNDREDS and hundreds of years, perhaps millennia, the favorite food of man on the steppes of Asia and Europe was horse. Expert that he had become in the herds' migrations, man soon learned to startle a band of horses into stampeding over the edge of a precipice and to finish off the beasts by stoning them to death, then to drink their blood, suck out their brains, and devour their flesh.

Once man became a shepherd, a keeper of goats and oxen, the domesticator of the dog and that poor relation of the horse, the slow and patient ass, the day dawned when, fascinated by open spaces and the lure of the unknown, man realized that only the swift and slender hoofs of the horse could translate his ambitious dreams into reality. Then, after he had mounted and become master of that back and sat high above the earth as if on a fatal throne, man discovered within himself hauteur and pride and vanity, and they were never to leave his heart.

Migrations that had been slow and tedious and often pacific suddenly became tragic epics engendered by a thirst for conquest and power. At one and the same time, the horse became protagonist and victim: on one hand the faithful, amiable, and prized companion, and on the other the heroic and aggressive inciter to violence and destruction, to the point of being melded with man in the myth of the centaurs and provided with wings to attempt the heavens. "Descend, Eagle, or I rise to thee," is the horse's challenge to the predator in an Arab song.

Here we have the diverse and seductive destiny inherent in the horse's character, his conformation, and his adaptability to every clime and terrain. From the moment man chose him to be the companion of his infinite enterprise, the horse was quick to reflect the style, taste, and inclinations of each civilization in his own physique, gait, and even in his color.

If man did not hesitate to adapt the horse to his service, the horse, in his turn, suggested the various and appropriate forms he could assume in the unbeatable game, becoming opulent, almost arrogantly blown up with pride, like a dragon, to suit the fancy of the Chinese; splint-legged and stylized to complement the mode of the Assyrian kings; stark and stupendous in compliance with the Greek aesthetic; fleet and flawless for the mathematically minded Arabs; a powerful war machine for the armed might of Rome; loose-limbed and mettlesome for the Renaissance sires; barrel-chested and baroque in the academies and affrays of the seventeenth-century courts; and fine-drawn and testy, to match the rationalism of the English.

When this astonishing transformation of an animal began, there were, or had been, two basic breeds—possibly three.

The Mongolian strain was spread over the steppes of southern Siberia and the Mongolian plateau, and became the vehicle for the most terrifying invasions carried out by the human race in the process of asserting its mastery, when the world was still unconfined and all stood open to the ferocious dreams of insatiable conquerors—from the Hyksos who overcame the Egyptians, the Hiung-nu who vanquished the Chinese, Rome's Vandals, and finally, to the bloody epics of Genghis Khan, Tamerlane, and Muhammad II.

The Aryan strain, coming from farther west, most probably flourished on the steppes of southern Russia. The last offspring of this breed, the tarpan, was still to be found up to the end of the last century. This was the horse that, in one instance, bore the Indo-Europeans to their conquest of India and, in another feat, carried them to occupation of the Mediterranean, Anatolia, and Mesopotamia.

The Mongolian breed was angular, thickset, and sedate, utterly resistant, the ideal mount for the bandit of the steppes, while the Aryan was more agile, fine-drawn, and impressive in bearing, of more marked individuality and provocative beauty, the strain that must have shone in the vigor of the Assyrian steed, in the divine lightness of Phidias's horses, and in the surpassing geometry of the Arab, from whom, in a miracle and enigma of genetics, was to descend sometime later the prodigious Thoroughbred.

There might have been a third wild horse, the European, raw and heavy, sacred to the Celts, the Gauls, and the Iberians. With the chunky build of a work horse, he was relegated to humble toil during the period of the Roman Empire, and came into his own with the advent of cavalry and the prevalence of the armored warrior. This, however, is solely a hypothesis, predicated upon discoveries and reconstruction.

I

ORIGINS

Where shall we begin? Shall we start with the antecedents of *Equus caballus*, the creatures that roamed the earth during the Eocene epoch, or those of the Pliocene, or the animals in those first drawings left us by the man of that savage past? Should we commence with the related species, the boar, hippopotamus, and tapir, or the horse's family relations the zebra, onager, and ass, or even take up those wild relics the mustang and tarpan?

Heavy skull, thick neck, powerful shoulders and crupper,

with short, slim legs, as limned in the drawings in the caves of Lascaux in southern France, the horse, whether totem or game, has the look of a suspicious layabout, ready to bolt, to rear; willful and hotheaded, and always full of fear and distrust. Yet, he is already possessed of a certain harmony of line that certainly must have fascinated the Paleolithic artist, with those fleshy contours that made him desirable game and such easy prey. All that was necessary was to frighten him, and he instantly fell victim to his own terror.

For years, phosphates have been taken from the foot of the Solutré cliffs, near Lyons. These come from the bones of horses that precipitated themselves over the edge of the bluff; and it is said that there are more than twenty thousand skeletons!

Let us attempt, therefore, to discover what that creature was, what sort of animal, this beast belonging to the order of Perissodactyla, the family Equidae, of the genus *Equus*, and species *caballus* in Linnaeus's system.

The horse *(Equus caballus),* then, is a perissodactyl, which means that it is a mammiferous quadruped that, having lost four toes (the first, second, fourth, and fifth), stands upon one alone, which is the third, and this too, in compensation, is sufficient to the weight of the animal and is protected by a nail called the hoof. The history of the evolution of the horse is one of the most consecutive and best known. The sole missing link is the horse's five-toed ancestor. All the others are known.

At the beginning of this century, studies of the evolution of the horse reached their peak when William Whitney, following the lead set by Wartmann (1882), provided the resources for the Zoology Department of Columbia University and Professor Henry Fairfield Osborn to undertake the most exhaustive researches in the Mississippi Basin and at the foot of the Rocky Mountains.

As a result of these explorations, more than eight hundred fossils of Equidae were brought to light, of which about fifty were in a complete and perfect state of preservation, permitting documentation of their evolution.

As recently reviewed by the American paleontologist G. G. Simpson, the history of that evolution can be summed up as follows: sixty million years elapsed between *Hyracotherium* and *Equus,* covering passage through eight genera, with an average of 7.5 million years in each; about thirty species, representing two million years each; and 15 million generations (considering four the age of sexual maturity).

Fossils of pre-Equidae have been discovered in Tertiary Eocene strata, polydactyls such as *Phenacodus* (discovered by Wartmann in 1882) in the United States; *Eohippus* (or *Hyracotherium),* which had four toes on each foreleg and three on the hind, and was not much larger than a fox; and *Orohippus,* about the size of a sheep.

Two fossils of the American Miocene epoch, *Mesohippus* and *Miohippus,* are consistent in showing only three toes and a structure that is the same as that of the modern pony. *Protohippus, Parahippus,* and *Pliohippus* all date from the American Pliocene. There are still three toes, of which only the middle one rests on the ground and is ungulate, while the other two are extremely short. The stature is almost that of the standard horse.

A fossil discovered in the American Pliocene stratum, *Equus parvulus,* has only one toe, and is similar to the horse as we know him today. In the southern United States, a monodactyl, *Hippidium,* was found, resembling the tapir, with its elongated snout, but recalling the ass in the similar conformation of its vertebrae.

From these prototypes, others derived during the Quaternary period: *Equus pacificus, E. occidentalis, E. curvidens,* species that all became extinct in the wake of cosmic upheaval, so that when the Spaniards arrived in the New World, they could find no trace of a horse.

In the Old World, the first of the pre-Equidae fossils comes from the Eocene, and is *Paleotherium,* but it is more recent than its American counterpart. *Anchitorium,* found in the Miocene, was about the size of a dog. It is only in the Pliocene that *Hipparion* is encountered, in Africa as well as in Europe. Discovered in 1882, it is considered to be the ancestor of all present-day Equidae. With three toes, and only the middle one touching the ground, in physique, shape of the head, and bearing it anticipates today's horse.

At the beginning of the Quaternary, Equidae were everywhere. There were *Hemionus fossilis* in Germany, the Val d'Arno's *Equus stenonis,* and the *E. quaggoides* of Otranto. Finally, in the province of Costantina, in central Asia, to the northwest of Hammal Meskhoutin, an equine fossil having very slender extremities and, therefore, presumed to be very swift, was found: *Equus caballus. Equus silvanensis* was discovered in Russia-in-Asia, and *E. nomadicus* was found in India.

These numerous discoveries confirm the theory that postulates a multiplicity of foci of generation or, rather, of appearance of organized beings on earth. Hence, the diversity in the equine family, which has been influenced by climate, the nature of soil and forage, and, in the domesticated state, by work.

With changes in the feet came simultaneous evolution of the dental structure, and one can observe how the older species ate tree foliage, while the more recent types fed on herbage.

Humid areas and steppes, where the grass and grain grow tall, favor the development of an animal's stature and the growth of hair, while dry, desert regions stimulate a refinement in line, lightness in structure, and, as a consequence, extreme speed in action, so that infrequent water holes and grazing can be reached as fast as possible.

It is apparent that the horse, soliped and herbivorous, and under the constant necessity of changing his pasturage, had found his ideal habitat in that broad band of rolling grassland that begins in Mongolia and reaches across Europe to the Pyrenees, skirting the craggy line of the Himalayas, the Karakoram range, the Caucasus, the Taurus Mountains, the Balkans, and the Alps.

It was the horse that made the fortunes of the nomadic Mongolian tribes, the Turks, and those Indo-Europeans who crossed from the steppes of central Asia toward conquest of the territories where they founded their kingdoms and empires. It was thanks to the horse that these pastoral peoples and occasional farmers became hard-riding warriors and conquerors.

While among the Indo-Europeans, particularly the Scythians, the horse became a cult object, he was brutally treated by the Mongolians and Turks, who looked upon him purely as a means to power. Perhaps that accounts, in part, for the rawness of the Mongolian breed, while the care and attention given by Scythian and Sarmatian, the continuous improvement and refinement, brought the horse to a perfection of structure.

II
DOMESTICATION

To capture an animal and break him to your will is not an easy thing. One needs not only the means of dominating him but also a proper place to keep him, as well as patience of a kind different from that required to break rocks or break ground with a plow. One must be disposed to take a dynamic attitude toward considerations of time and space, inasmuch as a great effort is being made without immediate result. Though the exhilaration of the chase is lacking to a point, since there is not the catharsis that comes with the kill, there is compensation in the pleasure of possession.

Architecture is the youngest of the plastic arts, but Stone Age man—who knew how to draw—had no experience of construction techniques. It is doubtful that he would have known how to build a corral. The other "lead" that he might have used to bring the animal to him, a lasso or rope, also was a development that came relatively late.

During the Paleolithic period, man did not know how to braid; and with a vine, one can leash a small animal but not the big ones. Leather thongs were to appear later, when bone needles came into use; and that tremendously important invention, the knot, did not exist until the Neolithic period.

If domestication is a form of coercion, becoming domesticated is a psychic process and, in a certain sense, a bilateral one. A lasting effect is achieved only when fear or the ease of his new life has brought the animal to complete subjugation. Then only is the thirst for freedom, the essence of wildness, repressed once for all. It is at that point that the master begins to analyze the character of his captive and establish some rapport with him. There must, therefore, be some enduring change that occurs in the animal's brain to transmit the same mentality to its offspring.

Among the animals that have been subjected, the horse is the one that offers the greatest resistance to domestication, but he has been man's greatest triumph, for the horse shortened distances for man, and brought the added gift of speed.

Domestication, like farming, was one of the first activities of man having no connection with his destructive instinct. In compensation, this exercise of power over the herd contributed toward the fostering of a sense of property. An ancient echo of that beginning is heard in the word "capital," derived from *capite*, wealth reckoned in terms of the number of head of cattle.

Many uncertainties persist in reference to the domestication and utilization of the horse at the dawn of history, and of course, many misconceptions that remain to be repudiated, such as the idea that the horse was harnessed before he ever was mounted.

Less strong than the ox, but fleeter and more agile; less dangerous than the stag or elk, the horse came to be subjugated long after the ox and ass and even later than the onager and the reindeer or, precisely, not until man finally possessed the means (fiber cords or leather thongs, not to mention understanding and authority) to bridle and dominate him.

There are some who maintain that, first of all, the horse was harnessed, and by a yoke not designed for this structure since it was similar to that used for oxen. To support this theory they point to those most ancient representations of the animal on rocks and stones, all of them showing carts. This, however, is erroneous, for those drawings date from the Second Bronze Age, and no evidence from earlier periods exists.

Notwithstanding, while a horse's harness represents an extremely complicated technical accomplishment (straps and bands, the wagon, and study to determine the precise point of junction at which its inertia can be overcome), to mount him appears to be simple enough: just pass a cord over his muzzle or through his mouth and everything is fine. While the cart does appear to be a mere problem in reasoning (fibers were perhaps the first aids after the sail utilized by man to turn a natural force to his own ends), equitation, even in its rudimentary state, is a highly complex art that calls for gymnastics, the ability to balance, and for preparation and a spirit of observation in no mean degree.

On the other hand, at the dawn of civilization, man had no idea of what to make of speed, a necessity linked to the growth of civilization itself. Probably, after the slow-moving ox, man next yoked the wild ass or onager in order to secure more mobility and be able to drive the animal from his cart, as shown in the standard of Ur or in the first Sumerian seals, and he controlled their wildness by a ring in the nose, as he had done with the ox. How he passed from that method of torture to the bit, how he ever guessed of the existence and discovered the "bars," that "apposite" space (as a military regulation had it) in the gum of the lower jaw devoid of teeth upon which the bit rests and reacts, no one knows.

Perhaps it happened when the horse tossed his head, making man aware of the excessive sensitivity of the horse's nostrils; or did a cord passed through the horse's mouth and embedded in the bars suggest that point of encounter between man's will and the horse's submission?

In any case, even if the horse's "yoke" was copied, and badly, from that of the ox, the idea of harnessing the horse burned in the imagination of young men in a hurry who no longer were satisfied with the old, slow ass—it was on an ass's back that Abraham went from Mesopotamia to Egypt—but the horse, ridden bareback, filled the requirement. There was no need for anything more. Neither saddle nor stirrups were necessary. It seems strange to us that the Chinese, Assyrians, Persians, Hittites, and Greeks, all superb horsemen and horse fanciers, had never suddenly been inspired to improve their stability on horseback by using a saddle.

The lack of saddle and stirrups for a long time restricted the use of the horse and his employment in war, so much so that cavalry was long in coming, and appeared only when those prodigious horsemen, the Hiung-nu, introduced the charge. Formerly, the horse had been used bareback only to carry a foot soldier to the place of combat, while the horse's speed was turned to good account for surprise attacks, but these were limited to bearing down on straggling remnants of enemy troops or to pursuit and harassment of them by riding circles around the troopers, much as the Indians do in a Western film.

Actually, man became complete master of the horse when the invention of saddle, stirrups, and metal shoes made the animal an instrument that could be easily and immediately employed.

Although utilization of the horse and the esteem in which he was held varied through the centuries, the connection between rider and mount has always been the very same: a study of determinate material and moral means that would lead to better mastery of the animal, which is an attitude that even the horsemen of today should maintain if equitation is to represent something more than just a simple pastime, and be a discipline and a true sport. Riding a horse should signify that one is conscious of one's own limitations and ability to command, and aware of the capacity of the animal to understand and obey.

Consequently, equitation is one of the pursuits that most tends to form the character and personality inasmuch as it continually demands subtle and perceptive observation of an animal. It is also one of the most revealing of activities, for on horseback, as in art and love, it is impossible to fake.

By "wild" horses, we understand those that have always run free. Herodotus speaks of the wild horses of the Dnieper; Aristotle, of the savage herds branded by Alexander on the march to India; and Strabo, of the wild bands in Spain. Varro, Pliny, and Julius Capitolinus all refer to the wild horses of Germany. *Ferales equi* are cited in the eighth century as devastators of crops, to such an extent that in 732 St. Boniface advocated their extermination in Thuringia and Westphalia. Their presence in Noricum was noted in the eleventh century, in Russia in 1240, and in Prussia in 1518. Gaspard de Saunier, in 1711, makes mention of them as interesting game of the Düsseldorf forest.

The tarpans, cimarrons, and mustangs were among the wild horses. In America, shortly after 1535, at the time Buenos Aires was founded (1536) by Pedro de Mendoza, a number of settlers went on to Paraguay, leaving behind their sick and spent horses, which promptly ran wild again and reproduced themselves to such an extent that when, in June, 1580, Don Juan de Garay returned from Paraguay to recolonize Buenos Aires, he found the immense herd of horses that became the wealth of the country. These *alzados,* or rebels, as they were called, did not lack a certain missionary spirit, and approached tame horses with neighing invitations for them to leave home. As a matter of fact, in many regions it became necessary to hunt the rebels who were corrupting their hard-working tame brethren!

While *Equus przewalski,* native to Mongolia and the Gobi Desert, is the last extant type of wild horse (and you can still see specimens in capivity in the larger zoological gardens around the world), the tarpan, *Equus przewalski gmelini,* became extinct at the end of the last century, a victim of intensive hunting. The very last of the breed had a dramatic end. This was a mare that had joined the string on a farm in Rachman, with her colt. The farm's owner, Count Alexander Durilin, had an idea that he might keep her to use in experiments in cross-breeding. Once imprisoned in a stall, however, the mare, who had already lost an eye, managed to flee, with her colt coming after her. Tracked down and surrounded, in her attempts to save herself from a new captivity, the animal fell and fractured a joint. Carried on a sledge to a farm in Lepetisha, where the leg was amputated, the mare died two days later.

"Who first tamed the horse?" asked Albius Tibullus, without ever expecting a documented response. An answer is very difficult to give, for neither the Chinese, Sumerians, nor the nomadic peoples of the steppes have left any traces or evidence of their passing.

In any case, with the new shortened chronology of the Mesopotamian and Egyptian dynasties, the honor of being first must fall to the Chinese. In China, ceramic statuettes dating from 3500 B.C., side by side with symbols of deified horses of the Fu-Hsi dynasty, were found, along with the first remains of two-wheeled chariots, complete with shafts for the harnessing of a pair of horses.

Among the nomads of the steppes (Mongolians, Sarmatians, proto-Turks, and Scythians) as well as among the Chinese, the horse was the object of a cult, for the very possession of the animal allowed these peoples to extend and maintain their dominion.

Definitive transmutation of the horse into a symbol was somewhat affected by the figurative idealization given him by painters and sculptors, who altered the animal's conformation to some degree. In fact, the horse soon began to represent one of the most telling signs of luxury. The imperial stables, beginning with the Chou dynasty—before the tenth century B.C., had thousands of horses selected for different purposes: draft, hacking, hunting, parade, and war. These were not big animals, but massive, barrel-chested, sturdy, and muscular, with slim legs and heavy skulls, evidencing the Mongolian strain. We see them at a rapid trot or ambling or racing in that so-called "flying gallop," represented as they are with hind quarters and forelegs in an almost horizontal position.

Still, perhaps only in connection with China can it be asserted that there is any foundation to the theory that the use of the cart, signifying the harnessing of the horse, might have preceded equitation. Recently, a royal tomb of the Shang dynasty was discovered in which were found the emperor's car, horses, charioteer, and all the gear used for a two-wheeled chariot, perhaps even a four-wheeled vehicle, drawn by a pair. The Chinese ideogram for a cart or wheel is actually the outline of one of these vehicles, viewed from above.

Since the Shangs could afford to finance and assemble such a large collection of vehicles, their fortune must have been considerable. It is highly probable that three persons took their places in a chariot of wood or wickerwork: the driver, a warrior armed with a bow, and another with a long lance, a penetrating weapon similar to that used by the medieval knights to increase the striking power of a frontal attack.

III

SUMERIANS

Meanwhile, in Mesopotamia, the Sumerians, who were, perhaps, of Dravidic origin, and of sedentary tendency, were using carts drawn by oxen. Although they had known, as far back as 3000 B.C., of the horse, which they called the "mountain ass," a name which leads us to believe that they had found the animal in the mountain passes of Armenia or Persia, whence they had come from the meadows or the plateaus of what is Kazakstan today, it was only around 2800 B.C. that they felt the need of a more dashing span.

The standard of Ur, the famous shell mosaic dating from 2600 B.C., depicts a four-wheeled cart drawn by equines with long ears, either asses or onagers. At Kish, the royal seat, a seal belonging to King Meskalamgud (2600 B.C.) was discovered in which the sovereign appears in a four-wheeled cart drawn by a pair that could very well be, not onagers, but horses at full gallop.

Little clay models of carts, votive objects (or toys?) with teams of four or, perhaps, five horses have been recovered from tombs in the larger Sumerian cities. Princes and nobles of the country recognized in these vehicles an area formerly unsuspected for ostentation and a display of wealth. In one clay tablet, the king appears, from the waist up, emerging from amid the assembled populace.

Other evidence is given by a krater found in Khafajiyeh, Iran, that shows, precisely, a chariot followed by a colt, a sweet touch that says a good deal about rural customs.

In the copper chariot of Tell Agrab, a team of four draws a car with two full, round wheels. The animals must still be onagers, testy and quarrelsome beasts, for the reins extend to a ring meant to go through the nose, in the same style as for oxen.

It is known, however, that as early as 2000 B.C. the Sumerians were using armored cars, with two and four wheels, from which the leaders fought. Since these appear to be standard models, equipped with a lance, shield, helmet, and back protectors, one supposes that there was a regular and permanent corps, as the cars are all exactly alike, as if mass-produced.

IV
HITTITES

The ones who brought the horse to half the world were the Aryans, peoples recognizable not so much through a unity of race as through a constant grammatical and linguistic similarity. Nomads of the steppes, they became masters of the horse long before using the animal to leave their own region in attempts to gain new territory.

It has not been ascertained whether one of the oldest of the Indo-European peoples, the Luwi, brought their horses with them when they circled the Black Sea and descended into Thrace, from whence they penetrated Anatolia about 2450 B.C.

The second wave of immigrants, which advanced shortly prior to 2000 B.C. from the steppes of southern Russia, going around the western arc of the Black Sea to enter Thrace, was furnished with horses, quite possibly to a considerable extent.

Here we are dealing with two related currents, the race of Minni (as they are denominated by the archeologists) of whom one part, the proto-Achaeans, invaded Mycenae; while the Minni of the Troad, in particular the Hittites, followed the route of the Luwi and settled themselves in the eastern part of Anatolia.

Although they were rough and cruel, the Grecian Minni did not wipe out the civilization and population they had overcome, but, following a typical Aryan pattern, preferred to dominate them and make them serve their needs. The myth of the centaurs probably springs from these events, testifying, as it does, to newcomers, the proto-Achaeans, who had come and fought on horseback, spreading terror among the Pelasgians.

Their cousins in Anatolia spoke a language related to Greek: Hittite. The word "horse" appears as *ippos* in Greek and *iqquios* in Hittite. Destroyers of Troy V and the presumed builders of the splendor that was Troy VI, the Hittites introduced the horse. As a matter of fact, the sign of an equine head, recurrent in Hittite hieroglyphics in Cappadocia from 1900 B.C., and the frequent mention of the horse in correspondence of Assyrian merchants of that time, testify to the need the Hittites had to supply themselves continually with horses from the famous studs in the north of Mesopotamia, and does not indicate, as some hold, that the Hittites had first known of the horse in the Orient, that is, once they had come into contact with the Mesopotamian peoples.

This latter theory is contradicted by the finding of horses in Thracian tombs of the twentieth century B.C., by the legend of the centaurs, and by the ritual that was still in use in the time of the Hittite king Muwatalli (circa 1300 B.C.), in which is mentioned the sun that rises from the sea, a thing that would be manifestly impossible for folk settled in Cappadocia, but which proves their memory of that migration toward the south along the western coast of the Black Sea.

That the horse was an instrument of power for the Indo-Europeans can be deduced from the predominance of a few Aryan clans over the numerous Semitic populations in Asia Minor. For the Semites, on the other hand, the horse became a means of swift transport, of which the merchants took advantage, making trips into Babylonia until it fell to the attack of the Assyrian army.

The singular stance of the Aryans in confrontation with the Semites they had overcome is shown even in their use of the cuneiform alphabet, which they took over for writing Hittite and Mitanni, consummately Aryan tongues to which a system of syllabic writing is not really adequate.

Peoples actually of inferior culture, but more vigorous, powerful, and quicker to assimilate ways of life and combat than their opponents, both the Hittites and Mitanni played a great part in the evolution of military tactics that went on from the sixteenth to twelfth centuries B.C., even though they were quite weak politically, as they tended to form federations of city-states, rather than a true empire (as the Etruscans were to do almost a thousand years later).

The Hittites and Mitanni were quick to see in the Sumerian cart a most effective instrument of combat. Although it was a cumbersome, heavy-wheeled vehicle, with a protected body (the Sumerians put their trust in a phalanx of foot soldiers), the Mitanni and Hittites could see how, once made lighter, the chariot would give them a means of bringing about a revolution in military tactics, permitting them to use the determining factors of surprise, speed, and shock. As a matter of fact, the light car made its appearance during the period that followed the fall of the Amorites in decimated Babylonia and, at the same time, among the Mitanni in Egypt during the eighteenth dynasty. It was the Hittites, however, who brought to perfection the construction and employment of the chariot.

Its use must already have been general even in the old Hittite Empire if eighty of the vehicles took part in the siege of Urshu and the battle conducted by King Hattusili (the report of this feat of arms, however, dates from after the siege, which took place a bit before 1600 B.C.); and the chariot contributed to the extension of Hittite power to Syria, and the Euphrates and Orontes rivers.

It was, however, around the fifteenth century B.C. that utilization of the chariot was brought to perfection to triumph in the celebrated Battle of Kadesh, when the Egyptian king Ramses II was routed by a surprise maneuver of horse-drawn Hittite forces. This was a tremendous defeat, even if the Egyptian chronicler who passes it on to us attempted to transform it into a partial victory.

The king's reproaches to his captains and soldiers reveal a very different reality: "What errors, what a crime you've committed, my commanders, my soldiers, to let yourselves be surprised without fighting. Only Victory, and Thebes, and Contented Nura, my unsurpassable horses, gave me any help when I was alone amidst my enemies. When I am back in Thebes, in my palace, I will continue to feed them with my own hands, for in them and in my charioteer, Menna, I found support and salvation."

To have arrived at that state of tactical perfection, the Hittites must have called upon experience and ingenuity and, above all, they must have gone into the technical aspects of employing horses. Dating from that time is a text, written in cuneiform characters on four clay tablets, *The Training of Horses* (its actual title), ascribed to Kikkuli, a master and probably a famous riding instructor from the country of the Mitanni. It was discovered in the archives of the Hittite capital Khattusas, near the modern village of Bogazkoy (about thirty miles from Ankara), and translated in 1930 by Professor Hornzy. It is a very detailed work on the breaking, acclimatization, and training of horses, dedicated to King Suppiluliumus the Great who, following the custom of many Hittite sovereigns, asked artists, experts, and specialists at neighboring courts to "make his reign splendid."

The text is in Hittite, but the technical terms are in Mitanni, a language that shows an affinity with Sanskrit, thus confirming the eastern provenance of the Mitanni, a group that detached itself from the Indo-Europeans who had gone to India, and a people who brought with them a profound knowledge of horses. They worshiped Indra, Varuna, and the twins Nasatya.

In the text, one reads, for example, terms such as *tera vartanna* (three turns), which is *tri vartanam* in Sanskrit; *navartanna* (nine turns) in Sanskrit would be *nava vartanam,* terms that were, as a matter of fact, deciphered through recourse to Sanskrit. The text is of exceptional precision and scrupulousness. It recommends that a horse be trained through a course of 148 days of progressive work and, for each day, Kikkuli describes the operation of the stables, management, the quality and quantity of food, even dressage.

Once the horses are selected in a trial gallop, they are to be purged and exercised in blankets to help them lose excess fat (as the English did in the eighteenth century), the first part of the work done at a walk, then at the amble, a gait very much appreciated in antiquity for its ease, and finally, at the gallop, the horses being made to run over increasingly longer distances until about a hundred miles a day were covered.

A *summa* of that type is evidently the fruit of centuries and centuries of experience in dealing with the animal. This knowledge, as set down by the Mitanni, had been collected by the Hittite princes who wished to take advantage

of expert training of horses to give their new weapon, the chariot, greater striking power and greater durability over long and arduous service.

The Hittite chariot, made lighter, but still solid and with sides that offered good protection for the combatants, carried three men, the charioteer and two warriors, one with a shield and lance, the other with a bow and lance. This provided for a greater number of mobile fighters to multiply the force at the front line, thanks to the rapidity with which these vehicles could get around. At the decisive moment, they could leave their chariots and fight on foot, like infantry.

There was no real cavalry, but only messengers and mounted patrols. The true mounted troop came later, but as an auxiliary corps, armed with light weapons, and used for surprise attacks.

V

ASSYRIANS

Even the conquest of Mesopotamia by the Assyrians was facilitated by the use of horses. Only in this way can one explain the conquest of such a vast territory so rapidly. Looking at the splendid high reliefs of Nineveh and Asshur, one sees that the Assyrian kings used the horse for war and sport, including the hunt. It is appropriate that the saddle horse assumed a preeminent role with these kings, and not only with royalty but also with dignitaries and the royal train, all of whom, till then, had used carts.

Chests out, proud, arrogant, with their barbarically refined hairdress, these Assyrians mounted horses of rare beauty. These were of the Aryan type, with convex foreheads, sinewy and muscular, and with their hair dressed as exquisitely as that of their riders.

What is curious is the fact that often, when hunting, a squire would lead a completely caparisoned horse. The bridle is perfect; the bit, with triangular pieces, such as appear in the first Greek and Etruscan renderings; the reins, short and passed through a species of martingale and held fast by a clasp behind the neck, which sacrificed the horse's shoulders but gave the rider more stability. The collar, one notes, worn high on the neck, is still in use in Macedonia today. The elaborate saddle-cloth appears to be fastened, not by a band at the girth, but by a complicated collar coming from the withers and passing around the shoulders.

The horsemen ride leaning forward slightly (possible only with a padded saddlecloth and with broad-backed mounts). The image gives an impression of intense dynamism and, above all, of the great mastery and easiness of the horsemen, intent on letting fly their arrows or hurling their javelins while their steeds are at the full gallop.

To be a fine horseman was a mark of distinction among these people, and that tradition persisted in Persia. Darius I, who had absorbed the art of equitation, and hunting on horseback as well, from the Medes, wanted the following

1 *Hunting cart of the pharaoh, Ramses III. Note the plumed head-dresses worn by the horses and the reins tied at the king's waist to free his hands for the bow. Abu Simbel, Egypt.*

1

epitaph inscribed on his tomb: "I loved my friends, was an excellent horseman, an excellent hunter, and found nothing impossible." A proud declaration, and one that seems to foreshadow the knightly attitude destined to flower in Persia a bit later, and then extend to Europe.

Both the Assyrians and their successors, the Persians, were lovers of choreography; and polo and the hunt, from the time of the Achaemenidae, had assumed the aspect of festive ceremonials requiring hundreds of horses for every match and meeting. At the time of Cyrus the Great, the satrap of Babylonia owned eight hundred stallions and six thousand mares.

VI
EGYPTIANS

The horse was introduced into Egypt around 1600 B.C. by the Hyksos, the famous "shepherd kings." Supporters of the Hurrians and Hittites, these Asiatic barbarians who penetrated Egypt from the north remained there for two centuries, without, however, becoming assimilated into the Egyptian population. Nevertheless, their civilization continued to flourish at Thebes until King Ahmose I led an uprising, hunted down the Hyksos, and, pursuing them, wiped out their conquests up to the Euphrates.

The Hyksos, however, had left behind them in Egypt vast herds of Mongolian horses that were scattered throughout Africa, coming from the north and descending into the south, where they also formed part of the Dankala breed. Thus it was that around 1500 B.C., at the time of the eighteenth dynasty, the cart supplanted the litter as a means of transportation for the upper classes. Nevertheless, it should be remembered that the Egyptians, who were good handlers of carts, were never great horsemen. Herodotus tells us that Egypt could be traversed on horseback up to the seventh century B.C., at which time the country had become so threaded by a network of innumerable irrigation canals that the use of the horse became limited to the open desert or the cities.

Egyptian artists almost invariably show the horse harnessed to a very light cart. The driver is usually alone, with the reins wrapped around his waist to allow his hands to remain free to use a bow or lance. The few depictions of horsemen do not offer any idea of the horse's trappings, from which we assume that the animal was mounted bareback. It is inconceivable that those artists, stylizers as few have been, but lovers of detail, would omit the design of a

2 *Assyrian carts and horses. The collar worn at the crest is like those still found in Macedonia today. Unusual in the harness are the checkrein and the complicated "neckpiece" worn between chest and neck to distribute the pull. It is attached at the withers, where the W-shaped "yoke" is connected. The horsemen's bare thighs present the only vulnerable target, which was the case even hundreds of years later, recalling the order of Pompey the Great to "strike at the thighs" before engaging Tigranes' cavalry. The horses wear rugs of tooled hide to protect them from attack by lions. Nimrud (ruins of the ancient city of Calah in northern Iraq).*

saddlecloth, since they took delight in rendering every element of gear in their reliefs.

The Egyptian horse differed from the Hittite and Assyrian in being long and gangling and definitely Mongolian in type, though he was, nevertheless, shown as slim and rakish.

VII
JEWS

The Jews were not a race of horsemen except, possibly, much later on. Hunted down, hounded from country to country, keepers of flocks in impoverished lands, obdurate moralists, they viewed the horse as another element of oppression and privilege.

It was only after they had returned to the Promised Land—through which they had already passed without realizing it—that, as rather peaceful precursors of the Hyksos, they began, of necessity, to form any herds of horses.

Not sportsmen by nature, they never became true horsemen or hunters. Even when the horse became a civil and military necessity, the Mosaic laws prohibited leaders from owning more than a certain number. For that reason, the Jews at war never took their enemies' horses as booty (perhaps, too, because they would be expensive to maintain) but limited themselves to hamstringing them.

All their hunting resolved into simple defense of their flocks through the use of nets, ditches, and snares. There was, accordingly, no chance for the chase to flourish, even in deference to neighboring peoples.

Solomon, their one king who did have the manner worthy of a great Oriental potentate, did restock the royal and military stables with a good twelve thousand mounts and some forty thousand cart horses.

VIII
CHINESE

The predominance of the Shang (eleventh century B.C.) over the agricultural peoples of China was due, in great part, to the superiority of their arms, that is, to the swift battle cart they had inherited from the central region of Asia.

Up to 300 B.C., China had remained faithful to that military style calling for a main nucleus of troops, about a thousand, in carts, with about fifty soldiers to each. With the indiscriminate increase in the number of carts, the army, encumbered by excessive troop movement, found itself at a disadvantage when confronted by the hard-riding cavalry of the nomads. The Chinese then saw that they would be constrained to change tactics. What really forced this decision was the attacks launched against them by the Hiung-nu (or Huns, as we know them), the proto-Turks from the northern steppes. The emperor Wu-ling decided to substitute armored cavalry similar to that used by the Hiung-nu, armed with lance and sword, in addition to the double-arc bow, for his cart-borne infantry.

Kao-ti, the founder of the Han dynasty, had already been sorely discomfited by the Hiung-nu. The real creator of the new cavalry, however, was the emperor Wu-ti (141–87). For the bow, he substituted the two-edged broadsword, and replaced the javelin with the long lance (a weapon that appeared in the West only around the ninth century), and, finally, adopted from the nomads the use of the saddle and, perhaps, the stirrups. Thus, if the Chinese ideograms are not in error, which is a possibility, the stirrup originated around the second or first century B.C.

The use of heavy cavalry led to a subsequent strengthening of the army. That innovation presupposed a breed of horse capable of carrying the weight of rider and equipment, as well as armor that would be solid and flexible at the same time.

Up to that date, only indigenous breeds had been employed in China, derived from the Mongolian Prezwalski type: stocky, powerful, the withers low, legs short, and back muscular. This type was replaced or, better, bred with a strain of horse deriving from the tarpan (an Aryan horse?), found near Fergana, and probably stemming from the Persian, out of the Parthian.

From that time on, it was this type of horse that was depicted in art: fine head, long neck, with a beautifully elegant sweep toward the front, arched back, and muscular hindquarters. At the same time, flexible armor such as the Persians had used, made of linked metal disks and covering not only the rider but the horse as well, was adopted. One can assert, therefore, that the cataphracts were extant in China from the first century B.C.

By fitting their arms and tactics to those of their adversary, the Chinese became victorious, thanks to better organization and a more subtle tactical mentality. As the bearer of this triumph, the horse was glorified, even in art.

If war for the Hiung-nu, like the Parthians, was solely mad and violent attack, like a hunt (the Hiung-nu beat their adversaries to death after they had thrown them into confusion and circled them closely as they would a wounded beast, falling upon the enemy as if possessed by some mystic frenzy), it was against these Hiung-nu that the Chinese employed the catapult, which became a defensive weapon; and, to protect their cultivated fields, they began to build bulwarks, walls that we can find in Iran and, at the very same period, already in use in Rome, the *limes*.

The use of the war horse spread, at the same time, to Korea and as far as Japan, where discoveries dating from the first to seventh centuries have been made of horses with their riders, saddles and, of more recent date, stirrups and long swords.

IX
HIUNG-NU

The Hiung-nu's tactic of fighting on horseback stemmed from their mode of life as shepherds and hunters. It was their emperor, Mao-Tun, however, who developed that technique to the utmost. The initial volley of arrows that opened the battle came to be regulated in every particular. Instead of crowds of horsemen charging in disarray, there was a disciplined and articulated cavalry in ordered unity. Alongside the light cavalryman already we find another, armored, and with heavy weapons and a lance. Combat technique, reduced to a system, had acquired more striking power, but it was now susceptible of imitation, and we have seen that China did not hesitate to follow suit.

X
SARMATIANS

The victory of Kao-ti over the Huns (190) provoked a chain reaction that had its repercussions in the West. The Huns moved against the Tocharians (of the Scythian race), who, in their turn, marched on the Sakians, beaten by Mithridates in 139 B.C., and inhabitants of the region known as Sakistan. Ten years later, the Tocharians reached Sogdiana and Bactria, snatching them from Greek rule, and invading Parthian territory. In turn, the Sarmatians, natives of the region of the southern extent of the Volga, attacked the Scythians, pushing them to the other side of the Danube. Withal, there were still no stirrups, which negates the claims of antique Chinese manuscripts that they were an invention of the Huns and Sarmatians.

If the migrations that precipitated the future of the East were, in the second century, provoked by the foundation of the Hiung-nu Empire, later they stemmed from the Huns' defeat by the Chinese; and things were much worse.

In 54 B.C., the chieftain of the Hiung-nu was forced to make an act of submission to the Emperor of China, and settle himself in a permanent location. Then, in one movement, around A.D. 170, the Hiung-nu disappeared from the Far Eastern scene under pressure from the Sien-bi (from whom Siberia takes its name), and stormed the West.

In A.D. 374, commanders of Roman fortresses along the Danube had reports of forceful movements manifesting themselves among the barbarians to the north. Very soon, it became clear just what had happened: the vast but fragile realm of the Goth Hermanricus, in southern Russia, had collapsed under the attacks of the Huns.

Ptolemy (Claudius Ptolemaeus), around A.D. 160, had already received news that the Huns were in the region between the Don and the Volga. In 260, the Huns were mentioned in Persian documents as mercenaries serving with auxiliary Sassanid troops. A raw race, nomads to the core, they had been unmindful of the rules and regulations governing their existence as a subject people in China and, furthermore, had flouted them, as nomads naturally would do, and had not been influenced in the slightest by the modes and manners appertaining to horses current at the Sassanid court.

XI
PERSIANS

Around the end of the first century B.C., three empires, the Roman, Persian, and Chinese, formed a bloc that placed itself counter to the peoples who were making their entry onto the stage of history: the Germans, Arabs, Huns, Berbers, and Slavs.

3 *Chinese horse in glazed earthenware of the T'ang dynasty. Note the set of the head, the padded saddle, and the type of horse: strong, fleshy yet sinewy, making him adaptable, as well, to the transport of heavy loads, a product of intelligent crossbreeding. British Museum, London.*

3

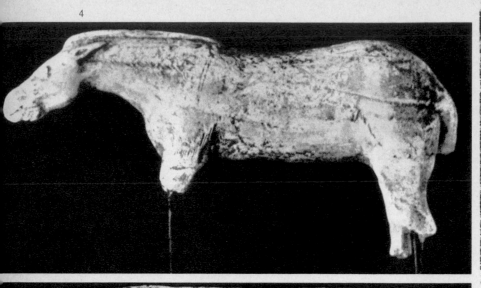

7

4

5

6

8

Viewed as a whole, those three empires constituted a continuous zone that extended over the whole of the ancient world, east to west. One can recognize in these three organisms a common rhythm of historic evolution, but no man can see in another their common destiny, nor could he in the third century A.D., when the three great faiths of messianic origin—Christianity, Muhammadanism, and Buddhism—that actively seek converts (unlike the mystic and particularistic religions of classic stamp) overtook the three great empires, to be spread throughout each one and mark its limits.

For a long time, Rome and Persia had found themselves united in defense of the Caucasian countries against the Huns and Alani, but otherwise, a state of continual hostility existed.

The sole tie holding the three empires was the Silk Route, which began in the valley of the Hwang-ho, or Yellow River, and Loyang, ran through the Tarim basin, then across Bactria, Media, Iraq, Syria, and Asia Minor. This was a road later traced by the messianic faiths, but one almost never traversed by armies or migrants.

The only exception was a patrol from a Chinese expeditionary force that suffered losses when, at least twice, it attempted to capture "blood sweaters" (a type of Aryan horse) in the region of Fergana. These were needed to introduce new bloodlines into the imperial stud, which had been decimated by the Huns, and to improve the breed of the Celestial Kingdom, stemming from the mediocre Mongolian types.

While the Silk Route lost its importance for some hundreds of years subsequent to the third century, the road to the north, conversely, was opened by Iranian nomads, the first Turks, the Arabs, and wandering Berbers, who covered the broad belt that extended from the steppe region of Eurasia through central Mongolia, Dobruja and on to Altföld.

This was the path of the great migrations, and it was followed by the Eurasian nomads: Tocharians, Sakians, Sarmatians, and Aorsians, from east to west. The Alani got as far as the Danube and the plains of the Tisza, whence they passed into Gaul and Spain. The first people, however, who could boast that they had covered the entire route, from the Ordos Desert to the Tisza, were the Huns, followed by the Magyars, Hungarians, and Mongols.

In the south, on the other hand, riding the sea lanes before the monsoon, as they had recently learned to do, came the Berbers. The Arabian dromedary had given them a new way of fighting which the Arabs had mastered. Their migrations had been going on for centuries, long before the

advent of the followers of Muhammad, just as it should be emphasized that the very first movement of Berbers along the North African coast had begun in the third century C.E.

XII
AUXILIARY AIDS

There has been a great deal of argument over the invention of the saddle, stirrups, and metal shoes, auxiliary aids and recourses that today appear to be not only indispensable to equitation and the breaking of a horse, but of natural and spontaneous origin.

On the contrary, not only are the mechanics of fitting a saddle to a horse complex; the problem of using a saddle is also difficult when one takes into account the fact that, after riding bareback, the feel of a saddle is disagreeable; for instead of giving a sensation of greater stability, as one might think it would, there is a sense of bewilderment and a feeling of almost having lost contact with the animal and of being separated from him because of the intrusion of the gear.

Yet if it is easy to achieve a certain stability mounted on a broad-backed horse, it is more difficult to maintain balance on narrow ones. Long military marches that necessitated the rider being up for hours and hours and at every degree of heat and cold suggested to the horseman that he might place something between himself and the horse that would cushion the friction of the ride a bit and prevent the animal's sweat from impregnating his clothes with its stench.

From a simple throw probably secured by a band over the chest, progress was made to a blanket fixed by a girth until, finally, the saddlecloth arrived. This was soon decorated with costly motifs and even extended by elements to protect the horse, as well, until the animal was visually transformed into a species of mobile trophy.

During the Islamic period, refinements grew to the point where horses carrying great ladies were fitted with small structures in the guise of miniature pavilions whose style was drawn from the litter.

We can establish neither who the first people were to adopt the auxiliary aid of the saddlecloth and girth nor in what period they came into use, since representations are always imprecise in these particulars, while being strongly stylized. Nevertheless, it is probably true that one of the peoples who lived on horseback first discovered these means for better subduing the horse; but it is difficult to establish whether it was the Scythians, whose veterinary technique was extremely advanced, or their cousins, the Sarmatians, or the Hiung-nu—the Huns the Chinese knew—who invented the saddlecloth.

Most likely, it was the Hiung-nu, since the Chinese, after constant contact with them in war, were able to introduce the saddlecloth and bring it to perfection through the application of very thick padding and rolls of cloth that created a soft and comfortable "mold" to accommodate and support the thighs, giving the cavalryman a prop while handling lance and sword. These saddlecloths, however, while affording greater stability and security, obviated the use of legs and spurs, which aids were replaced by a long riding whip.

4 *Paleolithic "horse" in ivory that could be a tarpan. Musée du Saint-Germain, Paris.*

5 *Stone slab showing schematic representations of horses in motion. National Museum, Stockholm.*

6 *Horse and sun cart, a votive object in gold in which the image of the wheel is likened to the sun. Danish National Museum, Copenhagen.*

7 *Wild horse in cave drawing. Note triangular shape of the head and the brawny neck. Lascaux, France.*

8 *Hittite horse and horsemen in relief, showing Indo-European characters. Archaeological Museum, Ankara.*

The first stirrup came in the second century C.E. in India, and is shown in the reliefs at Muttra. It was not adopted there universally, however, but solely by the Hindu aristocracy who were accustomed to going barefoot. This round stirrup, a ring of iron (still in use in certain regions of Asia) was carried on the wave of Buddhism to China, Timor, the Philippines, Polynesia, and to the west as far as Ethiopia.

In China, after its diffusion in countries to the south, upon arrival in the north where horsemen were booted, the stirrup underwent a needed transformation, the ring becoming larger to accommodate the whole of the foot, thus marking the birth of a genuine stirrup as early as the beginning of the fifth century, an era in which it reached Korea and Japan. The stirrup quickly passed into use in central Asia and, in the sixth century, was taken up all over the steppes, coming to Turkestan and Iran, so that the troops of Muslin (694) employed it.

In the meantime, the stirrup had reached Byzantium, where we find it mentioned in the military works of the emperor Maurice. From there, it went to Germany and France, where it was adopted by Charles Martel for his army. He quickly saw in the stirrup a means of giving his horsemen not only more stability in the saddle but also a way of utilizing the lance as the javelin had never been used: as a piercing weapon that would take advantage of the force of the cavalryman's arm and of the weight of the horse behind it as well, on striking.*

XIII
GREEKS
(Achaeans, Dorians, Cretans)

The horse was unknown in Crete until the last Minoan period, or around the sixteenth century B.C., as was also true in Cyprus and Argolis. The animal probably came to that island from Egypt, for the word *hiqquia,* for "cart" (an adjective deriving from the noun *iqquos,* "horse," and clearly of Hittite origin), in use in Knossos and Pylos, could indicate that the horse reached Crete from the north.

We find the animal superbly represented in a seal: spirited, standing close to a ship from which he appears to have landed. The head is short, the forehead convex. There is a long, thin mane; he has a round, slanting rump; and the lines are typical of the Beriberus horse, which is of Mongolian derivation. Since this is a royal seal, it is probable that it commemorates the arrival of the first horse on the island, perhaps the gift of one sovereign to another or an acquisition made by the King of Crete from the Egyptian stud.

The yellow in which horses are generally rendered leads us to believe that sorrel must have been the predominant color among the island breed. We find that the horse was used for draft, hitched to a light, two-wheeled cart with a fender to accommodate two people, and also as a pack animal. Finally, he also came to be a substitute for the bulls in the famous Cretan acrobatic displays.

The arrival of the Cretan horse or one from Anatolia in Argolis is attested by the myth that has the animal rising from the sea after the trident of Poseidon had struck the rocks of the Peloponnesus. The Cretan inventories list a cart encrusted with ivory, and painted purple and red. They also tell us that the wheels were made of elm, willow, and cypress, bound with metal. The inventories from Knossos are the fullest, listing complete carts and extra wheels. We know that around 1400 the lord of Knossos could account for some four hundred carts, some of which had been furnished by his vassals as a form of tribute.

The symbol for "horse" in the Linear B script of Knossos has a mane curiously dressed in three locks, a characteristic that reappears in frescoes on the Grecian mainland that are certainly more recent than the date of the destruction of Knossos, 1400.

The horse's shining era, however, actually began in Greece, even though that country's uneven terrain, not really appropriate for large solipeds, appears to be less favorable to a great development in equitation and cavalry than, say, that of Persia, and because the horse was introduced by a conquering people who had previously been established in Thessaly, the proto-Achaeans.

Actually, the profoundly agonistic spirit of the Hellenes caused them to see the horse almost as a symbol of challenge, competition, and speed. Perhaps they also loved the animal because his thirst for liberty, his rebelliousness, and his very restlessness held for them something of the mystic and sacred. They had understood that the horse must be continually rewon, just as must any being that demands respect first of all for his own individuality and, accordingly, is destined to become either a great ally or an implacable foe.

It was for these reasons that the horse soon began to form a part of the heroic sphere of Greek life and, for artists, the symbol of plastic and dynamic perfection. The first image of a living being on an amphora of the protogeometric period is, justly, that of a horse, and plastic representations of the animal served as handles on drinking and other terra-cotta vessels. With the advent of monumental sculpture there soon appeared those superb equine figures that testified to the consummately important role played by the horse in Greek life and myth.

Never has the horse been portrayed with greater knowledge of his body or more understanding of his character. From the great models of classic Greek sculpture descend all later masterpieces like the bronze horses of St. Mark in Venice, the remains of a monument cast by artists from Rhodes, in Alexandria, brought to Trajan's Rome, thence to Constantine's Byzantium, carried to Venice in 1204, carried off to Napoleon's Tuileries, to be returned to Venice in 1815.

---

* It is interesting to note that the Italian word for stirrup, which is *staffa,* was introduced by the Lombards, among whom it had the meaning of "step." The French *étrier* derives from the Old French *estreu,* coming from *streup* for "strap." The English "stirrup" derives through Middle English from the Old English *stigrap,* composed of *stig,* meaning "ascent," and *rap,* "rope."—TRANS.

9 *Carts in procession on Attic vase dating from 675* B.C. *and clearly proto-Corinthian. Louvre, Paris.*

10

11

12

There was also the war horse of Marcus Aurelius, as well as, one may add, the magnificent equestrian statues of the early Renaissance.

Though in Grecian art and religion and war the horse supplanted the bull (relic of the Aegean culture), and, harnessed to a war chariot, served as a mark of the aristocracy, achieving its full brilliance a bit before the First Trojan War (thirteenth century B.C.), riding a horse was an activity that gained in importance slowly, and solely after the Doric migrations, though there has been found at Mycenae the figure of a warrior mounted on a horse sculpted in the fifteenth century.

Among the Achaeans, the cart was an object of luxury and a symbol of caste. One can be seen that was used to carry a hunting party of two ladies, dressed in the Cretan fashion, in a mural in Tirinto. The cart cannot be Cretan, but must be an improved version of the Anatolian type, judging from the way it is built.

Carpenters, who were very numerous in Achaean Greece, constructed a cart with four spokes (instead of the six employed by the Hittites and Egyptians), exceptionally light, drawn by two horses hitched to the shaft by a leather girth knotted on the exposed flank of the animal, as well as a collar all of leather, about nine inches high at the center, which passed between neck and chest, with the ends connected to a wooden yoke shaped like the letter W.

During the preclassical age in Greece, the extra horse—hitched with the pair for steep or particularly difficult terrain—was already employed. That custom, which probably led to the use of the quadriga, is documented in the Iliad (Book XVI) when Patroclus joins to Achilles' two immortal steeds, Xanthus and Balius, the mortal horse Pegasus, who falls when killed in battle, and puts the other two into peril.

Why Patroclus ever added a third horse, throwing the car off balance in a hard-fought engagement, when he had two unbeatable horses like Xanthus and Balius, is not easy to understand. Perhaps he preferred to have his own horse, from home, and upon whom he could count as being obedient to him. Or did he want to be able to make better time over open country? Or did he want to have a replacement ready, should one of the pair eventually be wounded?

It is worthwhile remembering that the Greeks of the classic age considered Homer an authority even on the art of war (Aristophanes has this said to Aeschylus in *The Frogs*). Notwithstanding, as a military manual the Iliad is more confused than one could believe possible, for the battles tend to be conducted in accordance with hoplite tactics, which were current throughout Greece at the end of the eighth century, but the decisive encounters seem to be the duels, like the feudal type of the fifteenth century.

In his *Introduction to Homer*, Fausto Codino says:

What is worse is that these descriptions do not give any idea of the size of those Homeric battles, at times hand-to-hand combat involving a few champions, then again engagements of multitudes, so that Hector (Book IX) does not know anything at all about how many are to the left of his array.

The chariot seems to be the basic weapon, but the record is vague and confused. Nestor, for example, before the battle, explains what is the best way to fight with cars, insisting (in a suspect manner) that "so it was done by the ancients" (Book IV). Agamemnon recommends that the horses be fed before going into the field (Book II), and Hector incites the Trojans to send the chariots against the Achaeans (Book XI). When the battle is in progress, however, the poet gives us the slip and does not tell us how one fights with chariots, which merely serve, as John Cherwick has said, as taxicabs for carrying the heroes over the longer stretches. They make haste to leave them so they can fight on foot, so much so that when a warrior on the ground encounters one in a chariot, it is usually the latter who gets the worst of it.

As a rule, nothing is said about when the chariot was abandoned or sent back, so that we do not know if Hector and Patroclus fought on foot or in chariots. Evidently, recollections of the system used in Mycenaean Greece have been sketchily interwoven with what was done in feudal and democratic Greece.

The chariot remains as a symbol of archaic valor in the sacred trains and as a typical element in competitions, so much so that at the Olympics, the cart races always precede the riding contests.

One can begin with Greece in tracing the history of horse racing, for even though it was obviously practiced among other peoples, only in Greece were the contests followed with such assiduity and the intense interest of people who not only love the entertainment but also insist on expertise in all its technical aspects, from genealogy to tactics.

In the Iliad the same Nestor offers precious advice to Antilochus for winning the race in honor of Patroclus, clever tactics and techniques that presuppose long experience with the sport; and Menelaus pours out complaints against Antilochus himself, who, after the curve, had pressed him unfairly.

The winners of the greatest races are glorified and mentioned not only by Pindar, the poet laureate of the Olympic games, but also by such writers as Pausanias and Plutarch.

There were games to celebrate religious festivals: the Isthmian, Nemean, Panathenaic, Pythian, and Delphic, not to mention the Olympic games, at which, by the time of the XXV Olympiad (680 B.C.), an event for quadrigas had already been instituted and won that year by a certain Pagondas of Thebes.

The race for saddled horses was established at the LIV Olympiad, held in the year 564 B.C., and won by Callias of Athens, who had already come in second in the quadriga event during the same Olympiad. At the XCVI games (396 B.C.), quadriga races for colts, run over a short distance, were programmed for the first time; subsequently, there were races for boys on horseback.

Up to the Achaean period, two types of chariot courses were in use: from a city to some sacred place, with the dis-

10 *Funeral procession. Seventh-century B.C. tomb relief from Xanthus in Lycia. Note the saddle blanket, the height of the fleshy horses, the plaited tail, and the sketchy "harness" of the two horses hitched together. British Museum, London.*

11 *Horse of the fifth century B.C. Acropolis Museum, Athens.*

12 *Racers at the gallop, shown in an archaic relief. Museo Nazionale delle Terme, Rome.*

tances varying between 50 and 150 miles; and the closed track, either grassy or sandy, with curves, generally four of them, marked by metes.* It has been recorded, for example, that in 404 B.C., Listhenes, a Theban, won the horse race run between Chaeronea and Thebes, a distance of some hundred miles.

From Pindar, we learn that the entrants went twelve times around the squared course formed by Olympia, Delphi, Pylos, and Corinth. The track at Olympia measured about 740 metres; therefore the total circuit was about fifteen miles. The same distance was run in the horse races in which riders used saddles, but they were less popular, possibly because they were not so spectacular as the chariot races.

In the list of Olympic champions, we find many famous names: Alcmaeon of Athens (in 592, at the XLVII Olympiad), a very rich man who had connections with Croesus, from whom he had the horses; Clisthenes, the tyrant of Sicyon, who won at Olympia in 572 (LII Olympiad) and at Pylos in 580 (L Olympiad), driving the same quadriga; the Athenian Militiades, the one from the Cheronese, not the Marathonian, who competed in 560 (the LV Olympiad); Evagoras of Sparta, who won three times (between 580 and 536), and ended by building a sumptuous tomb for his horses. Cimon of Athens, victorious in 536 (LXI Olympiad) while he was in exile, ceded his second win to Pisistratus, to obtain permission to return to Athens, then won twice more; but a few months after his third victory, he was killed in Athens by the sons of that very same Pisistratus. Pisistratus himself won the quadriga race in 532 (LXII Olympiad), obliging Cimon, in the year in which Pythagoras experimented with a diet based on meat rather than dried figs for the athletes.

A celebrated victory was that of Phidolas, the Corinthian in the horse race of 532 (LXII Olympiad). His horse, Aura, fell at one of the curves, but then recovered and picked up speed at the sound of the trumpet announcing the last circuit of the track. A statue of the steed was erected with public funds. In 508 (LXVIII Olympiad), Phidola's son won the event, riding the same Aura.

In 500, a race for mule-drawn quadrigas was instituted, but was later discontinued because such teams did not have much speed. In 495, we find Empedocles of Agrigentum, grandfather of the philosopher of the same name, winning the race and offering a feast to the populace, just as Alcibiades was later to do. A trotting race, instituted in the same year and subsequently abolished, was won by Pataikos of Dyme.

It was during the sixth and fifth centuries that the Sicilian tyrants Panthares, Gelon, Hieron and Dionysius, who sported superb teams of horses bred in Syracuse, began to win.

In 464, the Thessalian Echecrates won the horse race with a pregnant mare. We find the laurels going to Agesilaus IV, King of Cyrene, in a quadriga with an African team in 460, while Leonidas of Sparta won in 424 with a chariot drawn by Venetian horses.

In 416, there was the sensational success of the teams of Alcibiades, the Athenian. That megalomaniac had sent seven quadrigas to Olympia, and took first, second, and fourth places. "His stables were renowned throughout the world, as was the number of chariots he owned. Never had anyone, private citizen or monarch, entered seven teams in any Olympiad, and no one had ever placed first, second, and fourth simultaneously with his own equipages," raved Thucydides. "Such a triumph is the most splendid ever had by anyone at the races and is glory and honor."

Alcibiades, the most ambitious and cunning man in all Greece, because of his love of winning ended in court when he was cited by a certain Diomedes. A friend of Alcibiades, Diomedes longed for nothing more than to win at least once at Olympia. Since he knew that in Argos there was a particularly fast chariot owned by the state, he prevailed upon Alcibiades to take advantage of his extremely good relations and the many friends he was known to have in that city and buy the car in his name. Alcibiades did buy the chariot, but he entered it in the race as his own, disregarding their agreement.

Furious, Diomedes called upon heaven and earth to witness how he had been duped. The case finally came to court; but since Alcibiades had won so many victories for Athens, it was easy for him to gain the decision.

In 408, Evagoras of Elis won the two-horse chariot race, which was run for the first time, while Archelaus, King of Macedonia, took the quadriga event, just as his nephew, Philip II, the son of Amyntas, would do in the same competition in 356. Philip of Macedonia held that day the most auspicious of his life, not only because his troops had taken Potidaea, the Illyrians were conquered by his general Parmenion, and his son Alexander was born, but above all because he had won at Olympia. To commemorate that feat, he immediately had coins minted that showed him driving his victorious chariot.

Alexander the Great, on the contrary, refused to participate in the event: "I would enter gladly if the contestants were kings." Later, Philip attempted to win other races, but never succeeded, for he always found himself trailing the unbeatable quadriga of Arybas, the former King of Epirus, whom he had deposed and who entered every race for which he saw Philip enrolled, just to spite his great enemy.

Following these names, we find those of professionals and others that are not Greek. Finally come Tiberius, Germanicus, and Nero. Tiberius won in 4 C.E. in his own chariot. In 67 C.E. Nero won everything, taking 1,808 crowns! (He had already added ten-horse teams, poetry contests, and a cither competition.) The Olympic Games were no longer to be taken seriously.

XIV

XENOPHON

By creating a corps of two hundred cavalrymen, Solon established a new social class in Athens and defined its character.

---

* Three conical posts set at a turning point or goal.—TRANS.

13 *The gods at the nuptials of Peleus and Thetis. Quadriga with four-spoke wheels and double shaft. The horses' manes and tails are dressed in the Corinthian fashion. François Vase, Museo Archeologico, Florence.*

13

Pericles raised the number of horsemen to a thousand and the mounted palace guard to two hundred, very modest figures in comparison with the strength of the Persian cavalry, for instance.

We know that the Thessalians and Macedonians were very fine cavalrymen, while the Spartans suffered from a "horse complex," viewing the animal with a certain suspicion. It was in the colonies, however, in Sicily and, above all, at Syracuse, that equestrianism particularly flourished. The tyrants of that country developed horse breeding to such an extent as to win the series of Olympic victories already mentioned. In Athens, the horse was a sign of distinction, a symbol of beauty, and even of vanity. We need only recall Pheidippides' mad passion for horses in *The Clouds* of Aristophanes.

On horseback, one traveled, hunted, traded, and even began to do battle. In such an atmosphere, it was natural that a need was felt for the publication of horsemen's manuals. Two texts of the many that were probably written remain to us from that era, one by Simon of Athens (mere fragments) and the complete work by Xenophon, his *Peri Hippikes*.

Simon of Athens was a professional, an *écuyer,* trainer of colts for gentlemen, and a riding master who gave lessons in equitation, becoming rich enough to be able to have a bronze statue dedicated to himself in Athens, upon the base of which were carved his equestrian exploits. Of his book, we have only one chapter and some odd fragments, so it is difficult to assess its technical worth. Its literary value, however, is nil, yet Xenophon did cite it three times, though not without a certain detachment that almost approaches disdain.

Simon, in any case, established that for a horse the essence lay in proportion, as is true for any athlete. He advised whoever wanted to acquire really good horses to waste no time in getting to Thessaly. He discarded the theory that a horse's color might determine his quality, yet suggested that one select an animal of a solid color, short on top (that is, from withers to croup) and small below (he probably meant short-shanked). He recommended that the legs be perfect, the hoof neither too large nor too small, with the horny wall "thick and resonant as a cymbal." The pastern should be "elastic, sloping, the tendons lean; the chest not too broad, but the shoulders as long as possible. The neck, thick at the base, should be light and flexible where it meets the lower jaw, and sufficiently long to allow the crest to be carried high."

From the description of the tail and the way it should be held, "long and high," the expressiveness of the head, the mobility of the small ears, and the broad back, there emerges the image of a horse very close to the Arab or, better still, to the stupendous steeds of Phidias.

One does not find in Simon those banal errors or certain superstitions that irritate us in the writers of the fifteenth and seventeenth centuries, but some assertions that are open to question, such as his statement that a horse should be "fleshy," which is the carping of a faultfinder and a reflection of the riding master, and different from that of Xenophon, who dealt with the horse consummately on the plane of sport.

Xenophon was a horse lover by family tradition and through his own love of equitation; and horses positively pursued him through life. It was on horseback that he overtook Proxenos, to march with Cyrus the Younger against Artaxerxes, in 401. The March of the Ten Thousand was made, in large part, on horseback, on animals taken in raids. At the end of that eventful expedition, dreaming only of returning to Athens, but without any money, sick at heart, he was constrained to sell his horse. His joy was as great as his grief had been when some friends of his later made him a present of that very same horse, which they had gone to recover in Thessaly, finding him in the hands of a trader.

It is probable that Xenophon, a bosom friend of Agesilaus, the King of Sparta, served in his cavalry. Thus, the decree that caught him unawares, ordering his exile and ending his career as an officer, did not cut short the vocation of the cavalryman who loved horses. After he was given an estate by the Spartans at Scillus, near Olympia, he continued with equitation, but now as a civilian, and when he decided to dedicate part of the free time he enjoyed as a country gentleman to books and his memoirs, he did not neglect writing works in which the horse was the subject. After the *Hipparkikos* and his *Cynegeticus,* he wrote *Peri Hippikes*.

He had no wish to write a manual, but rather a sort of pleasant *causerie,* almost a compendium of advice and counsel for his own children, his friends, and for the Athenians. For that reason, he moves from one subject to another as the spirit, mood, and memory move him, creating a book that is fascinating for its freshness, for the immediacy with which he describes methods, devices, and precautions that we use even today in dealing with our friend the horse. Above all, he demonstrates that he understood the fundamental nature of the beast and, therefore, the most appropriate way of handling the animal in order to dominate him. To this end, he insists that horses should be dealt with kindly and not in anger, because the important thing is to become master of his "psyche," which happens only if you treat him well. It is also essential to obtain "the best disposition of the horse's points" so that his every movement is beautiful. He adds, "A dancer really dances well when he does so with enthusiasm and not when he is forced to perform."

Xenophon apologizes for repeating points already made by Simon of Athens, but consoles himself "that, nonetheless, they will have just that much more value, concurring as they do with the affirmations of an expert on horses such as he." He is quick to add, "We shall seek to discuss problems that he has omitted."

In examining a horse, Xenophon recommends always beginning with the feet, "for no matter how beautiful it may be, a building is good for nothing if it does not have a firm and strong foundation." He examines the hoof and the relation between toe and heel, and explains the way the horny wall should be to obviate "that soft and delicate triangle at the frog." The pastern should be "sloping, just enough to avoid the joint's brushing the ground on cultivated or stony terrain, but not too straight, to avoid a stiff walk."

14 *Young horsemen parading at the Panathenaic games, by Phidias. Parthenon frieze, Athens.*

15 *Tiberius and his wife (?). She is seated sidesaddle* (Muliebriter Insidere?). *The horse's frontlet is swallow-tailed. Museo Nazionale delle Terme, Rome.*

The cannon, or shin, should be solid, yet lean enough to forestall varicosities. As for the gait, "a horse that 'lifts' [a high-stepper] is less likely to stumble and tire than one that just grazes the ground." (Simon, on the contrary, noted that horses that skim the ground are faster.)

"High withers afford the rider a firmer seat, and permit him to hug the shoulders and body of the animal more closely, just as a broad back gives him a more commodious seat. Full ribs, well sprung toward the belly, assure that the horse will provide a more solid seat..."—indications that are particularly interesting because they give an insight into the style of riding and the seat used at the time. The rider's firmness up, we can assume, was achieved through hugging with the buttocks, thighs, and calves, and, only occasionally, using the knees; or what every horseman does who mounts bareback, and the one for whom the wide, rounded back offers an advantage, a point that Homer had emphasized (Iliad, Book II).

For a man as wrapped up in his subject as Xenophon was—among other things, he had put words and phrases into Socrates' mouth (in The Economist) that would have done honor to a truly well-grounded horse fancier, something that astonishes us, for Socrates was never a horseman—for a man so dedicated, Xenophon gives short shrift to the training of colts, maintaining that anyone in a position to indulge in equitation surely is a person of means and merit and, accordingly, the sort who might better devote himself to politics, government, or the learned professions rather than horse-breaking. "Leave it to those who have to do it for a living and who know something about it."

Nevertheless, he does suggest taking certain precautions, and writes that "you proceed as you would if you were sending your son to learn a trade, stipulating in writing what he should know when he comes home." Turning to the treatment of a colt, he notes that "a horse does not merely love a man, but feels the need of him when he realizes that it is he who takes care of feeding him, doesn't let him go thirsty, and protects him from pests." He advises petting the horse often, and talking to him, and putting him in the care of a groom who is calm and prudent, one who will accustom him to being among people and to face with confidence all aspects of our life: its noise, lights, and so on. Whenever the horse takes fright, "there is no reason for you to become angry; but show him that there is nothing terrible in that object or that noise."

He suggests that before buying a horse, the animal should be walked back and forth, continually switching direction, to see whether he has deformed bars.* Misshapen bars and a dead mouth are the great preoccupations of Xenophon, reflecting the ease with which the Greek bit, which was very hard, could injure a horse's mouth.

"It is also necessary to check whether a horse going at a brisk gait knows how to pull up promptly and come to a collected halt. A horse that does not obey is not only useless, like a careless servant or absent-minded soldier, but frequently acts exactly like a traitor."

In the fourth book, Xenophon discusses the stables, how they should be situated, aired, and protected "so that the manger isn't emptied by thieves." In short, keep an eye on your horse "to cure his illnesses quickly, and know when he

is tired or stale." The stable ground should not be damp or slippery, and should consist of stones about the size of a horse's hoof. "As much effort should be made to see that the stones are hard as you put into seeing that the mouth is soft."

During training, "clean the head with a damp rag but the back only with your hand, not with any hard instruments, in order not to injure the rider's 'seat'"—and Xenophon uses the Greek word ἕδρα, which signifies the back of a mounted horse, rather than ῥάχις, meaning "bareback."*

The horse should be courageous, nimble, manageable; able to sidestep holes, jump walls, take banks, and go down escarpments either on a straight or diagonal track. When he hesitates, lead him gradually over these rough spots, "for a well-trained horse will do anything, on the condition, of course, that he is in good health and not slacking."

As for skittish or timorous animals and bad-tempered ones, he suggests that one get rid of them, "for if they bump into other beasts or rush against someone, they can cause a great deal of trouble and even legal complications for their owner." Evidently, the Greeks employed horses that had not been altered, and these might easily leap upon others, but they were reluctant to use geldings, of which Xenophon speaks well in his Cyropaedia, praising their adaptability, when discussing the Persian cavalry, "the best in the world."

He not only counsels against lazy horses, who force the rider to do too much legwork, but also against those that are too hot-blooded and, taking the bit in their teeth, force the rider into dangerous situations.

Rather touching is his advice to wash the crest, mane, and tail, those "ornaments bestowed by the gods," frequently, and not to shave the mane at the top of the neck but to leave the hair long to afford a good handhold for the rider. It would seem, therefore, that it was customary to grasp the mane (done by us only exceptionally) to keep one's balance. As a matter of fact, because the bit was so hard, the horse must have had a tendency to raise his head. (With the neck in the natural position, the rider would be likely to hang on to the mane at the withers.)

Xenophon dwells upon the splendor of the mane and tail, and to illustrate his assertion that they are god-given, adds: "Because this is so, mares running free in pasture will not let themselves be approached by an ass, to be mounted, so long as their hair is left full, which is why mule trainers clip in the spring." Curious, quaint, and unlikely that these proud mares could be violated through the snip of a shears!

Nevertheless, "when they see themselves so dishonored," insists Pollux, one of the commentators on Xenophon, "they lose their aloofness and permit the ass to approach." Actually,

---

* To indicate the rider's place to sit.—TRANS.

16 Preparations for the contest between Pelops and Oenomaus, who is on the right, while Pelops is to the left of Zeus. East tympanum, Temple of Zeus, Olympia Museum, Greece.

17 Detail of Pelops' chariot.

18 The Battle of Issus. Alexander is at the left, on Bucephalus, while on the right, Darius flees in a cart with knurled wheels. Archaeological Museum, Naples.

---

* The toothless portion of the lower jaw where the bit rests.—TRANS.

16

17

18

19

20

what was probably true was that the tail impeded coupling, given the difference in stature between the two animals.

But how Xenophon hits the mark when he insists on a gentle hand to calm nervous horses and gradual pulling up on the reins to halt them! "A long and easy canter soothes a fractious horse," he notes, "much more than frequent changes in direction. With such edgy animals, avoid galloping in company, as spirited horses are more apt to vie with others. Use your voice to quiet irritable and sensitive animals, and humor them by speaking your commands. Also, in battle, when the trumpet sounds, do not drive the horse on, but instead hold him back so that he loses his nervousness and does not bolt.

"If you want your animal to shine," he suggests, "refrain from alternately spurring him on and then dragging on the bit, for by doing so you upset him.

"You require a very light hand to teach him to raise his neck. When he tosses his head, take him behind the bit, which will provoke elegant, elastic movements on his part that he will also like. There is proof that horses do like this, for whenever one wants to be admired by other horses, and particularly by the mares, he will arch his neck and tail and pace proudly and pompously.

"Working at the noble gait" (χαλλοπιξω) is the precise phrase used by Xenophon for *haute école*—"all exercises that stupefy spectators and cause them to murmur the adjectives 'fiery,' 'impetuous,' 'spirited,' 'terrific,' because on horseback a man appears to them to be a god. In reality, such adjectives describe only the negative aspects of true equitation. But aren't the statues of a god or hero on horseback marvelous? When you see a beautiful horse, well schooled and well mounted, doesn't it give you an aesthetic pleasure such as nothing else can?"

The descriptions of how to bridle a horse, how to approach him are moving: "Advancing from the left side, look him straight in the eye, and resolutely cup up beside his shoulder"; how to leave him: "Leave the stall without hurry or disturbance." It is as if time had stood still.

He recommends mounting by the Persian method, what we call "getting a leg up," or by using a block, while taking a great deal of care to maintain correct tension on the reins; but he disdains making the horse kneel or bend at the rear, methods still used today by the Bedouin.

Finally, he comes to a discussion of the cavalryman's armor: a breastplate that fits perfectly, a well-made gorget to offer protection up to the nose, a Boeotian helmet "that covers well but does not interfere with the view, a gauntlet going over shoulder, arm, elbow, and hand that folds and telescopes enough to protect the area at the armpit left

exposed by the body armor. As far as the right hand is concerned, he suggests that it be left free and protected as much as possible by hinged "wings," while the forearm should be fitted with an independent iron *cnemide*, that is, a vambrace.*

He recommends that the horse, as well, be shielded by a frontlet, a plastron, rump pieces (these are very difficult to identify, since Xenophon describes them as serving to protect the rider's thighs, as well). Finally, he talks of the saddle and of the fact that it is padded to give the rider more support and prevent injury to the horse's back.

Xenophon suggests that the cavalryman wear boots and a saber rather than a sword, since "cutting strokes, coming from above, are more effective than thrusts," indicating that the Greek cavalryman was firm in the saddle; otherwise he would not have been able to handle a saber. He further recommends the javelin rather than a lance, even both of them, in the Persian style. "Going at a brisk gallop, you hurl the javelin, rising up on the thighs; then suddenly have the horse make a half-turn to reenter the lines."

Evidently, there were no stirrups and no shoes. To dismount, he proposes that, besides the support, one make use of the lance, keeping the left hand at the withers (a sort of pole vault).

There is talk of a bedecked and padded saddlecloth, but one cannot really call it a saddle. In the *Cyropaedia*, Xenophon speaks of the *ephippia*† the king had distributed to his officers for a military parade. The *ephippion* did exist, but was not always used. There is yet another interesting passage in the *Cyropaedia* in which Xenophon refers to the Persians, "who use more blankets on their horses than on their beds, because they take particular care to have a soft seat for someone who is not really firm up." The *ephippion* in the bronze equestrian statue of Alexander appears to be extended toward the rear to protect the horse's belly, while it is flared in front in order not to touch or constrict the withers. It is true that Xenophon was fearful of sores on the back but not of festering withers, which is much more serious. Perhaps this was because the *ephippion* could not irritate that very delicate part of the horse's body.

XV

GAUL

The people who knew how to exploit the horse, and to the highest degree, were the Celts and their descendants, the Gauls of the Orient and Occident. (All else aside, without the horse, how would they ever have been able to extend that singular sway of theirs, which was not precisely political, but more ethnic and spiritual, over the territory of that vastest of empires?)

If theirs was not the strongest cavalry from a numerical point of view, it was highly operational. These people were expert inventors of vehicles, and many of their models were later adopted by the Romans. The town of Carrono in Lombardy memorializes in its name the existence there of a great cart factory.

19 *Head of a horse, dating from the fifth century* B.C., *by Phidias. From the Parthenon. British Museum, London.*

20 *Bronze head, the famous "Horse of Vergil," which during the late Italian Renaissance was believed to be the work of Donatello. It is all that remains of a colossal statue, later partially melted down, that stood at the entrance to the hippodrome in naples. The head was presented by Lorenzo de' Medici to Diomede Carafa. Museo Nazionale, Naples.*

* The Greek word actually means "greave," which is the analogous piece for the shin.—TRANS.

† Horse blankets or trappings.—TRANS.

The great passion these people felt for horses ultimately found its singer in Vergil, whose Celtic origin really came to the fore in the loving treatment he gave equestrian subjects and descriptions, and also in the nocturnal and lunar tone of some of his poetry.

The Gallic horses must have been of the European type, rather large, fleshy, and heavy, even though they were not very tall. This is the same horse that gave rise, in the Danube region, to the Noric horse, the breed much sought after by the Romans for heavy draft work. We recall that the first Gallic invasion of the Po Valley, in the sixth century B.C., was accomplished by hordes on horseback.

XVI
ETRURIA

The mysterious Etruscans, whose unleashed passion for horses seems to have been almost morbid, judging from murals and certain evidence, were probably the ones who taught the Romans the equestrian art. That same enthusiasm and the same way of racing (over natural terrain on horseback, on special tracks in two-horse chariots), as well as the care they gave their horses, all might give us an insight into their customs so that we could retrace the much-disputed origins of this people that landed in Italy from the sea.

History would end by agreeing with the legend that has them coming from the Troad, that identifies them with the famous "people from the sea" so feared by the Egyptians, that has them disembarking near Carthage, real pirates who carried aboard their ships horses ready for attack and battle, and, finally, that transports them to the low-lying coastal area of that land that was called by those of Teucrian origin Tuscia (Tuscany), and Etruria by the literate.

On the other hand, didn't Aeneas fight on horseback against Turnus? Paintings show us horses of the mesomorphic type, nervous, high-strung, undoubtedly of Eastern and Aryan strain, and close to our ideal Arabian horse.

The races, more than ceremonials, must have been precisely regulated, and the public (whom we see crowded and tense in the grandstand) must have gone wild, and bet a good deal, while the contestants committed plenty of fouls, and hooted and bickered after every race, and at the intervention of the judge, who was trying to make peace—that is, if we can draw conclusions from what is handed down to us in the murals.

XVII
ROME

The relations between Romans and the horse were of the most varied and complex, naturally influenced by the times, the political, military, and social situations, and the expansion of power, but were always rather lacking in depth, imperfect, and never really warmly genuine, determined, as they were, by utilitarianism.

Regarded with a certain diffidence at the beginning, considered an emblem of luxury, ridden by mediocre, or more accurately raw, horsemen, certainly not polished riders as were the Tarantines and the Neapolitans, the horse was not considered as being basic war matériel, but merely auxiliary equipment for many hundreds of years. Nor were the Romans able to recruit a strong and substantial body of cavalrymen in Latium so long as the knights (so called because they had sufficient income to permit maintaining at least one horse to bring with them when called up for military service) little by little came to form an élite corps, but they were not technically competent, and were lacking in esprit de corps and any tradition.

Only the necessities of war—in other words their confrontations with nations that had large numbers of men on horseback—impelled the Romans to provide themselves with strong contingents of mounted troops. They recruited units of Numidians, widely renowned cavalrymen from North Africa whom Caesar himself had credited with the success of a number of battles.

From reliefs and statues, we can see that, contrary to the Assyrians, Greeks, and Etruscans, the Romans, following a tradition of southern Italy, demonstrated in vase paintings, used very long reins, sat rather far to the rear, above the animal's kidneys, using the buttocks as a cushion, with their legs hugging the horse's trunk, so as to be shaken as little as possible when going at a fast pace.

There is reason to think that the women rode in a manner different from that of the men, keeping to the dictum *muliebriter insidere* (sit like a woman), perhaps on a saddlecloth. But without stirrups or hooks, how did they stay on?

With time, many riding academies grew up in Rome, and we know that the gilded youth gathered at the Campus Martius to ride and jump obstacles. At last, riding became so necessary to gentlemen that they installed "hippodromes," large and small, at their villas. So generalized did this custom become that we have a letter written by Pliny in which he described villa gardens traversed by paths, called *gestatii* because they could be covered in a litter, which led to the hippodrome, of which there remains clear evidence alongside the Domus Flaviana on the Palatine Hill, built by Domitian (81–96 C.E.), and surrounded by porticoes during the reign of Septimus Severus (193–231).

In Pliny's villa, in Tuscany, the hippodrome, next to the stable *(equilia)*, is situated in part of the park, a large area surrounded by myrtle shrubs, tall-trunked trees, a veritable private park for riding, as one gathers from Martial's epigram "… and the flying hoof makes ring your dusty drive…"

21 *Young man with a blue-and-white colt. Tomb of the Couch, Tarquinia, Italy.*

22 *Troilus, on horseback, draws near the pit, a detail from a seventh-century* B.C. *wall painting depicting the ambush of Achilles. Tomb of the Bulls, Tarquinia, Italy.*

23 *Three-horse-chariot race, from the Chiusino stele, sixth century* B.C. *Museo Nazionale, Palermo.*

24 *Fallen horse. Tomb of the Olympiads, Tarquinia, Italy.*

25 *Fight between warriors and Amazons from the "Sarcophagus of the Amazons," an Etruscan painting showing Hellenic influence. Museo Archeologico, Florence.*

21

22

23

24

Naples had a hippodrome when were still no races at Rome, or, rather, when they still raced in the Etruscan manner, on improvised tracks, and when horse races were, perhaps, more frequent than contests for two-horse chariots. The hippodrome at Naples, which was huge (the longitudinal wall was over 1,300 feet), was situated between the present Piazza Mercato and Corso Umberto, a bit outside the Paleopoli district.

From all this, one understands how important it was felt to be, during the empire, to keep up appearances and how equitation represented a sport and a pastime for a certain class of society. Once they became lovers of luxury, tradition, and style, the Romans also piqued themselves on their expertise in horse breeding, thus emulating the Greeks and Persians. (An extraordinarily massive bay, said to be a descendant of one of Diomedes' mares, was acquired from the consul Dolabella for 100,000 sesterces, and became the property first of Cassius and then of Antony. It was born in Argos, in the stud of Cnaeus Scius.)

"To breed" does not merely signify raising a good animal, but improving him and, above all, selecting him for a specific purpose, seeking in the parents those traits that can be emphasized through crossing. If they were not great horsemen, the Romans certainly were magnificent horse breeders, instituting public registries *(acta)* for inscribing the studs *(admissari in acta ferre)*, along with their characteristics and bloodlines, including their wins or how they finished all through their racing careers.

The best horses in Italy were found in the Veneto; the fastest ("and if you see a victorious chariot," wrote Pindar, "it will be drawn by Venetian horses"... but he was paid) came from Puglia, solid horses, but rather raw; and from the Campagna came the ones that were, above all, elegant.

When the Romans got their hands on the studs in the Campagna, they used them to improve the Latium breed and to strengthen the postal network that they had recently initiated. Bit by bit, on all the roads, *stationes* and *mansiones* began to appear, each one about ten or twenty Roman miles (the Roman mile equals about 2.6 English miles) distant from the next, where horses were changed.

Later, they imported stallions and dams from Spain and the Orient to create a hunter *(venaticus)*, horses for short draft (the *itinerarius*), and slow *(manuus,* a little horse for buggies and the country), the walking horse *(gradarius* or *ambulator:* compare the American pacer) for long trips (Incitatus, Julius Caesar's horse, was of this type), the trotter *concussator* or *succussator* or even *cruciator*,* evidence of just how uncomfortable trotting was for those horsemen who had neither saddle nor stirrups; horses for parade and sport (the *cantherius*), the warhorse *(bellator equus),* and the race horse *(celer equus).*

The popular passion for horses, then so prevalent, found an escape valve in the races at the circus. "Yes, I am renowned throughout the world," wrote Martial, "but why so much envy? I'll never be more famous than Andremone." Andre-

mone was a horse, a noted winner, but not so well known as Victor, who won in 1429, or Tusco, first in 1386.

Horses of such quality had the right to burial and a stele recording their exploits. On the cippus erected by Claudia Erica for her beloved husband, Aulus Dionisius, charioteer, she had inscribed the names of his most famous horses, "Aquilo, son of Aquilo, first, 1,300 times; second, 88; third, 37; Hirpinus, son of Aquilo, first, 114 times; second, 56; third, 36." Performances like those are still used today to show that a champion is fit to go into stud.

Very soon, a need was felt to build hippodromes, first of wood, later of masonry, and ever more sumptuous, among which the most famous was the Circus Maximus, for the magnificence of the statuary that adorned it and for its great size, being larger, perhaps, than the renowned circus at Antioch, and equaled only by the one at Byzantium. The great extension of the Circus Maximus is traced along the valley lying between the Palatine and Aventine hills for about a third of a mile, the *carceres* (cells) lying below the quondam Palace of the Muses, and the curved façade is at the entrance to the park of Porta Capena.

Tradition has it that it was erected by the Tarquins, Tarquinius Priscus, to be precise, in the place where the rape of the Sabine women had occurred. It is probable that, in that open and level vale, races had been run over tracks marked for each occasion, in accordance with the Greek and Etruscan custom. The masonry edifice must have gone up not earlier than the second century B.C. Caesar held a mock battle there in 46 B.C., with a thousand foot soldiers, six hundred cavalry, and forty elephants. Augustus constructed the stand under the Palatine. Nero's fire and another occurring during the reign of Domitian destroyed it completely.

The new circus was terminated under Trajan at the beginning of the second century. Caracalla enlarged it even more, and Constantine restored it after a part had collapsed in Diocletian's time. At that period, it could hold 300,000 spectators. The last races were held there in 549, and we have evidence of the event in a pathetic letter written by Cassiodorus.

If there are remains of Domitian's circus beneath the house that fronts on Via Zanardelli, and whose perimeter gave rise to that Renaissance and Baroque masterpiece that is Piazza Navona, and if one side of the Circus Flaminius, constructed in 221 B.C. by Gaius Flaminius, gave a start to Via Botteghe Oscure, where the medieval bottle dealers settled themselves between the arches, we have, in the Ager Vaticanus, near the Porta Santo Spirito, the little that remains of Caligula's circus, where St. Peter was killed. This was later enlarged by Gaius and Nero. Little, however, remains except for a few steles.

In a much better state of preservation is the Circus of Maxentius, on the Appian Way, which was built in 309 and dedicated to Romulus, the emperor's son, who had died very young and whose tomb rests there. This circus, which is approximately 1,600 feet long and 260 wide, could hold 18,000 spectators in ten tiers. Among the decorations was Domitian's obelisk, which Bernini later moved to the Piazza Navona. This circus was used for races when the Circus Maximus was under repair or otherwise unusable.

The Circus Maximus, which was a little under 2,000 feet long and over 650 feet wide, was circled by three marble

---

* "Crucifier" or "tormentor."—TRANS.

26 *Samnite warrior in battle dress. Pompeii.*

arcades that supported the tiers *(cavea)* where the public of fanciers and rabid fans *(iubilatores* or *plauditores)* sat in places *(loca)* that were numbered and divided among vertical *(scalaria)* and horizontal *(praecinctiones)* sections. The longitudinal wall was about 700 feet long, and determined the tour of the track *(curriculum)* in the arena, which was about 285 feet wide, with an extent of about 1,930 feet,* which was made tricky by the narrow curves at the two metes *(metae)*.

Under Augustus, twelve races were run each day. This figure rose to thirty-four with Caligula, and finally reached a hundred with the Flavians, going from morning to sundown. The distance was seven turns of the track, reduced to five under Domitian, and came to about fourteen furlongs or 1.75 miles.

The equestrian competitions *(equestria certamina)* that were most appreciated were those for two-horse chariots *(bijuga)* and for quadrigas, until the stunt of hitching up six-, eight-, and ten-horse teams became common. There were also races for saddle horses, with jockeys *(cursores)* up, some of whom *(desultores)* gave shows of equestrian acrobatics and, in a certain type of race, hung on the underside during the last circuit of the track for the final dash.

On race days, which were held in celebration or sponsored by a patron *(editor spectaculorum)*, the program opened with a processional rite *(pompa)*. The races were run in heats *(missis)* and a final. Usually, there were four formations for four heats and four at the finale. From time to time, however, six or even eight cars competed.

There were four stables *(factiones)*, indicated by the color of the charioteer's mantle and the chariot: *alba* or *vinaca*, which symbolized winter; *russata* for summer, *prasina* (green) for spring, and *veneta* (blue) for autumn. Domitian added two: *aurata* and *purpurata*. There was a commissioner-general, the *magister*, who supervised the races and compiled the programs *(libelli)*, which were hawked among the crowd and which carried the names of the horses and charioteers.

Every faction had its own supporters who, in time, ended by attracting people of the same shade of political opinion, as well as breeders *(agitatores)*, veterinarians, tailors, saddlers, and more or less famous charioteers, who were usually people of humble origin.

The charioteers rode standing in their cars, their heads protected by casques, with whip in hand, buskined from ankle to thigh, wearing a coat in their faction's color, with the reins wrapped around their middles, which permitted them to throw their full weight on the horse's mouth at the curves by leaning backward. At the waist, the charioteer carried a dagger so that in the event of a fall he could cut the reins *(habenae)*, whence come the expressions *adducere, premere habenas*, meaning to drag on the reins or slow down, and *dare, effundere habenas*, to give rein or accelerate.

The best charioteers usually became rich and famous, for in addition to the large fees they received from their supporters, they had gifts from the emperors and the magistrates. *Milliarii* was the name given those who had won more than a thousand victories, like the celebrated Scopus, who had 1,043; Pompey Epaphroditus, with 1,467; Pompey Musclosus, called Diocles, who won 3,559 times in a two-horse

chariot and 1,442 in a quadriga, and had 35 million sesterces in the bank when he retired at forty in 150.

It was customary, during the races, to distribute *panem* (bread), gifts, sweetmeats, travel tokens, farms, houses, in fact, anything to distract and quiet the more turbulent of the spectators. As a matter of fact, violent altercations between the supporters of the different factions were forever breaking out, and even the emperors did not hold themselves aloof.

Caracalla actually killed the charioteer of the hated Green team. Vitellius, who had lost a packet on the Green, had a few of the Blues murdered. Upon the death of Domitian (Juvenal's "Bald Nero"), Martial, a fan who was lost (as was his money occasionally) to all but the Greens, since he bet on them continually, wrote to the effect that, Domitian alive or dead, the same people are winning the palms. So the Greens won even without the threatening intervention of Domitian!

It is said that Caligula passed days at a time inspecting the Greens' horses in their stable, and even dined there, then ended by poisoning the Blues' charioteer. Finally, Theodosius was forced to pass a law that forbade doping, whether to stimulate a horse or keep him back.

A good deal of betting, at the Circus and off-track as well, must have been done if, as Varro tells us, there were people who came to the races with a cageful of carrier pigeons, which they released after each event, with a slip giving the results tied to a leg.

It got to the point where the State held about fourteen thousand horses, all of which were distributed to the various factions, which were responsible for their upkeep and employment. The regulations were precise and strict, and a second offender could even be put to death. There is a letter from Simmaechus to one of his agents in Spain, ordering him to find some new horseflesh, as the public had grown tired of always seeing the same animals running.

Horses raced with their tails done up in a knot, the mane ornamented with bows and beads, with amulets at the ends. The race began near the *carceres*, on a line diagonal to the track, to give an even chance to the two-horse chariots on the outside; and the start was given by the *designator*, or marker, who in early times waved a torch. Later, a white flag came into use. The stewards at the finish *(moratores)* waited at the white line *(alba linea* or *calx*, so called because it was marked with chalk). To count the laps, there were markers called *delphini* (dolphins), in homage to Neptune, of *falae* and *ovaria*, egg-shaped marble counters, to honor Castor.

Not only speed, but the ability to negotiate the curves determined the winner, as well as the use of the right tactics. One way, *occupare et vincere* ("get in and win"), was to take the lead and hold it to win. *Superare et vincere* ("beat 'em and win") involved overtaking and passing the field after the halfway mark, to come in first. *Erumpere et vincere* ("break out and win") called for holding back and then making an all-out effort, coming down the homestretch, to finish first.

Turns were made to the left, and the curves were very strait. Going into one, the horses on the inside (called *funales*, since they were hitched with ropes, *funi*), had no bits, and the reins connected to a nose-band, or muzzle, that might have had "Sicilian barnacles" of knurled iron pinching the nose, knew how to wheel the car around (the two on the left brak-

---

* A little under three furlongs.—TRANS.

ing), while those on the outside swung around with enough momentum to counteract the centrifugal force of the inside two harnessed to the shaft, turning their force centripetal inasmuch as the shaft was connected by a belt to the girth of the horse to the right. If the turn were too narrow, the chariot could crack up. Were it too wide, the car could be overturned by the one behind it or, in any case, lose ground.

The chassis of the chariot, which was very heavy at the outset, was improved technically, bit by bit, to make it as simple and light as possible, until it was reduced to the essentials: a framework with a shaft, running boards, two wheels, and a wickerwork dash for the charioteer's protection.

Every horse was provided with a certificate of origin. The colts were trained at the *Basilica equestris,* a covered ground near where the Palazzo Farnese now stands. After being broken at the age of two, they started, at three, being broken to harness, and schooled so as to race when they were at least five years old. For each stage of work and diet, there was an exact and scrupulous procedure that was passed on by word of mouth from one trainer to the next. Above all, when a race was imminent, care was taken to assure the animals' absolute tranquillity. As evidence of this, one need only mention that, on the eve of a race, Caligula forbade the Praetorian Guard to sound its trumpets so as not to disturb their faction's horses.

A turning point in ancient times was marked by Cannae (216 B.C.), for that battle showed that popular conscription was a social and economic waste. From that time onward, the army of professional soldiers was to prevail. Never again did Rome resort to an army of citizens and farmers after the defeat it suffered at the hands of Hannibal. Of course, the conscript army did not fade away at one fell swoop, but by 202, at the Battle of Zama Regia, the victorious outcome was decided by the Numidian cavalry.

Thenceforth, though, cavalry victories were to mark the setbacks of the Roman army throughout its history. At Carrae, in 53 B.C., the heavy infantry of Crassus crumbled before the Parthian horsemen. Munda, Caesar's last battle, was a triumph for Bocchus' Mauretanian mounted contingent. Again, near Mysia, in 260, the Mauretanians routed the bellicose Pannonian legions and, in a second fight near Mysia, Constans' *clibanari,* armored warriors, defeated Magnentius and his half-German army. Finally, a single cavalry charge by the Goths and Alani decided the issue at the Battle of Adrianopolis in 378.

Notwithstanding, the Romans insisted upon their type of fighting, with cohorts drawn up in serried ranks, flanked by lightly armed cavalry, or else they established the *limes,* palisaded earthworks to halt the onslaught of the barbarians, while refusing to modernize their offensive and defensive warfare.

Rome, rather than learning the new ways of war from the East that it so much feared, and instead of attempting to understand the needs of the new society that pressed against its confines, at a given moment, with the arrival of the Eastern emperors, imported the custom of dynastic succession to replace the adoptive system, which was so fundamental to Roman thinking and which had awarded the right to the throne not only upon the basis of heredity but also upon grounds of capability and intelligence.

After the defeat of Valerian by Shapur, it was actually the armored troops of an Arab, Odenathus of Palmyra, that recouped Roman prestige in the East. He routed the Sassanid cavalry and restored Rome's power along the old frontier between Persia and Egypt, thanks to his hard-riding and superbly mobile mounted troops.

Failure to defend the frontier during Valerian's reign had demonstrated that the Sassanids' military tactics could not be withstood by using methods that had been previously effective. It was to Diocletian's credit that he provided for border defense on new bases, creating an adequate system of fortifications that not only extended along the frontier but also went deep enough into the surrounding area to present an obstacle to the Persian cavalry. At the same time, he organized new cavalry units, and even enlisted the services of the Bedouin, Goths, Burgundians, Syrians, Itureans, and Commageni, as well as the Mauretanians and Numidians. Thus, it was the East that imposed upon Rome its own peculiar methods of combat, while the Illyrians continued to provide the empire with their indomitable force and unremitting valor.

It should be noted that the Germans, in combat, had always struck the Romans as madmen gone berserk. Rome was convinced that the apparent lack of cold calculation and ordered discipline would always deny their enemies the final triumph. With time, however, it dawned upon them that the German attack, which was based upon the interaction of cavalry and infantry, could be effective.

If Caracalla and Maximinus owed their major successes to their shrewd use of the catapult, it was Alexander Severus who equipped his cavalry with arms and armor copied from the Persians. After his first happy experiment, he ordered his cavalry into *catafracti* and *clibanari,* the first being armored warriors, and the second, armored warriors on horses that were armored, as well. Alexander Severus led these units to the Rhine, and there inflicted heavy losses upon the Alemanni. When Maximinus stormed over the Venetian plain with the legions of the Danube, there rode on the flank squadrons of cataphracts supported by Oriental guards, Mauretanian lancers, and German cavalry.

It is odd to reflect that in the period immediately following, nothing more was heard of armored, mounted troops except in the battles between Odenathus and the Sassanids. We see, however, that Aurelian introduced a new tactic against the army of Zenobia of Palmyra. The Dalmatian cavalry was given the mission of tiring the armored troops that were trying to strike with full force by feigning flight and drawing the Palmyrans into pursuit, which they did. When their pursuers were exhausted by the heat, their own efforts, and the dust, so that their resistance was utterly gone, the Dalmatians rounded on them and put their pursuers to rout.

In a second great encounter, however, the Palmyran cataphracts were on their guard, and after long temporizing, inflicted such damage on the Dalmatian cavalry that only the intervention of the Roman infantry saved the day. By that time, the cataphracts had become indispensable. The reliefs on the Arch of Galerius in Salonika show them side by side with the *clibanari,* whose armor not only covers the horsemen but also reaches down to the horses' knees. A detachment of *clibanari,* disposed in a wedge, halted the march of the Gallo-Germanic troops of Constantine when he appeared in northern Italy.

For the first time, then, we have caught up with the medieval knight, for there is only a short step to go from the armor of the *clibanari* to that of the King of Sweden. The later Roman *clibanarius* is easily recognizable in his Germanic heir.

King Arthur, archetype of the hero of the age of chivalry, was nothing less than the leader of a troop of cataphracts, and in the most ancient of traditions, bore a Roman title. His armor was a helmet with a golden dragon and a cuirass, its Roman origin apparent even then in the Celtic model.

Since the most responsible portion of the empire's population had been decimated by war, Rome was forced to resort to peoples beyond its borders to serve in its army. The Germans were an intact power, a reserve of bold men whose natural inclination made warfare their trade. If, up to that time, foreign barbarians had been opposed by others who were within the confines of the empire, thenceforth there was the risk of confronting foreign elements with others equally foreign. It was, therefore, inevitable that an encounter would take place between the foreign barbarians and the traditional elements of the army.

Marcus Aurelius and Commodus had already made use of Quadi and Marcomanni in the army, but it was Caracalla who raised an élite guard, called "The Lions," from German troops on the Danube frontier.

Maximinus, who had Gothic blood in his veins, used Germanic cavalry, and employed them in the riskiest engagements and in every mission that was particularly dangerous. Even his rivals, the emperors nominated by the Senate, Pupienus and Balbinus, had instituted their own bodyguard made up of German soldiers to counterbalance the strength of the Praetorian Guard garrisoned in the city.

Gordianus III conducted the Persian campaign with contingents of Gothic and Germanic cavalry, while Postumus depended upon Frankish units. Claudius established colonies of conquered Germans, and incorporated these people into his own army, but when they proved unruly, he divided them into groups of fifty or sixty under each centurion. Under Constantine, the ancient Illyrian courage ran out at Pons Milvius before the Gallo-Germanic cavalry. Thenceforth, Roman coins were to bear, not the old motto *virtus illirici*, but *virtus exercitus gallicani*.

In contradistinction to the border defense *(limitanei)*, stable and monolithic, detachments of mixed nationalities, *vexillationes*, began to be formed under direct command of the emperor. In these, the cavalry comprised the nucleus and shock troops, a professional, specialist corps *(comitatenses)* that cost a good deal to maintain.

Even the Mauretanian lancers were mounted, and they were disposed in open formation. Their fame went back a long way. Habituated by violence and rapine to the trade of arms, the Mauretanians, who were nomads like the Scythians and Sarmatians, were taken captive with difficulty. Such expert horsemen were they that they could ride headlong without using a bridle, utilizing just the weight of their bodies or a twig to direct the horse, which was a small, high-spirited animal, ridden without saddle or bridle, with only a neck strap. The Mauretanian cavalry broke the resistance of the Carpi under Philip the Arab, who lived in Dacia. If it had not been for a terrible epidemic that decimated the Mauretanian contingent, perhaps the Battle of Carrae would not have had the disastrous outcome of which we have read.

Under Gallienus, a new role was found for the Mauretanians. He combined them with the Illyrian cavalry to form a large reserve of mounted troops attached to the headquarters command at the emperor's base camp. Wearing short cuirasses and carrying long lances, the Mauretanians and Dalmatians fought side by side for a long period wherever it became vital to decide the turn of the battle. They crushed the legions of Pannonia and Mysia that had rebelled against Gallienus,* and supported the emperor on the outskirts of Milan when he besieged Aureolus. The Mauretanians formed the contingent picked to spearhead the reconquest of the Oriental provinces.

Another African nation that supplied cavalry forces was the Belmi, from the region of the Upper Nile, whom we can readily identify in the friezes of the Arch of Constantine because they carry their arrows stuck through a headcloth rather than in a quiver. Thus, Orientals and Africans were aligned with Illyrians, and acquired a certain distinction among the components of the Roman army. Notwithstanding, the greatest rivals of the Illryians were the Germanic troops.

Ultimately, the ranks of the Roman army included Alani, then Huns, and finally there came the time when the infantry no longer felt sure of itself in combat without the support of the crack cavalry of the Goths. It was the well-organized cavalry that decided, for instance, the Battle of

---

* Shortly afterward, Gallienus was killed at Milan by his own troops, in 268 c.e.—Trans.

---

27 *Commodus hunting. Note the ancient way of holding the reins. The inner side of the sandals is flat, possibly to permit a firm hold on the horse's barrel. Museo Nazionale, Naples.*

28 *Caligula and his horse Incitatus, looking like a Thoroughbred. The rider is seated very far back. Museo Nazionale, Naples.*

29 *Bronze head, noteworthy for the complicated, ornamented bridle. Castellamare di Stabia, Italy.*

30 *Bronze statuette of Alexander the Great. Note the breastplate and girth securing the* ephippion *that flares at the withers. Museo Nazionale, Naples.*

31 *Parading youth group of Virunum, mid-second century c.e. The horses foreshadow the medieval Germanic type. Note the padded saddlecloth, the crupper, and breastplate. Museum Klagenfurt, Austria.*

32 33 34 *The Arch of Constantine. Note the saddles, cruppers, and breastplates detailed in relief. The horsemen are fairly erect, mounted on their thighs, while those shown in Trajan's Column are seated on the buttocks and in simpler saddles. Rome.*

35 *A Noric horse, from the stele of Silius. The saddle already has a pommel and cantle, though it lacks stirrups. Museo di Magonza, Italy.*

36 *Trajan's Column: the Moorish cavalry of Lucius Quietus, riding bareback. Rome.*

37 *Trajan's Column: the roman cavalry routs the Sarmatian cataphracts. Note the horses' eye protectors. Rome.*

27

29

30

28

31

32 33

34

35 36

37

38

39

40

Adrianopolis. A contemporary author wrote: "[The cavalry] shot like a bolt of lightning among the enemy, and everything before it was struck down by the charge." Just twenty years before, like a bolt of lightning, the King of the Goths had routed the Roman army, and even at that time, the strike had been spearheaded, with savage fury, by the cavalry.

The cavalry had always been too costly inasmuch as it called for a period of training that was much longer and more complex than that required by any other arm of the military. Also, it was difficult to keep it up to strength should men and animals be lost. Horses, furthermore, are animals that have always been particularly vulnerable to epidemics and the wear and tear of service. For these reasons, Roman generals tried to restrict cavalry engagements to favorable terrain and to those instances where they would be supported by other arms of the service. There is no doubt that cavalry demands a situation tailored to its style of combat and to tactics studiously developed upon the basis of the terrain and the disposition of other forces available.

Perhaps it was these limitations that underlay Rome's lack of enthusiasm for mounted troops, considering the cavalry as an arm to be used only when success was virtually guaranteed. On the other hand, it was a unit that, badly used, could act to the detriment of the infantry itself.

Rome was cautious in its employment of the cavalry, and preferred to borrow when it could. Some consideration had been given to integrating the mounted troops on loan into the regular army by improving their equipment, training, and discipline, and giving them experienced commanders, but even this possibility was limited in the proportion that available funds could cover the additional expenditures. The ever-growing arms appropriation had increased fiscal pressure to a point where it was well-nigh intolerable. When the last financial reserves had gone, it was inevitable that the quality of the army would suffer and, with it, the soundness of the cavalry.

XVIII
THE WHEEL

The invention of the wheel as an element of terrestrial locomotion undoubtedly was an outgrowth of agricultural activity in an area so well demarcated as to be identifiable as western Asia, whence it spread to the Mediterranean, thence to Africa, and, only some time later, in the Age of Bronze, to reach the extreme fringe of the Asian Orient. An invention of capital importance, the wheel so stupefied people that it came to be considered a gift of the gods.

38 *Four-wheeled wagon with arched staves and cushion seat, a traveling coach of the fourth century. The heads of the horses are stylized, a convention that was to be followed in Germany during the High Renaissance. Church of St. Mary of Saal, Klagenfurt, Austria.*

39 *Large wagon from Vaison-la-Romaine. Musée Calvet, Avignon, France.*

40 *Harness with possibly a species of collar, harness saddle, breeching, and straps. The heavy Noric horses wear what appears to be a sort of sandal held in place above the joint.*

In the Near East, means of transport with wheels appeared during the prehistoric era, as necessity demanded, for farming, commercial, and ceremonial use. The oldest types of Mesopotamian carts are known to us through the discovery at Tepe Gawra of terra-cotta statuettes (end of the first quarter of the third millenium B.C.). Some of these have two wheels, an open box up front, and a ledge seat and footboard for the driver. Other carts have four wheels, and some, a covering that was probably of leather. Other little clay models, from Kis (third millenium B.C., probably protodynastic), have either two or four wheels, with the rear of the cart higher than the sides.

A votive object from a temple at Tell Agrab is a cart drawn by four horses (perhaps onagers). The two in the middle are harnessed, while the ones at the sides are hitched to the collars of the other two. The four wheels are made of wooden segments bound and clinched by four double pegs, and the rims are reinforced by metal strips, such as one sees in the protodynastic seals and in the famous standard from the royal tombs at Ur (2500–2350 B.C.). The Ur standard shows a four-wheeled war wagon that is quite complex, as it has a protected rear platform jutting out behind. There are four harnessed beasts at whose feet lie slain warriors.

Even in India and China, two-wheeled carts were used, but there, the wheels were of enormous diameter, because of the marshy or sandy terrain. Such huge wheels were not needed over the flat, hard, rocky land of Mesopotamia. Besides, in China, the horse came long after the ox. Carts such as those depicted at Mohenjo-Daro (West Pakistan) or at Astara (Asia) or those of the Liang dynasty are still in use today in Pakistan and in many Indian villages.

The cart with solid wheels used by certain aristocratic castes in Mesopotamia was replaced by the war or hunting cart introduced around the middle of the second millenium by the "mountain people," the Assyrians. This type had a platform with a ledge sufficiently high to provide support for the one or two occupants who were busy fighting or driving the team. The spoked wheels were attached to the underpart of the platform, so that the weight of it was almost wholly sustained by the horses. The war carts were finished in bronze, while those for hunting or touring were somewhat lighter.

In northern Syria and Anatolia appeared a cart that had a long shaft stemming from the upper part of the box, which was generally rectangular and was carried on four-spoke wheels. These carts are similar to those we can see in the Hittite reliefs dating from the first centuries of the first millenium, although the Hittite carts had eight-spoke wheels and two crossed quivers affixed to the box. These quivers also appear in the Egyptian reliefs of the New Kingdom. Of particular interest are the crossed boards that support wooden panels, and the eyelets above the shaft to accommodate the reins.

XIX
HARNESS AND CARTS

The horse-drawn war cart was introduced into Egypt, as well, from Hittite and Syrian territory at the beginning of the XVIII Dynasty. The first mention made of it is in the Carnarvon tablet, which records the defeat of the Hyksos. The foreign origin of the cart, which had a semioval box with wide lateral openings, a shaft coming from the rear of the box, and four-spoke wheels, is attested by the Semitic names given it: *mrkbt* for a hunting or war cart drawn by horses, and *grt* for the same, pulled by oxen.

Besides the reliefs showing the manufacture of carts, like the one from Tomb 86 of Menkhepere-Seneb at Seyh Abd el-Qurna (reign of Thutmose III, circa 1475 B.C.) and the Saitic relief in the Archaeological Museum in Florence, there are some war carts from the Theban tombs of the XVIII Dynasty, such as the one made of oak, ash, and hornbeam, covered in leather, at the same museum; and the magnificent treasure carts of Tutankhamen, richly decorated with gold relief and inlays of enamel and semiprecious stones. Syrian war carts appear in temple reliefs of the XIX Dynasty (Karnak, Abydos, Abu Simbel, Thebes), celebrating the exploits of Seti I, Ramses II, and Ramses III.

One of the oldest examples of a Cretan cart is a clay model from Palaikastro (Middle Minoan), which has a large rectangular box whose four sides have painted polychrome panels. This cart has solid wheels painted with three concentric circles over crossed lines, showing the active transition toward the spoked wheel. The most ancient Cretan carts have two four-spoke wheels and a very long shaft that comes from the upper part of the box. Starting with Late Minoan I (1450 B.C.), a cart appears with a pole that springs from the bottom of the box, which is arched, in the Syrian and Hittite style.

The war cart was introduced into Greece from Anatolia (according to some authorities, it came from Crete) shortly after the middle of the second millenium, but after its heyday during the Homeric Age, it rapidly fell into disuse, and remained as a heroic and mythologic emblem in legendary scenes on Corinthian and Attic vases and Clazomenaean sarcophagi, but just as a light racing vehicle.

The Homeric cart (ἄρμα, ὀχεία) has a box (δίφρος) poised on two wheels (τρόχοι, κύκλα) held together by a plank and reinforced by metal plates. Usually, there are spokes, and the sides of the cart are reduced to a curved wooden bar. The shaft (ῥυμός) is integral with the box and joined to it by a fixed connector. Only at the time of the black-figured vases did the Greek cart adopt the fork (στήριγμα) to support the shaft; otherwise, the shaft is connected to the *antyx* (rail around the front of the chariot) by a leather belt that already had been depicted in Assyrian reliefs and is distinct from the reins held in hand by the driver and from the harness that hitches the horses to the shaft.

The Greek *biga*, that is, the war chariot with a box closed in front, on two wheels, and having, at the most, a panel highest in front and decreasing in height on both sides going toward the rear, resembled the most popular Etruscan vehicle, which had, perhaps, a period of practical use much longer than it had enjoyed in Greece, in view of the rolling plains of Roman Etruria.

With the development of the cavalry, the use of the chariot became more and more restricted to chieftains and military leaders, who could better command the field of battle from such a vehicle and be more easily seen by their men.

The last appearance of the cart in any artistic depiction of war is in the mosaic in the House of the Faun, in Pompeii, which shows the Battle of Issus. At the time of that event, although the chariot had already fallen into disuse in the

Mediterranean region, it still preserved an emblematic significance in Persia.

Using carts in the city was complicated because it was difficult to turn around. The streets were one-way, and only at intersections and squares could one manage to change direction.

XX
SLEDGES

The use of vehicles that slide along the ground, for all that they are of the remotest origin, seems always to have been somewhat limited and sporadic, even in the Arctic. Egypt, in its earliest days, had sledges that ran on wooden runners, serving to transport even boats from one canal to another. The practical development of the sledge, however, came in northern and eastern Europe. Among the most ancient examples in use in the Western world are the four sleighs discovered in 1908 in the tomb-ship of Osberg (Folk Museum, Oslo). Each of these has a small rectangular box set on two high skate runners with barbaric decoration, and they probably date from the second century B.C.

There exist examples of sixteenth-century processional sledges, richly and heavily ornamented. One, belonging to the emperor Maximilian I, has decoration, hangings, and harness combining to form a harmonious whole. Others were completely transfigured by allegorical scenes ("Justice with Sword and Balance," "The Treasure Ship," and so on), like the sleigh from the court of Dresden. There were also the vehicles used by the court jesters, but since these had decorations of papier-mâché, they have not survived. Then there were the baroque sledges of Frederick I (the Centaur, Samson, and Apollo sleighs), and the rococo models of the eighteenth century in southern Germany, Venice, and Leningrad, which had clusters of figures at the rear of the sleigh.

At the end of the eighteenth century, the vogue for the sleigh as an elegant plaything declined, and around 1770, the architect André Jacques Roubo designed a simple, practical type that had little decoration, and completely eschewed figurative fancies.

XXI
TOURING

People did a good deal of traveling during classical antiquity. The Romans, including magistrates, soldiers, noblemen, traders, and artists, voyaged even more than the Greeks, and they preferred to go by sea, since travel by land was rendered even more inadvisable by the absence of decent inns. Despite stricter and stricter laws applied to innkeepers, these continued to know how to take advantage of their guests, as they still do.

One traveled in a *lectica* (litter) or a sedan chair *(sella gestatoria)* borne by two to eight liveried slaves. These were the only means of transport tolerated in the cities, where the

41 42 43 44 *The four factions of the Circus Maximus. Museo Nazionale delle Terme, Rome.*

41

42

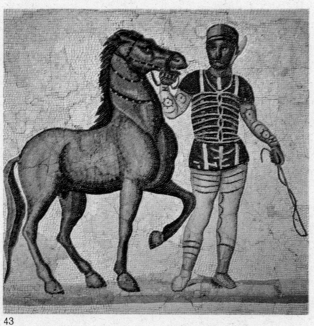

43

44

45

46

law prohibited the use of carts on the streets during the daytime. As for vehicles, there were three kinds: processional, touring, and freight. Of the parade and sport models, the two-wheeled *currus*, lumbering and heavily decorated, continued to be used for triumphs, while there was the lighter, more dashing *biga* for racing.

Among the vehicles used in ceremonials was the *tensa*, a two-wheeled cart with a very large rectangular box, pilastered and corniced; the *pilentum*, which was of Etruscan origin and had four strongly rimmed wheels. This cart was first reserved for the Vestals and priests, but later, with the laws of 359 B.C., was permitted to matrons, as well.

Vehicles for touring included the *carpentum*, originally Etruscan, which had a covering all around, and was an elegant cart that was generally drawn by mules. Since only ladies of the imperial family could use the *carpentum* in town, it is undoubtedly this turnout that we see on the coins of the empire depicting women.

The *reda*, imported from the Gauls, had four wheels and a number of rows of benches for passengers. It was drawn by pairs. The *petorritum* was also Gallic in origin, but a bit smaller. There was the *carruca*, of which we know of one type used by the magistrates, having a throne in the middle, behind which stood two lictors, and another, for traveling, that was closed on three sides and had seats for two persons in the rear.

The *carruca dormitoria* was covered by an awning that also curtained off the driver's station in the rear, a species of bed curtain. Of British origin was the two-wheeled *cisium*, a light hack that was stationed at the gates of the city. Driven by a *cisarius*, it could be rented with or without the chauffeur. Finally, there was the *essedum*, another light carriage; fast, with twelve-spoke wheels, Gallic in origin, and driven by an *essedarius*.

For freight, there were such vehicles as the *plaustrum*, which was used to transport farm produce, having two solid wheels and a trellised top going over the sides; the *carrus*, four-wheeled, the two in front spoked, and the sides of the cart composed of planking; the *arcera*, which was a species of stretcher-cart for the sick; the *serracum*, which had small, solid wheels and carried heavy cargoes; and the *corvinus*, of Celtic origin.

It should be remembered that, from 45 B.C., vehicles were prohibited within the confines of Rome (Lex Julia Municipalis). In other cities, they were allowed to traffic only at night. Claudius extended the prohibition on the circulation of all means of transport and of quadrupeds to every city in Italy because of a number of incidents arising either out of a lack of respect for pedestrians or because of traffic jams. Regulations were also in force to limit the maximum load that could be carried over certain arteries of traffic and on specified roads and bridges.

45 *Races at the Circus Maximus. Detail showing a quadriga. Museo Lapidario, Foligno, Italy.*

46 *A stunt man's acrobatics during a chariot race. Naturally, the harness simulates the ancient type that would have been used, but the wheels are equipped with foot brakes. Still from the film* Ben Hur.

On the other hand, we know that in Byzantium, a city that had been built as an entity and with the benefit of more sophisticated city planning than had been provided for the old cities of Italy, the "carriage way" was very busy. There were gilded carts, painted in a variety of colors, preceded by liveried eunuchs. In such carts ladies sat or even reclined on palliasses. One of the models might have been suggested by the cart of Cybele and Attis, having a box with a high, almost semicircular backrest, the outer edges of which were decorated by sculptured figures. The cart had six-spoke wheels, and is the one incised on the silver dish of Parabiago (ninth century, Milan, Museum of Castello Sforza).

We know from the Trier Ivory (sixth century, from the cathedral treasures) that luxury carriages were used. This shows a cart with a high quadrangular seat supported on four eight-spoke wheels, with no backrest, the edges high and richly carved, a high stool for one passenger and a lower one for the driver.

There were also mail carts, but we have no idea what they were like. The racing cars, however, were similar to the Roman ones, but more opulently decorated and brightly colored.

XXII
THE POST

A state postal service, operating regularly and continually, was organized for the first time by Darius of Hydaspae in the fifth century B.C., a facility that endured even in the Hellenistic states that sprang up after the fall of Alexander's empire. The most sophisticated mail system, however, was that of the Roman Empire, both for its efficiency and for the security of its lines of communication. Along the military roads raced postal cars and couriers as fast as they could go. From the Augustan period on, the mail service had various designations: *cursus publicus, cursus vetricularis, cursus fiscalis,* and *res verediaria.*

Direction of the post offices was the responsibility of the prefect of each *praetorium*. Under Constantine, the service was even more refined. In the provinces, the *praesides*, or governors, of each one had a magistrate reporting to him charged solely with running the postal system. He was required to maintain the roads and keep the bridges in good repair. The provinces, in turn, were divided into a number of postal districts, each under a director *(manceps)* who had working for him a number of functionaries *(apparitores)*, some of whom *(stationari)* took care of changing the post horses, while others, *muliones* and *hippocomi*, handled the animals or, if *mulomedici* and *veterinari*, treated and doctored them; some worked in the stables *(stratores)* or repaired the carts *(carpentari)*.

The post horses were strong and swift, and their drivers did not hesitate to whip them up to make them run faster. Some drivers even used clubs, which led to a law in defense of the horses, prescribing severe penalties for any who resorted to that method.

Only occasionally could private citizens avail themselves of the state system. Instead, they formed their own services, using slaves, *tabellari*, to carry the mail within the city limits, and *cursores* for long-distance deliveries.

XXIII
BITS

Xenophon describes and recommends the use of two bits: one, a soft type with "wide little disks," and the other, hard, "with a sharp and pointed mouthpiece, so that when he [the horse] has been trained with the hard bit, and then switched to the soft, the pleasure that he feels will incline him to obey and do willingly all that he learned when the hard bit was used."

The bit of antiquity was different from ours. If the parts that held it in place, presumably of leather, were similar to what we use today—headstall (κορυφαία), cheeks (κατατείνοντα), and browband (κεκρύφαλος), the metallic parts were different, since there was neither curb nor snaffle.

Since there was no snaffle, there was only one rein and one cheek. But how was the bit held? Perhaps the cheek was forked or a split leather band came from the middle of the headstall and was able to support the bit and prevent it from slipping out of the horse's mouth.

The reins were attached—and Xenophon states this clearly—either to two rings or two hooks that could be detached or fixed to the mouthpiece. So adjusted, the action of the bit must have been similar to that of our snaffle, exerting pressure primarily at the corners of the mouth. One can, however, imagine types of rigid bits (and Xenophon mentions these) that multiplied the pulling force. As a matter of fact, when the bridle is attached to the lower ring, there is a very strong pull; the "little disks" press on the tongue, and the teeth of the mouthpiece upon the bars. A bit like that must have been a veritable instrument of torture. No wonder Xenophon insists so strongly upon a light hand. If we bear in mind, however, the fact that the Greek horseman was relatively unstable on horseback, we can understand that he would have need for something in hand with which, without ceremony, he could control his animal. Nevertheless, that bit, and the unattached one, as well, forced the horse of ancient time to keep his mouth half open, as he is usually depicted in sculpture.

In the Middle Ages, the bit became a sort of lever with a small plate that pressed against the tongue and on the palate, and had cheekpieces as long as eight inches. In the High Renaissance, the snaffle and bit came into use, with the four reins they required, since better breeds were being ridden by that time.

XXIV
STIRRUPS AND SADDLES

"Were it not for man's unprogressiveness, it would be inexplicable that, though so important a military invention as the bridle bit dates from the early Bronze Age, if not still farther back, saddles were unknown in Europe until the fourth century c.e., and then remained without stirrups until the reign of the Emperor Maurice (A.D. 582–602)." So wrote J. F. C. Fuller in *Armament and History*.

That delay does have an understandable motive. Try changing from an English saddle to a military one and then to a Western tree, and you will feel as if you had lost all contact with the horse, as well as the unpleasant suspicion that you cannot control his actions. The same progression obtains in going from riding bareback to a saddlecloth, *ephippion*, and padded saddle. These accessories that come between horse and rider definitely change the horseman's seat, and he finds himself constrained to regain his equilibrium and make a slight adjustment in the way he uses his leg muscles. It is like starting to ride right from the beginning all over again.

On the other hand, the advantages that stirrups offer the horsemen are such that one is hard put to believe just how slow was the progress of this aid, which appeared in India in the second century c.e., emigrated to China, and arrived at Constantinople at the beginning of the seventh century. It is even more perplexing when one considers that riding with the legs swinging free produces specific circulatory disturbances, mentioned by Varro and other writers.

Once Maurice became acquainted with stirrups, he introduced them into the massive force of the Byzantine cavalry, thus completing the saddle, which had already come to the Western world around the fourth century—as we learn from Johannes Zonaras, chronicler of the wars between Constans and Constantine.* It was in Byzantium that an order was issued forbidding cavalrymen to use saddles weighing more than 286 pounds, such had become the vogue for piling them with covers and cushions, embellishing them with encrustations of metal and stones, and hanging them with bags for booty. The *ephippion* had taken six centuries to become a saddle, right and proper, but it still lacked stirrups.

The *ephippion* is probably portrayed with particular exactitude in the small bronze statue of Alexander the Great on horseback, at the Museum of Naples. While the horse, who could be Bucephalus, hindquarters bent, lifts his forelegs in an attitude similar to the *courbette* (a stylized rendering, modish at that period but, nevertheless, undoubtedly deriving from a real air that must have been much appreciated at the time), the rider sits well over the horse's kidneys, his left leg hugging the end of the ribs, and his right directly over the point of the hip. Alexander is about to let fly the javelin in his right hand while his left pulls on the reins, and he seems to be clinging to the front of the *ephippion*. This looks as if the *ephippion* were made of leather; it has a very high breastplate and a broad girth. The bridle, which also must be of leather, has worked metal closures holding the various parts together, and a split headstall to secure the bit.

In the celebrated "Battle of Issus," to be seen at Pompeii, Alexander sits astride his horse close to the withers, as if to drive the animal forward just as fast as possible in pursuit of the fleeing Darius.

---

* Youngest and eldest, respectively, of the three sons of Constantine the Great.—TRANS.

47 *Chariot race. Roman terra cotta of the first century* c.e. *British Museum, London.*

48 *Quadrigas at the meta. Still from the film* Ben Hur.

49 *Detail from a Roman mosaic showing the names of the charioteer and his horses. Note the woven reed body of the quadriga. Museo Arqueológico, Barcelona.*

47

49

48

50

51

The sculpture on Trajan's Column (A.D. 113) and the Arch of Constantine (A.D. 315) show the evolution of the saddle during the Roman period. On the first, we see a saddle-cloth firmly held in place by a breastplate, crupper, and girth. The horseman appears merely to be perched among the folds of the saddlecloth, which seems to flutter at the bottom, as if it were made of some very light fabric.

On the Arch of Constantine, the saddle has a girth, a very ornate breastplate, and a solid crupper, as we can deduce from the strongly curving relief; and at the very edge the effect is of a wooden core, while small pads of quilting in high relief descend from the forehand, seeming to form a sheath from the forearm down to the knee.

As a matter of fact, saddles were already being made of a rigid wooden frame covered with cloth and stuffed with fleece. The trees were, increasingly, acutely arched and padded to give the rider more stability. They became so heavy that Emperor Theodosius had to limit their weight to sixty pounds.

The Orientals had already introduced the West to the use of the lady's saddle.

Stirrups and horseshoes do not appear illustrated in Western documentation before the ninth century. Nevertheless, we have reason to believe that, in the instance, depiction of these aids was well behind their actual application. A stirrup was found in the tomb of Charles Martel (690?–741), which shows how rare an object it was, at least in France, at that time. The stirrup, however, as well as the horseshoe, became solidly established under Charlemagne.

The stirrup also brought with it a revolution in the handling of the lance. There were two methods, the old and the new. In the old way, the lance was used like a javelin; it was carried high over the shoulder, by the horseman, so that it could be thrown, even if not very far. Using the new method, a very much longer and heavier lance was employed. It was first carried with the hilt underarm; shortly afterward, it was suspended and balanced against a hook called the rest. "Lance at the rest" quickly came to signify a cavalryman ready to charge.

XXV
BYZANTIUM

It is to be supposed that the first true creators of systematic, virtuoso equitation—and by that we mean "school riding"—were the Byzantines, whom fate led to model their equestrian manners on those of their eternal enemies, the Persians—a people who by the fourth century B.C. were already the most finished of horsemen.

The Persian aristocracy had royal riding academies at its disposal in the capital and in every satrapy, and the academies were required to see that every horse was put through the particular dressage that would fit him to compete in the intricate and arduous games of polo that were the chief delight of the Achaemenid and, subsequently, the Sassanid courts. It was from the Persians that the Byzantines learned how to deck and groom their horses so magnificently. From the Persians, too, they took an aesthetic and precious mannerism, which was quite in keeping with their own character. Given that, the passage to equestrian virtuosity was an obvious progression.

In a riding academy, where speed is impossible, there is a natural tendency to kill time on virtuoso effects, ever more studied and elaborate, in dogged emulation of professional riding masters and dashing young men of the *haute monde*. Looking at some Byzantine mosaics, one might almost believe, and with reason, that the horses they depict are executing the passes, croupades, pirouettes, and other figures that, a thousand years later, were to form the repertoire of school airs. (School riding almost always represents the stylization of social and mental attitudes.)

While *biga* and *quadriga* racing at Rome began to decline because of the increasingly prickly political and economic situations, the sport flourished exuberantly in Byzantium. The Blues and the Greens had arrived at a point where they constituted veritable *demoi* (families) in themselves, with their militias and followers enrolled under definite political and religious platforms. The Blues were the more orthodox, linked to the throne, while the Greens were in opposition.

When the emperor, Justinian, sought to weaken the influence of the two groups, they combined, and on a Sunday in January, 532, in the packed hippodrome, to the cry of "Eternal happiness for the Blues and Greens," proclaimed a new emperor. This was rebellion, and Justinian, then and there, would have fled had it not been for the fiery words of Theodora, who well knew the temper of the heroes of the arena, raised in the circus, as she had been, the daughter of a circus guard. Acting on Theodora's advice, Justinian dealt with the Blues and then moved against the Greens. The insurrection was quashed with the massacre of over thirty thousand people right there in the circus.

The charioteers of the fifth and sixth centuries were the idols of the city, such as Porphyrius during the reign of Anastasius I. Hippodrome intrigues could shape imperial policy. Around the ninth century, however, this state of affairs changed profoundly. The professional charioteers were forgotten or pushed aside, and the amateurs became the crowd-pleasers, men like Basilius the Macedonian and Philoreus, a stableboy, who became the toast of all Byzantium when he galloped around the circus, standing on his horse and brandishing two swords.

Certain aspects of Western "horsemanship," introduced by Manuel Commenus, made the circus, for a time, the byword for exciting equestrian tournaments. It was precisely here that the equestrian art developed, and was later transported to Naples.

Even though the chariots were seen no more in the hippodrome, it continued to draw the princes and nobles who wished to learn the equestrian art and to enjoy a bit of polo.

50 *Sassanid plate, showing a warrior lion hunting, without stirrups, his horse in the attitude of the Chinese flying gallop.*

51 *Arabian horseman, in stirrups, hunting gazelle. The painting shows Persian influence deriving from the Sassanid tradition. National Museum, Damascus, Syria.*

Roads

The Byzantine government did not encourage travel throughout the empire. Communities that stayed put were much more easily controlled and available to the tax collectors. The only migrations that were undertaken, or rather solicited, by the government were the mandatory transfers of the Armenians, who were sent toward Europe, and the Slavs, who were marched in the direction of Asia, to isolate insubordinate tribes. Notwithstanding, permission could be obtained to journey throughout the empire to consult teachers and spiritual advisers or to go on pilgrimages.

Long voyages, generally, were undertaken by sea, but there were excellent roads, kept in perfect condition, although they were closed to civilian traffic during troop movements, which were frequent. The cost of maintaining the roads was met by tolls, from which only civil servants, foreign emissaries, and a few aristocrats were exempt.

The Army

Although they were not naturally bellicose, the Byzantines, eternally surrounded as they were by enemies, were obliged to maintain an active military establishment.

After the debacle at Adrianopolis (378) when the Roman legions demonstrated their utter impotence before the cavalry of the Goths (the victory of Julian over the Germans at Strasbourg in 357 had been the last triumph of Roman infantry over German mounted troops), Theodosius decided to recruit German cavalry to confront the Persian horsemen. These troops were good enough to stop even Attila, but the *foederati*, as they were called, ended by bringing down the empire in the West, under Odoacer.

In the East, the *foederati*, under Leo I and his son-in-law Zeno, were counterbalanced by tribes from the empire that were even more savage than they, the Isauri and Armenians. Subsequently, these latter were offset by the cataphracts from Asia Minor that Procopius so much admired, the very same armored troops that were to decide Justinian's victories.

Since the general, and not the state, was the one to recruit and pay the troops *(bucellarii)*, the system became a perilous affair. What with Justinian's meanness and his reluctance to give his general either authority or funds, the army suffered. Confronted by this situation, later emperors, Tiberius and Maurice, seized the opportunity to reform on new bases of recruitment. Side by side with the *bucellarii* and *foederati*, Tiberius and Maurice trained private citizens, who were called up to serve with the soldiers in border defense. This was the army that Heraclius led to victory in the long campaigns against the Persians, but that same army, sapped by fatigue, was ultimately routed by the force of attack of the Arabian light cavalry, which had better horses.

After that, the *temi* or *regionali* were organized, which were territorials, and the *closure* detachments for permanent duty at the more vulnerable of the mountain passes—troops that proved to be of the utmost value in the guerrilla warfare against the Saracens under the command of the epic Digenis.

Under Nicephorus I (ninth century), the *tagmata*, troopers of the Imperial Guard, grew in importance. They were all mounted on selected horses. There were five regiments of sixteen hundred men each, under command of a *domestico* whose headquarters were in Thrace. They accompanied the emperor on his military sorties—campaigns that became offensive actions under the leadership of Nicephorus II. When the emperor was on maneuvers in Asia, he was accompanied by at least six thousand horsemen, and foot soldiers as well. It was the mounted *tagmata* who literally undid the army of the Saracen general Omar, near the Halys.

Notwithstanding, prudence was the outstanding characteristic of Byzantine strategy. Attacks from barbarians and infidels were so frequent and sudden that an expansionist policy was almost impracticable. Every Byzantine military treaty (one was made in the twelfth century by a woman, Anna Comnena) stressed the empire's right to take precipitate and headlong action, to guard itself against surprise attacks and its troops against ambush, to be able to have its army cover its flanks, and, most important, gave it the option to employ ruse and stratagem. A base military code it was, upholding the stricture of keeping one's word when given, while warmly recommending subterfuge and equivocation to gain time to spy on the enemy, and keeping morale of troops high by giving them news of imaginary victories.

From Byzantine military treaties, one comes to the conclusion that the empire's real force lay in its intelligence and astuteness. Thus, it was easy to fool the Franks; but when it came to the Turks, who were just as clever and had an army that consisted of rank after rank of light horse, the Byzantines were constrained to move cautiously, even though the imperial heavy cavalry could confront that adversary with a maximum of tranquillity.

The Saracens were more to be feared because they had a tremendous number of troops, and were highly mobile. They were, however, less organized than the Byzantines, and did not have the morale to sustain them in defeat. They were also highly sensitive to climatic conditions: the cold and rain depressed them excessively. Night attacks threw them into a panic. Summing up, a chronicler wrote, "The Saracen horsemen could not resist the Byzantine attacks, so the latter had no fear of meeting the Saracens on the field of battle so long as the enemy's forces were not overwhelming in number."

52 *The miracle of St. Florian and St. Lavrenty, a fourth-century icon of the Novgorod school that preserves the most archaic Byzantine characters. Tretyakov Art Gallery, Moscow.*

53 *The quest of Ali and Harousa, eleventh century. Note the short stirrup leathers. Royal Asiatic Society, London.*

54 *"The Three Sons of Shah Jehan," a painting of the Mogul school dating from the sixteenth century. Victoria and Albert Museum, London.*

55 *Engagement of Arab and Norman cavalry. The coats of mail and helmet with nasal recall the Norman crusaders. Painting of the Fatimid dynasty, Egypt, 1160. British Museum, London.*

56 *Knights besieging a fortress. The horsemen have no stirrups; they ride light, brilliant mounts, and employ the lance like a javelin. Byzantine miniature from the "Evangel 74." Bibliothèque National, Paris.*

53

54

55

56

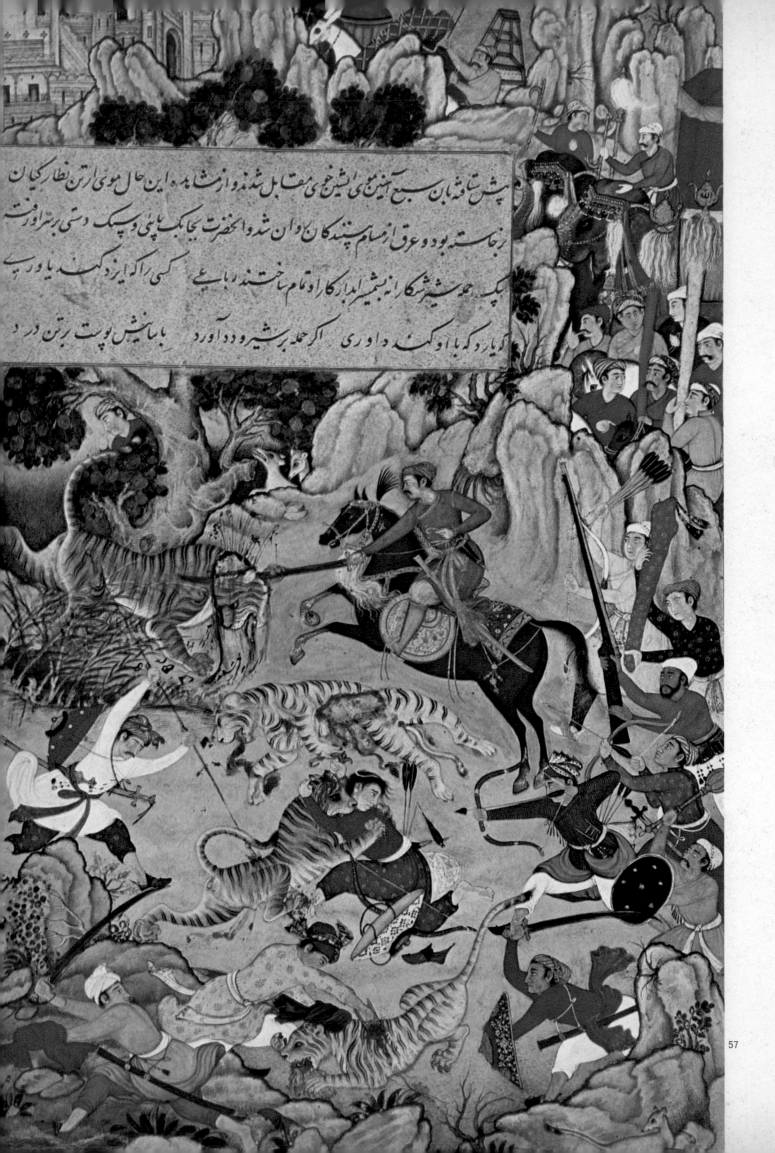

Byzantium's strength, therefore, lay primarily in its horsemen, the *caballarii*. These troopers, who from the eighth century onward were generally recruited from among the small landholders, were upon their return to civilian life exempt from all taxes except those for defense.

In 1071, however, the Roman emperor Diogenes, acting contrary to every canon of Byzantine military strategy, led his troops to disaster at Manzikert. From that day, the Byzantine Army never regained its former status. The empire lost a large part of Asia Minor, and the entire organization of the *temi* disintegrated. Successive emperors managed to put together an army of mercenaries, but this became an ever heavier burden upon the state's resources inasmuch as the government was not always in a position to exact tribute because of the misfortunes of war and domestic difficulties.

One can say that, for all practical purposes, long before the fall of Constantinople the Byzantine army was no more.

XXVI
PERSIA
(Parthians)

Just when do our Middle Ages begin? Some would have them commence with the fall of the Roman Empire in the West, in A.D. 479; actually, the medieval period, at least viewed as the age of chivalry, of fable, and of feudalism, began in China around the second century B.C. It filtered, by osmosis, into Persia, there to flourish and influence both Goths and Alani, and to an extent, even the refractory Huns, finally passing over into Europe with the Germans.

The young Ardashir, called to court by the King of the Parthians, associated with the sons of knights, frequented the royal stables, and right there, among the horses, met the king's daughter: a typical theme of the cavalier life, which had a formal code that was the sum of the customs of the Parthians, quondam nomads of Scythian stock coming from the Turanian steppes, and the luxury and strict etiquette of the Persians.*

By nature, the nomad is restless, given to rapine, violent and despotic, a man who travels over vast expanses, and considers them his own domain. He is the heroic figure that wagers his life in combat, and who has found in the horse the means to lead his fiercely stark existence, to sack and plunder, the core of his cruel life as a marauder.

Wearing long coats of mail, "they are always on horseback and, mounted, they ride off to war," wrote an ancient historian, "and on horseback, they go to banquets, fulfill their public and private obligations, do business, and converse among themselves. In short, what distinguishes the servant

from the master is the fact that the former is always on foot while the other is never seen unless he is on a horse."

From this springs the social significance of the "horsy" life and the concept that a member of the aristocracy takes his proper place as the man with the upper hand because of his possession of a horse. To the time of Darius, things were more or less this way. Darius himself had called Persia a "land of wonderful horses," and a man's wealth was reckoned by the number of horsemen he had at his disposal or how many he could muster to send off to war (and is that not already feudalism?).

The Parthians, like the Huns, the Sarmatians, the Avars, had no taste for hand-to-hand combat or for sieges. Their strength lay in sudden cavalry charges, in pretended flight, and in the unexpected return to the attack, in a body, to fall upon an enemy confused by surprise and uncertainty.

Mounted archers, who had so much mobility, who could advance, then wheel about, disperse in droves, then return to the attack unexpectedly, cannot be considered as anything other than light cavalry. Yet, it is here, among these troopers of central Asia, that one finds the origin of scale and plate armor.*

Armor was already in use at the time of Alexander the Great (the left flank of the Persian army at Gaugamela, in 331 B.C., wearing scale armor, fought against Bactrian and Scythian troops); later, some consideration was given to protecting horses, as well. Then, in order to engage enemies at close range, the long assault lance was introduced.

Light and heavy cavalry complemented each other. Just as soon as a hail of arrows had been released by the light cavalry to break the ranks of the enemy, the cataphracts came up in frontal assault. The general who perfected this tactic, which resulted in the complete rout of hostile troops on foot, was the Parthian Surenas, who was responsible for the notable defeat of the Romans at Carrae (53 B.C.). Surenas, at his own expense, was able to maintain a force of a thousand armored cavalrymen and nine thousand archers—all this, long before the knightly tradition of medieval Europe!

Corresponding to the Persian cavalry in the military sphere was a counterpart civilian political regime extremely well endowed financially, for the Parthian kingdom was noteworthy for the existence of a number of powerful families possessing extensive properties and numerous dependents. On the other hand, these families represented a strong check on the power of the throne. Recognizing this immanent danger, the Sassanids attempted to offset the influence of the feudal Parthian nobility by instituting a new aristocracy that was closely linked with the Sassanid dynasty.

As in China, where a cavalier and courtly culture developed under the T'ang dynasty (618–907 C.E.), women in Persia were not ashamed to be seen in the saddle. A little gem of its type is a statuette of a polo player, a young girl, mounted on a pony.

This civilization that, on the one hand, was to have an influence upon Europe through its impingement on German customs, was also to make its mark upon the Arabs, though not so much in those early times as later, during the period of the caliphate in Baghdad.

---

* Ardashir is known to Western historians as Artaxerxes, the founder of the Sassanid dynasty, who served the Parthian King Artabanus, then rebelled against him, and ruled from 226 to 240 C.E.—TRANS.

57 *Akbar the Great Tiger hunting, a sixteenth-century Indian miniature. Victoria and Albert Museum, London.*

* The basis of the heavy cavalry.—TRANS.

Chivalry and nobility, a quasi-tyrannical priestly caste, universal orthodoxy and authority—all these presaged the characteristic shape of the historical evolution that was to bring about the Middle Ages in Europe, and all this came about in an age of crisis, at a time when Rome still did not know that it would have to choose that same direction, with the same decision and the same outcome.

XXVII
THE ARABS

Lacking land they could cultivate, the Arabs became breeders of sheep and camels to make up for deficiencies in their food supply, and to such an extent that their whole existence depended more and more upon their flocks and herds.

The Bedouin, who were moved, above all, by the promise of plunder, formed the nucleus of the Arab armies. Most of them rode dromedaries, but the sheiks were privileged to use horses. The riders carried long lances, bows, and a small round shield. Horses were given the care due a rare and precious possession.

At the outset, however, it was the dromedary that constituted the mobile force of the Arabs. When the Romans disembarked in Egypt, this two-humped camel was still a great rarity. In time, however, it became more common and, ultimately, gained its importance in war. Nomads mounted on dromedaries became a part of the Roman standing army. Two squadrons of these troops formed part of the regular armed forces under Diocletian (284–305).

Meanwhile, the Arabs were on the move. Certainly, long before the coming of Muhammad they were penetrating into Egypt, Iraq, and Syria. The Nabateans, the people of Tammuz, the Sassanids, and Palmyrans were all of Arab stock.

If the dromedary represented the wealth of the Bedouin, their national glory was the horse, which was the basis of their existence as warriors and free men. The Arabian horse, which descends from Persian and Syrian strains selected from the dry desert regions, utterly sinuous and fluid in motion, fiery and proud, responsive and swift, became the basis of the Bedouin's life, and his fixed point of reference in appraising beauty, wealth, and ease.

Contrary to the Romans, who had gone about improving the breed through crossing and rather rigorous and particular selection among the circus winners, the Arabs did not look solely for the fleetest specimens, but for those that would also best suit their style of warfare, which was based on audacious action, surprise attack, and ambuscade, deriving from the primordial instinct to raid that ruled these poor and primitive people. It was adaptability to these specific requirements as indices to quality in a horse as well as physical harmony, that attracted the Arabs. As well as his instrument, a horse must be a man's faithful companion. While the Arab considers the dog a filthy beast, he looks upon the horse as the perfect being that Allah has given into man's keeping.

The horse's history (in the Arab view) is strange, however, for if the origin of the equine race is to be found in the choosing of the first five mares from the eighty-five sent to Mecca by Muhammad, this purely feminine beginning confuses the issue a bit by making it impossible to trace the male line. From these mares, nevertheless, sprang the strains and subspecies whose export the Koran forbids.

Muhammad himself was a skillful horseman. Although his early experience, acquired as a caravan master, was with camels, when he chose the calling of a prophet, he supplied himself with fiery chargers, among which his favorite was the miraculous Borak, as well as his five celebrated mares.

The horse was not indigenous to Arabia. When the animal was introduced there, it found an arid land, sparse forage, and a climate that was torrid but dry and that would reduce its stature. The dry, soft ground caused the horse to develop a small, strong hoof and, consequently, legs that were slim, flexible, and fast. Forced to sudden sprints by the Arab raider who rode him, he became a tremendously fast runner, and with further training, he still maintained his lightness and gained a sleek, slim belly like that of a greyhound.

The Koran lays down the law to the Arab, who relies upon the horse as a necessity of life and conquest, saying that he must be loved like "a part of your own heart." Since mares are precious possessions, for "a treasure grows in their wombs," the most pious Arabs, in order not to menace such prizes, rode only stallions in battle.

As Muhammad forbade naming horses after men, the Arabian imagination devised the sweetest of names for their horses, taking inspiration from the color, attitude, gentleness, and grace in motion of their mounts.

It is a curious fact that Muhammad's predilection for liver-colored chestnuts carried the word *alezan* to France, where it is used to specify the color "chestnut," although the word, in Arabic, indicates that a horse is a Thoroughbred.

"If they tell you they have seen a horse fly, ask what color it was, and if they say, 'chestnut,' you can believe it."

The great horse Eclipse was a chestnut. On the other hand:

"Iron-gray and Judean yellow, if his master returns, cut off his hand for me."

Of all colors, however, the dappled and Isabella were considered unlucky. This might appear to be merely an aesthetic preference of an imaginative and indomitable people, individualistic and loyal. Actually, it is a practical attitude, based on long and perceptive observation that science today has reaffirmed, for it is a fact that light-colored horses do not stand up well to hard work; that bays, on the other hand, need a great deal of exercise, since they tend to put on weight; and that a chestnut keeps in shape longer, since he is strongly influenced by the secretion of the suprarenal glands, which keep him from growing wan.*

The Arab's treatment of his horse has become axiomatic: "In the stable, he treats him like a treasure; in the saddle, as though he weren't worth a cent." There is, however, another saying that trainers of today might do well to consider: "Train early and use late."

From his earliest days, the Arabian horse shares the life of the tribe, staying next to the tent of his owner. In this way, he becomes accustomed to noise, learns to understand com-

---

* This is probably opinion, not fact. There have been many good light-colored horses; but since there are fewer of them, there is less evidence upon which to base statistics.—Eds.

mands, and is taken care of by the women up until the time that his training begins, at the age of three. For centuries, his ration has consisted of eggs, sheep or camel's milk, dates, and barley flour, a diet conditioned by the fact that no oats grow in the region of his birth.

The horse learns to keep a bit in his mouth, to carry a weight on his back, to be among other horses without becoming skittish. In other words, he learns all the exercises that comprise the course of the Arab fancy, which training consists of a series of actions necessary to skirmishing and warfare: the galloping getaway from a standing start, the abrupt stop, the sudden turn to the left or right, the headlong run, the halt and leap forward, hindquarters in air, outstretched against the enemy, outflanking an adversary by making a swift break and coming over, as if to join his side, then to rear and plunge off through the hostile lines.

Finally, the horse would kneel, stretch out on the ground and play dead; then, of a sudden, get to his feet and streak off. The Arab even taught his mount to refuse food touched by any hand but his and any weight other than that of his master.

Driven by religious fanaticism and a thirst for riches, the Arabs, riding in small bands, attacked the Persian army. For three days, the mighty columns of elephants resisted the assault of the Arab horsemen, but at Kadesia, amid the uproar of horrendous trumpeting, their flight began.

Three thousand Arabs and seven thousand Berbers, all on horseback, composed the force large enough to invade Spain. It was only in 732, at Poitiers, that the Arab cavalry was stopped, for the first time, by the armored horsemen of Charles Martel.

The Arabian horse and his descendants have stocked five continents, and the strain is present in all the more prized breeds. The Arabian, however, cannot be traced to one founding sire or to a single stud. The Arabs themselves make a distinction among some fifteen strains, and each of these has about ten offshoots. The most celebrated strain, the Kochlani, comprises about thirty families.

XXVIII
VETERINARY MEDICINE

The history of veterinary practice has its origin in the domestication of animals. Obviously, epidemic disease—despoiler of flocks and herds, illness that ultimately was transmitted to man—would be the first to be diagnosed upon the evidence of recurring pathological manifestations.

Since the life of the community was dependent upon animals, whether they were used for sustenance or as a means of production or transport and, in the case of the horse, in war, as well, these indispensable companions forced the more progressive peoples to take an interest in providing for their wants, their hygiene, and their health.

As early as 1800 B.C., we find stipulated in the Code of Hammurabi, with all that minute detail of which the Mesopotamians were capable, the duties of the *munai-su*, the veterinarian, as already distinguished from the medical doctor and the witch doctor. Veterinary medicine was a profession that had its risks, for although every animal cured was worth a fee of a sixth of a silver shekel, if one should die under the

ministrations of the Mesopotamian veterinary, he was required to pay over a quarter of the beast's value.

In Egypt, the veterinarians were divided according to their specialties, among them, the care of oxen and the treatment of cats. Still guided by primitive instinct, these men were able to employ herbs and other natural substances to cure sores, arrest hemorrhages, and clear up inflammations. They were also sufficiently skilled to repair fractures and treat the respiratory and digestive tracts through the use of specific potions.

As crude and brutal a nation as they were, the Scythians, stockbreeders and legendary horsemen of the steppes between the Danube and the Don, could, nevertheless, cauterize and geld, and protect a horse's hoof with a rudimental leather fitting so that the horny portion would not become soft in the dampness of that marshy region. It also appears that they could perform laparotomies.

Not otherwise particularly able technically, the Greeks managed, however, to organize and analyze what the Scythians had achieved empirically. By calling the specialist in veterinary medicine a *hippiatra,* the Greeks revealed their sole interest in that field, the horse. Through codifying their knowledge of the life and needs of the horse, they evolved a rather sophisticated system of hygiene, and suggested ways by which it might develop beyond mere prophylaxis. The Greeks were able to make accurate diagnoses of hepatic, renal, and intestinal disturbances, tetanus, hernia, typhoid fever, and foot inflammations, and even cure these with some success.

The Romans' practical sense turned them to the study of parasitic disease and contagious illness (they were the first to make mandatory the inspection of meat in public slaughterhouses), while adding to surgical expertise through the perfection of certain operations. When it became necessary for them to take an interest in all aspects of the horse, an exigency of their building and control of an empire, the Romans attempted to assimilate Greek science, certain traditional skills of the Spaniards, and the acute observations of the Carthaginians. Their old *mulomedicus* became the more distinguished *equorum medicus,* until the office acquired the name *veterinarius,* coming from *veterinae,** draft animals and beasts of burden, the name deriving, probably, from *vetus* (old), weary, sickly creatures in need of a cure.

The Middle Ages sank to witchcraft, and fell into ignorant darkness for centuries. Meanwhile, in India, the tradition of animal hospitals continued, establishments that were a cross between a zoo and a harem, where a Hindu of a particular sect cared even for beasts of the forest. With the advent of Islam, however, these hospitals were destroyed. The Muhammadans restricted their mercies to horses, in accordance with the strictures of the Koran, which were extremely detailed on the subject, though not too reliable in theory.

In the fourteenth century, a work on farriery appeared in Padua that, bit by bit, became the manual of veterinary science. Then, a collection of observations and rules for the treatment of horses and dogs, in a book on hunting by Gaston

---

* Literally, "old hacks."—TRANS.

Phoebus, the Count of Foix, became famous. In 1598, a magnificent volume, *Anatomy of the Horse,* attributed to the jurist Carlo Ruini, and illustrated with plates by Leonardo da Vinci, was published in Bologna.

The great forward surge in veterinary science, however, was to come from enlightened France, and was impelled by Claude Bourgelat, an attorney of Grenoble who, disgusted with his "false and lying" profession, turned to equitation and founded a school at Lyons, an activity that gradually led him to the practice of veterinary medicine.

Bourgelat's studies, which were fascinating, brought him the patronage of Bertin, one of the ministers of Louis XV, who bestowed upon him the largess of fifty thousand francs to be used in fighting cowpox. Supported by the Encyclopedists, Bourgelat founded the School for the Treatment of Disease in Large Domestic Animals.

Veterinary schools became even more important in the nineteenth century, not in small measure because of the benefits that finally began to accrue from the invention and advancement in the use of vaccines and serums for the treatment of animals, and horses in particular. For the whole of the nineteenth century, however, veterinary science, apart from that practiced in the cavalry schools and state universities, was restricted to the stables and the treatment of race horses.

With the advent of the twentieth century, associations began to be formed, in England and France, to coordinate the activities of all who were interested in veterinary medicine as it concerned itself with race horses. Such foundations, like the Animal Health Trust, established in England in 1924, had as their purpose the support and aid of any study and research in the field, such as inquiries into sterility, parasites, and the diseases of colts, as well as the employment of electrotherapy, including the use of cardiography in diagnosing diseases of the heart. These foundations and the research they sponsor are designed to give breeders, who are often confronted with situations requiring the best information available, the best counsel in the shortest possible time.

As recently as 1966, the Grayson Foundation was set up in the United States with the intention of organizing an annual conference of the leading lights in the field of veterinary science on every continent so that every clinic, every university could be kept abreast of the progress made by the hundreds of research projects undertaken throughout the world in connection with race horses.

The principal problems that remain to be solved by scientists have to do with influenza, infectious anemia, and viral abortion, three ills that cause great loss every year to breeders, owners, and horse racing generally.

XXIX

THE GOTHS

On the far side of the Don, which the Huns managed to cross only in 375, extends a vast region that was dominated by the Goths and the Alani. The Goths, who came from southern Sweden (when they had reached the Baltic coast by sea, they went up the Vistula to penetrate into the vast region to the north of the Black Sea), had mixed with their new neighbors, the Alani, a vigorous people of the Aryan strain, who had served the Sarmatians as guides.

"The Alani have no huts, nor are they familiar with the plow," wrote a historian of the fourth century. "They eat meat and clabbered milk. Living in carts, which they protect with a roof, often made of cowhide, they travel the steppes. When they find a pasture, they arrange their wagons in a circle and eat as if they were wild animals. When the grass is finished, the community goes on its way in the carts in which the people live, eat, and bring up their children. All their care is given to the raising of horses."

When they came to southern Russia, the Goths already knew how to ride; and their armies, as was the case in all the Germanic forces, had cavalrymen fighting in mixed formation with foot soldiers. After their contact with the Persian nomads, as a result of which equitation achieved a notable maturity and refinement, the horse assumed decisive importance among them, and the cavalry became the fulcrum of the army.

The Goths adopted their equipment from the Sarmatians and Alani—held to be bad soldiers in hand-to-hand combat, while irresistible when assaulting in squadrons of serried ranks. This equipment consisted of a plate-mail breastplate or a coat of mail reaching to the feet, a conical helmet, long lance, leggings, and a shaped and fitted saddle without stirrups. They also learned to manipulate lance and saber with hands while on horseback.

Once the horse had become the prime essential for war and power, he became identified among the eastern Germanic peoples with the same regal dignity he had symbolized in Persia and China. The Middle Ages had already begun on the steppes of Eurasia. There were, nevertheless, unusual incidents, such as occurred when a troop of Alemanni, preparing for an attack before the Battle of Strasbourg, obliged the nobility to dismount and fight hand to hand. Again, in the sixth century, we find that the army of the Franks (actually, western Germans) was made up principally of foot soldiers, with only a few elements on horseback, surrounding their commander.

The Franks believed that hand-to-hand combat was still necessary to instill and encourage heroism. For the nomadic tribes and the eastern Germans, however, warfare was based on wiliness, surprise, and the simulated retreat of troops that turned back upon their pursuers, en masse, throwing them into confusion and disarray.

Combining both types of fighting was the charge, which had already been adopted in savage form by the Huns, and was used as a tactic by the Goths to resolve an issue, particularly during the reign (350–376) of their emperor, Ermanaric, who later saw his empire overthrown by the Huns. The Germans had no love for Ermanaric, who surrounded himself with luxury, like a Persian, according to legend, but considered him something of a tyrant inasmuch as he had every intention of fixing the nomadic tribes on the land, in an effort to consolidate his realm.

Ermanaric made good use of a huge number of horsemen to keep within his clutches a domain that extended from the Black Sea to central Russia. It was these mounted hordes, in their continual comings and goings, who carried far and wide and deep into the heart of Russia the arms and customs of the man on horseback.

XXX
THE HUNS

The ferocity, the untrammeled, bloody violence that ruled the Huns, and the awesome reputation that has always surrounded their name help us to understand how armed cities, well-run armies, and fortified countries fell before the thrust of those implacable invaders on horseback. Poor, starving, unencumbered by the impedimenta of war, they had a crack military organization, and were not without a certain talent for strategy and diplomacy.

If the Huns were able to destroy entire nations in little time, they owed their success, above all, to the stamina and sureness of their small, bony horses. Like all the nomadic peoples, they ate little meat, since animals at pasture were looked upon as wealth and a medium of exchange, but never considered as food. From mare's milk the Huns made kumiss, a fermented beverage of extremely high nutritive value, which they reinforced with warm blood taken directly from the horse.

It was precisely the Hun's poverty, their sparse equipment, and their consequent need to prey upon others that gave them the advantage in their encounters with the Goths and the other Germanic peoples who had become almost sedentary in habit, weighed down by chattels, as they were, and with insufficient means of transport.

Better to understand the mentality and character of the nomads and their relations with the horse, we should consider some of their tribal customs.

It is known that the emblem of the clan figured as a brand on the rump of a horse, and only on horses, as if the animal were actually a member of the clan in his own right. In Turkish inscriptions of the seventh and eighth centuries, horses taken as booty in an engagement in which the Turks were victorious are listed under the clan names of the conquered tribes, as if they were a race apart. Frequently, it happened that the strain of horses bred by a tribe gave its name to a clan.

A captain of the fourth century, one of the Alani who had joined the Goths for their invasion of the Balkans, was known as Safrag, a Latin transliteration of the Alanic *saurag*, which means, literally, "black line" or "black troop," the same name applied to a race connected with the Xalas.

The Cumani, or *qumans*, as they are called in Turkish—known in Russian as *polovtsy*—are a Turkish people who controlled the steppes of southern Russia. They took their name from the color they favored in horses, Isabella, since *qu* has the significance "yellowish" in Turkish, the precise translation of the Russian *polovtsy*. There were instances of whole squadrons of cavalry mounted on horses of a given color in the nomad armies, like Genghis Khan's famous guard, the thousand *baghatur*, all of whom had blackish horses. The horse's color very often was patent evidence of an underlying religious motive.

For peoples such as the Scythians, Alani, Huns, Turks, and Mongols, the horse was something more than a mere means of transport. He was a friend and a companion who shared both life and death. It is for that reason that a dead warrior was followed by his horse to the tomb.

Herodotus tells us how, one year after the death of a Scythian king, fifty of his young attendants and fifty of his handsomest horses were strangled at the royal tomb and their bodies stood upright, held erect by wooden supports, each man on a horse, to form a macabre guard of honor. Strangulation was the preferred manner of dispatch in such cases, to obviate any shedding of blood, which was held to come from the soul of a man, and from a horse's, as well. Clumsy or inefficient killing would have destroyed the soul.

The system most frequently used, however, among Oriental populations, and employed to save the soul of the victim, was to break the spine, the method, for example, of the shamans of the Altaic Turks right down to the nineteenth century. Among the Mongols, that was the system employed until the fourteenth century to execute princes of the royal blood found guilty of treason.

PART TWO

MIDDLE AGES,
RENAISSANCE, AND SCHOOLS

I
THE DARK AGES

DURING THE HEIGHT of the medieval period, what with the decadence of the Roman roads and the continuous necessity of defending oneself against Arab, Hungarian, and Norman invaders, whoever owned a horse had the means to flee from death or take the initiative and seize upon anything he could steal or carry off with him. For that reason, little by little, the horse became identified with the power of the individual and, subsequently, with political power, as well as military strength. One could say that the feudal system was founded upon the availability of the riding horse.

In the West, however, it was strictly the aristocracy that was in the saddle, while in the East, whole populations advanced on horseback. In Europe, the horseman's armor, heavy and costly, an inheritance from the final years of Rome, ended by imprisoning its wearers, for it kept them from having the mobility and fulminating effect that characterized the Arab cavalry, as well as influencing their taste in mounts. This was the period when big, strong, powerful horses began to be bred. They were derived from the Noric strain, which had become famous as packhorses during Roman times, and formed the basic stock in crosses that led to chargers capable of carrying as much as some 650 pounds.

We learn, nevertheless, from the letters of Gregory the Great (Gregory I, pope and saint, 590–604) that, in Sicily, the pope himself was forced to give up horse breeding—which he engaged in for his own account—evidently because the market price was so low (perhaps he was raising horses that were too small) that the cost of maintaining workers for the stud was about twelve times more than receipts. The pope ordered that any of his handlers who were left without animals be distributed among the various large holdings in the area so that they could work on the land—all this at the end of the sixth century.

In the meanwhile, not only the nobility was going into the cavalry, as we can see from a law of 750 made by King Astolf, in which for the first time men of affairs, the *negotiantes,* appear as a social class, divided into three categories in the event of a call to arms. There were the *maiores* or *potentes,* who were equated with landholders owning at least seven houses for tenancy. These merchants, like those large landholders, had to equip themselves with a cuirass, shield, lance, and horse. The *sequentes* were required to appear with a horse,

shield, and lance, but no cuirass; while the *minores*, probably local small tradesmen, needed only a bow and arrows.

II
MARCO POLO

Marco Polo, his father, Niccolò, and his uncle, Matteo, traversed Asia from one end to the other, at least four times. During that period (1260–1295), the greater part of that continent pertained to the vast empire of Tartary founded by Genghis Khan, a conquest that the Great Khan owed solely to his masterly employment of the greatest cavalry force of all times. Infantry and combat elephants had fought, as well, but the cavalry reigned supreme in those battles.

Marco Polo makes a particular point of telling us of the different breeds of horse he encountered, giving special praise to the merits of the numerous herds bred by Persians and by the Turcomans.

The following, for example, is what he had to say about the horses of Balashan (eastern Persia):

The horses raised here are of superior quality and capable of great speed. Their hoofs are so tough that they have no need of shoes. Urged on by their riders, they gallop down the sharpest declivities that no other animal could possibly negotiate.

They say that not long ago one could still find direct descendants of the famous Bucephalus, Alexander the Great's favorite steed, all of whose foals were born with a distinctive mark on the forehead. Every one of this particular breed belonged to one of the uncles of the Khan of Persia who, for refusing to give them to his powerful nephew, was put to death by his order. His widow, irritated [*sic*] by such cruelty, had all the horses killed, and the world lost all of what was certainly the best breed it had ever known.

58 *The feud of the Sogo brothers. Detail of an eight-panel Japanese screen of the Tosa school, seventeenth century. Museo Orientale, Venice.*

58

The Tartar invasions, however, which started in eastern Mongolia and continued to the very confines of Europe, were based upon the use of hundreds of thousands of Mongolian horses. Referring to this, Marco Polo writes:

> Every Mongol army had eighteen horses, mares and stallions, who ate only grass, requiring neither oats nor any other grain. The men are accustomed to staying in the saddle for as much as two days and two nights in succession, sleeping while their mounts pasture. If necessary, they can go for ten days on the march without halting, nourishing themselves on blood drawn from an opened vein of their own horses.

An invading force must be able to count upon a perfect logistics system and quick, sure communications. According to Polo:

> Two hundred thousand horses are employed in the mail system. Every post has four hundred good horses always on hand so that imperial couriers and the Khan's ambassadors can always find fresh horses and leave their spent mounts at any of these stations. Not all of the four hundred horses assigned to a post are ready for immediate use, however, but just two hundred, while the other half of the complement is put out to pasture in the neighborhood before returning for service.
>
> When a great Mongol chieftain rides off to war, he puts himself at the head of a hundred thousand horse, divided into units of ten, one hundred, one thousand, and ten thousand cavalrymen.
>
> In combat, these troopers do not mix with the enemy but ride circles around them, harrying them, like wasps, with flights of arrows, and attacking first at one point, then at another.
>
> From time to time, the Mongols pretend to withdraw in disarray, all the while shooting arrows behind them as they go, to kill off their pursuers and their horses, achieving the same effect as they would have if they stood and fought their enemy face to face. In this way, they give the adversary the feeling that he is victorious when, in reality, the battle has been lost. At that moment, the Mongols round on the enemy and, surprising their adversaries with a new and unexpected frontal attack, finish them off.
>
> Their horses are so well trained that at even the slightest signal they change direction, ready to attack wherever and however they may be ordered to do so.

On a visit to a part of China that had just been conquered by the Great Khan, Marco observed:

> The horses here stand high. The youngest are sold in India. These people ride with their stirrup leathers very long, as the French do among us, while the Mongols and almost all the others draw them up short so that they can use a bow better, for it is standing in the stirrups that they shoot their arrows without a miss.

An item particularly touching to followers of Caprilli's teaching on "natural equitation" is Marco Polo's observation that these horsemen gave their mounts the utmost freedom in the mouth, permitting them to seek their natural balance. Those rapid changes in direction must have been controlled more through knee action and the rider's shifts in weight than through his hand.

III

THE HUNGARIANS

A Mongolian tribe, the Hungarians first reached the limits of Europe in 883, and by 886 had destroyed Moravia, the only powerful principality in the eastern part of the continent that was already officially Christian. In 899, the Hungarians poured into the plain of the Po.

Their raids were incredibly fast. They must have had exceptionally resistant and speedy horses, but certainly not very large animals, if they were able to take even crossing the Alps in stride. As well equipped as nomads could be, having saddles, saddlebags, and stirrups, the Hungarians brought with them packhorses to use for carrying their plunder. Soon, however, their rapaciousness was attenuated perforce. Always greedy for booty, the Hungarians had begun to use carts to carry away their plunder, but these proved slow and cumbersome when they made their withdrawals, and certainly less secure than the Normans' ships. Besides, their horses were not always able to find enough to eat in fields that had been so heedlessly devastated.

Byzantine generals were very much aware that "the great obstacle against which the Hungarians had to fight was the lack of pasturage." In addition to the continual skirmishes, they had to combat disease, which spread rapidly, gradually reducing their numbers. A chronicle dated 924, kept by the cleric Flodoard of Rheims, notes with joy the report of a "plague" of dysentery among the raiders in the region around Nîmes.

Some of the Hungarians stationed along the Danube lost the habit of riding out over long distances. The work of harvesting a crop kept them from making bandit sorties. It is curious to see the Synod of 1012, which met after the conversion of the Hungarians to Christianity, threatening to fine those villages that were too far distant from a church.

It was not without reason that ibn-Khaldun, the Arab historian, noted that, given two adversaries of equal forces and strength, the one more accustomed to the nomadic life would be victorious. It was so in the conflict between the Hungarians and the West and with the Arabs against the Persians, the Byzantines, and the Spaniards.

Though the Hungarians won on the open field, they found it difficult to force well-armed cities to capitulate. Pavia was the only important city that they were able to take, but they failed against the wall of Kiev. Like the Huns and the Hiung-nu of Chinese extraction, who also went on long peregrinations, the Hungarians, or Magyars, were also typical people of the steppe. They were all nomads, and though they differed in language, all led similar lives, imposed by their common condition. Handlers of horses, they were bandits

59 *Head of a horse from a mural of uncertain date. Baptistery, Poitiers Cathedral, France.*

who lived on mare's milk and game, and were declared enemies of, above all, the tillers of the field. Also, they had adopted much of Turkish life and language.

IV
NOMADS AND THE BARBARIAN KINGDOMS

The successes of the nomads were enhanced by the difficulty experienced in the barbarian kingdoms in recruitment, where the system was ever more burdensome for an administration that grew less and less capable of performing its bureaucratic functions.

In Italy, except for the Romans and the Lombards, weakened by misery and desperation in the ranks, there was no one capable of wielding a sword. While the Germans were attached to the land and were now more farmers than warriors, the old Roman settlers* were a thing of the past, although men could be called up, in case of need, for organized legions that gave them some training.

In France there was no standing army except the royal guard and household troops maintained by overlords. How much recruits lacked training and experience, and how difficult it was to arm them, can be assessed from the fact that in Charlemagne's time, a man was required to have only a club when he presented himself for service. These defects gravely influenced the Merovingian military system, but they became even more apparent as the balance of power on the battlefield shifted from the foot soldier to the cavalryman, equipped with considerable offensive and defensive armament.

To keep a charger and equip himself from head to foot, a man really had to have means or be subsidized by someone wealthier than he. According to the Ripuarian Law,† a horse was worth twelve cows, or the same amount as a *broigne,* a leather breastplate reinforced by metal plate armor, or twice the price of a helmet. In 761, a small property owner in the territory of the Alemanni gave his family holdings and a slave for a horse and sword.

Furthermore, long training was necessary to learn how to handle a horse effectively in combat and to fight in heavy armor. A document in the Abbey of Saint-Gall reads, "You can make a horseman of a boy at the age of puberty, but never later." That saying was to become proverbial in the time of the first of the Carolingian monarchs.

Just what was it that caused this decline of the infantry, whose sociological repercussions were to be so great? It is believed that it stemmed from the effects of the Arab invasions. In order to withstand the attacks of the Saracen cavalry and to give chase, Charles Martel was to transform his Frankish troops into troopers. The exaggeration is obvious. Even supposing—and this conjecture, has, in part, been disputed—that the cavalry had the decisive role to play in Islam's armies,

surely the Franks, who had increased their mounted troops, would not have delayed giving them a mission of importance until Poitiers.

When Pepin I, in 775, transferred the date of the annual reunion of the great lords and the army from March to May, the season when horses were turned out to pasture, that significant change marked the terminal point of an evolution that had taken centuries.

V
THE NORMANS

The Normans came from Norway. Extremely skilled at working in wood, they were the creators of those masterpieces that sailed river and sea, the fearsome "long ships," which were about sixty feet in length, and struck terror into the hearts of coast watchers all along the North Sea. Built without decks, the long ships could run under sail or be rowed, and they accommodated some fifty men.

Thanks to those ships, the Normans were able to penetrate into the heart of the West, going up the rivers. In France, they got to Orléans, and then went on to Lyons. In England, they reached London and York, exacting tribute and ransom as they went, and putting cities to the torch, or, if these appeared to them to be too well fortified to attack, as was Paris, they skirted them by marching cross-country, their light boats on their shoulders, taking to the river once more at a point farther along the way.

In 860, the Normans arrived at Fiesole. Of necessity, they had begun to use horses, which they managed to excellent account in their military operations, just as those great horsemen, the Arabs, subsequently became first-class seamen, in order to scour the Mediterranean.

In the countries they invaded, the Normans took the horses they would need for their campaigns (in 866, for example, they made a great raid on the eastern part of England) or else they brought horses from a country they had sacked to another, as they did when they went from France to England in 855. In this way, they put themselves in a position where they could strike inland, away from a river, and even take fortified cities by surprise, an advantage they had over Hungarian cavalry.

The Normans instilled terror wherever they went, and their raids were unpredictable. In 860, they went so far as to sell in Ireland Moorish prisoners and horses taken in Morocco. In 1012, they pelted the Archbishop of Canterbury with the bones of the animals they had devoured at his own banquet, after having cannily held him until that time for ransom. One Icelander in their ranks was known as "the man who loves children," because he refused to spear them on his lance, "as was the custom among his companions."

Born predators, the Normans were ever moved by an insatiable thirst for conquest, which led them to fight Islam

---

* Retired soldiers given land as a form of pension in return for their service as militiamen or territorials.—TRANS.
† The code governing the Franks dwelling along the bank of the Rhine, near Cologne, during the fourth century C.E.—TRANS.

60 *Episode in the war of Gen-Pei. Detail from a six-panel Japanese screen of the seventeenth century. Museo Orientale, Venice.*

60

61

62

in Spain, to their conquests in southern Italy, to service as mercenaries under the Byzantine emperors and, finally, to the search for a route to the East, on the pretext of seeking the Holy Sepulcher. These wanderings served as a vehicle of culture, particularly that which was French, and occasioned the encounter of two civilizations on horseback that was to yield significant fruit in the twelfth and thirteenth centuries.

VI
TRANSPORT AND COMMUNICATION

The sole postal link that continued during the feudal period was that between Venice and Constantinople, thus excluding the West. The last attempts to maintain a mail route on which horses were changed in the fashion begun by the Romans died with the collapse of the Carolingian Empire. That the German sovereigns, the authentic or presumptive heirs of that empire and its ambitions, did not have either the authority or the intelligence necessary to revive an institution so patently indispensable to the governing of vast territories is a significant indication of their general disorganization.

While it was possible to make nearly ninety miles in a day's sailing, given favorable winds, on land the distance that was normally covered in a day was between eighteen and twenty-four miles. There were, however, couriers and a handful of determined men who managed to travel twice that distance.

A letter written in Rome by Pope Gregory VII in December 1075, arrived in Goslar, which lies at the foot of the Harz Mountains, on the first of January 1076. Its bearer had covered around thirty miles a day. Since one traveled on horseback, food for one's mount was a prime consideration. Many of the periodic stops mentioned in accounts of such journeys were not caused by bad weather, but by a lack of forage. Under the Carolingians, couriers waited until after the first haymaking before starting on their rounds.

Notwithstanding, in certain areas pedestrians in good form could cover astonishing distances. Charles the Bald* thought of assuring communication with Transalpine Gaul by using swift runners in top condition.

In order to maintain contact so that control could be exercised over a country—in other words, governing, collecting taxes, issuing orders, and seeing that they were respected—it was necessary to ride continually back and forth between its borders. In the early part of the feudal period, it was not uncommon for kings to die, worn out by the effects of their endless travel on horseback.

* King of France 840–877, and Emperor of the Holy Roman Empire 875–877.—TRANS.

It is curious to note that, in the universalistic medieval age, relations were maintained with nations far from home, while there was no communication (or what little existed is difficult to verify) between neighboring countries. Ever on the move were groups of refugees forced to take the road by the misfortunes of war and famine, adventurers, renegade soldiers, and peasants in search of a better life.

Finally, there were the pilgrims to whom were entrusted letters that often never reached their destination, for on the way the devout travelers frequently were set upon by bandits and highwaymen or impoverished gentlemen who demanded outrageous tolls and tribute, forcing them either to run for their lives, if they could, or live out their days in slavery.

The roads in Italy were rebuilt around the thirteenth century, first between one community and the next and then within individual regions. Generally, these roads were laid in the plains, for all conveyance across the Alps and the Apennine range consisted of carrying burdens in hand or loading them on the shoulders of a bearer or, at best, on wheelbarrows of minimal capacity.

While roads came to stretch across canals in the plains, conditions were bad in those areas lacking the development fostered by large communities or a rich mercantile bourgeoisie. The journey from Florence to Naples, which merchants sometimes succeeded in making in eleven or twelve days, riding on horseback from morning to evening via Terni, Aquila, Sulmona, and Teano, was bristling with difficulties and danger. Abruzzi was traversed over paths, and where it bordered Campania, the area was infested with brigands. Between Rome and Naples, the most direct route—by way of Terracina—was unsafe, so commerce took to the sea, exclusively. Beyond Naples, the only highway traveled by traders and covered by small wagons was the ancient one linking Campania with Foggia and Manfredonia.

Even greater difficulties beset overland traffic headed from Italy to the fairs in the Champagne, Paris, and in Flanders, perils that usually were aggravated by political complications. Travelers, therefore, preferred to make their way to Provence by ship, whence they proceeded up the Rhone or Saone.

Contrasting with the slowness of transport—six days from Chiavenna (northern Italy) to Chur (eastern Switzerland)—was the relative rapidity in transmitting news by land. Beginning in 1300, monasteries, universities, communities, and merchant companies made extensive use of couriers, most of whom covered either the whole route or a part of it on horseback, each stage being marked by posts where horses were changed. Traveling in that way, the journey from Venice to Bruges took from seven to eight days.

VII
CHIVALRY

It is said that chivalry has always existed. Perhaps so, if by chivalry one means that ideal, bordering upon the utopian, of wishing to play a role in life, to take a noble, courteous, and somewhat mannered part. Bayard, Cyrano, and Don Quixote are consummate examples of a concept of life so persistent as to appear even ridiculous in respect to certain rules that be-

61 *The Four Horsemen of the Apocalypse in a miniature by Petrus Clericus illustrating a history of El Cid, 1086. Burgos Cathedral, Spain.*

62 *Luxury at a Burgundian court: serving table on horseback. State Archives, Coblenz, Germany.*

came absurd once the conditions of life out of which they had sprung no longer prevailed.

It is certainly true that the chivalry of the medieval period had the merit of adding a strong dose of sentiment to the mixture of heroism and belligerence that passed for virtue. Chivalry gave life to a marvelous reality in which the warrior spirit turned upon Christian principles of succoring the poor and being obedient to the rule of an order, so that mere fervor was transmuted into practical action of real import at a time when everyone was threatened by violence and the abuse of power.

It was a new and unique way of life and, as it spread, new orders of knighthood were created, to a point where it became the fashionable mode of life. That life degenerated, however, as it stimulated unhealthy desires, espoused privilege, and created a caste system. It expired, finally, in the mere profession of arms or in bitter nostalgia for an ideal no longer attainable.

So long, however, as one gentle act was done, performed as the expression of a rite, chivalry remained and was, perhaps, the most extraordinary development of the Middle Ages.

VIII

THE DAWN OF EUROPEAN CHIVALRY

A German poet, repeating an old Carolingian truism, had this to say: "Whoever stays in school until the age of twelve without ever mounting a horse is fit for nothing but the priesthood."

The image of the knight the Middle Ages carried in its heart was that of an athlete: rawboned, sinewy, his body well marked and signed with the scars of honorable wounds, broad-shouldered and wide, likewise, in the crotch, as befits a horseman. The knight, furthermore, was expected to have the covetousness sufficient to his constant craving for victories, reinforced by enormous courage. He was supposed to show devotion to his lord and, were he involved in a holy war, devotion to a cause, as well. He had to have a passion for glory and (when things went badly) show a calm acceptance of destiny; and he must be heroic to the point of pigheadedness.

Accustomed to fearing no danger, the knight found in warfare an extra attraction: a cure for boredom, which was needful, in fact; for the life of those gentlemen of scant culture and few, if any, administrative preoccupations, was on the brink of falling, inevitably, into the deepest monotony; hence, the urge to flee the confines of one's own land and search for adventure elsewhere.

While the Spanish knight had the involvement of his holy war against the Moslem, the Frenchman, once the waves of Norman fury had subsided, was forced to wander to find excitement adequate to his pride. Under the Carolingian monarchs, a knight was anyone who, by virtue of wealth or a successful raid on another's property, could put his hands on a horse, all considerations as to the nobility of his line being swept aside. If he made a career of his arms and horse, the knight might be rewarded with a holding, which became a fief as soon as he was able to provide the armor for his own son, as well. Even if he lost his fee and keep, if he kept his horse and armor the knight remained a respectable lord forever, as he kept his privileges, so there was always a chance that he

might recoup his fortune either as a renegade knight, a knight-errant, or as a jouster.

It was a hard life and a toilsome one, and its customs cruder. In winter, the warmest place in the castle was the stable, so a knight often preferred to sleep on straw shared with his own horse rather than lie on a straw pallet in his own icy bed.

With the advent of the Middle Ages, the use of the horse became universal, and the employment of armored cavalry gave rise to experimenting and breeding to produce chargers capable of bearing enormous weight. In those days, a horse was considered a good one if he could carry about nine hundred pounds. In the country, however, and for festive races, another sort of horse continued to be a favorite, a light, bright animal of smaller stature.

Thus, various types of horses were identified: the charger, a big war horse, which a knight rode only in battle, leading him on the right of the horse he rode when traveling; the palfrey, sometimes called the ambler (the Roman use of the amble for hacking continued), when it was not necessary to break into a trot under the full weight of the arms being borne; the courser, the lancer's horse, ridden in pairs into combat, where the horse's speed was turned to account as the force of attack against an adversary; the jade, a nag used as a beast of burden; the docked, a horse whose tails and ears had been cut short, used to carry baggage for horsemen and archers. There were also the hackneys and ponies, animals of small stature ridden by women astride or seated upon a sort of packsaddle with a footrest.

63   *Detail from a series of frescoes by Pietro Lorenzetti that most charmingly illustrate all the ways a saddle horse can be employed. Note that the lady rides astride. Palazzo Publico, Siena.*

64   *Scene from the Bayeux Tapestry, twelfth-century record of the Norman invasion of England, in 1066, led by William the Conqueror. This work catalogs all the uses of war horses. Of interest here are the heavy, unprotected horses, the knights in coats of mail, and the handling of the lance in both the new and old fashions. Bayeux Cathedral, France.*

65   66   *"The triumph of death." Details from the mural by Francesco Traini da Volterra, an extremely realistic interpretation. Note the accuracy with which the horses' grooming has been rendered and the easiness of their bearing. Campo Santo, Pisa.*

67   *"The Journey of the Magi," a mural by Gentile da Fabriano. In the same work, one can see leashed cheetahs and monkeys carried on the croup, and velvet rugs. Uffizi Gallery, Florence.*

68   *Tournament armor and trappings, of Can Grande della Scala (leader of the Ghibellines). The rein is a fine chain having none of the usual reinforcement. The knight leans backward, his foot arched to secure the tread of the stirrup iron. Arches of the Roman arena, Verona.*

69   *A miniature by Niccolò da Bologna, illustrating the* Bellum Pharsalicum, *in which the horses' heads are curiously stylized. Biblioteca Trivulziana, Milan.*

70   *"Guidoriccio da Fogliano," a painting by Simone Martini. The horse is ambling. Note the four reins in the same ring, the absence of stirrup guards, and the horseshoes with calkins. Palazzo Publico, Siena.*

71   *"St. Hubert," by Pisanello, showing the utmost in luxurious trappings for the hunt. Art gallery, Verona.*

68

69

70

71

72

Equitation, like everything else medieval, was a brutal and violent thing. The horse was expected to be able to halt instantly, even with some six hundred pounds on its croup, and then be ready to start up again immediately. He had to make narrow turns, a difficult exercise for an animal of any great size, but a feat that the horseman guaranteed through the application of leverage on the bit and extremely long, pointed spurs.

The knight, who was lowered into a deep, padded saddle, called a *selle à piquer*, his lance at the rest under his arm, used the horse's speed to overturn his opponent or spill him out of his saddle on impact. Usually, however, he "charged" at the trot or, better still, at an amble, since it was exceedingly difficult to aim the lance at a specific target at the up-and-down motion of the gallop. Notwithstanding, the cavalry charge never became one of the more common combat tactics.

Where the condition of the terrain made it imperative, a knight dismounted, thus becoming a foot soldier for the nonce. Lacking roads, however, and without the trained troops for coordinated maneuvers that had been the strength of the Roman legions, only the horse made it possible to bring to any advantageous conclusion the long marches that characterized those wars between princes and the brief skirmishes with which the majority of the overlords contented themselves.

The horse permitted knights to arrive at the scene of battle without untoward fatigue, after traveling over plowed fields and marshy bottoms, and to surprise the enemy by unexpected action, as it allowed them to flee their adversaries, just as the Saxon nobility escaped in 1075, after defeat by Henry IV of Germany, saving itself solely because of the speed of its horses, while the poor country folk who served as their infantry were cut to shreds.

All this contributed to the formation of a cadre of professional soldiers, trained in the tradition of a class, which was that of the knights. These men were not, necessarily, those who were rich enough to assume the burden of long service to the king's profit (generally the first and foremost requisite, right down to the end of the ninth century); but men in armor, professional fighters, who followed their leaders for the love of plunder.

The Merovingian kings had a guard, always mounted, called the *truste*. Even bishops thought it necessary to provide themselves with similar mounted "gladiators," as Gregory of Tours called them.

The knight of the Middle Ages needed war, a practically permanent state of war. One has only to read Girard of Roussillon and the biography of the emperor Heinrich IV to understand how humiliating a return to peace would have been for the "poor knights." They feared the snubs that were already shown them by great lords who no longer needed

their help; dreaded seeing the dashing charger replaced by the heavy workhorse; the golden spurs turned to iron; and nothing but critical loss of economic and social standing.

On the other hand, for the farmer and the trader, a return to peace signified a return to life, to work, and the feeding of oneself. It was the nobleman Girard who recalled the time when he himself, having taken to the road with his wife, fell upon some traveling merchants. His duchess, thinking it prudent to convince these traders that her husband, whom they thought to be the bandit, was dead, insisted: "Girard is dead. I saw him entombed."

"God be praised," was the merchants' response, "he did nothing but wage war and more war. From him, we had nothing but loss and misery."

Girard, hearing this, as he wrote, turned black in the face with anger, and had he sword in hand, would have killed those "miserable ones."

It is a clear and incisive episode he gives us, taken from life, illuminating the disparities inherent in the existence of the different classes of society, antitheses that were two-edged, for if the knight, from the pinnacle of his courage and his superior ability as a warrior, scorned the people, *imbellis*, to whom arms were a mystery, he came, later, to detest the bourgeoisie, whose economic power appeared the more odious to him because it was acquired by means that, to him at that time, were mysterious and directly in opposition to his activities. Even though the inclination to violence was widespread (think of the murders and of the atrocities in the cloisters), the concept of war as a fount of honor and a means of subsistence made of that little society of "nobles" a caste in and of itself.

Actually, three systems of city life flourished in Europe. There was the Italian which was the pattern in Provence and the Languedoc, Rheims, and Trier, where Roman civilization had left enduring traces and where urban life was more intense and revolved around an overlord or bishop. Then, there was the Netherlands fashion, which was also the style in Germany across the Rhine, Bruges, Ghent, and Lübeck, where the walled cities harbored only rich merchants; and finally, there was life as it was led in the regions that had become subject to the conquering Normans and other barbarian peoples, carried on within fortified *villae*, towns and small cities that had been built around the time of the fourth century, as in the Gallic countryside—testifying to the dissolution of the *pax romana*, which flowered in the Frankish period, even while the greater number of courts inhabited by rich proprietors and, perhaps, even the royal palaces, had remained without permanent defenses right down to the time of the Norman and Hungarian raids, as had been the case in the south of England and along the Adriatic and Tyrrhenian coasts.

Because of the exigencies of defense, castles and fortified rural towns became nests of petty nobles, and well answered their rudimentary needs: "for those men, forever involved in fights and massacres, protecting themselves from their enemies, triumphing over their equals, and oppressing their inferiors" were their principal occupations in life.

At first, there were the small castles, built of wood, situated on a hill or rocky peak where "the lord lived, ate, and slept with all his followers." Next came the stone castles, as Bertrand de Born, a troubador of the time, tells us, slowly introduced in the twelfth century; these were to become the

72 *Piero della Francesca's "Defeat of Maxentius." Of interest are the very long stirrup leathers and the reins and chain running from the same leather strip to the withers in order to hold the rein taut and keep it always within reach, while preventing its being snatched by an opponent. Church of San Francesco, Arezzo.*

characteristic dwellings of petty knights and lesser noblemen. Here, the lord lived and breathed the same air as his warriors, vassals who had no homes of their own, and young noblemen, for as an English code of conduct of the thirteenth century put it, "It is not fitting for a lord to eat alone."

Even though these lords lived in the country, they did not lead the lives of country gentlemen or, even less, that of gentlemen farmers. Such knights did not exercise their power directly over the village, but delegated it to their "sergeants." Aside from meting out justice, the knights' chief diversion was the chase, which was not pursued solely as a sport but as a means of sustenance, as well. For that reason, the populace was forbidden to hunt over their lord's land. (In England, that is, in conquered territory, the strongest and most stringent regulations were put into force to prevent trespass and poaching.) Overlords forced those who paid tribute to them to raise hunting dogs and even horses, and when the custom of hunting with falcons was introduced from the Orient, they had another resource, more dependents, and even more wealth.

"He made more of a fuss over a goshawk and his flight than over a fine preacher," wrote a chronicler of the Count of Guines. "He was a gentleman, and his dogs loved him very much," was the epitaph on his murdered master pronounced by a jester who saw him surrounded by the yelping pack.

The hunt and the horse had the merit of poetically bringing together knight and nature; and so, besides knowing "the woods and the river" through the tradition of his class, he began to love the beauty of them, which was to be reflected in the figurative art and literature of the period.

Now, to the tournament, an institution that the codifier, Geoffroy of Preuilly, who died in 1066, would have us believe (as was thought in his own medieval period) was a relatively recent one, at that time. However, the tourneys, qualified as "pagan games," were mentioned at the Council of Trier, held in 895. As a matter of fact, they derive from the usual catch-as-catch-can fights indulged in between young men of every clan, tribe, country, and city, traditional rites of spring and fall that the barbarians revived. They are universal elements of folklore that, bit by bit, in the barbaric climate of the high medieval period developed along a precise line in which the horse, already a basic element in war, became the absolute protagonist.

At the same time as they served to amuse the court, these exercises that were an imitation of war became a necessity for training horsemen who had to learn to move, wearing armor that grew heavier and heavier over the years, and the horses that had to carry them. Charles the Bald and Louis the German had no hesitation in taking part in such manifestations under the Oath of Strasbourg (an alliance in 842 solemnized by the two against their brother Lothair I).

The original touch of the feudal era lay in recasting those military or popular tournaments into a type of mock battle that was relatively well ordered, and provided an occasion of pomp and spectacle when knights could go through their paces. It was the amusement of a class; and the nobility was not to know another that attracted it more in all the centuries to come, with the possible exception of the hunting party and the great balls.

These meets were expensive and could be organized only when kings or barons were holding their grand courts, so that a special class of knight came into being, men who traveled the world, going from one tournament to the next, professional players of a dangerous game. These knights were not only penniless, perhaps banded together in a "company" in search of prizes and booty, but great lords as well, like the Count of Hainaut (Baldwin IV) and the "young king" Henry II (1133–1189), who did not, however, make a very brilliant showing.

In these competitions, the young knights were usually grouped by regions, and if the teams were mixed, Flemings with Burgundians, say, that gave rise to scandal, as it went against custom. Often, the tournament "ended badly," as the poet Raoul of Cambrai put it, for which reason it was outlawed by the Plantagenet King of England, Henry II, and proscribed by the Church, which refused burial in consecrated ground to any knight, "even penitents," who died as a result of the tourney.

Inevitably, any class so neatly defined by its way of life and its social supremacy must end by formulating its own code of conduct. The rules, which began to develop a little after the year 1000, formed that composite of noble qualities designated as "courtesy," a word deriving from "court," since that etiquette had grown out of the gatherings of followers surrounding the barons and kings.

In France, the term *prud'homme* was born, a word—according to King Louis IX (St. Louis)—that "filled the mouth," so great and good it was, intending, as it did, to vindicate the virtue of the secular man confronted by that of the cleric. "There is a great difference between the brave man and the gallant one," declared the French King Philip II, who considered the second much superior to the first. The new code of courtesy came from France, and more precisely, from the land around the Meuse. It was imitated in Italy and in Germany, where Wolfram von Eschenbach called its birthplace the "land of knightly rectitude."

It was in France, however—where the distinctions between the courtly class and the unarmed mass of the populace was accentuated—that society, as a whole, remained united to a considerable degree, without the harmful schisms that existed between Guelph and Ghibelline, between papacy and empire, as was the case in Italy and Germany.

Under feminine influence, responsible as ever for a man's refinement, worldliness, too, reared its head. Knights fell subject to the civilizing effect of "courtly" love, a consummately idealized concept of the tender sentiment that moved the cavalier to become a litterateur (the first of these knightly poets was William of Aquitaine, who died in 1127), and the pinnacle of this rather suddenly acquired art was the asceticism of the troubador.

73 74 *Details from "The Battle of San Romano," by Paolo Uccello. Here there are four reins, armored horsemen, and unprotected horses. Louvre, Paris.*

75 *"Home from the Hunt," by Andrea Mantegna. The detail shows a selle à piquer realistically depicted both as to construction and ornamentation. Palazzo Ducale, Mantua.*

73

74 75

The knight, as cavalier, was a species of rough-and-ready gallant who followed a code of love that had nothing in it whatsoever conducive to matrimony. On the contrary, standing diametrically opposed to the law, the knight paid his court to a lady above his station and beyond his expectations and, accordingly, unapproachable.

One suspects, today, that there was a definite Arabian influence reflected both in courtly love and in the lyric poetry that served as its mode of expression. Certainly, it had not the remotest connection with the Roman *ars amandi*, and even less than nothing to do with the Greek art of love, even though pederasty was rife among both monks and knights.

The fact that knights were greedy for booty and ransom abroad, and bled their dependents white when they returned home, shocked no one. Their spoils were considered legitimate tribute because they were soon spent, and prodigally so. Acts of profligacy became legend: there was the incident at a Limousin court, where one knight had a freshly plowed field sown with silver coins; so another, not to be outdone, ordered that thirty of his horses, or all that he had in his retinue, be burned alive.

This was an arrogant class, a class that held the point of honor as the mark of distinction between it and every other group. It was ripe to crystallize itself into a caste, a group that stood apart, not by virtue of custom alone, but also in regard to its unique legal and hereditary rights. The consistently more frequent use of the term "gentleman," the man of fine *gens,* or family, of superior stripe, attests to the growing importance given the quality of the blood.

Ultimately, it was around a ceremony, the dubbing of a knight, that this class did effectively crystallize, fated, all too soon, to become a parasitic growth upon society.

IX
THE EDUCATION OF A KNIGHT

During his early childhood, the future knight was entrusted to the women of the household. One of the cadets of a noble line, he represented a threat to the eldest son, heir to the title, until that moment of decision when he was offered the opportunity of making his way in life independently, to become a source of pride to his family and, finally, that poignant, adventuresome, and infinitely ambiguous figure, the knight-errant.

Once this had been decided, soon after his seventh birthday the boy began to follow his father on jaunts and accompany him about the fief, learning first to ride correctly, then to fence and, eventually, to hunt, tutored by instructors rich in practice and experience.

At the age of twelve, the boy was sent to live in the household of a baron of greater consequence than his father or even to the court of the king himself. There he found rivals of his own age against whom he competed and whom he strove to best, at least in some of his acquired skills. Engaging

76 *Detail from "The Drink," by Hans Memling. The light and sinewy horses have four reins; the upper ones are rigid, the lower, fine. Art gallery, Antwerp.*

with his fellows in mock assaults or galloping, swimming, and fencing, the day passed quickly for him and was rich in incident.

As a page, the youngster was expected to wake the household, carry water to his lord, and serve him as valet. At mealtimes, he was required to serve bread, pour wine, and carve. Beyond all his other duties, however, the page was supposed to take a passionate interest in the stables. From the manner in which he learned to present his lord's horse and his own, the more the animals glistened and were kept at the top of their form, the more he would win of his master's regard.

When hunting, the page was expected to be able and even cunning, but he also had to know the etiquette of the chase without thinking, and was expected never to be guilty of breaches of form. It was his duty to train falcons and dogs, and exercise them when hunting was impossible.

All this was a great deal for an adolescent boy to have to do, particularly when he was also required to become proficient in the arts of war, keep his lord's arms and his own bright and shining and in good repair, and—not the least of his travail—practice bearing them hour after hour.

Once promoted to squire, the young man followed his lord at all times everywhere, to the chase and to war. He served his master, carried his arms, led his charger, and learned the difficult art of hearing, understanding, and learning, while appearing to be self-effacing, standing apart, silent, and unobtrusive.

The squire had also to remain behind the lines with the remounts, for no one who had not been dubbed was permitted to confront a knight. As a matter of fact, the squire did not even carry a sword. The most that was permitted him was a pike, although he was more commonly supplied with just a club.

All the while, the day of his investiture was drawing closer and closer. He counted the hours, just as soldiers today count the minutes until the moment of their mustering out, down to the day of the ceremony, a day whose pomp bespoke its almost sacramental reality and inevitability.

"Dubbing," the ceremony by which a man becomes a knight, is derived from the Old High German verb *dubban,* "to strike" (the French and medieval Latin verbs *adober* and *dobbare* come from the same word), and equates the investiture as a knight with the tap on the young man's shoulder given him by a bishop or the overlord as the culminating act of the rite. That tap was given either with a closed fist, the *collata,* or an open hand, the *paumée.*

The dubbing ceremony usually took place in the village square or in the castle courtyard. Sometimes, squires were invested on the field of battle, while in other instances, when there was a desire to stress the religious significance of the act, the rite was performed in church.

On the eve of his dubbing, the squire bathed, confessed himself to a priest, then went into retreat to pass the night in vigil and prayer. On the morning of the great day, after taking communion, he received his arms: sword, baldric, and spurs, blessed by the priest. Next, he vowed to obey the laws of chivalry and to uphold its ideals, fighting for them.

Though bound by these pledges and his own conscience, the knight, however, became a free man, and gained his independence even though he was obliged to defend the weak and perform certain religious duties. As had his confirmation, this new investiture served to remind him that he was born anew into life, and in token of this, an old knight, or the priest, tapped the young squire on the shoulder, using the flat of the hand or a clenched fist, in accordance with the old tradition.

That done, the new knight left the church, leaped upon his horse, which stood waiting, bravely caparisoned, and joyfully galloped off toward freedom. He rode to honor, to combat and tourney, proud, generous, and noble, and to his encounter with his fated lady, his own *belle dame sans merci,* that lovely, austere, and unattainable creature upon whom he might occasionally dare to cast an eye.

X

THE CRUSADERS

The medieval world, exalting class and privilege in every aspect of life, encased its warriors in armor and ended by encapsulating them, more and more, in their individualism and their rigid idealism, turning them deaf and blind to all that was new and on the rise in the East.

Combat had an etiquette of its own—not always respected—and, with an eye to the *beau geste,* when a lord fell, his troops were disbanded, for only personal confrontations between leaders were held to be important and could resolve an issue. These European nobles could not understand the mobile, wily warfare waged by the Byzantine Empire, the combination of shock and surprise—carried to the maximum consequence—that was the tactical resource of Constantinople, which even went so far as to adopt, in the seventh century, that primitive flamethrower called, appropriately enough, "Greek fire." It was the Crusaders who occupied Constantinople during the Fourth Crusade, who managed to lose the secret of that weapon, which they eschewed in a proud burst of misplaced loyalty.

Despite the efforts of the Crusaders, Constantinople did not succeed in saving itself from the new firearms that had already taken a heavy toll of knights from the West. Appearing outside the highly fortified city on the morning of April 12, 1453, Muhammad II pounded its mighty wall with the balls shot by fifty-six cannon and thirteen bombards, until he opened the fatal breach, thus finishing off the Empire of the East, which had long been in its death agony.

That event marked the beginning of the end for the chivalrous cavalry, which still constituted two thirds of the army at the end of the fifteenth century but which by 1528 did not represent more than one eleventh of the troops, and was limited then to the strength in the Spanish forces. Still the "parfit gentil" knights fought on in the name of their innocent ideals, obstinate champions of their code of purity, to the point of falling into the pathetic folly of a Don Quixote. The cannon and the harquebus nullified courage, and treacherously struck down knights prepared to resist and oppose the trend of the times. It did not matter that a knight could harass harquebusiers he had taken prisoner when just one of these men, with a lucky shot, could send to his Creator that invincible adversary, the sublime Bayard, who fell at the Battle of Stesia in 1524. That knight *sans peur et sans reproche—* tales of whose courage fill the last legends of chivalry and who

was honored to the point that Francis I wished to be dubbed by his sword on the eve of the Battle of Marignan—was struck down by a shot fired by an unknown harquebusier.

XI

TOURNAMENTS

The ties that linked rider and horse in the late medieval period were not unlike those that induced Scythian leaders to have themselves interred with their chargers. The barbarian chiefs of Germania and Pannonia also had their horses' company in the tomb until the Church intervened and forbade the practice. Nevertheless, the custom continued for a long time. Not only Chilperic's personal treasure was found in the Frankish King's tomb, but his horse as well, fully decked in his finest trappings.

With the passage of the years, the tournament assumed not only a mystic value (the judgment of God) and a martial significance (the challenge) but a social character as well, a mingling of gallantry and sport that existed despite the fact that the knights were forced to employ the strongest of horses because of the extreme heaviness of their armor. At the early tournaments, one could see as many as two thousand knights take the field. During the Hundred Years War, the English and French often confronted each other in tourney, one might say in *hors-concours,* or side-effects activity, since these encounters had nothing to do with settling the war.

Tournaments offered a knight a good opportunity to keep in trim, win a suit of armor, or perhaps even the amount of a ransom. It was Geoffroy de Preuilly who stipulated the rules for tourneys in a code that was meant to be scrupulously observed. In the course of events, a knight who entered tournaments was tantamount to a professional athlete, as he went from castle to castle, picking up purses for his skill. Finally, it came to a point where two types of dueling weapons were used in these contests: the points were either blunted and draped with cloth for mere tests of skill or left bare and sharpened for fights *à outrance.* In equestrian dueling, the knightly contenders, protected by heavy breastplates and armed with long lances, lined up at the two ends of a broad, grassy field divided into lists and enclosed at the sides by a palisade, behind which were the grandstands for spectators.

At a signal from the trumpet, the knights gave rein to their palfreys and spurred them into a brisk trot. Bit by bit, the pace was quickened so that when the two opposing sides came face to face, the impact was violent. Any knight who could not manage to dodge or withstand the blow from a lance aimed at him by his adversary, and was unhorsed, was declared beaten, and considered to be a prisoner of the man who had unseated him. The winner immediately set about

77 *"St. George and the Dragon." Church of San Zeno Maggiore, Verona.*

78 79 *Details from "The Meeting of the Queen of Sheba and King Solomon," by Piero della Francesca. It is curious to see how the artist always depicts the hoofs of hunting and war horses as being very flat, evidently a distortion for artistic effect. Church of San Francesco, Arezzo.*

77

78

80

81

taking possession of his victim's armor and horse, against a price to ransom them. Thus, a sort of crude professional athleticism developed not unlike the sport in the circuses and arenas of late antiquity. In time, the tournaments attracted even the newly rich bourgeoisie, providing an opportunity for the old nobility to safeguard its prestige as a class. With the death of Henry II of France, who took a mortal blow from a lance at a tournament held in 1559, these contests were outlawed, and innocuous jousting and carrousels took their place.

XII
CHIVALRIC CUSTOMS

When, somewhat more than a hundred years ago, medieval history began to assert itself as an object of interest and admiration, the first element of it to draw general attention and to become a source of enthusiasm and inspiration was chivalry. To the epoch of romanticism the Middle Ages and Chivalry were almost synonymous terms. Historical imagination dwelt by preference on crusades, tournaments, knights-errant. Since then history has become democratic. Chivalry is now only seen as a very special efflorescence of civilization, which, far from having controlled the course of medieval history, has been rather a secondary factor in the political and social evolution of the epoch. For us the problems of the Middle Ages lie first of all in the development of communal organization, of economic conditions, of monarchic power, of administrative and judicial institutions; and, in the second place, in the domain of religion, scholasticism and art. Toward the end of the period our attention is almost entirely occupied by the genesis of new forms of political and economic life (absolutism, capitalism), and new modes of expression (Renaissance). From this point of view feudalism and chivalry appear as little more than a remnant of a superannuated order already crumbling into insignificance, and, for the understanding of the epoch, almost negligible.

Nevertheless, an assiduous reader of the chronicles and literature of the fifteenth century will hardly resist the impression that nobility and chivalry occupy a much more considerable place there than our general conception of the epoch would imply. The reason for this disproportion lies in the fact that, long after nobility and feudalism had ceased to be really essential factors in the state and in society, they continued to impress the mind

as dominant forms of life. The men of the fifteenth century could not understand that the real moving powers of political and social evolution might be looked for anywhere else than in the doings of a warlike or courtly nobility. They persisted in regarding the nobility as the foremost of social forces and attributed a very exaggerated importance to it, undervaluing altogether the social significance of the lower classes.*

The reason that chivalry and its spirit endured, even though it was already surpassed and superseded, was the fact that the pattern of life of the nobility continued to dominate society even long after that same nobility, as a social force, had lost its predominance and because the position of the bourgeoisie as a class had begun to be misconstrued and undervalued.

In his *Temple de Boccace,* Georges Chastellain (fifteenth century) excuses himself for having to mention the great financier Jacques Cœur, while he makes no bones, thanks to his gentle birth, about defending Gilles de Rais despite his crimes; nor does Chastellain think it worth his while to give the names of the bourgeoises fallen at Ghent.

The picture of a world guided by chivalrous principles gives the world a certain color, and writers took pains to present that society in the light of its beauty, although, in reality, the true story is an account of crime, horror, and outrageous abuse of power, a world in a chronic state of dispute, invasion, and war. In substance, the chivalric concept is an aesthetic ideal, composed of fantasy and the emotion of heroism. It intended, as well, to encompass an ethical principle, but since the Middle Ages could honor a concept of life only if it were set in terms of piety and virtue, chivalry was doomed to fail, based, as it was, on sin and violence, the core of the ideal remaining "pride exalted to the point of beauty." Chastellain himself asserted: "The glory of princes rests on pride; all princely powers are in strict accord on one point, and that is: pride."

Not the least of the elements responsible for this attitude was the horse. Pride stylized and exalted gives birth to honor, the staff of life for the nobility. Just as profit is the stimulus of the middle and lower strata of society, according to Taine, pride is one of the great motivations of the aristocracy. The chivalric aspiration toward glory and honor is inseparable from the cult of heroes. The chivalrous life, perforce, is continuous *imitation,* and in this emulation of heroes not much difference is drawn between those of the Arthurian cycle and those of antiquity.

At the time the "romance" was flowering in the most exalted spheres of chivalry, Alexander was already a major figure. However, when one comes to the romance, *Le Jouvencel,* based upon the life of Jean de Bueil, who died in 1477 (?), one finds realistic features touched with the sort of glorification of war that is an early anticipation of the spirit of martial France, the same spirit that was later to create the stereotypes of the *mousquetaire,* the *grognard,* and the *poilu.* Here, one senses the metamorphosis of a universal figure—the medieval Euro-

80 *"Tournament in Honor of the King of Denmark," by Marcello Fogolino. Knights contending, two by two, in the lists, which are separated by a fence, while others stand by, awaiting the signal from the trumpets that will send them into action. Castello di Malpaga, Bergamo.*

81 *Illustration from* Le Livre de Tournois du Roi René, *by Giron le Courtois, showing a very old type of tourney in which two groups of knights, sometimes as many as a thousand or more to a side, opposed each other in extremely bloody and costly entertainments. Bibliothèque National, Paris.*

* John Huizinga, *The Waning of the Middle Ages* (New York: St. Martin's Press, Inc., 1948).

pean champion—into a national military hero. As a matter of fact, the hero of the book releases his prisoners on the condition that they "become good Frenchmen."

Above and beyond heroism and pride, the chivalrous life was a dream of love. The more it obeyed those imperatives, the more accentuated became the ascetic element that already pervaded the great religiomilitary orders of the period of the Crusades. But in the measure that reality belied the ideal, the ideal retreated into the realm of fantasy. Nevertheless, in the great champions, the chivalrous ideal was warmed, on one hand, by the heat of religious conscience, compassion, justice, and fidelity, and on the other, by the flame of love despairingly offered a lady who was, on principle, absolutely unattainable. Undoubtedly, the raptures of amorous sentimentalism found dramatic release in that magnificent spectacle, the tournament.

The tournament was the medieval sport par excellence, since it was highly dramatic, and carried a heavy charge of eroticism. Actually, the sports of any age have this same amalgam of dramatic and erotic elements, but, while modern sport has returned to a linearity that is almost Hellenic, the medieval joust, particularly that of the late Middle Ages, was a sport supercharged with ornamentation, heavily draped, in which the dramatic and romantic elements were intentionally supplied in order fully to realize the very function of the exercise.

Furthermore, one of the most important turnings taken by the medieval spirit was that for the first time it put forth an idea of love having a negative basis: courtly love, in which the feeling of painful sadness stemmed not so much from a lack of erotic satisfaction as from a prior conviction that an unhappy outcome was inevitable. Accordingly, love became the ground in which any perfection of art or morality inherent in a knight could flourish, while reality compelled the spirit increasingly to forswear the chivalrous ideal.

For a long time, the art of war had shown no conformity with the protocol of the tournament. Warfare in the fourteenth and fifteenth centuries was waged on a basis of ambush and surprise attack, raids, and bandits' tactics. The English were the first to reintroduce the custom of knights dismounting before a battle so that they might fight on foot, a practice that was soon adopted by the French, as well, leading to the sarcastic observation by the balladeer Eustache Deschamps that it served to make flight more difficult.

In the *Débat des hérauls d'armes de France et d'Angleterre*, written about 1455, the inadequacy of the chivalrous ideal as a military principle is ingeniously presented, that is, an effort is made to save appearances while announcing the changes that firearms have been making in the conduct of war on horseback. After all this, the fact that Jacques de Lalaing, the very model of a proper knight-errant, would be killed by cannon fire sounds like the irony of fate.

The profession of arms had its economic charm for the nobility, and they spoke of it with utter frankness. Every stage of the history of the early Middle Ages makes it obvious how much importance was attached to the fact of being able to take distinguished prisoners, with a view to a large ransom. Froissart never omits mentioning just how much the perpetrator of a felicitous "strike" managed to make. Aside from these immediate profits, the nobility could also look to receiving pensions, revenue, and administrative posts. Chastellain found it perfectly natural that a man who wished to acquire earthly glory be greedy and calculating.

XIII
PAS D'ARMES

In the fifteenth century, to organize a *pas d'armes* one simulated a romantic adventure, and upon that foundation artistically constructed a joust.

In the midst of a romantic setting, *la fontaine des pleurs* or *l'arbre de Charlemagne*, a lady would stand with a unicorn bearing three shields. Any knight who tapped one of those escutcheons or had it touched by his squire committed himself to fight in a particular duel and in accordance with the conditions—stipulated in every detail—in the so-called *chapitre* (literally, "chapter") that was both the announcement of the joust and its regulations. The shields were always struck on horseback, and knights found horses there available for that purpose.

For an *emprise du dragon,* on the other hand, four horsemen would station themselves at a crossroads, and no lady would be permitted to pass until a knight had broken two lances for her; otherwise, a forfeit would have to be paid. (Our games with forfeits derive from these courtly exercises.)

One can read in one of these *chapitres* that a man who is unhorsed during the duel must wear a golden handcuff for the rest of the year or until he finds the lady with the key to it, when he may be released by her if he vows to place himself at her service.

All these games are hazed by a mist of melancholy. The shields are white, violet, or black, dotted with pearl tears. Whoever strikes them does so in the name of the *Dame de pleurs*. In the *emprise du dragon,* the king, René of Anjou, appears in black mourning, mounted on a black horse. His shield is black, with golden teardrops, for he has come to take his leave of his daughter, Margaret, now Queen of England.

XIV
DEVELOPMENTS IN EQUITATION

Equitation in the Middle Ages was rude and sketchy, and comprised exercises designed to put an adversary at a disadvantage so that he could be attacked and overcome. Nevertheless, those maneuvers did require notable coordination and timing, for a knight who betrayed through the action of his hands or legs what his next move might be would leave himself open to being struck or even unseated by a quick and clever opponent.

With these considerations in mind, therefore, the seat that developed positioned the rider so that one arm had complete freedom in wielding a weapon. His legs hung down, almost straight, so that the horse could be contained by the heels and the extremely long and sharp spurs, allowing the horseman to move the upper part of his body in whatever direction he might need to go in striking or parrying blows. For that reason, the hand that held the reins, firmly enough to control the horse and his movement, was not supposed to act in any way that might neutralize this natural impulsion or prevent the horse from following through.

This was unsophisticated, utilitarian equitation. It should be noted that the tournaments called for turns, pirouettes, quick half-turns, and unexpected maneuvers from horses that were extremely massive, heavy, and with little sensitivity. Furthermore, these animals were carrying anywhere from six hundred to eight hundred pounds on their backs, not to mention riders rigid and unyielding in armor that restricted their every movement. Such conditions called for a very strong bit and spurs that carried more than a hint of authority, even though it was only at rare times in a tourney that a knight would have his horse break into a gallop—a gait highly uncomfortable for a man in iron armor, which would inevitably ride up and down on his body to give him something of a drubbing.

The fast gait of the Middle Ages was the amble. Usually, one traveled and fought at the walk, not in the least because dignity demanded a certain sobriety in behavior that the walk was able to confer.

The disasters of Benevento (1266), of the Teutonic knights (1280), and at Crécy and Agincourt, in 1346 and 1415 respectively, all manifested the defects of chivalric concepts of warfare and hastened the end of the old ways of thinking that had grown out of feudalism. The old chivalrous military caste was exhausted, and it was time for new ideas. With the advent of gunpowder, the change would be complete.

It was this break of the chivalric life that served to open two new roads to the horse: on the one hand, equitation came into its own as a pure art, school riding; and on the other, the horse was to emerge as the incomparable runner as breeds were improved through the importing of mares and stallions of Arab blood—two ways, two paths to the delightful, entertaining life that would come only with the evolution in customs that the Renaissance would bring.

XV

THE RENAISSANCE

The knight's inevitable passage from ideals more or less religious to worldly was a gradual but irresistible progression. Both society and the horse beckoned to him to ride, to mount the animal that had, bit by bit, evolved from an instrument and means of war to an object of pure beauty and a delightful sporting companion in the hunt or in the virtuosity of games and manège.

Despite their equivocation and errors, the Crusaders had realized in their time just what valuable assets the speed and manageability of the Arab horse were, and from the Orient they had imported into old Europe good specimens of the breed regarded, notwithstanding, with a certain diffidence because of their small stature. At the same period, the Arabian equestrian world of Spain—which had the famous jennets, elegant, spirited steeds—was to contribute its creation of the Andalusian breed, the root stock for the finest of saddle horses.

Inspired by Arabian experts, by the writings of Abubekr-ibn-Bedr, who had lived at the court of the Sultan of Cairo in the thirteenth century, and stimulated, above all, by fragments from the writings of Varro, Cato, Columella, and the poetic passages in Vergil's *Georgics*, a whole new European equine and equestrian literature came into being. There were the works of the Sicilian Giordano Ruffo, who

was at the court of Frederick II; the writings of the Bolognese Pietro de' Crescenzi, and the Roman Lorenzo Risio, who were the first to offer a rational study of the horse's good and bad points, his diseases, and his feeding, which gradually did away with a good deal of medieval superstition. To these might also be added the perceptive studies made by painters and sculptors, rediscovering the anatomy of the horse, of which an outstanding example is the earlier-mentioned essay by Carlo Ruini with marvelous anatomic sketches attributed to Leonardo da Vinci.

Meanwhile, the great Italian princely families were spurred to develop their own breeds—horses that were faster, more beautiful, and more resistant than those of a neighboring prince. These breeds became the glory of their house, and were sent all over Italy to be ridden by pages in livery* to compete with and, if possible, outdo the horses shown by rival princes. Very soon, the outstanding breeds were those raised by the Estenso, and then by the Gonzaga families, splendid examples of which dominate Giulio Romano's frescoes in the Palazzo del Tè.

To speak of horses was a pleasant and cultured thing to do, like talking of books, paintings, and philosophy, and the most elegant of all was conversation about bloodlines and breeding, as well as favorites, as today the *raffinés* discuss sports cars and GT models, cylinders and horsepower! If one wanted to make a career in certain courts, like that at Mantua (Isabella d'Este was mad about beautiful horses), one had best be up on chargers, racers, and palfreys. Hence, the unquestioned value as a courtier of Baldassarre Castiglione, who was a man of letters, a diplomat, and a very astute horse breeder. He took the horses of his lord, Federico Gonzaga, to race meetings all over the peninsula, and saw them win, giving strict written orders to the jockeys so that if they lost, there was always evidence of what his instructions had been.

In some lines of *The Courtesan*, there is a certain boredom evident, for example in the passage where Castiglione complains: "The great lords are like that. Above all, one has to give them news of their horses, and chat with them for hours about them, then listen, without tiring, to whatever it pleases them to say on the subject."

From Castiglione, one recalls the famous episode of the Roman race, when one of his master's horses was cut off just before the finish line by an armiger of the pope, whose horse won. Baldassarre was furious and out for blood, despite a soothing letter from His Holiness who, finally, not to lose the support of the powerful House of Gonzaga, sent them a copy of the first prize, a magnificent silver fruit dish wrought by Cellini. It was Baldassarre Castiglione who unwittingly contributed to the creation of the thoroughbred the day he suggested to his lord that he send Henry VIII of England a painting by Raphael and a few mares from his celebrated stock. Though it is difficult to retrace that Italian blood in the bloodlines of the famous Royal Mares, someone has attempted to do so.

In Henry's letter of thanks to the duke, one can read of his gratitude for *illo equorum genere*. Just what does he mean

---

* The first jockeys as we know them today.—TRANS.

by "that kind of horse"? Race horses, naturally. Henry was also lucky enough to receive in that same year of 1533 a gift of some outstanding mares from Catherine of Savoy, the daughter of Philip II of Spain. The mares came from the great stud near Turin, possibly one of the finest in all Italy. Those mares also must have had Oriental blood, since the Italians had long since discovered that such lineage was the best for winning races. That Eastern horses were used as racers is amply borne out by the fact that certain events, like the "barb races" (for "barb" read "Berber"), were named for the breed that competed in them, in this instance, those imported from the Barbary Coast of Africa.

To realize just how much the rest of the world prized the Italian breeds during the sixteenth century, one need only recall that in 1595, when Vincenzo Gonzaga left with a crack detachment for Hungary, joining the forces of Rudolf II against the Turks, he had the admiration of all as he passed through the Tyrol, Austria, and Bohemia with his troop of one thousand horsemen mounted on select horses. This was a cavalry force such as no country, not even the Spain of Philip II or the France of Henry of Navarre, could put into the field. (At that time, England was just beginning to elaborate its plans to develop a horse that would be swifter and more manageable than any other type then in use for civilian purposes, that would be, primarily, for use by the cavalry.) Fine specimens from the celebrated stud of the Gonzagas, these Mantuan horses elicited admiration wherever they went. They were ridden by the court horsemen, who put them through their paces as they went from one city to the next, one country to another, making them rear up and prance in an extravagantly fanciful display. The Gonzaga riders wore scarlet hose and scarlet doublets laced with golden yellow and ornamented with yellow-and-white ribbon bows. All of them wore caps with long yellow-and-white plumes. At the head of the company rode Duke Vincenzo on his favorite horse, the celebrated Armellino, extraordinarily fiery and high-spirited.

Among the statutes of republican Padua, one can find an ordinance establishing that a *palio,* or race, three turns around the Prato della Valle, would be run each year on the twentieth of June to mark the end, in 1236, of the tyrannical rule of Ezzelino da Romano (1194–1259). It provides that the owner of the winning horse receive twelve lengths *(braccie)* of scarlet cloth, the runner-up, a hawk, and the third, a pair of gloves. No horse worth less than fifty lire would be permitted to enter.

As a matter of fact, long before this event was decreed to celebrate the victory over Ezzelino, it was customary to race at the old Prate della Valle. Later, races were run along the road going from Voltabarozzo to the Piazza delle Erbe, and this route was first decreed for the race of July 25, 1318, the day on which the citizens of Padua conferred seignorial rights upon Jacopo I, Duke of Carrara. The ancient records of Padua also show a race for August 3, 1338, to the glory and honor of Marsiglio I, Duke of Carrara, and another, on May 8, 1338, to celebrate the commencement of the seigniory of Jacopo II. Another *palio* was decreed by the Venetian republic to commemorate the spontaneous alliance to it of the Paduans on November 17, 1405. The course ran from the Bassanello bridge through the gate of Santa Croce to the church of San Martino, which was demolished in 1811, but

then stood in front of the main portal of the university. From 1509 to 1560, the Strà Maggiore—today, via Dante—was the designated track for the race decreed by their excellencies.

In 1608, on the fourteenth of June, the barb race was revived. It began on the Pontecorvo road, about a mile outside the gate, and passing the San Lorenzo bridge, terminated in the Piazza del Vino, now the Piazza delle Erbe, in front of the Spitieria del Lion d'Oro. In 1638, a proclamation announced new races for June—and a very attractive event in which women would be substituting for men in the footrace, the winner to receive a length of crimson cloth.

Interesting details are given in the documents that refer to the races held in June, 1657. Barbs, jades, and asses ran from a point outside the Pontecorvo gate, "il luogo del Rovere," to the "Pomi d'oro," the name of the apothecary shop located at the end of the via Beccherie Vecchie, today called via Cesare Battisti, while the race for women began at the Pontecorvo plaza.

A horse race was held in 1765 that started at Santa Croce, a short distance from the church, and terminated there after going three times around the Prato della Valle. The splendid spectacle was again repeated in the following year, 1766, in the only outside enclosure of the Prato. In that year, on June 11th, the great square was festively decked for the horse races that were to take place on the morrow. Rugs, brocades, and tapestries were draped from the windows of all the houses adjoining the course. The sixteen riders who were entered for the event made three turns around the Prato della Valle. The winner was the horse entered by the nobleman Ciera, who carried off thirty lengths of velvet as his prize. After the race for barbs, there was an event for men on horseback, which called for jockeys riding bareback at the gallop, three turns around the track, for a prize of thirty ducats.

XVI
ORIGINS OF THE THOROUGHBRED

While the Italian nobility was creating fine breeds that were confined to a duchy or a region, the English kings were able to operate on a much wider scale and with economic resources two or three times those available to the Italians. Even so, we know that the English monarchs' horse-breeding activities were haphazard for lack of competent direction, to the point that Elizabeth I, at the suggestion of the Duke of Leicester, called to her court from Naples the man reputed at that time to be the leading specialist in the field, Don Prospero d'Osma.

In 1576, d'Osma wrote his report, in Italian, on the English royal stud, a manuscript that lay lost to the world in the library of the Earls of Leicester, until brought to light by a bookdealer; it is now in New York. Don Prospero's account can be considered as the first documentation of the English Thoroughbred. Among the brood mares that Don Prospero mentions and evaluates, the outstanding ones are those with Italian names, like "Brilladoro" and "Savoia," given, precisely, to indicate their origin. Of capital importance is Don Prospero's admonition not to cross two different breeds, as the offspring would be bastards. The statement is even more valuable as testimony when one considers that those prized mares were always covered by Oriental studs, which is sufficient evidence to establish that the mares, too, must have been of Eastern origin.

From these indications, Federico Tesio, in his valuable *Purosangue, animale da esperimento,* deduces: "The horse that wins the great classics in any part of the world is probably almost wholly descended from Oriental bloodlines."

Tesio adds that, in 1655, Cromwell wrote to Longland, his diplomatic agent in Leghorn, asking him to send thoroughbred Orientals from Naples and the East; Longland then shipped him six horses, paying the equivalent of $2,400. He also tells us that the first book of systematic genealogy, published by Reginald Heber in 1756, and regularly by James Weatherby from 1793, besides giving data on the most prominent winners of that remote period, attempted to trace their origins. It was discovered that almost all these horses were of Oriental provenance, with very few being of unknown origin—which does not exclude the fact that they may well have had Eastern beginnings, too.

This *General Stud Book,* together with the *Racing Calendar*— the race results that have been published regularly since 1727—provides a means of checking on millions of horses, which are described minutely as to physical and temperamental characteristics, along with their lineage and racing performances. It was a scientific patrimony that Tesio knew how to put to good use.

Nevertheless, there always remains the biological mystery inherent in the creation of a type of horse that can do three fifths of a mile in less than a minute and maintain that speed for about thrice the distance, while the Arab horse, extremely fast, cannot keep that pace for more than about a half mile. On the other hand, going by the running time registered for Eclipse's races over the quondam classic distance of 6,400 meters (about four miles)—6:42 as a maiden and 6:00 in a subsequent race—we must consider that champion a nonpareil whose descendants are the palest shadows of their great forebear. That he was a phenomenon is confirmed by the records, which show that he led the field, all hand picked, by some 400 meters (about a quarter mile). In any case, the running times registered officially from 1846 on guarantee some progress in the Thoroughbred, at least in connection with speed; but the very fact of such horses as Eclipse and the other two great sires, Herod* and Matchem, is still something of a biological enigma.

One wonders if those three prodigious progenitors would ever have been born and if the breed would have been equally fast and as much esteemed if three great Arab sires, the Godolphin Barb, the Byerley Turk, and the Darley Arabian had not been imported into England, and if the selection of the descendants of these three had continued from among the preceding eighty-two Arab stallions, forty-six Barbs, and thirty-eight Turks that appeared registered in the *General Stud Book* and the various pedigrees.

Undoubtedly, England artificially managed to create a masterpiece, so that the cream of the turf outdid the cream of the desert, or the original strain. We are given proof of that in a curious incident. Once the breed was established, the English Jockey Club, convinced of the purity of that breed—

---

* Often known as King Herod.—TRANS.

but, actually, in error—definitively closed the *Almanach de Gotha* of the Thoroughbred.

It was only at the beginning of 1800, in France, that it was reopened as a result of this reasoning: if the Arab created the English Thoroughbred, surely, if we inject new Arab blood into the line, using select mares, we should be able to get an even better breed. The result was a fiasco. The offspring not only lost ground, but speed as well. The new Arab blood was eliminated, for since the horses were incapable of winning, they were weeded out.

What then, is the Thoroughbred? He is a magnificent bastard, according to Tesio, selected not on the basis of Mendelian characteristics, but on the perfection and resistance of the material.

XVII
SADDLES AND BITS

The *selle à piquer* (literally, the "spurring saddle") is peculiarly connected with the equitation of the Middle Ages. One need only observe the development of the tree and the cantle *(troussequin)* to understand that these elements formed a sort of cradle into which the knight was set securely so that he could better resist the shock of his adversary's lance blows, in jousting, in the carrousels, or in the tournaments. It was a saddle built precisely to satisfy the needs of the rider of that period.

According to some authorities, the *selle à piquer* received its name because it was used by the *picadores* of the bullring. Others maintain that it served to fix the rider's position when he spurred his horse on, *piquait le cheval avec l'éperon.*

Later on, when heavy armor was abandoned, the saddle became lighter, as horsemen looked for fast, manageable mounts. The revolutionary changes in the cavalry would never have come about without the influence of equitation itself, and proof of this can be seen in the changes made in the saddle by La Guérinière, who abolished the *battes* (batts) and *troussequins* to make the saddle lighter and more appropriate to the needs of a horseman who wanted to be unrestricted and free to manage his mount with ability, speed, and precision.

The *selles à piquer,* which preserved a sort of rudimentary cantle, were called *royales* or *demi-royales.* The *selle rase* (the close-fit saddle), also called the *selle à la française,* does not resemble the *selle à piquer,* except for very short and low *battes* that surmount the front arch of the saddle. These were the saddles used in French manège for all of the nineteenth century. There is also a *selle à piquer* for wild horses, buckers, and unbridled jumpers that assures the rider's stability against the risk of being unhorsed.

While the French saddle is built with the intention of facilitating the positioning of the horseman and his movements in control of his mount, the English saddle is made to burden the horse as little as possible yet allow the maximum freedom of movement to the rider and the greatest contact with the animal.

Bits became more and more complex, both in the mouthpieces and cheekpieces—more goldsmith's creations than anything wrought by a blacksmith—decorated with an agglomeration of dragons, monsters, and leaves; the imagination ran riot to create such contrivances as "chicken-leg snaffles,"

"Calabrian snaffles," and so on. The one thing they all had in common was that they were instruments of torture, even though equitation had become more refined. They were particularly in vogue among the Spaniards and those influenced by Spanish fashions. In England, on the other hand, every effort was bent toward reducing the weight of the saddle, harness, and vehicle, so that everything was much simpler and more appropriate to riding.

XVIII
ARMOR

The eternal conflict between arms and armor, between offense and defense prior to the invention of gunpowder, was brought to its maximum consequence by the cavalry of the Middle Ages. It was a time when the horse functioned simultaneously as an arm of penetration, at the charge, and as a living bulwark when, protected by the same armor as his rider, they awaited the enemy's attack.

The "new method" of employing the lance, and the use of the ironclad mace by cavalrymen, rendered the *cotto*—the hauberks and cuirasses derived from the Roman *lorica*—inadequate as protection. Reinforced with metal bands that grew wider and wider, designed to protect the most exposed parts of the rider's body, armor reached the point where it became a veritable shell encapsulating both man and horse, isolating them from all external contact—serving to aggrandize pride, as well.

The armorers needed an extraordinary knowledge of anatomy to construct such protective gear that would constrict neither the horse nor the rider's arms and that would allow them freedom of action. Authentic masterpieces in metal were made in which technology and art were admirably blended.

This craft flourished particularly in Milan, where even today street names such as Armorari (Armorers) and Speronare (Spur-makers) give evidence of all that activity. Knights from France, Germany, and even England came to Milan to have themselves measured for custom-made armor, armor that was constantly being improved and perfected.

The Missaglia and Negroli families were the master armorers of the fifteenth century, and were knighted for their skill by the duke Filippo Maria Visconti. They reached the pinnacle of their art in the virtuosity shown in their damascened armor, which they were making around the start of the sixteenth century.

Besides the Negrolis and Missaglias, who owned an ironworks in Brianza, there were other prominent armorers around the end of the fifteenth century, like the Barmi Negroli, the Figino, and Mola families, who went from Florence to Rome, as well as Pompeo della Cesa, military tailor and armorer to Philip II of Spain, the Farneses, and the Gonzagas.

The horse's accouterments and all the accessories used for war and the hunt were also ornate with arabesques and chased design. Milan was so full of armorers and their stock was so extensive that Filippo Maria Visconti was able, in just a few days, to reequip four thousand cavalrymen and two thousand infantrymen that Francesco Bussone da Carmagnola's army had stripped of everything after having taken them prisoner at Maclodio in 1427.

The Helmschmied clan of Augusta (Sicily), who availed themselves of the talents of such artists as Dürer, were rivals of the Milanese.

Examining suits of armor, we can see that the knights were usually very wiry, muscular, not very tall, with the broad shoulders and slim legs common to jockeys, because they did little exercise on foot.

During the whole of the medieval period, the success of a battle depended exclusively on the cavalry, an extension of the social order that set its sights by the noble knight. Since riding well was the fundamental requirement of a gentleman, along with knowing how to handle arms, there was no need to write texts on equitation, as these principles were passed on orally and through practice and emulation from father to son, from knight to page.

Generally, for important engagements, the knight wore plate (or coin) armor, but he often carried a coat of mail in his saddlebag to don for protection should he be caught by a surprise attack unarmored. Otherwise, he might wear a brigandine, a short coat of velvet interwoven with bands of overlapping steel or silver plates, a handsome garment that the elegant young men liked to wear to impress the ladies.

In the thirteenth century, knights began wearing over the coat of mail a surcoat that bore their blazon, a custom that often saved their lives, for their arms served as a guarantee that they could pay ransom. Later, however, sovereigns were constrained to send "doubles" wearing their arms onto the field so that they themselves would not present the obvious target. In Shakespeare's *Richard III,* the king exclaims:

"I think there be six Richmonds in the field;
Five have I slain today, instead of him."

Still elegant, and perhaps even more elegant than in battle dress, knights participated in tournaments and carrousels, and tilted at the quintain to show their skill and to keep themselves in training for combat. The tournament was a team competition, while the joust was a duel between two adversaries who confronted each other, using either real weapons or blunted lances.

Before the tourney or joust, it was customary for a knight to display his plumed helmet and his escutcheon for inspection by the judges, who were empowered to disqualify any entrant if he was not considered worthy of participating or lacked the necessary quarterings.

During the Middle Ages, knights used a large, double-edged sword with a cross hilt, a solid, resistant weapon for duels that consisted mainly of slashing strokes. At a later period, the Italians came to realize that the point of the sword

82 *Pisanello's studies of the horse's proportions.*
83 *"The Months: April," by Fr. del Cossa, showing riders racing bareback, using light bridles, followed by others mounted on asses, a somewhat grotesque touch. Palazzo di Schifanoia, Ferrara.*
84 85 *"Lorenzo de' Medici as One of the Magi." Details from the work by Benozzo Gozzoli show a single rigid rein, richly decorated. Palazzo Riccardi, Florence.*

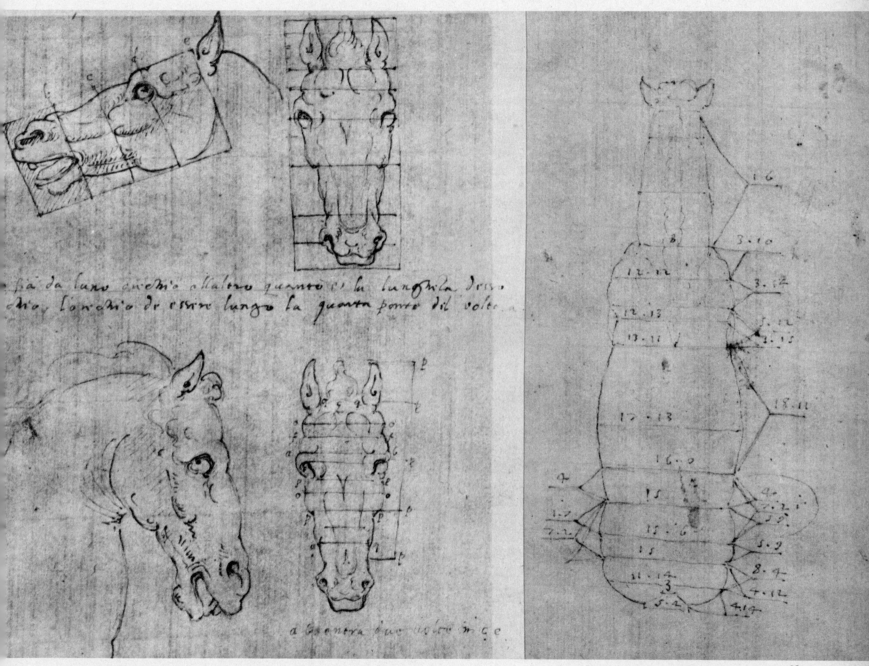

86

87

was more important than the edge; accordingly, they devised a lighter weapon, the sword that gave rise to the art of fencing.

While the horseman dominated an age when war matériel was scarce, with foot soldiers armed only with clubs or pikes and, therefore, easily undone by a cavalry charge, that situation was quickly reversed with the Battle of Crécy, when the peasant infantry took to the field armed with bows and arrows to put the cavalry into serious difficulty. These archers aimed for the horse, for even a light wound would make an animal disregard his rider's hand on the rein, causing him, perhaps, to become unseated, and a knight unhorsed was a man irremediably lost.

In 1487, Maximilian I armed his lansquenets with halberds, a weapon that was a cross between a lance and a pike. It could be shafted or used for slashing, and had a beak or hook employed against horses to make them rear and unseat their riders.

Maces, mallets, and halberds were nothing more than derivatives of the arms used by peasants while serving their feudal lords. Later, the crossbow reappeared on the scene. Since it could pierce armor, the knights reacted by wearing thicker plates.

In 1460, firearms began to replace the crossbow, but rather than make the use of body armor obsolescent, that development led to its increased use and, as late as the seventeenth century, military technicians continued to bend all their efforts to finding a new type of armor that would be proof against musket and pistol shots. Things got to the point where some horsemen were wearing two sets of armor, one over the other, which, naturally, considerably curtailed the mobility of the cavalry as a whole.

According to Stephen V. Grancsay in *Arms and Armor*, even the soldiers were equipped with the heaviest of armor until they refused to wear it. At first, the men asked for more compensation, because of the extra fatigue they suffered on the march; then, they just "lost" their armor, and got rid of it that way.

Armor was worn right down to the middle of the seventeenth century in combat, but it was, actually, more parade dress than anything, and it was still worn, as well, in the carrousels. A reflection of those times continued to be seen in the helmets of such mounted troops as dragoons and uhlans and in the steel helmet of the modern soldier.

XIX

SCHOOL EQUITATION

During the period of the Italian Renaissance the *crème de la crème* of French and German nobility were drawn to the Peninsula to learn there the sophisticated manners and graces of the Italian princely courts. Besides learning to handle the sword and to dance, they ultimately took up a certain style

86 *Head of a horse in sixteenth-century Milanese armor. Museo Stibbert, Florence.*

87 *Head of a horse in sixteenth-century Nuremberg armor. Museo Stibbert, Florence.*

of equitation that was taught in Naples, and subsequently in Ferrara, and was a fashion no gentleman could afford to ignore.

It would appear that there were riding academies in Naples from about the twelfth century. These, most likely, were schools of equitation maintained by Byzantine emigrants come to seek their fortunes in a city that had always maintained cultural links with the ancient capital of the Eastern Empire. The first great school of which we have evidence, however, is that which was opened by the nobleman Giovan Battista Pignatelli, a gentleman belonging to a family of Lombard stock, a school which he opened after returning from a voyage to Constantinople.

Pignatelli gets the credit for being the first to train a horse using a breaking cavesson and a pillar, although some mosaics dating from the period of Rome's decline would seem to indicate that the pillar was already in use at that time. It was at Pignatelli's academy that Federico Grisone, who gave us the first complete text on equitation, was trained. The work, entitled *Gli Ordini de Cavalcare* (The Rules for Riding), was published in 1561, a fundamental work on which other Italian riding masters from Fiaschi to Caracciolo, Curzio to Santapaulina have drawn.

In substance, the brutally utilitarian equitation of the Middle Ages was transformed into a passionate, rigorous study—mathematically and physiologically supported—of the horse and rider as a dual entity at the various gaits, both natural and artificial. It was viewed in the light of a new aesthetic and rationale: the influence of the rider's seat and action on the comportment and reactions of the horse, along with the interplay of balance between horse and rider. The decline and demise of the tournament, the changed role of cavalry in battle, the growing refinement in manners, and the evolution and improvement of breeds of horse are all factors that combined to modify the training criteria and even the very concept of equitation. It is due to those various modifications that, even today, Grisone's training methods are still characterized by firmness and even brutality, at times, while Antoine de Pluvinel and the Duke of Newcastle's systems tend toward a type of domestication that is softer and employs more persuasive and gentle means. François Robichon de la Guérinière's method emphasizes regularity and kindness, while somewhat later, Vicomte Pierre Marie d'Abzac was to call for precision and energy, decision and vigor in his style of training.

As we have said, Grisone's brutality cannot be justified, unless we consider that the horses of his time were still heavy and unresponsive, lacking, as they did, spirit and sensitivity, necessitating violent means if they were to obey instantly. Shortly after, however, with the appearance of lighter, more sensitive breeds and finer gear, trainers were much more cautious in their use of "aids," possibly because of the greater delicacy of the horses or possibly because this new employment of the animal was designed to display the horseman's ability, grace, and deftness rather than his courage and valor. La Guérinière wrote:

M. de la Broue, who flourished during the reign of Henri IV, wrote a book that affirms the principles of Jean-Baptiste Pignatelli, the illustrious master who had a riding academy in Naples. That school had such a great reputation that it was regarded as the best in the world. All of French and German nobility who wished to perfect themselves in equitation were obliged to go and take lessons from that famous teacher.

In the *Dictionnaire d'hippiatrique* (The Horseman's Dictionary), written by François Cardini, one can read: "It was from Naples that La Broue and Pluvinel brought those principles of the art to France, where academies were founded in Paris, Tours, Bordeaux, and Lyons, and such establishments later multiplied all over the kingdom. In Germany, it was Eisenberg who broadcast those same principles."

Furthermore, at a time when the cavalry fought by "profound" orders instead of successive waves of "subtle" ones, and riders confronted each other in tournament, the style of equitation used was clipped and cadenced, always that of the parade ground, with little or no speed, but calling for the instant submission of the horse to the demands of the rider, which explained the strong bits and the cruel spurs.

From the day that the tournament was abolished and armor became lighter, when the cavalry became the fighting arm that was looked to for quick, surprise attack and rapid withdrawal, there was no longer any call for horses that were "set" at cadenced paces, but a need for more brilliant subjects.

Equitation *raccourcie* was replaced by a style that was more relaxed, free, and flashy, whose technical bases might be summed up as follows: Strive for speed and changes of gait while continuing, nevertheless, to control the horse, guaranteeing the means of command.

What one had, therefore, was an application of measures and methods that responded to the necessities to be satisfied, while maintaining, unaltered, certain principles that are fundamental and valid at any period. It has always been difficult, no matter what the time, to apply principles in the most convenient way, that is, *in the measure* most appropriate. In other words, what is always required is just enough of the proper means and impulsion to arrive at the desired result.

XX
FEDERICO GRISONE

Thus, Grisone, to achieve a brilliant result and simultaneously render the massive horses of his time submissive, counseled against "making flexible" the neck of the horse. He understood that animals so built would lose all their forward force if their necks were to give; and so he revived the method of achieving the horseman's requirement through violent use of the spurs in order to engage the animal's hindquarters for turns, pesades, courbettes, curvets, and half-turns.

To give adequate lightness to the horse's back, a quality completely lacking in these heavy animals—to their disadvantage—he advised riding in freshly plowed fields, over rocky roads, through torrents, and on the seashore, in order to force the horse to lift his legs and give his back and shoulders a good workout. He sought to give fire and speed to these horses by riding them "all out" for fairly long distances, but since they were always lacking in vigor and were, by nature, coldly unresponsive, he recommended that they never be allowed to "flex," realizing, as he did, that no horse would ever make a good war-horse if he lacked firmness and solidity

in the neck, for, as a matter of fact, excessive flexibility in that part of the body would give rise not only to uncertainty in the horse, but defensiveness, as well.

Let us quote some of the passages from Grisone's book so that we can see how advanced that master was in his understanding of the play of equilibrium and force. In a dry but lively style, although not always very clear, he writes:

In order to make you understand how to aid a horse with the spurs, at the beginning of the "promenade," if you wish to turn to the right, you must aid him from the opposite side, with the left spur, and with the right, increase the pressure in order to make the turn a rounded one, so that the horse turns exactly on his track . . .

It is necessary to aid him at the beginning of the turn, then at the halfway point, but the inside spur must make contact farther to the rear than the other one (which hits in the region of the girth straps), almost at the groin.

At this moment, you will have a great deal of difficulty in knowing the feeling and disposition of the horse, and consequently in giving him the spur at the precise moment and to the right degree. It is here, gentlemen, that practice, example, and experience are worth more than words. . . .

I am warning you that the horse will use any trick he can, like tossing his head, resisting the aids, or champing the bit. When he resorts to this, however, or to any such maneuver, you must reprimand him in a stern and angry tone of voice, shouting roughly and menacingly, using whatever words come to mind, like: "Come on, get on, get going, you traitor, rebel! About-face, turn, stop, turn this way, turn that . . ." and more of the same, so that your shouts are tremendously intimidating. Keep on with this until he gets it right.

Dressage for horses, as Grisone and his predecessors understood it, was intended for a common, heavy sort of horse, destined for combat. When Pluvinel and Newcastle were teaching, saddles and the accouterments of war were being made much lighter, and lighter breeds, such as the Barbs and Spanish horses already employed, were coming to the fore. Not only could work be more refined as better horses appeared and were put to better use, but also, because of the fashion for carrousels, they were supposed to show finesse more than raw courage.

Grisone understood perfectly the action and opposition, the resistance and support that served to get a horse moving properly and maintain him at the desired cadence. He also had a profound comprehension of the horse's character. Another interesting passage:

But do not think that the horse, no matter how well made, well proportioned, and endowed by nature, can do things himself and go through his paces without help from a man and the proper discipline.

88 *Milanese armor of the sixteenth century, made for a horse lighter and more agile than the medieval type, foreshadowing those adaptable to school equitation. Armeria Reale, Turin.*

89

It is, therefore, necessary to give him a thorough "workout" and bring to light all the hidden virtues that he may possess and, in proportion to the skill and mastery with which he is treated, those good points will become apparent; just as it is possible, with art, to compensate for certain deficiencies in the animal.

The ancient Romans called him *equus* (what a sweet philological blunder!) which has no significance whatsoever unless the horse be correct in everything, and through everything, in every respect, correct and balanced: correct at the walk, at the trot, and at the canter, and correct at full speed; correct at rest, correct at work, and correct while jumping. Finally, his head must be correct, also his stance, and he must be just as correct, in the same measure, as the man who mounts him.

Furthermore, his walk should be high-stepping, his trot easy and elegant, his canter vigorous and powerful, his jump elastic; and he must appear light, and his movements swift and sure.

One must know, working him, that he will pick up agility at the trot, vigor at the gallop, and speed at full gallop, and power when jumping...but the neck and the set of the neck should be incredibly firm and the mouth should be soft and held correctly, which is the foundation of the whole theory.

That is a rather splendid passage, in its technical crispness and the elegance of its style, in some ways worthy of Xenophon.

XXI
SALAMON DE LA BROUE

La Broue advises:

After having obtained the desired suppleness with the cavesson, it is time to employ the false reins,* but it is recommended that the curb chain be removed so that the horse will fear the bit less and accept it more steadily. Later, when the horse is worked with a normal bridle and the curb chain is replaced, the action of the bridle will make him light enough. This holds true equally for horses that seek too much support and for those that will not take the bit. The use of false reins gives the neck the same curve that is obtained by using the cavesson; but whereas the cavesson works upon the nose, the false reins work on the bars of the horse's mouth, and make them very sensitive. This is all to the good, for the horse becomes so used to it that when he is placed in a normal

* "False rein" means a "running," or "draw" rein, which went from the girth through the curb ring and back to the rider's hand.—EDS.

89 *"The Gattamelata." With the statue of Colleoni in Venice and the Marcus Aurelius in Rome, this work by Donatello ranks as one of the three most beautiful equestrian sculptures in Italy. It is the first free-standing group, a statue that was not designed as part of an architectural scheme, and dates from 1445. The horse, at the amble, is derived from classic models. Padua.*

bridle with a curb chain he will move beautifully, freely, and without causing any difficulties.

Once you have made the horse supple, and have given his neck the right curve with the cavesson and with the false reins, the bridle reins, working upon the bars, are used to continue training his body, for this calls solely for the action of the regular bridle. Holding one rein in each hand and pulling on the inside rein on turns will make the horse very supple. This is the right way to work a horse through the three steps; cavesson, false reins, and finally the regular bridle, in order to bring him to perfection.

La Broue also had the following to say:

If a horse is restless because he has been punished or restrained too much, he needs all the gentleness and patience you would give a foal.

Horsemen should remember that big, sharp spurs are not appropriate to the training of young animals. The punishment these give can frighten a horse and make him suspicious and timid, and, as a result, even more skittish, while those animals that are hot-blooded or choleric may be easily driven to desperation instead of learning obedience.

It is such treatment, more often than not, that is behind the rage and terror of horses that fling themselves against a wall, or halt suddenly, or fall to the ground, or madly bolt, dragging their riders behind.

It should be noted that in those days only unaltered stallions were trained; but if such measures had been applied to mares, three quarters of them would have become restive or rebellious. La Broue then advises that a mistreated horse be purged and left to rest so that he can regain his *premiers esprits,* his strength and good spirits, for as long as his indisposition continues to make him irritable or sad.

Once restored to health, the horse should be taken to the country, ridden over open land, and without spurs—care being taken to avoid anything that might agitate him. Nevertheless, every time the horseman feels that his mount is about to halt or act up, he should discourage him, if necessary, give him a touch of the whip between the barrel and the hindquarters. It is a good idea to have a man on a pony follow behind who will get off his mount whenever needful to whip the animal on the rear and the legs, every time he is recalcitrant or kicks out.

On the other hand, you should be just as quick to pet him immediately he decides to obey, for kindness is the best thing to convince a horse to learn.

The school of La Broue, Pluvinel, and Newcastle lasted for a century, even though it tended to become modified. The equitation of the tournament and the carrousel imperceptibly gave way to the equitation of the hunt and military riding, a development that provoked a period of transition, bringing certain disorder to the principles of horsemen, and a conflict among masters—which La Guérinière tried to smooth over— with some carrying Newcastle's principles to a point of exaggeration, while others realized the necessity of simplifying them.

Saulnier, riding master of the University of Leyden,

wrote: "If one wanted to curve a horse's neck as used to be done in the old days, the breaking cavesson would be the best means for arching his neck and bringing his head down. That might have been a more difficult time with the bridle, but today, no horse should have his neck curved like a bow, as the old-timers believed."

Though the schools of Grisone, Pluvinel, and Newcastle employed the spurs as an aid, and recommended their constant use, nevertheless, in certain circumstances, with particular types of horse, they all disapproved of that practice.

XXII
PLUVINEL AND NEWCASTLE (WILLIAM CAVENDISH)

Antoine de Pluvinel has left us one book, published posthumously: *Instruction du Roy en l'Exercise de Monter à Cheval, par Messire de Pluvinel, Escuyer Principale de Sa Majesté, Imprimé à Paris, au Dépense de Crispin de Pas le Vieux à Utrecht, avec Privilège du Roy très Cristien, 1629.*

The king was Louis XIII, King of France and Navarre, and it was to him that the man who wrote the introduction, René de Menou-Charnizay, addressed himself. When the time had come to surround the Dauphin with worthy men, the choice had fallen upon Gilles de Souvre, a man advanced in years but, nevertheless, quite a fellow. He had saved the city of Tours for Henry III (1551–1589) during the disturbances of the Catholic League.

Among the other advisers chosen was Pluvinel, "the most excellent riding master of his time, who in instructing the youth of France in the best manner kept them from going to Italy—as had been done in the past century."

Louis XIII was was devoted to every sort of hunting, and was an outstanding school rider as well as a fine horseman in the field. It can be said that he was one of the first of the fox hunters, instituting that dashing, brilliant diversion to protect his great preserves of deer, roebuck, and stags.

Pluvinel, who had been at Pignatelli's school in Naples, does not mention that in his book. In his opinion, the true equestrian science was born in France and at his instigation. As a matter of fact, France did develop a type of equitation that was logical, elegant, and refined.

The king once asked Pluvinel what size would be the best for a saddle horse, and was told a medium-size animal:

> THE KING: "What do you desire, above all, of a pupil of yours?"
> PLUVINEL: "That he be a handsome horseman."
> THE KING: "What difference do you draw between a handsome horseman and a good horseman?"
> PLUVINEL: "I call a handsome horseman that man who has grace and elegance, in addition to science and intuition."

When the king asked Pluvinel why a horse more willingly turns to the left, Pluvinel replied, "Because, in his mother's womb, he is curled to the left."

Immured by Pluvinel in the manège, equitation became an exquisitely technical and recherché activity, the work complicated by the variety of airs and all that was then required of the horse—requiring the horseman to have him well enough in hand so that the animal could go through collected gaits, giving him a good deal of suppleness, as a consequence. It was for that reason that Pluvinel—contrary to Grisone, who was completely concerned with the foreparts of the horse—took pains to give smoothness and suppleness to the animal's posterior. While Grisone, to conserve the horse's impulsion, recommended not letting him arch his neck, the minute one wanted to diminish that force to shorten the gait, it was natural to do just the opposite of what Grisone had advocated.

During the lesson that Pluvinel gave Louis XIII, when the king requested "…the procedure and order that he [Pluvinel] uses to train horses and make them easy to handle, with that immense facility that is seen in everyone from his school," the master replied:

> Since I know from long experience and practice that one cannot call a horse "trained" unless he is perfectly obedient to the hand and the two heels, I need do nothing more than bring a horse to that point. One thing is sure: Any horse that permits himself to be led by the bridle, who will go in one direction and another, and who will raise his forehand and hind quarters, as his rider wishes, I consider well trained and must handle precisely in accordance with his strength and vigor.
>
> Now, as to getting to achieve these two points, I believe that I have, by my method, cut the working period by more than half the time; but since the perfection of an art lies in knowing where one must begin, I have been very fortunate in that it was I who gave the horse his first lessons, before anyone had ridden him.
>
> Then, knowing that the most difficult thing is turning, I take him round a pillar, as I will explain to your Majesty, so that, by making him walk for a few days, he will show us his amiability and all his inherent qualities, so that we can decide to what use he should be put and how he should be brought along.
>
> All this I do much more easily in a place where the horse is restricted, for one has the advantage of being able to see all his movements, far better than if he were mounted; all a horse's energies at this period of his training are generally turned toward defending himself against men, a thing which he is very apt to do if you employ a method other than mine.
>
> It was this, Sire, that made me search most carefully for the system I use, for by following any other method, it would be impossible for me to break the great number of horses for which I am responsible, and the greater part of them valuable animals.

The use of the pillars, from Pluvinel onward, was in the interest of flexing the horse's neck and giving suppleness to it and to the hindquarters. After working the horse for some time

90 *"The Battle of Pavia," by Bernard van Orley, a masterpiece of Flemish tapestry. This detail shows Charles, Constable de Bourbon, in his splendid dress armor. Museo Nazionale, Naples.*

92

with the reins and just one pillar, he moved on to two pillars to achieve a deeper and more telling effect:

After having begun the lesson around the pillar, I attach him between two pillars, as below, and using the handle of the whip, I make him go this way and that so that the horse feels himself more constrained by the cavesson in one spot than in another. Once the animal has been submitted to this work, one can return him to exercise going round the pillar, and by shortening the longeing rein attached to the cavesson and keeping his head close to the pillar, one can have him walking on his haunches by touching him up with the switch.

Then he turns to the two pillars when he needs to do so:

These means are very fine in that they permit the prudent and judicious horseman to observe what his horse is capable of doing and what his temper is when he is not under the influence of any man.

The horse learns, through combining these means, how to walk, trot, and canter; how to go on a single track and to move back and forth. He also gives himself more punishment, because of the cavesson, than any man would, should he go off the track.

In addition, by continuing with this lesson, three important things are achieved: first, they are never strong in the mouth; second, they are never restless; and third, they rarely turn stubborn or willful or resist turning to the right and left, which is the most common fault one finds in unschooled horses.

While Newcastle (1592–1676) was to go well beyond Pluvinel in achieving all those flexions in the horse, Pluvinel is, nevertheless, the codifier of the Neapolitan method. He put a man on horseback as soon as the animal willingly (and *avec gaillardise*) could go through the lesson with saddle, bridle, and stirrup leathers, for while the greatest difficulty for the horse is turning, the hardest thing for the rider is breaking the horse to the bridle. Pluvinel, therefore, began with the most difficult part: he put the bridle on the animal and worked him around himself.

It should be repeated that the equitation of the seventeenth century, which was intent on developing movements that were elegant and brilliant, was very slow-paced and, of necessity, must have been very "seated." There was, accordingly, no way of achieving a worthwhile result without the continual use of the spurs.

Then how was the horse schooled to give him a perfect understanding of the heels as an aid? To that question from the king, Pluvinel responded as follows:

I will tell your Majesty what you wish to know: finding

a horse responsive to the heels, to begin to make him obedient to them or more so, according to what is necessary, begin the lesson with only one pillar or make him go round in circles. While he is moving, I try, very gently, to prick him, as delicately as I can, with one heel or the other, as is required, or with both at the same time once or twice, if he bears it, and then, with a pat, show him what is desired.

If he does not endure this, I have him placed between two pillars, with the reins short, and lifting him, I have him gently squeezed together. If he resists that treatment, I give him a taste of a switch on the haunches and have him pushed, until he sees that he must respond to the aid of the heels, as he did to the switch, a thing he soon learns....

Pluvinel goes into detail on how to induce a very sensitive horse—as well as the horse that is rather indifferent—to take and respond to *le pincer de l'éperon* (a touch of the spur):

"What do you mean," asks the king, "by a touch of the spur?"

Sire, giving a horse a touch of the spur, when he can be handled, is to press him very gently with the two spurs, or one of them, against his barrel, not brusquely, but squeezing lightly or tightly as is necessary each time or whenever called for, so that, being accustomed to this aid, he picks up a bit or a great deal, as the horseman indicates.

This aid has really all the subtlety of true science, both for the horse and for the rider, and I consider it the most refined of all the aids, calling as it does upon the man's intelligence as well as that of the horse. Without it, it would be impossible for a rider to manage a horse handily, since the horse, not recognizing, understanding, or suffering the heels as an aid, there would be no means at hand when he had to be picked up, urged on, or chastised. The touch of the spur, however, is for punishment, while the legs and steady nerves are the aids; but when a horse does not respond as he should to the aid of the legs, one must stop there and, if the horse does not respond, apply a touch of the spur, as I have said, and which very few people do well, through ignorance.

Naturally, the people to whom Pluvinel referred were those who used the horse as a means of transport and, therefore, employed the animal in the simplest and most forthright manner, perhaps even brutally, but without subtle inquiry into the art. It is this duality of use—the contrast between the riding academy and the road, between the school and improvisation or even experience—that determined the frequent ruptures with, but also the frequent return to, the most natural style of equitation all through history.

Notwithstanding, it is impossible to define the use of the spur as an aid better than Pluvinel does it. The same cannot be said of La Guérinière, who for the next period has not left us a definition equally clear and valid, but only what was appropriate and adequate for his time, when the principles of Pluvinel and Newcastle were still in effect.

There is no question about the definition of *rassemblé*, "collected." Just what does it mean to "collect" a horse if not

91 *Illustration from the fourteenth-century* Traité des Tournois, *by Louis d'Aryon, showing the Duke of Brittany.*

92 *Knight on horseback in sixteenth-century Japanese armor. Museo Stibbert, Florence.*

to contain him between hands and legs? Is it possible to find a better definition than that given in Pluvinel's book?

> This lesson, properly applied, lifts and lightens the horse, fuses and firms him on his haunches, and gives him sureness in his cadence, making him freely receptive to the aid of the hands and the heels, which renders him more agile in performing all that is desired of him and, consequently, makes everything easier.

There are many who believe that Pluvinel's definitions and ideas can serve as a basis for all equitation, present and future, or, in a better sense, that he deals with principles to which one must necessarily turn now and then.

In contrast to Pluvinel, we have Newcastle, with the air of an innovator. He maintains that only his method is good, and damns all horsemen who do not do as he does; and to cap the climax, everything that existed before he came along counts for less than nothing: "I write for those, who, like myself, make it their profession to be among horses; it is enough that I make myself understood by them, by a proper use of the terms of Art, in which I presume I have pretty well succeeded."

The title of his book is: *A General System of Horsemanship in All Its Branches: containing a faithful translation of that most noble and useful* WORK *of his Grace William Cavendish, Duke of Newcastle, entitled, The Manner of Feeding, Dressing, and Training of Horses for the Great Saddle, and Fitting them for the Service of the Field in Time of War, or for the Exercise and Improvement of Gentlemen in the Academy at home: A Science peculiarly necessary throughout all Europe, and which has hitherto been so much neglected, or discouraged in England, that young Gentlemen have been obliged to have recourse to foreign Nations for this Part of their Education.*

To achieve such results and so prodigiously, at that, calls for a certain vanity and a good dose of presumption. The marquess must have been remarkably deft. To anyone who asked him how long a time was needed to train a horse, he replied that it depends upon the animal's strength, the age, the spirit, and the disposition; his agility, memory, sagacity, and good or bad temper; that you cannot find the same quality everywhere, just as no artist paints like another, and dancers don't all perform in the same way. Nevertheless, he believed that if a horse is tractable, and has spirit and vigor, a quick disposition, judgment, and memory, and is without faults, he could be trained in three months; but he guaranteed that with his method, one schools a horse in half the time, and that the horse will be more nearly perfect than those trained by other teachers.

What, then, are the miraculous means employed by Newcastle? To begin with, to position the head of the horse, to make the neck supple immediately after the preliminaries for making the colt docile and tractable; for the horseman to "set" the horse's head in the best position and, bit by bit, as he gains possession of the mouth and head, increasingly limit his freedom, dominating the animal to the point where the head has been positioned as desired. Then the horse should be maintained in that position and worked with the hands low. He continues:

> Trot him upon large circles at first, holding the inward rein of the cavesson tight, that he may not only keep

within the circle, but have his haunches rather without than within it.

> The main point is to manage a horse's head and to give him a proper weight upon the hand; for it is very easy to manage his haunches. I have therefore been often surprised that some horsemen should begin by managing the crouper or tail. If the head of a horse is well regulated, you may afterwards manage him as you please, provided his nature and strength will admit of it; for should you not secure his head, it is impossible ever to make him a complete horse, since you have only your hands and your heels to manage him. Otherwise the most essential parts will fail you.... Have a gentleman appear on horseback without stiffness or formality.

Newcastle believed that no school attitude could give results to equal those coming from a simple and instinctive posture, which is a belief of capital importance in helping to understand how modern the marquess' concepts are. Still, he says, "He who does not fit genteelly upon a horse, will never be a good horseman."

As to the management of the bridle reins and cavesson, he claims that he will teach more concerning them "than has been hitherto known."

Newcastle begins with the way to use the cavesson:

> Take a long rein, with a small ring fastened to one end of it, and pass the other end of the rein through this ring, which bring over the pommel of the saddle, and fix it

93 94 95 *Founders of three schools of equitation: Fiaschi, Pluvinel, and Newcastle, respectively, Italian, French, and English.*

96 *Flandrin, one of the most famous French horsemen.*

97 98 *The natural gaits of a runaway; a horse, annoyed by an ill-fitting saddle, has slipped from the hand of the groom leading him.*

99 *The aubin, an irregular gait, in which the forelegs canter while the hind legs trot.*

100 *School walk.*

101 *Tail to the wall.*

102 *Passage.*

103 *Piaffe.*

104 *Collected canter to the right.*

105 *School canter, or galopade.*

106 *Pirouette, canter to the left.*

107 *Redoppe (canter on two tracks).*

108 *Levade: the horse lifts the forehand while keeping the hind legs planted on the ground without advancing or retreating.*

109 *Courbette, executed in the style still followed at the Spanish Riding School in Vienna. At Saumur, the horse is lifted higher over the haunches.*

110 *Pirouette to the left.*

111 *Croupade, a jump in which the horse lifts himself higher than in the courbette. At Saumur, the croupade is a double kick, with the forelegs on the ground.*

112 *Ballotade.*

113 *Capriole, one of the most spectacular school jumps.*

114 *Shoulder-in, the basis of advanced equitation.*

101

97

98

102

103

106

107

108

110

111

112

99

100

104

105

109

113

114

there in such a manner that it cannot move; then draw the rein downwards, and pass it under the fore-bolster of the saddle, and then put the remainder of the rein through the ring of the cavesson directly before, bringing the same end of the rein into your hand. Then do the same by the other rein.... This sort of cavesson is exceedingly useful, both to settle a horse's head, to make him steady in hand, to give his body a proper bent, to preserve his mouth, to stop him, make him go backwards, or to turn him easily to either hand....

Newcastle insists on the horse being agile and flexible:

It is not sufficient to keep the head and neck of a horse within the circle, but give an entire pli or bent to his whole body from the nose to the tail.... For although some object that his neck will be weakened by this method, I can answer that objection in no other manner, than by saying that such horsemen do not understand the art they pretend to profess who would make a horse stiff-necked by their management, and not able to turn or wheel about....

If one continues to consult Newcastle, who can be considered an advocate *à outrance* of *assouplissement,* as well as the power of suggestion, one will see that, notwithstanding the fact that he advises dominating the horse, he insists that he be trained right away to make him sure in his foreparts well up front— a prime and indispensable condition, no matter what the work to which the horse will be submitted.

When a horse is trotting, the rider ought to press him a little faster before he stops, and stop him immediately after by drawing the inward rein of the cavesson a little stronger than the other, and move towards his body, putting his body a little back that he may be obliged by the weight to put himself upon his haunches; but particular care ought to be taken that he does not advance, by which I mean that he should not rise before, but only stop without rising; for a sure way to spoil a horse is to teach him to rise before he trots and gallops freely, for he would be apt to rise and be restive, instead of advancing. Particular care ought therefore to be taken never to make him rise until he answers freely the spurs both in trotting and galloping. But the spurs in the beginning should be given with great care and but seldom, and then gently. He should be stopped without suffering him to rise.

This proves that Newcastle thinks, and rightly so, that the horse's first taste of the spur should come with his being urged forward, while he considers that the aid of the spur is indispensable in sustaining the hindquarters and conditioning them to bear stops that tend to pull the horse up, seat him, and collect him.

Trotting and stopping a horse is the foundation of all

115 *Capriole from the ground, one of the most difficult exercises.*

airs; they settle his head and croup, put him well upon his haunches, and make him light before. Reining back settles the horse's head, puts him upon his haunches, and makes him light before....

It is by placing him against a wall that Newcastle taught him to understand the spurs as an aid, to learn to use his haunches, and to sit.

Here, the wall takes the place of Pluvinel's two pillars. Newcastle does not approve of pillars, in fact, he detests them; but the results are the same. One must impede the horse in order to accustom him to interpreting the action of the spurs and to go forward. Any method at all can be of worth in teaching him that; either put the horse between pillars, or against a wall, or with a man in front of him in the middle of the manège or on the road.

Above all, Newcastle concerns himself with the flexibility of the neck, and achieves it by his own peculiar method: instead of using pillars, he begins to flex and limber it on the spot with headstall and noseband, then in motion, working, first of all, on the cavesson.

XXIII
LA GUÉRINIÈRE

School equitation inevitably invaded the field of hunting, hacking, and even military riding, as did the equitation of the carrousels. It had a troubling effect and led to a confusion of ideas and unavoidable argumentation among horsemen of differing opinions.

It was these discussions that François Robichon de la Guérinière attempted to resolve by formulating a more inclusive and informed system of school equitation, one that remained, notwithstanding, thoroughly academic. In substance, what needed to be decided was whether, to a greater or lesser extent, one should practically break a horse's neck to dominate him. La Guérinière was of the opinion that not all horses could or should be subjected to the same work, nor should or could they all be trained at the same time. What he did was discard all that he considered worthless in the teachings of La Broue, Pluvinel, and the famous Lord Newcastle, bitter opponent of Pluvinel's pillars.

La Guérinière (1687–1751) was the most able student of Geneval Monpoint Vendeuil, but he was never part of his manège at Versailles, even though he bore the title of *Ecuyer-Royal.* He had his own academy, and a very noted one it was, in Paris, from 1715 to 1730. Considered the real father of French equitation, which is still loyal to him today, his theories spread throughout Europe, and it was under his influence that the celebrated Vienna riding academy was founded in 1729.

La Guérinière wrote two books: the *Ecole de Cavalerie,* published in 1735, and, in 1740, the *Eléments de Cavalerie,* which signaled a new era in the history of equitation. This master wrought great changes in the horse's tack by removing the padded seat and roll from the *selle à piquer,* turning it into what is virtually the saddle still in use at the Saumur cavalry school. He taught the rider to seek his own equilibrium in the seat, in the "rightness" of his posture, which became an attitude more natural and less mannered; and he simplified the proceedings in dressage.

Let us hear what he has to say about the grace and elegance of the rider:

> Grace is a great ornament to a rider and, at the same time, a great path to science, which all horsemen must, first and foremost, employ as long as necessary to achieve that status.
>
> By grace, I understand an air of ease and freedom that must be conserved in a correct and relaxed posture, whether while maintaining one's seat and controlling the horse, as necessary, or while purposely letting go, still keeping, as much as one can, through all the horse's paces that exact balance that comes from properly applying the counterpoise of one's body. Furthermore, the rider's every move should be subtle, so that each serves that much more to complement his seat and his aid to the horse.
>
> Since this concept has been neglected, and nonchalance, together with a certain air of sloppiness, now attracts the attention of the man who in the past might have been concerned to acquire and maintain that beautiful seat—which so charms the eye of the onlooker and infinitely embellishes the good points of a handsome mount—it is not in the least bit surprising that riding has lost much of its old luster.

Then he begins, as every manual in the world, in every age, has begun:

> Before mounting a horse, one should inspect all his gear. Such attention, which takes but a moment, is absolutely necessary to obviate the inconveniences that may occur if one neglects this small task.
>
> The majority of those who ride do not have anything more than a confused notion of the movements made by a horse's legs at his different gaits. Without such knowledge, however, which is essential to the horseman, he will be unable to take proper action, being ignorant of the mechanics of the operation.
>
> Horses have two types of gait, that is, their natural and artificial paces. Among the natural gaits, one can distinguish those that are perfect: the walk, the trot, and the canter, and the imperfect, which are the amble, the broken walk, and the rack.
>
> The natural, perfect paces are inherent, and require no art to improve them, while the imperfect gaits result from the horse's feeble or spoiled nature.
>
> The artificial gaits are those that an able riding master knows how to give the horses he trains in order to teach them the different airs of which they are capable and which should be practiced in a well-run academy.

From the manège at Versailles came great teachers, among whom we should mention M. de Nestrier, *premier écuyer* of Louis XV; M. de Salvert, who wrote a study on equitation; M. de Neuilly, who was riding master to Prince de Lambesc, the last great *écuyer* of the old monarchy, and, finally, the Viscount d'Abzac, who was an *écuyer* at the age of nineteen, and still teaching when he was eighty-three. A master of equitation and all its fine points, he served three kings, Louis XVI, Louis XVIII, and Charles X. It was d'Abzac who carried to its epitome the academic tradition in the amenable climate of the Restoration.

XXIV
EVOLUTION AND DEVELOPMENTS IN MILITARY EQUITATION

In the middle of the eighteenth century—precisely at the time that the Duke de Choiseul, the French Minister of War, going ahead on a program that had not been completed by the famous minister Colbert, had founded five schools of equitation, among them, the cavalry school at Saumur—the Seven Years' War was revealing the inadequacy of school equitation, manifest in the defeats of the French cavalry by the German.

Horses trained in the *haute école* were performing bravura exercises in the midst of battle. Furthermore, the introduction of firearms had shaken the cavalry. In the absence of the lance, the cavalry had substituted a charge based upon the caracole, involving the advance of a platoon, drawn up in lines, followed by a salvo of musket shots at the enemy, then a half-turn to allow the next rank to take their place, another salvo, and so on, while the first line to attack reloaded its guns. Gaspard de Saunier tells us that the horses from the academy at Versailles were absolutely unable to adapt themselves to these new conditions in the campaign of 1691, and could barely drag themselves, dazed and stupefied as they were, along the paths of war.

It was Marshal Turenne who carried the charge to its apogee by tripling his cavalry and instructing it to advance *au galop en sauvages,* truly "at the charge." Thanks to the troops employed in this way, he won some battles and resolved some desperate situations in his favor; but despite these prodigious successes, the French cavalry, faithful to its academic tradition, immediately returned to fighting in a style more appropriate to the carrousel—and lost their engagements.

Frederick the Great, however, who also had heavy artillery, created a highly mobile and maneuverable cavalry capable of taking to the most uneven, broken terrain, and charging the enemy. Just such a detachment, brilliant and fast-moving, inflicted a terrible defeat upon the French at Rossbach in November 1757, where thirty-eight Prussian squadrons overwhelmed fifty-two squadrons commanded by Marshal de Soubise.

Voices were raised against academic equitation, but in vain. Meanwhile, in Paris, Jacques d'Auvergne was heading the military riding academy that had been established in 1751. By modifying the rider's position in the saddle, he brought the horseman to an easier and more natural posture. He also

116 *Drawing of the school airs practiced at the Spanish Riding School in Vienna.*

117 *A German woodcut showing the breaking and training of a horse by a rather brutal method.*

116

117

Wie das Füllen auß dem Gestüd zusü:
en / vnd etzliche tag zam vnd gehorsam
machen.

managed to strip equitation of all the superfluities burdening it and, in an effort to achieve a natural gait, discarded all that was artificial and flashy for the "correct horse," to the point where he could be considered the man who created French military equitation.

At the same time, Ludwig Hünersdorf, a Württemberg riding master who served the Duke of Hesse, rebelled against the practices of the Spanish Riding School in Vienna and strove to balance the horse in an attitude that was less "set" and more favorable to work in the open.

This evidently was not merely a conflict over techniques and methods, but also against tradition and caste, baroque preciosity, and complacent class pride in virtuosity, all pitted against the necessity for daily practice of handling geared to military ends.

The French Revolution was to make a clean slate of the schools of equitation. The manège at Versailles disappeared, and its riding masters emigrated, most of them to Germany. The tradition of Saumur, then a vital center of equitation, and even biological and genetic research that had begun in 1771, were interrupted; but the need for an operative cavalry forced the Directory to form a national school of equitation at Versailles in 1796. Despite the fact that it drew on the remnants of the old academy, the school gave disappointing results, until Napoleon had to establish eleven schools with his decrees of May 17, 1806, signed at Schönbrunn, of which the school at Rennes was to become the most famous. In 1809, he created the special cavalry school at Saint-Germain.

With the Restoration, Louis XVIII ordered the reestablishment of the Versailles academy, which endured vicissitude and alteration before it truly began to function in 1825. However, it operated in the midst of difficulties created by its commanders and the instructors themselves, each of whom had his own techniques, and with a school doctrine more or less antiquated. So it continued until the advent of Count d'Aure (1799–1863), who was to be the great adversary of François Baucher, another fine horseman, but of humble origins.

XXV
ANTOINE D'AURE

Count d'Aure had been a pupil of d'Abzac. He founded a manège in Paris that had a very chic clientele, attracted by the repute of its owner. Among his students was the Duke de Nemours, who supported his candidacy for head *écuyer* at Saumur, despite the opposition of Marshal Nicolas Soult, who wanted to eliminate civilian instructors at the school. It was only with the death of Soult that d'Aure acceded to the post, once experiments with Baucher's methods had ceased. It was all a history of intrigue, gossip, support, and influence worthy of Stendahl's best.

D'Aure did not return the school to the orthodoxy of Versailles, but followed a line that d'Auvergne had tried a century earlier. The count wanted the horse to be utilized

118 *A perfect column of riders leaving the manège at the Spanish Riding School in Vienna.*

"as Nature has made him," and his intention was to employ the animal's innate resistance and opposition, pitting one against the other, to achieve results—arising out of the contrasting forces—that would lead the horse to follow mechanically the orders given by the rider.

Instead of having the horse flex, cracking himself in two to negotiate a curve, d'Aure wanted the horse to turn *d'une seule pièce,* like a ship. The opposition of the withers to the haunches was the principle on which he based the new method. It called for great sureness and straightforwardness of impulsion, the horse shooting ahead and well in hand. For this, d'Aure advocated the *rêne d'opposition.* In his *Traité d'équitation,* he discusses his methods for maintaining a free and easy gait, developing speed, and making the horse, as he puts it, *perçant* (alert).

At that time, all horses were worked in the same way, and instruction to riders consisted in teaching them which aids they should use to achieve the movements necessary to their horse's employment. Opposed to this, to utilize a horse "as Nature has made him," to understand the motives for and origins of his defenses, and to train him to achieve desired results would have called for a long series of repeated exercises with many different horses. This, of course, was most inconvenient, although it did have the virtue of putting young horses into service quickly. For that reason, Count d'Aure greatly encouraged work in the open air, and for this purpose used the uncultivated land around Saumur. His virtuosity on horseback won the admiration of all who saw him, while his style of teaching was incomparable. He excelled at practical demonstration, and always used to say, "Watch me and imitate me."

Perhaps the most elegant definition of equitation is that given by d'Aure: "Breaking a horse to obedience, appropriating his means to our necessities, conserving and developing the qualities inherent in him, these comprise the art of equitation."

A horseman's talent lies in knowing how to employ his own action in proportion to the horse's potential and capability, his nature and instincts, so that the animal accepts, without resentment, his rider's domination, and becomes quietly obedient, while yet simultaneously preserving just enough initiative to permit him to show his best qualities and his "personality."

In order to achieve such a response from a horse, all constriction that tends to make a horseman a mere executer of forced motion must be proscribed from any system of rational equitation, the more so because its effect is solely to brutalize and ruin the animal.

A horse reacts in proportion to the stimuli he feels, going whither he is directed, accepting the aid offered him, and giving way in the face of resistance and pain. It is, therefore, the way that he is made to feel sensation that determines how much of his effort is brought to bear and the movements of which he is capable. That is the key to his performance, and it is an invariable, mechanical, and thoroughly scientific one.

In accordance with the effects desired, the actions that produce those demands upon a horse are quite simple, but they do not come quickly and naturally because the novice rider is inevitably stiff and given to worry and is subject to a certain amount of fear—tending to paralyze him somewhat and make his actions awkward and his reactions slow. It is therefore necessary to work on the rider's seat and to give him such balance as to allow all his aids sufficient strength and freedom of action to produce the movements desired from his horse.

The legs find their *point d'appui* in the fixity of the knees, so that the rider can produce the effects he wants with precision and without undesirable consequences. With students of a certain stature, the instructor forces the position of the hips, to make them roll so that the knees are not open but cling to the saddle as much as possible, for without this adhesion, the legs would lose all their value as an aid. Generally, the position of the knees and legs is dependent upon the position of the hips.

To attempt to turn in the toes, the knees, and the legs without moving the hips would be wrong, since this would cause a contraction that would nullify the action of the legs. Knees that turn in too much, however, are just as bad as knees spread wide. Neither of these two positions can be assumed without strain, which would mean a loss of comfort and ease in the seat. With the knee turned in, the leg, which no longer clings to the horse's body, loses its normal means of action. If the knees are wide open, the hips lose their contact with the saddle, and the legs—hugging the horse's body—act independently of the horseman's will, which certainly results in uncoordinated movement.

All these adjustments of the position can come only with time. The instructor should not content himself merely with explaining the seat, but should seek to correct the defects caused by the student's own physique. Thus, for instance, if the student is rather stiff in the small of the back, he will inevitably tend to rigidity and to seating himself on the crotch. In such case, one should recommend that he relax the small of the back and bend forward slightly; but be careful that he does not exaggerate, or he will end up making his original mistake. To correct that posture, it would be a good thing to force him to seat himself well into the saddle, making him understand that the first prerequisite for a good seat is to sit well, right in place, comfortably, and lightly, and to have agility and unrestricted freedom of action—impossible when the small of the back is stiff and concave.

If, on the other hand, a pupil is slack, if he slumps and curves the small of his back, his chest will be thrown in and his shoulders forward. One must then see that he sits up straight.

These things should be left to the intuition and intelligence of the instructor, and cannot be given as set principles. The instructor, furthermore, should take care to bring the other parts of the student's body into a position of harmony and good rapport. He should be particularly attentive during the first lessons to the position of the arms and legs, making sure that arms and hands are loose and free and never stiffen, which would cause reflex action leading to a stiff back and too heavy a pull on the horse's mouth. After having let the rider's hips and legs fall naturally of their own weight, the instructor should also see to it that the knees are well fixed against the saddle.

A fundamental principle of equitation, and one that can never be repeated too often to students, is to make good use of one's horse but to spare him, and never to exert undue force and wear him out.

If we are to train enthusiastic riders, we must make them prudent and even shrewd. It is not galloping madly or jumping over obstacles badly that produces ardent, able riders. That system just creates reckless horsemen, devoid of any idea whatsoever of how to use a horse properly—those who ruin an animal after taking him out a few times. The proverb is right: "Qui veut voyager loin ménage sa monture." ("He who wishes to travel far takes care of his mount.")

When returning to the walk, after doing the canter and trot, one can at this point attempt to have the student lengthen and shorten this gait. It will serve to demonstrate to him that acceleration of the pace comes rather more from the way in which the mass is balanced than through increased muscular activity, which, on the contrary, is what happens when you attempt to reduce this gait.

Ancient and medieval equitation never regarded the extended trot as a gait for a saddle horse, greatly esteeming the amble. To the end of the eighth century, no gaits were acceptable but the walk, the canter, and the passage, a cadenced, collected school trot, nor were any rules given for preventing the horse's reactions to paces not in use. In the same team, the postillion horse would be going at the gallop while the others trotted.

With the nineteenth century, whether because of the physiological changes made in the breeds or because of different necessities and, consequently, the different uses to which the horse was put, the extended trot became the gait most desired of a saddle horse; however, the longer and more brilliant the trot, the harder and more fatiguing it is for the rider.

There arose, therefore, the need for a way to attenuate the reactions to a gait a horse could sustain more easily in the majority of instances, and for longer than the gallop, while achieving the same swiftness of pace. When you wish to press a horse onward at such a gait that he falls into a *traquenard*,* you should lean back, so long as you do not have to oppose or attenuate the reaction—since the gait is broken and the reaction not very acute—and then, because the mass is strongly displaced toward the rear, you must avoid overburdening the haunches with too much of your own weight. Furthermore, since you are toward the rear, place your arms and hands in the best position to support the horse and permit him to take maximum advantage of the gait.

As for the English trot, d'Aure adds:

> This work should not be considered an exercise, since only on rare occasions can and should it be of practical application in the cavalry. Furthermore, it would be absurd to attempt to eliminate the bumpiness from a trot in military exercises, for on maneuvers, no one ever moves at such an extended, direct pace.
>
> The rhythm of the ordinary trot cannot be taught successfully unless one proceeds quickly in a straight line and unless one is certain of continuing on the same track for a given length of time.
>
> These innovations will come in good time if horses that have developed the trot continue in general esteem

---

* A broken or running trot.—Trans.

and if they are produced as the taste and necessities of the time demand.

On the subject of taking jumps, d'Aure's words give us an idea of how obstacles were negotiated in his time. First of all, he says: "The first condition is that the horse be obedient to the aids, so that he will not refuse." As to the way of using the horse, however, he notes that that depends, essentially, upon the manner in which the animal is disposed to take the obstacle. There are, therefore, no fixed rules or absolute principles.

According to d'Aure, there are horses, "…that go freely toward the obstacle, and they themselves assess their strength." With such horses, the rider "…should leave off doing anything and place himself in rapport with the horse's means." Other horses fling themselves over with such rapidity that "…the weight is upon the shoulders at the moment of clearance so that the reaction of the forehand upon the hindquarters results in insufficient elevation and quickness, and the horse balks at the obstacle instead of clearing it. "In that case, the rider should avoid any leg action, and secure and lift the hand in order to maintain and prepare the forehand to rise at the opportune moment."

There are other horses that approach an obstacle uncertainly, all their weight being on the hindquarters so that once the foreparts are over the jump (lacking enough strength to get the weight of the rear over), they stumble over the fence.

D'Aure continues:

The jump made by a horse in clearing an obstacle should have the action of a bascule. As the forehand is the first part lifted over, it should be the first to regain the ground, to land so as not to hinder the hindquarters as they lift, in their proper turn.

Generally, the rider should increase the action of his legs to put as much of his weight as possible on the forehand, unburdening the hindquarters. The hands should remain still and low, in order to avoid any action that might shift weight to the rear.

In all these cases, at the moment when the horse has lifted his rear to clear an obstacle, the hands must remain low to obviate any action from front to rear that would shift weight from the forehand to the hindquarters, making it difficult for them to pass over. Not until all four hooves have hit the ground once again should the rider use the hands, either to slow down or to halt.

The different examples we have given should suffice to show that the means to be employed for clearing an obstacle should be modified according to the conformation of the horse and his character.

As one can see, this is very different from the method already in use in England, which consisted in carrying all the weight on the haunches so that a fence could be taken with security, at least as far as the forehand was concerned.

In answer to those who maintained it was impossible to train a Thoroughbred, Count d'Aure expressed himself as follows:

If, however, a horse comes out of training and you subject him to the same conditions as a horse that will not run, and should you, instead of letting him stretch his neck forward, lift it and bring it to the position in hand, and engage his haunches, you will then see that horse, which looked so ungainly, take on the most elegant lines, and he will also gain the lightest and most collected paces, for actually all your care has produced the elements of those factors that determine speed.

These you will find are also the horses that will give you the airs above the ground, since the articulating angles—upon whose prime condition speed depends—are in their best condition equally for pulling up, elevation, and brilliance of movement.

Running, the horse will appear to have his croup high and the forehand low; while in practice, on the contrary, his forehand will appear to be raised and his hindquarters, low.

D'Aure then cites some forty horses he had ridden in the races (winning Thoroughbreds, for the most part) that, shortly after entering his manège—which they had never attended before—and taking a few lessons, were as "supple and easygoing as any Spanish horse."

XXVI

FRANÇOIS BAUCHER

Some say that François Baucher (1796–1873) may well have been one of the forerunners of "the system," since he introduced some motions that coincide with natural equitation.

Baucher indubitably was the man who best knew how to advance the evolution of equitation. Developing at least five styles after having followed for years the way of the *tout ensemble,* the basis of school equitation, he scandalized all the faithful adherents of school work with a dictum they came to understand only with the passage of time: "Hands without legs; legs without hands.

Baucher also advocated the use of the snaffle, an invention of his, although that did not represent an advance for equitation. He had no experience of equitation in the field, and was unable to solve the problem of freeing the neck and withers; therefore his training systems were always those of the classic school, which was also true of Cesare Paderni. We should not forget that Baucher had been director and ringmaster of an equestrian circus, for which he prepared and presented his own horses. He was also a teacher at Versailles during its period of crisis over its teaching staff, and there he found himself pitted against the *écuyers,* of whom Count d'Aure was the leader.

Baucher presented a method of equitation that was quite logical and reasonable, a method that spread throughout Europe and gave rise to criticism that was more or less justified. General Nicolas Oudinot even wanted to try out Baucher's method with the army, having Baucher himself serve as instructor. This, of course, emphasized the disparity between him and d'Aure, who could not tolerate Baucher and, even more, despised him because he had come from an equestrian circus. It is a matter of record, however, that Baucher was a horseman of rare ability, logical in his theories, and masterly in the training of his circus horses. Notwithstanding, in no way was he the author and gentleman to merit consideration as the head of a school.

Here we have his thoughts on the seat:

> *Posture of the Rider:* The rider should throw out his chest as much as possible, aligning each of the upper parts of his body in relation with the others so as to achieve a position that will augment the action of the buttocks in the saddle. The arms should fall naturally at the sides.
>
> Through their force of adduction, the hips and legs should seek to discover the maximum number of possible points of contact between the saddle and the horse's flanks. The feet will follow the action of the legs naturally.
>
> From these few lines, you can gather what the posture of the rider should be. You should then teach the student never to have recourse to the aids intended to serve him in keeping his seat for directing his horse; nor should he employ, to maintain his seat, those aids that act as a guide toward distinguishing cause and effect.

Finally, to demonstrate that the basis of training a horse rests upon respect for his natural equilibrium and the perfecting, rather than the opposing of it, for the purposes of handling a horse, he writes:

> Any sentient being is subject to the laws of motion in maintaining his balance and the liberty and sureness of his own movements. More than any other animal, the mounted horse is sensitive to these laws inasmuch as he not only has to proportion his movement in relation to the displacement of his own mass (his body) but must also take into consideration the additional weight of a rider who tends continually to adjust his own natural balance.

Discussing the causes of resistance by a horse to the will of the rider, Baucher had this to say:

> Everyone has spoken of the resistance and opposition to the demands of the rider occasioned by the imbalance of the horse, but no one has known enough to say what determines such resistance nor how it can be combated and destroyed in order to achieve necessary lightness, and that is just the exercise that is so much sought. It is this serious lack that has left the art of equitation with so much to be desired, and it is precisely this lacuna that I believe I have managed to fill.
>
> At the outset, I offer as a thesis my opinion that every demonstration of resistance offered by a young horse stems, in the first place, from a physical cause, and that resistance will not become a personality trait except through bad schooling, or as a consequence of the rider's brutality or ignorance.
>
> If only the methods of those who base their systems upon hackneyed principles were to die out—in the light of the great number of bad horses one sees! That there are so many horses that remained unspoiled because of their perfect conformation or the ease with which they could be trained only contributes to the perpetuation of the old methods—systems so deleterious to progress in the art of equitation.

A few glimmers of natural equitation appear in all the foregoing, but in substance Baucher's system is based upon the seat, the bend, and the principles covering work in the classic school manner. It is essential to remember that the concept of equitation in the field was not what it is today, for the horse was taken out into the open with just the instruction he had received in the manège—all flexion and collection.

It would seem that in hunting and cross-country riding, La Guérinière can be credited with having caught something of that spirit of natural equitation. In the few short pages he dedicated to the subject, he writes: "It is imperative to let the horse gallop without holding him back or urging him on, as he would go himself, *were he riderless.*" A wonderful bit of insight, but let us not delude ourselves; rather, recall how closely linked was La Guérinière with the French school—built upon dressage and the exercises of the *école;* and it was to this that France remained faithful for some three centuries.

According to Baucher, "collecting" a horse served to correct whatever slight defects an animal might have, whether it was a badly set neck or a slight weakness in the forehand; but what if he were weak in the hindquarters or his conformation poor? Not all horses can be well "collected," according to Baucher. To achieve collection, a horse must be strong in the loins and firm in the hocks; otherwise, the hindquarters will not be able to carry that portion of the weight that the forehand cannot bear. Only after an efficient and complete position in hand has been attained can collection be attempted. To obtain the desired effect when the horse is going at a walk or at the trot, or working on his haunches, one attempts, through the counteraction of the hands and legs, to obtain lightness and mobility, without advancing or retreating. It is with the aid of this "suspension of movement," prudently employed in the proper measure, that one manages to bring the hindquarters down and under, toward the center of gravity. To this effect, however, one must use the hand well, for if the horse balks while his hindquarters move forward, he will not be collected. Collection of a high degree, judiciously practiced, will inevitably lead to the piaffe.

In essence, for Baucher, collection is understood to mean the act of bringing the horse's center of gravity to the center of his body in such a way that he vibrates only a very little from forehand to hindquarters, and vice versa, while his posterior is drawn up toward the midpoint. Baucher defined *le ramener* as "placing the head of the horse in a perpendicular position." The idea for this came to him through watching horses at rest in the stables, where they did not put their noses into the wind (a position that requires contraction of the upper neck muscles) but carried their heads quite low.

119 *"In Peril": little hope for the girl. A French print.*
120 *"The Lady and the Soldier," by Dürer. She is seated in a saddle that has a bolster to support the feet. At that time, saddles were virtually miniature upholstered chairs, yet even so early in the sixteenth century, the fork had appeared, foreshadowing the side-saddle.*

119

120

121

122

123

In Baucher's system, the farther removed from perfection a horse's conformation, the greater will be the resistance offered by the neck and jaws. Once all muscular rigidity has been overcome, the muscles must be brought into harmony, like the strings of an instrument, so that each helps the other. We must, therefore, work first on foot and then on horseback, with the animal standing still and then walking, to give the maximum possible suppleness to his neck and jaws. All horses can achieve the "flexion" that will make them light in hand and well balanced, giving them grace and ease in their movement. The flexion is the foundation upon which everything rests.

At this point, Baucher paraphrases the saying "The style is the man," and observes:

> The horse is the man, man in his physical and moral aspects, for the horse's movements, like his speed of comprehension and his readiness to act on command, depend entirely upon the rider. To this end, therefore, the flexion must be perfect. If not, the horse will contract his neck and jaw muscles, and the efforts of his rider will count for nothing in the face of such resistance, and the animal's action will be labored and uncertain. Thus, everything comes down to the flexion "which instantly gives the rider a sense of coordinated effects and provides the horse with the necessary means to execute them."

XXVII
GENERAL L'HOTTE

France found next, in General Alexis François l'Hotte (1825–1904), the man who managed to make a perfect synthesis of the teachings of d'Aure and Baucher, and brought to his work a more modern view of equitation.

L'Hotte received his first instruction, as a garrison lieutenant at Lyon, from Baucher, and also from Louis Rousselet and Beucher de Saint-Ange. Though L'Hotte remained Baucher's friend, at Saumur he became convinced of the validity of Count d'Aure's principles. L'Hotte combined the two methods, discarding those elements he believed superfluous, and when he became director of the academy at Saumur, in 1864, he established his own doctrine, which favored Count d'Aure in material covering equitation in the open air, and Baucher in what related to *haute école*. His intention was to perfect the school exercises where they dealt with the simplest movements, and to substitute, as much as possible, work in the field for work in the manège.

121 *"Tournament in Piazza Castello," by Antonio Tempesta. The point of view is midway between the tourney, joust, carrousel, and the choreographic spectacle. Art gallery, Turin.*

122 *"The Battle," an imaginary engagement painted by Salvator Rosa. In the artist's time, the cavalry was in the minority, and operated upon the basis of the caracole or charged either at the trot or intervened on the fringes of the battle. Galleria Pitti, Florence.*

123 *"The Battle of Wagram," by Horace Vernet. Napoleon, round-bottomed and short as he was, was not much of a horseman, but his limners have usually portrayed him in more or less correct postures. Palais de Versailles.*

His principles continue to be quite elemental; and his standing order was, "Keep calm and go straight ahead." He is outstanding for the clarity and elegance of his writings, like the *Questions Equestres,* where he has set down his system brilliantly, leaving his own teachers far behind in his discussions of the theory and philosophy of equestrian art. It was L'Hotte who initiated the modern period of equitation in France and gave it the stature that permitted a decisive orientation toward the sporting equestrian activity of our own time. L'Hotte introduced the posting trot—the English trot—into the cavalry and also gave the cavalry its Regulations of 1876, which, except for modifications of a few details, remained in force right up to the eve of World War II.

Besides L'Hotte, others who continue to be cited in France to this day are Comte Louis Edmée de Montigny, an instructor at Saumur, Alexis Etienne Guérin, a commander, and, most of all, General Faverot de Kerbrech, author of a book of particular interest, *Dressage Methodique du Cheval de Selle d'après les Derniers Enseignements de F. Baucher.*

After the Franco-Prussian War, Saumur turned itself toward the equitation of sport, and dressage was directed more toward the practice of the extended gaits, using d'Aure's method as a basis. Military races were also encouraged. A student of L'Hotte, and an *écuyer* of great talent, was another commandant of Saumur, Montjou, a first-rate organizer who not only wrote a manual on equitation and dressage but also founded a society to foster the breeding of war-horses. Captain Saint-Phalle, an instructor at Saumur, and James Fillis, a civilian teacher at the Russian court, were remarkable personalities on a par with the commandants Champsavin, Bossut, Horment, Crousse, Royar, and other noteworthy horsemen, and remembered for the encouragement they gave sporting equitation.

This brings us to the period after World War I, when General Wattel, as commandant, reorganized the manège at Saumur, giving pride of place once again to academic equitation. He organized regional and national dressage competitions, resulting in 1932 in the French squadron—comprising Marion, Lesage (a magnificent horseman who became *écuyer en chef* in 1939), and Jousseaume winning the dressage event at the Olympics, crowning a long and scrupulous preparation. Nevertheless, Wattel also gave equitation at Saumur a strong push toward sport by instituting racing, various competitions, polo, and so on, and founding a training center to prepare for international competitions.

Wattel's successor was the celebrated Colonel Danloux, who brought Federico Caprilli's principles to the notice of the French and also eliminated some of the errors that arose through misinterpretation of those same principles.

XXVIII
DRESSAGE

Here we have the classic principles of dressage, taken from the writings of La Guérinière, generals L'Hotte and Wattel, commandants Licart, Susanna, and Nomis de Cossilla, and others.

Since the horse should be properly framed between the legs and the hands of the rider, one says that a horse is "in hand" when his hindquarters are placed in such a way as to allow for even distribution of the weight of his body, when the neck is raised in relation to the gait, the mouth is light, and the head is always at the same angle.

The haunches should be the instigators of the impulsion, but the horse must have that prerequisite for being brought "in hand"—the *ramener,* a deconcentration of the jaws, resulting in a lightening of the hindquarters through the raising of the neck. This is the action that is the basis of *équitation savante*—school or academic riding.

Such exercises should first be done standing still, even on the ground, and then in motion. The horse, however, must already have the proper equilibrium and the proper impulsion so that this very delicate movement does not turn into a withdrawal. Press down with the seat from back to front, to engage the hindquarters, which will be framed by the legs, while the hands maintain contact with the mouth to permit the horse to support himself there as strongly as is desired, proportionately to the gait and the cadence.

One speaks of "support," but it is to be understood as being a high degree of conscientiousness and delicacy on the part of the rider and as resulting from the balance and attitude of the horse, the rider's seat, and the degree of understanding between horse and rider. When these conditions obtain, the horseman's will and his actions, the prompt response of the horse, the impulsion of the horse's body, and the rider's contact with him become melded into a single coordinated force.

Collection is the foundation stone of all dressage, since from it, in particular, and from the position in hand, springs that lightness of action that is the goal and purpose of dressage. Collection has been defined as the line of demarcation between elementary and advanced equitation. It consists of making the horse dispose the various parts of his body in the manner best suited to the distribution of his own weight, thereby rendering his every movement more flowing and functional. This is very hard work, and it is not for every horseman to do, nor are all horses in the proper condition for it.

A basic rule is that it is not the hands that determine collection but, rather, the action of the legs, which are capable of regulating the rhythm of the horse's movement so that it becomes intense, brilliant, and infinitely light, while the hands are meant simply to control and contain any excessive impulsion, measuring and apportioning it as necessary. All this can be achieved only when the horse has learned to use the muscles of his back, neck, and shoulders properly.

This, too, is very hard work for a horse, and therefore it should be done in small doses. The horse should move decisively at the three gaits, in smooth, vigorous action, holding himself ready for any change in cadence. His neck should be raised, the head in an almost vertical position, and the extension of his movement should be less than usual for the cadences, while for impulsion it should be as strong as it ordinarily is, thereby adding vigor, with the haunches engaged.

Just what purpose does collection serve? A horse whose body is extended more or less naturally cannot immediately change from a slow gait to a fast one, but must accelerate his pace until he gets up to the required gait. The same is true in attempting to go from a fast pace to a slow gait. Dressage trains a horse so that he can change instantaneously from one pace to another effortlessly, and puts him in the proper equilibrium to do so without strain.

To obtain a cadenced gait without effort, whether the horse is starting from a halt or is changing gaits, it is necessary to resort to gathering the horse, from his haunches to his forehand. This is collection, achieved by pressure from the legs and restraint from the hands in proper coordination so that the horse moves forward, taking short steps. The curb chain is brought toward the neck (his head raised by the snaffle rein), his hindquarters at the center of gravity. In that manner, the horse is distributing his own weight properly over his four legs and is, therefore, ready to go into any gait, given a good horseman in the saddle. Since the horse should be in hand, that is, going forward, the action of the legs should prevail, relatively, over the restraint imposed by the hands.

The first condition for having a horse correctly collected is proper flexion of the neck. This flexed or "in-hand" position, together with collection and the lateral gaits, will bring forth maneuverability—at any pace—and perfect obedience to the rider's wish—whatever the cadence. This flexion is the action that one obtains, letting the hands give way lightly and with simultaneous aid from the legs, when the horse moves his head and arches his neck, bending it at poll, or between the second and third vertebrae.

For this flexion, which is first executed when the horse is standing still, the animal must be in perfect balance. Next, at the lightest of signals, he should champ the mouthpiece of the bit. Should the horse fail to respond to the hands, one need only apply pressure with the legs, repeatedly, to make him obey. The horse's head should come up, bit by bit, until it assumes the flexed position: the frontal line, from the poll to the nose, should be almost perpendicular to the ground; and the point where his lips join should be lined up so that it is about two inches lower than his dorsal line.

If the horse tucks his head in, the rider should stop acting on the bit and, by lightly drawing on the right rein of the snaffle, have him lift his head to the desired position.

After an initial period in which the flexion of the neck is practiced, within limits, and the horse becomes accustomed to bending at the two vertebrae, one should be able to achieve a perfect straight flexion of the neck. At that point, one can pass to the right and left flexions; that is, when the horse has his neck perfectly curved, looking straight ahead, one can call upon him to turn his head to the right or left, in the flexed position.

The curve to the right or left will have been perfectly executed when the rider, sitting erect, can see either the right or left eye of the horse. It is not right if the horse just twists his

124 *"Cossacks in Pursuit," by Kivschenko. Fast, natural riding, even though the horses are worn and on their last legs with fatigue. Here we have horsemen capable of any sort of acrobatics, undoubtedly derived from the most ancient habits and customs of the steppes, where even a fall was of little account. Art gallery, Moscow.*

125 *An attack by light horse of the guards, the golden age when such action almost invariably resolved a desperate situation, but at a tremendous cost. It was Frederick the Great who introduced the charge at the gallop as both a shock and surprise tactic. From a painting by Schipov. Leningrad.*

124

125

126

neck. The neck and shoulders should remain straight while only the head turns.

Once this flexion of the neck has been achieved standing still, it should be practiced at the walk, and then at the trot. As it is much more difficult to do, the faster the pace, it should be attempted progressively. When calling for the flexion of the neck while the horse is in motion, the horseman, holding the reins taut, should be careful that the horse does not stretch his neck out, and should repeatedly "call" to him by constantly pressing his legs against the barrel, in such a way that his aids prevail over his restraint.

Once the horse is able to achieve the flexion of the neck at the walk, trot, and canter, one can attempt the collected walk. Holding the horse to the flexed or in-hand position, one aids him with the calves. This action of the legs will bring the hindquarters down and under, and the action of the hands will bring the forehand back, closer to the center of the body. Thus, the horse will go forward with more energy than he would were his body extended naturally, and will proceed at shorter, collected steps, lightly and vibrantly, and will become so sensitive to command that he will be able, instantaneously, to change to whatever gait the horseman may desire.

In order to increase the horse's suppleness, once he has mastered the collected walk, the horseman should post in the saddle in rhythm to the trot (the school trot), and by giving him more energetic aid with the legs, bring him to the collected trot. The school trot is necessary to impress one's weight on the center of the horse, as well as on his shoulders, in work in which the horse will distribute his own weight equally over his four legs. The collected trot, which is slightly shorter and more active than the regular gait, at the beginning should not be held for too long a time.

The Rider's Actions

To break into a canter, when the horse is trotting on an inside diagonal, what is needed is action by the outside leg in perfect synchronization with the action of the horse's outside rear to force the animal to accelerate; also needed is pressure from the inside leg on the barrel to support the back as it receives the weight projected from the rear, and to encourage the inner fore to extend itself, along with action of the hands to aid in balancing the neck and shoulders and to maintain constant contact with the mouth.

Should the horse have a tendency to raise his head, the inside hand should be lowered to encourage him to extend his head and relax the cervical muscles. At the same time, to avoid pressure or shock to the loins, the rider should be on the fork, moving in coordination with the play of muscles in the horse's back, the knees tending to descend, and the bottom just grazing the saddle.

In advanced equitation, breaking into a gallop should come after the horse has been collected to a fair degree, with the rider going at the school trot—favoring a lightening of the

forehand and engaging the hindquarters, thus encouraging the horse's forward movement. Besides the action of the legs, there is the action of the pelvis coming from the oscillation of the horse's loins, all actions that should be brought to bear upon the animal in just measure.

Furthermore, the horse's head should come into play as a balance weight, swinging easily and high, and ready, along with the neck, to act like a pendulum, redistributing the horse's weight to keep it in perfect balance—an action typical of the gallop, a gait that requires the stretching and slackening of the animal's dorsal muscles, the first condition for succeeding in the work on the flat. If this development of extension is not achieved, the horse will never be truly collected, for like a spring, he must be able to lengthen himself as well as to collect himself.

To go from a canter to a slower gait, the rider should lean back a bit, sit lower on the fork and deeper in the saddle, and prepare the haunches—through the action of the trunk—to receive more weight as the forehand is lightened. Using leg pressure, one causes the horse to draw his rear nearer to his shoulders, shortening his back. With the elbows close to the body, the rider's hands should exert subtle yet elastic resistance, and even pull on the bars, to contain the neck, but they should never drag or yank on the reins.

Once the change has been made to a slower gait, the rider should return to the action necessary to assure the freest continuance of the horse's movement, without his losing impulsion.

From the foregoing, it should be understood that one must have constant contact with the horse. Even when finally halting, the hands should not provoke the action because of "having exhausted the horse's vitality and forward movement"; rather, the horse should still be eager to go forward.

Extended Canter

When one wants a horse to lengthen his gallop, and he has been badly trained, stabled too long, or is not well mounted, he will take advantage of the opportunity to work off a bit of his natural exuberance and will be skittish and, perhaps, even hard to handle.

One should arrive at the extended canter after serious work at the three gaits, and obtain it through increasing the action of the buttocks and the pressure of the legs, while the hands remain ready to give the measure of support necessary to the mouth to assure the proper increased extension of the neck. This extension should be achieved by the horseman progressively, while in the saddle, through drawing back his chest, and by moving his trunk so that the horse is collected, working all the time with the hands, easily, to obviate any imbalance.

To go into the collected canter, then, all that is necessary is for the rider to move the upper part of his body slightly to the rear, increasing the pressure on the pelvis and the legs, and balance this with light action from the hands to prepare the horse to strike off to a collected canter. In substance, the mechanics are these: the horse raises his head and neck from the shoulders, lifts his loins, and engages his hindquarters.

126 *"The Light Cavalry," by Giovanni Fattori, who generally depicts rough, scraggy Maremman horses. Galleria di Capodimonte, Naples.*

A fundamental task in training a horse is to cause him to make those modifications in his attitude that are necessary for him to regain his proper balance, as well as the proper distribution of the weight between forehand and hindquarters, particularly in consideration of the fact that the weight of the rider will fall—about two-thirds of it—on the horse's forehand.

Training, therefore, tends toward engaging the hindquarters, elevating the neck and shoulders so that the head is in the vertical or in-hand position. This prevents the horse's weight from going on the forehand—toward the shoulders—in which case the horse would lose control of his own weight and rebel against the added weight imposed by the body of the rider.

The impulsion or forward movement, which should be controlled in any case, produces the action; that is, the slight extension that sustains the horse's body and posture—his distribution of his own weight over his four legs. When action affects position, one has movement; when position prevails over action, one has nothing.

From these principles we derive the concept of instable equilibrium and the dynamics of movement. We have the constant loss and regaining of balance, which are the gaits, or, in other words, the proper distribution of the animal's weight over the different parts of his body in accordance with the movement and position required.

XXIX
HAUTE ÉCOLE

If dressage is the training particularly indicated to give a horse the utmost harmoniousness of movement and demonstrate his perfect susceptibility and obedience to the will of his rider, *haute école*, in its airs above the ground, is truly schooling for virtuoso performance.

While it is true that, in the wild state, a spirited horse will execute certain acrobatics, with a man in the saddle those movements must be done on command and in accordance with certain definite rules of style. This calls for a punctilious and complex performance, much as is required of someone playing a violin concerto: for either the work is done in a sublime manner, when it has a fascination that few things possess; or the execution is slipshod, in which case it is worthless and tiresome, and every aspect of the performance is either raw or overdone.

Naturally, there are always horsemen for whom equitation is solely school equitation, all other aspects of it considered merely tentative or vulgar, just as for some music lovers there is only Bach or a string quartet, while for some riders there is only hacking or the rodeo. There is no disputing personal taste, and therein lies a great deal of the fascination of equitation: there is something in it for the instinctive roughrider, or the pedantic, finicking horseman who is a devotee of *haute école*. Now there is a tendency to synthesize both the system and the employment of means for every specialty.

Federico Tesio, who was a practical man, gifted with a ready, quick mind, expressed himself in these terms in discussing *haute école:*

In certain special situations, the horse's intelligence has appeared to me to be superior to that of man. Among the many experiments that I've tried during my lifetime, one was that of teaching a horse, while still young, the principles of *haute école*.

These are artifical movements learned in the manège, which were very much in vogue about sixty years ago and made a furor in equestrian circles, and which, even today, are much applauded, particularly abroad.

If I had to make an analogy, I'd compare them to dress-parade figures executed by soldiers. As an experiment, I bought a young colt and the best book on *haute école* that I could find on sale in the international market at that time. The horse was a gray half-bred; and the book was the *Traité d'Equitation de Haute École,* written by Etienne Barroil, and published in Paris in 1889.

I read, studied, and began experimenting, following that book. I'll tell you right away that, after a month, I closed the book and sold the horse.

Had I wanted to, I could have resorted to the means employed by the *gauchos* and, at the risk of breaking my neck, dominated the horse in about fifteen minutes. He took fences and, at times, had some dreadful falls, but all that rather amused me. On the other hand, it would have sickened me to continue over a period of months, without any personal risk, to torture an animal who would look me in the eyes to try to understand why I was putting him to such torment, and attempt to interpret it and obey me.

Here, let us transcribe and translate a chapter from that thick volume of Barroil's of which Tesio speaks, covering the *jambette,* the *pas,* and the *trot espagnol:*

Jambette: to do a *jambette* is the expression used to describe the complete extension, above the ground, of one of the forelegs. The first *jambettes* are done in place, with no rider in the saddle.*

One prepares the horse for this action by accustoming him to raising each of his front legs in succession, by touching each one lightly at the cannon with the whip. One facilitates the lifting of a foreleg by holding down the opposing member. For instance, one engages the near foreleg by a half-flexion of the neck to the right, and does the opposite by engaging the off fore.

Continue in this way until the horse's weight is on one foreleg; then have him lift the other by tapping him lightly on the cannon with a whip until he raises it. At this point, stop and pet the horse, then have him lift the other leg, reversing the procedure. Progressively, the play of the whip should become more severe: keep striking each of the forelegs on the cannon alternately until the extension of the legs becomes longer each time. When that extension has reached the maximum possible, the horse has performed the *jambette*.

---

* These are not part of *haute école;* they belong to circus (trick) riding.—EDS.

Tesio continues, in his own words:

> ... and so on in this style for two hundred ninety-nine pages, not to mention another volume. I make you a present of the rest, but I pray that you read over the few lines quoted, a great philosophical lesson for any man. You will see instantly that the aim of the text is to teach a horse movements that are, for the most part, unnatural, difficult, balletic, and acrobatic. The method of instruction is extremely complicated and consists, in the main, of both petty and monstrous torture.
>
> Following that method, given time and enough drubbing, every horse would end by learning how to be a dancer. Stop and think, however, to just what intellectual effort the poor beast would be put to interpret man's cruelty and satisfy his complex demands.
>
> Were an Italian drillmaster to attempt to teach an Eskimo with no knowledge of our language how to march on parade, using the system outlined in the *Traité d'Equitation de Haute École,* I don't know that the Eskimo would do much better than the colt at learning the game. While it is certain that men know all about horse's complaints, the horse knows nothing of man's; but it is undoubtedly true that a horse knows more about a man's psyche than the man understands his horse.
>
> The horse interprets the very sound of a man's speech. He interprets the significance of certain tonal motifs: awakening, saddling, galloping, and so on. He interprets the punishments and the petting, as he interprets the very lightest touch of the hand that guides him, and he forms a reasonable assessment of the psyche of the man who masters him.
>
> Man, on the other hand, does not study, does not interpret, and therefore, rarely knows his horse's psyche.

That is the opinion of an outstanding horseman, the greatest the Italian turf has known. Everyone, however, is not of the same opinion; and even today, people are turning once more to school equitation.

Xenophon had already spoken of the collected horse who "carries his rear down and under and engages his hindquarters." Thus, through collection in school work, it is not the forehand that engages the hindquarters, but vice versa: the hindquarters impel the fore, causing the forces to converge at the head, which is held by the reins. "Thus, the horse goes forward without supporting himself on the bit, and reaches perfect lightness in his gait."

The difference between *haute école* in the Renaissance and that of Xenophon's time lies in the fact that while the latter, in line with Greek concepts, was concerned only with rendering the horse's movement beautiful and harmonious, dressage technique was designed to give the horse the utmost suppleness and maximum ease in executing, immediately and without effort, all desired changes in gait. The horse of which Xenophon was thinking as he wrote was the animal trained for processions, reviews, and festivity.

Haute école, which the French refer to as *équitation savante,* is the exaltation and consequence of dressage. By exercising the horse's joints, ribs and spine, and neck and shoulders as much as possible—necessary to obviate the least rigidity—the animal is made supremely supple and obedient to the will of the horseman, and, above all, becomes extremely light, with only the simplest of aids employed in the airs on the ground and, with perhaps just a bit more urging, in the airs above the ground, as well. In sum, *haute école* dressage allows a horse to move at an elegant, rhythmic gait and perform difficult acrobatics effortlessly.

Haute école is virtuosity and an end in itself, a luxury to which horsemen of exceptional will may aspire if they possess that particular sensitivity that will permit their forcing an animal to such effort without alienating him (calling, as it does, for assiduity and extremely fatiguing work). Such work will sharpen the horseman's knowledge of his mount and refine both tact and contact with the animal.

Haute école, which was born in France and flourished in Austria, was taught in the Italian Cavalry School at Pinerolo by Wagner and Paderni—both alumni of the Spanish Riding School in Vienna—to twelve cavalry lieutenants each year, beginning in 1868, posted to the school to receive this instruction. *Haute école* calls for at least six months' training of a rider already strong in dressage, and at least the same amount of time for teaching his horse the airs on the ground. Horses for such training must be docile, well built, strong, and completely developed.

Because of the evolution in the equestrian art brought about by the teachings of Federico Caprilli (1868–1907), *haute école* in Italy was abandoned in 1892. As a matter of fact, even dressage was dropped.

The most important work that we have on *haute école* is the first volume of the *Ecole de Cavalerie* by François Robichon de La Guérinière, *écuyer* to Louis XV, pupil of Vendeuil, and director of the riding academy at Paris. La Guérinière is considered by the French to be the "father of French equitation."

Among the great adepts of *haute école* who have left their mark, we can mention La Broue, Pluvinel, La Guérinière, De Nestrier, Lubersac, Viscount d'Abzac, his pupil Count d'Aure; Cordier, the instructor of the Cadre Noir; Baucher, Aubert, and General L'Hotte, who, as has been noted, synthesized the work of d'Aure and Baucher. The general, who was the teacher of a whole generation of *écuyers* and cavalry officers, is the author of the methods that still prevail today at the school at Saumur.

Haute école distinguishes among low, intermediate, and high airs. To the first category belong those airs in which the horse does not leave the ground, comprising the *pas d'Aure,* passage, piaffe, collected canter, flying changes of canter leads, the pirouette, and *terre à terre;* the second category includes the pesade and the courbette; and the third, the capriole, ballotade, and levade.

At this point, we must clarify the action of the reins and the hands as they affect the forward movement and direction of the horse. The hands act upon the hindquarters, but reflexively, together with the legs and the weight of the horseman, that is, the seat, upon the rear. In *elementary equitation,* it is obvious that if one pulls on the right rein, the horse will turn to the right. To execute the manège figure called the *serpentine,* however, it does not suffice if one pulls from the side of the pillar that is to be half circled. One must also yield the opposing hand, working with the inside leg to shift the hindquarters toward the inside. Thus, the same technique is used as in the volt, which may be performed by inclining the horse toward the inside, bringing the weight upon the inside shoulder, flexing and arching the spine toward the direction in which the volt is to be made, or it can be performed by maintaining the neck and shoulders in the normal position and, through the action of the inside leg, switching the trunk and haunches toward the outside.

In the serpentine, as well as the volt, the horse should respond to the commands with just the right amount of suppleness in neck, shoulders, and back. Above all, the serpentine emphasizes the shoulder-in and hindquarters-in action.

In *advanced equitation,* however, to bring out the "steering" action of the neck and shoulders, to obtain certain movements, and to eliminate resistance interposed by the hindquarters and achieve complete control over the haunches, the rider must learn to use the reins in various ways to obtain different effects. Thus, we have, besides the *direct* or *opening* rein, the *counter-reins,* also known as the "reins of opposition" or "support," which oppose the shoulders to the haunches, and vice versa, and which can be direct of opposition, counter of opposition, and intermediate. They must be used with discretion insamuch as they act upon the impulsion.

Lateral effects are produced through the opening rein and the direct rein of opposition; diagonal effects with the intermediate, supporting, or counter-rein of opposition. The action of the opening rein is the most natural and straightforward, but should be upward to obviate in some measure the complete imbalance of the horse upon the inside shoulder, that is, upon the shoulder on which the rein acts.

The supporting, or counter, rein will make the horse turn, for example, to the near side, if the right rein is brought forward on the near side, thus forcing the horse to turn his head to the right but to carry the weight of his neck on the left shoulder to the point where he must turn to get his balance once more.

The reins of opposition cause the shoulders to work against the haunches, acting upon the horse's weight and causing a strong reaction. Since the reins of opposition tend to contain the impulsion, they call for greater leg action. The direct rein of opposition swings the shoulders from their normal position, through the action of the hands, almost parallel to the axis of the horse, and switches the haunches to the opposite side, so that they are forced to cover more ground. In relation to the greater force of the propulsive action, the horse becomes heavy in the shoulders.

The counter-rein of opposition acts diagonally and behind (right toward the left, left toward the right), flexing the neck to the right and shifting the shoulders to the left in direct proportion to the impulsion, while the haunches flex slightly to the right. This involves a decisive opposition from the hand, forcing the horse to put his weight on the haunches in order to turn on the hindquarter that acts as pivot, which would be toward the left, should the action come from the right rein. Naturally, lively aid from the legs is required to complement the effect of the reins.

The intermediate rein of opposition is midway between the direct and counter-reins of opposition, acting as it does on both shoulders and haunches, and more strongly on one or the other in accordance with the angle. The right intermediate rein engages the off rear and lightens the right shoulder, consequently causing the left side to lengthen; and because the horse shifts slightly from that side, the leg action must be fairly strong. In all these actions, the other rein, called the "opposing rein," should limit the curve of the neck to the point desired.

All the foregoing, which looks complicated in print, is actually quite simple and, in practice, is reduced to actions that are natural, almost instinctive, once the rider has learned the interplay of both his own and his mount's balance. To maintain his balance, the horse must keep his center of gravity before the center of gravity of his total weight. Thus, when the rider shifts the horse's neck and shoulders, or his own weight, he forces the horse, as well, to shift in the same direction, diminishing, accordingly, all other aid, in particular that of the hands, which should be kept to the minimum both in elementary and advanced equitation.

If the fork and buttocks, which dominate the horse's trunk, can always keep the musculature under control, there should be no stiffening in the horse's back, a sign of defensiveness, nor any slackening, indicative of a loss of forward motion; also the hands should achieve such sensitivity that they can anticipate the horse's intentions when they feel any stiffening or relaxation in the animal's neck and jaw.

To exercise the horse's trunk, haunches, and withers, commence by working the horse in the volt and the double volt, first at a walk, then at the collected trot, changing the flexion at every change of direction. The rider, flexing the horse lightly in the direction that he is to take, should describe a circle twelve paces in diameter, keeping his inside leg at the girth and the outside leg on the ribs, directly behind the girth, to oblige the horse (whose body is flexed) to ease the flank around. To change direction, three paces before completing the circle, the rider turns to the opposite direction, changing the flexion, and switching the position of his trunk and legs.

The double volt is a figure eight, a figure that need not be insisted upon if it is going to cause adverse reactions. Some horses, while performing the first exercises in flexion, attempt to escape the hands by raising and lowering their heads. In this case, one must insist by placing the hands at the withers, so that the horse, to avoid hurting himself, will cease to resist. Notwithstanding, it is principally the rider's lightness of hand, his delicacy and sensitivity, that will make the horse obedient, and obtain from him the perfect execution of whatever is requested.

The lateral gaits are those in which the horse moves to the side, or, rather, on two tracks. These comprise *shoulder-in* and *shoulder-out,* *haunches-in* and *haunches-out,* and the *half-pass-in* or *half-pass-out.*

Shoulder-in is the key to dressage inasmuch as it confers upon the horse maximum suppleness and independent action of every part of his body. It prepares him to perform any change of direction in the correct manner, and gives him the ability to execute any movement with a broad, elevated, and elastic leg action, enabling him to pass one leg over the other. Furthermore, it loosens the horse's shoulders, gives lightness to the hindquarters, and a suppleness to the haunches that comes with obedience to the legs, as well as the lightness that springs from obedience to the hands. Shoulder-in further engages and conditions the spinal column, which acts as a transmission between the forehand and hindquarters. The axis of the spine should form an angle of thirty degrees with the track to permit easy, cadenced movement over two tracks.

It is best to begin the shoulder-in exercise by making the horse move in a circle, pushing him toward the perimeter when he is well flexed. To request the off shoulder-in, one must first use the right opening rein, then the rein of opposition to swing the shoulder to the left (here the neck and shoulders must be firm so that the horse does not become heavy in the hand, yielding the head and the off shoulder) on a track parallel to that covered by the hindquarters. At the same time, while the inside rein—the intermediate of opposition—acts, the external or supporting rein controls and contains the curve of the neck and shoulders, and seconds the degree of looseness and compliance reached by the horse.

Similarly, and always in proportion to the degree of the animal's physical conditioning and his understanding of what is requested, the inside leg, slightly retracted, should act to aid the displacement of the haunches, contain the trunk, and activate the horse's movement; the outside leg, slightly advanced, balances the movement from the outside toward the inside in a continous impulse from the seat, particularly upon the outside hindquarters—which must come forward to achieve the broad and elegant movement of the inside fore. The trunk, accordingly, must flex toward the inside, but not excessively.

Shoulder-out is executed like shoulder-in, the actions, of course, being reversed. It is frequently a necessary exercise to eradicate the imbalance and rigidity that certain horses have because of imperfect conformation or certain defects or limping or wobbliness. (Almost all horses, to some extent, lack perfect conformation, have some fault, and are, inevitably, more or less unsure.)

Haunches-in is performed through the use of the outside counter-rein of opposition, with pressure of the outside leg, drawn back slightly, to induce the haunches to proceed along a track farther in than that over which the forehand continues to go in the normal manner. The outside hind leg crosses over the inside hind leg at every step, while the rider's inside leg controls the mass of the horse's body and calls for forward movement whenever this tends to slacken, using the spurs, if necessary. The inside hand should control the inside shoulder so as to continue to advance with decision and in complete equilibrium without letting it slip toward the longitudinal axis and close the angle with the track—which should remain at thirty degrees. (Therefore the slight flexion of the neck should permit the rider to see a bit more of the inside eye.) This is the basic figure for rotating the haunches around the shoulders.

In shoulder-out, contrary to the preceding figure, in which the horse looks in the direction in which he is going, he should look slightly toward the outside for the effect of the similar but naturally reverse action of that for haunches-in.

These, then, are all the exercises designed for making the horse supple, each with its own particular mechanics and purpose. The horseman must learn to choose the one that is appropriate to the needs, balance, and education of his horse.

The haunches-out at the three gaits (when achieved through containment of the hindquarters so that they extend more to the outside than is strictly necessary, they render the exercise futile) induces the horse to take deep, rhythmic breaths, moving roundly and supplely, which is necessary to the proper execution of the *volt with haunches-out,* done with action from the outside rein. It is one of the most useful figures for dressage work.

The next step along is the half-pass, in which the horse moves along two parallel tracks with the forehand and hindquarters; proceeding straight ahead, with head and neck slightly turned in the direction in which he is going, while he looks, almost imperceptibly, at the road ahead. The inside opening rein is used to indicate the direction, to request flexion of the neck in this direction, and to sustain the inside shoulder. The outside hand uses the counter-supporting rein toward the inside, and the leg first swings forward to displace the forehand toward the inside, and then backward, to induce the outside rear hind leg to cross over the inside one, while the rider's inside leg, slightly behind, contains the haunches and the whole mass of the horse's body; the hindquarters are engaged through the seat to guarantee constant forward movement for the decisive crossing of the outside lateral over the inside.

The fundamental difference between shoulder-in and the half-pass lies in the fact that in shoulder-in the horse is curved and the movement is provoked primarily by the hands, while in the half-pass the horse remains straight, the spinal column is responsible for the posture of the head, the regulated parallel movement of the hands shifts the forehand, and the legs displace the hindquarters.

XXX
AIRS

The shoulder-in is the foundation of all movements on two tracks. The horse is bent around the inside leg of the rider, which together with the inside rein has a strong influence, and induces the horse to move sideways and forward. The rider's outside leg, together with the outside rein, acts in a restraining way, and prevents deviating of the hindquarters to the outside. The horse's body is bent away from the direction to which he is moving. The object of this exercise is to increase the collection and the engagement of the hocks. The bend of the horse is more or less accentuated according to the degree of lateral suppleness the rider seeks to attain. Two tracks are frequently performed at the canter.

In the half-pass, the weight is on the inside stirrup of the advancing leg, thus freeing the outside diagonal, giving it ample space to cross the inside diagonal. Neither of these two exercises should be practiced at length.

To execute these airs, the animal's head should be elevated, shifting the center of gravity to the rear. The degrees of elevation of the head vary from the natural position, with the bars of the jaw on a line with the chest, the usual stance of wild horses, to an elevation of the head by the rider. Thus, the shoulders are relieved of the weight of the neck, with the bars of the jaw at about 15 centimeters below the dorsal line. A third degree of elevation of the head places the bars of the jaw even with the dorsal line, at a 70-degree angle to the ground.

The low airs, such as the *pas d'Aure,* can be executed either on foot or mounted, with the animal held close in hand, by increasing collection and making use of a long whip to switch the hindquarters. The extra length allows the rider to retain his grasp on the reins, maintaining control.

The horse can also be worked between pillars, usually two sturdy padded posts about 2 meters high and 20 centimeters in diameter, the invention of Pluvinel, so criticized by the Duke of Newcastle, who considered them instruments of torture, designed to exhaust a horse and subjugate him to the trainer's will. He believed, on the other hand, that a threat would make the horse raise his forehands and stand on his haunches or bend at the hocks without advancing, supporting himself on the shanks while on the halter.

Low

The *pas d'Aure,* invented by Comte d'Aure, requires the horse to move forward while raising and extending the front hooves, which are propelled forward by a down-and-under movement of the hindquarters. At first it is best to work the horse on foot, holding him close in hand, standing near the right shoulder and touching the shoulders alternately with the whip, thus causing the horse to raise his forehand at each tap. An assistant, standing in front of the horse, takes each hoof alternatingly, extending each leg until it is almost horizontal, and then releasing it. In addition to this work on the forehand, the assistant, standing even with the haunches, touches them up with the whip so that they move energetically, without restraint. When the horse sufficiently understands what is required of him, the air can be executed mounted. After collecting the horse under him, the rider signals him to move forward both with a tap of the whip on the shoulder and with the reins, at the same time using decided leg pressure on the side opposite to the shoulder so that, for example, if the right forehand begins the walk, the signals will come from the right rein, the whip on the right shoulder, and leg pressure on the left side, bringing the left hind leg under.

The passage is a slow, shortened, highly collected, very elevated and very cadenced trot. It is characterized by a pronounced engagement of the hindquarters, a more accentuated flexion of the knees and hocks, and the graceful elasticity of the movement.

There is a great difference between the school and circus passage which is attained by touching the forelegs with the whip. There is no proper bending of the hocks, and the hind legs are stiff and the steps irregular. Swinging the hindquarters from side to side is a serious fault in the school passage, whereas it does not matter in the circus passage.

The preliminary training for the Spanish trot is done on the ground. The trainer, by light taps of the whip, induces the horse to raise one foot after the other and replace it lightly. Some trainers employ ropes to achieve the desired elevation, but it is best not to use any mechanical aids if possible. The most difficult idea to convey to the horse is not that he must raise his feet but that he must bring them down lightly while moving forward. When the animal finally understands what is desired, the trainer mounts, and, still using taps of the whip on the shoulder and croup—accompanied now by a gentle swaying of his body and heel pressure directly behind the girth—leads the horse into the new air. Every attempt should

be made to ensure that the hind legs as well as the fore are lifted.

The piaffe is the collected trot in place. The horse's back is supple, and the hindquarters, with active hocks, are well engaged, giving great freedom and lightness to the action of the forelegs. The horse's body should move up and down with a supple and harmonious movement, without any swinging of either forehand or hindquarters from side to side. "Piaffe" (or "piaffer") are correct terms.

The pirouette in classical dressage is the turn on the haunches in four to five strides at a collected canter. The horse, with his hocks well engaged, does the turn with its hind legs completing the smallest circle, almost on the spot, and with the forelegs describing a wider circle around the hind legs. The correct cadence and proper sequence of the strides must be maintained. The hind legs should never twist around each other. The twisting of the hind legs or forelegs around each other is frequently seen in the circus. I would call these airs pivots, but never pirouettes!

To execute the changes of leads in the air at a canter, the horse must first learn to do simple changes of leads from the walk. The horse is placed in a collected canter for a few strides, then brought to a walk. Then, with the proper aids, the horse should again canter, but on the opposite lead. The intervals between the changes of lead should be shortened until only a second elapses before the horse automatically changes leads on signal. Practical ways of achieving this come through teaching the change while cantering on a circle, or on the serpentine, clearly establishing, at all times, when the change of leads is to occur. The rider must remain perpendicular to the animal to ensure maximum lightness on the forehand, though the change must be begun by the hindquarters followed by the forelegs, in consequence of the dynamics and balance of the horse. If the rider weighs more on the stirrups than on the fork, his mount will break his gait.

Maximum adherence of seat and legs is necessary to impel the proper actions to engage the horse. If the gallop is on the left lead, for example, the rider's right leg should bring the left hind leg back by increasing the pressure on the left haunch, while slightly releasing and raising the right hand, elevating the head. From the moment the left forehand receives the total weight, the change of leads begins with the hindquarters, followed by an instant of suspension, with the forehand then descending, and the left diagonals supporting the weight.

The Duke of Newcastle has precisely defined the *terre à terre* as a gallop performed in double time on two tracks. In this air, the forelegs are raised to the canter position and touch the ground together, the hind legs following the forelegs in like manner, thus achieving a slow but accelerated cadence very much like a series of short jumps near the ground, with some forward impulsion from the haunches. Although the *terre à terre* is classified as one of the low airs, since it is performed near the ground, it is considered the basis of all the high airs executed in double time. This is an exercise of violent motion that few horses are capable of performing with the required exactness. A supple, spirited animal has the potential for this difficult air. True horsemen consider its execution a touchstone in *haute école,* exhibiting the real skill and capability of both rider and horse.

The structure of the horse, as well as his disposition and

character, determines whether or not he possesses any potential for performance of any of the airs. A short-legged animal can be taught to execute the piaffe, but a horse with poor conformation will hardly be able to do a half-pass or courbette. To keep a horse in show condition, he should be exercised daily at least 30 to 40 minutes.

If the horse has the necessary training, he can perform the *terre à terre* effortlessly, with only the slightest movement of the half-haunch-in; but since this air is so exhausting, it should not be performed for more than a few steps.

The last of the low airs in the circus is called the pirouette (but, as I explained above, these airs are really pivots), executed at a gallop in place. In this air, the horse's haunches describe a circle and the forelegs serve as a pivot. Its performance requires the rider to bring the horse to a collected gallop and then to apply pressure of the inside leg close to the girth, as well as using pressure from the outside leg behind the girth, near the chest. The pressure should alternate from the outside to the inside with quick lateral movements on each beat of the gallop, and at the same time using the rein of opposition, keeping the forehands in place, induce the animal to move his croup away from the pressure. If the horse is well trained, he can be persuaded to really wind up his legs so that they are actually twisted around each other. This is known as the spiral pirouette, and is performed only by highly obedient, supple horses.

A pivot is no more than a volt around the hindquarters or forehand, and is quite similar to the pirouette, though not to be confused with it. By holding one hind leg in place while side-stepping with the other, the rear pivot is performed, while in the croup-around-forehand, the horse is made to move away from the pressure of the rider's legs, as in side-stepping, while the forehand is kept in place by use of the reins.

Intermediate

In the levade, the horse is elevated with his forehands tucked in without moving forward, keeping his hind legs in place. When the horse feels secure in the piaffe, the rider has an assistant tap the horse with the whip on the shoulder near the withers, and the horse, if he is well trained, will raise his forelegs. On a further signal, he will lean lightly on his haunches. The levade is not to be confused with the action of the rearing circus horse who bends his forelegs at the knees, extending the hooves in a climbing movement. In the air, however, the horse must bend and rest on his haunches, keeping his head in place and almost touch his elbows with his hooves.

High

The pesade is performed by raising the forelegs and drawing them in while balancing the body on bent hind legs. This exercise cannot be taught between pillars because of the elevation and the freedom of movement required. The horse, collected and advancing at a slow gait, is signaled by the reins and strong leg pressure, thus causing him to lean on his haunches and thrust upward and forward with his forehands, as if he were jumping an obstacle, but keeping his hind legs planted on the ground.

The courbette is an air that evolved from the levade. In this air the horse raises itself from the ground with the forelegs well drawn in, and then jumps up and lands on its hind legs without touching the ground with its forefeet.

For the croupade, the horse raises his forelegs slightly, then brings them down and immediately raises his hind legs, and draws them under. Such an air is, of necessity, taught between pillars. The horse is secured by a halter and shanks, and then is collected. When he responds well, the trainer taps him with the whip on the right shoulder, and as soon as the horse has risen he taps him behind the girth. The forelegs come down and the hind legs are thrust upward. A croupade, in which the horse draws in its hind legs so that the shoes are visible, is called a ballotade, and is the first stage of the capriole.

A horse is trained for the capriole as he is for the croupade, except that, in the capriole, the horse is tapped with the whip on the point of the shoulder and then immediately on the haunches so that he raises all four legs, the hind legs kicking out to the rear.

The *pas et saut* is executed in three phases, the first the *terre à terre*, the second, the pesade, and the third, the capriole, and continuing in this order.

Kneeling, lying down, and volts on the shoulders with legs crossed, are not airs of the *haute école*, but exercises designed to teach obedience or stunts of the equestrian circus.

XXXI
VERSAILLES AND SAUMUR*

The oldest riding schools and academies or, as they were generally referred to in their day, manèges—where masters were able to establish the principles of their doctrines on equitation and maintain a tradition through the practice and teaching of them—are those of Versailles, which gave rise to Saumur (as we know it today), the famous Spanish Riding School of Vienna, and the school at Hanover, which descended from the older academy of Göttingen.

When the academy at Versailles was created, in 1680, it was established in the large and small stables in front of Louis XIV's palace. Three hundred saddle horses were stalled in the large building, and in the smaller, there were six hundred draft and cart horses. The two establishments handled the training and working of all horses destined for the king and the service of his court. Generally acquired in Normandy and the Limousin, the better animals—if posted to royal service after eighteen months of training in the "reserve"—were promoted to the ranks of the "silver bridles" or to the superior "gold bridles."

As for students, the riding masters taught any young men of good family who showed a talent for becoming *écuyers* and assistants—as well as four élite guardsmen sent by their regiments to receive training as instructors, a few "scholarship" pupils admitted as a special favor, twenty-two of the king's pages, future cavalry officers who had already seen

---

* Taken from *L'Encyclopédie du Cheval.*

three years of service, and also men attached to the stables who were to become mounted huntsmen. The courses were rigorous, and a great deal of emphasis was placed on achieving the correct seat as the basis of equitation. For three years, the pages rode with neither stirrups nor spurs.

The riding academy at Versailles was disrupted by the French Revolution and reestablished in 1814 under the direction of the d'Abzac brothers, but it had dwindled to practically nothing by 1830 without having made any significant contribution, its directors being too formalist for all practical purposes.

During the sixteenth century, a riding academy had been founded at Saumur—next to the school of liberal arts— by the regent of Henry IV. In 1763, after a regiment of carabineers was garrisoned there, construction of the school and manège that we know today began. Differences of opinion and rivalry among various factions did not permit much progress in the art of equitation until a commission, comprising an inspector and a number of cavalry colonels, sitting at Paris in 1766, examined a group of top students and announced that, henceforth, for their excellence, established principles of the school at Saumur would prevail. This led to the reestablishment, once again, of a riding academy at Saumur, under the command of the Marquis de Poyanne, in 1771.

Thus, the bases of French equitation were laid, and the tradition continues today. Saumur, however, was shut down in 1788. Subsequently, a national academy was established at Versailles in 1796, and in 1809 a special school was created at Saint-Germain-en-Laye. Little was accomplished by either of these institutions. Finally, on the first of May, 1815, Marshal Nicolas Soult reopened the establishment at Saumur as a cavalry school.

After some conflict between the military and civilian factions, the school was again shuttered in 1822, mainly because some of its students had involved themselves in the conspiracy headed by General Berton; but it was again reopened in 1825 as a cavalry school, with the course of instruction oriented solely toward equitation for military purposes.

In 1837, Jean Charles Cordier was named *écuyer en chef*, and the school acquired twenty-five Irish horses for work in the open, as well as a supply of English saddles. Also, a school for farriers and a breeding research center were created. In honor of a visit by the Duchess de Berry in 1828, a carrousel was staged, a pleasant custom continued right down to our day.

Under the tenure of Count d'Aure, racing was introduced. In 1852, an obstacle course called the Chemin Vert was laid out in the surrounding countryside. A veterinary corps to improve hygiene and the treating of horses was also created under d'Aure, and in 1860 a special corps of handlers was established.

Broken up in 1870 by the Franco-Prussian War, then reestablished in 1872 and confirmed in a ministerial regulation the following year—which gave it 850 horses—the school at Saumur was made responsible for the training of sublieutenants of all branches of the armed forces and the officer-candidates of Saint-Cyr. The riding masters continued to be known as *écuyers* and the course of instruction as "manège." The name *Cadre Noir* for the student body comes from their

black uniforms, with gold buttons, and first included a redingote, then a short jacket, and, finally, a close-fitting tunic for regular duty. For dress wear, there were white trousers, gold epaulettes, and a bicorne (at one time the regulation hat for all students), nicknamed the *lucerna* or "lamp."

After the war, Saumur turned its attention to sport: racing, polo, and the three-day event, without, however, forgetting the traditional manège. It was Colonel Wattel who brought about this extension of activity, enabling Saumur to take a lively interest in various ways of employing the horse, while assuming the prime function of training horse cavalry and motorized units—during the era between the two world wars. It was during this period, under the command of Colonel Lesage, that Saumur reached its heights, but World War II ruined everything.

After the armistice of 1940, France managed to save a bit of her equestrian tradition with the national academy of equitation that had sprung up at Fontainebleau under the

127 *A jump by Cesare Paderni. The important thing is to clear the obstacle. To do so, the forehand must be lifted and held on the bit, the rider's point of support. In that way, his own balance is assured when he moves his legs forward.*

128 *Lieutenant Della Noce, riding more on the fork, but still substantially like the rider in the preceding illustration, although he is pulling on the reins with one hand, rather than two.*

129 *Guido d'Oucieu de la Batie. A period of transition, when the rider began thinking about the need to sustain the horse. Note, however, that he still is planted well over the horse's loins.*

130 *Lieutenant Lanzi. Still in a period of transition, the rider's efforts to "follow" the horse awkward, clumsy, and unnatural. He bears down on the stirrup, and raises his body (which is a step forward), but still remains behind. He cannot liberate the horse's neck, which the French had already managed to do through the use of the snaffle.*

131 *Lieutenant Lanzi. Evolution continues with the rider's attempt to "follow" the horse, permitting the horse to adopt a better and safer position, although still not complete extension.*

132 *How obstacles were taken when Cesare Paderni was instructor at Pinerolo (1880–1890). This squad is practically committing a crime in the name of school equitation and* haute école *applied to open and cross-country riding. The horse is contained by the rider's legs; the rider dramatically to the rear, chest back, with the horse on the bit and ferociously seized in the mouth, all intended to help raise the forehand and sustain him. The horse, hardly managing to see the obstacle, takes off furiously against it to be free of the "impulses" received from ill-considered "aids" and the torture to his mouth by the rider's hands.*

133 *See how much calmer and more extended both horse and rider appear in this international squad led by Captain Caprilli. Almost all the horses are on the snaffle. Although the Russian officer, second from the right, still seems a bit awkward in the hands. In general, the appearance of the group is natural and relaxed.*

127

128

129

130

131

133

132

134

136

137

138

135

139

aegis of the Haut Comité des Sports. In 1945, however, a tank and cavalry school was reestablished at Saumur, and the manège was reorganized by Colonel Margot, the commandant of the academy. So, once again, the French equestrian tradition and *l'esprit cavalier* was preserved—the spirit of the cavalry, we must note, not the spirit and tradition of pure equitation of Versailles or Vienna, but a cavalry school looking to the widest utilization of the horse.

XXXII
THE SPANISH RIDING SCHOOL OF VIENNA

In the heart of Vienna, in the very center of the city, in that museum of dusty memories that was the Imperial Palace where Maria Theresa held sway and Marie Antoinette passed her sunny girlhood, where the spurs of Eugene of Savoy (defeating the French at both Oudenarde and Malplaquet) spiked the wit of Voltaire and the spice of Casanova, and where old Franz Josef put an end to the history of the Habsburgs, one hears every day now, in passing, lively neighing, and those who are nostalgic for the parades of another day stop to see the beautiful white horses of Vienna as they are ridden out for their exercise in the Prater.

These stallions trace their ancestors to Spain, and for four centuries have been pure-bred in Vienna. How this line came from Spain, to be reproduced in Austria, is not quite certain. Some authorities maintain that the Spanish Habsburgs sent some of these horses to their Austrian cousins as gifts. Another hypothesis is that the Spanish stud and riding academy passed to the Austrian Habsburg court through the Bourbon rulers of the Kingdom of the Two Sicilies who maintained their famous stables, which still exist today, near Naples, and which, at that time, were full of Spanish horses. On the other hand, Ernst Marboe writes that these horses are called Lipizzaner after Lipizza, near Trieste,* and from 1580 on were sent by the bishop of that Adriatic city to the court at Vienna.

* The site of the Austrian imperial stud.—TRANS.

134 *Lieutenant Campello takes a steep one in the old style, with his chest parallel to the horse's back and the action of the reins concentrated on the mouth.*

135 *An exemplary descent by Lieutenant Lugli. The horse is so much at his ease that he does not even seek a foothold nor does he drag, but comes down perpendicularly as if he were walking a ramp.*

136 *Captain Caprilli on Melopo, winning the Turin competition (2.08 meters), a record that stood until 1909, when beaten by General Ubertalli (2.20 meters) on Vissuto.*

137 138 139 *Demonstrations of the validity of the Caprilli system. Obstacles that would have been refused were school-equitation methods used are now taken in complete tranquillity. Captain Bolla goes over two bicycles on Blitz, the sort of strong, tough horse he preferred. Lieutenant Lizzato takes an automobile neatly, in perfect application of the system, while Sublieutenant Bognetti has no trouble jumping a set table. Forty years later, Major Odetti would not hesitate to jump two light-armored cars.*

The Austrian school of equitation, known as the Spanish Riding School, was popularized by Charles VI (Emperor of the Holy Roman Empire 1711–1740). During this time there was a "Spanish manège" within the palace dependencies, so called because its horses came from Andalusia. The purpose of the school under the emperor's aegis was the preservation of the equestrian art in its most noble form, *haute école*, in accordance with the precepts established by eighteenth-century masters. To this end, it recruited students to fill gaps in its enrollment, and selected horses particularly suitable for advanced dressage work—the Lipizzaner breed.

The instruction given at the school, limited at one time to court officials and imperial dignitaries, was later made available to young men of the bourgeoisie and foreign officers. The first commander in chief of the school was Count von Regenthal, while another still remembered was Commandant Niedermayer, who was head of the school when General l'Hotte visited it in 1884.

The horses bred at the imperial stud in Lipizza had Andalusian, Neapolitan, and even Danish strains, as well as Arab blood. The Lipizzaner breed comprises five families, descended from the following sires: Pluto, gray, Danish, 1765; Conversano, black, Neapolitan, 1767; Neapolitano, brown, Neapolitan, 1790; Favory, flea-bitten gray, Andalusia, foaled in Lipizza, 1779; and Maestoso, gray, Spain, 1779. Between 1840 and 1869, there was an infusion of Arab blood.

The Lipizzaners, which stand about fifteen hands high, are characterized by their extremely docile temperament and magnificent bearing. The school at Vienna proclaims its fealty to La Guérinière's principles, and even considers his mantle to have fallen on some of its own illustrious horsemen, such as Maximilian von Weyrother and Colonel von Oeynhausen.

The course of instruction has been passed on by word of mouth, rarely through texts. Colts are subjected to two years of work on the longeing rein, then are mounted. The horseman seeks only a good response to the hand, and a low neck. Dressage continues by hand, with the longe or long reins used between pillars or along the wall.

Among the airs practiced at the Vienna school, the piaffe, the trot in place perhaps is the one most characteristic of its strict and perfect style. Even that very regular and brilliant passage, a highly collected trot with very slow forward movement, is frequently gone into from the piaffe, the bridge between these two airs being almost imperceptible, and provoking not the slightest change in the regularity of the beat.

At the Vienna school, the school leaps are still practiced as they were at Versailles, and following the very same patterns: the "levade," with the horse seated on the hocks, hindquarters flexed, and forehand well raised; the "high pesade," with the horse in the same attitude as for the levade, but straightening himself on the hocks; the "courbette," in which the horse raises his forehand, balancing on his haunches by a spring from the hocks; the "cabriole," in which the horse kicks out with his hind legs to a horizontal position, with the forehand raised.

Thanks to the dedication of its director at the time, Count von Straten, the school did not succumb with the fall of the monarchy in 1918. The count used his own fortune to bring together once more horses and personnel that again were to flee after the catastrophe of World War II. At that time, thanks to the understanding of General Patton of the American Army, the school evacuated its establishment in Vienna, and found refuge in the American zone.

XXXIII
THE HANOVER SCHOOL

Baron von Münchhausen, son of the Elector of Brandenburg's great riding master, and himself a fine horseman, founded an equestrian academy in Hanover in 1734, as one of the schools of the University of Göttingen. It was directed at first by Valentin Trichter, and later by the Ayres family, father and son; Trichter's efforts were subsequently engaged, at Seidlitz, in the reform of the Prussian cavalry.

The academy was intended to preserve the equestrian art in its purest state. Horsemen such as Oehlmann, General Mayer, Major Kampe, and Major Schweppe added luster to its name and reputation. Transferred from local jurisdiction to the city, it was superseded in 1866 by the military institute of equitation created by the emperor, Friedrich Wilhelm III. Shortly after moving to the town of Schwedt, on the Oder River, the course of instruction was oriented toward work in the open air, with particular emphasis given the *chasse à courre*.

After World War I, the Treaty of Versailles provided for the establishment of a military riding academy, and this school took the name of the Hanover Cavalry School, with its command given to General Seiffert, who oversaw its reorganization, a difficult task, in view of the limited number of horses available, and those all intended for officer-candidates of the cavalry.

Major von Flotow, however, along with Sublieutenant Gerhardt, a graduate of the Vienna school, managed to reestablish one section of the school and, shortly thereafter, bring hunting once more to its place of honor, while developing other sporting activities—races, steeplechasing, and cross-country riding, all favorites in Hanover.

In particular, the section devoted to such events as horse shows, dressage, and so on grouped under the "Tournament Section," won fame throughout the world during the years preceding the Second World War.

In 1939, Hanover ceased to be the seat of German equitation with the transfer of the school to Kranowitz. After the war, the German Equestrian Federation established a school at Warendorf, in Westphalia, to develop the breeding of saddle horses and to provide training for equestrian events that would preserve the classic German tradition.

XXXIV
THE SPANISH SCHOOL

A school of equitation, part of the military academy at Valladolid, was created in 1882 to train instructors for all mounted units. In 1902, it was replaced by a new military school in Madrid, which had a wonderful obstacle course, owned by the Racing Club, at its disposition. The course was located near the Prado, as well as the difficult Zarzuela track, full of natural and artificial pitfalls.

Instruction at the school was based on the classic French principles of equitation. Around 1910, the Italian method was introduced by two sublieutenants, Gregorio García Astrain and Federico García Balmori, and officially adopted by the mounted services after a competition between two groups of horsemen—one following the classic method and the other, Caprilli's.

In 1920, the school was greatly enlarged to the point where it had 384 horses, of which twenty were Thoroughbreds. Instruction was primarily in equitation appropriate to campaign and rough riding; the slide at Zarzuela, an almost vertical drop of some fifty feet, became famous.

In 1928, the Spanish team, comprising Captains Julio García Fernández, José Morenes Navarro, José Alvarez de Bohorques, and the Marquess de los Trujillos, won the jumping event at the Olympic games held in Amsterdam. After the formation of the republic in 1931, the school adopted the name School of Cavalry and Equitation. Then, with the advent of motorization of the armed forces, the school changed its aspect and course. But Spanish horsemen still maintained their tradition and place of honor at the Olympics in 1948, in London.

The school is commanded by a brigadier general, has a staff of 80 officers, 1,000 men, and a complement of 266 horses. There are three principal sections: general instruction, military studies, and equestrian training. Equitation is divided into the following studies: breaking of colts, dressage and *haute école*, work in the field, jumping, vaulting, racing, polo,

140 *Lieutenant Bonacossa comes down an escarpment in accordance with the system: chest forward, the merest support to the horse, heels low, riding well on the fork, and with the center of gravity naturally low.*

141 *The rider is seated and dragging on the reins, so the horse cannot possibly stretch his neck.*

142 *One of Caprilli's countless falls while riding Vecchio. The master, nevertheless, is at the peak of his form and the height of his researches, but still continuing to experiment. Photographs of Caprilli are so familiar that there is almost no point in reproducing them here. Take, for instance, the one in which he is at the Roman fence on Piccola Lark, where one can see how the horse, completely at liberty while still an extension of his rider, takes a difficult obstacle with utter naturalness, giving an impression of infinite agility. When Caprilli jumped a wagon, it was not mere exhibitionism, but a stunning demonstration of the possibilities of his system; such a jump was taken during his experimental period when he was testing the practical and technical improvements he advocated. He arrived at the point where the horse was providing the impulsion for his own weight, putting his own center of gravity forward, while the rider was advancing to stay with him, that is, following through on his movement in the best possible manner by moving his hands forward to give the horse maximum freedom on the bit, and permitting the animal to lower his head, getting some weight off his back to enable the horse to attain maximum elevation in his jump. Through proper use of the stirrups, using his knees as a fulcrum, the rider moves his weight toward the forehand, freeing the horse's loins completely in what is referred to as "giving way."*

143

144

145

146

147

148

149

150

and hunting. The school's installations are situated at a magnificent site near Madrid, in Carabanchel Alto.

Memorable figures at the school have been Captain Adolfo Botin—*"maestro de maestros en el arte ecuestre"*—and Sublieutenant Manuel Rivera, a fine, classic *haute école* horseman. The most celebrated of the horses at the school during recent years have been Quorum, who was world champion jumper in 1953; and Amado Mío, who set the record for the jump (1.83 meters, or approximately 6 feet), when ridden by the commandant, López del Hierro.

143 *Three at a time: Ricca, Caffaratti, and Moro. The first officer's hold on the reins is rather odd, but note the elegance of the third, where impulsion and following are perfect.*

144 *Sublieutenant Francesco Baracca on Lord at Tor di Quinto. Here was a horseman of great physical and moral attributes, brilliant and aggressive. His temperament can be judged by the dash with which he follows and his smooth employment of the Caprilli system. He was one of the first to transfer from the cavalry to the air force.*

145 *Count Alessandro Bettoni on Judex. He was famous for his drive in showings throughout the world and for having commanded the charge of the Savoy Cavalry near the Don at Izbuschensky in 1942. Possessed of a style very much his own, he was one of the first horsemen to attempt to have the horse completely "in hand," that is, to understand him and control him, and therefore not too generous in following.*

146 *Major Guido Borsarelli, the unforgettable rider of Don Chisciotte and the little Crisp. Here he is with Don Chisciotte in London in 1923. A horseman with a great competitive spirit, he was, as no other rider, able to bring out the same spirit in his mount, but over the jump, he still left the horse completely at liberty.*

147 148 *Captain Gutierrez on Osoppo when he set the high-jumping record. Fig.148 shows him at the fence in preparation for the 2.20 meters: a perfect seat, the horse calm, and with just the proper amount of extension after his takeoff. In Fig.147, which shows the record jump, the tremendous impulsion required to carry a weight of almost a half-ton over a 2.44-meter obstacle has indubitably impaired the rider's balance, but Gutierrez tries to overcome it without affecting Osoppo. This record was beaten by the Chilean Captain Laraguibel on Huaso at Santiago, in 1949, with a jump of 2.47 meters.*

149 *The Dowager Duchess of Aosta in the saddle on her favorite gray on a hunting run during the period when the Caprilli system was first being disseminated. While still not completely "lightened" in the saddle, the duchess does follow rather handsomely, at the expense of the reins, which are permitted to slip through the fingers. (Memorable among Italian horsewomen are Countess Jolanda Calvi di Bergolo, a brilliant and technically sound rider who was extremely elegant in her stylistically perfect use of the system; and the wife of General Pino Cacciandra, Signora Alma Cacciandra, gifted with wonderful hands, who with rare competitive spirit overcame the limitations of the sidesaddle.)*

150 *General Tommaso Lequio, of whom General Ubertalli wrote: "Flexibility and balance were the rare gifts that Lequio possessed to a high degree, and he used them in an extensive and*

XXXV
WOMEN IN THE SADDLE

In ancient times the name Amazon was given to mounted female warriors. Derived strictly from the Greek *amazos,* meaning, literally, without one of the breasts, the name arose from the belief that these women fighters on horseback bound or caused one of their breasts to atrophy in order to make it easier for them to handle their weapon, the bow and arrow. Actually, the women whom the Greeks thought were Amazons were probably not women at all, but Nordic warriors wearing long tunics that appeared as feminine garb to the Hellenic eye.

Rome gave us few women on horseback to remember. There was Camilla, who fled from Porsena's camp on horseback and crossed the Tiber. Cesonia, Caligula's wife, in full warrior's kit, rode at the head of troops.

Oriental woman on horseback is shown in splendid statuettes of rare beauty, and Persian women appear in ceramics and miniatures.

In Europe, during the medieval period, women rode in the same style as men or else were seated on a packsaddle with a cushioned seat that could be drawn up by two chains. The horse was usually led by a groom. With the growing fashion for heavier and heavier garments of stiff brocades and velvet, and with skirts growing longer and more enveloping and, possibly, with a new morality, women sought to find another way in which to sit on a horse. As a result, a saddle was introduced with two supports that forked over the pommel and turned outward so that a lady could place her right leg between the supports, pressing the knee around the upper "tooth," while her left leg hung naturally with her left foot in the stirrup.

Catherine de' Medici introduced this *selle à rampe* into France around 1533, and it was later improved through the addition of a third "tooth," against which the upper side of the left knee could be supported to give more security in case the rider were thrown forward by the force of momentum.

The position of a rider using such a saddle can be seen in Dürer's picture (page 125) "The Lady and the Halberdier," in which the lady sits to the near side and lets her right hand fall on the shoulder of the thin but stalwart soldier in a somewhat dallying way.

The riding skirt, which was supposed to cover the feet, was lengthened until it flowed to the ground and became something of a threat to safety. Around 1900, during an upsurge of feminism and a return by women to active sport—with an accompanying change in fashion to lighter skirts—women also returned to trousers, and took to riding in breeches

original way. These are the gifts that bring one what is called 'the sense of the natural', a feeling for the horse's natural equilibrium. He was the horseman for any and all sorts of horses, particularly the difficult horse. He was the horseman for any obstacle, no matter how fast the approach, no matter how high.... He was not the horseman to break an animal to his will through continuous, persistent exercise, but with perfect intuition and subtle intelligence, created a partnership with the horse...."

that permitted them better control of their mounts, although it did take from the woman in the saddle some of her poetry and grace. In 1902, an American organization of women, led by a Mrs. Landenburg, moved for the abolition of the sidesaddle; and women throughout the United States took to riding astride, like men.

From the sixteenth century, equitation has been taken up by great ladies accustomed to hunting with their men. Celebrated horsewomen were Diane de Poitiers, Anne Marie of Austria, the mother of Louis II of Hungary, Marie de Bourgogne, and Valentina Visconti. There are also records of flat races and jumping events exclusive to women. In a letter written in 1723 to the Harley family of Oxford, a Mrs. Bateman had this to say:

Last week, Mrs. Aslibie arranged a flat race for women, and nine of that sex, mounted astride and dressed in short pants, jackets, and jockey caps participated. They were striking to see, and there was a great crowd to watch them. The race was a very lively one; but I hold it an indecent entertainment.

Even in France, around the middle of the nineteenth century, obstacle races for women were instituted. There are some interesting prints of these, in particular one showing a steeplechase at Longchamps reserved for women.

In Italy, ladies of the aristocracy rode to hunt and even in cross-country meets over the brush. From 1931, they have been permitted to enter special races for women riders.

In England, a number of women are licensed as trainers, while Russia has a great many employed as stable hands and handlers. Alexandra Burdova is famous in Moscow for her wins with the American trotter Apex Hanover, but she has not been able to get permission to drive her champion in France or in the United States in competition.

XXXVI
THE FRENCH AND THE "FILER"*

Before discussing the revolution in equitation brought about by Caprilli, it would seem opportune to observe the changes made by French horsemen in the sport of jumping. To begin, let us consider what d'Aure had to say upon the subject of the martingale:

The running martingale serves to fix the horse's head and maintain it in the normal position. The device is particularly used for hunting, when the snaffle is not employed, in order to leave the horse's neck completely free while jumping. After a jump, if the horse assumes a bad attitude, the use of the snaffle along with this martingale will bring the head back to the correct normal position. It is a very useful piece of tack, but one that must be employed with the greatest discretion.

Something of the same thing that occurred in the evolution of language happened with equitation: the academic was

* To comb the reins.—TRANS.

supplanted by the popular; *équitation savante*—that high-flown hyperbole of the saddle (if such can be imagined)—was brought down to earth occasionally by the infusion of a fresher and more ordinary style of riding. Naturally, school equitation remained the prerogative of a few masters, nobles, officers, and troopers, but those who had to use a horse just to get from place to place rode in a very different manner indeed. Even though the army continually sought lightness

151 152 *Major Ayroldi di Robbiate and Major Formigli on Suello. In each case horse and rider are in perfect form as they take a fence and a ditch, calling for entirely different techniques. From this period, we recall Colonel Ferdinando Filipponi on Nasello, a very durable pair (Filipponi spent long hours exercising him on the longeing rein). There was also Gherardo Conforti, an excellent competitor and fine instructor, who could include Saba as one of his triumphs. Lieutenant-Colonel Francesco Forquet was a cool horseman, a rider in the classic style but one with great sensitivity who carried that most difficult animal, Trebecco, to international honors. Lieutenant Giorgio Bianchetti, a direct heir of Caprilli's, can be seen in masterly jumps in his photographs, demonstrating how yielding becomes a suave movement and firmness in the saddle is achieved from firm yet flexible knee action that permits the body the maximum flexibility so that the rider can keep with his horse in the animal's rapid changes of balance. There was also Captain Morigi, the great rider of La Mi Carezza, a gray mare who won the fancy of the crowd at all the shows. Also, there were General Lombardo di Cumia, a horseman of notable manners, even though he was thoroughly competitive, and General Raffaele Codorna, a keen competitor and sportsman, who viewed equitation as an extremely fine means of education. Another general, Badino Rossi, a brilliant rider and defender of Caprilli's system, demonstrated that one could jump without a bridle, thus proving complete dominance over the horse whether through personal authority or through the perfect containment of the animal through a firm and precise position of the legs. Another celebrity was Francesco Amalfi, who got a lot out of his riding but was not, perhaps, always convinced of the validity of the system. Fabio Capasso, a fine horseman who was at his best in the races, gave something of the system to the steeplechase. He was killed in a racing accident in 1928. General Pino Cacciandro, a superb horseman, was less exuberant than his brother, Giulio, but equally gifted with a solid seat and remarkable style. Colonel Renzo Bonivento, one of the public's favorite riders, sometimes accentuated the characteristics of Caprilli's system, but always with tact and elegance. He participated in the Olympics at Berlin in 1936, and in the postwar period was consultant and sports director of the FISE. Finally, there was Count Ranieri de Campello, an incomparable guide and consummate gentleman, who won flat races, steeplechases, cross-country events, and other competitions, thanks to his spirit and his fine, intuitive horsemanship.*

153 *International Horse Show, Turin, 1902.*

154 *Austrian officers.*

155 *Two representatives of the Turkish delegation.*

156 *German officers.*

157 *Victorious Russian officer.*

158 *Caprilli wins the City of Turin Grand Prize.*

153

154

155

156

157

158

159

160

161

and agility in the saddle, it was always influenced by masters of classic systems who ended by smothering the greater resources of the cavalry—its mobility and element of surprise.

The fact that the recently formed Revolution cavalry, made up of elements which casually took to the saddle during marches, showed itself to be more maneuverable and expeditous than the regiments of veteran cavalrymen trained under the old systems opened many minds to the advantages of having a mounted force free of any stylistic conceits and mannerisms.

The fact that a simpler and freer style of riding had developed apace with school equitation was shown in point-to-point meetings, the hunt, and other such riding for sport, whenever stiff cavalry officers had to admit bitterly to themselves that the burghers had more stamina than they, that the burghers overtook and passed them with greater speed and lightness, and that they tripped and spilled much less often. With the Restoration and the return of the suppressed "schools," complete with wigs and trappings, more than one person was heard to murmur that he was riding a dead horse.

The masters knew that the school was an end in itself, but for reasons of punctilio and prestige they continued to give lip service to the idea that it was fundamental to all riding, even hacking, and that it was the basis of any proper military utilization of the horse.

Much was written and much argument ensued in support of such ridiculous statements as those of Captain M. Horace Hayes, perhaps the most highly respected expert on equestrian matters in England in the nineteenth century. He had ideas about the horse's mouth that leave us with strong feelings of dismay—ideas about the bars being calloused so that they are well able to sustain the horseman's weight without any negative reaction. Can such things ever have been?

We can, perhaps, reason that such a way of thinking arises out of the fact that a great many people in England do ride, and, rather than bothering about equestrian niceties, their chief concern is in having a useful, solid mount about whom they do not have to worry. Furthermore, even Baucher found it necessary to mention that among the French, "equitation is the art of controlling and directing the muscular force of a horse," one of many definitions he gives; but it is particularly vague in showing that where rules governing the anatomy and mechanics of the horse were observed, these rules varied, evidently, in accordance with the sort of equitation in which one indulged.

It is precisely, and only, after becoming aware of such concepts that one can appreciate the value of Caprilli's insight, and see how it represented a complete break and a thunderous close to the aristocratic and cavalier tradition.

It was not coincidence that Caprilli's ideas came to the fore exactly at that period when the Italian bourgeoisie was beginning to shine, when that class finally came into its own and became conscious of its worth, and started to become the dominant class—the class that directed the progress of the country.

Notwithstanding, to implant the "system," Caprilli's system, took nine long years of setbacks and dissension, despite patent evidence of a real clear-cut advance to be gained by equitation—for sport or otherwise—through the adoption of a method based on principles of balance, forward movement, and support. This does not mean to imply that school riding, as well as *haute école*, have no place in equestrian art. Like the style of equitation of any given period, they all have their place, for they represent an effort to develop skill and artistry in accordance with certain determined rules, and upon the basis of definite principles.

Thus, we may conclude that equitation is not just a matter of getting up on a horse, but, necessarily, knowledgeable activity designed to achieve a desired and calculated effect through the conscious use of deliberate force and means, all within the framework of a precise and intelligent concept.

General Ubertalli, for example, arrived at the conclusion that equitation should be understood as "...the exercise of riding at the point where it goes beyond the limit of the elementary, and becomes subject to some rules, and, above all, gives the horse a bit more than just a healthful workout."

Even today, in England, one can see gentlemen (of the old school) taking the jumps while hunting, their chests well back. If the English jumped walls and fences with the sole preoccupation of getting the animal's forehand over and on the other side, it was to avoid the so-called *panaches* (the most dangerous sort of fall, in which the horse's fore gets stuck on the obstacle, and his hindquarters fall across the back of his unhorsed rider). Count d'Aure taught in the middle of the nineteenth century that the horse was to be used in the field as nature had made him, thus placing himself squarely in opposition to the most rigid adherents of the "school."

From these principles and others, the French in 1892 introduced a system designed to free the horse's mouth (contingent upon permitting the fingers of the left hand to comb [*filer*] the reins)—just as much as the horse indicated he needed by thrusting his head forward to clear the jump. The reason for supporting the horse in this manner is set forth in Count de Gontaut-Biron's *Travail à la Longe et Dressage à l'Obstacle*, published by Berger-Levrault of Paris in 1893. The count writes as follows:

1. The horse draws his head and shoulders back to shift the weight to the rear and unburden the forehand so that he can lift himself easily. The movement is preceded by an extension barely perceptible, but which nonetheless occurs. In the play of head, neck, and shoulders, the horse is doing just what a man would do to throw a stone: first extend the arm and hand holding the stone, then draw the arm back as far as possible, bringing it forward once more to let the stone fly.

2. Free the loins, the croup, and the haunches of the rider's weight at the precise moment of confronting the obstacle, so that the horse, free of his burden, can exert

159   *Captain Piero d'Inzeo wins the Royal International Horse Show in London in 1958 with His Excellency: a perfect team, the rider assured, the horse calm.*

160   *The mighty fallen: Captain d'Inzeo in 1953 on Uruguay at the Prix des Nations in Geneva.*

161   *Piero d'Inzeo takes a high, spread fence on The Rock, the Irish horse that later passed to Graziano Mancinelli.*

himself in complete freedom to lift himself as high as possible with minimal effort.

3. See that the rider, through his body, has such contact with his mount and, through his hands, with the horse's mouth that there is never any uncoordinated action between them, but that they move forward as a single unit—in a complete and delicate union between horse and rider—in perfect equilibrium.

4. Get forward movement going over the fence, whether through the gait taken or by urging on the horse.

Though it was the French who perceived the way to yield by "combing the reins" and giving the horse's mouth some freedom, there can be no doubt about where they got the idea.

At the great horse show held in Turin in 1902, the eight *écuyers* from Saumur performed this maneuver to perfection, but Caprilli saw what was lacking in the action of those decidedly elegant horsemen. They did not accompany their horses' surge forward at the peak of the jump, but remained planted on the haunches. The difficulty lay in the fact that they used long stirrup leathers, as if for dressage work. When raising themselves from the saddle, the higher the fence, the more they had to turn their toes toward the ground in order not to lose their stirrups. Once over the jump, the right hand, engaged in bringing the reins toward the body to get the stirrups back to normal length, could not coordinate with the left hand to control the horse as he took up his pace. The horse had the whole weight of the rider on his propulsive parts: loin, haunches, and hocks, through every stage of the jump.

When the stirrup leathers are too long and one attempts to secure the tread of the stirrup with the arch of the foot, besides using the knee, the tendency is to press against the barrel with the calves in order to stay in the saddle. The action is disturbing to the horse, who will speed up and buck at the next jump because of the involuntary touch of the spur. This, in sum, was the French school's style of jumping: freedom to the mouth at the cost of the reins—allowed to slip through the fingers, with the rider recovering them after the jump—and the body of the horseman leaning back.

It was only after 1923 that French horsemen became convinced of the necessity of freeing the horse's loins. That was the period of the followers of Xavier Bizard, Laissardière, Gudin de Vallerin, and the rest—in those early days considered to be dissidents (as far as the French school was concerned). Actually, they were adherents of the principles first expounded by Colonel Danloux, the father of the new system of French equitation after 1910, during which period he paid a visit to Tor di Quinto.* One must say, however, that Caprilli's system, the essence of it, was never really understood by the French, who just took up the superficial "yield."

"The error into which school horsemen fell," emphasizes General Ubertalli, "and into which they still fall when they consider natural equitation, is extremely easy to explain. If in school riding the so-called coordination of the aids was an end in itself, thought these horsemen, then natural equitation

had no preoccupation other than substituting for those aids others that were simpler, easier, and less liable to change the horse's natural attitude; but they stopped there. While previously one had been taught that, to stop a horse, you held him back with the hands while urging him on with the legs, subsequently one was advised that one need only use the hands, forgetting the legs—which corresponds to the formula of Baucher and Champsavin, not to mention many others."

All this signifies that no new doctrine was created. There were merely some simple logical modifications in some principles of school equitation, but those principles were still a part of school equitation nonetheless.

XXXVII
NINETEENTH-CENTURY ITALIAN EQUITATION

If horse and rider do not know how to jump, they'll never do much of anything. If at least one of them knows how to go, the trained horse will teach the novice rider.
—CAPRILLI

In Italy, during the seventeenth and eighteenth centuries, there were no courts sufficiently affluent to be able to give time and money and attention to cavalry schools, as had been the case in France, where there were Fontainebleau, Versailles, and Saumur; in Austria, with the school in Vienna; and in Germany, with schools in Munich and Hanover.

Despite the fact that these schools were the custodians of an unnatural and captious course of study, they did have the virtue of keeping alive a passion for the horse, considered as something other than a means of transport or a military necessity, which he was at that time. The schools preserved a taste for that exquisite diversion that was a symbol of a circumscribed but definite social group.

In Italy, as in Spain, the Counterreformation and the economic and intellectual decline it brought had put the horse as an element of entertainment in a bad light, and all sixteenth-century tradition had been lost. The Napoleonic Wars then revived a certain feeling for things equestrian to a point where Carlo Felice, in 1824, at the height of the Restoration, decided to found a cavalry school and locate it at Pinerolo. The Independence campaigns gave the school an opportunity to serve as a recruiting center for troopers and a remount post for horses that were distributed to the various cavalry regiments. These, incidentally, bore themselves bravely, but the school did not really become an educational institution, in the real and proper sense, since it created no cadre of instructors.

What was lacking was unity in orientation, for although there were some rules and some styles, there was no nucleus of masters capable of teaching and passing on a definite style peculiar to the school. Accordingly, at the beginning of 1867, a committee headed by Colonel Count Lanzavecchia di Buri, commandant of the school, was sent to Vienna to try to find an officer who could instruct and direct Italy's school of

---

* One of the two cavalry schools in Italy, the other being Pinerolo.—TRANS.

162–167 *Raimondo d'Inzeo with Posillipo at the Hamburg Derby: agility, elegance, and precision.*

162

163

164

165

166

167

168

169

170

equitation. The choice fell on the talented Austrian Lieutenant Cesare Paderni, born in Cividale del Friuli in 1833. Upon his graduation from the Wiener Neustadt academy, passionately addicted to equitation, he became a pupil of Colonel Edelstein, a celebrated instructor of *haute école*, who also knew open-air equitation, according to the systems of that time.

Paderni, who had tact and a special feeling for horses, along with desperate courage in the field, was promoted to captain, then major, and assumed direction of equitation in general at the school, personally giving instruction in *haute école* and campaign riding to cavalry officers in the advanced course. He was truly a master teacher when following the classic line, but in the field he followed the systems of the manège without perceiving the practical uses of equitation in the open air nor its possibilities for military and sporting purposes.

Paderni has left us three short works and a short set of instructions, dated 1890, covering the training of young horses. The set begins: "The new method of training young horses could be called 'elevation from the base,' and is divided into the first, second, and third degrees of elevation, successive stages that denote in the horse and in the attitude of his neck and head a marked change." This is a species of progressive torture to bring "... the horse's neck to an S, from front to back, in a graceful and elegant attitude...." Paderni wanted the horse, at the end of his training, to have the metal part of the snaffle at the height of the withers.

As for jumping, Paderni wrote, "If the fence is high, the gallop should be neither too short nor too extended and free, for the rider would need great skill and strength to raise a horse suddenly and at just the right moment with his forehand out of control as he speeds toward a fixed obstacle of considerable height."

We should mention that the "considerable height" was about three feet or a little more! It seems incredible that Paderni, a sensitive horseman, well rounded and with a profound knowledge of horses, did not understand the animals' mechanical needs when confronted with an obstacle and while jumping.

Not even when Savoiroux—a great horseman on the track—and Baralis succeeded Paderni, introducing a more advanced style of equitation, did things change. When a horse refused, it was customary to bring him back to the fence, and, leaning back, urge the horse forward through pressure on the loins. Furthermore, the rider's chest was still well back in the last phase of the jump in order not to put any weight on the forehand (sic). If the horse hesitated, the rider leaned back and used a sidewise action of his fists to call him to attention and avoid any swerving.

168 *A prodigious pair: Mancinelli on Rockette.*
169 *Mancinelli on Turvey in a somewhat acrobatic jump, but one that gives impulsion and permits maximum freedom to his difficult, powerful mount.*
170 *Mancinelli, again on Turvey, coming over the double bar. His exceptional jumper suffered an aneurysm right after jumping a difficult wall at Aachen.*

Instruction in jumping started with fences about thirty inches high, with the instructor at the ready with a whip. The fence was usually set up on one side of the manège. In 1889, Prince Amedeo, Duke of Aosta, in his capacity as cavalry inspector, ordered that the bars be set twelve feet from the rail. Notwithstanding, through the help of a kindly Providence, the students of the school at Pinerolo managed to overcome all the obstacles strung in the path of aspiring cavalrymen.

Paderni was relieved of his post in 1892, not because his instruction had become ineffective or obsolete, but because of the hostility of certain superior officers who were annoyed at the fact that the guard had to snap to when a "bourgeois" passed by, and for other such petty reasons. Thus was born the "Paderni Case," which ended by giving the General Staff at Rome quite a headache.

When we consider the development of equitation in Western Europe (excluding Italy) and certain recommendations of the more enlightened French masters—such as Baucher, who wrote, in 1870, "As the horse goes along the parabola of his jump, leave him free to do as he pleases with his head, his neck, and the way he lifts himself, as nature intended"—one might really be led to conclude that Caprilli and his system appeared in Italy as an inevitable reaction to the obtuseness of Italian military schools, the inexpertness of Italy's horsemen, and the backwardness of Italian equitation throughout the whole of the nineteenth century, paralleling the artistic and political spheres where certain revolutions and ruptures showed that the country's artistic expression had too long remained somnolent and academic and that its politics had become reactionary.

XXXVIII
CAPRILLI

Federico Caprilli (1868–1907) was born in Leghorn into a wealthy family. His mother came from Pisa; his father was a rich Livornese shipbuilder who died when his son was still a boy. Caprilli was given real paternal affection by his stepfather, the engineer Carlo Santini.

Perhaps it was the stories told him by Santini, who had been an officer of Garibaldi's and a volunteer at Mentana (where Garibaldi was defeated), that fanned the sparking passion he felt for the military life. In any case, he was admitted to a military academy in Florence in 1881, and in 1886 he enrolled in the military school at Modena as a cavalry officer-candidate. The school's medical review board, however, did not think he was fit for equitation since his trunk was too long and, conversely, his legs too short. Fate ruled otherwise, and when a vacancy in the ranks occurred, Federico was admitted to the cavalry.

He soon surpassed his classmates in enthusiasm, tact, and diligence. In 1888, after being promoted to sublieutenant in the Royal Piedmont Regiment, on garrison duty in Turin, he attracted a bit too much attention for his successes in sport and the social world, so that the was posted to Nola to the Milan Lancers Regiment. His name, however, was already known throughout Italy. General Luigi Berta, a future inspector, followed his work (still lacking a great deal of theory) on the horse's body and weight displacement during a jump, to the point of introducing his own new method. Several young men who attempted to imitate him failed miserably in trials before the public.

Caprilli kept on working, and, with Berta's support, arrived at the point of clearly delineating his own theory, comprising three stages: (1) when going over the fence, sit well in the saddle and keep the hands firm at the sides of the withers, with the reins taut; (2) when going over the jump, lift yourself about eight inches above the saddle, maintaining the hands and reins as above; (3) when going over the jump, rise a bit over the saddle, keeping the crotch over the pommel, with the hands following forward toward the horse's mouth so as to permit the horse to extend his neck and shoulders as he needs, while constantly preserving the lightest of tensions on the reins running from the rider's hand to the corners of the mouth.

During the first and second phases of his work, which covered a period of five years, Caprilli suffered so many falls that in 1900 he was obliged to ask for six months' leave. His back ached, his whole body pained, but his passion carried him forward.

In 1904, General Berta gave him thirty recruits for the Fourth Squadron of the cavalry school at Pinerole to work with, and after only four months a review board could see the difference between the men trained according to Caprilli's method and all the rest. The old guard, however, was still not convinced; nevertheless, the system spread of itself, and riding masters from all over the world came to hear the new gospel preached at Pinerole. The last to come were the French, Belgians, Germans, and Austrians.

Caprilli's system contributed toward "relieving the horse of the suffering brought by a bad rider, making the horse more responsive, while saving the rider from falls, those falls that are at times so harmful to the body and always to the spirit."

Caprilli was famous for his exploits before representatives of the world's cavalry. He astounded the audience at the Turin horse show in 1902 and at an exhibition he gave at Saumur. At thirty-nine, two years after his system was put into use by the entire cavalry, Federico Caprilli died at Turin on December 7, 1907. Overcome by a sudden vertigo he fell from his walking horse.

Caprilli's secret basically was simple, but it took some time to discover it. His secret was to observe and study from the ground the way a horse moved at every gait and, above all, when jumping, and to consider the way in which he could be supported and spared any suffering or undue effort, while remaining under control. Caprilli envisioned a rider who would follow with his horse, accompanying him in his movement and seconding him completely with his arms and chest, while keeping his knees firm and his legs, as they fell naturally, riding solidly on the fork.

He realized that it would be necessary to bring the crotch down, which led to the "heels-down" style, with the sole of the foot turned out—merely a means of imparting firmness to the lower part of the body and, consequently, permitting the maximum flexibility above the small of the back. Firmness, support, and yielding made an ensemble of horse and horseman, and were the tenets of the system of "natural equitation," that is, of the Italian school. Natural equitation teaches the way to make a horse adaptable, in the shortest time, to the varying exigencies of war and sport. By "natural equitation" one understands equitation that permits the horse to find his natural balance once he is carrying the added weight of rider and tack, with his neck and head remaining in a natural attitude.

The difference between natural equitation and what is known as school equitation lies in the fact that while the latter strives to adapt the horse to the horseman, the former is designed to fit the rider to his mount. Fitting the rider to his mount is a much easier task, and once you have got the idea of natural equitation, you will be convinced that it is simpler and will see how useful it is—getting results that formerly could not be achieved in thrice the time. In natural equitation, the horseman wants his mount to extend his neck and shoulders and carry his head in the oblique position of the ordinary trot, the horse's most "natural" position.

Caprilli has left us few notes, yet they are sufficient for us to be able to reconstruct the bases of his method and, brief as they are, they have the value of an equestrian and possibly spiritual testament, for he went far beyond questions of balance of horse and man, or the equilibrium of a horse with the added weight of a more or less stable man on his back. He touched upon fundamental ideas regarding rapport, cohesion, and a deeper "dialogue"—both instinctual and logical at one and the same time—that the rider must bring to the act of riding.

Caprilli revolutionized equitation even more profoundly than we might think. In Italy he shook the foundations of that unnatural, baroque military aristocracy instituted around 1500, which waxed until the French Revolution made it tremble, but not topple. Caprilli threw wide the windows that had been closed for centuries in the riding academies, and let in the fresh air. He gave the horse his rightful stance as an animal of flesh and blood and not a symbol of a caste or a heraldic device or a pretext for pedantry. He brought equitation back to the simple, logical, and affectionate lines that Xenophon had given it.

Caprilli saw the horse as more than a means of practical locomotion—as a companion in sport and the field, and as a friend who, though mute, is eloquent in his own fashion and who leads you to reason and to inquire into his ways.

XXXIX
CAPRILLI'S WRITINGS

Let us give some extracts here from rules dictated by Caprilli during January–February, 1901, in Parma:

I believe that one must lean toward having the horse as he is in nature: with natural balance, with a natural position of the head, for if there is any necessity of changing

171 *Pierre Jonquères d'Oriola on Pomone B.*
172 *D'Oriola winning at Tokyo on Lutteur.*
173 *D'Oriola in a characteristic attitude on the flat on the celebrated Pomone B.*

171

172

173

174

175

176

the equilibrium, you will see how the horse, by himself, will make the modification while he is working, if he is left free to do so.

The two types of equitation, for show and for the field, are, in my view, contrary to one another, and mutually exclusive and destructive.

Let us now examine the prerequisites for a rider and horse in the field. To me, a cavalry horse is one that is good-tempered, calm, confident of his rider, fast and resistant, accustomed to galloping for long periods over any sort of terrain, cool and alert in emergencies, and instantly responsive to the demands of his rider. This is the horse for field work and he is the war-horse.

Long years of practice and continuous observation have convinced me that, generally, a horse effortlessly acquires the qualities that I have just enumerated if his rider gives him a logical and continual course of training, during which the rider makes an effort to attenuate his own actions as much as possible so as not to disturb the development of the horse's natural attitudes and forces.

By this, I do not mean to indicate that one should let a horse do just as he wishes. On the contrary, he should be persuaded with firmness—energetically, if necessary—to do what the rider wishes, but he should be given complete freedom to muster his strength and means as best suits his balance and force.

On this fixed and fundamental principle, I base all the practical rules of equitation discussed below.

Once the horse has been freed, in this way, of all other preoccupations, he will turn his attention to all that he must do, and little by little learn the best way to employ his own means and perfect his action. Contrariwise, when the horse is held subject by his rider and restricted in his movement, he is forever looking for a way to free himself of these constraints, and, in consequence, spends all his time thinking of this, giving no attention or interest to the work that he should be doing.

When we study the jump, we have patent evidence of this. The horse that strains himself taking a jump, or, better, has a rider who does not yield going over, gets a sore mouth and a pain in his loins. To see that it doesn't happen to him again, he will either refuse a jump or learn to take a fence without extending his neck, jumping foursquare. Furthermore, he will approach a fence completely disoriented and most unwillingly, and turn all his attention to judging the moment that he can plant himself before the hurdle, running off; or another time, he may fling himself desperately against the bars, losing all control.

When the rider overly aids the horse before the jump, the horse, fearful of this action, rushes the hurdle. We have another example in the horse that has become accustomed to being held back at the takeoff, so that he

hurls himself forward furiously, in an attempt to overcome the hand that inflicts pain upon him. Usually a horse that breaks and bolts does so in reaction to the reins.

Actually, the bolting will cease when tension on the reins is eased, and a horse on the bit, usually mounted with a snaffle, given a light hand and no trouble from the legs, will not bolt.

If you consider the horse in his rightful equilibrium, his rightful impulsion, you will discard the flexed neck, collection, lateral gaits, and so on and you will not prescribe the bit as a normal mouthpiece for every horse and every occasion, but using it exclusively when necessary and with two reins; and even then the horse will go well if he is held lightly and not annoyed in the mouth.

It remains for me to say a word now about the belief, held by many, that work in the field is hard on a horse. This is absolutely untrue. First of all, there is nothing that says in the teaching of horses and riders in the field that one must do extraordinary things or fatiguing work. All that is needed is easy, daily, continuous exercise, short rides, and short gallops; and such work, well regulated and proportioned to the abilities of our horses, will not only be harmless but beneficial to the keeping of a good cavalry horse.

*Rules for the Method
of Preliminary Instruction of Horses
and Riders in the Field*

We have seen that in order to habituate horses to work in the field without ruining them or making them bad-tempered, you must always take advantage of the animals' natural instincts, second his movements and paces, and give him as little annoyance as possible in his mouth, loins, and back. You should also get rid of all curved necks, forced positions in unstable equilibrium, and all action from the legs excepting that which is necessary to urge the horse on. Let us get into the saddle and stirrups right away to make everything from the very beginning—especially at the beginning—as easy as possible.

To teach how to mount and dismount, the thing is to have the student imitate someone who knows how to perform these actions. Once in the saddle, see that the recruit has his knees firmly against the shoulders and that the stirrup leathers are the proper length to permit the rider always to rest the arch of his foot comfortably against the tread of the stirrup iron. (On the road, when going at a walk or trot, to relax the feet, it is permissible to have just the toe against the tread of the stirrup.) If the leathers are too short, the seat, too often, will be a shaky one, while if they are too long, not only will the seat be insecure but the horseman will also have the annoyance of having to reach out for his stirrups, and this preoccupation will put him out of balance, and neither his legs, knees, nor, consequently, the rest of his body, will be firm.

Remember that proper adjustment of the stirrups

174 *Stylized following by Captain Fresson on Grand Veneur.*
175 *Lieutenant Durand at the horse show in Rome in 1963.*
176 *Captain Lefrant at Rome in the 1964 competition.*

is prerequisite to the instructor's achieving for his students firmness in the saddle and a solid seat. If the instructor remembers, especially at the outset, to make few corrections in position, the recruit will not fall into the habit of stiffening his body; and in working toward the proper position for the student, the instructor should bear in mind the student's stature and physique.

The reins should always be held, either one or two, or all four, in one hand. Riding with four reins, as described in the Regulations, is one of the main reasons, I believe, that some soldiers never learn to control a horse well, and therein lies the reason that the squadrons have dropped restive and indecisive mounts.

Actually, if we assume that the horse is naturally led to turn by the inner rein and that he turns when the outer rein is eased to a proportionate degree, what happens when we have four reins, divided? The soldier moves his hands to the left to turn to the left and to the right to turn to the right, and in this way, comes to pull on the rein opposite to the direction in which he wants the horse to turn.

Now then, wouldn't it be better and simpler to have him hold all the reins in one hand, or even two reins in each hand, but teach him to use the other hand to pull the right or left rein so that later he can do so even when he is carrying a weapon?

To sum up, the horseman should learn to turn mechanically to the right by pulling on the right reins while yielding on the left hand, and vice versa. Should any horse be indecisive in responding to that command, the rider will have to turn him by pressing with his inside leg, and, if necessary, giving the animal the spur.

That is the way the rider should turn every time, even when he is carrying side arms, for then if he does not manage to turn on the action of the inside rein, he can bring his right hand (even if he is carrying a lance or saber) over the reins he is holding, to employ them at that moment, as explained above.

While the rider learns to keep his balance at the various gaits and gets the feel of the saddle, the instructor should teach him that the hands should be held naturally and as closely and quietly as possible at the side of the withers. He should also be taught that in every movement and in his every reaction, he should keep his hands low and ready to give way in the direction of the horse's mouth. They will allow the animal to position his neck comfortably without receiving a yank in the bars, but rather always enjoying the same support.

That is the most important thing, and, at the same time, the most difficult always to do well and properly, and the instructor should not weary of insisting on this point right from the beginning.

This primary instruction of the recruit should be carried on for about a fortnight in the manège until there is no danger, in the slightest, in taking him outside. During this period, as much as possible he should be left to his own devices, practicing using one hand, then both, in turning the horse, so that one day it will suddenly be clear to him just what the proper action of the hands should be on the horse's mouth.

After the student has been on the horse for a few days, he should be made to go back and forth over a very small, adjustable obstacle that can be gradually elevated to a height of about twenty inches to two feet. This exercise is the only one done regularly, without being replaced by any other even for a while, that will make the rider free and easy in the saddle and get him to the point where he instinctively finds his balance—even when the horse takes him by surprise—while simultaneously bringing home to him that the horse's mouth should never serve as a support to keep him in the saddle. The instructor should not bother at all with the school trot; at the most, he should see that it is done a few times, raising the stirrups, so that the student does a bit of gymnastics, which is just the right thing for obviating any of that harmful rigidity that comes from using the school trot and riding without stirrups.

Accordingly, the recruits will be kept in the manège about two weeks, learning to ride with saddle and stirrups at the different paces, and will be taught how to make the horse turn, go forward, pull up and halt. They will be left on their own except during the first two or three days, when it is better to have them under the eye of an expert horseman.

It should be borne in mind that group practice is to be avoided as much as possible, as well as any exercise that tires the horse to no useful purpose. The rider will not be in command after such work, for the horse will end by obeying the orders given by the instructor rather than those of the man riding him.

The reins should be long enough to allow the horse to keep his head, neck, and shoulders in the position most agreeable to him, and to maintain at all times the lightest bit of pressure on the snaffle mouthpiece.

The instructor should see to it, from the initial phase of training, that the rider uses light aids to make the horse go forward and that he gradually increases them to the point where the horse takes up the proper gait, but, at the same time, moving calmly and at an easy tempo.

Remember that heavy and sudden aids throw the horse off and make him take off precipitately, which is always bad, and particularly so in the ranks or in a squadron, for such starting is always followed by a drawing back and halt that wreaks havoc on mouth and loins.

Just this and nothing more should be taught in the manège, and work should be continued in the open air along these lines to develop facility. When you have got to the point where a rider has absorbed these few simple principles and applies them properly, you can rest assured that you have a good horseman and an excellent horse, good-tempered, willing, and responsive.

The application of the rules—so simple under normal conditions—I have set forth at moderate gaits over easy country, are to be remembered when the pace is fast and the going rough. Then, very often, the rider loses his seat and tends to hang on with hands and legs. Besides losing his head, instead of remaining still and passive, he has an urge to do something—anything—because he is afraid that the horse will not know what to do or will not do enough.

Some defects are lost only through gradual, continual, and well-directed exercise in the field. Any pat rule or theoretical reasoning in this connection that differs in the slightest from the brief remarks I made at the outset, if not harmful, is utterly useless.

The cavalry perfects the rider's seat by working in the open, for it is in the field that he can best learn to adjust his balance, providing him with the necessary firmness in the saddle in every position taken by the horse and through his every movement. He does not build himself up, as is the general belief, by long exercise without stirrups. As a matter of fact, that is precisely what makes a rider stiff and leads him to use force when it is not called for, while the secret of being firm in the saddle lies in being flexible and knowing how to use force only when it is required. Furthermore, a rider's balance without stirrups is entirely different from his balance with them. A rider should learn well how to employ the stirrups to save the horse jabs in the back, and to lighten himself.

Accordingly, if exercise without stirrups is used in certain cases and done in moderation, it can have a certain usefulness; but too often, it is not only futile but harmful as well.

Riders are made through practice and natural progression, and the instructor should seek to lessen his difficulties, not add to them. During exercise, it is necessary that the instructor take great pains to correct any stiffness, no matter what form it takes or in what part of the rider's body it manifests itself. Otherwise, rigidity will finish by being transmitted to the hands, consequently giving the horse a great deal of pain in his mouth, which, in turn, is transmitted to the loins.

Rules for Cross-Country
Riding and Overcoming Difficulties
in the Terrain

After a fortnight of well-absorbed work in the manège, the instructor will be able to put the recruits on horseback, knowing that it will not be dangerous for them to work in the open. During that preparatory period, he will have taught them how to turn, pull up, stop, and go as indicated, according to the rules set forth. After that period, he can take them out, at first working over flat and level terrain. Here, he can leave them in a group, at ease, taking particular care to work individually and frequently with each one.

The moment has arrived when the trooper must be made to understand how he must comport himself so that his horse works well in the field. At this point, I find it my duty to repeat once again what I have already stated and reaffirmed: A horse works well and willingly when the horseman takes the trouble to make all his actions as little annoying as possible and, while insisting that his mount be subject to his wishes, permits him complete freedom to employ his own force and keep his balance.

The instructor should now have the recruits work at the trot and take short gallops, having them advance at the proper progression and, during these exercises, work to have each rider control his horse and make him go straight ahead at an even tempo; also, when turning, to use the method already prescribed.

Above all, the instructor should be attentive to any attempt to maintain the horse on the proper track by moving the hands out of position, and he should not allow them to be moved laterally. The thing he must not tire of repeating is, "Pull up on one rein and ease up on the other."

He should also continue to insist, as he has taught, that the hands be kept still and low and that the reins be sufficiently long to give the lightest support, while the hands remain ready at any time to yield and advance when the horse shows that he wants to extend his head and neck further.

The upper body should be kept still and as upright as possible, inclined very slightly when galloping, the legs firm and not clinging too much to the barrel, and the feet completely in the stirrups. Finally, the quick trot should always be used.

The purpose of this first phase of instruction in the open air is to make the rider learn to keep calm, keep the proper rhythm at each gait, and to let the horse work with his neck extended, giving him light support and knowing how to yield and to let the hands move forward when the horse indicates that he needs to extend even more. This will happen whenever the horse, changing his balance, has to move his center of gravity forward, and at times is an indication that his attention is absorbed (particularly if he moves his ears forward at the same time)—which is what happens in a most peculiar way when the horse looks at a spot of ground over which he must go.

That alertness should not be combated, but seconded, and the rider should be attentive to it, for that movement very often precedes any indecision on the part of the horse or even his refusal to pass a given point. In such cases it becomes necessary to help him along by using the legs without even to the slightest degree pulling back with the hands, to avoid his balking. The hands, though, should be prompt to take any action to keep the horse from bolting.

Notwithstanding, the horse should always be permitted to stretch his neck, since it is also his way of watching where he is going, and if he cannot see well, obviously he can't keep moving.

The position in which the horse's neck is extended parallel to the ground, besides being extremely practical, permitting the horse, as it does, to see better and give his attention to the ground to be covered, is also highly advantageous for another reason: In this position, the horse can arch his back and take some of the weight off his loins and withers. Since these are the parts of his body that tire most easily when working hard, the more they are eased and spared, the more efficient his performance. With his back arched, the horse can support a heavy weight with a minimum of fatigue. This should be obvious, for even men curve their shoulders to ease a heavy burden on their backs.

In sum, the greatest extension of the neck is required for every move the horse makes; for every action that he takes makes it necessary for him to move his center of gravity forward as he advances. When a horse is galloping on his own, he falls into that position of his own accord, and he will continue to take it, as the most comfortable position, if the reins are kept long, the support light, and if the rider sees to it that he moves his hands forward whenever the horse shows him that he needs more neck extension. At times, it is useful to lean forward a bit, making oneself lighter in the saddle, but without bringing up the hands, keeping the reins in the left, and conveniently supporting the right on the horse's shoulders and keeping it there.

The instructor should see to it that the riders aid their horses without brusqueness, using just the control that is necessary, in just proportion to their mounts' sensitivity. He should see to it that the riders never stiffen their hands during the interim between one action and the next, but that they keep them relaxed and, even more, avoid any muscular tension. They should be taught that, in general, and when dealing with nervous horses in particular, it is very useful for the body to be loose, especially in the legs, and if they must pull on the reins at one time or another, they should never lift their hands. Remember that a horse often will precipitate himself forward in reaction to an overly strong pull on the reins; by easing up on the hand, the rider can obtain the desired cadence.

When you have reached the point where the horses work quietly, watching the ground where they are about to put their feet and where the riders are not in conflict with their horses, the moment has arrived when you can take them out for a short stretch, with hope of success. But before this, do anything else you can to give the riders encouragement and to fill them with resolution; also, relieve them of any apprehension they may have, but see that you do not cause them any trouble while doing so, or you will just worry them more.

When taking them out for rides, as in everything else, observe a logical progression, and begin by insisting that the horse go quietly and with the least expense of energy possible, not only to keep him from undue effort but also to avoid creating any aversion to work. To assure this, take care that the rider sees to it that the horse pays attention and watches what he is doing and that the horseman does not interfere with his horse or annoy him as he performs.

Apart from obstacles that may have to be jumped, which I shall cover in another chapter, in the field one may encounter ditches, uneven terrain, slopes, rises, bad patches, and paths difficult to follow where the horse will have to watch carefully in placing his feet. When these are not too difficult, where permissible, it would be useful to have the riders learn to take them at the different gaits.

Before going out, in no instance whatsoever should the horse be alarmed by being held too much on the rein or aided where there is no necessity for it; otherwise, as the rider will be interfering with his ability to watch where he is going, he is liable to refuse or bolt. The horse should go ahead resolutely, always with the same contact on the reins, and he should not increase or diminish the cadence of his gait.

Steep descents should be taken at the walk, and always on a straight line. When approaching them, the horse will extend his neck and lower his head so that he can observe the terrain better and also be able to carry his hindquarters well under his center of gravity. If the horse is opposed at this point, he will almost invariably balk or bolt, enraged. It is essential, therefore, that the rider let him do as he pleases and second the horse's extension of his head and neck by moving his hands forward without moving them laterally. The body should be kept firm and erect; and, if necessary, the legs should take up the rhythm, with increasing force, up to the point where the horse begins making his descent, not forgetting, however, that while doing this, contact should be maintained, as always—and very light it should be.

Once the horse has started to go down, the rider should lean back to offset the angle of the grade and, if the horse is doing well, cease leg action, dropping the heels a good deal to avoid spurring the horse, while keeping the hands still and low, maintaining light contact with the mouth.

Should the horse for any reason precipitate himself down the slope, the rider must try to pull him up by gradually moving his hands back toward his own body while taking care to see that the impetuous animal does not take an oblique path. That is a most dangerous thing that one should strive to avoid at all costs, just as one must discourage the tendency some horses have of doing an about-face and going off in the opposite direction.

Remind the rider that he must be calm and cool-headed, and to think clearly, for only in this way will he be able to avoid contretemps. Do not forget that when a horse rushes down a hill or takes it on the diagonal, it is almost always a fault of the leg or hand action and sometimes a result of the annoyance he feels over the strain on his loins and withers when descending. Turning about generally comes from the same things, but turning may also happen when the horse has not truly observed the terrain before going over it.

When going uphill, one should also move in a straight line. Such slopes, however, should be taken at a moderate gait, especially if they are fairly extensive, so that the horse does not use up all his energy at the beginning and have nothing at the finish. At times, it is better to take a rise at a brisk gait, particularly if the distance up is short, for then the horse will combine his own muscular effort with the force of impetus and momentum.

On approaching an upward slope, the rider should lower his hands and move them up forward somewhat so that the horse can extend his head and neck, thus shifting his center of gravity to the fore. You will observe, however, that in taking the slope, the horse takes consecutive galloping jumps, and at each one he extends his neck anew and even more than the previous time, especially toward the end, when he has lost his initial impetus. Because of this, the rider should be sure that he always has enough rein in reserve to be able to give the horse, when he requires the added extension, a bit more.

When going up a slope, the horseman should lean forward and if necessary he may grasp the horse's mane with one hand. If the horse refuses to go onward, the rider should resort to vigorous leg action and use the crop over the barrel. If the horse gives any indication that he is about to turn around or go off at an angle, instead of pulling on the rein, the rider should whip him across the nose or threaten him with the crop.

It is a useful thing to train a horse to go into ditches and come out of them—so long as the ground in the ditch is fair and without sharp stones—and to have them do this at different gaits. When going down into and coming up out of such ditches, the rider should take them as he does downward grades and upward slopes, taking care, when descending, to curb any tendency the horse may have to jump to the opposite side. In this connection, you will note that when the horse lowers his head quite a bit and looks into the ditch, it is unlikely that he will jump, or if he does attempt it you need only signal him with a rein, laterally, or completely let up on your contact with his mouth.

To get out of a ditch, one should strive energetically to turn the horse so that he is perpendicular to the bank by pulling on one rein and yielding on the opposing one, up to the moment that the horse is about to lift the forehand. Lean forward suddenly and markedly and let the hands second the usual neck extension, which in this instance will be very pronounced because the horse has no impetus to carry him forward and because the sides of a ditch are usually quite steep. At that moment, it would be a good thing to aid him with the legs.

When the horse has to go up a jagged bank or one that has been bricked over, if it is not too steep, he will elevate the forehand, placing it right on the bank; poised on his front legs, he will move his body as far forward as he can and, lowering his head, gather his muscles to bring his rear under. In this case, the rider should yield completely and, if necessary, aid the horse with his legs, but only after the horse has his forelegs on the bank.

The horse will now learn of his own accord to master all types of track, taking difficulties in his stride as he works in the open, providing the rider does not conflict with him but seconds his action and stimulates the animal's natural habit of watching where he is going. Once the horse has looked over the terrain, he will deal magnificently and successfully with any difficulty encountered along the way. All the rider need do is go forward, leaving his mount's mouth free, and with his body second the animal's equilibrium. The first, basic rule, therefore, is always to permit the horse to observe the terrain; never force him to go on before he has had a chance to do so. Leave him at liberty and do not oppose him, and yield to him at the opportune moment.

I must now say a few words about horses that become difficult when one wants to put them to work. In the first place, as a general rule, bad horses are that way because they have not been able to adapt themselves progressively as they should to the demands made upon them and because their attempts to do what was expected of them were accompanied by useless suffering. To go as they should, horses that are like that need only be mounted by riders who will not cause them pain.

On the other hand, there are horses that are naturally lazy and those that are bad-tempered, although these are rarer than you might think, and there are also those that have been made bad by poor methods, so that they have fallen into the habit of disobeying and doing everything defensively. With such spoiled and captious animals, one must resort to punishment, applied with force and ever-increasing insistence, until the horse yields.

Once they have yielded to the rider and done the work required, should these horses suffer at his hands they will revert to their former state and become more rebellious than ever.

On the other hand, if that does not occur, and the horse, after yielding, has nothing more than the fatigue of work to bear, he will soon learn to submit in order not to have to bear the pain that comes with punishment. Thus, for example, when a horse balks, it is necessary that every touch of the whip and the spurs be followed by an easing of the reins, so that the horse can go forward without having to support pain in his mouth.

You can take it as a rule that when you can use good manners and persuasion, things will go better; but should you obtain no results in this way, you will just have to resort to punishment, and not let up until the horse has given in, even if just a little or for just a moment. This is the least you should get before stopping.

Once the horse's calmness in action has been developed through long gallops at cadenced gaits and over progressively more difficult stretches of ground—and once the rider has a good seat, balance, and good judgment in dealing with his mount—you can crown the instruction of both rider and horse by teaching them to jump.

In order that this exercise give good results, however, it must be well done, and not attempted in the empiric way usually employed, for in such a case, besides being of no value to the rider, it can seriously damage the horse. When jumping exercises are done properly, the horse learns to overcome those obstacles in the field that he could not otherwise take without squandering his energy. The greatest benefit, however, accrues to the rider. The jump, as a matter of fact, is the one action of all the horse's movements in which, in the brief space of a few seconds, he most changes his balance and his position—radically so. The horseman, therefore, requires a certain tact and firmness in the saddle in order to second the horse and not distract him with his hands or the weight of his body.

When the rider supports his horse in the execution of a jump, he has more than enough expertise and tact not to annoy him in any other action whatsoever. That will become clear after the brief study I am now about to make of the jump itself.

I shall try to analyze the jump in all its details, both in light of the advantages to be gained when it is well done as well as the dreadful results that redound when the jump is not well understood; furthermore, I shall do this because I am passionately interested in the subject! What I have to say will not be grasped by the trooper, but it certainly should be by the instructor to the point where he can oversee this exercise knowledgeably, correcting errors as they occur and anticipating them, and seeing the real reasons for difficulties or the horse's refusal.

Jumping

Contrary to what many believe, the jump* is as natural a movement to the horse as the walk, the trot, and the gallop. To improve his ability in jumping and to perfect himself in it, the horse needs the proper exercise, always based on the same principles of not requiring anything of him that is forced or artificial, but solely a seconding of what comes naturally, while being left at liberty, and not caused any unnecessary discomfort.

---

* Federico Tesio held that the jump was an unnatural action for a horse, deducing this from the fact that colts he had observed never jumped, not even over a fence or ditch, although they might be driven by hunger or impelled by the desire to join another horse of whom they were fond. He also saw three famous jumpers who were incapable of jumping the paddock, even though they were impatient to get back to their boxes. This convinced him that the jump is contrary to the horse's natural means and that it is performed only when the horse is forced to do so by man, his implacable master.

"Of course, you can teach a horse that is running free to leave the corral by jumping the gate, but even this is training, the result of domination. Naturally, he would prefer to wait until the gate were opened, once he knew a man was coming to get him each evening. Left on his own, the horse avoids large obstacles and, often, even the small ones."

On the other hand, cats and lions jump with facility. Tesio continues:

"The physical structure and mental orientation of the feline are organized for jumping: the long supple back, low-slung shoulders, flexible paws, excellent vision, and power of concentration. The horse, on the other hand, has a structure and orientation that are diametrically opposed to that of the cat: short and rather rigid back, withers far from the ground, hard hooves, short sight. Considered as a mobile machine, the horse has four speeds forward: walk, trot, gallop, and full gallop. The fourth speed, the headlong gallop, is the ultimate defense, even for trotters, when beset by danger.

"The jump is a bit of acrobatics imposed upon the horse by man, but without any natural origin; thus its attitudes cannot be transmitted to offspring. In the same way, fifty generations of acrobats can do nothing to assure that a child will be born who can perform a high jump without training—but that same baby will learn to walk without anyone teaching him how."

At this point, Tesio remarks that the great natural and instinctive jumpers are the deer, gazelles, chamois, antelope, and ibex, all of which have long shinbones, rigid backs, not very flexible hoofs, and true of any animal in flight, little power of concentration.

These jump in a manner completely different from the felines, springing from all four feet at once. When the feline jumps, it is to reach another spot, a branch, the back of another animal; while the ruminant jumps to get over a crevasse, a ditch, or any other such irregularity in the terrain, in order to continue his flight.

The horse finds himself between these two species because of the complexity of his articulation. At times, one sees him jump like a deer, when he has to cross a ditch, for instance; while on other occasions, and more frequently, his jump is parabolic, as he basculates over a high obstacle.

Who has not heard that the less you jump with a horse, the better, and that every jump depreciates him a bit, so that you should have him jump only when it is absolutely imperative? Just how absurd these conceits are, I am not about to demonstrate here; but these people have formed their ideas upon the basis of jumping exercises that are badly done, so that the horse, fatigued and hurt by the rider, learns to jump badly and gets into the habit of refusing. Furthermore, the rider's bad habits, and the false, forced balance the horse is constrained to achieve and maintain because of them, will certainly wreck him in time. Naturally, the jump will cause him harm, just as any other action done badly will do, as we have seen.

Thus, the first condition for assuring that a horse become a good jumper is not to put him through any useless suffering. The rider should never forget this and should remember that the most unpleasant thing for the horse, and what annoys him most, is any action that runs counter to the natural movements—I might almost say the mechanical movements—he makes during the jump.

What should be given more thought than any other aspect is the horse's mouth, for the actions performed on this part are the most painful, and they can modify the whole of the animal's natural balance. Since this is such an important consideration, we shall briefly look into the manner in which a horse executes a jump, and take for our purpose a jumper on his own.

When he nears an obstacle, we can see that the jumper puts his nose forward, thus extending his neck. This move, which makes it easier for the horse to observe and measure the obstacle, is of prime importance, even for the mechanics of the jump.

As a matter of fact, while the horse extends his neck and shoulders he plants his forelegs squarely on the ground to take the weight of his body, ready to shift it the moment the hindquarters are conveniently disposed to receive it. By so doing the horse can more easily bring his hindquarters under the center of gravity, and best arrange them to take the major part of the weight of his body, so that he can then fling that mass forward into the air at the takeoff.

Next, the horse pulls in his head and neck, and contracts the trunk muscles, bringing the center of gravity behind. In this way, along with the forward counterthrust he makes, he is able to lift his forelegs, thus combining the spring of the hindquarters with the added impulsion given the entire mass during the last paces of the gallop—to give himself the needed elevation.

177 *P. Fresk (Sweden), on Kastad at Rome, yields a bit too much.*

178 *Frank D. Chapot (United States) on Trail Guide at Rome in 1960.*

179 *William Steinkraus (United States) on Ksar d'Esprit. His leg has slipped back a bit.*

180 *William Steinkraus (United States) at the Rome Olympics in 1960, showing the same defect.*

181 *Nelson Pessôa (Brazil) on Grande Geste, his greatest "creation."*

177

178

179

180

181

182

183

At this moment, the horse has marshaled the forces that will take him off the ground, so we have caught him in a very important movement. As a matter of fact, as well as providing for the necessary height, this movement quickly displaces the center of gravity forward, once again lengthening the neck and head markedly, and simultaneously stretching the forelegs forward. These, after having contributed toward pitching the center of gravity forward, take the weight upon themselves.

As the center of gravity is shifted forward, there is also a contraction of the trunk muscles from rear to fore. As a result, it becomes easy for the hindquarters, which have been lightened, to clear the obstacle. As soon as the forelegs have touched down, the rear legs are brought up to assume the weight and permit the horse to continue in his gait.

The first rule that the rider should draw from all these observations is to see always that the horse is permitted to execute a jump precisely in this way.

Thus, the horse should always approach an obstacle at right angles to it and at a cadenced gait; the rider should maintain the same contact, with the horse's head straight, and the rider's hands still and low at the level of the withers. Take care that the body is not set too far back or too far forward, and do not give any aid with the legs that is not absolutely indispensable to keeping the horse going at the same speed and gait.

The horse should proceed willingly toward the obstacle, calm and attentive, and the rider, accordingly, should avoid making any move or doing anything that might give him pain. Don't seize him excessively in the mouth; wait for him to come to hand of his own accord. You will give him confidence if you let him observe the obstacle well, and if you can, even let him smell it. In this exercise, as well, it is important to follow a definite progression, beginning always with very low jumps, and never rushing to take the next higher one until the horse has performed ably over the last obstacle.

When dealing with young horses being trained to jump, the rider, after making them understand what it is that they have to do, should try, above all, to develop the eye, and by "eye" I mean the horse's ability to see with precision and confidence just when to jump. As far as I am concerned, this is the most important trait to look for in a jumper, and it is an ability partly natural and partly acquired. Actually, the horse develops this ability through long practice, working over an obstacle that can be raised gradually, but never too much at a time. The horseman should leave him pretty much on his own, allowing him to approach the jump at a moderate gait, seeking only to calm any fears he may have or forestall any tendency toward rushing the obstacle.

It is necessary that the horse should learn not to fear any action from the rider when approaching an obstacle, but rather to have confidence that the rider will always give him the freedom to jump without interfering or hurting him to no purpose. Unless the horse learns this, he will not concentrate on doing his work well, but will turn his attention to avoiding pain.

For that reason, to accustom the horse to trusting his rider, without fear of his actions, it is preferable to exercise the horse mounted (if you are sure you can ride well), even though you may be shaken up a bit.

Do not forget that in jumping practice, except to correct downright laziness, bad temper, or wandering attention, you should be chary of too much punishment. At times, when the horse is uncertain at the obstacle and advances indecisively, it is essential to aid him energetically with increasing force and in just proportion to what is called for, but never do so nastily, so as not to provoke an adverse reaction from him. It is in knowing just how much of himself is needed that the rider reveals his qualities.

With the understanding that balance and firmness in the saddle are the *sine qua non*, let us now look at what, in my opinion, is required of a rider in the jump: to accompany with the weight of his body—with the hands, especially—every movement the horse makes, offering him no interference. Furthermore, and more particularly, as the horse approaches the obstacle, the rider should permit him to stretch his neck and head forward, and the rider should move his hands up so that the animal can do so without losing contact or slackening on the reins, but maintaining a constant light tension.

Next, when the horse draws back his head and neck and shifts his center of gravity back, putting the weight on the haunches, the rider should bring his hands back a bit, taking care not to increase tension on the reins too much.

Just as soon as the horse has sprung, the rider should let his trunk follow the displacement forward of the center of gravity, without, however, lifting his seat too far out of the saddle. At the very same instant, he should allow the horse to stretch his neck and shoulders, which is an extremely important movement, and essential to the horse's completing the jump without being hurt, by moving his hands forward as far as possible, and giving the horse full rein, letting the reins slip through his fingers, should that be necessary.

You will see that this "following" when the horse is in the air is of prime importance. The slightest bother the rider causes the horse at this moment will not only prejudice the jump but inflict pain that will go from his mouth to his loins and might even, as often happens, make him hit the obstacle with his hind legs.

If the rider does not yield when he is in the air, and does not follow the horse's shift in weight by moving his trunk, the animal will be disheartened, and innumerable difficulties are bound to arise out of his attitude. Furthermore, he will learn to land foursquare, which is very hard on the loins and calls for greater effort from the horse than does hitting the ground correctly. The rider's shifting his upper body forward, therefore, should be slight, but sufficient to permit him to be ready to take control of the horse should the animal hit the obstacle or stumble when he hits the ground.

182 183 *Trial obstacle course at the Villa Borghese, adjacent to the famous ellipse of the Piazza di Siena.*

In conclusion, I believe that following by the rider when the horse is off the ground is the most important action of all on his part, and it is therefore the movement the instructor should insist upon and see that every rider achieves.

Aiding the horse systematically, a thing many would like to see during the jump, is something that cannot be done at times; and in some instances, in my view, it has bad consequences. It often happens that the horse, fearing the aid, rushes during the last part of his approach to the obstacle, and seriously compromises the jump.

A good jumper does not have to be aided in his jump, for once he has gauged the obstacle, he knows just how much force he needs to get over it without the rider demanding it of him superfluously. Mediocre and inexpert jumpers can become good ones through rational and continuous practice, but never through the employment of aids or violent means.

Occasionally, in exceptional cases, aid may be useful in the last two or three beats of the gallop and at the moment when the horse is just about to take off, if he shows signs of holding back by hesitating. One must, however, always be cautious in giving aid, and do so in the appropriate measure.

You must cease any aid the moment the horse indicates that all is well. At all cost, avoid moving the hands out to the sides. Instead, move them up, easing up on the reins. Remember that moving the hands is extremely harmful, since this keeps the horse from being able to observe where he is going, and therefore gives him an excuse to balk or to be off in his timing.

Never put a timid or fearful horse over a high obstacle. Such horses should practice with low obstacles, preferably at a slow gait, and given the opportunity to see the obstacle clearly, even smelling it, if necessary. Do your best to discover just what it is that frightens the horse or makes him timid, and try to eliminate that factor. When that has been done, but not before, you can begin, gradually, to increase the height of the obstacle. With nervous horses, the rider should even avoid squeezing them at the fork or alarming them by taking them up too much, for this will make them bolt or confuse them.

I have limited myself in this study to outlining a few basic principles, and have certainly left many lacunae, but the principle that I have sought to place in evidence and what, as I see it, is the fundamental rule for all equitation in the field, is always to second and favor the horse's natural instincts and attitudes, and avoid giving him any undue pain while working.

With rigorous application of that principle, which comes through the simple employment of a few uncomplicated rules, the horse, submissive by nature, will not regress, but will display all the many gifts that have made him a precious instrument of warfare throughout the ages.

I close, then, with the fervid hope that these few thoughts, fruit of experience by no means brief—that have received even the approval of many foreign officers with whom I have had occasion to exchange ideas—will receive the dissemination and approbation throughout our cavalry that they seem to me to merit and that they become touchstones of military equitation to pass on to the men.

XL

DEVELOPMENT AND DIFFUSION
OF THE CAPRILLI SYSTEM

The following periods mark the development and diffusion of Caprilli's system:

1888–1900: During this time, the new ideas caught on, were approved, and began to spread.

1900–1902: Caprilli's ideas continued to spread, and bit by bit were adopted, until the system finally was recognized officially. Both the generalized use of the snaffle for the horse's mouthpiece and the great increase in equitation in the field already were responsible for permitting the most devoted and advanced horsemen to achieve good, logical results. Although 1902 did not see wholly vigorous activity and the complete triumph of the system, it did mark the beginning of its total acceptance and the point of departure for a new orientation of the method.

1903–1907: Through the efforts of General Berta, the Caprilli system was presented to the Italian Cavalry School, where it was taught and applied, and more widely adopted.

1907–1911: These years marked further diffusion of the system and the training of numerous good instructors, and an ever-growing group of students, which meant more good horsemen.

1911–1920: Further adoption of the system, which was disseminated outside Italy, with the preparation of more instructors and training of more students. These could be called the system's "golden years."

1920–1925: The years following World War I marked a return to racing in Italy and throughout the world. The best Italian horsemen had many successes abroad, and their primacy as horsemen in international competition was virtually undisputed.

1925–1939: During this period, for a number of reasons, the great mass of horsemen were oriented toward the international horse shows, and tended to think of horsemanship in terms of sport. Accordingly, there were the first signs of degeneration and infiltration into the system of the first bits of school work.

Young instructors who were, in general, excellent horsemen and who had been, in the main, trained by instructors who were not direct recipients of the teachings of Caprilli brought to their own teaching certain personal variations and added touches that were not true to the spirit of the Caprilli method. Some of these grew out of the fact that Caprilli had not spoken of how one was to train horses for natural equitation.

After World War II, for lack of direction—many cavalry regiments were disbanded—and because of competitive necessities, with events and races becoming ever more spectacular, the system took a good deal of punishment, particularly in the schools, and could not be maintained in its pure form as it had a few years earlier.

XLI
VARIATIONS ON A THEME

The belief that Caprilli would have changed his opinions were he alive today has been current even in Italy, and highly qualified people have said as much. However, no one has defined exactly what Caprilli might have kept and what he might have discarded from his system, or even added.

It appears that even Caprilli would be having his difficulties and that General Ubertalli and others of his line would no longer be sufficient to save him from criticism. Though the great horseman and master freed Italian equitation from its old bonds by freeing the horse's loins, neck, and shoulders (after having observed the animal's natural attitudes), he has, nevertheless, left the sum of his observations—a series of acute, inspired, and fascinating notes—full of gaps.

For instance, Caprilli did not speak of preparing horses for the track, nor did he indicate the means and direction that should be taken to train a horse gymnastically to jump by his system. Evidently, he thought all this was obvious and therefore superfluous, given the fact that a basic preparation would come naturally from the hours and hours it was customary to spend working in the manège. For the same reason, probably, he did not say anything about the formulas of dressage, which naturally excluded all the strain of the high and low airs. This work, this practice of dressage, from Caprilli's point of view, would probably have to be discounted as well.

On the other hand, Caprilli refers almost wholly and exclusively to equitation in the field, which was employed in his day for sporting purposes, that is, hunting, and for military use. Caprilli, we must not forget, was concerned with teaching cavalrymen to handle a horse with deftness and skill so that they could get the animal to go where they wanted and do what they wished, according to the exigencies of the moment. In the light of these requirements, his system was just the thing for attaining that absolute dominance over the horse, for getting him to be light and eager, workable over any terrain—as can be seen from the way he could go over obstacles of any type and difficulty in the most relaxed and composed way, with the horse going forward in his natural way and not with all his potential impulsion in the hindquarter.

Truly, today one remembers that the crowning technical feats of Caprilli are represented in the photographs of him jumping with Piccolo Lark, each jump a masterpiece of composure, with the maximum result and the minimum strain either upon the horse or upon the rider.

The necessities of competition—plus back trouble from too many falls—led Caprilli to force his position and double himself up too much, so that the system and the natural method became somewhat mannered. Meanwhile, racecourses were becoming more and more complicated and the hazards greater, either to give the public more of a spectacle or, possibly, to prove just how good (or bad) riders and horses were.

The first to realize that the system functioned within certain limits was Alessandro Alvisi, who commanded the squadron of the Militia, and had such horsemen as Pogliaga, Mangilli, Coccia, D'Angelo, and Kecler at his disposal.

Alvisi came to the conclusion that a return to school work was indispensable if he wished to continue the series of victories won by Caprilli's followers; the rules of the game had changed somewhat, and even the horses one had to work with were of a different stripe, ever more difficult to manage and dominate.

Abroad, Caprilli's system, half understood, had already created problems, particularly in England. We remember how the English jumped traditionally: the old school was designed for the courses used in England at the time when, for the most part, obstacles were vertical and highly shifting; the time counted for nothing, while what really mattered was the precision with which jumps were taken. At the point of approaching the obstacle, the Englishman kept his horse to the gait until the takeoff. Then, however, when the English rider saw the success the Italians were having, and when he was confronted with obstacles more solid and deeper than those to which he had been accustomed, and entered in races where time was important, he decided to shorten his stirrup leathers. This change permitted him to gallop faster over obstacles, but he still insisted on interfering with his horse's action, as always, with the result that he was never with his horse and, consequently, either pounded on the animal's loins or dragged on his mouth.

While the French, with the exception of Danloux, have always shown a certain diffidence toward the Italian system—preferring to stay with the principles expounded at Saumur, and practicing the *demi-arrêt*, whose most extraordinary exponent today is Pierre-Jonquères d'Oriola—the Germans studied Caprilli. While following his principles, in some measure, for their own purposes, the Germans extracted from his theory and practice the work in connection with the parabola of the jump—precisely Caprilli's most masterly insight—but as to the athletic preparation of the horse and the gymnastics done in the manège, they have preferred to stay with the rules of their own Hanover school.

Today, it is said that if it had not been for the war and for the changes it brought, the finest of the Italian riders would have lost because, over complicated courses, with their horses in the forward position, they could never have overcome the superb technique and rigorous preparation of the German horsemen. Tommaso Lequios, the noted Italian international competitor, lectured in the manner of Caprilli, but as soon as they left the riding academy, young riders sought to return to school riding. Because of all this, Italian equitation underwent an evolution that was different from any other.

The man who began to seek a synthesis of the two methods—natural and school equitation—after watching the German riders, was in 1936 considered a turncoat by adepts of the Caprilli system. After Alvisi and his group (let us not forget that Mangilli was the first Italian to attempt the grand prix dressage event at the Olympics, riding the thoroughbred gray Guerriero de Capestrano), it was Francesco Amalfi who headed the new line of innovators. He was followed, among the young officers, by Gherardo Conforti, the one who developed, at first with some awkwardness, the new tendencies. He did his work in a somewhat empiric way, precisely because practical application is always rather prickly for the Italians, and then in greater detail.

Today, all riders who really shine have arrived at such

equitation through their own sensitivity, having made a balanced choice from old and more current traditions and the newest of tendencies, without actually defining any particular school of their own. Such a course is followed at the military and sporting equestrian center in Italy, headed by Colonel Manzin who appeared in the three-day event at the Helsinki Olympics. The new tendency is to have the horse light, going forward naturally, but athletically developed, and to achieve this last, some outline of work must be fixed upon.

Those favoring simplicity at all costs, who are guided by the few, sparse notes on the subject by Caprilli, would like to leap on the back of an unbroken horse and teach him to jump without making him an athlete, without even having put him through a bit of gymnastics. That would be like taking a strong and husky country boy who doesn't know how to walk and expect him to run the hundred meters. (What should be followed is a course of preathletic work so that the boy can learn how to use his muscles to do what he wants and with precision; then he must do special exercises to develop those muscles for sprinting and speed.)

As a matter of fact, you see many horses that cannot trot in the proper rhythm or take off in a gallop to the right or left. A great deal of preparatory work is needed, work done shrewdly and conscientiously. What is needed even more is to take our old Caprilli style of equitation and orient it to the exigencies of today's horse—that is, combining impulsion and forward movement with lightness, or, better still, in essence combining exceptional impulsion with constant equilibrium.

While in the seventeenth century one performed the pirouette, croupade, courbette, and the cabriole, and put everything into executing these difficult exercises with beauty and elegance, today these figures, particularly the pirouette, should be performed with enough forward movement and surge to permit a horse, after a half-turn of no more than a few yards in radius, to take obstacles as much as five and a half feet in height.

In substance, what must be done is a great deal of gymnastics to develop the horse's hindquarters to an exceptional point. Putting him on his haunches diminishes his ability to put weight on his forehand, and the haunches become placed well underneath the horse.

What is indispensable here is discovering the mechanism of the *apparade,* a strong half-halt that Fritz Thiedemann, for example, practiced to the excessive point of executing it at every three beats of the gallop.

As for curves, Caprilli wrote: "Pull up on the inside rein and yield somewhat on the outside rein," but today's technique, in place of this principle of the direct rein of opposition, tends to the indirect rein of opposition, since the first method puts the horse too much on his shoulders (the hindquarters cover more distance than the forelegs, and tend, therefore, to make themselves lighter, and consequently shift the impulsion to the forehand), while the second method has the horse covering more ground with the forelegs, consequently shifting more to the rear. This method is the one instinctively used by cowpunchers here, who, like most other cowboys, generally hold the two reins in one hand. These riders generally turn a horse more through the shifting of their own weight than anything else.

Amalfi used to watch a rider at the trot, and from the way he performed while going at this gait, decided whether or not he would be able to jump. "You're not trotting," he would protest whenever he saw a rider put his horse on the forehand, or if the rider posted excessively, shifting his own body from rear to front. Conforti, inspired by Amalfi's principles, applied them to himself, and found in the horse Sabà a perfect performer, and in Popilio, a Thoroughbred not too gifted by nature, a notable winner.

The first Italian team to benefit from these revisions in the theory and technique of equitation was the one that competed in the 1948 Olympics, held in London, and consisted of Conforti, Bettoni, Piero d'Inzeo, Azais, and Ricci.

XLII
THE D'INZEO BROTHERS

Succeeding the number of great horsemen active between World Wars I and II, were three riders of international class—perhaps the best Italians of all time—who brought their country a new period of splendor in the equestrian field. They are the d'Inzeo brothers, Piero and Raimondo; and Granziano Mancinelli.

While Mancinelli is a champion apart, considering his equestrian verve and style, his character, and the fact that he is a civilian semiprofessional rider, the d'Inzeos must be considered together, not merely because they are brothers but also because, paradoxically, their completely contrary characteristics have brought them both to the very same heights.

Piero and Raimondo were born, respectively, in 1923 and 1925, in Poggio Mirteto, in the province of Rieti, the sons of Costanzo d'Inzeo, a marshal in the cavalry, and an extremely brilliant and meticulous riding instructor. Not surprisingly, the boys had superb private schooling in equitation—rigorous and precise training from their own father. Piero, immediately eager to learn, and the more disciplined of the two, was riding in private shows by the time he was eight, and cutting quite a figure. Raimondo, however, was no more than a spectator for about ten years. While Piero, profoundly influenced by his father's instruction, gradually became the incarnation of Caprilli's manual, Raimondo rode as he pleased, rather sloppily and shoddily, despite spankings and his father's despair that one of his sons would never be a horseman.

Actually, it was Piero's first successes in those early competitions that put Raimondo on his mettle and moved him to emulate his brother, which has been the basis of his

184 *At the horse show: A rider shortens his stirrups.*
185 *Two horsemen watch the competition from the trial ground.*
186 *Taking the measure of an obstacle.*
187 *Last-minute work on the rope before the competition.*
188 *Called out onto the field.*
189–192 *In competition.*
193 *Going to receive their prizes, symbolic recompense for difficult work; prizes for equestrian skill have no more than token value.*

184

185

186

187

188

189

190

191

192

193

194

success. It was an open imitation that had nothing in it of envy or rancor, but rather, we might say, amusement. In their formation as horsemen, this difference can be seen when the two are in the saddle, for while Piero became an incomparable stylist who would refuse a jump rather than take it haphazardly and incorrectly, Raimondo became a consummate competitor who picked up his medals and titles quickly, winning a silver medal (a bronze went to Piero) at the Stockholm Olympics in 1956, a gold (a silver to Piero) in 1960, at Rome, and in addition to his Olympics victories was world champion in 1956, riding Merano, and in 1960, on Gowran Girl.

What fascinated observers of Piero was his style, the perfect unit he formed with his horse, the perfection of his extremely supple back, shoulders, and arms, his vibrant, harmonious bearing, completely contained—the fruit of his physical training and attitude. It was his physique and bearing that gave Piero d'Inzeo optimum results; his wonderfully supple body beautifully followed his horse's changes in equilibrium, while his legs never lost their firmness.

As far as work was concerned, Piero believed that jumpers should be prepared and exercised on the flat, for only on the flat, he believed, could the rider dominate the horse's impulsion and equilibrium, while if he were to take him over every fence in existence, he would not be accomplishing anything more than the usual gymnastics, of questionable value, and possibly harmful.

Piero d'Inzeo also insists that schooling should be successfully completed with the use of the classic snaffle and simple bridle. Any other bit, any other type of rein, no matter how well designed, is an admission of weakness on the part of the man who uses it, since he depends upon the effect rather than upon the cause, and therefore obtains results that are merely provisional, erroneous, and probably dangerous. D'Inzeo's assertion merits consideration by those who seek to find the secret of success in a bit or put themselves to the trouble of taking jump after jump after jump without ever stopping to pause and reflect.

Piero d'Inzeo remained the most brilliant and constant star in the equestrian firmament until 1955, when his brother, Raimondo, began to come to the fore. Raimondo, though playful, was rather timid, while Piero was serious and reserved. Never, however, has there been any animus between them, despite the fact that each is preeminent in international equitation and that their followers and fans have not hesitated to attempt to create rivalry and discord between them. Raimondo has always admired and respected the class and style of his brother, and has always affirmed that no one would ever match Piero because no one "would be more horse" than Piero. Nevertheless, he has observed that if Piero is the paradigm of equitation, his metamorphosis is Raimondo.

Piero d'Inzeo, then, is classicism in the saddle, even though today the hypercritical may see him as a bit of a humpback, and somewhat laughable (though the hunchbacks

do better than those who sit on a horse too stiffly and erect). He is wisdom in the saddle. Raimondo, on the other hand, is all invention, the impulsive horseman who has managed to transform the canons of the Caprilli system into a singular, instinctive art. His daring has earned him more and harder falls than Piero has ever suffered, not to mention eighteen stitches, a punctured eardrum, and aches and pains that come with every change in the weather.

While Piero insists that he has a classic system of schooling a horse that is valid for all, and does not believe that there is a horse that would not submit to his control and will, Raimondo, more impulsive and pragmatic by nature, works by getting to know the horse, penetrating to his very soul, seeking his obedience through real cooperation. This, in practice, means years and years of work, but hardly any monotony, for one horse is never like another. Raimondo would never be content to go into competition riding a horse he didn't know inside out, without knowing that he understood the horse, and had made himself understood. To achieve all this takes the patience of an acrobat, the cold calculation of a gambler, and the sensitivity and delicacy of an artist.

Notwithstanding, Raimondo d'Inzeo, a horseman of a very personal style, and an inordinate competitor, with his mount Merano has become a "classic," with certain of his performances standing as examples of technical perfection and masterly tactics. In the same way he has reached the heights of artistry on Gowran Girl, improvising and taking each fence as it came, keeping that madcap filly always under control from one flurry to the next, always adjusting to the situation, and keeping up with the spirit and response of his mount.

For Raimondo, an obstacle course is a series of surprises, a race to be run from one obstacle to the next, "played by ear" over every stretch. This is Raimondo d'Inzeo's peculiar quality, this ability to improvise, to renew himself over each stretch of a course and with each horse, even while knowing that his restless hands and his legs that slip back are bound to earn raised eyebrows from the keepers of the classical flame. Raimondo knows that you do not take to the field to give a demonstration of style, particularly today when a speed class is decided by a tenth of a second, when fences are always more difficult, courses more tortuous, and when every horseman is restricted to the limit of the balance of a man in a saddle and the animal's athletic potentialities. It is a combination that always makes for unlimited risk.

Piero, very much to the contrary, has always worked with the almost abstract precision and punctilio of the great masters of another day—*écuyers* who knew that it took two years to put a horse through *haute école* figures. (For Piero, jumping is almost another high-school figure, only more difficult.) His style, however, seems to spring from a hard obstinacy carried within himself and that he would impose upon the horse to the point of disrespect or overriding the horse's personality; the animal must become a machine, a means to an end, rather than a companion in sport.

In preparing a horse, in attempting to get the animal on its haunches, Piero has become so exasperated (like the Germans, but more dramatic, and painfully so) that now and then a horse has rebelled. Those animals whose nature is such that they have been receptive to Piero's schooling have become unsurpassable instruments of his genius; horses such

194 *Major Svend Truelsen (Denmark) falls at a jump during the three-day event. The horse was unhurt, but his rider was taken to the hospital with a broken collarbone.*

as Uruguay, Sunbeam, and The Rock carried Piero d'Inzeo to perhaps insuperable heights of classic equestrianism.

Nevertheless, it is Piero who insists that the horse participates in the competition, that he is a sincere collaborator; while Raimondo is convinced, contrariwise, that the horse, no matter how good-hearted, faithful, and demonstrative he may be, has no intelligence whatsoever. That opinion was his father's, and is shared by the many who judge the horse's intelligence without taking into account all the unnatural and exasperating work they force him to do. The horse's intelligence is that of an animal on the run: remote from our way of thinking, this animal intelligence is ruled by a hypersensitivity capable of exciting him to the point where he will put down his own life in jeopardy. Such a state of mind permits little of the concentration required in competition. Raimondo forgets that his own Merano, at the end of every jumping competition, when the prizes were awarded, would buck if he had won, but if a mistake had been made, merely looked sheepish. (Raimondo suspects that a horse, either intuitively or telepathically, is sympathetic to his rider's feelings.)

That every horse reacts to a competition is undeniable. Some are frightened of competitions; others go into them courageously, while some are even downright aggressive. Merano, according to Raimondo, was not the "most gifted" horse of his time, but was certainly the most willing, the most attentive, the most responsive, and the most tenacious. Yet, when he was a colt, no one would have given a plugged nickel for him, he was so ugly. When Raimondo saw him for the first time at the Morese stud in Ponto Cagnano, it was love at first sight, for although Merano was the most unprepossessing colt of all, Raimondo felt he could see in the animal a certain skeletal conformation, a certain disposition of the joints and play of the members, a certain "humanity" in the eye that made him decide to choose that "ugly duckling."

Piero and Raimondo d'Inzeo are of average height, thin, as if made spare and dry by riding, with narrow, triangular, actually equine faces. They both possess the art of achieving perfect harmony with a horse of their choice—through totally different methods. Raimondo is intent upon making the horse a faithful, passionate collaborator; and even though he thinks the animal has little intelligence, he does everything possible to understand the horse's nature and attitudes. Piero, on the other hand, begins by deciding to mold the horse in accordance with a personal model he has in mind, his own concept of the perfect jumper.

For some twenty years, elbow to elbow, these two have met without rivalry but bound by a spirit of fraternal emulation—a feeling strong enough to surpass rivals named Thiedemann, D'Oriola, Winkler, Pessôa, and a few others.

XLIII
GRAZIANO MANCINELLI

Graziano Mancinelli is the most extraordinary Italian civilian rider of our period. He is a rider who moves, presses, takes risks, and wins.

Mancinelli's style, at least in the field, is not usually that of the manual, but instead is enthusiastic, exciting, devilishly inspired, and in its own way perfect, even though his hands may move in a manner not altogether orthodox (busily, though with extreme coherence, so as never to contradict the horse). Mancinelli's hands, their action completely independent of his shoulders and the rest of his body, preserve the precise inclination calculated never to change the horse's equilibrium or to affect his forward motion. At times, one can see him place his inside hand against the horse's withers, working with the other hand, but without ever "nailing down" the horse, merely keeping his exuberance in check without resorting to the nasty riskiness of the French *demi-arrêt*.

Mancinelli's method is a determined effort to impose and obtain the proper cadence for confronting each new obstacle. Then, going over the fence, his leg may fly back at times, and halfway through the trajectory he will crumple in the saddle. The fact of the matter is, however, that Mancinelli is never "away" from his horse, never ahead of him or behind, but always part of that one unit of rider and mount. This unit exists not only in the physical sense; but is also present in the forward movement, the coordination of action, in the very dynamics of equitation. It is a psychic unit, as well.

"When I work, my leg is where it belongs," explains Mancinelli, "but when I'm competing, that's another thing"; and he is right. "You have to keep moving at all costs, and you can't do that stylishly. On today's courses, style just leads to refusals, and you're left in the lurch." Mancinelli adds, "You always have to be ahead, and there is not the chance or the time at each jump to control yourself at the moment of the spring."

On the other hand, there is always time to control the horse, certainly, surge by surge, but for Mancinelli his own self no longer exists except as an implacable force, the force of will, the precise calculation of time, the measure of the rhythm and power needed to "get over there." For that reason, Mancinelli gets the most out of every try, even though, at times, perhaps because the horse is weary, or perhaps because he is unduly on edge, the results are a bit feeble. These are Mancinelli's off moments, the times of which he doesn't speak, nor does he wish to. Perhaps all that he has lacked at such moments is just a bit more of that demoniac spirit that usually drives him.

In 1960, an acute observer wrote: "Were Mancinelli, the most perfect imitator of Winkler's defect of bending his leg—the heel is brought up to the buttocks at the height of the parabola of the jump—to observe Winkler attentively, he would realize that the defect has completely disappeared, and that Winkler's legs, now in the proper position, keep to the spot they were assigned to in the first place."

In truth, Mancinelli is an extraordinary competitor, cool in appearance but actually highly nervous because of a strong temperament; tough on himself, but still capable of great ardor, and imposing a profound intensity of purpose upon his collaborators and his students: the Italian team Federazione Italiano Sport Equestri placed in his care for the European championships. He is a hard man, incapable of compromises that affect his art and skill, at one and the same time affable, yet detached, quite capable of dropping a curtain between himself and people who would like to make use of his expertise and professional knowledge.

The rough professional rounds gave Mancinelli the opportunity to make a good deal of money in a short time, but it was "work in the salt mines," and time spent on mediocre horses (not worthy of his talents), turning them into jumpers, much as one might work to teach a fat old lady to dance ballet, and succeed.

Possibly fresher than the d'Inzeo brothers, more ambitious, and more sophisticated, Mancinelli still is a very hard and tireless worker, a man nudged on by the memory of a difficult childhood, a hard apprenticeship, and desperate, ceaseless training. There is something bitter in him and something ingenuous as well, a dramatic quality that lends a hallucinatory aura of high tension to his every performance.

One might say that he possesses characteristics of both the d'Inzeos: he resembles Raimondo in the way he handles a horse, though he is less the improviser, less peremptory, less lyrical than he. When working with a horse, he shows a particular insistence, a coercion that is much like Piero's, but only to a point, for he also has a good deal of respect for the nature and character of the animal. With the Thoroughbred Turvey, for example, he has a perfect understanding—to the point where horse and horseman seem to be happy to be working together and agreeing upon what they should do. This is quite different from Piero d'Inzeo, who acts as though he suspects his horse were up to something, which the animal sometimes confirms by refusing a jump. What is significant in Mancinelli's relationship with his mount is the liberty he gives this "pupil" when going onto the field, so that the horse may have a chance to look around, see the obstacles, observe the crowd, take it all in. Only when that look around has ended, and the horse has overcome his first alarm, do the two of them start working together as a team.

Mancinelli's first great horse was Ussaro, a huge sorrel raised by Prince Odescalchi. It was Mancinelli himself who broke him, taught him to trot, to gallop, and to move like an athlete. Ussaro had a miserable temper, and it got him into plenty of fights and difficulties, marked by incomprehension. Crotchety, neurasthenic, and hypersensitive, Ussaro obeyed one person his whole life long, and that person was Mancinelli; this parallels Raimondo d'Inzeo's experience with Merano.

Then there was Elke, a German gray mare, powerful, uneven in performance, and difficult because she was extremely edgy. "We say 'difficult,'" notes Mancinelli, "but the fact is, at a certain point, all horses, inevitably, become difficult. It was Elke who first put me into the big time, getting over 2.18 meters. I made my debut with her at Lucerne, in the Prix des Nations. From twelve countries, only two were left after the trials: Winkler (Germany) with Halla, Thiedemann (Germany) with Meteor, and I (Italy) with Elke. My heart was in my mouth."

In 1959 came Rockette, the other gray mare, and Mirtillo, a fiery Sardinian chestnut who, in 1960, out of forty-eight speed classes won forty-four and even won puissance competitions at two meters. This horse is like a pet dog, something like the legendary Crispa di Borsarelli.

As a study in balance, Graziano Mancinelli is a masterpiece. His knees appear to be nailed to the saddle, and at every single moment of the jump's trajectory they are fixed at exactly the same point. This permits Mancinelli utter freedom of movement, maximum sureness in action and balance, and the guarantee of not interfering with his horse. His hands, which are less mystifyingly ordered than Piero's in their action, and less dramatic than Raimondo's, are like an orchestra conductor's, always ready to take up the beat of each surge of the horse and to give the animal the proper rhythm, relieving him of weight as if he were ready to take him to the skies.

Mancinelli's ultimate creation is a twelve-year-old Thoroughbred from Ireland, Turvey—another horse with a difficult character, extremely sensitive, and richly endowed with natural ability, but with very little in his head. As an example, he entered and left a starting gate without breaking stride and without touching a bar; but the truth of the matter is, no rider could stay in the saddle with such violent impulsion from a horse. The wrong approach to Turvey was to err, to fail to take him into consideration, to show him a moment's hesitation or timidity. He would not tolerate this, as he would not rude treatment in the stable. He permitted himself to be taken in hand only by Mancinelli, whose empathy he sensed. He respected him as if he had understood that this horseman, first of all, was severe with himself.

There is in Mancinelli a quality that, despite his will to win, permits him to be a very close friend of his greatest rival, Raimondo d'Inzeo. (The stupendous purity of this sentiment has nothing of jealousy or rancor.) Furthermore, it permits him to stimulate his friend, to proclaim his worth, and cheer him on in competition—but also to attempt virtuoso flights never seen before, in order to emulate Raimondo and to surpass him. He is reserved and solitary by nature, and it is difficult not to feel sympathetic and benevolent toward him, as difficult as it would be to find a man more simple, straightforward, and honest—a man about horses, an untiring winner, a great gentleman, and the perfect teacher.

Mancinelli made his way in the world with a strength of will that is almost crude, but with the openness of one who has also known the somber side of life.

XLIV
THE FRENCH

The school at Saumur did not only dedicate itself to preserving and perfecting equitation in the manège. By 1822, General Oudinot already had acquired twenty-five Irish horses for work in the open air. He also had English saddles made to order. General F. de Brack, in 1838, developed work in the open and jumping over obstacles. In 1850, an obstacle course, known as the *Chemin Vert*, was created.

When the school was reestablished after the events of 1873, teams were formed for competitive sports. From the school's preparatory center, instituted in 1922, came the team comprising Commanders Marion and Lesage and Captain Jousseaume, which made a great showing at the Los Angeles Olympics in 1932. From this same center came such great horsemen as Bizard, Gaudin de Vallerin, Carbon, De Breuil, Cavaillé, Bertrand de Balanda, and others.

In 1922, polo was introduced at Saumur. In the spring of 1922, Saumur took up and continued the tradition of the Cadre Noir, while the preparatory center was transferred to

Fontainebleau under the name of the Centre National d'Equitation.

Naturally, the weight of tradition and that taste for rendering homage to the past so notable in the French inevitably came to have a conspicuous influence upon equitation. The French, who considered themselves the first to advocate "freedom of the mouth," began to ride in keeping with the spirit of that system only in 1923; but, system apart, they had already become holders of the record for the high jump. In that same year, the officers of the Cadre Noir ceded their place of honor to the expert regimental officers who engaged in competition and had finally become aware of the fact that the reason the Italians were picking up the laurels was that they followed the system.

With Xavier Bizard, Gaudin de Vallerin, and Laissardière, the French began to demonstrate their great qualities as equestrians, qualities that nevertheless stemmed from their rich heritage of school equitation—making it difficult for them to enter into the spirit of the system since they preferred to follow the teachings of Chevalier Jean d'Orgeix, using a horse more tortured (as being more responsive) than trained. In that fashion, however, the horseman, never really with his horse as part of a single unit, demands that the animal sacrifice loins and mouth. He gets a great deal out of the animal notwithstanding, even though it is from the French that we derive that species of equestrian Esperanto that results in each school not understanding the other. To the French, usually, riding Italian style is leaving the horse on long reins and staying behind over a fence.

Indubitably, D'Orgeix's *demi-arrêt* (the Italian *regolare,* or manner of controlling a horse when going over an obstacle) has disoriented a whole generation of horsemen. The *demi-arrêt,* however, is a consequence of a seat founded on the teachings of the school, that is, calling for natural equilibrium, to obtain which one must resort to acrobatics, as D'Orgeix always does. The *demi-arrêt* is adopted by those who are unable to go with the horse, so they bring the horse to them.

Classic French equitation has always been understood by the French themselves as *haute école,* "based upon the sensitivity, the delicacy, and the composure of horse and horseman, the precise action of hands held low, with full response from the mouth to the supple neck and shoulders and, above all, upon a perfect seat, true to the application of the prescribed standards—which are very different from those of the Italian system."

Even Danloux was sympathetic to the Italian system, but he did not understand its essence, and, like Gaudin de Vallerin, shortened his stirrup leathers, rested his hands near the horse's shoulders, and was hampered by the concepts of *haute école.* Furthermore, no Frenchman (or Irishman, either) has ever attended any of the Italian schools of military equitation, although a total of some 141 foreign students have been at Pinerolo and Tor di Quinto, coming from thirty-two nations: Albania, Argentina, Austria, Bolivia, Bulgaria, Czechoslovakia, Chile, Denmark, England, Ecuador, Finland, Germany, Greece, Hungary, Japan, Lithuania, Mexico, Montenegro, Norway, The Netherlands, Persia, Peru, Poland, Romania, Russia, Serbia, Sweden, Switzerland, Turkey, United States, Venezuela, and Yugoslavia.

The French, then, as a result of the success enjoyed by D'Orgeix, De Fombelle, and the theories of Gaudin de Vallerin, spread that type of artificial equilibrium used in *haute école* and brought it out of the manège into the field of competitive riding with the addition of that half-stop, or *demi-arrêt,* designed to rebalance (at least, that was their intention) before each and every obstacle. On the other hand, Captain Fresson is a rider of great dash and admirable style, especially when it comes to speed—where he best demonstrates the collaboration between horse and rider in his calculated jumps made without any change in gait.

The phenomenon of French equitation, however, is Pierre-Jonquères d'Oriola, who was a gold-medal winner at Tokyo, a rider who can spend as little as an hour a day in the saddle and who works his horses quite superficially, but a rider, when he is at his best, who shows a competitive spirit almost unequaled (perhaps Raimondo d'Inzeo was his equal in this), and who in his hard, tough, and provocative spirit is second only to that magnificent competitor Graziano Mancinelli.

D'Oriola probably believes that he rides in the Italian style, being a bit more broad-minded than is considered proper, leaving the horse extended and the reins long, but actually remaining a bit behind over the obstacle or recuperating his balance by lowering his body toward the fore, bending into an arc.

D'Oriola is not the product of a school but an exception to the rule, having the exuberant personality and natural ability that bypass the technical rules. D'Oriola is a true and proper equestrian acrobat, and that is a quality held to be indispensable in competition today, particularly where speed is called for, as well. But though his way of riding looks wonderful, it ends by costing the horse a great deal.

XLV
THE ENGLISH

The English seat, which depends upon rather long stirrups, provokes constant oscillation and balancing of the whole of the body and the legs. This seat comes not from a school, as does the French, but from the hunting seat and the necessity of bearing down on the saddle, with the legs brought forward, to attenuate the gait effect of strong and testy hunters.

The English, therefore, are accustomed to confronting fences in an attitude of "prudent defense," even if the obstacle is one that can be surmounted with a margin of abso-

195 *The three-day event at Helsinki, a fall by Rubaek-Nielsen (Denmark) riding Sahara.*
196 *Ted McCoy at Melbourne, completing the parabola.*
197 *Keith Campbell on Star Dust, off balance at the Royal Show in Adelaide.*
198 *John Lanni (Great Britain) goes beyond all limits on Huntsman at Dublin in 1956.*
199 *H. Smith on the Sea Hawk at Badminton making a rather unorthodox landing.*
200 *The Diver, ridden by Len Wilcox, takes the plunge at the Royal Meeting in Sydney.*

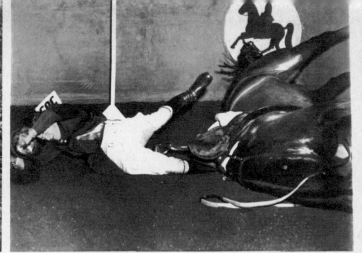

195

196

197

198

199

200

lute security. Intervention from the legs, the action always authoritative and vigorous, is considered as a second line of defense and security.

The English usually use the fixed martingale that the Italians believe should not be employed, but for them, accustomed as they are to putting young horses over obstacles of considerable size, the martingale is held to be necessary for preventing the horse's assuming the "head-to-the-wind" position. Even in this case, the matter of the proper seat has secondary importance. What is important is getting beyond the obstacle, which is the reason for the intervention of the swinging legs in the ultimate surge, even though they broaden the seat and take no account of stability in the saddle.

We must not forget that the cult of the horse is more alive than ever in Great Britain. There are more than six hundred stables breeding saddle horses, and each year there are more than three hundred competitive horse shows. Excluding Ireland, there are more than two hundred packs of hounds for fox hunting and twelve polo clubs with a total of some five hundred players.

Nevertheless, Great Britain, which has been furnished with horses since Roman times (the Romans left us a description of a species of quadruped very similar to today's New Forest pony), and a country that has been a great improver of the breed of every type of horse, considered the traditional equestrian sport to be fox hunting, as would be natural in a country which offered such magnificent terrain for open-field riding and which is still rich in natural obstacles. By comparison, such pursuits as dressage and horse shows, dear to the hearts of Europeans, were in the past held in disrepute, and considered no sport for an English gentleman.

Although today the majority of horsemen sit more or less in accordance with Caprilli's principles, if not his style, there is everywhere a good deal of doubt as to whether it is possible to apply his method at all times, including confronting all the obstacles in today's races. These doubts arise because of the necessity of intervening, the need to "adjust" the horse, the time a horse spends in front of obstacles that are badly placed, the need to reduce speed to surmount certain oxers—all these factors make it impossible for a horse to be compressed like a spring yet always straight and in the forward position, except perhaps in the last three strides.

The fact is that horsemen usually put the horse's hindquarters under through the action of the legs, but the contrast of the hands generally held high provokes, not the arching of the back, but a bend in the opposite sense that produces a concave back. This puts an enormous strain on the loins, is harmful to the withers, and, in general, results in a very bad distribution of the animal's weight.

We have noticed that riders with a physique that is not the most felicitous for horseback riding—John Kidd, for instance—manage to compensate for the excessive length of their limbs by achieving an extraordinary suppleness of body, to the point that they get to know exactly where to position their legs, which is not always the case with very tall people.

201 *Equestrian competition in the snow, which has become the fashion for winter meetings in Switzerland, Sweden, and Italy.*

The English have two gifts that are peculiarly theirs: great competence, which derives from habitual association with horses and an inherited passion for them (you can see in a squad of English juniors—fifteen-year-olds—how they understand horses, sympathize with them, care for them, and second them); and their other capacity, good timing at obstacles. The English concentrate their attention on each obstacle, taking one after the other, as it comes, rather than considering the course as a whole. Accordingly, each fence is a problem in itself, and must be resolved. This leads the English to break the rhythmic continuity of their gallop before each obstacle. From this attitude and practice, the English have come to the point where they habitually take the fixed obstacles in the field, a habit that has influenced their equitation in every aspect.

It was Captain Joseph Dudgeon (now director of a renowned riding academy in Dublin) who introduced the Italian system (Caprilli) into the English military school, in 1922. This action was roundly criticized, since at the time, Cesare Paderni's system was at the height of its popularity and was considered the only possible one for military and field equitation. It did not take long, however, for the Caprilli system to be generally accepted and adopted. The English set about adapting their tradition, their style, their types of horses, and their equestrian education to the exigencies of the new system, which resulted, of course, in their introducing into it certain variations, some of them necessary because of the differences between the Italian and English builds.

Notwithstanding, this system has produced such horsemen as Captain Dalla, the excellent David Broome, an Olympic bronze-medal winner at Melbourne and in third place at Venice for the world championship; Henry Llewellyn (with his celebrated mount Foxhunter, an example of sheer symbiosis), all of them first-rate. David Broome made a tremendous impression at Rotterdam in the European Championship of 1967 in two competitions riding Mr. Softy, coming in before another Englishman, Harry Smith, on Harvester, the German Alwin Schockemöhle on Donald Finshed, and Nelson Pessôa, the Brazilian, riding Grand Geste.

Nevertheless, there are still some in England today who are not hostile to the system but are of the opinion that it needs to be evolved so as to fulfill the exigencies of current employment of horses. Such English experts sustain the theory that one should no longer ride in either the English or Italian styles, but in a way that is a cross between them both. The old English style, where one approached the obstacle with the horse keeping cadence and very much in hand, and in which the rider acted to control the horse's rhythm, right down to the moment of the takeoff, was useful for the courses that were run at that time in England, where the obstacles were vertical, difficult, and the time of a race was no object.

Caprilli's system, based on the forward seat, relatively short stirrup leathers (compared with those used by the English), a quick, though cadenced gait, and the horse free to find time in the gallop to carry him correctly over the fence, was adopted by the celebrated Italian teams in international competition, made up of such horsemen as Antonelli, Lequio, and Borsarelli, in the period between the First and Second World Wars.

Today, English horsemen have shortened their stirrups, but they still control the horse, even over the obstacle. Many of them insist that the Italian riders, like the D'Inzeos, *did* control their horses, as well, and definitely intervened in their mounts' action when taking a fence. Nor is it exact to say that in the Caprilli system the horse is completely at liberty to pace himself in order to get over the obstacle. Actually, horse and rider must work this out together, as a unit and in coordinated action. This is the most difficult part of the classical Italian system, according to General Ubertalli, who notes that there is no system that will make every rider a champion any more than any university will make every student a genius. These days, perhaps, it is more fitting to talk of a "manner" rather than a "system," which is what always exists for all but a few champions to the manner born, the majority lacking true inspiration, while a system implies respect for precise rules.

Among Englishwomen, Patricia Smythe is unforgettable: thrice European champion, and extraordinary competitor in the three-day event, as well. Courageous and infinitely poised in the saddle, the superb Miss Smythe had a magnificent mount in Flanagan.

XLVI
THE IRISH

At the moment the Irish school is still going through a transitional phase, which began after the last war, and its members are renewing their squad of competitive riders. This is not surprising even in a country rich in horses and in a taste for things equestrian. After World War II most of Europe was constrained to salvage what was worth saving after the disaster that had struck not only European equitation but also the class and the mentality that had been most involved with it. In these circumstances, even international teams were made up of whatever riders were available to compete, and not too much thought was given to such subtleties as seat and style.

Nothing else could be done, since neither the old instructors nor the old academies were available. Everywhere the rule was to do the best one could and get over the obstacles. The problem for Ireland, as for other countries in Europe, was to set about reorganizing her competitive apparatus and recapture her ancient prestige in the field of jumpers.

Ringrose, that phenomenon, must be taken as the connecting link to a glorious past, a period before the war when Ireland had such horsemen as Lewis, Aherne, Cory, Dudgeon, and O'Dwyer, and horses like Limerick Lace and Burney Castle, who beat the finest of the German horses, then in their golden era. Years ago, Irish horsemen used short reins, and their horses were always on the defensive. Nowadays, taking Ringrose as their model, almost all use long reins, even though he seems to be the only one who knows how to use them well. He always uses his legs, no matter how fast the horse is going, with his neck and shoulders stretched forward, an action that other riders do not know how to manage or, perhaps, do not dare attempt.

When a horse is galloping quickly and freely, his hindquarters are not engaged. The horseman's legs do engage his mount, but by so doing he leaves it to the horse—acting without the hands to communicate—to resolve the most difficult problems on his own. If, however, the rider does not use any leg action, the horse is able to take advantage of his

complete freedom and natural equilibrium either to stop himself or to take off.

XLVII
THE GERMANS

It is common to hear that a horse that has been trained in the German manner will have lost all his personality and his natural equilibrium as well. German horses, which are less spirited than others, but extremely strong and athletic, reflect the iron training routine—almost military—to which they are subjected.

They execute orders with precision, like trained soldiers, and they wait for these orders, convinced of, rather than resigned to, the necessity for obedience. They seem delighted to submit themselves to a hard disciplinary rule. The horses as well as the German horsemen seem assured that they can make a good showing, no matter how difficult the course to be covered.

Fritz Thiedemann, the last great contributor to the grandeur of German equestrianism, serves as a perfect example, in that he was a bit rigid, not the slightest bit superficial, but severe, disciplined, extremely orderly, and highly intelligent. He left little to improvisation; all was method.

However, the German rider who has most struck the fancy of the public recently is Hans Günther Winkler, together with his famous mount, the mare Halla. We know that Winkler, who was one of Thiedemann's pupils, spent a good deal of time observing the D'Inzeo brothers at work, Piero, in particular, the same Piero who, when he rode at Stockholm, at the height of his powers, excited so much

202 *Taking a gate at the three-day event in Paris in 1924.*
203 *A German competitor goes into a stream during the three-day event in Berlin in 1936.*
204 *A German officer jumping a very rough ditch at Berlin, 1936.*
205 *Della Noce on Fiske at Paris.*
206 *The ditch at Berlin: One competitor jumps, while another, who has slipped to the bottom, watches.*
207 *Soare (Romania) riding Cabale, takes a spill at the Melbourne Olympics in 1956.*
208 *Raimondo d'Inzeo on Posillipo at the Olympic Grand Prix of 1960, which he won.*
209 *Molinar falls at the bars at the ditch, riding Uccello, during the three-day event at Stockholm.*
210 *Piazza di Siena in Rome, scene of the equestrian events of the 1960 Olympics: the Grand Prix Dressage event, with Patricia Galvin in the ring.*
211 *Klaus Wagner (Germany) in the Dressage phase of the three-day event at Stockholm.*
212 *A Russian officer at the Stockholm Grand Dressage event.*
213 *The winner of the Grand Dressage event at Stockholm, Captain St. Cyr on Master Rufus.*
214 *Sergeant Kastenmann (Sweden), winner of the Stockholm three-day event, kisses his horse after their victory. (The Swedish Ministry of Defense presented the horse to the sergeant.)*
215 *A perfect turn by St. Cyr on Master Rufus.*
216 *Rosemarie Springer (Germany) in a piaffe.*

202

203

204

205

206

207

208

209

211

212

213

214

215

216

217

219

221

218

220

222

223

224

admiration that the other competitors dismounted to watch him perform.

At the outset of his career, Winkler attempted to imitate the Italian system, but his legs kept going back, the same trouble that Mancinelli and D'Oriola had, and his jump was quite acrobatic, even though his very agile hands carried Halla over the fence with maximum precision. He had exercised Halla long and patiently on the flat so that she was capable of responding to any impulsion, with the right amount of impetus, and in perfect relation to such impulsion, so that she "basculated" over the obstacle with rare effectiveness and in perfect time, as required.

Notwithstanding, although he had the spirit of the system, Winkler could not apply it exactly because his feet were not properly positioned in the stirrups, which meant that his legs went back too far, almost to the horse's croup. Despite this, he won out. Gradually he corrected his error until his legs were more pendant, although he had a constant tendency to slip a bit at the fork. Consequently, when he brought his chest forward, he seemed to feel less secure in his seat, which hampered his arms and kept them from being completely independent, so that they could not stretch out to the maximum. Even though he was correct at the highest point of the parabola of the jump, he lost that correctness right afterward, since he was constrained to draw back a bit and resettle himself to regain his balance, with the result that, while he looked to be somewhat before the horse at the height of the parabola, he soon was seen to be behind his mount.

Winkler is a winner and a champion by virtue of his great intuitive understanding of horses and the assiduity and methodicalness with which he prepares himself and his mount. He is possessed of an observant, thoughtful nature, and a competitive spirit, not to mention wisdom in choosing his horses.

The Germans have established a great number of riding academies, but only the one at Warendorf is in charge of preparation for the Olympics. This school has created a group of fine young riders, but none of really championship stature as yet.

217 *Filatov (USSR), on Absent, magnificent winner of the Grand Prix for Dressage at the Olympics held in Rome in 1960, and a bronze-medal winner at the Tokyo Olympics.*

218 *Le Goff (France), on Image, in the final stretch of the three-day event in Rome.*

219 *A turn at the canter by Captain Guy Lefrant on Nicias, first in dressage in the three-day event in Rome.*

220 *Lawrence Morgan (Australia), on Salad Days, winner of the three-day event at the Rome Olympics.*

221 *Steeplechase course: Captain Nava on Arcidosso.*

222 *Cross-country phase of three-day event at the Rome Olympics: Lucio Tasca on Rahin comes to the twelfth fence at the end of an excellent round.*

223 *The Italian team that won a bronze medal for jumping at the 1960 Olympics: Raimondo d'Inzeo on Posillipo, Piero d'Inzeo on The Rock, and Antonio Oppes on The Scholar.*

224 *Lieutenant Bertoli in trials for the three-day event.*

XLVIII
THE SPANISH

Spain trains its competitive horsemen and dressage teams at the military school at Carabanchel, where civilians also study. The Spanish style derives from the Italian, though the stirrup leathers are a bit longer. Yielding to the horse is generally in proportion to the height and depth of the obstacle to be taken.

There has been a strong interest in equitation among the young people. Francisco Goyoago, one of the stars of the Spanish international team, is a finished horseman, blessed with a fine seat, courage, style, and competitive spirit. Some of his performances have been marked as perfect. Goyoago has had two wonderful jumpers in Quorum and Quonian. Goyoago's wife is also a fine rider, not reckless but intent, and showing the results of her husband's excellent instruction. He is considered one of the world's finest horsemen, for his sensitivity, acuteness, and capacity. José Alvarez de Bohorques, Carlos Figueroas de Castillejos, and Angel Alonso Martín are all fine riders who show little of that lamentable Latin tendency to improvise.

Spain's great moment in equestrianism came in 1954, but now she has to look to training new horses, for on an average the Spanish horses run to about fifteen years of age.

The great Goyoago marked the end of his career as an international competitor in 1966, with a stupendous victory at Aquisgrana.

XLIX
THE HUNGARIANS

Of all the teams behind the Iron Curtain, the Hungarians showed most that old fire in their appearances in the West. Their spirited horsemanship, however, is not always profitable, and at times a bit uncontrolled and overly reckless.

István Suti, Imre Karcsu, Josef Baranyai, Lászlo Móra, and the horsewoman Melinda Szakal are none of them suave or sophisticated riders, but they are all spirited and capable of winning unexpectedly on the basis of their great competitive drive, even though their technique is sketchy. Outstanding as a competitor is Miss Szakal, who has unrivaled courage.

L
THE POLES

The Poles have produced a young, untrammeled team including Marciu Szopa Stepiniewski, Marian Babirecki, Janusz Nowak, and Wlaslav Byszewki, all passionate horsemen (true of many of their countrymen, being horse lovers by tradition). Perhaps a bit raw, they are nevertheless sure and firm in the most dramatic situations.

While they do not yet have another Adam Królikiewicz among them, they have good material to draw upon, for equitation has been added to the sports curriculum in a number of state schools and colleges. In the European Championship of 1967, Jan Kowalezyk placed fifth, riding Drobnicka.

LI
THE ARGENTINIANS

In Argentina, equitation is still very much an everyday pursuit, part of life for a great many people, and therefore quite straightforward and almost instinctive. There is a notable selection of riders to choose from for competition, and they are finished in the style of the Italian school. The Argentines pride themselves on not importing horses but on mounting animals bred only in their country. They would like to develop a breed that is well proportioned and sturdy for European conditions. They have many riding clubs and horsebreeders' associations, and some five million horses. They hope to bring this number to about eight million.

The Argentines' desire to emulate the Irish in creating show horses is not a vague aspiration, though it may well prove to be difficult to accomplish. Just as they have produced a polo pony, the Argentines would like to be able to select a big, solid, powerful horse for competitions. There is, however, a substantial difference in the way the Argentines and the Irish regard their horses. For the Irish, the horse is a part of the family, and selling him is an occasion for tears; Argentines generally regard their animals with diffidence, considering them servants, and no more. Thus it is hard to see how their selection can be as profound or subject over the years to the complete involvement required in dealing with every horse.

LII
THE SOVIETS

The Russians have been watched with a good deal of interest recently. Apart from affirming their worth in the person of Sergey Filatov (they have preserved a masterly line in dressage), the Russians stick to the traditional Cossack style of riding—with a very firm leg—adding a slightly pronounced displacement of the chest, and moving the center of gravity toward the forehand. On a course where galloping is easy, and where the obstacles are at some distance from each other, with no double jumps, the Russians' energy and competitive spirit make their teams efficient and effective, despite the fact that stylistically they are somewhat open to question. When the course is tortuous and complicated, however, their lack of polish becomes very apparent. They are nevertheless great natural horsemen, instinctive and brilliant.

LIII
THE BRAZILIANS

The most extraordinary rider today is the Brazilian Nelson Pessôa, who could be called a Teutonically trained Latin. An elegant, supple rider, Pessôa, born in Brazil, was educated, and underwent his technical preparation, in Germany and Switzerland. He knows his dressage to perfection; he applies his knowledge with the fluidity and verve of a Latin who has absorbed the principles of Caprilli.

Between Pessôa and Hans Winkler there is a difference, Pessôa being light, easy, and genial, and capable of improvis-ing on the spur of the moment; Winkler is much harder, even rigid, though he does tend toward a certain Caprillian smoothness—not for nothing has he spent a good deal of time studying the work of Raimondo d'Inzeo. Pessôa, in turn, has followed Winkler's work, adopting his way of changing gallop in the air, certain training exercises, and routines for developing specific muscles.

Few people have an idea of the intense amount of work Pessôa goes through in preparing for competition. He is masterly at conditioning his mounts for shoulder-in and quarter-in, the basis of the athletic preparation of a horse. (The Germans have got to the point of punishing a horse that is distracted enough not to step out on the right or on the left foot when necessary, even without being signaled to do so.)

We can see, then, that there is an evolution taking place in equitation, even though the public may hardly be aware of it. There are two factors behind this evolution: first, the exigencies of competition, with courses constantly becoming harder and more complicated; and second, the continual improvement in the horse and the constantly growing percentage of athletic animals in comparison to the continually lessening amount of time that both civilian and military horsemen are prepared to devote to work in the manège. This is bothersome for the superficial horseman but sublime for the more speculative.

Pessôa dedicates his free time to horses. He began to ride under the guidance of his father, a passionate horseman and breeder. An acute observer, Pessôa has profited from what he has studied in Mexican riders and their seat, the German way of working on the flat, and the sure way of riding in competition exhibited by the Italians. From all this he has drawn conclusions that permit him, today, to show the solid Mexican seat, with a deep fork and heels decisively turned down; the willing submission of his mount to even the most minimal action of his hands, and sacrificing a bit of the attitude of the neck and shoulders according to the German method of schooling; and, finally, a marked forward projection of chest and arms in the parabola of the jump, which is an action and attitude typically Italian.

In working, Pessôa always employs a snaffle bit, and has tended to pass from one with a heavy metal mouthpiece to a rubber one, showing a respect for the horse's mouth that speaks volumes. Notwithstanding, during preparation, Pessôa utilizes a collecting rein, which is not in the orthodox Italian style, inasmuch as the collecting rein is employed for the flexion of the neck and shoulders; the Italians prefer a *consistent* neck, even if it is exercised on occasions. For this reason, the first reaction of a horse to the hand action of Pessôa is an arching of his neck, with a simultaneous lessening of speed, an attitude that is neither spontaneous nor natural.

Another characteristic of Pessôa is seeking impulsion at the last measure of the gait before the obstacle. Pessôa has got to the point where he confronts even a wall at the walk, allowing the horse only one measure of the gallop. This favors exercising the spinal column and engaging the muscles and the withers so as to basculate over the obstacle with facility. Furthermore, to oblige the horse to give all his attention and to respect the obstacle, Pessôa leans two crossed barriers against the edge of a wall, making the horse jump within the angle they form. He never resorts to speed to increase the impulsion, but engages and strengthens the horse's parts to achieve his ends.

Working on the training field, Pessôa places a fence about fourteen feet from the obstacle to allow the horse to anticipate the basculation, thus securing the horse's concentration, and achieving more precision when he finally basculates over the obstacle itself. During the jump he gives the horse free rein, and will even abandon the reins if necessary. As aids, he uses his legs effectively, restricting their shift behind, and he does not use spurs (which give authority to the legs when they are unauthoritative or inopportune in their intervention).

After preparing the horse at the pace and trot, Pessôa works the animal at the slow canter, except in cases where his mount shows laziness. He does not use a standing martingale (as the English and Germans do), but prefers the running type in which the rings are adjusted, not to the height of the withers, but to that of the hip. After having obtained the horse's submission and his response to the slightest action of the hands, Pessôa, even when competing, keeps his hands up high or almost in contact with the withers, and by simply rounding his wrists toward the inside and in the direction of the stride easily diminishes the cadence of the gallop, and assures himself of the exact distance suitable for the jump to be made. The play of his hands therefore is the most interesting part of his riding style, for he uses neither his forearms nor his elbows, not to mention his shoulders.

By always engaging the hindquarters a bit more, and by liberating the forehand to the maximum possible, and striving to achieve a slow canter immediately after the jump has been taken, Pessoa increasingly leans back, then bends forward again at two measures before the obstacle, to follow perfectly.

LIV
THE AMERICANS

In recent years, the United States has selected a group of excellent horsemen of international caliber: William Steinkraus, Frank Chapot, Kathy Kusner, and the very young Jim Day. Unfortunately, this team could not participate in the last world championship competition since the American Horse Show Association was short of funds and could do no more than appeal to the generosity of the public. It should also be remembered that many of the horses at the Olympic training center in Gladstone, New Jersey, belong to private individuals or have been bought by people precisely to place them at the disposal of the Olympic team.

The Americans are trained by Bertalan de Nemethy, who was born in Hungary. He is competent, endowed with great ability, earnestness, and love for what he is doing, and above all, has an exquisite horsemanly quality. A man of great prestige, Nemethy has a great deal of influence over his students, who enter every trial as if they were taking an examination, and with the ingenuity that distinguishes every American. That talent is a compond of cleanness and correctness, correctness not only in the seat but in form and sportsmanship, as well, correctness in concern for the horse's mouth, correctness in chest carriage and in employment of the legs. True amateurs, the Americans have no "star complexes" or the jealous rivalry that goes with them.

They are easy in the saddle, affect no airs, and ignore the philosophy of the new dressage. They do not project themselves forward, diving, in the parabola of the jump, nor do they saw on the horse's mouth to hold him back. They gallop with their horses and jump with them, striving to harmonize their actions with the horse's needs; and because they do, every performance has an air of ease and lightness. This reflects well on their instructor, who, furthermore, has managed to obtain just the right horses: attentive, well conditioned, and light. Nemethy begins work in the manège, having them work at the walk and using the collecting reins. Even at the trot and canter, his work is methodical, always done with the collecting reins.

In the open, Nemethy uses snaffle reins on the horses, and initiates work that is mathematical in nature and designed to put the animals into condition to confront obstacles. Finally, always methodically, the horses are worked over the jumps and stopped whenever necessary, since all the horses are Thoroughbreds or highly spirited mounts, and therefore generally intolerant of precise controlled commands from their riders.

This is scrupulously progressive preparation, with much work on the longe, sometimes with the horses mounted; with constant employment of bars, some elementary dressage, little lateral shifting, and much work at the trot and pace on hills. Captain Nemethy's objective is not necessarily to win—but to ride well.

We must mention the victory of Miss Patricia Galvin in the grand dressage event at the Pan-American Games held in Brazil, as well as the taking of the three-day event by Michael Page, Kevin Freeman, and William Haggard.

Since they use highly bred horses, the Americans sometimes use a gag below the snaffle bit, a cruel device that rests on the lowest part of the nose, near the nostrils. When the rider pulls on the reins, two effects are produced: Respiration is impeded and pain is produced in the bars.

Because of their imperfect foot position in the stirrups, some of the American riders tend to have their legs swinging even in the trot, and when they lower the point of the foot in a jump, their legs in consequence slide backward. It was in the United States the theory arose that it is advantageous to force down on the stirrups at the moment the horse takes off for his jump and to proceed independently out of the saddle in order to allow the horse to get maximum elevation, getting together with the horse during the descent. The consequence to the forehand is easy to imagine. Nevertheless, this idea is now being taken up in England. For example, Patricia Smythe usually jumps in this style, and not (we insist) just accidentally.

LV
THE MEXICANS

A fleeting, ephemeral phenomenon was the fabulous success of the Mexican riders around 1954. They arrived in Europe with solid, athletic mounts (a famous one was Arete), guided by Colonel Mariles, put in the saddle by German masters, and displayed a beautiful interpretation of the Caprilli system.

The horses were of Mexican origin, more strong than elegant, and accordingly more rugged than slender, but beautifully muscled. They certainly did not represent the ideal of the show horse envisioned by the experts and lovers of the classic. Very much "forward," they had a tendency to fling themselves forward, and usually changed gallop, but their equilibrium at the opportune moment was perfect. They managed to turn in a minimum of space, thanks to their German schooling, and to change gait and rhythm. Prompt to respond and powerful in their takeoff, they were more able to achieve elevation than spread.

Their riders had mixed the best of all the schools and added the ferment of their own natural and instinctive *charro* style of riding. As far as legs and back are concerned, their seat was Italian, but their hands moved with extreme obvious freedom. The chest often moved brusquely to the sides. The hands, which gave the horse's mouth complete freedom when going over the obstacle, persistently bothered the horse on the flat with empty gestures that were designed to keep the animal under pressure without permitting him to hurtle, and to keep him supple and brilliant and at all times with his hindquarters under full impulsion. On the flat, as a matter of fact, it looked as if a constant battle were being waged by horse and rider, a fight that ceased near any obstacle. Going over the fence, the Mexicans held their hands very low, their legs going back, just as with the Americans, and the chest shifted forward. They yielded completely, and their horses jumped with heads low, while generally cantering with their heads to the wind.

The Mexican style can be considered a product of great physical training in equitation and jumping, extraordinary confidence in the saddle, unlimited faith in the mount's capacities, and quick reflexes that keep the rider, from one moment to the next, master of the problems of balance. Their acrobatic attitude deprives them of the classicality that characterizes the Italian style, but it gives them a touch of robustness and picturesqueness that attracts the general public. It is interesting to observe that the Mexicans, following the German custom, use a running martingale, but one with a strap so short that its effect is more restrictive than that of the standing type.

LVI

COMPETITION

The fact that competition and show riding allow for some compromise and adaptation in style should not lead one to equivocate between there being a correct way to jump and the idea of horse and rider as a unit and, on the other hand, the desire to take a jump no matter how. The rider should not fool himself into thinking that he can win without style and that in the hurry-scurry of taking the same mount over the same jumps in the wrong way, the horse will finally adapt

himself to the rider's errors and assume unnatural attitudes to compensate for his defects. What about yielding?

The horse learns to contract his neck and shoulders and lower his head to avoid suffering. If he is ridden correctly, however, he will take any obstacle, and can go months before jumping again because he remains in condition. On the other hand, equestrian events are competitions, and the man who makes the fewest mistakes will win, whether or not he has ridden well. A good horseman, though, has above all the responsibility of respecting the needs of his horse. Notwithstanding, because show riding is becoming more and more an exercise in sophisticated acrobatics, many people sustain the theory that a more complex style is now called for, combining Caprilli's principles with some concessions to dressage techniques. Actually, Caprilli considered the horse as an element in field maneuvers, and therefore did not bother himself with conditioning the horse, except perhaps to exercise those muscles that were necessary for straightforward locomotion. Thus was show riding born.

Since the first requirement of a hunter is to know how to take obstacles in the field surely and with ease, to evaluate horses destined for work in the hunting field, the Irish at the end of the last century—followed by the English, then the French, and then almost all the rest of Europe—organized horse shows and obstacle races. These shows, besides serving as a means of selection, also served to carry to the sphere of sport the work done in the cavalry regiments, which by that time had their only outlet on the racecourse; they helped determine new ways of riding in order to take artificial obstacles that imitated the natural ones found in the European countryside.

When these competitions began, errors of the forehand were penalized more heavily than those committed by the hindquarters, since the first were considered to be more serious in the hunting field, with its fixed obstacles more damaging to the horse. Later, every effort was bent toward making the horse-show events more spectacular, more varied, more arduous, and as fast as possible, until the point was reached where the races became an end in themselves, their original purpose forgotten. Tracks became more difficult and obstacles more impressive. This led, of course, to the gradual formation of a class of riders who specialized in jumping.

Celebrated horse shows and competitions today are those held in New York, Toronto, London, Dublin, Paris, Zurich, Stockholm, Rome, Siena, Geneva, Nice, Aquisgrana, and Viña del Mar. Competitions include the fault-and-out, the American relay race, the test-of-endurance race, and various hunting-class events. Penalties are marked in points, where time is optional; or in seconds, where errors are converted into seconds and then added to the total time needed to complete the course. The stopwatch was so instrumental in revolutionizing the final preparation and selection of jumpers that various types of courses were added to accommodate unique mounts, the *à barrage* course for the powerful horse, the hunting-class courses for the well-balanced, poised horse, and timed courses for fast, manageable horses.

PART THREE

EQUESTRIAN OLYMPIC GAMES

I
DEVELOPMENT

The end of the nineteenth century saw the advent of the railway and the steam turbine, and the consequent loss of any valid reason to train a horse for speed and endurance over a long distance. But because the spirit of competition had not died, nor had horsemen changed, riders continued to perfect their skills; and their horses were conditioned to show the stamina and style needed to win in national and international meets. Such contests, as well as international competitions in other sports, naturally set men to thinking of the oldest international meet of all, the Olympic Games.

The man primarily responsible for the modern cycle of Olympic Games was Baron Pierre de Coubertin, a Frenchman. Through his efforts and those of interested sportsmen throughout the world, an International Olympic Committee was organized in 1894. In 1896, the first of the modern Olympic Games was held, appropriately enough, in Athens, dedicated to sport, physical fitness, and international amity. As is invariably true when many nations must live by one rule, the International Olympic Committee's greatest difficulty occurred in establishing the rules for each of the Olympic events, as each country considered any variation from its own regulations an affront to its sovereignty.

The inclusion of equestrian events came at the instigation of Count Clarence von Rosen, Master of the Horse to the King of Sweden, who proposed them to the meeting of the International Olympic Committee held at Athens in 1906. His suggestion was not well received, for little general interest was shown in the events and it was felt that the expense of mounting equestrian events would be out of all proportion to their attraction. A year later, however, the committee decided to include them in the program of the 1908 Games at London, after preparation of the necessary rules and regulations. Polo was to be an optional event, since it was an expensive sport, and there were few nations with high-caliber teams to compete. In time, it was dropped completely.

Just prior to the London Olympics, the International Horse Show Committee dropped the entries for the equestrian events; therefore these contests were first included in the Games at Stockholm, in 1912, with eleven nations participating. The equestrian events really came into their own after the First World War, and were a notable success in Antwerp in 1920, when a modified program was offered. This success encouraged the Baron to urge the International Committee at Lausanne to draw up a definitive program for the events, which was done, and is still followed today.

The equestrian events comprise three phases: the first, formerly called The Military and now known as the Three-Day Event, is the competition of competitions, an equestrian marathon divided into the Dressage Test, Cross-Country (including Speed, Endurance, and Steeplechase trials), and Show Jumping, all open to teams and to individual competitors. The second major event is the Prix des Nations, a show-jumping competition for teams and individuals; and the Grand Prix de Dressage, also for teams and individuals.

Individual jumping competitions evolved into team endeavors, with the first three contestants to finish receiving medals, as in the Three-Day Event. The number of participants from each country in each of the competitions was increased from three to six in the individual and from two to four in the team contests, the latter becoming a firm three.

The Three-Day Event is so spectacular that it is sometimes included in the programs of national and international horse shows. It has gained wide popularity in England, Ireland, Germany, France, the United States, and Australia. The first day's event, the Dressage Test, held in a 60-by-20-meter regulation arena, lacks the variety or complexity of the classical Grand Dressage, but does require the animal's absolute balance, obedience, manageability, and responsiveness. Time allowed for the course is 7½ minutes, with a half-point penalty for each second in excess. Penalties for first, second, third, and fourth faults are points 2, 5, 10, and elimination, respectively. Movements are scored from 0 to 6, with a maximum score of 138 points.

The second day's program includes the endurance and speed tests, the steeplechase, and the cross-country test to be completed without a break over a total course of 32,700 meters, covering swamp roads and tracks, which riders are allowed to survey on foot the day before the event. Exceeding the time limit for any of these trials results in elimination, while extra points are earned for better time over the steeplechase and the cross-country courses. On the latter, two penalties, of from 2 to 8 points, are also incurred for falls, refusals, disobedience, and deviation from the course itself. The steeplechase (3,600 meters), with its various obstacles (ditches, spa rails, fences, and walls), is largely judged according to the rider's time and general performance, while the more difficult cross-country route (7,200 meters), which can be taken at any gait, tests the skill of both rider and horse under the natural conditions of open terrain.

The show jumping, usually held on the third day, closes the Three-Day Event. On a 1,000-meter course of 12 obstacles to be taken at 400 meters per minute, it is noted more for its test of the horse's stamina and suppleness, after the grueling events of the previous day, than for any peculiar difficulties. Penalties are for errors in direction, disobedience, falls, and refusals, with elimination for four refusals.

Although the competitions of the Three-Day Event may be spread over four days, if there is a large number of entrants and if the order of the tests is rearranged, according to the Rules Committee, the title given to this Olympic event is no misnomer. Formerly, contestants were always accommodated within the prescribed period.

The following is the sequence used in the Dressage Test in the 1964 Olympics, held in Tokyo.

1.	A	Enter at a collected canter.
	x	Halt. Salute.
2.	x	Proceed at ordinary trot (sitting).
	c	Track to the right.
	MXK	Change rein at extended trot (rising).
3.	KAF	Ordinary trot (sitting).
	FXH	Change rein extended trot (rising).
4.	HCMB	Ordinary trot (rising).
5.	B	Turn right at ordinary trot (sitting).
	x	Halt. Immobility five seconds. Move off at collected trot (sitting).
	E	Track to the left.
	EKAF	Collected trot (sitting).
6.	FX	On two tracks.
	XM	On two tracks.
7.	c	Ordinary walk.
	HXF	Change rein at extended walk.
8.	F	Collected trot (sitting).
	KX	On two tracks.
	HX	On two tracks.
9.	c	Halt. Rein back six steps. Move off at ordinary walk without halting.
10.	CM	Ordinary walk.
	M	Collected canter to the right.
11.	F	Half circle ten meters' diameter.
	BCS	Counter-canter.
12.	s	Ordinary trot (sitting).
	V	Collected canter to the left.
13.	K	Half circle ten meters' diameter.
	ECR	Counter-canter.
14.	R	Ordinary trot (sitting).
	P	Collected canter to the right.
15.	KHC	Extended canter.
16.	CM	Ordinary walk.
	MXK	Change rein at extended walk.
17.	K	Collected canter to the left.
	FMC	Extended canter.
18.	CHE	Ordinary trot (sitting).
19.	E	Collected canter to the left.
	A	Down center line.
	G	Halt. Salute. Leave the arena at free walk.

225 226 *Part of the cross-country event at Pratoni del Vivaro, near Rome. The riders are in correct and elegant positions.*

227 228 *Mauro Checcoli, gold-medal winner of the three-day event at the Tokyo Olympics, on Surbean in the jumping and dressage trials and the third and first events respectively. The Italian team, which also included Paolo Angioni on King, and Giuseppe Ravano on Royal Love also won the team award, and was followed by the United States, Germany, Ireland, USSR, Argentina, Australia, France, and Mexico, in that order. The Italian team owed its exceptional performance to the solid, painstaking preparation, both technical and moral, given it by its Captain, the Marquis Fabio Mangilli.*

229 *Le Goff (France), on Léopard, at the Tokyo three-day event.*

230 *Michael Page (United States), on Grasshopper, at the three-day event of the Tokyo Olympics.*

231 *H. Wiley (United States) on Master Williams.*

232 *Carrying a saddle in the proper way, with stirrups run up on their leathers and with the girth (buckled to the billets on the right) lying over the seat.*

233 *How to bridle a horse: With the bridle over the forearm, bring out the horse and, having removed the halter (if used), pass the reins over the horse's neck so that he can be restrained if he should attempt to get away. Bring your right shoulder even with the horse's near shoulder. With the right hand, slide the crownpiece of the bridle along the top of the horse's nose and, with the palm of the left hand, place the snaffle between his lips. If he resists, make him open his mouth by sticking your index finger between the bars. To check the length of the cheekstraps, see that the snaffle lies just at the corners of the mouth, without strain (the mouthpiece of the curb bit lies just underneath). Then buckle both crownpiece and throat latch.*

234 235 *The proper way to hold the reins when leading a horse.*

236 237 *To saddle (standing on the near side), after smoothing the hair of the back, place the saddle pad and the saddle a bit forward of its proper position; then slide it into place, thus smoothing the hair of the withers. Make sure that neither pad nor saddle presses against the withers.*

238 *Remove the girth from the seat from the far side, attach it first to the billet straps on the far side, then pass it under the barrel to the near side. If the horse wears a martingale, attach it to the girth (attaching the other end of the martingale to the noseband or running the snaffle reins through its rings, as required).*

239 *Buckle the girth to the billets on the near side, but do not pull it too tightly. The girth should be just loose enough to allow you to insert three fingers at the ribs and slide them down easily to the brisket, where the strap should be snug.*

240 *Stretching the forelegs to smooth any wrinkles away.*

241 *Readjusting the girth after walking the horse a bit.*

242 *Measuring the stirrup leathers.*

243–247 *Mounting, and the correct seat.*

248–251 *Mounting with assistance, or "getting a leg up."*

252 *Adjusting the length of the stirrup leathers while in the saddle.*

253 *Trying the stirrups.*

254 *Walking.*

255–257 *Trotting.*

258 259 260 *Galloping.*

261 *Vaulting from the saddle.*

262 263 *Fastening the curb chain is done by turning it to form a flat chain, then hooking into the "s" curb hook one of the first links of the chain. Three fingers should be able to pass freely between curb bit and chain.*

227

228

229

230

231

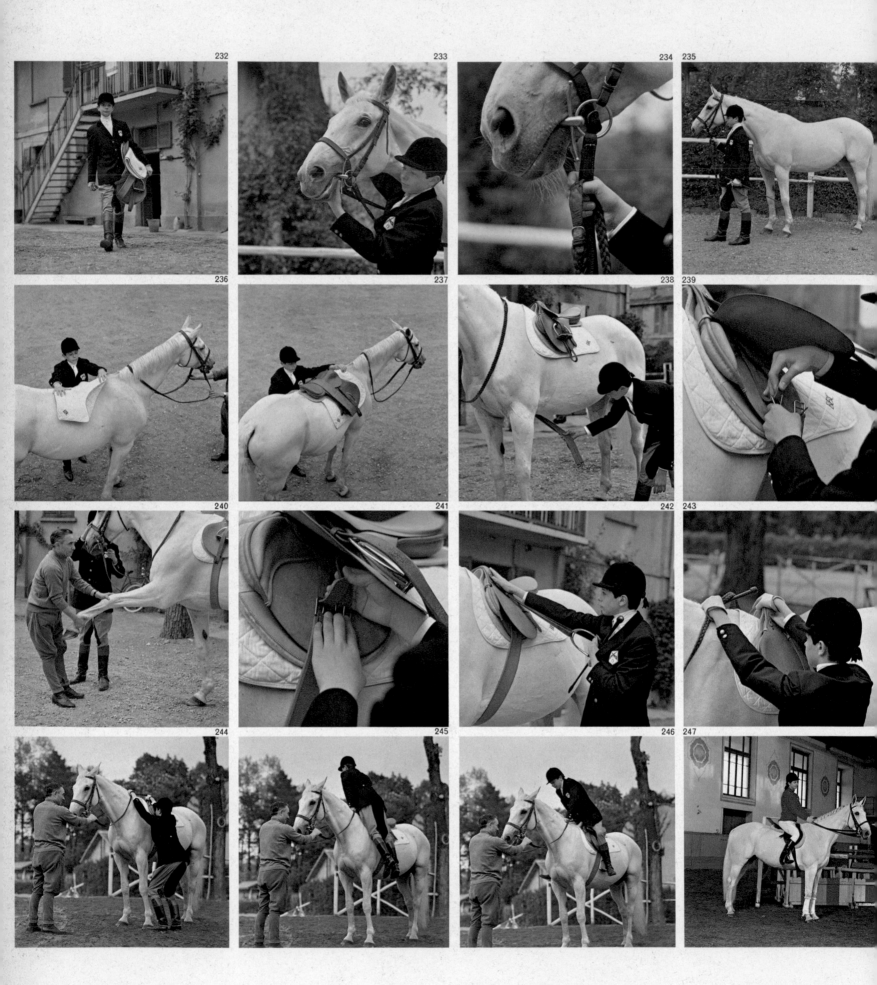

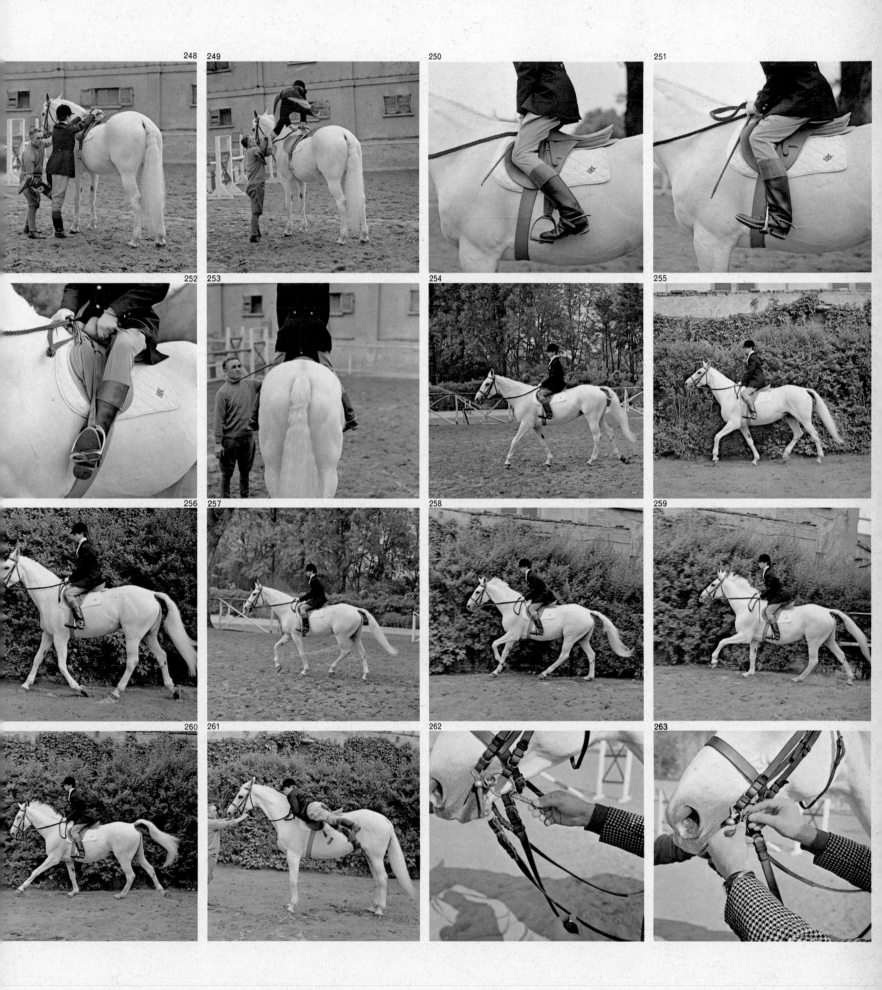

264 265

266

267 268

The Grand Dressage is performed in a 60-by-20-meter arena for 13 brilliant minutes, displaying the animal's calmness, keenness, and manageableness, as well as his freedom, and his lightness of paces. The walk should be free and easy; the work at the trot, both slow and extended, including the slow trot, the halt, run back, advance, ordinary turns and those on the haunches, as well as small circles at that same gait, should be performed with little visible effort on the part of rider and horse. The work at the canter, slow and extended, should include ordinary turns and small circles, canter from a halted position, figure eight, with and without change of leg, a flying change of leg on a straight line at least four times, and a turn on the haunches at an extended canter. The horse at all paces should be light, balanced, and on the bit, carrying his head with composure and steadiness. At all turns and circles, the animal should be flexed to the inside and bent around the rider's inside leg. Failure to execute any of the above-mentioned movements is penalized by one point the first time and five points each time thereafter with the judges reserving the right to ask a contestant to execute any movements and to repeat movements already executed.

The Prix des Nations or the show-jumping competition is the last event in the equestrian Olympic Games, and is followed by the Closing Ceremony. The obstacles, 13 or 14 in number, necessitate 16 to 20 jumps at a minimum height of 1.30 meters and a maximum height of 1.60 meters (against a maximum of 1.20 for the stadium jump), with only 2 upright obstacles at the latter height, and a water jump with a spread of 4.50 meters, including a low fence on the takeoff side. Spread obstacles (open ditch, bars, spa, and oxer) should have a span of 1.50 to 2.20. The length of the course depends on the dimensions of the stadium but it should not exceed 1,100 meters. Exceeding the time limit is penalized by a quarter of a point for each second over, but completion under the time limit offers no premium. Performance penalties are for disobedience, knockdowns, falls of horse or rider, and elimination on a third disobedience. A jump-off over six obstacles from 1.40 to 1.80 meters in height is mandatory both for individual competitors and for teams, in case of a tie, with no penalties for time except in the event of a tie, in which case the better time will determine the winner.

Unlike all other Olympic competitions, equestrian events were for many years military in character, with only cavalrymen entered. Gradually, as the cavalry disappeared, the emphasis shifted to the civilian, where it has remained. The transformation is dramatized in the large increase in the number of national horse shows held in all equestrian-minded countries, as well as in the equestrian events of the Games, which constitute the supreme international championship competitions. In addition to the sporting interest, the events have served to demonstrate the level of equitation of the various countries and, to some degree, their methods of training and instruction. The standards and methods of the winning countries at the Games have always been studied with great interest and, in particular instances, have been partly or wholly adopted by other countries. A certain degree of uniformity and progress, especially in the show-jumping seat and the general concept of dressage, has been noticeable since the first equestrian events in Stockholm in 1912.

264–268 Trotting over poles laid on the ground, a basic exercise for learning to maintain balance.

OLYMPIC INDIVIDUAL GOLD MEDALS

YEAR	THREE-DAY EVENT	JUMPING (PRIX DES NATIONS)
1912	Nordlander (Sweden)	Cariou (France)
1920	Mörner (Sweden)	Lequio (Italy)
1924	Van Zijp (The Netherlands)	Gemuseus (Switzerland)
1928	De Mortanges (The Netherlands)	Ventura (Czechoslovakia)
1932	De Mortanges (The Netherlands)	Nishi (Japan)
1936	Stubbendorf (Germany)	Hasse (Germany)
1948	Chevalier (France)	Mariles (Mexico)
1952	Blixen-Finecke (Sweden)	D'Oriola (France)
1956	Kastenmann (Sweden)	Winkler (Germany)
1960	Morgan (Australia)	R. d'Inzeo (Italy)
1964	Checcoli (Italy)	D'Oriola (France)
1968	Guyon (France)	Steinkraus (United States)

OLYMPIC TEAM MEDALS—THREE-DAY EVENT

YEAR	LOCALITY	GOLD	SILVER	BRONZE
1912	Stockholm	Sweden	Germany	United States
1920	Antwerp	Sweden	Italy	Belgium
1924	Paris	The Netherlands	Sweden	Italy
1928	Amsterdam	The Netherlands	Norway	Poland
1932	Los Angeles	United States	The Netherlands	—
1936	Berlin	Germany	Poland	Great Britain
1948	London	United States	Sweden	Mexico
1952	Helsinki	Sweden	Germany	United States
1956	Stockholm	Great Britain	Germany	Canada
1960	Rome	Australia	Switzerland	France
1964	Tokyo	Italy	United States	Germany
1968	Mexico	Great Britain	United States	Australia

OLYMPIC TEAM MEDALS FOR JUMPING (PRIX DES NATIONS)

YEAR	LOCALITY	GOLD	SILVER	BRONZE
1912	Stockholm	Sweden	France	Germany
1920	Antwerp	Sweden	Belgium	Italy
1924	Paris	Sweden	Switzerland	Portugal
1928	Amsterdam	Spain	Poland	Sweden
1932	Los Angeles	—	—	—
1936	Berlin	Germany	The Netherlands	Portugal
1948	London	Mexico	Spain	Great Britain
1952	Helsinki	Great Britain	Chile	United States
1956	Stockholm	Germany	Italy	Great Britain
1960	Rome	Germany	United States	Italy
1964	Tokyo	Germany	France	Italy
1968	Mexico	Canada	France	Germany

N.B. The Olympics were not held in the years 1916, 1940, and 1944.

II
SCHOOLS

In the United States, schools have been founded for young people who wish to specialize in dressage. Similarly, in Belgium, France, and England riding schools and equestrian associations have recently enjoyed a marked increase in students and memberships. The most important British associations are the British Society and the British Show Jumping Association, while West Germany counts 1,500 equitation societies, of which 136 are affiliated with the International Equestrian Federation (FEI). At Dortmund and Aix-la-Chapelle, the shows attract over 50,000 spectators yearly.

Unlike the other nations that participate in the Olympic equestrian events, the Russians have no formal associations for training horses or riders for the Games, but instead have enormous sporting societies that boast fine horses and riders of international quality. Among the best known of these Russian groups are Spartak, Bureviestnik, Urasgiay, and Dinamo. Equitation enthusiasts manage to keep abreast of the latest happenings in international equestrian circles, but still cling to some of their own traditional methods.

PART FOUR

THEORY

THIS SECTION, actually an appendix to the preceding material, explains the concepts and ideas presented in Caprilli's notes, which, written as they were for instructors, naturally presumed an understanding of elementals.

Riding is a discipline that becomes a sport and an art when the horseman, through the application of established rules, arrives at a perfect understanding with his horse so that he can make the animal sense exactly what is expected of him. At the same time that he exploits the horse's forward movement, the rider eases and seconds his exertions. According to our principles, he achieves this by striving constantly to maintain his fixed center of gravity in vertical alignment with the changing center of gravity of his mount.

It should be remembered that the horseman, the prime mover, is so much dead weight as far as the horse, who performs the action, though subservient to the will of the rider, is concerned. No proper understanding, therefore, can ever be achieved unless it be through effectively maintaining the seat, that is, through employing a particular disposition of the body in the saddle, as prescribed by a given school. To paraphrase Caprilli:

The horse has a natural center of gravity that shifts as he changes gait and as changes occur in the terrain. The average mount weighs between 900 and 1,200 pounds, while the average rider tips the scales at about 160. Thus, the horse finds himself carrying upon his back a weight equivalent to about one sixth his own, a burden more or less unstable and having a tendency to displace his own center of gravity. For that reason, the rider's concern must be to reduce to the minimum the disparity between those two centers of gravity, the natural one and that resulting from his own weight in the saddle, so as to cooperate with the horse as he moves, rather than oppose him.

Since all equitation, at any time, is predicated upon propulsive force, everything reduces itself to the problems of equilibrium and seat, with the horseman's legs commanding the forward movement or a change in direction through the haunches, which impulsion the hands must act to control and distribute. The objective, therefore, is to provoke movement and direct its effects.

In substance, the principles are simple enough: the horse's neck and shoulders are a lever at whose extremity the head acts as a mobile, suspended weight. Any retraction or extension of this pendulum causes the horse's center of gravity to move from the forehand to the hindquarters or vice versa, modifying the balance of his entire body. As the haunches are the fulcrum of the propulsive force, the source of the motive power that is distributed throughout the body, the hindquarters are the part of the body vulnerable to the variations in the animal's center of gravity, compounded with those of the rider.

Riding a horse still remains an activity that carries a social cachet. The trouble, however, is that people want to master it quickly, get showy results, do something spectacular, a failing that has always been apparent in every field of endeavor, and even more so today, in this age of speed. On the other hand, the idea of learning to ride a horse in a short time and master one's mount quickly is not a new one. *Equitation des gens pressés* is an ironic book written at the beginning of this century by that man of the world and man about horses, the Count of Comminges.

In Italy, as well, some decades prior to that publication, volumes were appearing that purported to teach riding in three hours, in five days, and so on. It was not without bitterness that Count d'Aure, one of the most perceptive and polished horsemen that France has known, unhesitatingly qualified his own riding academy as "an industrial establishment receiving men of all ages and types desirous of becoming horsemen in twenty lessons."

On the other hand, if, up to a certain point, it is impossible to separate the training of the horse from the education of the horseman, paradoxical though it may be even today, one can say, in the celebrated phrase of Gustave le Bon, "By the sole fact of being on horseback, one is unconsciously breaking in or breaking down."

A horse that is stiff and rigid in action is a torment to the rider, just as the unyielding equestrian, tense and jerky to his movements, provokes rebellion on the part of his mount, which, in his turn, tends to become taut in order to mitigate the irritation he is suffering. In such conflict, the horse is always the stronger, for while the rider has only saddle, stirrups, and reins to support him, aside from his mount, the horse has four very firm points of contact with solid ground.

Above all, remember that a man can never prevail over a horse by using force, but only through the seat, through balance, by choosing his time and using his intuition and, once more, that profound knowledge of the character and spirit of the animal. It is for just that reason that horse and horseman develop a relationship that goes beyond the reins, the knees, the legs, the shift in weight or even, in extreme instances, the whip. There is a sentimental rapport that is based upon reciprocal esteem and trust.

It should also be remembered that the hands, our hands, are a vexation to all animals, a boon to us that terrifies them. We should approach a horse without gesticulating, and win his confidence—once assured he hasn't the nasty habit of biting—by bringing the face up close to his head and letting the animal rest his chin on our shoulder. By whistling to the horse, we can start him getting acquainted with us and accustomed to the pleasure of our company.

A pernicious habit of instructors, stemming from the military, is that of vaunting oneself before the pupil, almost as if to accentuate the pupil's deficiencies and throw his inadequacies in his face. On the contrary, a teacher should avoid any humiliation of a student, see that he does not fall, and never let him get into a state where he is afraid to do anything rather than make a mistake. Remember that the beginner in the saddle is completely defenseless, since he lacks a firm seat and feels ill at ease with the animal and movement. What is necessary, therefore, is to give the novice faith in himself and in the horse, and make him understand the animal's character and characteristics, his exigencies and limits—things that are just that much more strange to the student if he has been brought up in the city, away from any possibility of becoming familiar with animals and of studying and understanding them.

It is important to inculcate in the student, gradually, confidence in the horse, and to teach him to approach him gently. In describing the seat, the instructor should make the student understand the precise function of the knee and the mechanical necessity that calls for keeping the heels low, as well as respect for the horse's mouth and loins. Finally, the student should be told how he is to employ his hands, legs, and trunk.

Avoid incorrect positions from the very outset of instruction, and try to analyze just why the student assumes one attitude in the saddle in preference to all others, which must be due to his physique (tall or short, heavy-legged, full- or flat-hipped, flat- or full-bellied, long- or short-waisted, and so on), his conformation to the saddle, the set of his back, the horse's position, or the relative speed of the gait.

A horseman without a proper seat will never be master of his horse, but at his mount's mercy. The seat is, in truth, an attainment of no mean worth, for it represents constant control over the coordination of all movement while always maintaining flexibility, that is, never *relaxing* into rigidity, even though one particular action—keeping the heels low—does require a bit of effort. One's position in the saddle is conditioned by the knees and the thigh muscles, particularly those that are used to fix the knees and keep the heels low.

By keeping the heels low, maintaining the sole at such an angle that the lowest part of the foot is that nearest the horse, by taking care that the toes are turned slightly inward, toward the horse, a rider flattens and stimulates the muscles of the hips, thighs, and knees, which keeps the fork from drawing up short, holds the calves in place, and obviates the heels' jabbing the spurs into the horse's barrel. To me, all this does not entail rigidity, but firmness, and it is firmness in the saddle that is wanted. Firmness in the saddle comes from balance and from the resistance offered by the thighs and

knees to the flaps, and the support given by the stirrups.

Keeping the heels low, therefore, apart from any pressure upon the tread of the stirrups, is up to the rider, and depends upon his conscious effort. He must, accordingly, exercise the lateral and anterior leg muscles and move the tibiotarsal joint. Such exercise over a long period of time will strengthen the leg and thigh muscles, so that the proper position in the saddle can be maintained.

As for trotting without stirrups, which many believe indispensable toward the acquiring of a firm seat, this is useful in special cases, where done in moderation. On the other hand, this is often not only useless but even deleterious, since it can become an activity sufficiently annoying to the rider to make him stiffen in the saddle. Actually, the best way of attaining one's equilibrium in the saddle is by riding out over somewhat uneven terrain. The continual slight variations in equilibrium will teach the rider to seek his balance and know when he has found it, besides building his confidence through accustoming him to the horse's movement.

The rider should exert as little pressure as possible upon the horse's mouth, keeping his hands light and advancing them whenever the horse must extend his neck and shoulders. In these conditions, nothing can keep the horse from drawing his head back, which is all to the good, but too often the hands may interfere when the horse extends and stretches his neck, which is disastrous, and most annoying to the horse, who must then modify his balance.

This is the basis of all riding in the field, and you cannot insist upon it too much. The novice should advance his hands every time the horse finds it necessary to extend his neck. This should be done during every ride, no matter how easy or difficult it may be. It should be done in the air, while jumping, and it should even be done, lightly, when you wish the horse to quicken his gait or shift his weight forward.

To sum up, a rider must have a seat that permits him: (1) to have certain parts of his body in absolutely fixed position so that he can control his own equilibrium and create the proper forces required to overcome inertia; (2) to leave his arms free for the reins and therefore disengaged from the action of his trunk; (3) to position his weight, when necessary, over that portion of the horse's body that will least suffer from it, that is, over the forehand, the transverse plane, going from the base of the withers, or the plane of the stirrup leathers; (4) to free the horse's back of his weight, so that the contractions of the animal's dorsal muscles (the most important in transmitting impulsion) are not hindered; (5) to aid, rather than impede, the horse's changing his equilibrium through the shifting of the upper part of the body; and (6) to resist exploiting the pulling force exerted by the bars, but rather employ them in a flexible, measured, and timely way.

The rider should also learn to move his hands in such a manner as to: (1) communicate his wishes to the horse's mouth in the most direct, simplest, and clearest way; (2) give the horse sufficient support to enable him to make a particular muscular contraction (in response to the force exerted) without impelling him to efforts that might damage his spine; (3) permit the neck and shoulders sufficient play to allow their maximum extension.

Once the horse is in motion, to keep with him requires knees to be fixed firmly in position (also necessary to a good seat); but also, the knees must be flexible (while remaining in one spot). The knee joints must bend so as to permit the hips, which are slanted forward, to lift the rider's weight. The knees and pelvis forming the fork are the intermediaries between legs and chest, while the thighs are in contact with the saddle, and function both as hinge and shock absorbers.

General Ubertalli wrote: "One might say, to give the final idea on the seat, that from the knees down, the rider's body is at his disposition, to assure his firmness and stability, while from the knees up, his body is at the disposition of his mount, since the horse imposes his exigencies here."

It seems to me opportune, at this point, to mention something perhaps not sufficiently considered by riders and riding instructors—the diversity in force and strength shown in the saddle by different riders owing to differences in physique. For instance, it is generally maintained that a very tall person will never make a good rider, which is not true, since it is not height but suppleness that counts, and which can, further, compensate for any lack of equilibrium resulting from the extra length between head and shoulders and the center of gravity. Because of these physical differences in riders, their saddles must be adapted to them. This is an important consideration.

According to General Ubertalli, a fine horseman and a great theoretician on Caprilli's system: "Physical anomalies cause abnormal sensitivity and, consequently, confused thinking. Such defects can lead a person to the point of thinking that he is right and believing that he understands the system perfectly and is putting it into practice while he is, actually, doing just the opposite"—a very delicate situation, as is also the psychological rapport between student and horse. The student should pet his mount, talk to him, and accompany actions with words and any objects identified with them so that the horse learns to trust him, even in the stable. Few of us have any idea just how much of what we are saying concerning him the horse can understand.

To lead a horse, one cannot repeat too often that he should be held on a short rein, that is, held about four inches from the bit, with the index finger held between the two reins and the fist closed. Never look a horse in the eye when leading him, as this tends to make him halt, but do talk to him as you go. If the ground is uneven, stony, or dangerous, give him a bit more rein and point out the difficulties to him, while leading him firmly, without frightening him.

In the saddle, a rider should always maintain his seat, never abandoning himself to the movement of the gait even when at the walk, but keeping agile and not stiffening, following, with his pelvis, the almost rotary and undulating motion of the horse's back, while his hands accompany the movement of the neck and shoulders, maintaining constant contact with the horse's mouth. The rider, however, should at all times be ready to follow the horse if he takes any liberties. Only after working should the reins be abandoned, to make the horse understand that the walk or pace is not to be held as a steady gait but is used merely to let him stretch himself and work out.

The sitting trot, in which the crotch touches the saddle each time a diagonal pair of legs hits the ground, is to be used only in exceptional cases. It is employed to collect the animal, which is a complex exercise not to be attempted under any circumstances by a novice. The standard trot used is the posting or English trot. In this, the rider brings his chest up when the hooves touch ground on one beat and relaxes into the saddle on the second beat. The movement should be easy, the rider taking up the rhythm of the horse's back in action. Since the knees serve as the fulcrum, the chest will obviously move on an oblique line. The rider should come up to the trot on the left or right diagonal motion and touch the saddle when the near or off fore touches ground. On curves, it is better to post when the inner fore touches down, to facilitate the horse's action.

The gallop, or canter, is on a right or left lead according to whether the horse touches ground with the off or near fore on the third beat. The disunited canter comes from the horse's galloping to the left on the fore and to the right on the hind, or vice versa. The false trot is when he gallops with the left lead, turning to the right, or vice versa.

Descents should be taken at the pace, and moving straight down, while if they are very steep you should slide down. Bear in mind that, going downhill, the horse will lower his head and arch his back, bringing his hindquarters under. If you do not let him do this, he will either refuse or bolt. The horseman, therefore, should be ready to intervene to avoid starts, halts, and hesitation. Accentuate the inclination of the chest during the descent, leaning well forward, in order to free the horse's reins; ease up on the reins, but be ready to use them if necessary to keep the horse from going off the track.

Long jumps should be approached at a moderate gait. If they are short or steep, they should be confronted resolutely and at a pace sufficiently fast to provide adequate momentum to diminish the effort needed to get over them. Even when jumping—rather, *particularly* when jumping—the chest should be well forward and the hands forward, as well, to give the horse all the extension he needs from neck and shoulders. Lift yourself up out of the saddle and, if necessary, hang on by grasping the horse's mane or by throwing an arm around his neck.

The action of following the horse, which is the basis of Caprilli's system, begins with the feet and correct employment of the stirrups, then goes to the legs, the knees, the fulcrum of the seat, and then centers upon the small of the back, the point of transmission for the chest, divides over the shoulders, runs down each arm to the hands and, through the reins, connects directly with the horse's mouth at the bars.

It is through this following or yielding action that horse and horseman achieve a perfect harmony of natural equilibrium and become a "unit," according to Caprilli. This, however, will only be achieved through the correct seat, with the thighs oblique, the legs hanging down, the heels low, and the sole of the foot turned outward.

269 270 *Tightening the girth in the saddle.*
271 272 *Adjusting the stirrup irons in the saddle.*
273 *How to hold the two reins.*
274 *Correct seat and position (riding with legs "on the girth").*
275 276 *How to hold four reins.*
277 *The correct position for foot and leg.*
278 *Bridle with bit and snaffle.*
279 280 *Four reins held in one hand.*

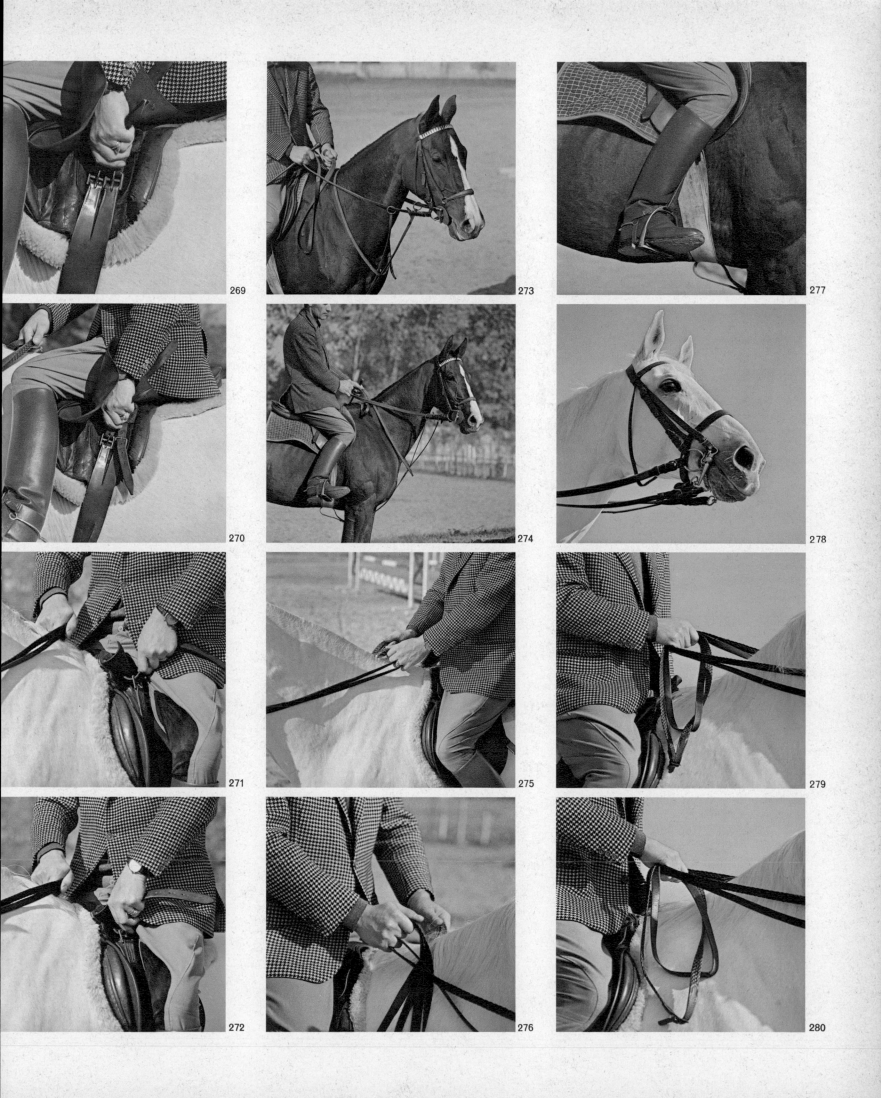

269

270

271

272

273

274

275

276

277

278

279

280

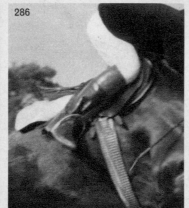

I

THE RIDER'S AIDS

The aids a rider has to communicate his wishes to a horse, move him to action, and to render him obedient are divided between natural and artificial aids.

The natural aids are precisely those that the rider provides himself: his seat, hands, legs, chest, and voice. The artificial aids are the mouthpiece, martingale, headstall, spurs, and crop. The rider should make tactful use of these aids, progressively, without undue show of activity, simply, clearly, and above all, in a manner comprehensible to the horse and to the degree commensurate with his sensibility and no more, to avoid misunderstandings. The aids should be indications to the horse, and only rarely controls imposed upon him.

A horse's resistance is reduced through tact, and it is the measure he possesses of this quality that defines the flair and capacity of a horseman.

II

NATURAL AIDS

The correct seat is the *sine qua non* in any stage of equitation, and permits the rider to freely use the aids he possesses.

The horseman will enjoy the benefits of employing these aids only if his seat is solid, and this stability in the saddle comes when his chest is inclined forward and the adductor muscles are working, his knees tending to stay low and adhering closely to the saddle, his legs firm, and hanging naturally, while clinging lightly to the horse's barrel.

The knees should be firm but flexible, so that the joints can move freely, as required. The descent of the knees is limited to the extension of the stirrup leathers, while its firmness is conditional upon the amount of pressure exerted upon the stirrup irons to thrust the heels down and activate the leg and thigh muscles. The rider will adhere to the saddle more easily if the soles of the feet are turned outward.

The Hands

The hands are the rider's natural aids in transmitting his wishes to the horse and receiving his mount's nervous and muscular reactions.

While maintaining constant contact with the horse's mouth through reins and the bit, the rider's hands must also allow the horse to move his neck and shoulders as he needs to do. He must also collect and regulate the animal's natural

281   *Chest too far forward and leg tending to slip toward the rear.*
282   *Toes turned out too far.*
283   *Insecure seat; hands hanging on the reins, leg too far forward.*
284–287 *Incorrect leg positions for jumping.*
288   *Leg hanging, rider half seated in a vain effort to follow.*
289   *Leg forward, rider sitting, horse jabbed in the mouth.*
290   *An attempt to respect the horse's mouth, but the rider is too far back, the knee is out of place, the leg forward—all hard on the small of the back.*

forward movement, as well as the impulsion deriving from his own signals, while making it pleasant for the horse to step out as he wishes, thus guaranteeing the animal's prompt obedience.

Hands that always have respect for the horse's mouth and the movement of the animal's neck and shoulders will help, after a time, to strengthen the muscles of the neck and shoulders, and their action will become so consistent that the rider's commands will have an almost instantaneous effect upon the horse's whole body. Actually, the neck should not serve only as a pendulum but also as the horse's transmission and, as such, should never be drawn in to the snapping point.

Delicacy and a sense of proportion in using the hands, depth of perception, and an ability to interpret every variation in impulsion, equilibrium, and the horse's temper make up that almost instinctive faculty of a true horseman, called "good hands." When a rider has good hands, his horse becomes easier and easier to handle. The animal either will not make errors or they will be quickly correctable; he will work calmly, obediently, effortlessly, and with a will, particularly if he is a spirited animal. Good hands are a gift of the gods, but they can also be created through application and intelligence, practice and experience.

One says that the hands "go" with the horse's mouth when they accompany all his movements and that they "act" on the mouth when they are used to hold him back or direct him. In every action of the hands, the horseman must perceive the precise moment in which the horse responds and obeys, so that he can then cease to act. For the hands to move in the best way, the arms should hang naturally, slightly bent at the elbows, with the hands in a line with the forearms, the wrists kept supple and flexible, and the hands slightly open, without stiffness.

The hands should always go with the horse's mouth. Avoid resting one hand on the neck and pulling with the other, for this will make the horse stiffen and, in time, create serious difficulties.

The Legs

The legs solicit forward motion from the horse, remove the opposition his hindquarters can interpose against his impulsion, and determine or contain the animal's lateral motion, thus directing the rear.

The legs should always cling to the barrel of the horse, lightly, and in such manner that their action does not have to be too improvised on the spur of the moment. The inaction should vary in intensity according to the result the rider wishes to obtain and the horse's sensitivity. Every action should have its own particular meaning. Naturally, the action of the legs is intensified if spurs are used.

To make a horse go forward, the action of the legs must be coordinated with a yielding by the hands. The hands and the legs are the rider's two natural aids toward employing the horse in various ways.

The Chest

By shifting its weight forward or to the side, the chest seconds the horse when he is advancing, changing gait, taking an obstacle, or turning.

The slightly inclined position of the chest at the half or when the horse is pacing becomes more definite at the trot, a gait at which the rider integrates his action with the horse's movement through the play of knee joints and hips. At the canter, the chest is inclined slightly more, and also lifted, and this action becomes even stronger when going into the faster paces, while taking a jump, and in any displacement of weight to give the horse more freedom in his back and loins.

The chest can also be held more or less erect when the horse is still; with an animal that shows some hesitation or reluctance to go ahead; and when one needs to reinforce the action of the hands when pulling up a horse very much in advance of the hands.

The chest uses the hips as a fulcrum. A simple shift in the chest's position is enough to get a horse's obedience when the animal has been well schooled. When the chest is inclined forward slightly, the hands are lowered, bringing them closer to the knees, thus putting the horse in a corridor, of which the hands and legs form the walls.

The Voice

The voice is a most effective means of getting the horse to act and to obey the rider's indications, so much so that it can almost act as a substitute for other aids.

His acute ear, memory, and facility in associating cause and effect (even when wrong) permit the horse to learn quickly what words mean and interpret a tone of voice, if the rider has conditioned him by suiting voice to action and avoided using his voice in the same way for different actions. In working in the open field, it is a good rule not to use your voice, so as not to disturb others.

Coordination of Action and Aids

In the conventionalized and figurative "language" that men adopt to obtain a horse's obedience, one of the indispensable things is precise and harmonious coordination of the aids that predispose and decide a horse to execute obediently whatever is required of him.

One should not, therefore, go on to using more aids until the horse understands those already employed; nor should one perform any action that negates or conflicts with another. For example: the hands should not pull back on the reins when the legs are urging the horse forward, or vice versa. This is permissible in *haute école*, it is true, but to a definite end.

It should be remembered that for young horses or those that have not been fully trained or worked for some time, work in company with other horses, steady animals on the flank or behind, and either in the manège or in the open, can be very advantageous. However, one must be competent to judge at what point such company no longer acts as a stimulant but incites the horse being worked to stampede, calling upon an instinctive reaction, a disagreeable and dangerous tendency in the animal that must be put down with energy and subtlety, but never with anger or extreme punishment.

That can only provoke rebellion and precisely that atavistic sense of self-preservation that engenders stampeding.

III
ARTIFICIAL AIDS

The Bit

The bit is that complex of aids applied to the horse's mouth to transmit through the reins the action of the hands to the horse, communicating the rider's wishes. The bit should be chosen in consideration of the sensitivity of the horse's mouth. One that is too strong will pain the animal, and he will react adversely, while one not strong enough will not guarantee the horse's prompt obedience to the rider's hands. It should be remembered that a horse's manageability does not depend upon some particular bits, but upon the appropriateness and quality of the rider's actions.

The bits most commonly used are the snaffle, the curb, and the Pelham bit, or pelham. Other types are used only in exceptional cases, and are best left to the skilled horseman and his judgment as to when they should be employed.

A snaffle of medium thickness is the bit in general use, and with it, one can school and control almost any horse. The snaffle does not constrict and is rarely painful, so it gives the horse complete trust in his rider. It is used with two reins and, once in a while, with four. In particular cases, the snaffle may be covered with leather, rubber, or cloth to soften its action. The snaffle is the mouthpiece most likely to win the horse's complete and willing obedience and it has the added advantage of keeping edgy riders from harming the horse's mouth.

The curb has a more acute action than a jointed mouthpiece and is, accordingly, more suitable for a fine horseman. It comprises the curb with the curb chain and the snaffle bit. The curb amplifies the efficacy of the hands and, for that reason, a good deal of care is needed in adapting it to the horse's mouth, both in relation to the thickness of the cannon (or bar) —as well as the length of the cheeks—and the amount of freedom this permits the tongue. The curb is the aid one has recourse to when the action of the snaffle seems to be inadequate. Only an able horseman can properly use this mouthpiece, harmonizing the action of the snaffle with that of the curb, whose effectiveness he can regulate by varying the length of the shanks and the curb chain. This provides many combinations of varying control. In natural equitation, the curb should be used only in exceptional conditions, with a definite effect in mind. Once that effect has been achieved, it is advisable to return to the normal mouthpiece, that is, the snaffle.

The jointed Pelham, or straight Pelham, is an aid whose effect lies somewhere between that of the snaffle and the curb bit, but is less suitable for fine, rigorous equitation. Notwithstanding, the Pelham is easy to use, and gives adequate results.

The Martingale

The martingale comprises a breastplate and strap with rings through which pass the snaffle reins, if it is employed with a

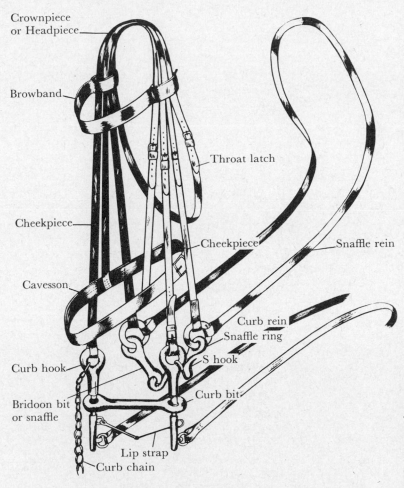

Crownpiece
or Headpiece

Browband

Throat latch

Cheekpiece

Cheekpiece — Snaffle rein

Cavesson

Curb rein
Snaffle ring

Curb hook — S hook

Bridoon bit
or snaffle — Curb bit

Lip strap
Curb chain

inadvertently, and they should be so attached to the boots that there is no possibility of their becoming loose and digging into the horse. There are various types of spurs; those used for open-field riding and competition, with plain shanks; while in dressage work, roweled spurs are used; and for grand dressage, they are curved into an "S," with a slight rowel. When using the spurs, they should be applied with no great pressure, but rather in short, light jabs, just behind the girth, and should not be scraped over the horse's ribs. If the horse reacts defensively, the rider should spur him again lightly, taking care that the horse does not become aroused, and making it easy for him to understand just what is required of him. Only while giving the horse complete freedom in the mouth should the spurs be used.

The Whip

The ordinary riding whip or crop is useful in getting the horse better to understand the aid of the legs, to incite him to action, or to correct him. It should not be longer than about two feet and should have a smooth surface. In inciting action, the whip should be used behind the rider's leg, to provoke the horse to an impulsion that will make him extend himself, but should be used delicately and at the proper moment. In jumping, the whip occasionally may be used to aid a horse who hesitates before an obstacle, the rider realizing that just leg action will not be enough to persuade him over.

As a means of correction, the whip is used as a defense against a bad-tempered or ill-trained horse. In such cases, the whip should be used repeatedly and energetically, and at brief intervals, applied alternately to the flanks and shoulders, but never around the head. It should be remembered that all corrective action with the whip in natural equitation should be taken only exceptionally, calmly, and with discernment.

snaffle alone or with a curb bit as well (with a snaffle and four reins, the lower reins pass through the rings; with a jointed bit, the upper reins go through the rings). As a rule, the length of the strap is determined by lifting the rings to the height of the withers. The strap serves principally to prevent the reins going over the horse's head when he turns or tosses it, as well as to offset any trouble that might arise were the hands suddenly to be raised abnormally high. At times, the regular strap may be substituted by a strap about five inches long with a ring at each end through which the reins run, making an Irish martingale, as it is called.

The Cavesson

The cavesson noseband, with two independent cheekpieces adjusted so that they are about two fingers' width above the bit (so that the lips are not pinched or injured) is used with young horses. The action of the cavesson is felt by the horse only if he should open his mouth to offset the action of the hands and the bit.

The Spurs

The spurs add authority (more or less, according to whether or not they are sharply pointed) to the action of the legs. They should not be so large that the rider spurs the horse

IV
THE HORSE WELL IN HAND

"Going with the horse's mouth" does not mean *supporting* a horse but having him, through impulsion, *come under support*. Support and contact must be continuous, not constantly of the same intensity, but variable in accordance with the work to be done.

There are horses that can be ridden without support, but only those with a good deal of heart. A horse is well in hand when he responds to our actions with precision and as if he were at liberty; one who obeys without defenses or starts, and is tranquil at all times. Naturally, there are some horses, by blood, who are testy and show a quick response to signals, while others are lazy and slow on the uptake or even downright slackers. The horse who is well in hand is always decisively inclined forward under impulsion and is prompt to react to the commands of his rider—in whom he must have complete faith, knowing that he will not be subjected to brusque or stiff action or conflicting movement.

Spirited horses, true Thoroughbreds, or those who are ill-schooled or timid, tend to defeat the action of the hands so that one finds animals that are before the hand, on the bit, heavy in the hand, out of hand, set to the near or off side, or rigid. On the other hand, when a horse attempts to evade support, he is said to be *behind the bit* or, if he attempts to slip out only occasionally, he is said to be *against the hand,* or else he may take false support and attempt to avoid this, for the slightest cause, by starting, halting, acting defensively, bucking, or tossing his head.

In the manège, a false impression is given because of both its limited space and its curves, banked in such a way as to rebalance the horse and to prevent him from extending himself. The rider may delude himself into thinking here that he has achieved reasonable mastery over his mount, and over equitation as well, for the horse feels light to him. He probably has a horse who is half asleep, moving automatically and by habit, and whose equilibrium will be lost as soon as horse and rider get out into the open.

Even though it is advisable that at the beginning a novice mount the same horse so that he can develop the animal's confidence in him and keep him calm, later on he should constantly change horses in order to learn to develop his own sensitivity, and a proper habit of observing his mount.

The different ways in which a horse employs his legs to proceed are called his *gaits. Cadence* is the rhythm of the gait, while *action* is the power and style of the gait under impulsion.

The walk is developed at a cadence of one hundred meters a minute (approximately 330 feet per minute). The stride should be as long as possible, and for that reason always calls for action from the hands and the aid of the legs. This pace is ideal for putting a horse into condition without straining his legs. The long walk, however, is no restful gait.

The cadence of the standard trot is 200 meters a minute, or about 660 feet. It can be increased to 250 meters a minute, or about 825 feet, since this increment comes from lengthening the stride without increasing the measure of the trot. The horse should alternate the beats of the trot if it is kept up for some time so as not to tire one pair of diagonals. The trot, if well cadenced, can be prolonged for some hours. It is, however, good practice to intersperse this gait with about ten minutes of walking.

The cadence of the standard gallop is about 350 meters per minute, or a scant 1,200 feet. The slow gallop, or canter, runs about 300 meters, approximately 1,000 feet per minute, while the extended gallop can go as high as 500 meters per minute, approximately 1,650 feet. A good horse can cover from about twelve to eighteen miles, even over difficult terrain, so long as it is not too heavy a track, without stopping. With good training, however, he can do as well twenty-four or even thirty miles, with brief intervals of rest at the walk or trot.

When galloping, the horseman, slightly lifted above the saddle, with his upper body inclined toward the fore, seconds the horse's movement with his hands, and accentuates the fall of the knee and the pressure of the feet against the stirrups; his heels, those elemental shock absorbers, are down low to guarantee his balance and security.

To slow down, to pass from a faster to a slower cadence, from a quick gait to a less rapid one, one must use gradual, progressive action, proportioned to the animal's impulsion and sensitivity. Also, when yielding or following—an action that the rider must perform without leaving the horse out of his control or leaving the reins hanging loose, even at the

walk—the tension on the reins should be lessened gradually to induce the horse to seek support and, accordingly, stretch his neck and shoulders.

To turn, the action should also be gradual, and rhythmically synchronized to the horse's movement. Pull on the inside rein, wrapping it around the wrist and bring the hand toward the crotch, simultaneously yielding on the outside rein just enough to keep it taut. The chest, which should always be slightly inclined toward the forehand, shifts to the inside. The inside leg acts to induce the horse to shift his hindquarters toward the outside, while the outside leg serves solely to maintain the horse's forward movement.

Intensity of action should vary in accordance with speed, the broadness of the curve, and the horse's resistance. With a well-schooled horse, just the displacement of the chest toward the inside and light action from the hand to achieve a curve of the right width should be all that is necessary. With colts or horses that are not too good, it might be better to bring the inside hand out, always at the level of the withers, to act laterally, taking the outside hand away from the neck and thus producing a sliding action on the bit rather than traction upon it. The most common way a horse will oppose this action is by stiffening his neck and shoulders and attempting to turn the neck in the opposite direction or by placing all his weight on the trunk. This comes from bad conformation, bad character, or bad schooling.

It is important to remember that a horse is generally more willing to turn on the near side, since when he is led the man always stands to the left of him and has him turn in that direction. For that reason, sometimes, and also because of defects in his conformation, the two bands of muscle on each side of the horse's spine are not equally developed.

At times, particularly with colts, a horse will toss his head, moving his shoulders and neck laterally, but resisting with his body. In that event, the inside hand should limit his action, and the outside should act to resist the flexion of the neck. The inside leg should remove any inertia or opposition from the hindquarters.

Backing is an exercise of notable moral importance for the horse. It is usually done as a punishment or even to settle the horse and get him better in hand. With progressive intensity, using the same actions employed to pull up and halt, the horse will be brought to move backward, and should be well framed between the legs and hands. After reversing, the horse should be allowed to go forward so that he again becomes light and extended.

It is obvious that to achieve desired results, a solid, precise seat is not enough. The horseman also needs sensitivity, self-control, patience, and the ability to remain relaxed and never to stiffen, for if he goes rigid, so will the horse, and more so if he is highly bred and sensitive. Bad schooling may have contributed toward making the horse go *behind or before* the bit, a bad habit that appears in some animals only at certain gaits, so that they tend to turn a walk into a trot, hurl themselves forward at the gallop or slow a trot, bolt, or go off on a tangent. They must, therefore, be corrected at the gaits in which they make these errors.

If the horse is behind the hand, at the first hint of defensiveness, the rider should cease following the mouth with his hands and aid the horse with energetic leg action until he again takes up the support through the bit. Should the horse attempt to go off to the right or left instead of going with the hands, the rider can always return him to the proper forward motion with the legs.

There are two types of horses that are before the hand. One type tends to support himself on the bit while increasing the cadence of the gait, withal remaining in balance, while the other stiffens neck and shoulders, pulling on the reins, and, not tolerating the bit, settles too much weight on the forehand, and loses his balance. To correct a horse of this type, he must be returned to the proper cadence through light support while being worked in a circle, at half-turns, and with frequent halts. The horse is before the bit because he wants more freedom in the mouth and because he is trying to find a natural position, which will vary during the work as he becomes tired.

With a horse that carries his head low, it is advisable to work with the hands a bit higher than usual and, when working in a circle, to move the hands sideways. If the horse puts his head to the wind, tossing his neck, it is best to keep the hands low, but not too much so, and to pet the animal often. Putting pressure on the neck or the crest, as some riders do, does not give results. By using the voice and petting the horse, you will always be able to get him to trust you and to calm himself. To work with such horses, one needs a solid seat and a calm atmosphere.

V
DEFENSES

Defenses are those actions or reactions of a horse bent on getting rid of his rider. More than bad character, such action usually springs from sudden mistreatment, from bad schooling, or because the horse is feeling pain or strain in his loins, heart, or legs. Sometimes a sudden recoil or bent hindquarters come from a weakness in the loins. In that case, the best thing is to walk the horse for some time before getting into the saddle, mounting him lightly and slowly. At other times, a horse will act defensively because he has been badly saddled. Check to see if the girth is too tight, if something has not been caught under the saddle pad, and so on.

To free himself of his rider a horse will buck, or attempt to throw his rider, or rear. Sometimes bucking is just a sign of exuberance and high spirits from a healthy animal or one who has, perhaps, been in the stable too long. The horse will lower his head, and, flinging his hindquarters high, will extend them repeatedly. It is not difficult to remain in the saddle if you avoid fighting the horse and give him a bit of liberty. To keep him from bucking, all you need do is make him lift his head and keep it high.

Tossing is a violent defense in which the horse will halt, lift all four legs off the ground and, thrusting his head down between his forelegs, arch his back at the loins, and then throw up his hind legs. The repetition of these quick and violent movements can throw the rider, particularly if he loses his seat. This is what one sees broncos do at rodeos. To avoid all this, the horsemen should take care that the horse does not stop and lower his head.

Rearing is the most dangerous of these defenses, for the horse may turn around and fall on his rider. At times the cause of this turning may be the fact that the rider, losing his seat, instinctively grasps the reins while, if anything, he should grasp the horse's mane. The novice should remember that he must never whip the horse on the head, since such treatment may make him rear; if the animal is not hindered, he will very rarely lose his balance.

VI
THE JUMP

Any horse is capable of going over obstacles about a meter or 1.10 meters high (approximately 40 to 44 inches) and about 3 meters (10 feet) wide. Some horses can even take a fence about 1.30 meters (52 inches) in height and with a spread of 4 meters (13′ 4″). Only horses with certain definite attitudes and powers can take more difficult obstacles, and these are the stuff of which horse shows are made.

Training for jumping begins with placing a bar on the ground that the horse takes at a walk. Results will be even better, the more the rider can inspire his horse's confidence in him. The horse should be quickly relieved of any fears he might have. Even horses that have a talent for jumping are put off or become hesitant if they have suffered pain as a result of bad or violent handling.

Once the horse can walk over a bar or hurdle without agitation, you can take him over at the trot and then at the canter, raising the height of the bar gradually. Do not rush this work; go about it slowly, and do not bore the horse by insisting too much on the exercise. Jumping at the trot is good exercise for the horse; however, the rider must be an able horseman so that he can soften the brusque movement of the animal. Jumping at the gallop is less bumpy, and therefore easier; furthermore it trains the horse's eye.

Once the horse can take isolated obstacles with assurance, you can begin to make use of the cavaletti, which are necessary in forcing the horse to bascule, that is, to make use of his neck and shoulders to aid the play of the loins and back. Seven-meter spacing teaches a horse what we call style—to take off at the right distance from the obstacle with a correct distribution of force and a proper utilization of his momentum. This work can be carried on for a week or more, according to the horse's capability. After that, you can move on to more difficult obstacles. Whenever a horse consistently refuses to take any given obstacle, it is better not to insist, but to lower the bars on that obstacle and also to take him over others to restore his confidence and trust, as well as to distract him a bit.

If the rider must be able to accompany the rapid and sudden change in equilibrium in the horse as he jumps and to second the horse's extension of his neck with his arms and chest, he must, even more, be careful not to return to the saddle before the horse has taken a few strides after the jump. When the horse comes down, the strain on his back is great, for his hindquarters are much higher than the fore—which must take all the horse's weight and the weight of his rider as well—while the loins contract to bring the rear under, and the line of the horse's back goes suddenly from convex to concave.

In any case, a horse can behave himself in various ways upon confronting an obstacle. He can take it correctly without any command from his rider if the fence is not beyond his powers and his schooling, and if his rider sits him firmly and suppley, that is, according to the rules of natural equitation. Jumps can also be taken according to Paderni's system or in the old English style, where the poor horse acted more in terror than in enthusiasm, but in those days, we must remember, a jump was more in the nature of a test of strength between rider and horse.

The animal can also take the jump through fear or (if he has that vice) hurl himself over the jump. The vice, however, usually comes from fear. He can also approach an obstacle with diffidence, indecisively, and end in a brusque refusal (in which case, too often, only the horseman takes the jump!), or he may shy more or less suddenly. Finally, a horse may crash into a fence, through a lack of courage or because of his failure to time himself correctly, or even because he was interfered with by his rider.

Riders tend to accelerate the cadence as they bring a horse up to an obstacle of some extension like a ditch or brook, oxers, or triple bars, which displaces the animal's center of gravity, first to the rear, and then forward. When he feels this imbalance, the horse takes his own measures: either he starts or he balks, if he feels that this sudden speed will lead him to take the jump too far from the obstacle; or, if he is too far under, jumping at a complete disadvantage, everything goes wrong—the rider will lose his seat, being thrown on the horse's loins and then upon his neck, and the effects on the animal's mouth will be terrible.

If the horse has a tendency to accelerate or precipitate himself forward when he nears an obstacle, the rider must pull him up with a very flexible hand, but be ready to yield when the horse does jump. It is advisable while practicing to make the horse take a couple of turns to the left or right, fairly near the obstacle, to slow him down and put him behind the bit. In extreme cases, put the horse at a walk and bring him up to the obstacle, halting him at the bar.

One must distinguish between the horse that accelerates and the horse that hurls himself forward. Usually, it is the enthusiastic horse that accelerates, imagining that he can better take a fence in a burst of speed or at a faster cadence than that requested by his rider; a horse that is fearful of the obstacle or of his rider's intentions will hurl himself forward and, as we have already noted, find himself in a position that makes it difficult, if not impossible, for him to take the jump, so that he ends by shying or balking.

If a horse starts, he should be halted and brought back to the obstacle, but to the side opposite to where he shied.

If he balks, it may be for lack of sufficient impulsion, in which case bring him back some distance behind the obstacle to attempt it again, and be ready to provide sufficient leg action to maintain sufficient forward movement. If the horse balks because he has not had enough training, reduce the dimensions of the obstacle and let him see it from close up, at a halt. If his refusal comes from bad temper or laziness, he should be brought up at a right angle to the fence and punished with a few jabs of the spurs and touches of the crop, then invited to advance until he gives an indication that he will do so willingly. Now, take him back and make a large circuit at the desired gait, gallop naturally, and advance toward the obstacle, being sure not to start too far back.

To prevent a horse from getting the habit of going over an obstacle on the oblique (something he does to take off at the distance he thinks proper), it is a good thing to make him jump as you ride him in a circle, continuing on the circular track after the obstacle has been negotiated.

Finally, remember that there is no sure way of judging what obstacles a horse can take, what his attitude will be, and his potentialities. These things will come to light only through schooling and practice.

A horse's attitude about jumping has nothing to do with size, physique, or blood. It is an inclination peculiar to those animals with a certain eye, courage, desire, and strength. Even small horses, and some of little breeding and less blood, have been exceptional jumpers. Remember that small horses should be ridden by light riders, and those with not too much class or background should be kept to a moderate cadence and not put over too many jumps or too many difficult ones.

Some riders attempt to use English Thoroughbreds as jumpers, but these horses are too nervous and sensitive for today's complicated courses, all twists and turns. This Thoroughbred also finds it difficult to concentrate, and is hard to control; he is apt to scramble over a fence and get out of hand. However, when an English Thoroughbred can be turned into a jumper, he is possessed of such impulsion as no other horse has.

When we look at photographs of Bianchetti, Lequio, and Caprilli in his earlier years, we see that they establish and affirm these classic principles, each forming a perfect team with his mount. Today, however, we see many riders who take it upon themselves to jump with their horses, but *at the very same time,* lift themselves in the stirrups, shooting their arms forward, and shifting their center of gravity to help the horse basculate over the obstacle. It is said that it would be better to have dead weight in the saddle, as long as it were secure, than a lighter, unstable burden. This is true.

Show riding today, though, is a form of sophisticated acrobatics and, that being the case, it is the rider who makes the horse jump and get over in cases where the horse would have refused. Out of this situation arises the constant conflict between the rider's hands and the horse's mouth—always abrupt and violent. Also, there is vigorous use of the legs, which, because it is the horseman who is jumping the horse, are placed horizontally, while the hands are thrust forward. Furthermore, the rider no longer looks beyond the obstacle, but at the fence itself—too often because he is hunched over. But we must admit that it is just the riders who double themselves up this way who get over better and more often, perhaps because they approximate the position of an athlete taking a jump on foot!

VII

GYMNASTICS ON HORSEBACK

Even from the first lesson, it is extremely useful for the novice rider to do exercises on horseback.

The first thing to have him try is to wrap his arms around the horse's shoulders when at the walk, reaching as low as he

291 *Raimondo d'Inzeo jumping a wall: classic seat and perfect balance at the height of the jump.*

292–294 *Correct seats, right "from the book."*

295–298 *No one should sit like this.*

291

295

292

293
294

296

297
298

299

300

301

302

303

304

305

306

can and forcing his heels down. He should push his bottom back and arch the small of his back. By doing this, the rider will discover a new way of balancing himself without falling on the horse's neck, and will come to understand the importance of the fork, as well as the fact that when he is mounted he is, in a sense, divided into two parts, from his heels to his pelvis (which portion of his body must follow every one of the horse's movements, sticking to the animal as closely as possible) and from his pelvis up. The upper part of his body must be solidly based on the lower and must move with lightness and ease, elegance and suppleness, so that the arms move independently of the trunk, the head of the shoulders, and the small of the back functions as a flexible but firm articulation.

Gymnastics on horseback are designed to strengthen the rider's seat, adding lightness and agility, and provide for independent functioning of the chest, arms, and legs. Good exercises to practice are swinging the arms out, behind, and then swinging them alternately, rotating forward and backward, bending the chest forward and back; and—of great importance to give a rider maximum confidence with his horse—vaulting into the saddle.

In conclusion, it might be well to remember that riding a horse properly is the synthesis of the will of rider and horse. If the horse wants to do one thing, and the rider is bent on having him do another, these conflicting wills cannot produce anything satisfactory. The rider should not make the mistake of putting too much faith in force and his ability to limit the horse's action. To know how to educate and convince are the two greatest skills the man in the saddle can have.

The fascination of equitation lies partly in the fact that it is a continuous interpretation by the horseman of the horse's gestures and movements, while the horse, for his part, must interpret the rider's signs and requests. One speaks to the other in code but with perfect understanding of the language on both sides—arrived at solely through clearness of expression and logical action in degree and progression.

One does not correct or persuade a horse by violent opposition to his instinctive reactions and sensory perceptions, but by seeking the cause of his action—often a false relationship between cause and effect—and gently pulling him back to reality. Bear in mind that the horse, whose senses are more highly developed than ours, also possesses instinct, which in us is minimal. We should, therefore, admit to ourselves that in certain matters (firmness of the ground, the safety in a step, and so on) the horse is much better able to judge correctly than we are.

It is our good fortune that the horse is very frank, perhaps too much so. All we need do to know what he is thinking is to watch his ears, which show the direction of his attention, the temper of his feelings, and his apprehensions. This is

the only way we can forecast a horse's actions. The horse, on the contrary, at any given moment knows precisely what we want of him, our mood, our feelings, even our indecision. He constantly takes our measure and, through the conducting wires that are the reins, the contact of our thighs, and the feel of our weight and how it is balanced, he guesses when we are feeling courageous or timorous, skillful or incompetent, our indecision or certainty, even our happiness or our sorrow, feelings that particularly sensitive horses are quick to catch.

There are nasty, vicious horses that at times enjoy themselves at the expense of inexpert riders; taking advantage of the slightest annoyance, these novices may cause them to toss them from the saddle. Sometimes it must be admitted they have reason to do so, given the rider's heavy-handedness. As a rule, however, the horse is just looking to remedy a critical situation, acting upon his instinct.

Equitation is muscular exercise only in part. It is also an exercise in delicate intuition and subtle reasoning. Naturally, athletic and technical problems exist, but they must always be seen in terms of the horse's physiology and the horseman's psychology. Equitation, then, is a complex sport in which technique and style have value only in the measure that they take cognizance of the sensitivity, the nature, and the physique of the horse. There is a never-ending play between the elements of domination and intelligence and resistance (or momentum) and enthusiasm (or laziness) of the horse. The old cavalryman's talk of "being on horseback by force" is an antique concept that today does nothing more than reflect the lack of horsemanship of whoever first pronounced it.

A saddle has been devised that reproduces a horse's movement. It may be useful in keeping an old hand in trim, but it will never serve to train a novice rider, since only on horseback can one train and exercise that properly apportioned muscular control—actions and reactions that are not merely constants as they are in almost all other sports.

Nor is it possible in equitation to reach a certain level and then rest on one's laurels, for the horse is always an imponderable element to some degree, and can never be completely sounded. These are the elements of change that make the novice stiffen in the saddle and grow heavy on horseback. Only when the rider's senses and intuition are attuned to the inconstant action of the horse, and he is close to seconding the proportioned play of muscular effort that creates balance and stability in the seat, only then will there be that interplay between horse and horseman that cannot exist without a mutual sensitivity and perfect coordination of movement.

The tacit transmission of our desires to a horse requires an appropriate course of action, calling not only for force but also for ready reflexes, vitality, and quick reactions. Herein lies the difficulty in equitation. It calls for intelligence and nervous energy and physical strength as well, and no mere athletic training will suffice for it all. The reactions to any movement in equitation are so diversified and specific that they cannot be learned except through long practice.

Working on a longe or rope is useful to avoid overburdening the loins of young or delicate horses; for disciplining difficult horses without arousing their hostility, saving the horseman from spills; for conditioning horses that have gone soft; for making a horse supple before entering him in competition on narrow tracks or rough courses; and also for schooling young horses in jumping.

299 300 *Breaking cavesson in correct position.*
301 *Working at the walk.*
302 *Working at the trot.*
303 304 *Working at the canter.*
305 *Taking a rather narrow ditch.*
306 *Another ditch, a bit wider.*

To do this work, you will need a cavesson, a whip, and a long rein or rope. As aids, you will need your intelligence and quickness, your voice, the action of the rope on the cavesson, and the whip. When the horse succeeds in working on a fairly taut rope, he can be considered well schooled. By tugging gently on the rope, you can get him to moderate his gait. The whip serves to make him move farther away from the center of the circle traced by the rope.

VIII
TACK

If you were to ask a saddlemaker the secret of a fine saddle, he would tell you that it is the quality, dependent upon two things: the leather of which it is made and the skill of the maker. These are the elements called for according to saddlemakers, and they contribute to the beauty of a saddle's design. Many saddlemakers believe that because of the particular pains taken in its preparation, English leather is best for saddles. Not too long ago, hides intended for English saddles were still tanned in a process employing English oak, thought to impart resistance to wear and a suppleness impossible to achieve with any other tanning agent. Saddlemakers say that the best-quality pigskin—the preferred leather for the seat—comes from Scotland.

The saddler's craft is ancient, and mention is made of it in the Bible. By 1115, in London they were so numerous that they were able to form one of the first companies in that city, a company that soon became one of the most privileged.

The frame over which the saddle is built is called the tree. Generally, it is made of wood (often beech) and metal (usually steel), with many saddles nowadays having a solid light-metal construction. The tree is undoubtedly the most important part of the saddle, which is why the finest saddlemakers have their own shops for their fabrication. A custom-made saddle is truly made to measure—the shape and dimensions of the tree must conform to the height and weight of the rider, and to the conformation of the horse at the withers and back.

Saddles are of varying design, in accordance with the purpose for which they are intended. Among the most common types, we have the general riding or hacking saddle, hunting, jumping, cavalry, flat-racing, show-ring, stock, and sidesaddles. One London saddler produces about forty-three variations. Walsall, in Staffordshire, produces more saddles than London, but the London saddlers are perhaps the most famous of all, undoubtedly because their Worshipful Company of Saddlemakers keeps them to a very high standard. Fine tack is an investment, and can easily last the rider a lifetime, if well taken care of. In addition to the saddle, the tack includes the girth, stirrup leathers and irons, saddle pad, generally of wool felt, and the bridle, with all its parts and accessories.

To be comfortable, a saddle should be fairly soft, and its flaps sufficiently slanted in front to permit the rider to place his thighs and knees correctly. The tree should be flexible enough not to cause discomfort to the horse, to avoid pain or sores, particularly at the pommel, and it should be perfectly fitted to the animal's contours, as should padding and lining.

The average flat saddle, together with the girth, stirrup leathers and irons, weighs from fifteen to eighteen pounds, but a Western saddle, even without its usual silver trappings and decorations, can easily come to thirty to forty pounds! On the other hand, the weight of a racing saddle can be expressed in ounces.

The girth, which can be made of leather or fabric, generally of canvas for saddle horses, should be just tight enough to keep the saddle in position. String girths, which are often used as standard equipment by the military and also the mounted police, are often employed when a horse is tender.

Stirrups, often called "irons," when used with flat or English saddles ordinarily are made of metal, although those used with stock saddles are usually of wood, with leather hoods and wrappings on the treads. Stirrups are made in various sizes and weights, but they should be wide enough to slip from the feet in case of a fall.

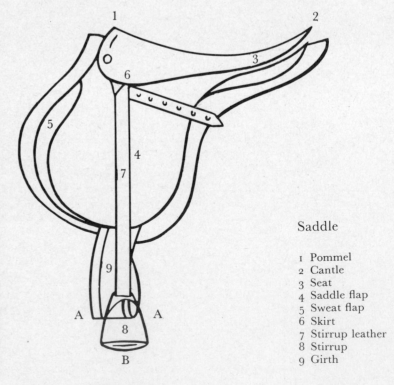

Saddle

1 Pommel
2 Cantle
3 Seat
4 Saddle flap
5 Sweat flap
6 Skirt
7 Stirrup leather
8 Stirrup
9 Girth

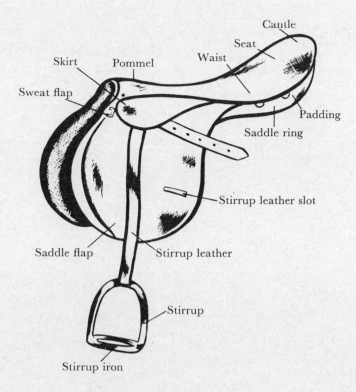

Skirt Pommel
Sweat flap
Waist Seat Cantle
Seat
Padding
Saddle ring
Stirrup leather slot
Saddle flap Stirrup leather
Stirrup
Stirrup iron

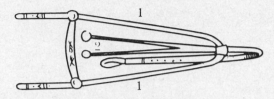

1 Hunting breastplate attachment
2 Running martingal

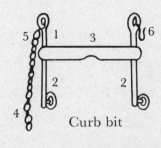

Irish martingale

Cavesson

1 Cheekpiece
2 Noseband

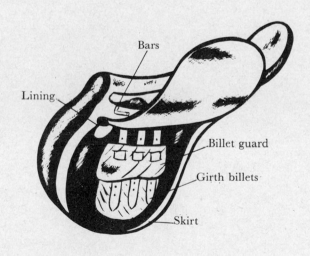

Bars
Lining
Billet guard
Girth billets
Skirt

1 Bar
2 Shank
3 Port
4 Curb chain
5 Eye
6 Curb hook

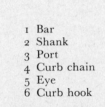

Curb bit

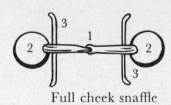

Full cheek snaffle

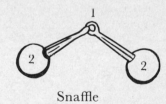

Snaffle

1 Mouthpiece
2 Rein rings
3 Cheekpieces

1 Mouthpiece
2 Rein rings

PART FIVE

THOROUGHBRED RACING

I
INTRODUCTION

The fascination of horse racing lies in its complex appeal to man's varied interests and emotions, catering as it does to his scientific bent, irrational enthusiasm, pleasure in method, delight in change, knowledge of the past, and search for the future. Its appeal blends patience with the lucky break, certainty with hope, and tension with relaxation, linking them to the name and figure of an animal (that has its own genealogy and history, in which man shares) as if that animal and its fate were man's very own. No less attractive is the physical setting, the racecourse itself, where natural beauty combines with the color and excitement of the spectactors.

A racehorse is the focus of tremendous attention, which is not fully explained by the fact that wagers are placed on his performance. More than betting is to answer for this.

There is a different sort of gamble, which to many people is far more important than wagering. This is the kind of gamble involved in owning, purchasing, selling, and breeding racehorses. A horse is subject to many hazards in racing. He may be bumped and injured in a race. A racehorse's legs are rather fragile, and it is not uncommon for them to become sore or swollen, for him to break or injure a bone in his leg and thus become unable to race; he may even have to be destroycd. In such cases, the owner suffers a considerable loss.

But the greatest gamble is in breeding. A stakes-winning colt may be purchased for a great sum of money to serve as a stud, and then prove to be impotent or ineffective or not prepotent (able to carry his notable racing characteristics forward.) Obviously, the purchase of such a stud was a losing gamble.

On the other hand, the owner of a valuable mare may pay as much as $10,000 or more to have her serviced by a famous stud, and then have a foal of poor quality. The owner loses not only the stud fee but also the breeding time of his valuable mare.

However, there is the sunny side. A man may purchase a horse for a modest sum and then develop him to become a great stakes winner or even a champion. And the great dream of a horse breeder is to breed a winner, and that happens often enough. To many people, the satisfaction, pride, and glory of owning a notable horse are far more precious than the financial rewards.

The attraction of the racehorse also derives from some mysterious inimitable force from within the horse that makes him a symbol, an object of a grand passion in an age of machines.

Throughout the world's myriad racetracks, each country has entered its finest horses, along with its pride, in races referred to as "classics," which are the highlights of the racing calendars each season. They are usually run over the same courses and distances, and always on significant dates, and are held not only for the sport but also to find the best specimens for subsequent use in improving the breed.

There are two main types of races for horses—free-running races and harness races.

Free-Running Races

By far the most important type of horse racing is thoroughbred racing. Thoroughbreds run both in flat races (from two furlongs—five furlongs in Britain—to four miles or more) and in jumping races (hurdle races—over moderately low hurdles, and steeplechase races—over rather higher shrubbery fences).*

In the United States, almost entirely in the Southwest, there is also quarter-horse racing. Quarter-horses, not pure-bred, are ranch horses capable of great speed for a quarter of a mile. At the present time, the race with the greatest amount of prize money is a quarter-horse race. In 1967 the purse totaled about half a million dollars.

Harness Races

Harness horses are not Thoroughbreds; they are Standard-breds. There are two types—trotters and pacers. These horses wear harnesses with special arrangements to control their gait, and they pull a light sulky in which the driver rides. Whereas in free-running races the horses may have all four feet off the ground, in harness races the horse may not have more than two feet off the ground. Pacers are trained and reined to have one side's fore- and hind legs off or on the ground at the same time. Their gait is sort of side to side.

---

* In flat racing in England, two-year-olds run in the five-furlong races until July 1; they can run six furlongs until September 1, and seven furlongs or more beyond that date.—Eds.

Trotters are trained and reined to have one foreleg and the opposite hind leg off or on the ground at the same time. Harness racing will be discussed in the next chapter.

The Thoroughbred is a clearly defined, registered breed of horse that originated in England. All the Thoroughbreds in the world stem from three great stallions—the Darley Arabian, the Godolphin Barb, and the Byerly Turk through their descendants Eclipse (great-great-grandson), Matchem (grandson), and Herod (great-great-grandson) respectively. About a hundred years ago, there were an estimated few thousand Thoroughbreds, primarily those registered in the English *General Stud Book*, with a few here and there in countries other than England. Today there are hundreds of thousands, and though the exact number is elusive because Thoroughbreds are spread throughout the world, it is possible to make a fairly precise estimate, based on some interesting observations.

It is obvious that the great increase in Thoroughbreds during the past century has brought with it changes in the relative quality of horses bred throughout the world. While a hundred years ago the English Thoroughbred was incontestably superior to horses from any other country, today, notwithstanding the fact that England may have more facility in selecting strains to produce the best breeding stock, other countries have equine resources rich enough, qualitatively and quantitively, to offer the English tough competition in the international market. Accordingly, we see France shipping horses to a large number of countries, Italy exporting its outbred studs sought in many countries to offset inbreeding in certain lines, Argentina, Brazil, and Chile furnishing horses to other Latin American nations and the United States, Australian horses going to Asia and the United States, and the United States selling horses to Japan.

Over the years, the Thoroughbred has been modified considerably, differing substantially from one age to the next, one place to the next, and particularly from one climate to the next. While the English Thoroughbred has kept the "classic broad structure, long dorsal line, and above-average height,"* the French Thoroughbred is much more rustic and compact and extraordinarily powerful; the Italian Thoroughbred tends to be smaller in stature.

Nevertheless, the lime-rich regions of England, France, and Italy appear to be the best places to raise Thoroughbreds because of the temperature and degree of humidity, the nature of the soil, and the fine hay and oats they provide. The same geologic and climatic conditions obtain in Kentucky, Virginia, and Tennessee; in the River Plate basin in Argentina, and, to a certain extent, on the shores of Lake Maggiore, near Dormello, Italy.

There are exceptional situations as Varola points out. Australia, which the English had thought would be a paradise for Thoroughbreds because of its fine climate and rich pasturage, has not been as good a place to raise racehorses as New Zealand, for example. New Zealand is hilly country mostly,

* Franco Varola's *Foundation Series*, Derby Editions.

and though it was poor in pasturage when the first settlers arrived it is now rich in grazing land. In the River Plate basin, the Thoroughbred has been brought to such excellence (through the import of such excellent stallions as Ormonde and Cylene) as to attract attention even in the United States. Despite the Argentine Thoroughbred's gain in stature and strength, however, in the course of three or four generations a definite heaviness of line and bone has become apparent.

In Brazil, on the other hand, the Thoroughbred has preserved his original characteristics, and tends to be a fine, elegant animal, even demonstrating a particularly even temperament.

In the United States, possibly because he has been adapted for racing on dirt rather than on grass tracks, and to speed trials, the Thoroughbred racehorse tends to be massive—powerful in the quarters and haunches, and somewhat heavy. Perhaps it is the rich diet of the American horse that has contributed to his being big and sleek rather than elegant in the exquisite, characteristic style of the English Thoroughbred.

Good breeding depends upon four fundamental factors: fine stallions, fine mares, fine weather, and an amalgam of care, hygiene, and discipline that are lumped together by experts under fine organization. Then, of course, there is the delicate process of breaking and training, an undertaking that at times can be a love's labor lost if even a single error occurs. (Tesio's belief that "observation is the basis for good results in selective breeding of racehorses" is confirmed by Varola: "It is useless to be dogmatic, for what is of value and what must be done are to observe and understand.") There are also special circumstances that lead to good horse breeding. Because Italy is a country with long experience and sophistication in equine matters she has remained as up-to-date as England and France, so that even with a very short supply of broodmares, less than a thousand, she gets wonderful products. Most of the mares are English and French, and are bred with studs on the other side of the Alps, some of which have fathered their best foals in Italy. In every age, the horse has been an expression of the social ambiance in which he has developed. Thus, the Thoroughbred has become an instrument of idealized perfection through a routine and organization that presuppose extreme political and social stability. The period in which the English Thoroughbred developed was prosperous, and its social life orderly. In Italy, production of thoroughbred racehorses was certainly not always as lean as it is now. Even in the United States, the more favorable conditions obtaining in such states as Kentucky and Virginia contribute to the production of better horses than those of richer states like New York and Texas, despite the fact that the passion there for horses is fervid.

II
ENGLAND

The earliest report of racing in England dates from 1074, found in William Fitzstephen's *Description of the City of London*. He mentions that every Friday horses were brought by their owners to Smithfield for sale. With a large crowd in attendance, these horses, ridden by professional jockeys, were raced toward a marker, returning at full speed past a grandstand.

In that way, prospective buyers and others were able to pick the best horses, and would bet among themselves.

With the coming of the Crusades, European horsemen were provided the opportunity of becoming acquainted with Arabian horses, and of appreciating their fine points—which they did to such an extent that kings and princes did their utmost to bring Arabians back with them on their return to their own countries. The first two Arabian stallions reached England in 1121.

Richard the Lion-Hearted was the Arabian's most dedicated advocate, and it was he who first started spring racing over the Epsom Downs for horses imported from the East. (Chance has preserved a fragment of stone found near the town of Epsom, dating from the Roman occupation of Britain, on which stonecutters some two thousand years ago carved a message. One can still see the final letters of *princeps* and the initials of *optimus maximus*. Possibly the most famous racecourse in the world, Epsom Downs has a fitting cornerstone, worthy of its place in world horse racing.) It was Richard, too, who offered the first prize, a purse of forty gold pieces.

Henry VIII was a great racing fan. It was during his reign that organizers of the Chester Fair in 1512 decided to offer the winner a wooden bell, which was later changed to a silver bell. In 1609, the Lord Mayor of Chester, finding the silver bell badly made, ordered another, which also failed to satisfy him. He commanded a third to be constructed, and then, with three bells on his hands, decided to award them to the owners of the horses finishing first, second, and third, a custom that has survived to this day. A racing program was published, fixing dates for events at Chester and Mamford. Going back to 1074, we see that racing in England got off on an organized basis, while the Italians, for example, were still racing around their piazzas or up and down the town streets and along the roads. Not until 1465 did Pope Paul II start the Barb races in Rome.

Henry VIII deserves recognition for his positive efforts toward the development of horse breeding in England. He promulgated a number of edicts whose purpose was to increase the quality and quantity of native horses. One of his proclamations in part reads as follows: "No one shall take stallions more than two years of age that are not at least fifteen hands high into the forests, lands, or broads, cultivated or not, throughout the whole territory of Norfolk." The same order was issued for twenty-three other counties, but with a minimum height of fourteen rather than fifteen hands. Other decrees seem somewhat bizarre, such as requiring each archbishop and duke to raise at least seven stallions fourteen hands high; that clerics who enjoyed an annual living of a hundred pounds sterling and laymen whose wives wore hats made of velvet must keep a horse or be liable to a fine of £20.

During Henry's reign the passion for horse breeding developed with such great rapidity that the king himself soon realized that the royal studs at Eltham, Kent, and Hampton Court Palace would soon be inadequate. He decided therefore to establish breeding centers at Tutbury in Staffordshire and Malmesbury in Wiltshire; these served as collection stations for new and more consistent breeding nuclei. Elizabeth I's request that Prospero d'Osma prepare a report on the state of the royal studs at Tutbury and Malmesbury was part of her first business. After inspecting them thoroughly,

D'Osma wrote his report. (The manuscript was auctioned by Sotheby's in April, 1927, and purchased by A. B. Maclay of New York for £115.) We have spoken earlier of the modern suggestions in D'Osma's report that anticipate the most advanced methods and techniques of horse breeding today. His treatment of the care and caution that should be taken in choosing a location for a stud is extremely intelligent, going into particulars such as how quickly the land absorbs water, the different types of herbage it could support, the location of shady, marshy areas, suggestions regarding the necessity of keeping the colts in a cool spot during the summer and sufficiently warm in winter, and so on. D'Osma's report ends with a critical opinion of Malmesbury and a hearty recommendation, for its positive qualities, of Tutbury. In a final word, he counsels against intensive concentrations of horses.

When James I, the first of the Stuart line, was proclaimed king in 1603, the majority of his courtiers were Scottish noblemen. Because these men were traditionally great lovers of horse racing, it was not difficult to win the king's favorable attention to matters concerning the sport. On March 3, 1617, from a platform erected by the citizenry of Lincoln, James I had watched a great flat race that was run for a cup. At his order, the circular track (a quarter mile long) was fenced in so that the spectators would be kept outside its limits, in better order, and "one could better follow the progress of the race."

A significant appointment in James's reign that is particularly interesting because of its future effect upon the English Thoroughbred was that of George Villiers, Duke of Buckingham, as Grand Master of the Horse. Buckingham was given complete power to intervene in the royal studs, a concession that he handled with good sense, until his murder in 1628. Buckingham accompanied the future Charles I to Spain incognito, when the prince was courting the Infanta of Spain, with whom it was thought he might contract a marriage. Plans for marriage were dropped,* but the King of Spain, nevertheless, had taken the opportunity to present Charles with twenty-four horses selected from his stud at Córdoba, and he made a gift of twelve horses to Buckingham.

With civil war and Cromwell's victory, Charles I, and the monarchy, fell. The royal studs, along with members of the king's party, were sacked, the horses sold, and all the wealth accruing from their sequestration went into the coffers of the Commonwealth. Not the least of Charles's memorials before he ended on the block was the racing tradition he began: from the second year of his reign, he arranged for regular spring and Autumn meetings at Newmarket.

With the Restoration and the accession of Charles II, James d'Arcy became Master of the Horse, and in a fairly short time managed to collect a considerably good stock of horses to fill the gaps caused by Cromwell's confiscation and

---

* Primarily because of Buckingham's influence upon James I.— TRANS.

307 *Berber horses racing during a Roman carnival, from a painting by Géricault. Louvre, Paris.*
308 *"The Derby at Epsom," by Géricault. Louvre, Paris.*

307

308

309

310

sale. As a result of the dispersion of the royal stallions among private persons substantive harm was caused to the bloodlines of the English Thoroughbred. Many of the private parties who owned these royal studs started their own breeding farms, which were located all over the country. These new breeders also imported stallions from Turkey, Italy, Spain, and North Africa. Tutbury and Malmesbury, however, which were occupied during the Commonwealth and even after the accession of Charles II in 1660, were no longer used as breeding farms. But there was revived and renewed interest in racing, which formerly consisted of events in which were entered horses of the king's courtiers, ridden by themselves. Cromwell, in an edict dated February 24, 1654, had prohibited horse races, but that merry monarch Charles II was quick to bring them back in all their old style, and the public returned to watch them with even more interest than in the past. Charles II was also a gentleman jockey.

William of Orange, who reigned over England as William II from 1688 to 1702, did not raise many horses, and transferred the royal stud to Hampton Court, though racing continued and intensified under royal favor. His successor, Queen Anne, however, was a great sports enthusiast, rather unusually so for a woman of her period, and she also loved to hunt. In 1711, after deciding that her immense park at Ascot should be the scene of important races, Anne established the meetings at Ascot, instituted a number of prizes, and saw her own horses take a number of cups. However, no proper installations then existed. The construction of a track alone cost £559, according to Court accounts.

The House of Hanover did not have much interest in the turf until the time of William, Duke of Cumberland, son of George II, who had a deep and energetic influence upon the racing of his day. We are obliged to the duke for raising Herod and Eclipse, from whom descend in direct line two-thirds (including Matchem, the entirety) of all the Thoroughbreds in the world today. The duke was as fine a horseman as he was a horse breeder, and one of the founding members of the Jockey Club. The second duke, nephew of the first, had a genuine racing stud, with excellent horses that ran in the Oaks (1779) and the Derby (1780).

On a May morning in 1780, several noblemen left a hunting lodge at Woodmansterne to attend a horse race. Their host was Edward Smith-Stanley, twelfth Earl of Derby, who was twenty-seven at the time. The county from which he took his name was spread out some hundred miles to the north. Because of his unhappy marriage, he rarely visited the place. The young earl spent a good deal of his time in Surrey, living in an old brewery, the property of his uncle, John Burgoyne. It had been converted into a gentleman's residence, known as The Oaks because it was surrounded and shaded by a grove of oak trees. The name was to become immortal when it was given in 1779 to the first classic race for three-year-old

fillies.* It was pure chance, however, that gave Lord Derby's name to the race he and his guests came to see that May morning in 1780. His guest and close friend Sir Charles Bunbury, another racing enthusiast, tossed a coin to decide whether the race that was to become one of the most famous of all sporting events would bear his name or Derby's. As we know, Derby won the toss, but Bunbury had the satisfaction of seeing his horse, Diomed, win the first Derby. Subsequently, the mile track at Newmarket was named the Bunbury Mile to honor the owner of the first Derby winner.

There might have been as many as fifteen hundred spectators at this first running of the Derby, news of which was carried by only one newspaper, and at that in the report of a coach that overturned on the return trip from Epsom to London. Thus began the classic race that has become the most famous of all, and whose name is a synonym for an event that pits the cream of the competition against itself.

The Derby was soon imitated in Ireland and in Scotland, and its fame traveled to Britain's colonies as well as outside the empire. Now there is a Derby run at Sydney and Melbourne. The Bermuda Derby is over a hundred years old. The French Derby was first run at Chantilly in 1836. The German Derby has been run regularly at Hamburg since 1869, without interruption, even during the dark years of 1917–1921. The Austrian Derby, run at Freudenau, near Vienna, started just a year after the German race. The Spanish Derby, run at San Sebastian, was a tradition until the fall of the monarchy. One of the oldest of the South American classics is the Chilean Derby at Viña del Marrun, since 1886, followed by the Argentine Derby at Palermo in Buenos Aires, the Peruvian Derby at Miraflores in Lima, and the Brazilian Derby in Rio de Janeiro.

The classic in the United States is the Kentucky Derby, started in Louisville, Kentucky, in 1875 by Colonel Lewis Clark, but Americans have more than one derby. There are the Santa Anita Derby, the Louisiana Derby, the Florida Derby, the New Jersey Derby, the California Derby, the American Derby (Chicago), Arkansas Derby, and others. But the Kentucky Derby is the most famous and glamorous of all American races. Its 1968 running made a special kind of history. The winner was Dancer's Image. Bets were paid off, and the great victory over the favorite, Forward Pass, was celebrated. But a few days later it was announced that tests showed a pain-killing drug in his urine. By the rules of the track, Dancer's Image was disqualified and placed last. His prize money of over $100,000 was withdrawn and awarded to Forward Pass, who had come second. This was the first time such a ruling was made in such an important race, and the news spread throughout the world. It was announced that this disqualification did not affect the betting, and pay-offs of bets were unchanged. The owner of Dancer's Image, Peter Fuller, protested, and declared he would fight the decision all the way to the top court of jurisdiction.

While he was still Prince Regent, George IV gave his

309 *A print showing the racing at Siena, August 16, 1813.*
310 *"Barbs Racing Through the Streets of Florence," by Rossello di Jacopo Franchi. Museum of Art, Cleveland.*

* The first running of the Oaks, incidentally, was won by the Earl of Derby's Bridget, a daughter of the noted Herod. This classic, a distance of a mile and a half, is run at the summer Epsom meeting.—TRANS.

encouragement to all forms of sport and brought them to a popularity and perfection never before seen in England. His stud came to cost him some £30,000 a year, and he saw his own horses win about 313 races. In 1788 his colt, Sir Thomas, won the Derby. George IV instituted an annual dinner for members of the Jockey Club. The Royal Stud continued under William IV, and horse breeders had a happy and prosperous time during the long reign of Queen Victoria, with royal favor continuing under the reigns of Edward VII, George V, and George VI, but it was under Edward VII that both the English Thoroughbred breeder and the English turf reached technical and spectacular heights. Today it flourishes under Her Majesty Elizabeth II, a great turf enthusiast, with a considerable number of promising broodmares at Hampton Court.

All Thoroughbreds in existence today go back to about forty mares and the three stallions mentioned before: two bays, Matchem and Herod, and the sorrel Eclipse. In direct line, 204 stallions have sprung from Matchem, 401 from Herod, and 1,435 from Eclipse. In collateral line, there are 89 Arabs, 46 Barbs, and 38 Turks.

The Darley Arabian from whom the great majority of English Thoroughbreds derives was imported into England in 1703. This horse belongs to the Mu'niqua Hadruj strain of Arabians. The Darley Arabian was discovered in Syria by Thomas Darley, who got him in trade for a gun when the horse was eighteen months old. Manak, which was the horse's real name, was sent to England at the age of three. In 1715 he produced Flying Childers, out of Betty Leedes, a mare of Eastern parentage. The colt was to reveal himself as the fastest ever foaled in England until that time. The Darley Arabian was never raced. Instead, he began his career as a stud. The Darley Arabian's get (beginning with the rather undistinguished mares belonging to his owner and, later, others) included Almanzor, Cupid, Brigh, Daedalus, Dart, Miruka, and Aleppo, all of which took prizes despite their coming from inferior mares—a demonstration of how remarkable was the quality of their sire. Afterward better mares were bred with the great Arabian. Among the best (and best-known) of his immediate descendants were Flying Childers (Devonshire) and Bartlett's Childers (Bleeding), who were so called because they had been raised by a Mr. Childers of Carrouges. The first was sold to the Duke of Devonshire; the second went to a Mr. Bartlett.

Flying Childers was worthy of his name. He was a light bay with a spot on his forehead, and four stockings. Following the custom of the day, which prohibited the running of racehorses not yet adults, he did not appear on a racecourse until he was six. Flying Childers was so formidable a competitor that his long string of successes forced the Duke of Devonshire to retire him from the track fairly early because other owners refused to pit their horses against him. He was put to stud and sired a string of fine horses, including Plaistow, Snip, Commoner, Blaze, Poppet, and Steady, all fast, distinguished animals.

During the reign of George II (1727–1760), many light Eastern horses were introduced into England, including the Black Barb, the Cyprus Arabian, the Devonshire Arabian, the Belgrade Turk (taken at the siege of Belgrade by General Merci and sent as a gift to England), Sir William's Turk, and most famous, the Godolphin Barb, the true sire of speed. We can say that the best English racehorses spring from the Darley Arabian and the Godolphin Barb, introduced about 1728 from Paris, whose marvelous produce soon became mixed.

The Godolphin Barb's history is a series of peaks and valleys, recounted by Eugène Sue in his book on the Barb. The incredible Barb was offered, along with other horses, to Louis XV of France by the Bey of Tunis after the conclusion of a trade agreement negotiated for the French by Count de Mauty. According to Sue, "These eight Barbary horses (since we do believe that the Godolphin was a Barb), of brilliant gait, brusque and impetuous action, savage heads, angular in conformation, very little muscular mass and, what is more, very thin from the rigors of the journey, were received in the royal stables with pity, and soon after treated with infinite disdain."

The reason for this lack of sympathy was simple. Louis had a predilection for horses imported from England, usually raised in Suffolk, which served him very well in war and hunting. They were short-coupled and consequently not very long overall, with well-developed muscles and short legs, the sort of horses known in France from the Middle Ages as courtauds. The horses sent by the Bey of Tunis were soon put to the humblest service the palace afforded, and were so mistreated and ill cared for that they became vicious and unmanageable. As a result they were sold. The Godolphin went to a water-carrier who hitched him to his cart. It was in this miserable situation that he was fortuitously discovered on the Pont Neuf in Paris by the Englishman Coke. Despite the misery of the horse's condition, Coke was struck by his apparent nobility and beautiful conformation. Coke bought him for a song and took him to England. Upon Coke's death he was bequeathed to Roger Williams, who kept the St. James Coffee House in London. Williams, however, soon found the horse intractable, and sold him for twenty-five guineas to Lord Godolphin, by whose name he was thereafter known. Godolphin put his new horse to use as a teaser: The Barb had the job of discovering whether the mares on the farm were disposed to the stud Hobgoblin. Things went along in that way for some time until the day Hobgoblin refused to cover the Arabian mare Roxana, and the Godolphin Barb took his place. Their offspring was Lath, one of the finest horses of the age for his magnificent conformation. The Godolphin Barb's further irrefutable proof of his ability as a fine sire made him equal, perhaps even superior, to the Darley Arabian. As a matter of fact, among contemporary horses, those of the most distinction have his blood in their veins. After Lath came Cade, Regulus, Babram, Blank, Blassam, Sultan, Cripple, and still others that were to become turf immortals.

In 1738, three of the Godolphin Barb's offspring were entered in different races at Newmarket: Lath in the race for five-year-olds; Cade in the race for four-year-olds; and Regulus in the event for three-year-olds, and all of them won.

311 *An English print of 1843, "The Thoroughbred Sale."*
312 *A rather stylized rendition, in an English print, dating from 1850, of the Punchestown Steeplechase.*
313 *The finish at Ascot, shown in an English print of 1850.*

311

313

312

314

315   316

Lord Godolphin was so sure that his horses would win that he had ordered their sire brought to the track in great pomp to bask in the victory of his offspring. The great sire died in 1753 at the age of twenty-nine at Gogmagog in Cambridge-shire. He was buried near the stable, where one can still see his tombstone. Among the Godolphin Barb's descendants is Matchem, by Cade and the Partner Mare, a line that reached its apogee in 1834 with Melbourne.*

It should be noted that while it takes two generations to fix the Godolphin-Matchem line, it took four to go from the Byerley Turk to Herod and from the Darley Arabian to Eclipse. The Turk was a war-horse acquired in Turkey and owned by a Captain Byerly, who fought with Wil-liam II in Ireland. His most famous offspring is through Jigg, who produced Partner, from whom descends the famous Herod (originally King Herod). Herod was a son of Tartar and Cypron, foaled in 1758. From 1763 to 1767, he was un-rivaled on the English turf. All his produce were notable horses. In a sense, Herod was a forerunner for Eclipse, foaled as he was at the stud of the Duke of Cumberland.

The Story of Eclipse

The Duke of Cumberland, maternal uncle to George III, is not only unmentioned in the history of racing, but never had he the chance to enjoy the prestige after he raised two of the three foundation sires of all Thoroughbreds. The duke died in 1765, too early to share in the successes of his horses. Herod had just begun his career, and Eclipse was still too young.

Not much beguiled by the pleasures of the turf, the duke's heirs liquidated his stud farm. Among those going to auction was a dark stallion, a small bay called Marske. He was bought practically for nothing by a neighborhood rustic who put him out at stud for the ridiculous fee of a half-guinea (about $1.75 today), until the day the Earl of Abing-don, impressed by the success of Eclipse, bought him for a thousand guineas and reset his fee at one hundred guineas.

A young nameless colt excited a bit more interest than usual, the son of Marske and Spiletta, herself foaled in 1749, by Regulus, son of the Godolphin Barb out of Northern Western, by Smith's Son, a mare without any particular history (this was her first foal). The colt was a bright sorrel, with a rather long blaze and a single high stocking on one of his hind legs. He was poorly built, low in front, and with a neck that was too long, but he showed character, was some-what skittish, and such a powerful breather that he seemed almost tampered with. His strong points, however, were so remarkable and his legs so good that he brought seventy-five guineas at auction. A meat salesman named Wildman ar-rived at just the moment seventy guineas were bid, and in-

sisted that the sale had begun before the preannounced hour, and demanded that the horses that had already been sold be placed on the block once more. Wildman made his point, and when the colt again came under the hammer, he bid him in at seventy-five guineas. At about the time the colt had been foaled in 1764, a solar eclipse occurred, and thereafter he bore the name.

It was just by chance that Marske's sire, Squirt, was not destroyed. Falling into bad hands, he was put to work be-yond his strength, and became such a problem that his owner resolved to send him to the slaughterer. A stableman, how-ever, took pity on Squirt, and bought him. Through tender care and treatment, he built up the horse's strength until he was restored to health and vigor. Had it not been for this kind groom, Eclipse would never have been born, consider-ing that Marske was truly his father. Many experts believe that Eclipse's sire was Shakespeare, a horse that had the same color and markings and also served Eclipse's dam. Such a derivation would not appreciably alter Eclipse's descent because both stallions in question derive from the Darley Arabian to the same degree—from his grandchildren: Marske through Squirt, a son of Bartlett's Childers; and Shake-speare through Hobgoblin, a son of Aleppo. Eclipse might therefore be the offspring of the Montagues and Capulets of the equine world, for Marske's dam Spiletta was a grandchild of the Godolphin Barb who killed Hobgoblin in a jealous rage over the mare Roxana, a fight immortalized on canvas by Bonheur.

Eclipse was raised near Epsom. His qualities soon came to light but it became obvious that he was difficult and tem-peramental and given to sudden, unexpected reactions. Wildman, who had pinned all his hopes on Eclipse, despaired when he saw his horse's great qualities compromised by a rebellious, overbearing nature that made him almost un-manageable. He discussed his problem with a Captain O'Kelly, a great sportsman of the time. O'Kelly told him about his own stablemaster, another Irishman, named Sul-livan, who was nicknamed "The Charmer" because of his almost magical ability to dominate the most rebellious horses. O'Kelly offered Sullivan's services in return for a share (eventually acquiring complete ownership) in Eclipse, the exact price to be agreed upon after Eclipse's first public ap-pearance. The horse would continue in Wildman's care, and O'Kelly would lend Sullivan to him. Wildman accepted. Sullivan arrived, locked himself in Eclipse's box, clapped his mouth over one of the horse's nostrils, and like someone giving artificial respiration proceeded to fill the horse's lungs with his own breath, pausing now and then to murmur mysteriously to his patient. After a few minutes of this treat-ment, Sullivan left the box and Eclipse was a docile, gentle, well-behaved animal!

In Eclipse's day, racehorses did not race until they were at least five years old, not having acquired the precocity of today's animals. Eclipse made his first public appearance on May 3, 1769, at the age of five, at Epsom in a race for a £50 purse. This was after long preparation by Wildman, who had taken care to keep bettors ignorant of his horse's perform-ance, and had possibly given false information regarding the hour of the animal's last workout. By the time the spectators arrived, the workout was all over. Notwithstanding, they managed to get some information preserved in a letter from

---

* After his last race at fifteen, he retired as a stud in 1763. He is credited with Man o' War, among other noted winners.—EDS.

314 *"The Races," by V. Adam.*
315 *Gavarni's "At the Races."*
316 *The races were a favorite subject of Dégas. Here, a detail from his "Before the Grandstand." Louvre, Paris.*

an old man who had watched Eclipse work out: "I don't know whether it was a race or not, but I saw a horse with white legs who was a monstrous runner and went over a great distance, and behind him, another horse. The second horse could do anything you might want but he couldn't ever catch up to that horse with the white legs, even if he ran to the end of the world."

The field comprised the five-year-old Gower, owned by Fortesque; the six-year-old Chance, owned by Castle; Social, owned by Jennings; and Plume, owned by Quick. The distance was 6,400 meters, or the usual four-mile course of the time. Eclipse did the distance in six minutes, passing the finish line at a hunting gallop in front of the field. At the second trial, O'Kelly bet a thousand guineas against five hundred that Eclipse would not only win but beat all his competition by at least an eighth of a mile. O'Kelly won his bet. After the race, Wildman set Eclipse's value at £935.

Eclipse had a short but illustrious career. He ran two seasons and won every race in which he was entered, twenty-six in all, from May 1769 to October 1770. Eclipse began his career as a stud in 1771, and distinguished himself in this role, too. His services were in such demand that Captain O'Kelly kept raising his fee until it reached £1,000.

The English Jockey Club

Without the precise control of the English Jockey Club, it is doubtful that horse racing, as we know it today, would have developed as fabulously as it has in the past two centuries. We do not have exact details concerning the origins of the Jockey Club, but tradition, generally accepted, fixes it as being established by a group of respectable gentlemen at the Red Lion Inn during a race meeting in Newmarket (around 1750) when they discovered that irregularities were being committed. Newmarket had been a fashionable racing center from the beginning of the seventeenth century. James I had visited Newmarket in 1605 and, among the attractions the town afforded, enjoyed watching a race; and we have seen that Charles took an interest in racing there.

It was around the time of George II that the first regulations of the Jockey Club appeared, and the club, by virtue of its competence and the dedication of its members, quickly assumed its place as the ultimate indisputable authority over England's racecourses. Control of the country's tracks had always been left to a committee that was responsible to the Crown, but in 1758 the first regulation of the Jockey Club appeared, dealing with the weight of jockeys.

Probably the effective establishment of the Jockey Club can be dated from 1752, when two of its members, the Duke of Lancaster and the Marquis of Hastings, undertook a fifty-year lease from William Errat, a Newmarket horse dealer, for a property upon which the Jockey Club built its first home. They called it the Coffee Room of the Jockey Club, while the Dining Room of the Jockey Club continued where it had started, at the Red Lion, until 1771.

Thereafter, first by purchasing from Errat's heirs the land it had rented, and acquiring additional lots as well, the Jockey Club established its site in Newmarket High Street, and also took possession of extensive holdings on the outskirts of town. It was on this land that the famous exercise tracks were laid out and, later, the two famous racecourses, as well as the buildings and installations. The stewards of the Jockey Club, three in number, were first recognized by the *Racing Calendar* of 1770, and have been included ever since. No steward serves more than three consecutive years, with the turnover of one member each year. The *Racing Calendar* (first issued in 1727 by John Cheny) is published annually by the Jockey Club, and the *General Stud Book*, begun in 1791,* continues to come out every four years under the imprint of Weatherby and Sons.

At the beginning of the nineteenth century, the club's prestige reached a point where its regulations became obligatory for every race meeting at English racecourses. By 1879, no jockey could ride unless he had been licensed by the club.

The club has no president, but there are several standing committees concerned with finance, regulations, and so on, drawn from members of the club. Excluding honorary members, most of whom are foreigners and/or representatives of racing clubs outside England, the club today has about sixty members, including the entire royal family. One can say that the English Jockey Club has been, and continues to be, a sort of racing autocracy, serious, competent, and active. Clearly, no one would dream of questioning or diminishing its authority.

The Steeplechase in England

The English steeplechase derives directly from the cross-country, and in it are preserved some of the characteristic irregularities of that course—the frequent obstacles alternating with long, flat stretches, the general similarity of the fences, and, at Aintree, the slight passage before the brush. The most difficult fence in the Aintree course is Beecher's Brook, for besides the water-filled ditch, the jump is just a few feet from a right-angle turn. Of the forty or more horses starting in the Grand National, the majority fall, tripping over horses already fallen or stumbling along the way. There is no doubt that the Grand National presents the toughest steeplechase course in the world. It is four miles, 856 yards in length, and the "water" is fifteen feet wide, while there are thirty obstacles in all. Officially called The Grand National Handicap Steeplechase, a name that it has borne since 1847, the race was instituted in 1839 by William Lynn, who kept an inn in Liverpool. This most difficult of steeplechases had a variety of titles until it received the name by which it has since been known, although it is usually referred to colloquially as "The National."

Incidentally, the actual word "steeplechase" derives from the custom of outlining the racecourse by orienting it with church steeples. The original idea of a steeplechase, with the exception of the Grand National, is to simulate

* The *Introduction To A General Stud Book*, followed in 1793 by Volume I. —EDS.

317 *The Northampton Steeplechase, from an English print.*
318 *"The midnight point-to-point," an English print.*

317

318

319

320

natural conditions in order to test a horse's quality as a hunter. For that reason, steeplechasers are not necessarily Thoroughbreds. Allied to steeplechasing is hurdle racing, which differs from steeplechasing in that the course is usually run over a dirt track, at a racecourse, over open hurdles. For some time, because of the dirt and danger to spectators and participants from flying hurdles, this type of racing went into a decline, but it has been taken up again.

III
FRANCE

The earliest documentation of racing in France goes back to 1370 and Saumur, but this was no more than a local diversion such as those Breton amusements that were an old tradition on the occasion of any festivity. The first horse race per se of which we know was on May 15, 1651, resulting from a bet between Prince d'Harcourt and the Duke de Joyeuse, which altered the race from a public event to a court exhibition.

The real patron of French racing, however, was the Count d'Artois, brother of Louis XIV. The count imported Sphinx (through his father a half-brother of Eclipse) and King Pepin from England, and founded a racecourse at the Champ-de-Mars. The races quickly caught on, and so did gambling.

Following the fashion of private betting, the Marquis de Stallan bet against a syndicate headed by the Duke de Bourbon on a race that covered the distance between Paris and Chantilly four times (about 100 miles), which his horse won, with a time of five hours, thirty-three minutes; Lord Pascool won a marathon in 1754 when his horse covered the distance from Paris to Fontainebleau (about 35 miles) in an hour and forty-eight minutes.

Races, as we more or less know them, however, came into being under Louis XVI with the institution of a jockey club he organized in the Sablons with regular spring and fall meetings. The first races were those held at Fontainebleau in November of 1777 with a field of forty horses, followed by one with forty asses. There were other races at Vincennes in 1781. Marie Antoinette had the urge to keep stables, but was prevented from doing so by the king, who was particularly incensed by the "affair of the necklace" at the time the suggestion was made.

The Royal Printing House issued rules and regulations for horse races along with specifications on weight, certificates of origin, and weights to be carried by foreign horses. This was the earliest manifestation of racetrack protectionism, which still exists in many countries. This practice fortunately is balanced by the more sophisticated policies of others.

The races continued even for a time during the first days of the revolutionary period, under the aegis of royal patronage. This was the classic bread-and-circus pattern of attempting to divert the populace rather than ameliorate social conditions. Ultimately, these meetings were turned into a series of festivals, in the Greek manner, held on the Champ-de-Mars, and included not only horse racing but harness and foot racing as well.

Not until the Napoleonic period did France issue its first official decree referring to racing, which harked back to an old project of Bourgelat and Le Boucher of 1770. The two tried to demonstrate the usefulness of racing as a means of improving the equine breed, and recommended that France follow England's example in this respect. Napoleon's decree, dated August 31, 1805, covered racing beginning in 1808 in the departments of France that could produce the best horses, and he established three series of prizes in each departmental capital: for 4,000 meters three purses of Fr 1,200, the three winners then to participate in a race over the same distance for a prize of Fr 2,000; the winners of the semifinals were to race in the Grand Prix at Paris for a purse of Fr 4,000.

The criteria established for weights are extremely odd: age and height. If a horse were five years old and 14.2 hands high, he carried 100 pounds; if he stood 15.1 hands, he carried approximately 150 pounds; and at 16 hands, it went up accordingly.

The races were in somewhat of a decline in the period subsequent to the empire, but were once more as popular as ever around 1819, when there were regular races for five-year-olds and others. Local prizes ran from Fr 800 to Fr 1,200 with the big ones going as high as Fr 2,000; a Grand Prix Royal, run in Paris, offered Fr 6,000. Following the division of the country into northern and southern zones, total prizes distributed amounted to Fr 78,000.

The true renascence of equestrian sport in France came with Napoleon III, with foreign noblemen such as Lord Henry Seymour, Count Demidoff, and the Spanish rider Chevalier de Machado participating in races. (French sportsmen who frequented the tracks in England spoke of Britain's prestige in equine matters with admiration and envy.)

In 1833, the year the Duke d'Orléans through Louis Philippe helped create the French Stud Book, the Société d'Encouragement pour l'Amélioration des Races de Chevaux en France (the Society to Encourage Improvement of Equine Breeds in France) had been founded by MM. Fasquel, Cambis, Caccia Delamarre, and Rieussec, Count Demidoff, Charles Laffitte, Ernest Leroy, Lord Seymour, the celebrated horseman Machado, the Prince of Moscow, and M. Normandie. Soon afterward, the usual opposition arose to declare that the association did nothing whatsoever toward improving the breed. The members, therefore, changed the name to the Jockey Club, and so it has remained. The resources of the few founding members were not great and they established club headquarters in an upstairs room of a cottage in a corner of Tivoli in Paris which was owned by a British subject named Thomas Bryon. It was the first home of the very influential organization that exists in Paris today.

Among the first criticisms that taxed the new club was the allegation that it was not following the norms and principles that had determined its founding, the most important of which was that it would race English horses exclusively,

319 *The jockey Ginestrelli takes Signorinetta to the scales after winning the Derby at Epsom in 1908, two days after taking the Oaks, a rare exploit.* L'Illustrazione Italiana.
320 *Returning from the races at San Siro, a cavalcade of elegant rigs in 1901.* La Domenica del Corriere.

completely setting aside native stock. There was a great deal of fuss and furor in Paris over the imposition of English technical terminology and the aping of styles, customs, and usages in vogue in England, to the point of discussing track matters only in English.

Very soon, however, with the naming of the pretender to the throne, the Duke d'Orléans, as honorary president, the club developed greatly and increased in prestige, particularly so after it moved to elegant rooms in the Boulevard des Italiens, near the corner of rue Helder, where it became very much a social center (and even more so, when it was elegantly installed in the Boulevard Montmartre, near rue Grange-Batelière).

Members of the club came from the court, the world of politics and banking, and the press. The club soon began to publish an official bulletin with news of what was going in on its various departments. Three sponsors were required to propose a new member, who had to pay an initiation fee of Fr 500 and an annual subscription of Fr 300. Although no such restriction appeared in the Statutes, it was tacitly understood that those in the trades and arts, the businessmen and the literati, would be barred. A curious exception to this rule was made—not for registered stockbrokers, but for unlicensed amateurs who speculated on the Bourse. Later, of course, it became obvious that votes were cast more upon the basis of personal taste and preference than anything else, so that the much-bruited admission of M. Rambeteau, the prefect of the Seine as well as a sportsman, became a *cause célèbre*.

The clubhouse was very popular with the members, and the scene of brilliant social gatherings. It had handsomely decorated billiard and reading rooms, and in its luxuriously appointed salons any discussion of politics was forbidden, though in practice politics (and Jockey Club politics, as well) was the favorite subject of conversation, and the very reason that many of the members attended.

In those first years of the Jockey Club's existence, because of a complex of factors rather difficult to evaluate today, the Club's efforts toward protectionism in relation to the production of native breeds was nil. At that time there were some 2½ million horses in all of French territory, which was further reduced by about 150,000 over a period of fifteen years. From 1823 to 1840, Fr 87 million were spent abroad on remounts for the cavalry. Notable French breeds such as the Limousin and Auvergne were crossbred to such an extent that purebreds practically disappeared. The administration of the state studs, founded in 1665 by Colbert, suppressed in 1790 and reestablished in 1806, had required in the period from 1806 to 1840 Fr 80 million, mainly to import English horses and finance competitions for English Thoroughbreds. This only added to the despair in the mid-nineteenth century of those who proposed to improve native French breeds, and were doing everything they could to develop French horse breeding. Certainly, it is difficult to criticize their methods, but results were extremely modest, to the further disillusionment of all breeders and sportsmen.

Some years later, a change was made in betting rules, establishing that all wagers would be noted in a "book," giving the amount bet and the name of the bettor. For many years, contrary to the custom in England, bets were limited to a few louis, and a wager of twenty-five louis was considered big money, indeed. In discussing betting, it is well to remember that at this period bets were not made only at the track. Horses furnished many pretexts for gambling. The English, for instance, had a passion for arranging original competitive events for the sake of a wager. For example, there were long speed relay races along the highways, such as the one in which George Osbaldeston won a rich purse in 1831 after covering two hundred miles in eight hours and forty-two minutes, using up three horses. The Marquis of Waterpont wagered on jumping a 4½-foot obstacle in his own bedroom; the Jockey Club in Paris sponsored a game of billiards played on horseback; and de Brizzi, a French master of equitation, won a bet for taking off in a balloon from horseback!

If the cost of breeding (especially) and raising horses at that period in France's history was extremely high, we must remember that owners refused to employ French labor in any capacity, insisting that all employees with access to the stables be English. The daily cost of maintaining a horse was about Fr 6, which meant an annual expenditure of nearly Fr 2,200, far more than what a father needed to put his son through school. Three or four grooms assigned to each horse each received a monthly wage of Fr 125. Added to the cost of choice forage (very high), oats and grain, made it a very dear occupation to run a stable, particularly a racing stud. As a matter of fact, of all the charter members of the Jockey Club, only eight could put horses in the field: Lord Henry Seymour and MM. Fasquel, Achille Fould, Anthony Rothschild, de Beauveau, Lupin, Pontalba, and Perrégaux. By then, the Jockey Club had members whose original enthusiasm for horses had waned somewhat and who went to the track more out of habit than anything else; others, who had been staunch proponents of improving the breed, rested content to let any horse run just so that they could go to the track and mingle with the owners who were really making an effort. During these formative years of the club, the first hunt was formed, in 1840. England already had some two hundred hunts and packs.

Adding to the problems of future racing historians, the French studs had a penchant for naming their horses after celebrated English mounts, such as Plover and Reveler. Others, however, gave their products names of famous or even notorious actresses; lyric-opera divas were great favorites. Still following English custom, some studs gave their horses a simple genetic designation, like Bay Colt by Plenipo out of Black Filly, while others chose more poetic names that hinted at the horse's descent: Oak Stick, a son of Royal Oak; Sophisme by Paradox; and Révenant, son of Phantome.

In 1842, for trials the time fixed for 1¼ miles was reduced to two minutes and forty seconds from the 1822 maximum time of three minutes (and five minutes and five seconds for 2½ miles).

321 *The Godolphin Barb, foaled about 1724.*
322 *The Byerly Turk (Dk. b.h.), foaled about 1680.*
323 *The Darley Arabian, probably a Barb, foaled about 1700.*
324 *Flying Childers (B.h.), foaled 1715, by the Darley Arabian.*
325 *Matchem (B.h.), foaled 1748, by Cade out of Partner Mare.*
326 *Eclipse (Ch.h.), 1764, by Marske out of Spiletta, continuing the line of the Darley Arabian.*

321

322

323

324

325

326

327

328

329

330

331

332

In the period 1838–1848, the number of horses belonging to private owners increased by ten the original figure, and racing, through the club, had assumed a definite direction. (In 1854 there were still many owners of winning horses at the Champ-de-Mars and Chantilly who were not members of the Jockey Club. Nevertheless, the names of great owners and horsemen have been preserved, men such as Normandie, Vaublanc, Edgar Ney, the Prince of Moscow, Allouard, and Lord Seymour.)

The race analogous to the English Derby, the Prix du Jockey Club (the French Derby), was established in 1835, and from 1836 was run over 2,400 meters for a prize of Fr 7,500. This was raised to Fr 10,000 in 1847, and Fr 20,000 in 1855. In 1853, in imitation of England, a Criterium was instituted for colts, and another, a Grand Criterium, for fillies.

Around 1848, trotting races, always very popular in Normandy, were begun at Neuilly and then at Vincennes, but the purses were small, and the events attracted too few spectators, who mainly preferred races at the gallop. It was only in the next century that trotting races grew in public favor, finally to become the popular sporting event they are today.

The Longchamp racetrack, established by the club, was inaugurated in 1856. Races were divided into three meetings totalling twenty-nine days of events. In 1860, there was the first offer of big money for prizes—Fr 945,350 having been paid out for the year, of which Fr 510,000 had come from the state. When one considers that there was an additional Fr 357,150 in entry fees, one arrives at the formidable sum of over Fr 1.3 million in prize money.

In 1863, the Duke de Morny campaigned to have the Grand Prix launched as an international affair. Toward this end, the City of Paris gave Fr 50,000, and each of five railway companies gave Fr 10,000, thus establishing the richest purse of the era, a prize of Fr 100,000. Until then the prize was an *objet d'art* presented by the empire, along with Fr 10,000 and Fr 5,000 to the place and show horses, taken out of the stake money. From that point on, things went well for the French track, and from the last years of the nineteenth century to today there has been a continuous increase in the number of tracks and champions, as well as prizes.

It might be noted that the French imported English Thoroughbreds only after their failure to create a new breed from acclimated Arabians. Foundation sires were invariably English—stallions such as Master Waggs, Beggarman, Emilius, the renowned Gladiator, Royal Oak, and The Emperor. It was only in 1867 that a French stud, Monarque, succeeded

in making his mark. Naturally, the four great French families derive from the great English sires: Fitz Gladiator and Dollar come from the Byerly Turk, while the Monarque and Pluto lines spring from the Darley Arabian.

The French turf currently leads all Europe, and is threatened only by the United States as a competitor. As we know, however, the American track does not favor the development of the sort of horses needed for European racing. In the United States most races are short, chiefly six or seven furlongs. Very few are more than 1⅛ miles. Accordingly, American horses are bred and trained essentially for speed. In France, races on average are much longer, and endurance quality is the prime objective. Also, in the United States all tracks are flat, with simple circular turns. In France, as in England, there are occasionally slopes and sharp turns. Thus, when an American horse runs on a French track he may not be able to adjust to the differences.

The French turf has been exceedingly fortunate to have been blessed with Marcel Boussac, the industrialist and sportsman. He is a financial genius who has managed to put racing and breeding on a businesslike basis, bringing France to a point of economic leadership and extraordinary productivity. In 1966, for instance, Fr 6 billion were bet, representing an increase of 400 percent in four years. From racing alone, which has afforded the French government more revenue than any other state sport or theatrical activity, the Treasury received a net amount of Fr 840 million (exclusive of taxes on admissions, installations, and plant).

In addition to permitting the selection of horses that are stayers and fast at the same time, the traditional French racing program allows the French to cross the Channel and take honors from the English. In Britain, horses have been raised in the recent past that in the main lacked in stamina but in the last year or two have shown a great change in that direction. Of course, there has been a tendency to breed fast two-year-olds to compensate for the rising cost of training, but the leading owners still want Derby horses with stamina as well as speed. French racing is based upon about fifty flat-racing tracks scattered throughout the country both in the cities and in the provincial areas. French breeders are extremely active as exporters, shipping studs, trotters, and Thoroughbreds, including the winner of the Arc de Triomphe, a son of the American horse Dan Cupid, to the United States.

We have noted elsewhere that France takes a great interest in horses bred abroad; and while she seems to ignore Italian production (Nearco, Donatello, and others came exclusively out of French bloodlines), she is very much taken with American horses. Among the twelve horses qualifying to race recently are two that were born in America, Blue Tom, by Tompion, and Gazala, by Dark Star. There are also offspring of American studs by Dan Cupid.

327 *Melton (B.w.), 1882, by Master Kildare by Lord Ronald by Stockwell.*
328 *Ormonde (B.h.), 1883, by Bend Or by Doncaster by Stockwell.*
329 *Hampton (B.h.), 1872, by Lord Clifden.*
330 *Stockwell (Ch.h.), 1849, by The Baron.*
331 *St. Simon (Dk.b.h.), 1881, by Galopin out of St. Angela.*
332 *Touchstone (B.h.), 1831, by Camel out of Banter.*

Longchamp

Almost all the great French tracks scattered throughout the country have their model in the Longchamp racetrack, which was founded in 1859 and then completely rebuilt by 1966, in a singular way: The old glorious stands were taken down section by section, but the new ones, in reinforced concrete, came down the track at a speed of nine meters an hour to replace the old, moving a total distance of three hundred meters. This was the first time in the history of architecture that such a procedure was adopted for normal construction. Now Longchamp has a capacity for fifteen thousand spectators under a roof without pillars, with space enough to seat more than half. Sixteen escalators and twelve elevators are included in the modern addition. The entire project was realized both through the organizing genius of Marcel Boussac and the immense contribution of Jean Romanet, the director general of the Société d'Encouragement, who, at the same time, was responsible for the installations at the colossal breeding center at Chantilly and the extension of the straightaway at Deauville.

The Steeplechase in France

Steeplechase and hurdle racing have developed in France primarily at the Auteuil, Fontainebleau, Pau, Compiègne, Cagnes-sur-Mer, and Aix-les-Bains tracks.

The first steeplechase races in France were run about 1830. They took place in the Bois de Boulogne and the Bièvre Valley. From 1836 on, they were held regularly at the Croix de Berny, a track somewhat different from the one at Auteuil, but with a prescribed course. Taking part in these races were gentlemen riders on hunters. They attracted a group of fashionable spectators, but the great mass of the public did not attend. Despite the efforts made by 1850 by the studs interested in promoting such races, they would have disappeared had a few particularly enthusiastic sportsmen not taken matters into their own hands. Such men were the founders of the Société des Steeple-chases de France, which was established in 1863.

With the founding of the Société the history of French steeplechase racing became inextricably entwined with flat racing and equestrian sport. The Société followed the course it had mapped out at its inception, and what was at first a risky distraction for a few daring horsemen became a national sport as well as a magnificent spectacle, which attracts a vast public and is a pillar of France's equestrian activities. The new society had its first headquarters at Vincennes, where it held ten meetings in its first year of activity. This was a modest start, but its importance was almost immediately evident when a few years later it moved to the administration and control of all steeplechase courses in France.

The Franco-Prussian War in 1870 put the brake on all this activity and progress. In 1873 the Société moved its Vincennes headquarters, which had not been spared by the war. A new racecourse was built to order in the Bois de Boulogne, at that time on the outskirts of Paris. The track was Auteuil, and it is still the pride of French racing, with nothing to envy of Longchamp. It was from Auteuil that the Société took its giant steps, notwithstanding its ten-year existence. At Auteuil the great jump races came into existence—the Grand Steeple-chase de Paris, in 1874, and the Grand Course des Haies d'Auteuil. There were twelve meetings that year and several years later there were forty. By 1910, the number had reached forty-five, and there it has remained. Naturally, over the years there has been an increase both in the number of races and entrants. From four races, the

meetings have grown to seven or eight, and the average number of participants has gone from six to seven to ten to twelve.

By 1909, Auteuil had grown even more attractive. It was only with the outbreak of war in 1914 that the constant development of the course was interrupted. After the war, when racing started again, everything was renovated, from tracks to grandstand. The inauguration of the renovated track in 1924 was a festive day for the Société and steeple-chasing. In 1932 the Société managed, during a difficult economic period, to maintain the organization and installations at Auteuil, although on a somewhat reduced scale. During the war years 1940 to 1944, Auteuil was the only Parisian track that continued in operation. By reducing the dimensions of some of the jumps, a flat-racing track was improvised on which versions of the Derby and Grand Prix were run.

With peace, Auteuil took up once again its rhythm of continual improvement. Auteuil today can be proud of its irrigation system, its subterranean electric cables and plant, a new pavilion, and a fine system for photographing the races, all outgrowths of its efficient organization and administration.

The history of Auteuil races themselves is grand and glorious, full of rich incident and splendid detail. There have been many dramatic moments, especially because the course is an extremely difficult challenge for both horse and rider. It is also one of the richest in the world, and as unique in France as the Grand National course is in England. The Grand Steeple-chase de Paris offers a sure opportunity of testing and proving the ability of horse and jockey over the entire race; its course is designed and punctuated with fences of different types and jumps of varying degrees of difficulty so that a real race can be run, rather than just a series of trials and spectacular incidents. The perfection that has gone into the designing of this course is seen in a race in which a bit and bridle were lost at the third jump, but with the horse finishing first, without any further incident; as has also occurred at Aintree. The race takes place under superb conditions and, in addition, marks the opening of the traditional *Grande Semaine* (Great Week) of racing. This is followed by the Grand Course des Haies and the Prix des Drags, both fashionable occasions that add to the crescendo of racing fervor and social gaiety that culminates in the running of the Grand Prix de Paris, at the height of the Paris season.

IV

IRELAND

Imposing results that spring from modest resources justify our interest in the general organization of Irish breeding and racing. Ireland has a good part of the world market in horses. Naturally, special circumstances have contributed to the success of the Irish, such as the gift of important foreign studs, particularly those of the late Aga and Aly Khan and those that are maintained by the Aga Khan's grandson, Karim. These have given Ireland great incentive and tremendous prestige. There is also the fact that many important English racing studs have established themselves in Ireland. Adding to its appeal, apart from its natural resources that make it such a fine country for horses, and all the activity connected with them, is a receptive and hospitable atmosphere springing from an easy familiarity with horses and racing which helps make all this activity possible.

In past years, Ireland's interest in horses was almost exclusively in her jumpers. As racing material or show jumpers or cross-country mounts, they enjoyed a fine reputation throughout the world. In no country in the world, perhaps, is love for horses and equestrian sport so general and so much a part of the people as in Ireland. Notwithstanding, interest in Thoroughbreds and in flat racing open to the public is something comparatively new. As a matter of fact, after World War I, the situation was not particularly bright, and in 1926 things had fallen to a very low and alarming state because of the government's indifference, which had continued right down to the end of World War II. By 1938, race meetings had been reduced to a minimum, and very few tracks, mostly those in the vicinity of Dublin, managed to exist. Prize money for thoroughbred races was down to a grand total of about £80,000.

Export of horses of every type, however, was a very positive element in Ireland's foreign trade, and the raising of Thoroughbreds has contributed so much to the economy that races can be considered more an aspect of an industry than the guise of a sport. As a matter of fact, these races are much more trials to measure the quality of the product and, simultaneously, showcases—a spectacular type of advertising.

Alarmed by the economic situation of the horse market, the government finally began to interest itself more intelligently in the Thoroughbred and in thoroughbred racing. It gave economic aid to exporters, contributed to purses for thoroughbred races, and promoted a reorganization, which included subsidies and definite financial and economic privileges to a National Stud that was conceived not only as a speculative venture but also as a controlling organ and extension service for private studs. During the years of World War II, the government's new interest in racing expressed itself practically in a contribution of £10,000 for classic purses in each racing season and, finally, in 1954, was translated into a Racing Board and Racecourses Bill that signaled the start of a new era.

Among other provisions, this law instituted a voluntary commission comprising eleven unpaid members who were held responsible for taxing bets made with bookmakers and overseeing wagers placed at the track through the totalisator. At the start, the tax on bets was 5 percent, but after six months' experience and study, this was reduced to 2½ percent on bets placed with bookmakers, a most unusual and enlightened act on the part of any government. The government's attitude has resulted in honest and disciplined compliance by the bookmakers, who are conscious of their advantages under the system and, therefore, happy to assume their responsibilities. In addition, the Racing Board has a schedule of stiff fines to be applied to those attempting to evade payment of the tax, and repeaters can lose their bookmakers' license.

By 1966, Irish thoroughbred racing had made great progress and showed a substantial increment over previous years' activity. In that year, total prize money amounted to £763,369 as against £735,148 in 1965. The volume of betting on the course had increased by 15 percent, with an even larger increase in bets placed through bookmakers, estimated at £10,000,000.

V

ITALY

The first Italian imports of Thoroughbreds from England go back to three broodmares acquired by Prince di Butera in 1808; the stallion Jerry bought by Prince de' Medici de Ottajana in 1828; Ariel, purchased by Count Saint John in the same year; the five mares imported by the King of Piedmont, Carlo Alberto in 1830; and the ten mares that arrived in Naples for Giuseppe de' Medici. Also in 1837, some very high-priced stallions were imported for the royal stud.

This, however, is virtually prehistory, the days of the pioneers. However, there had been some isolated races in Italy prior to 1800, generally arising out of bets made by horse owners. One can talk of race meetings proper only in 1827, when these began to be held during the spring on the field at Quercione in Florence. Regular activity began in 1837, after the establishment of a Florentine racing society. In that same year regular meetings were begun at the Campo di Marte course in Naples, and meetings were held in Piedmont and Sicily.

One gets an idea of the tenor of this racing from contemporary announcements, like the one from Turin, dated 1809:

> The race shall begin on the great Rivoli road and shall be continued over the Via della Dora to the Piazza Imperiale where two columns shall indicate the finish. The riders shall wear tunics and white pantaloons, like the model on display near the Municipal Building and shall not use either spurs or whip. Each racer shall have a colored ribbon that may be worn as a scarf and upon which shall be painted or embroidered the number assigned by lot.

A few years later, still at Turin, we find two consecutive days of racing programmed, one for native horses, the fifteenth of November, and the sixteenth for horses of any breed whatsoever. In some Florentine regulations of 1837, we find provisions very like those of today concerning the start and the conduct of the race. In Naples, in some regulations dated 1840, there is this stipulation: "Each jockey must wear a shirt of silk or velvet in a color or colors most pleasing to the owner. The breeches shall be of yellow or white velvet or leather and the boots with tops." More specific and precise are the regulations for Milan, written in 1843. The same regulations, fourteen years later, are so complete that they comprise 105 articles, and detail the races for Senago and Garbagnate, over the flats there, stipulating that these are to be of "three types": (1) for horses of every breed, (2) for Italian horses, (3) for Lombard horses, that is, for horses foaled and raised in the nine provinces that made up the Kingdom of Lombardy.

We begin to have news of an association of racing societies in 1862, when Bologna, Milan, and Turin attempted to orient their meetings on a similar basis and establish technical regulations of a general character, such as those covering differences in weights in horses of different ages, which were to be graduated in accordance with the distance.

A few years later, in 1869, we find the constitution of a Lombard racing society, and then, in 1870, San Rossore comes into view, organizing two days of racing annually. For the first time, regulations were made for betting.

A bulletin published by the Jockey Club tells us that the following courses were in operation in Italy in 1881: Piedmont: Turin, Alba, Alessandria, Asti, Saluzzo, and Vercelli; Lombardy: Milan, Varese, and Monza; Veneto: Padua, Treviso, Udine, and Verona; Venezia Tridentina (Trentino-Alto Adige): Merano; Emilia (Emilia-Romagna): Bologna and Volta di Reno; The Marches: Pesaro and Sinigaglia (Senigallia); Tuscany: Florence, Leghorn, Pisa, and Grosseto; Umbria: Gubbio and Perugia; Latium: Rome, Tor di Quinto, Fregene, Monterotondo, and Nettuno; Campania: Naples, Castellammare di Stabia and Capua; Apulia: Bari, Foggia, Lecce, Lucera, San Severo, Andria, and Cerignola; and Sicily: Palermo.

Only Lombardy and Tuscany have maintained the position they had a little less than a hundred years ago; Piedmont depends only upon Turin; Veneto has a minor meeting at Treviso and Emilia, The Marches, and Umbria have disappeared from the list; Latium, Campania, and Apulia each has retained only one track; Sicily has stayed with Palermo, where racing goes on after having been discontinued for a long period, but Merano has inherited and improved the old autumn meeting.

In 1966, there were thirteen tracks in operation: Rome, with ninety-seven days of racing; Milan with eighty-six, Naples with fifty-three, Turin with thirty-five, Leghorn with thirty-two, Florence with twenty-seven, Merano with seventeen, Varese with seventeen, Pisa with nine, Treviso with nine, Grosseto with seven, Foggia with six, and Monza with four, in all, 399 days.

The first races were promoted by the hackney club. One of its documents reads: "The hunting season always ended with a race, which was repeated every year with great success." Another document, from 1844, gives us a picture of the sporting life of the day: "Today the long-announced races finally took place, so often postponed because of the bad weather we have been having, but they did not run at Ponte Lamentano as usual but at Roma Vecchia, outside Porta San Giovanni, on the left side of the Albano road, where there was a great parade of carriages and people on horseback and on foot. There were seven races, five of them only for the English, another for horses from the Roman countryside, and another for horses belonging to Roman owners, ridden by their grooms."

Thus, we can say that the fields of Roma Vecchia and the year 1844 saw the initiation of Roman racing. This area, with the Prati Fiscali, as well as the Torre Spaccata, served just for occasional racecourses that had to be marked out each time races were held. There was, however, a definite wish to give Rome a permanent racetrack. The choice fell on Capannelle, where work was begun under the direction of Prince Marcantonio Colonna who had made a study of tracks in England and France. The first official races at the new track were held on March 15, 1881. Capannelle (Little Huts) has its origin in the two shelters for shepherds at the crossroads of the Via Appia Nuova and the Via Appia Pignatelli, just a mile before the track that exists today.

The yearbooks report that the first running of the Italian Derby was under the aegis of the Jockey Club Italiano, but a derby was run at Milan, over the Arena course, on May 13, 1864, won by Weatherbow (owned by Elijah Carter) who beat out Cariddi (owned by Ercole Turati). The prize was for those days very tempting—10,000 lire to the winner and 4,000 to the horse that placed.

In comparison with the progress made by other Italian cities, Milan was late in getting its racing started, primarily because of political difficulties; but when it did finally get around to it, Milan was lucky enough to find such men as Count Durini, Count Turati, Marquis Fossati, and such families as the Cicogna, Trivulzio, Sormano, Ponti, Porro, Venino, Melzi, Negroni, Silvestri, Visconti, Litta, Scheibler, Locatelli, and Arpisella. Together they created on the outskirts of Milan, in the San Siro district, one of the finest racecourses and a great and well-organized training center. There were races in Milan, more or less organized, as early as 1807, patronized by the stables along the road and held on the present Buenos Aires course, then a long road in the middle of the fields. Two programs that year were preserved in the house of Count Gian Giacomo Durini, whose great-uncle had been one of the organizers of the races. Prints from 1822 depict races and jockeys around the Piazza d'Armi, which would lead us to think that, as was usual for such events, these were probably thoroughbred handicaps with horses imported from England. Only at Milan did racing proceed along scientific lines and with a definite seriousness and scholarly intent. The *Gazzetta Privilegiata di Milano*, as we learn from the Marquis Calabrini's *Storia della corse dei cavalli in Italia* (History of Horse Racing in Italy), gives notice of the founding of a racing association. The announcement is edited in typical Milanese style, with extreme precision, and gives a list of names that echo the society of the city in that day and its serious involvement in every form of scientific and sporting endeavor. The *Gazzetta* dated May 1, 1830, notes:

Count Ottavio Agosti, Prince Emilio Belgiojoso, Emanuele Brambilla, Duke di Cannizzaro, Count Lorenzo Castellani, Count Carlo Cicogna, Marquis Gilberto Porro, Marquis Raimondi, Giovanni Resta, Count Sola, Count Lodovico Taverna, Count Angelo Trivulzio, and Count Uberto Visconti have formed a society in Milan to organize each year until 1840, in the spring and fall, if possible, one or more horse races. The same organizers have also decided to admit annual members who would pay yearly dues of three louis and would, in return, enjoy full membership rights except that they cannot serve on the board of directors, and also ten-year members, who will pay annual dues of one louis and will not be permitted to enter horses in races unless

333 *Carbine (B.h.), 1885, in Australia, by Masket.*
334 *Common (B.h.), 1888, by Isonomy.*
335 *Persimmon (B.h.), 1893, by St. Simon.*
336 *Cyllene (Ch.h.), 1895, by Bona Vista by Bend Or.*
337 *Flying Fox (B.h.), 1896, by Orme by Ormonde.*
338 *Diamond Jubilee (B.h.), 1897, by St. Simon.*

333   334

335   336

337   338

339

340   341

342

they paid three louis in the year during which they would like their horses to participate. Those wishing to read the Society's statutes and inscribe themselves as either annual or decennial members may call at the home of Count Carlo Cicogna. The first race will take place, weather permitting, on May 18 at the Piazza d'Armi.

In 1842 the society was disbanded, as was the racing section, in 1848, by the government, because of political interferences. The races were also suspended, but there were some run in 1852 and then in 1857 under the auspices of an association that organized them on the fields of Senago. It was only in 1877, when Lombardy knew where she stood, and was going, politically, that the Milanese devotees of horse racing founded the Varese Society with a track at Casbeno. The main event in the racing calendar was the Gran Premio di Varese, a race that is still run at Bettole di Varese. Lombardy assumed a leading role in Italian racing with the formation of the Società Lombarda per le Corse di Cavalli, with headquarters at Via Monforte 23 in Milan. This society, which brought together those same names that had figured in the old association, mentioned in the *Gazzetta* for 1830, included many that had figured on the board of directors.

The first course sponsored by the new association was built at Castellazzo di Rho, outside Porta Sempione, for the Gran Premio di Lombardia, run over 2,400 meters, which had a donation of 7,000 lire for the three-day spring meeting. The success of this racing inspired the association to seek a site nearer Milan, and the final choice was San Siro. In 1888, on May 10, this elegant track had its inaugural meeting, and the basis for a permanent cycle of spring and fall meetings was established along the lines of the French and English, which would lead to a solid, prosperous Italian horse-breeding industry.

In 1889, the Premio del Commercio was established, with a prize of 50,000 lire for the 3,000-meter race, with weights assigned according to age. This later became the Gran Premio di Milano, the greatest race run at San Siro, a race that pits the best of the younger generation against the best of the veterans, a competition that is not included in the English or French racing calendars.

In 1904, the Premio Ambrosiano was established, the Premio Sempione in 1906, and the Oaks in 1910. Even though the Derby is run in Rome, the meeting at San Siro is the high point of Italian racing life. Planned in 1914 and inaugurated on April 25, 1920, the Lombard racing association's new, monumental track soon became the most trying field of selection for the Italian breed. At the same time, the association assumed the name *Società per l'Incoraggiamento delle Razze Equine* (SIRE). The great Italian horseman Federico

Tesio did most of his experimental work here in his efforts to bring the Italian racehorse to perfection.

The activity of SIRE, however, did not cease at San Siro. Because of the growing interest in racing and the increasing number of horses, the society projected the construction of two new training farms, at Trent and at Maura, and land between San Siro and Trent had been set aside for owners to build a breeding center. Furthermore, SIRE revived the very popular trotting, sponsored by the Società di Turro. In 1924, it arranged for a large winter meeting at the trotting track there which, although rather old, was still in operating condition. SIRE also rented an area at Monza to create the Mirabello track and built installations there for a stud. Thus owners could board their mares there and have them serviced.

Owing mainly to the efforts of the Milanese association and a number of breeders and owners, the young Italian stud has been able to compete with the great experienced French and English studs. Without SIRE's stud and the devoted interest of the Milanese racing public, Italy would certainly not have been able to make its mark in the international racing field.

Italy has about 125 to 130 studs, about fifteen or so in the first rank, with anywhere from twenty to fifty broodmares. In 1966, Italy had registered 3,911 thoroughbred racehorses; 2,333 flat races were run for that year, 644 steeplechases, and 6,650 trotting races; 1,295 Thoroughbreds and 2,547 Standardbreds participated.

In 1850, the races in Naples were transferred from the course laid out on the Campo di Marte to Agnano, and on that occasion English measures of distance and weight were dropped for the Neapolitan mile (1.85 km). In 1852, the Pisa track was inaugurated on the royal holdings of San Rossore, and in 1857, the Società per le Corse in Piemonte organized races at Turin and Asti, while the Lombard association held race meetings at Senago.

In 1862, Victor Emmanuel II imported a number of stallions and some fine broodmares from England. His example was followed by a number of noble horsemen; but though the House of Savoy and the aristocracy showed themselves ardent lovers of horses and the turf, there were not the government acceptance and support or the popular enthusiasm so characteristic at that time in England and the United States. Noteworthy in the history of the Italian breed was the import, between 1870 and 1880, of three foundation sires who were to have a great influence on bloodlines: Andred, Hamlet, and Melton, all English horses. A number of fine mares also arrived during that period.

Racing activity started in Rome around 1868, one might say, when Kettledrum won a race on an unofficial track. Ten years later came the first running of the Omnium, and in 1884, at Capannelle, the first Derby, instituted by Humbert I.

Toward the end of the nineteenth century, a number of studs and stables came into prominence. Among them was the Barbaricina stud, the Sansalvà stud, the Cologna stud at Ferrara, Prince Doria's stud, and the Volta stud. In 1906, the glorious Besnate stud was founded by the Bocconi brothers, and later went to Riccardo Gualino, the attorney who added to its resources a number of fine horses imported from Great Britain. About the same time, the Tesio stables began to make themselves known for their constant development

339 *Signorinetta (B.m.), 1905 in Italy, by Charlereux.*
340 *Mon Talisman (B.h.), 1924 in France, by Craig an Eran, by Sunstar by Sundridge.*
341 *Tulyar (Dk.b.h.), 1948 in Ireland, by Tehran.*
342 *Manistee (B.h.), 1925 in Italy, by Havresac II by Rabelais by St.Simon by Galopin.*

and numerous successes. In 1921 the Montel stud came into existence. This was the establishment that had acquired all the yearlings of the Montfort stud in France during World War II. Montel horses were Manistee and Cavaliere d'Arpino, the latter producing the famous Bellini-Tenerari-Ribot line, as well as Traghetto, a brother of Bellini. (Added to this development in Italian breeding was the change in training methods introduced by Frank Turner a few years later.) Another stud also to come into prominence was the Oldaniga stables, particularly because of the products of its stallion Munibe, a son of Rabelais.

At this time, however, there were signs of a coming crisis, provoked by the imbalance between fine stallions, of which there were many, and select broodmares, of which there were far too few, so that even though there were about 700 horses in training in the studs of that time, few were of any outstanding quality. In the face of this, SIRE intervened and purchased a number of broodmares in France which it distributed among its associated breeders. This generous undertaking, however, gave sparse results.

To encourage breeders, prize money increased, but this had little effect. Also, admissions fell off, since the public was interested only in seeing champions run. In 1929, however, Ortello, foaled and raised at the Montel stud, appeared to avert the crisis. This horse was truly the answer to a prayer, being the first Italian horse to win the Grand Prix de l'Arc de Triomphe, coming in ahead of such unbeaten champions as Oleander (German) and Kantar (French). Furthermore, Italian breeding had led to a handful of fine stallions like Michelangelo, Scopas, Senecio, and Salpiglossis, and later further strengthened by the import of such stallions from England as Sagacity, Captain Cuttle, and Spike Island. Another great stud also came into existence at this time: the Crespi's Soldo stables.

Those who can be considerd responsible for the improvement of Italy's breed are Count Felice Scheibler, the Bocconi brothers, Prince Doria, Federico Tesio, Colonel Chantre, De Montel, G. R. Cella, and the Crespi brothers. However, it is to Federico Tesio that Italy owes its most telling triumphs of its horses and breeding abroad. In 1932, in the wake of such great Italian winners abroad as Scopas, Apelle, and Ortello, Luchino Visconti's horse Sanzio had an easy victory at the Grand International in Ostend. In 1933, Crapom, from the Soldo stud, also won that event, and the Arc de Triomphe, in Paris, as well. Another new stud joined the front ranks in this year, the one founded by Professor Lorenzini.

Notwithstanding some difficulties encountered in the early thirties, 1934 was a fairly good year for Italian horses at home and abroad. Particularly in evidence were Navarro, Sorolla, Tofanella, and Tabacchi. The turf benefited from the renovation of the Agnano course, once more in operation; a year-long program at Romafi; and the institution of evening racing in Milan.

An exceptional horse came to light in 1936, Archidamia, a filly who won seven important races, and emerged as one of the best horses of her time, colt or filly. Outstanding colts were the Tesio-Incisa stud's Donatello II and El Greco, the first going to an English buyer the next year. Nearco, considered by many Italians to have been the best of their horses of any day, made his appearance on the horizon in 1935. He was to win the Grand Prix in Paris in 1938.

The Italian Jockey Club

The Jockey Club Italiano, founded in 1880 along the lines of the English Club, had as its objective, as it does today, the encouragement of flat racing to improve the breed. Among the charter members who established its statutes and regulations were the Duke di Marino, the Duke di Fian, and Prince di Rossano, representing Rome; the Marquis della Marmora and Count Colli di Felizzano for Turin; Count Cicogna and the nobleman Venino for Varese-Milan; Count Costabili, Count Talon, and Count Zucchini for Bologna; the Marquis Ginori Lisci and Count di San Giorgia for Florence; Prince Piedimonte and the Marquis de' Medici for Naples.

By 1879, a committee of deputies from the National Parliament had been organized to publish a stud book, including Baron Baracco, Count d'Arco, the Marquis delle Favere, and Count Sambuy. King Victor Emmanuel II was himself an enthusiastic turfman, and raced wonderful horses raised at Manduria.

In 1884, under the auspices of the club the Royal Derby was run for the first time at Capannelle, which had recently been completed. This race was instituted by King Humbert I. In 1890, the racetrack at Tor di Quinto was opened, and in the first decade of the new century, under the auspices of Count Scheibler, the Parioli track was opened. Also, old courses were expanded in addition to new ones being established, making great racing centers at San Siro, Agnano, Mirafiori, Cascina, Ardenza, and Varese. Each of these steps marked the club's progress, which was an uneasy road because there was scarcely any sympathy from the government toward horses and racing, and changing times and social patterns complicated affairs and aspirations already made difficult by war and political crises.

VI
BREEDING IN GERMANY

German thoroughbred breeding, which produced some noteworthy horses in the period between the two world wars, is now beginning to affirm itself for the first time since the destruction of the turf during World War II. In 1965, German breeders showed some thousand broodmares and foals registered. Notwithstanding, the German turf is a long way from the English, French, and Italian, but since at this time it represents a good market for breeders in the more advanced countries, it deserves attention. Germany has bought a number of broodmares from Italian breeders, and the Italian stallion Botticelli is let in Germany. Other stallions to serve in Germany recently have been Zank, Obermat, and, at the

343 *Ribot (B.h.), 1952 in Italy, by Tenerani.*
344 *Tenerani (B.h.), 1944 in Italy, by Bellini.*
345 *Big Game (B.h.), 1939, by Bahram.*
346 *Apelle (Ch.h.), 1923 in Italy, by Dardanapale.*
347 *Ortello (Ch.h.), 1926, by Teddy by Ajax by Flying Fox, one of the most famous Italian racehorses and sires, winner of the Prix de l'Arc de Triomphe in Paris.*

343   344

345

346   347

348   349

350

351   352

top of the list, Orsini, sire of twenty-seven winners out of forty-two offspring, for a total of fifty-nine victories in 1965. Orsini, foaled in 1954, has been one of the most extraordinary European horses of recent times, having won the German Derby, the Belgian Grand Prix d'Exposition, the Oslo Cup, and the Stockholm Cup. He also raced in the King George VI and Queen Elizabeth stakes and in the International in Maryland. Orsini is the son of Oranien, who was sired by Oleander, out of Nereide.

The most important breeding farm in Germany is the Erlenhof stud, founded in 1923 by F. M. Oppenheimer of Frankfurt, which included Nereide and Ticino. The founder based his breeding on Italian horses, importing a number of broodmares, including Nella, by Gubbio, who never raced, but showed herself to be a great mother of winners; and Angelina, who had foaled Apelle in Italy but was a disappointment in Germany. The foundation sire of the Erlenhof stud was Ticino. He was followed by Figaro, by Oleander, out of Flora. The stud currently has about thirty mares.

An important stable is the Ravensberg stud, founded by Paul Niemolle, which has followed a course different from that of the other racing stables by initiating its activity with mediocre mares and gradually improving production not only through using prime studs but also by making rigorous selections from the tracks, putting to stud only those horses that have proved to be of great solidity and tenacity. The leading stallion at Ravensberg, which is now directed by Niemolle's heir, Reinhard Delius, is Anzitz, a son of Aventin, by Teddy, out of Austria.

The oldest German thoroughbred stud is Schlenderhan, which for three generations belonged to the Oppenheim family, having been founded by Count Eduard von Oppenheim. Situated right outside Cologne, it was in the first rank as a producer of Thoroughbreds as early as 1874. Among its internationally renowned horses have been Sturmvogel, Schwarzgold, and Allgau. Its most famous product, however, was Oleander, sire of the Italian champion Orsenigo (1940), among others. As a matter of fact, as a result of an agreement between the Montel stud and the Oppenheim's, the services of Ortello were exchanged for those of Oleander. As a result, the Italian breeder gained Orsenigo, who won just about every Italian race on the calendar, whereas the German breeder got Allgau, winner of the German and Viennese derbies among other classic races.

348 *Bellini (B.h.), 1939 in Italy, by Cavaliere d'Arpino by Havresac II. He is the sire of Tenerani.*

349 *Niccolò dell'Arca (B.h.), 1938 in Italy, by Coronach by Hurry On, a powerful runner.*

350 *Donatello (Ch.h.), 1934 in Italy, by Blenheim II by Blandford, a sire of sires.*

351 *Nearco (B.h.), 1935 in Italy, by Pharos by Phalaris by Polymelus by Cyllene; undefeated.*

352 *Orsenigo (B.h.), 1940 in Italy, by Oleander.*

VII

RACING IN RUSSIA

In 1924, at the instigation of Budenny and other highly placed cavalry officers, the Soviet authorities permitted the reopening of the Russian racecourses. In addition to putting a number of the principal ones in order, some new ones opened, so that today seventy-eight racecourses have regular spring, summer, fall, and winter meetings. There is a Derby during each season, providing considerable diversity in track conditions: very heavy and muddy in spring, dry in summer, heavy in fall, and icy in winter.

The Soviet has been organizing a turf world that is vast, yet efficient. From the Ukraine to the Urals, the Caucasus to Siberia, racing fans get together every Saturday and Sunday at the local course, where races are programmed from noon to evening under lights. Even winter meetings are especially exciting, when the horses run on packed snow. Selection is rigorous in Russia, with winners of the various classics earning the right to compete in the Grand Prix that is run in May at the foremost course, in Moscow. The race draws as many as twenty thousand or more spectators.

The Moscow course has a trotting track within a two-mile flat-racing course. It has a well-lighted, sumptuous, commodious grandstand built by the czars, modernized somewhat, with accommodations for dining. The entrance decoration is late nineteenth century, with a wrought-iron gate that recalls the great stables of the era. The racecourse is administered by the secretary for horse breeding of the Ministry of Agriculture. The flat-racing calendar includes a series of such gala events as the Grand Prix Inauguration race, a spring Grand Prix, the Republic Stakes, a Russian Derby, the Marshal Voroshilov Stakes for three-year-olds, and races such as the Kalinin Stakes for two-year-olds, the autumn Grand Prix, and the Grand Criterium. The season ends in October with a closing-day stakes for three-year-olds.

Prizes are in money, part going to the stud farms and part to the trainers and jockeys. The majority of the horses, however, belong to state entities that are part of large collectives devoted to stockbreeding in general. At present, a number of racehorses belong to racing clubs, and a few are privately owned by high officials (Budenny had four Thoroughbreds, and Stalin raced two.) Placed above the prizes, however, is official recognition for improving the breed.

One of the most important stud farms, the Krenovsky, is near Moscow. It is 250 years old. It was from this stud that the Orlov breed derives. At the end of their racing careers, the best horses are distributed among the various studs to balance and improve their stock.

Local racecourses in the small towns and countryside are numerous, and local Thoroughbreds are raced. These courses come under the administration of a regional secretary of the Ministry of Agriculture, reporting to the central organization in Moscow, which is concerned with improving standards throughout the country. A journal is published by the Ministry of Agriculture. This is the principal source of information on horses and the turf, and, in a way, analagous to jockey-club bulletins in Western countries. A Moscow afternoon newspaper publishes charts, results, odds, and so on. Programs are available at the races. Every race meeting in Moscow has twenty-six races, fourteen for flat races and twelve for trotters.

Often, there are troika exhibition events, generally during the winter. In all, a day's racing brings up to 250 horses to the racecourses.

There are very few jump races, even though the greatest winners of the Pardubice Grand Steeplechase, a Czechoslovakian course almost as difficult as Aintree, are almost always Soviet horses. Epitaph, for example, was a fantastic champion who won that race three times. The quality of Soviet horses was shown by Zabieg (third at Laurel Park, first in Warsaw), by Zadornik (fourth at Laurel Park, first at Peking), and, above all, by Anilin (second at the Maryland International and, in the same year, first in the Grand Prix d'Europa at Cologne). In view of these encouraging results, the Ministry of Agriculture is proceeding on a five-year plan designed to stimulate thoroughbred breeding and training. Among other things, the plan provided for the importing of about eighty English mares and four studs, and includes increased shares in prize money for trainers and jockeys.

A curious thing in Soviet racing is the absence of handicaps. All horses run at the same weight, and are divided into categories according to points. Points are gained, proportionately, as a result of winning, or being placed, and higher points are given for races of greater importance.

VIII
UNITED STATES

All statistics connected with the American turf are almost fantastic. In 1966, some $3 billion was bet at the tracks; in addition, an incalculable amount, possibly as much as a billion dollars, went into the pockets of bookmakers, operating illegally, away from the track. There were 47,020,456 spectators admitted to the nation's tracks, which means that each one bet at the races an average of about $65. Total purse money distributed throughout the country came to $130,653,813. Adding the amount spent on harness racing, we arrive at a total of $4,614,602,369 bet legally, and an attendance of 62,887,478 for the year. The Internal Revenue Service took $88 million in taxes. There are some who insist that the total of bets placed illegally, through bookmakers, equaled the amount bet at the tracks.

All this has raised the value of a racehorse, and we find record prices paid for champions. Following the $1 million paid to lease Ribot for five years as a stud was the $1.5 million paid for Sea Bird, winner of the Arc de Triomphe and a son of the American Dan Cupid. As the value of champion studs rose astronomically, the practice of syndication grew. A single owner might hesitate to invest more than a million dollars for a stud. But a number of owners could get together, each buying one or more shares, with service privileges for his mares. The convenience of syndication helped to escalate the price for champion stallions. Stud fees for the leading stallions run as high as $20,000 per service.

Kauai King, the winner of the 1966 Kentucky Derby and the Preakness, has been syndicated for stud duty in Maryland for $2,160,000, representing about $70,000 per share. Broodmares, too, bring tremendous prices. The sale of nine-year-old Berio in 1966 brought $235,000 from John E. duPont, topping an earlier high of $215,000 for Rose Trader; and these prices are rising every day.

Betting and horse sales have brought an annual average revenue of $146 million to the State of New York, the greater part of the betting money, of course, coming from the flat races, but a good percentage accrues from the trotting race tracks. In 1966, there was a total of 1,349 days of racing at eleven tracks, including flat racing and the trotters, and the volume of bets rose to $1,412,306,405. Of this total, $147,704,390 went for taxes.

The record for a single day's betting at one track (for a nine-race program) is over $5½ million. On an important holiday, or when there is a great classic race, a mutuel "handle" (total betting) of over $5 million is not unusual.

Pari-Mutuels

The pari-mutuel (meaning "mutual betting") system has done a great deal to stimulate interest in horse racing. All the money bet on each position in the race is pooled. After the "take" is deducted, the winner or winners share the proceeds. The "take," amounting generally to about 16 percent, is the share retained for the state and the track. For example, let us say that $100,000 has been bet to win, $60,000 bet to place (2nd), and $30,000 bet to show (3rd). Horse 4 wins, 5 is second, and 6 is third. In the win pool, $84,000 was left after the "take." All this goes to those who bet on Number 4. Say $20,000 was the total bet on number 4, the equivalent of ten thousand $2 bets. Dividing $84,000 by 10,000, we see that each $2 bettor gets back $8.40 for his bet. For second place, $10,000 was bet on 4 and $3,000 bet on number 5. After the "take," there was $50,000 left to divide. The amount bet on the two horses entitled to place money ($13,000) is deducted from this $50,000, leaving $37,000. Half of this ($18,500) goes to those who bet on Number 4, half to those who bet Number 5, in addition to the return of the money bet. Thus, each of the five thousand $2 bettors on Number 4 to place gets back, besides his $2 bet, $3.70 ($18,500 divided by 5,000), a total of $5.70. Likewise, those who bet on number 5 (1,500 tickets) get back, besides the $2 bet, $18,500 divided by 1,500, or $12.30—a total of $14.30. The odd pennies over the even amount is called breakage, and becomes part of the take. The show (3rd) money is divided in the same way.

At most American tracks there are electric totalisators that show almost instantly the amount of money being bet as the betting proceeds, and the approximate current odds. The process is all in view, and there is no question about the accuracy of the division.

With the expanding interest in racing, new tracks are constantly being established, and existing tracks are being improved and rebuilt. Famous Belmont Park, rebuilt at a cost of $30,000,000, reopened in May 1968.

Naturally, all this wealth is reflected in the improvement of the American racing breed. (It doesn't matter that the great majority of races are run over small tracks and short distances.) In 1966, in Chicago's Arlington Park, Buckpasser, with Braulio Baeza up, broke the record for the mile made by Swaps, 1:33 1-5, with a new time of 1:32 3-5.

Generally, the careers of American racehorses are much more intense and longer than those of European mounts. The great handicap races with their rich purses, in which the big winners consistently appear, increase the champions' earnings tremendously. Some examples follow:

Foaled		Starts	Wins	Earnings
1957	Kelso	63	39	$1,977,896
1954	Round Table	66	43	1,749,869
1963	Buckpasser	25	22	1,462,014
1952	Nashua	30	22	1,288,565
1958	Carry Back	61	21	1,241,165
1945	Citation	45	32	1,085,760
1941	Stymie	131	35	918,485
1952	Swaps	25	19	848,900
1950	Native Dancer	22	21	785,240

	1950	1966
Thoroughbreds foaled	9,095	19,646
Horses auctioned	1,717	2,863
Average price	$2,944	$6,400
Days of racing	3,290	5,254
Races	26,932	46,814
Racehorses	22,554	39,604
Money wagered	$1,358,739,248	$3,526,778,409
Winnings per horse	$2,260	$2,675
Attendance	21,845,556	47,020,456

This balance sheet of a sort shows the tremendous financial activity in relation to the turf in the United States, and all of it has its basis and strength in American horse breeding.

The American turf is the child, more or less legitimate, of the English track. The first British governor of New York, in 1665, after the colony had passed out of the hands of the Dutch, had given a grant of land on Long Island to be used as a racecourse. In 1966, the Tercentenary of the first official race run in the States was celebrated at Aqueduct. The first established track came to be known as the Newmarket Course, and was installed on Salisbury Plain, near Hempstead, in 1668. By 1680, there were already five tracks in use in Virginia, all straightaways of a quarter-mile.

So that they could run more races, American interests early resorted to importing horses. As we run through their names, we find some celebrated horses, and others long since forgotten; the impressions are that they were acquired on a rather haphazard basis, just so that there would be a goodly number available, and that bloodlines perhaps esteemed at the time soon dropped from favor. Notwithstanding, we find that from the end of the eighteenth century to today at least twenty Epsom Derby winners crossed the Atlantic. The first Derby winner, Diomed, was imported at the age of twenty-one, in 1798. Perhaps a bit late in life for a stud, but he provided excellent products nevertheless. He was bought by John Homes of Virginia, and had a fundamental influence upon the breeding of American racehorses.

From Diomed sprang Lexington, the stud who become legendary in the history of the turf. Here is the line: Diomed, 1777; Sir Archy, 1802; Timoleon, 1814; Boston, 1833; and Lexington, 1850. What is strange is that Diomed left no trace in England of his twenty-one years at stud, while he became a great foundation sire in the United States. Boston was phenomenal for his stamina and his long career. He started forty-five times. From his third to tenth year, he won forty times.

Lexington was extraordinary as a runner and stud. His dam, Alice Carneal, was a daughter of Sarpedon (by Emilius).

Foaled in Kentucky, near the city whose name he bore, Lexington ran as a three-, four-, and five-year-old at distances of one to four miles. He crowned his career in a race against Lecompte at four miles. A short time later, the great horse went blind, and was put out to stud in 1857, continuing thus for twenty-one years, and producing 236 winners of 1,776 races, for a total of $1.2 million in prize money.

After Diomed came Saltram (Eclipse) winner of the Derby in 1738, imported at the age of nineteen by a Virginia breeder; John Bull (Fortitude, Herod); Speed Eagle (Volunteer, Eclipse); Sir Harry (Sir Peter, Herod); Archduke (Sir Peter, Herod); Lap Dog (Whalebone); Priam (Emilius); St. Giles (Tramp); Blue Gown (Beads Man); King Craft (King Tom); George Frederick (Marsyas); St. Blaise (Hermit); St. Gatien (The Rover); Ormonde (Bend Or); Rock Sand (St. Foin); Durban II (Rabelais); Blenheim II (Blandford); Bahram (Blandford); and Mahmoud (Blenheim II). It should be noted that both Blue Gown and King Craft died on the trip over. Ormonde came from Argentina. Sir Harry, Priam, Rock Sand, and Blenheim II had a tremendous effect on bloodlines.

Other celebrated imported stallions are Bel Aethel (Aethelstan); Boswell (Bosworth); Bull Dog (Teddy); Castel Fusano (Ksar); Easton (Dark Legend); Gino (Tetratema); Heliopolis and Hypnotist (Hyperion); Jacopo (Sansovino); Masked Marvel (McKinley); Rhodes Scholar (Pharos; Sickle Phalaris); Swift and Sure (Swynford); Hunter's Moon (Fox Hunter); Challenger II (Swynford); Leamington (Faugh a Ballagh); Rayon d'Or (Flageolet); Negofol (Childwick); Australian (West Australian); Teddy (Ajax); and Sir Gallahad III (Teddy). Both Australian and Sir Gallahad marked a new era in the story of the American turf.

Among the numerous offspring of Teddy, imported or born in the United States, pride of place must unquestionably go to Sir Gallahad III, foaled in France in 1924. Not only was this horse the sire and grandsire of Gallant Fox, Omaha, Happy Fox, Gallahadion, Sir Damion, Fighting Fox, Insco, and Count Gallahad, but also the producer of fifty stallions who in turn sired winners. We might also remember Bull Dog and his colt Bull Lea.

Another flourishing line in the United States is that descending from Touchstone through Orlando—the imported Eclipse, Alarm, Hymiar, Domino, and Commando, who, along with his sons Peter Pan, Colin, Celt, Ultimus, and Transvaal, produced Pennant, Black Toney, High Time, Stimulus, and Supremus, who in turn gave us Black Servant, Blue Larkspur, Bimelech, Equipoise, Equistone, Bolingbrooke, and others.

The third important group goes back to Polymelus through the Phalaris, Fairway, or Manna lines. The imported stud Pharamond II, sire of Menow; and Sickle, sire of Stagehand and Unbreakable, are among the greatest stallions American breeders have seen.

An up-and-coming line is that descending from Isonomy, which already has had such products as Challenger and St. Germans, reinforced by Bahram, Blenheim II, Mahmoud, Whirlaway, and Bold Venture. While the Herod blood in the Lexington line has been almost exhausted over the past fifty years, the blood in the Dollar line showed well in such horses as Castel Fusano and in some of the offspring of Epinard and Rodosto. But the horses of the Le Sancy line, notwithstanding Stefan the Great, Royal Canopy, Boscombe, Belfonds, Royal Minstrel, and their descendents, no longer shine. The German Mio d'Arezzo, excluding great success with Mioland, also seems to have been a flash in the pan.

Australian, however, who was foaled in 1858, has demonstrated magnificently the quality of the Matchem-Melbourne blood. The best product of the line undoubtedly was Man o' War, and then there were Display, Chance Play, and Chance Shot, who led to Discovery, Brevity, Chance Sun, War Admiral, Hard Tack, and Seabiscuit. The get of Hurry On do not merit our attention.

Breeders

Leading all other states in number of breeding farms and reproducers, Kentucky has a climate and terrain that make it ideal for raising horses. Rolling, luxuriant bluegrass meadows and pastures have been the basis of that development, further reflected in the establishment of racecourses in Louisville, Lexington, and Owensboro. Louisville, of course, is where the Kentucky Derby is run, at Churchill Downs.

Claiborne Farm is one of the greatest of the Kentucky studs, not only for its more than two hundred broodmares, but for its some fifteen sires, among whom have been Blenheim II, Boswell, Gallant Fox, Jacopo, Sir Gallahad III, Johnstown, and Rhodes Scholar. A. B. Hancock, Jr.'s, Claiborne Farm has nearly three thousand acres, and has been known for its production of famous racehorses.

The Calumet Farm, established by Warren Wright and now owned by Mrs. Gene Markey, had such studs as Bull Lea and Whirlaway. Among the champions produced by Calumet Farm were the unforgettable Citation and Armed. Calumet also dedicated a good deal of care and effort to the breeding of trotting horses.

The C. V. Whitney Farm is renowned for its dual success as breeder and owner. Its installations cover some 500 acres of some of the most beautiful and fertile land in Fayette County. From about 1924 down to shortly after the end of World War II, the Whitneys, Hancock, Widener, and Wright, all with farms in Kentucky, figured almost uninterruptedly in the first rank of American breeders and owners.

The second great concentration of breeding farms is in California, where there are not many important ones, but a great number of studs of interest. In compensation, some of these farms have huge properties running into thousands of acres.

Another prominent breeding place of Thoroughbreds is in Ocala, Florida, located in the central part of the state. In the mid-1950's it was discovered that the soil in that area is very rich in limestone, which is so important for the development of strong horses and nutritional needs. Many of the stud farms of Kentucky have annexes there. The Ocala Stud, headed by Thomas E. Wood, Jr., bred and raised Carry Back, who won the Kentucky Derby in 1961. The 3M Company (Minnesota Mining and Manufacturing Company) has a large farm there, Tartan Farms. W. L. McKnight is the owner.

Although Texas has no racetracks of the first rank, because of the King Ranch more than anything else, it is one of the country's most important breeding centers, and derives a great deal of money from it. Robert J. Kleberg, Jr., one of the owners of the King, directs activities at the one-million-acre ranch.

Next in importance among the states as horse-breeding centers come Maryland and Virginia. Maryland was the home of the famous Blair Stud of William Woodward, which raised Nashua, Gallant Fox, Bug Brush, and other great winners of classic races here and abroad. Also in Maryland is Alfred Gwynne Vanderbilt's 582-acre Sagamore farm, with stallions Kauai King and Native Dancer.

Florida is becoming more and more important as a horse-breeding state, though no real champions have been produced as yet. At the Florida tracks some races are run only for Florida-breds, and in some races there is a weight allowance for Florida-breds. There are about 110 major tracks in the United States, and myriad small ones.

The major tracks are near the big cities. Near New York are Aqueduct and Belmont Park, with Saratoga upstate near Albany. In New Jersey, Monmouth Park is near New York; Atlantic City draws from New York and Philadelphia; and Garden State is near Camden, across the Delaware River from Philadelphia. Delaware Park is near Wilmington. Pimlico, Laurel, and Bowie are near Baltimore in Maryland. Near Boston (and Providence) are Narragansett, Suffolk Downs, and Rockingham.

In Florida (all near Miami) are Hialeah, Tropical Park, and Gulfstream. In Kentucky there are Churchill Downs, Latonia, and Keeneland. In Chicago the major tracks are Arlington and Hawthorne. Michigan has Detroit and Hazel Park. Oaklawn Park in Arkansas is notable for its Derby. In California, Hollywood Park and Santa Anita are in the Los Angeles area; Bay Meadows, Golden Gate, and Del Mar are near San Francisco, and there is also Tanforan. With the exception of Hazel Park, all the above-mentioned tracks are at least one mile long.

Jumping Races

Steeplechases have never been very popular in the United States, and very few tracks program them; even these seldom have more than one jumping race in a day's program. However, there are a number of hunt clubs, more or less private, that feature and encourage jumping races. Notable among these are the Camden Hunt, Fairfax Hunt, Blind Brook, United Hunt (which holds its meetings at Belmont or Aqueduct), Malvern Hunt, Glyndon Hunt, Grand National Hunt, Middlebury Hunt, Pinehurst Hunt, Southern Pines Hunt, Warrenton Hunt, Unionville Hunt, and Whitemarsh Valley. These clubs each have only a few days of racing per

353 *Just a few hours old.*
354 *With disciplined care, the mare takes her foal through his first steps round the paddock.*
355 *One-year-olds running free in the fields near Pisa.*
356 *Lord Derby's stud: One of the first eagerly awaited offspring of Ribot plays with his mother.*

353

354

355

356

357

358

359

360

361

362

363

364

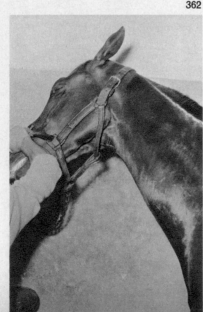

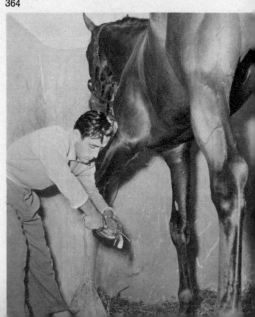

year, and the attendance they command, with a few exceptions, is quite small.

In an effort to encourage jumping races, hurdle races were introduced at a number of tracks. Steeplechases, with high barriers, are difficult and somewhat risky for most horses. But lower and simpler barriers, called hurdles, were more attractive to many trainers. Though these hurdle races increased the interest in jumping races, they are still far from popular.

However, there are a number of important traditional steeplechase races that, in their field, rank with the great flat races like the Kentucky Derby, Belmont Stakes, and the Travers. The Maryland Hunt Club Steeplechase, possibly the most renowned, has been run at Glyndon, Maryland, since 1894, the Beverwyck Steeplechase Handicap (Aqueduct) goes back to 1897, the Grand National (Aqueduct) to 1899, and the International (Belmont) to 1895.

In recent years there have not been any truly great steeplechase horses, with Bampton Castle, Mako, and Lumière showing the most quality.

IX
SOUTH AMERICA

In Brazil and Argentina, turf and horse breeding are given particular attention by both public and private interests. The discussion never ceases over which country has the better horses; Argentina has more of them; and Brazilian quality is claimed on the basis of Narvik winning the 1958 running of the Grande Premio de São Paulo.

In both countries, particularly in Brazil, the leaders in the field are generally owners and breeders who are socially and politically prominent, and racing is therefore looked upon as an expected activity for those in power. A great deal of scientific research is carried out, largely in Brazil, primarily to resolve the difficulties stemming from variations in climate from one racing center to another. The pioneer Brazilian turfman José Alfredo Martínez de Hoz did considerable valuable research to discover the best grasses and legumes for fodder grown in tropical and semitropical climates. He was also concerned with the adaptability of the Thoroughbred to the various terrains and climates. Along with the studies of De Hoz, another seminal work is that of Peru's Adolfo Vázquez on raising Thoroughbreds in the tropics. Since the horse is still employed in useful labor in South America, valuable research on workhorses is being done there; accordingly, a good deal of cooperative effort exists between racing associations and organizations concerned with improving the breed of draft horses, pack animals, and the like.

The establishment of the South American Horse Federation (FIS) led to a high level of racing, and has provided an enthusiastic public with international events of tremendous beauty, spectacle, and excitement. The federation comprises both public and private members, including, among others, the jockey clubs of the various Latin American countries, private clubs and racing associations, breeders' associations, and publishers and sponsors of various national and regional studbooks. These last are usually unattached to any racing or breeding societies, though often they have offshoots in associations dedicated to a particular breed or branch of activity, as in the United States. Members of the federation are Argentina, Brazil, Chile, Colombia, Peru, Uruguay, and Venezuela. Together, they number approximately 25,000 broodmares, as well as twelve racecourses of international rank and stature, and account for millions of dollars yearly in wagers. Since a good part of this money is untaxed or taxed at a very low rate, much of it has been invested to benefit racing.

The Jockey Club Brasileiro not only maintains and expands its track and installations but has also apportioned a large part of its winnings to social service. The track is one of the most beautiful in the world for its scenic setting and magnificent installations. The marquee over the grandstand is without a single support or pillar, and is the largest cantilevered reinforced concrete structure in the world. The Club provides scholarships and contributes to the homes, to schools, and health services of its employees and their families, as well as to others not directly concerned with it. In São Paulo the Club maintains a fine stud and breeding farm for servicing owners' mares. Both the Rio and São Paulo clubs encourage and sponsor a good deal of scientific research.

As in many Latin American countries, in Brazil the almost daily city, state, and federal lotteries are drawn on the pari-mutuel results. In these warmer regions, racing is almost a year-round activity. Rio de Janeiro, for example, is known not only for its Saturday and Sunday meetings but also for its evening meetings each Thursday, some of which are galas. Brazilian racing receives excellent, informed coverage in both the regular and the specialized press, and is broadcast and televised.

Some of the richest purses in the world are offered in Venezuela. The frenetic interest of the general public, however, does not derive from a concern with the track and its horses, but from the fact that in addition to the state and national lotteries depending on them, a pool on the winners of five or six of the races run over the weekend is the favorite diversion of the masses. The pool, which is similar to the English football pool and the Italian "Totocalcio," depends on guessing correctly a number of winners in stipulated races. "Guessing" is the proper word, for since the majority of Venezuelan races are handicaps run over 1,200 meters, with inadequate coverage (they are run at the national racecourse in Caracas), bettors all over the country are just playing hunches. Besides, in races of this sort, it is generally the start that determines the final result.

X
JAPAN

"Angels of the turf" are attractive uniformed girls employed at the track to answer the public's questions. They will look after a mother's children while she places a bet, explain to the novice how bets are placed or what the odds mean, discuss

357–364 *Work in a racing stud: opening the stable at dawn; taking the harness from the tack room and hanging it at each box, while the horses tell secrets; then, cleaning up and brushing down.*

any racing technicalities, and generally aid and comfort the novice as well as the racing fan, without charge; they are not even permitted to accept tips. These angels of the turf at ten of Japan's leading racetracks have brought nothing but praise since they were installed.

The Japan Racing Association, which was founded in 1955, does not miss a trick in popularizing the sport to which it is devoted; in consequence, it is building an ever-growing public for the Japanese tracks. The racecourse in Tokyo offers approximately forty days of racing; the track at Nakayama, fifty-one; Kyoto, twenty-nine; Osaka, forty-six, and the racecourse in Shuchi, thirty-two, a calendar modeled closely upon the American. In addition, there are sixteen days of racing offered at Sapporo, eight at Hakodate, fourteen at Fukushima; eight at Niigata, and twenty-four at Kokura. All these tracks are up to the minute, with the finest of modern installations, and are the "big ten" of Japanese racecourses. There are, in addition, thirty-six smaller tracks scattered throughout the country. Every Japanese track has seen an increase in the total wagers each year.

The great development in thoroughbred racing in Japan is owed in large part to the tremendously active and progressive Japan Racing Association and its dedicated president, Hiroshi Ishizaka. The technical facilities at the large racetracks include closed-circuit television systems that monitor all data on the illuminated infield boards and others showing odds, morning line, and so on, as well as horses' weights and other information. In fact, every inch of the large tracks is under surveillance, and a telemetric system based on infrared rays registers partial times.

XI
SOUTH AFRICA

While the national game of South Africa may be rugby, the races draw bigger crowds. In six cities of the Union, there are races twice a week, and in addition to these events are the innumerable trials at small local tracks through the country. Bets reach millions of dollars annually. At Durban in June of 1966, the totalisator for just one race registered a volume of £229,980, which, of course, excludes bets placed with bookmakers, about fifty of them.

Off-track betting, which is illegal, has been a problem to the authorities for many years, particularly in Johannesburg. After a clean-up campaign, Tattersall Clubs were established, practically eliminating the clandestine bookmaker. In the Tattersall Clubs, only members can bet, but there is nothing aside from conscience to prevent a member from wagering for a friend's account. Racing is under strict government control, with each bet taxed anywhere from 5 to 7 percent, according to the administrative district in which it is placed. Bookmakers are required to pay weekly taxes. A bookmaker's license is given for life, and is difficult and expensive to acquire because the number is kept to about the same few hundred. Only death or assignment of a license enables a newcomer to join this select group.

Horse racing not only is a major South African sport but also one of the country's most lucrative activities. About 1,500 thoroughbred foals are produced each year. Every part of the country prides itself on the horses it raises, and

any one of the classic races, like the Metropolitan at Cape Town or the Summer Handicap at Johannesburg, will attract the attention of the entire country and bring about half the population to the track. In Johannesburg, it has been shown, one person in two goes to the track on a fairly regular schedule.

XII
AUSTRALIA

Just as in the United States it was the first sport, historically, horse racing in Australia is about as old as the country's history. Unlike the States, however, where baseball, football, and other sports came to displace racing as the popular attraction, the track in Australia is still the greatest draw of all sporting events. The country does not lack for tracks, large and small. For example, Sydney has seven, Brisbane, three; Melbourne has seven, two of which are dedicated to harness racing; there are three in Adelaide, and Perth has two each, for flat and harness racing. Pacing, incidentally, rather than trotting, which is practically excluded, is the harness racing preferred in Australia. The race that makes for a virtual national holiday is the Melbourne Cup, which draws a gate of about 400,000 at the Flemington racecourse. This race is a handicap in which as a general rule the favorite is heavily bet, and usually loses. The public often shows less interest in the classic races.

XIII
GREAT PEDIGREES

The assertion by the Italian horseman, Franco Varola, in his *Stalloni Capirazza (Foundation Sires)*, that certain stallions reappear with overwhelming frequency in the pedigrees of the great winning racehorses may well persuade us to seek statistical confirmation. This can be done by giving a point for each appearance of any one of thirty-one stallions in each pedigree examined. Why thirty-one? Because that is the number of studs figuring in the first five generations of any pedigree. Why five generations? Because beyond the fifth generation an ancestor's direct influence is extremely problematical, and the sixth and seventh generations would provide fewer names, most likely the same ones; also, five generations, stretching from 1900 to date, is the most important breeding period of our century.

As many pedigrees should be examined as we believe necessary to the study. The point to establish is that the group taken as the whole are all champions. We might take all the winners from a given country during a fixed period, or the Epsom Derby, or the most important international classics, or even all these together. Whatever the selection, we shall find that for every horse the final result is invariably the same.

We have a group of studs with a greater number of mentions in pedigrees than does a second group, and that

365–368 *Ribot being cared for by his groom.*

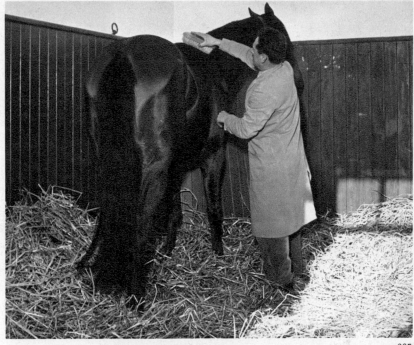

365

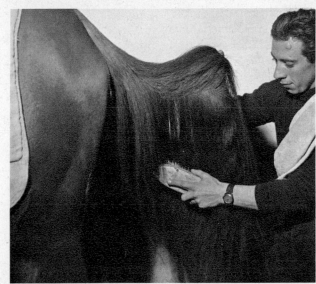

366

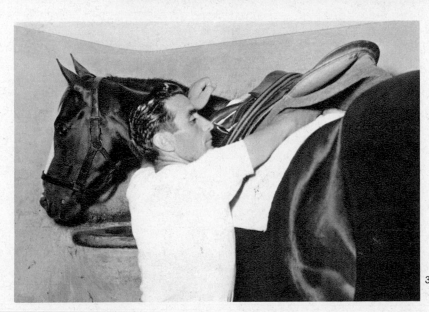

367

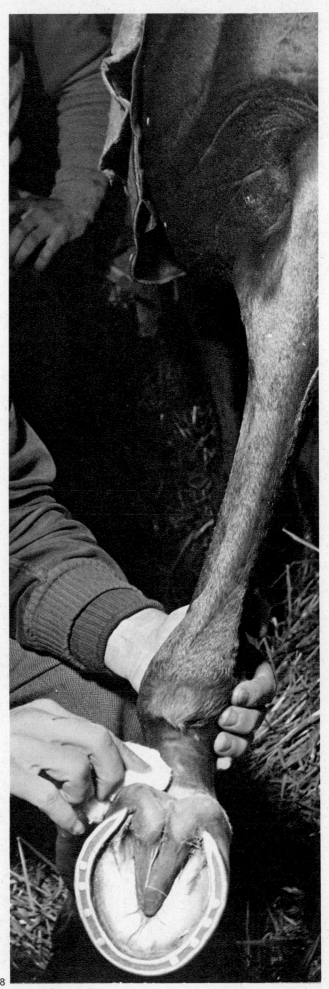

368

second group in its turn is mentioned many more times than a third group which is characterized by horses appearing once, twice, or thrice, and generally sporadically in the pedigrees studied. Thus we have three groups indicated for our study: the first comprising the great foundation sires of international importance; the second comprising important sires; and the third made up of average stallions. But for a few variations, this is Vuillier's system for blending (with its relative appendix on the calculation of discards), which is still used as a basic criterion in the operations of stud farms of international importance, such as the Aga Khan's. (Despite its carefully balanced blending of strains, the stud has failed to produce any of the usual exceptions that make for champion horses.)

Vuillier's calculations, however, for all practical purposes went only as far as the great stallions who flourished at the end of the last century, such as St. Simon, Hampton, Hermit, and Bend Or. More than seventy years have passed since then, sufficient time for us to attempt a new selection in order to isolate the male line that stands out today, covering a good part of the first half of our century.

Examining the pedigrees of today's great horses, we see that five generations cover just the period of time we are interested in, as we can observe from a pedigree taken of random: Braque (1946), by Antonio Canale (1941), by Torbido (1936), by Ortello (1926), by Teddy (1913), by Ajax (1901); or Ribot (1952), by Tenerani (1944), by Bellini (1939), by Cavaliere d'Arpino (1926), by Havresac II (1915), by Rabelais (1900); or Charlottesville (1957), by Prince Chevalier (1943), by Prince Rose (1928), by Rose Prince (1919), by Prince Palatine (1908), by Persimmon (1893); or St. Paddy (1957), by Aureole (1950), by Hyperion (1930), by Gainsborough (1914), by Bayardo (1906), by Bay Ronald (1893). In each case we can see that the period of the fifth sire (great-great-great-grandfather) coincides with our own century and time.

We can therefore choose any champion listed in the International Racing Book or any of the national annuals without fear of going beyond the time limit that interests us. For instance, in *Le Grandi Prove Ippiche (The Great Italian Horse Races)* we find a list of fifty horses that won the most important international classics in the years 1957–1959 throughout the world. This list is a revelation, and proves the thesis set forth: Adil, Alcide, Arctic Explorer, Bald Eagle, Ballymoss, Braque, Chitet, Cobetto, Cora Husker, Djanaa, Don Varela, Dushka, Escorial, Escribano, Espiche, Exar, Feria, Fomento, Fric, Gallant Man, Gladness, Herbager, Hillsdale, Ismone, Mahan, Malefain, Manantial, Mi Tocayo, Monteval, Nagami, Narvik, Oroso, Orsini, Pennsylvania, Round Table, Sailor's Guide, St. Crispin, Scot, Sedan, Senegal, Tanerko, Tanzhusar, Tatan, Tello, Tema, Terrang, Wallaby, Windfang, and Zarathustra. A count of their ancestors shows Phalaris leading (being included forty-three times), followed by Chaucer (forty), Swynford (thirty-five), Polymelus (thirty-two). We can now see how Phalaris, Chaucer, and Swynford, more than any others, clearly are the three sires

that form the genealogical substratum on which all the great racehorses of today rest. (We can discount the fourth, Polymelus, because he is the sire of Phalaris.)

An interesting sidelight on these three great sires is that they all were part of Lord Derby's stud, which confirms the fact that Stanley House even today is the most puissant single factor in the development of the classic thoroughbred racehorse throughout the world. This would never have been deduced by looking at the usual racing statistics, which generally record performances and earnings. The Derby stud's winners have never been in proportion to its importance, which is witnessed in the excellence of its selective breeding generation after generation, as we have seen.

After the sires mentioned above, in descending order, come Bayardo, Blandford, Gainsborough, and Teddy, each appearing twenty-six times in the pedigrees studied, and Ajax, Pharos, and St. Simon, mentioned twenty-three times each. Of interest is that Bayardo is the sire of Gainsborough, and Ajax of Teddy, while the already-mentioned Phalaris is the sire of Pharos, and Swynford of Blandford. It is curious, even fascinating, to observe how St. Simon still appears within the rather strict limit of five generations inasmuch as he was foaled in 1881 with the greater part of his activity as a stud occurring in the nineteenth century. The classic winner of today, Ribot, for example, does not have St. Simon in his fifth generation but more likely in the sixth or seventh, even though St. Simon appears much earlier in the descent of Fils d'Eve, the winner of the 1960 Italian Derby, by Wild Risk, by Rialto, by Rabelais, by St. Simon, by Galopin.

Up to this point, our examination has dealt with horses representative of the principal stud lines of our era, so it is natural that there have been no startling revelations. But if we go further down the list, we find some rather interesting data: Dark Ronald and John o' Gaunt are each mentioned twenty-one times in the pedigrees considered; Rabelais, twenty times; and Bay Ronald, Havresac II, and Son-in-Law each appear eighteen times. The Dark Ronald–Son-in-Law line, therefore, is much more important than one would have thought, and the discrepancy between the line's fame (little), among the racing public, and its true vitality (considerable) results from the sort of races programmed in many countries today, all being over relatively short distances, which do not permit such stayers to show what they really can do. As one American expert put it with a great deal of perspicacity, the success of a stallion is dependent upon the racing secretary at the track.

Havresac II has a flattering position on our list, principally stemming from the fact that he is Nearco's grandsire, on his mother's side, which accounts for twelve mentions in pedigrees. Continuing down that list, we find Spearmint mentioned seventeen times; The Tetrarch, sixteen; Hurry On, Persimmon, Tracery, and White Eagle, fourteen; Friar Marcus and William the Third, thirteen; Marcovil, Nearco, and Sundridge, twelve; and Desmond, Gallinule, Sans Souci II, and Sunstar, eleven; while Minoru appears ten times. We shall not go beyond ten appearances in a pedigree since, naturally, the list is much too long, going into the hundreds, and of course these studs are of less interest. The classification of The Tetrarch also is indicative of an importance not reflected in the rather considerable adverse criticism of this horse and his descendants. It is interesting to note

369 *Riding in wintertime in the enclosed paddock.*

that such criticism is not borne out by the records. However, no one can be surprised at the positions in our list occupied by Spearmint, Hurry On, and Persimmon, while it is a bit startling to see how well Tracery figures, since, in Europe at least, he has practically no male descent. Professionals accustomed to examining pedigrees from all over the world never cease to be amazed at how often the name of Tracery appears. The presence of White Eagle and Friar Marcus is due almost entirely to their respective colts who have been responsible for important studs, and the same is true of William the Third. Nearco is a different case, and with the passage of time he will figure even more frequently in the production of great winners because of his contribution, which is reflected around the world, and even more, that of his colts and fillies.

Of the final group mentioned, Marcovil, Sundridge, Desmond, Gallinule, Sans Souci II, and Sunstar belong to another era, most particularly Gallinule, who is well back in the last century. It is interesting to note that Nearco already figures as frequently as these great sires of another day; also of significance is how often Gallinule figures, when we realize that he was foaled in 1884. This horse is another that has had more detractors than admirers, but the record shows that he has made a great contribution. One might say that Son-in-Law, The Tetrarch, and Gallinule figure in this list as the three great rehabilitators of bloodlines, with Tracery as the vitalizing element, and Nearco, the great hope for the future.

XIV
GENETIC CURIOSITIES

Stallions and mares of four years of age rarely produce great horses. Nasrullah and Noor, however, were the get of four-year-old sires who proved exceptions to that rule.

Eight winners of classic races that did have four-year-old sires are Scottish Queen (1869 winner of the Thousand Guineas) by Blair Athol; Chelandry (1897, Thousand Guineas) by Goldfinch; Roseway (1919, Thousand Guineas) by Sternoway; Diophon (1924, Two Thousand Guineas) by Grand Parade; Turkhan (1940, St.Leger) by Barham; Commotion (1941, Oaks) by Mieuxcé; Ocean Swell (1944, Derby) by Blue Peter; and Arctic Prince (1951, Derby) by Prince Chevalier. The oldest stud to sire a winner was Matchem, who was responsible at the age of twenty-eight for the filly Teetotum, who took the Oaks in 1780.

The youngest broodmare on the list of producers of great horses is Monstrosity, who started as a reproducer as a two-year-old and gave us the 1844 winner of the Two Thousand Guineas, The Ugly Buck. Foaled by three-year-olds were the winners of the St.Leger of 1779, Tommy; of 1809, Ashton; of 1812, Otterington; of 1845, The Baron; the winner of the Gold Cup of 1860, Rupee; of 1935, Tiberius; and the winner of the Thousand Guineas of 1924, Plack. Among the veteran broodmares was Rubens, who foaled Firebrand, winner of the Thousand Guineas of 1842, at the age of twenty-five. Remember, however, that horses do not reach full maturity as sires and dams until they are between five and six years old.

XV
STALLION LINES

The fascinating material amassed on stallions and their offspring is very instructional and also, as we have seen, open to question. There is no positive way to establish precisely what would have been the best efforts of any given stud had he functioned in another country, for instance, if Nearco had been active in England rather than in Italy; or Airborne had been in a country that held no prejudice against a gray coat; if Khaled, by Hyperion, had remained in Europe and not been sent to the United States where he did so well that he was able to give us a champion like Swaps.

Alternately, stallions that had transmitted defects ended by being eliminated from the great pedigrees, even though they may have been responsible for valuable horses like Gallinule, for instance, who passed on a tendency to hemorrhage, or other studs who were incapable of making their mark to produce a dominant type.

In order to form a better, more precise idea of the situation that obtained in relation to stallions and their get, and to omit all of what appeared to be more myth than fact, Varola and a number of other students of the Thoroughbred have established the following bases from which the stallion lines developed during the periods in question:

1. The Byerly Turk, bay, foaled about 1680; the Darley Arabian, dark bay, foaled c. 1700; and the Godolphin Arabian (sic), dark bay, foaled about 1724. There are no known pedigrees for these horses.

2. Each of these three sires passed on his characteristics to one of his offspring who became what are considered the three foundation sires of the Thoroughbred: Matchem, a bay, foaled 1748, by Cade, out of the Partner Mare, by Partner, continued the line of the Godolphin Arabian (or Barb; either term is used, as there has always been some question as to just what he was); Herod, a bay, foaled 1758, by Tartar, out of Cypron, by Blaze, continued the line of the Byerly Turk; and Eclipse, sorrel, 1746, by Marske, out of Spiletta, by Regulus, carried on the Darley Arabian's line. From these sires, the true fixers of the characteristics of the Thoroughbred, derive those horses that Vuillier considers the most illustrious specimens at the beginning of the nineteenth century. The initials in parentheses indicate the line—(E) Eclipse, (M) Matchem, (H) Herod.

3. (H) Pantaloon, sorrel, 1824; (E) Voltaire, dark bay, 1826; (E) Touchstone, dark bay, 1831; (H) Bay Middleton, bay, 1833; (E) Birdcatcher, sorrel, 1833; (H) Gladiator, sorrel, 1833; and (M) Melbourne, dark bay, 1834. Vuillier also

370 *A daily ride in the open air.*
371 *The great esplanade at San Rossore, where, every winter, an uninterrupted cavalcade of old horses and colts from every imaginable stud spends the season, now including English horses.*
372 *Federico Tesio surrounded by some of his colts.*
373 *Camici about to dismount from Tissot.*
374 *The return to the stables.*

372

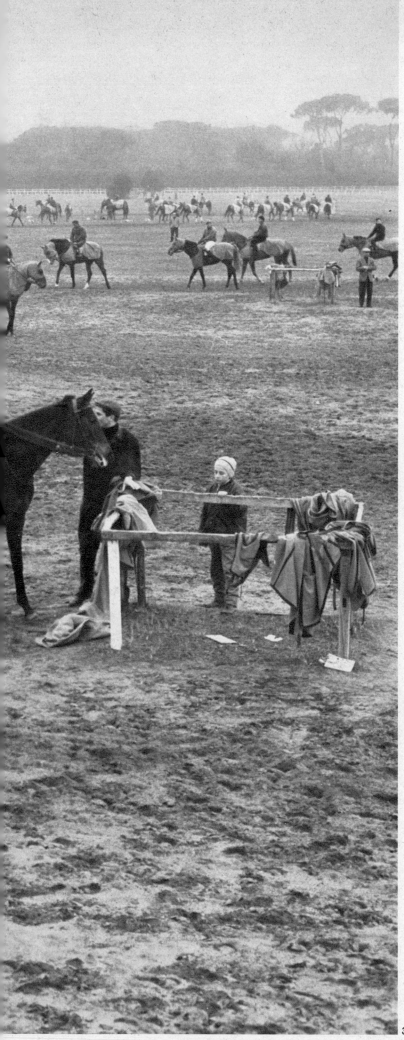

373

374

371

377

375

376

378

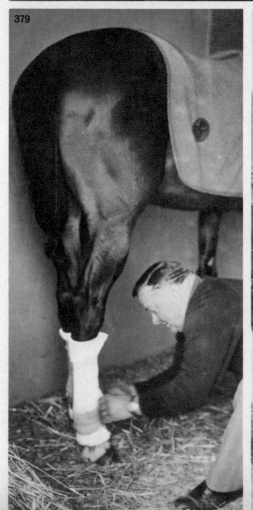

379

380

included Pocahontas in this list, perhaps the most famous broodmare of all time, who foaled King Tom, Stockwell, and Rataplan, and is the only female included in his "dosage" theory. Varola also noted the great concentration of important sires between 1831 and 1834. This was a phenomenon that was to occur in other periods in the future. Coming at mid-nineteenth century, we find:

4. (E) Newminster, bay, 1848, by Touchstone; (E) Stockwell, sorrel, 1849, by The Baron. Newminster gave rise to the Hampton strain, while Stockwell was responsible for the Bend Or strain. Vuillier's group for the third period, coming at the end of the nineteenth century, comprised:

5. (E) Hermit, sorrel, 1864, by Newminster; (E) Hampton, bay, 1872, by Lord Clifden; (E) Galopin, dark bay, 1872, by Vedette; (E) Isonomy, bay, 1875, by Sterling; (E) Bend Or, sorrel, 1877, by Doncaster; and (E) St. Simon, dark bay, 1881, by Galopin. Note that this entire group are descendants of Eclipse; the Herod and Matchem lines were to peak only after 1900, with the appearance of The Tetrarch and Hurry On.

The last twenty years of the nineteenth century are dominated by the exceptional individuality of St. Simon, whose presence was so ubiquitous that England was faced with the problem of avoiding excessive inbreeding, although the line did threaten to disappear, and was saved some fifty years later through the grandchildren being broadcast throughout the world. According to Varola, these are the modern foundation sires: (E) Son-in-Law, dark bay, 1911, by Dark Ronald, out of Mother-in-Law, by Matchmaker, England; (H) The Tetrarch, gray, 1911, by Roi Herode, out of Vahren, by Bona Vista, England; (M) Hurry On, sorrel, 1913, by Marcovil, out of Tout Suite, by Sainfoin, England; (E) Phalaris, dark bay, 1913, by Polymelus, out of Bromus, by Sainfoin, England; (E) Teddy, bay, 1913, by Ajax, out of Rondeau, by Bay Ronald, France; (E) Gainsborough, bay, 1914, by Bayardo, out of Rosedrop, by St. Frusquin, England; (E) Havresac II, dark bay, 1915, by Rabelais, out of Hors Concours, by Ajax, France; (E) Blandford, dark bay, 1919, Swynford, out of Blanche, by White Eagle, England; (E) Pharos, bay, 1920, by Phalaris, out of Scapa Flow, by Chaucer, England; (E) Astérus, bay, 1923, by Teddy, out of Astrella, by Verdun, France; (E) Congreve, bay, 1924, by Copyright, out of Per Noir, by Perrier, United States; (E) Fairway, bay, 1925, by Phalaris, out of Scapa Flow, by Rabelais, England; (H) Tourbillon, bay, 1928, by Ksar, out of Durban, by Durban II, France; (E) Hyperion, sorrel, 1930, by Gainsborough, out of Selene, by Chaucer, England; (E) Bois Roussel, dark bay, 1935, by Vatout, out of Plucky Liege, by Spearmint, France; (E) Nearco, bay, 1935, by Pharos, out of Nogara, by Havresac II, Italy; (E) Bull Lea, dark bay, 1935, by Bull Dog, out of Rose Leaves, by Ballot, United States; (E) Ticino, dark bay, 1939, by Athanasius, out of Terra, by Aciti, Germany; (E) Nasrullah, bay, 1940, by Nearco, out of Mumtaz Begum, by Blenheim II, Great Britain.

After commenting on the great concentration of exceptional sires in the years immediately preceding World War II, the return of the Herod and Matchem lines through The Tetrarch and Hurry On, and how the unusual number of stallions—Touchstone, Galopin, St. Simon, Son-in-Law, Phalaris, Havresac II, Blandford, Bull Lea, Ticino, Fairway, and Nearco—with dark coats were having a definite effect upon the development of the breed, Varola then attempted to spotlight those stallions that had a capital influence in this century upon the classic pedigrees, a prime necessity if one is to arrive at the proper "dosage" and balance of fundamental characteristics. Varola lists thirty:

Chaucer, dark bay, 1900, by St. Simon; Rabelais, bay, 1900, by St. Simon; Spearmint, bay, 1903, by Carbine; Orby, sorrel, 1904, by Orme; Dark Ronald, dark bay, 1905, by Bay Ronald; Fair Play, sorrel, 1905, by Hastings; Bayardo, bay, 1906, by Bay Ronald; Swynford, dark bay, 1907, by John o' Gaunt; Alcantara II, bay, 1908, by Perth; Sunstar, dark bay, 1908, by Sundridge; Tracery, dark bay, 1909, by Rock Sand; Black Toney, dark bay, 1911, by Peter Pan; La Farina, sorrel, 1911, by Sans Souci II; Solario, bay, 1922, by Gainsborough; Oleander, bay, 1924, by Prunus; Ortello, sorrel, 1926, by Teddy; Vatout, bay, 1926, by Prince Chimay; Château Bouscaut, bay, 1927, by Kircubbin; Prince Rose, bay, 1928, by Rose Prince; King Salmon, bay, 1930, by Salmon Trout; Admiral Drake, bay, 1931, by Craig an Eran; Fair Trial, sorrel, 1932, by Fairway; Precipitation, sorrel, 1933, by Hurry On; Panorama, sorrel, 1936, by Sir Cosmo; Pharis, dark bay, 1936, by Pharos; Big Game, dark bay, 1939, by Bahran; Count Fleet, dark bay, 1940, by Reigh Count; and Alycidon, sorrel, 1945, by Donatello II.

What Tesio defined as "laws of maximum instability," Varola considered as "limiting factors" that keep a product from going beyond a determined level of performance, that is, beyond a limit of natural characteristics. Thus, "if all the great winners were to produce horses equal or better than they, the Thoroughbred would ultimately reach supersonic speed." This limiting factor, which is apparent when a fine horse has mediocre offspring, and vice versa, leads to a median level of performance that should not vary much from first to last.

Examining Tesio's theory, Varola justly points out that to expect a stallion line to yield a Derby winner in every generation is a bit too much. The Derby at Epsom Downs is just one of some few thousand races run on the flat each year in England, and the horse that is being prepared to race there is just one of several thousand potential aspirants to the winner's circle. On these considerations alone, it is truly a marvelous thing when both a sire and his colt win, and even more wondrous if a grandson wins, too. As to the odds on four horses in direct line being winners, Varola asks if anyone has ever won on a number at roulette four consecutive times.

The six winners of the German Derby, Landgraf, 1917; Ferror, 1926; Athanasius, 1934; Ticino, 1942; Neckar, 1951; and Wilderer, 1958, make a unique but not too surprising exception considering that there is little strong competition in stallion lines. Actually, there are no obstacles to the same thing occurring in England or in some of the classics in the United States, but the number of contrary probabilities would be infinitely greater than in Germany.

Taber, who first set forth the limiting-factor theory, was

375–380 Back at the stables after a run, where the horses are led to their stalls, rubbed down with straw, dried of sweat, while food is prepared, legs are bandaged or wrapped, and shoes checked.

heartily criticized. The champion, like the genius, is abnormal, and cannot perpetuate his abnormality in just the proper balance required of an athlete. If the hindquarters are developed too highly, the forehand suffers; too much high spirit sacrifices the coolness of the racer; too much staying power leads to too little speed; and the truly stylish runner will have rough going on a heavy track. Outstanding characteristics disproportionately repeated in offspring can become veritable defects, and most probably passed on.

Varola notes:

> Without John o' Gaunt, there would have been neither Swynford nor Blandford, and without Roi Herode, no The Tetrarch, and now Hampton continues by grace of the modest Bay Ronald rather than through the exceptional Merry Hampton, Ladas, and Ayrshire. Barcaldine went on through Marc, not Sir Visto. That same Swynford lived on by virtue of Blandford and not Sansovino. Progress does not move in a straight line. The most unprepossessing runner may be the carrier of the most balanced hereditary characteristics or the sire of the most educable offspring. Examples are El Greco and Bozzetto, both sons of Pharos, the first, a tremendous runner who almost outdid Nearco, but a washout as a sire, at least of racing colts, but a fine father of excellent mares, as was the case with the trotter Muscletone, while the second, not much as a runner, was a sire beyond every expectation.

We might also consider the case of Nearco: three of his sons were exceptional runners: Dante, Nimbus, and Sayajirao, but his blood went round the world through Nasrullah, Royal Charger, and Mossborough, who were certainly not up to the measure of the other three on the turf.

It is impossible to compare horses of the eighteenth century with those of today. Probably their potential was the same, although external conditions were different, like feeding and training and tack. Only diverse conditions of history condition the flourishing of one or another strain. On the same basis, Varola observes that England, conservative and realistic at one and the same time, but rigorously class-conscious, at least until fairly recently, has maintained "a ritualistic character"—we might even say "hierarchic"—in matters pertaining to horses and the turf, particularly in the genealogical aspects, so that sprinters remain sprinters, intermediates, intermediates, and stayers, stayers. A transfer to another category would be unthinkable. So it happens that for stayers, for example, the gap between Son-in-Law and Fair Trial is not bridged. Too often today the demand for an immediate financial return forces small owners to spasmodic quests for the precocious fast horse.

Varola brought Vuillier's work up to 1960, through the two basic works, *Stalloni Capirazza dal 1900 ad Oggi (Foundation Sires from 1900 to Date)* and *Nuovi Dosaggi del Purosangue (New Thoroughbred Blends)*, in which he has brought Vuillier's original number of stallions to a hundred, with the stated intention of increasing the number by a score in the near future; more important, he has divided them into the five categories previously mentioned, thus adding a new branch to the study. Varola's work has been well received throughout the world, and his methods are being followed by a large number of breeders.

Notwithstanding the need for quick returns, in Germany the Thoroughbred is a precise, methodic, well-blooded animal showing only slight genetic variation, since there is little desire to breed for the unexpected. In the United States, the struggle is purely economic, an intermittent effort to get the best market price, hence the necessity of seeing that a horse has a short, brilliant career and retires from racing when he is at the peak of his glory.

France, much as she accepts every current of thought and culture and then assimilates it and makes it distinctively French, has done the same with her Thoroughbreds, which reflect this variety to such a point that it is difficult to orient oneself in considering French stallion lines. There are none that are truly dominant, or any families that really stand out. In France, contrary to the general pattern in England, one is too frequently confronted with the total failure of great runners at stud, just as relatively obscure animals, particularly robust ones, seem to do well.

XVI
GREAT CHAMPIONS

STOCKWELL by The Baron, England, 1849–1870. This horse was known as the "emperor of the stallions." As a three-year-old, he had started fourteen times to win eleven, but he did not finish in the money in the Derby because of some temporary indisposition. In the 1852 St. Leger, however, he left behind the Derby winner Daniel O'Rourke. Stockwell sired three Derby winners, six winners of the St. Leger, and four Thousand Guineas winners.

WEST AUSTRALIAN by Melbourne, England, 1850–1857. The first winner of the English Triple Crown (the Derby, St. Leger, and Two Thousand Guineas), this horse was beaten only once, in his first start, and came in first ten consecutive times. The American line that was founded by Australian derives directly from West Australian, and produced Fair Play, Man o' War, War Admiral, Relic, and others, while the European branch, founded by Solon, led to Hurry On, St. Albans, Lord Ronald, and Doncaster, sire of Bend Or.

381 *In England and France, racehorses often winter at beach resorts, where the climate is milder. They are often taken for a run along the shore.*

382 *A champion in the making: Surdi, son of Airborne, a great winner.*

383 *Colts taught to start by being trained with a tape. Now, with the use of automatic starting gates, they are made to go through narrower and narrower stalls to accustom them to the gate.*

384 *The fine track at Bolgheri, which belongs to the Marquis Mario Incisa della Rocchetta.*

385 *A view of San Rossore.*

386 *The private track at Bolgheri.*

387 *The main entrance to San Rossore.*

388 *Riding out at Bolgheri.*

381

382

383

384

385

387

388

386

389

390 391

BEND OR by Doncaster, England, 1877–1903. After six victories as a two-year-old, he won the Derby by a head. Bend Or's most famous descendant is Ormonde, who not only gave rise to the line Flying Fox-Teddy-Ortello-Astérus, and so on, but also to Phalaris, who sired Pharos and Fairway.

ST. SIMON by Galopin, England, 1881–1908. St. Simon did not run in the classic races because his subscriptions were canceled upon the death of his breeder. Bought at auction in 1883 by the Duke of Portland for 1,600 guineas (about $4,000 today), he retired undefeated but never really had to prove himself. An extremely nervous horse, St. Simon's temper grew even worse after he was put to stud. Among his get that achieved success, some thirty of them, we might mention particularly Florizel II, Persimmon, St. Frasquin, Desmond, William the Third, Chaucer, and Rabelais. Of these, the descendants of Rabelais and Persimmon are in the first rank today.

ORMONDE by Bend Or, England, 1883–1904. One of the greatest of all Thoroughbreds, not only because he won the Triple Crown but also because he was never beaten in sixteen starts. Through his son, Orme, he gave us Flying Fox, from whom came Ajax, Teddy, Sir Gallahad III, Astérus, Ortello, and a host of others.

ISINGLASS by Isonomy, England, 1890–1911. Another winner of the Triple Crown who ran as a two-year-old and until he was five, losing only once in eleven starts. He is the foundation sire of the Blandford line, from which derive Blenheim, Donatello, Brantôme, Bahram, Norseman, Big Game, and others.

CYLLENE by Bona Vista, England, 1895–1925. Despite the fact that this horse did not race in any of the classics for three-year-olds, Cyllene probably can be considered the best of his generation, having won nine times out of eleven starts. In 1908, he was sold and shipped to the Argentine for 25,000 guineas (about $63,000 today). His best products were Minoru, Lemberg, and Tagalie, but his greater fame lived on in Polymelus, sire of Phalaris, from whom descended Pharos, Manna, Nearco, Nasrullah, Dante, Sayajirao, and Pharis.

FLYING FOX by Orme, England, 1896–1911. As a two-year-old he won three times and placed twice, out of five starts. At three, he won all of six races, which included the Triple Crown. Flying Fox did not run as a four-year-old. After the death of his owner, the Duke of Westminster, he was sold at auction to Edmond Blan, a Frenchman, for £37,500. The new owner had made a fine purchase; Flying Fox sired Ajax, sire of Teddy, whose line then divides into two branches, the French, with Aethelstan and Astérus, as well as Sir Gallahad III and Bull Dog, who were successful in the United States; and the Italian branch, with Ortello and Salpiglossis.

389 *Training on the racetrack.*
390. *The splendid action of Surdi.*
391 *Marguerite Vernaut coming up in a burst of speed.*

AJAX by Flying Fox, France, 1901–1915. He had five starts as a three-year-old, and won all. For his record as a sire, see Flying Fox.

BAYARDO by Bay Ronald, England, 1906–1917. After seven wins in seven starts as a two-year-old, this horse had a bad period from May to June when he was a three-year-old, and did not finish in the money in either the Two Thousand Guineas or the Derby. Hitting his stride once again at the Ascot meeting, he won consecutively sixteen times. During his whole career, Bayardo started twenty-five times and won twenty-two, earning £44,533 in prize money. He sired two winners of the Triple Crown, Gay Crusader and Gainsborough, the first without any really outstanding get, the second, sire of Hyperion, a great stud in his time.

HURRY ON by Marcovil, England, 1913–1936. This colt ran only as a three-year-old, and was undefeated in six starts, all won by a large margin. Since he made his debut in the middle of June, he was not able to run in the two spring classics, so that his most important win was at Newmarket, where the St. Leger was run that year because of the war. His get includes Captain Cuttle (sire of Pilade), Nesiotes (sire of Fante), Coronach (sire of Niccolò dell'Arca, Daumier, and Corrida), and Precipitation (sire of Chamossaire and Airborne).

GAINSBOROUGH by Bayardo, England, 1914–1945. The fact that he won the Triple Crown and the Gold Cup, as well, makes him look like one of the greats but Gainsborough's claim must be discounted slightly when we consider that he had few rivals of real worth. Perhaps the best competition at the time was the filly My Dear, who won the Oaks and finished second in the St. Leger, and Prince Chimay, who came in third in the St. Leger and won the Jockey Club Stakes, ahead of Gainsborough. His great worth was as a foundation sire, having given us Solario, Singapore, Emborough, and Hyperion.

KSAR by Bruleur, France, 1918–1937. As a three-year-old, after having won the Prix Hocquart, the Lupin, and the Jockey Club, this horse had a bad day at the Grand Prix de Paris, and finished unplaced. He came back solidly at the autumn meetings, taking the Royal Oak and the Arc de Triomphe, ahead of Flechois, in the colors of Commendatore Perrone. As a four-year-old, he made six starts and won four times, including the Arc de Triomphe for a second time and the Prix du Cadran. As a sire, he did well, giving us Ut Mejeur, Amfortas, Thor, Le Ksar, the Italian Muzio, and, best of all, Tourbillon.

CORONACH by Hurry On, England, 1923–1949. A very fast horse, like most of his descendants, he lost only the Two Thousand Guineas, as a three-year-old, to Colorado, winning the other five races in which he was entered. As a four-year-old, he won the Coronation Cup and the Hardwick Stakes. The best of his get was undoubtedly Niccolò dell'Arca, but there were also Cranach (the French horse of that name, not the Italian), Call Boy, Precipitation, and De Albertis, and the phenomenal filly Corrida.

FAIRWAY by Phalaris, England, 1925–1948. With three successes in four starts as a two-year-old, he appeared to be due for all the honors, but the track at Epsom Downs presented such difficulties that he finished unplaced in the Derby, which Felstead won. Fairway did, however, win other great races: Eclipse, St. Leger, and Champion Stakes. As a five-year-old, he won five times and was beaten only once, in the Eclipse, by Royal Minstrel. He took the St. Leger, but could not manage the longer distances, like his brother, Pharos, and that is a characteristic in his descendants, although Blue Peter and Watling did win the Derby. The first gave us Ocean Swell and Botticelli. The best stud of the line was Fair Trial, sire of Court Martial, Petition, and Palestine, all fine stallions, and with rare exceptions sires of sprinters or, at best, middle-distance runners.

ORTELLO by Teddy, Italy, 1926–1947. Unbeaten in the spring meetings as a three-year-old, he took the Arc de Triomphe, followed by the French horse Kantar and the German Oleander, but only placed, after Gérard, in the Premio Chiusura. As a four-year-old, he finished unplaced in the Arc de Triomphe, coming in fourth, behind Motrico, Hotweed, and Filarete. The best of his get were Vezzano, Moroni, Sirte, Zuccarello, Macherio, and Torbido, who sired Antonio Canale, who in turn gave us Marco Visconti.

CAVALIERE D'ARPINO by Havresac II, Italy, 1926–1941. Raced only once as a three-year-old, and won; undefeated in his four starts as a four-year-old, but really had little competition (he never ran against Ortello, who was the same age). He was unlucky during the summer he prepared for the Arc de Triomphe. Put to stud in 1931, this horse sired two fine animals: Bellini, from whom we had Tenerani, Ribot, and Tissot; and Traghetto, who shone after World War II.

TOURBILLON by Ksar, France, 1928–1954. Unbeaten as a three-year-old until the Grand Prix de Paris, he won the Prix Greffulhe, Hocquart, Lupin, and Jockey Club. He finished third in the Grand Prix, behind Berneveldt and Taxodium. Thereafter he disappointed his public by finishing unplaced in the Arc de Triomphe. One of the great studs of modern times, he headed the French list in the years 1940, 1942, 1945, and 1946, bringing fame and fortune to the Boussac stables, and siring the notable Djebel and Goya.

HYPERION by Gainsborough, England, 1930–1960. As a three-year-old, he won four victories in as many starts: the Chester Vase, Derby, Prince of Wales Stakes, and St. Leger. Hyperion finished third, behind Felicitation and the French horse Thor, in the Ascot Gold Cup as a four-year-old. Pony-sized, but full of temperament, he was a first-class sire, with offspring on both sides of the Atlantic, among whom were Stardust, Owen Tudor, Alibhai, Rockefeller, Pensive, Khaled, Gulf Stream, and Aureole, among whose progeny were such horses as Swaps, St. Crispin, Ponder, and Tudor Minstrel.

BAHRAM by Blandford, England, 1932–1956. The last horse to win the Triple Crown and one of the last of the great English horses to remain unbeaten after nine starts. As a sire, however, he was mediocre but did give us a winner of the St. Leger, Turkham, as well as Big Game and Persian Gulf,

who were responsible for Zarathustra, Rustam, Combat, Zimone, and Tamerlane.

CLAIRVOYANT by Mon Talisman, France, 1934–1940. Unquestionably one of the most celebrated horses of the period just prior to the Second World War; by a technicality he is unbeaten (the first time out, in the Prix Juigné, he was left at the post). His other five starts and wins were the Prix Hocquart, Matchem Stakes, Lupin, Jockey Club, and Grand Prix de Paris. Clairvoyant promised to be the best stud continuing the line of Sunstar, but after only two years at stud the horse died, leaving no noteworthy offspring.

DONATELLO by Blenheim, Italy, 1934–1955. After two starts as a two-year-old, he easily took both the Gran Criterium and the Criterium Nazionale. A massive animal, he beat out the excellent filly Amerina, winner of the Premio Regina Elena and the Italian Oaks, as a three-year-old. Donatello again came in ahead of Amerina in the Gran Premio d'Italia and won the Gran Premio di Milano, beating Mousson, the French champion, who placed. This victory over Mousson decided Tesio to enter him in the Grand Prix de Paris, where he was beaten by Clairvoyant. Notwithstanding, Donatello made such a good impression that he was bought by a syndicate of English breeders and put to stud. Among his numerous get, the most famous was Alycidon.

NEARCO by Pharos, Italy, 1935–1957. One of the greatest, if not *the* greatest Italian horse, comparable only to Ribot, perhaps, if one can make a comparison between two horses that ran twenty years apart. Nearco was magnificently built and well proportioned, though he appeared to be small. His extraordinary career covered fourteen starts and fourteen wins, seven each as a two- and a three-year-old, taking the Criterium Nazionale, the Gran Criterium, the Premio Tevere, and the Premio Chiusura, a unique feat in the history of the Italian track. As a three-year-old, after running at Pisa, he took the five principal Italian races of the spring meeting, the Parioli, Emanuele Filiberto, Derby Italiano, Gran Premio d'Italia, and the Gran Premio di Milano. On June 26, 1958, Nearco won his last race, at Longchamp, coming in ahead of the winners of both the English and the French Derby. After this exploit, he was purchased by a British syndicate as a stud, and demonstrated his great quality by siring a string of winners, and worthy descendants of Pharos, such as Nasrullah, Dante, Nearula, Royal Charger, Sayajirao, Nimbus, and Mossborough, not to mention a number of fillies that became

392 *The fabulous extension in the gallop of Antonio Canale, a son of Torbido, which, of course, did him no good on a heavy track.*

393 *The finish at the Gran Premio di Milano in 1965. On the outside, wearing Number 1, is Marco Visconti, son of Antonio Canale, who finished second, beaten by Accrale.*

394 *Suspense at Epsom: Lester Piggott, swung round in the saddle, falls from his horse on the final stretch.*

395 *Sir Victor Sassoon's St. Paddy, with Piggott up, beats Beasley on Alcaeus and Hutchinson on Kythnos in the Derby, Epsom Downs, 1960.*

392

393

394

395

396

397

398

fine broodmares. Along with Hyperion, Nearco ranks as one of the pillars of international breeding over the past thirty to forty years, and over a hundred of his get are at stud throughout the world today.

PHARIS by Pharos, France, 1936–1957. This horse had had a very brief career, three starts and three easily won victories, the Prix Noailles, Jockey Club, and Grand Prix de Paris, when the Second World War broke out. A great sire, one of the best of his period in France; and among the best of his get are Priam, Ardan, Scratch, Talma, Stymphale, and Auriban.

DJEBEL by Tourbillon, France, 1937–1958. In twenty-two starts, this horse lost quite a few races, but he improved with age, to be undefeated as a five-year-old in seven starts, which included both the Grand Prix de Saint-Cloud and the Arc de Triomphe. The great French line that began with Dollar was continued brilliantly by Ksar, Tourbillon, and Djebel, down to the 1950's. Among the notable horses sired by Djebel are Arbar, Clarion, My Babu, Montenica, and Coronation.

LE PACHA by Biribi, France, 1938–1960. He did not run as a two-year-old, but the next season, in seven starts, he won every time, and his races included the Greffulhe, Hocquart, Lupin, Jockey Club, Royal Oak, and Arc de Triomphe. Le Pacha, however, was a failure as a stud, and no trace of him remains in French lines.

NICCOLÒ DELL'ARCA by Coronach, Italy, 1938–1959. A powerful horse. As a two-year-old, Niccolò dell'Arca was beaten three times, once by Ruwenzori, and twice by Zliten. In the Gran Criterium Tesio's horse did a walkover. From the Gran Criterium to the St. Leger, eleven months of activity, he had a series of easy triumphs, except for his last race in which Zuccarello rivaled him. He also took the Parioli Emanuele Filiberto, Derby Italiano, both the Gran Premio d'Italia and the Gran Premio di Milan, the St. Leger, and even picked up the summertime Berlin Grand Prix. Like most descendants of Hurry On, Niccolò dell'Arca was a pacesetter. Following World War II, having left a good number of offspring behind in Italy, he was imported into England, where he did not have the success he merited, although he sired many good horses and, more particularly, broodmares.

ORSENIGO by Oleander, Italy, 1940–1960. Here was a champion despite his small stature. As a three-year-old, he had some trouble getting started, but he impressed one with his overwhelming style and the records he set for the Derby Italiano, 2:27 1-5; the Gran Premio di Milano, 3:08 4-5,

equaling the mark set by Niccolò dell'Arca. Orsenigo was a good stud, but left no notable offspring to continue the line in Italy. Orsenigo was shipped to Brazil for breeding purposes, and sired some notable horses, one of which, Escorial, is now in France.

TRAGHETTO by Cavaliere d'Arpino, Italy, 1942–1962. Perhaps the best of Cavaliere d'Arpino's sons. He showed his quality over all distances, from 1,600 to 3,000 meters. As a two-year-old, he lost twice, but he took the Triennale, the Criterium Nazionale, and the Premio Chiusura. After this he was unbeaten, winning the Derby Italiano, the Ambrosiano, and Premio Turati, not to mention the Parioli. In preparation for the Gran Premio di Milan, he ran the 3,000 meters for the Premio Cavalchina, beating Luca di Leida in the exceptional time of 3:09, a mere fifth of a second over the record time of Orsenigo and Niccolò dell'Arca, but carrying almost 128 pounds. As a four-year-old, he had four wins in four starts and was then retired to stud, where he not only headed the list of stallions but also sired such classic horses as Nuccio, Zamoretto, Alberigo, Río Marín, Mexico, and Carolina.

CARACALLA by Tourbillon, France, 1942, retired. A great horse over the long distances, and unbeaten, he made his debut in a race of secondary importance in which he was entered by his owner, Marcel Boussac, at three, and then really showed what he could do in the 3,000 meters of the Prix Reiset. That race was the preamble to the Grand Prix de Paris, in which Caracalla showed great promise, realized in his winning of the Prix Royal Oak. As a four-year-old, he won the Gold Cup at Ascot, and then took the Arc de Triomphe. At stud since 1947, he accomplished nothing whatsoever, and was, accordingly, retired.

HAVRESAC II by Rabelais, France, 1915–1939. Importing Havresac into Italy was a stroke of good fortune. In 1916, the French turf was in difficult straits because of the war and the requisition of thirteen hundred Thoroughbreds for the armed forces. (The races, which had been suspended, began again on a small scale at the beginning of September, 1915, with some proving trials.) Some owners sent their best horses across the Channel, while others sold all or a good part of their stock. One of those sold was the Montfort stud, in the Sarthe, which disposed of all its yearlings to a M. de Montel. Among them was Havresac II, who belonged to the same generation that had its best representative in Teddy. Havresac was a rival of Burne Jones, and won the Ambrosiano and the Premio Principe Amedeo. Had it not been for the war, he never would have come to Italy, paralleling the history of his sire. (Rabelais was foaled in England in 1900 and exported to France because of the outbreak of the Russo-Japanese War in 1904. A Russian commission that had already bought Rabelais saw its purchase agreement annulled by the conflict.) Thus France obtained the services of one of St. Simon's (sire of Rabelais) best colts. Havresac was a chip off the old block, and while he was not a handsome animal, being rather angular, he was a very lively dark bay, the purest St. Simon type, and a valuable sire. The first of Havresac II's get started appearing on the tracks in 1923, and it would be too much to expect great things so soon, but from

396 *The Queen of England, in Calcutta for the 1961 running of the Queen Elizabeth II Cup, studies the form of the Maharaja of Baroda's Monkshood, with W. Snaith up, in the paddock.*
397 *A view of the paddock during the Royal Ascot race meeting.*
398 *Epsom: Approaching Tattenham Corner.*

1924 onward his name often headed the list of stallions for his great number of very fine mares and good colts. His successor was his colt Cavaliere d'Arpino.

FLORIZEL II by St. Simon, England, 1891–1909. Winner of both the Jockey Club and St. James's Palace Stakes, as well as the Goodwood, Florizel II sired Doricles, winner of the St. Leger, who was grandfather to Massine, who sired Maravedis, Souverain, Mieuxcé, Blue Moon, and Scot; also Volodyovski, winner of the Derby and maternal grandfather of Manistee, Vedas, winner of the Two Thousand Guineas, and of Floreal, who took the Russian Derby. Florizel II also sired a number of fine fillies.

PERSIMMON by St. Simon, England, 1893–1908. A full brother of Florizel II, this colt won the Derby, Prince of Wales's Stakes, St. Leger, and the Jockey Club Stakes as a three-year-old, and the Eclipse Stakes and Ascot Gold Cup at four. He won seven times in nine starts. A big, broad horse, Persimmon bore no resemblance to his sire except in being an excellent stud. Among his get were the phenomenal Sceptre, Zinfandel, winner of the Jockey Club and Ascot Gold Cup; Keystone II, who took the Oaks; Your Majesty, winner of the St. Leger, Eclipse and St. James's Palace Stakes; Perola, who won the Oaks; Prince Palatine, who won the St. Leger, Eclipse, Doncaster Cup, and the Ascot Gold Cup twice. Persimmon headed the list of sires of winners and of broodmares a number of times. Continuing his line was Prince Palatine, from whom sprang Princequillo, Prince Bio, Prince Chevalier, Sicambre, and Arctic Prince; later came Sedan and, subsequently, Ediar.

ST. FRUSQUIN by St. Simon, England, 1893–1914. The same age as Persimmon, this colt won nine races, among them, the Two Thousand Guineas. He was an excellent sire, twice heading the list, and always somewhere at the top of it. Among his get were Quintessence, winner of the One Thousand Guineas; St. Amant, who took the Two Thousand Guineas and the Derby; Flair, the One Thousand Guineas; Rhodora, the One Thousand Guineas; and Sarakrit, who won the Austrian Derby and the Hungarian St. Leger. Many of his offspring were fine broodmares, such as Quintessence, dam of Clarissimus; Bonny Bay, who gave us Burne Jones; Santa Fina, Galloper Light's dam; Sweet Briar, who foaled Sun Briar and Sunreigh; Angelina, who foaled Apelle; Salamandra, responsible for Salmon Trout and Sagacity. The stallion line of St. Frusquin is to all effects extinct.

DESMOND by St. Simon, England, 1896–1913. A colt that ran little and won little but sired The White Knight, winner, twice in succession, of the Ascot Gold Cup, and the Goodwood Cup; Sir Archibald, put to stud in Italy; and a number of other winners. Most of his European descent have disappeared.

WILLIAM THE THIRD by St. Simon, England, 1898–1917. A winner of five races as a three-year-old, he showed his great stamina when he took the Ascot Gold Cup and the Doncaster Cup. While he sired a number of winners, such as Willonyx, who took the Ascot Gold Cup; Rembrandt, the winner of the Derby Italiano, and the French colt Pilliwisckie, William

the Third did better with his daughters, among them, Dutch Mary, the dam of Duccia di Buoninsegna.

CHAUCER by St. Simon, England, 1900–1926. A half-brother of Swynford, Chaucer ran thirty-five times and won seven, but mostly in races of secondary importance, except for the Gimcrack Stakes, in which he started as a two-year-old. Indifferent, his breeders turned him out to stud at a forty-guinea fee, but Chaucer soon became very much sought after, and today his name is a part of many illustrious pedigrees: Scapa Flow, dam of Pharos, Fairway, and Fair Isle; Lady Nairne, mother of Colombo, and Selene, Hyperion's dam—all his daughters. The best of his sons were Steadfast and Prince Chimay. From the latter derive Vatout, Bois Roussel, Vatellor, My Love, Tehran, and Migoli.

RABELAIS by St. Simon, England, 1900–1928. He won four races as a two-year-old, and the Goodwood Cup at three. He was imported into France (under the circumstances of the Russo-Japanese War mentioned above) by the Montfort stud for 700 guineas, and proved to be an exceptional stallion, and three times headed the French list. Submitted to Voronov's gland operation at the age of twenty-eight to restore his youthful powers, he died a few days after the operation. Rabelais, through his colt, Havresac II, gave Italy many of its best horses, such as Cavaliere d'Arpino, Bellini, Tenerani, Traghetto, Nuccio, Ribot, Tissot, Zamoretto, Alberigo; while in France his sons Rialto and Biribi were sires, respectively, of Wild Risk, Rienzo (sire of Winston Churchill's Colonist), Worden, and Vimy (in England), and Le Pacha, Mat de Cocagne, and Al Mabscot. Florizel II, Persimmon, Chaucer, and Rabelais can be considered to be the colts that best inherited St. Simon's characteristics. Havresac II was not only sired by Rabelais but was crossed with St. Simon, his dam's grandfather. This saturation, plus the fact that he preserved the peculiar characteristics of the line, contributed toward making him a stallion of enormous potential. Confirmation of Mendel's law is seen in the fact that his best offspring were bays, tending toward dark bay.

399   *The modern installations of the totalisator at Tokyo's largest track.*
400   *The starting gate at the Tokyo track.*
401   *Tattenham Corner, taken during the 1964 Derby at Epsom, won by Santa Claus with Beasley up.*
402   *The finish of the Cesarewitch at Newmarket.*
403   *On the track during the Gold Cup at Ascot in 1957, won by Zarathustra.*
404   *Goodwood: the final stretch.*
405   *Four at the finish at Saratoga.*
406   *Three in a photo finish at Aqueduct.*
407   *A muddy finish on a dirt track.*
408   *Nashua, whose great rival was Swaps, works out on the turf.*
409   *A view of Belmont Park.*
410   *Hutchinson on Tavernier after winning the Italian St. Leger.*
411   *A photo finish of three quarter horses in a special event for their breed.*
412   *Trouble at the starting gate.*

399

400

401

402

403
404

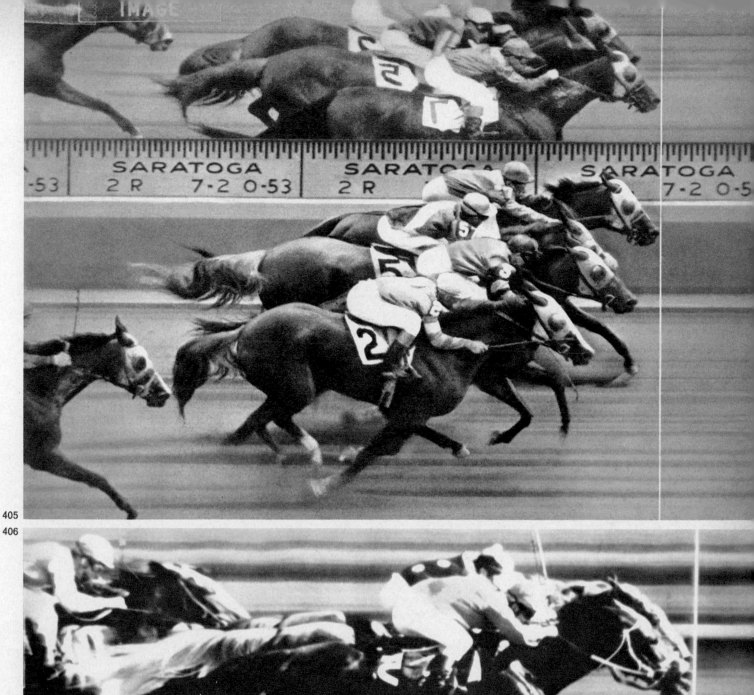

408

409

410

411

412

407

413 414

415

416

BELLINI by Cavaliere d'Arpino, Italy, 1937–1959. The eldest of the three best contemporary colts of Ortello since Traù was foaled in 1939 and Traghetto in 1942. A brilliant colt at two, Bellini made twelve starts as a three-year-old and won eight races, coming in second three times, and third once. In Italy, he won the Ambrosian, Derby Italiano, Nastro Bruno de Monaco, St. Leger, Jockey Club, and Piazzale. As a four-year-old, he had five wins and placed twice out of seven starts. Over his whole career, Bellini ran in twenty-three races and always finished in the money, fifteen wins, eight times placed. He could sprint only about 150 feet but that was usually all that was needed to get him home. A good-looking colt, a bit smaller than average, he was put to stud during the war and left his mark only in his colt Tenerani.

TENERANI by Bellini, Italy, 1944–   . He was not much to look at. An unsuccessful two-year-old, it was not until a year later that he was able to demonstrate his good qualities. He was beaten only once as a three-year-old, at Merano after winning the Derby Italiano, the Gran Premio d'Italia, and the Gran Premio di Milano, and subsequently, in the fall, the Gran Premio del Jockey Club. His career as a four-year-old was even better; he made eight starts and lost only one race, the run for the Gran Premio di Milano taken by his stablemate, Astolfina, adding to his victories the King George VI Stakes and the Goodwood Cup. As a stud, he sired the great Ribot and Tissot in Italy, then was sent to England and later returned to end his days at the Fonte di Papa stud, near Rome. Besides the two cited, his best offspring were Malhoa and Haseltine, the first of which has already gone into stud to take his sire's place. Tenerani's get on the average have been good horses, fighters with plenty of stamina, and usually successful on a heavy track.

RIBOT by Tenerani, Italy, 1952–   . Much has been written about this Italian champion, debating whether he is the superior of Nearco, bred at the same stud but foaled seventeen years earlier. Naturally, it is difficult to make comparisons between horses separated by so many years. It can be said in Ribot's favor, however, that he did win three races abroad as against Nearco's one foreign victory, that he has beaten more of the older horses and, finally, that he probably has had a more active career and been put to the test much more than Nearco. As a matter of fact, Nearco had only one real trial, in the Grand Prix de Paris in 1958, against Ribot's three great international races. Unbeaten in sixteen starts, Ribot won out over the best English, French, and American horses for two successive years in the Arc de Triomphe, including a formidable trio entered by Marcel Boussac. Ribot ran only three times as a two-year-old. In the Gran Criterium he came within a tick of losing to Gail, whom he finally beat by a head, having had a difficult run on the heavy going. But his other

fifteen starts were easy victories. Upon his return from the Arc de Triomphe to Italy, Ribot ran for the Jockey Club prize at the San Siro track, against a field that had such French representatives as Norman, Cordova, Savoyard, and Hidalgo II, as well as Stani from Germany. The race was a romp for Ribot, who came in first, fifteen lengths ahead of Norman. As a four-year-old, Ribot won the King George VI Stakes and his second Arc de Triomphe. After winning the Gran Premio di Milano, coming in ahead of Tissot, he went to Ascot, where he won by five lengths. At stud, first in Italy, then in the United States where he remained, Ribot sired, among others, Molvedo, Corpora, Romulus, Ragusa, Long Look, Tom Rolfe, and Ribocco.

BOTTICELLI by Blue Peter, Italy, 1951–   . This colt's garland of victories is one of the richest in the history of the Italian turf, for in addition to winning the Triple Crown of his country, he also took the Premio Emanuele Filiberto, the Gran Premio di Milano, and the Milan Gold Cup. Botticelli had difficulties when he ran on a heavy track, which occurred in the race for the Italian Jockey Club prize at San Siro, the King George VI Stakes, and the Premio Chiusura, to name just a few instances. He did, however, manage to take the Ascot Gold Cup. Botticelli was good at almost any distance, from one to two miles. As a stud, he did quite a bit of traveling. After a period in Italy at stud, he was let out in England, then returned to Italy to end, finally, in Germany.

NASHUA by Nasrullah, United States, 1952–   . This American champion was a reflection of the best American, English, French, and Italian strains—and a superb mixture it proved to be. Nashua had an active career of three years on the track, and topped the previous record as a moneymaker, held by Citation, earning $1,288,565, a record not surpassed until Roundtable topped it with $1,749,869. This handsome grandson of Nearco was of impeccable conformation, closely resembling his sire, from whom he also inherited certain quirks of character. Best of his generation as a two-year-old, he maintained that title as a three-year-old as well, even though he was up against a formidable adversary in Swaps, who beat him in the Kentucky Derby but over whom he had his revenge in a match at Washington Park. Nashua won twenty-two races out of thirty starts and achieved three world records. His principal victories were the Flamingo Stakes, Preakness Stakes, Florida Derby, Belmont Stakes, Wood Memorial Stakes, Arlington Classic, and the Jockey Club Cup twice. At the end of his racing career he was auctioned for $1,250,000 for stud purposes.

SWAPS by Khaled, United States, 1952   . Swaps was unfortunate in that he was racing at the same time as Nashua, who was the same age. While Swaps had neither the looks nor the brilliance of his rival, in any other season he would have been considered well beyond the rest of the field. Nevertheless, he did take the Kentucky Derby, keeping Nashua from picking up the Triple Crown (Kentucky Derby, Preakness Stakes, and Belmont Stakes). He had trouble with one foot, which recurred often enough to keep from winning when he might have handily had he not been afflicted. His bad foot eventually led to a fractured joint while racing at Garden State Park. Everything was done to save Swaps, not

413–415 *The notorious ford at Lambro being crossed during the Monza International Cross-Country race.*
416 *Racing on the solid ice of the lake at Saint-Moritz.*

with any hope that he would ever race again but so that he would be healthy enough to be employed at stud. He has proved to be one of the finest American stallions. Swaps was an Anglo-American product. His sire, Khaled, was a son of Hyperion, and exported to the States from England, while his dam had the blood of some of the best American families. Swaps made twenty-five starts and won nineteen times, his outstanding successes being the Kentucky Derby, the Santa Anita Handicap, the American Derby, the Californian Stakes, and the Hollywood Gold Cup.

CITATION by Bull Lea, United States, 1945–   . Bred on Calumet Farm, Citation was closely related to some of the best of the European champions, such as Caerleon, who had won the Eclipse Stakes; Colorado, who took the Eclipse and the Two Thousand Guineas; and Toboggan, winner of the Oaks. Citation had a full and active career, with forty-five starts and thirty-two wins, which brought him the record in winnings for his time, $1,085,760. Besides winning most of the prestige races, Citation was the last horse to take the Triple Crown. Citation attracted the fans like no horse since Man o' War. His career neatly divides into two phases: the first, from 1948 through 1949, when Citation started twenty-nine times and won twenty-seven; in the second phase, after a year of inactivity, he ran sixteen times but came in first only five.

MAN O' WAR by Fair Play, United States, 1917–1947. "Big Red" is possibly the best-known horse to women and children and those who generally never visit a race track or read a racing form. The famous chestnut was foaled in Lexington. His dam was Mahubah. Regarded as one of the greatest racers of all time, he was bought as a yearling for $5,000, won a lifetime total of $249,465 and a place in the official Hall of Fame. As a two-year-old, Big Red won 10 out of 11 starts, including the Belmont Futurity and the Hopeful Stakes. His career as a three-year-old is unblemished, with wins in the Preakness Stakes, Travers Stakes, Lawrence Realization Stakes, Jockey Club Gold Cup, and the Kenilworth Park Gold Cup, ending his career with 21 wins out of 22 starts as the world's leading money winner of the year. He broke either a track or world record in 8 of his last 11 races. Man o' War gave us Hard Tack and War Admiral, and he is the great-grandsire of Buckpasser, the third highest money winner in the world today. When Big Red retired from stud in 1943, he had sired over 300 colts and fillies. Over 50,000 people visited him annually in his retirement just for the opportunity to see the great Wonder Horse.

BULL LEA by Bull Dog, United States, 1935–1964. His sire is the French-bred son of Teddy who also gave us Sir Gallahad III and Ortello, and his dam was Rose Leaves. Bull Lea was a brown horse bred at the Coldstream Stud and purchased as a yearling by Warren Wright for $14,000, and raced for him. At stud since 1940 at Mrs. Markey's Calumet Farms, his sire record is outstanding in that he led the list five times— 1947, 1948, 1949, 1952, and 1953, with $1,630,655 in 1952 alone. In 1966, his 17 winners tied Alibhai as the leading sire of winners of $200,000 or more. Two of his famous offspring are Citation, former world's leading money winner with $1,085,760, and Armed, well up on the list.

NASRULLAH by Nearco, United States, 1940–1959. This spectacular bay out of Mumtaz Begum was bred by the Aga Khan at his stud in Ireland. He was sold by Prince Aly Khan for $50,000, but his father, unaware of the sale, proceeded to sell him also, to an Indian. The earlier sale stuck. Nasrullah was eventually purchased in 1950 by an American syndicate that brought him to stud at the Claiborne Farm, where he made a great name for himself. The price was $372,000. The stallion headed the leading-sire list five times in the period 1955 to 1962 (the last three posthumously), not including a second position. Nashua, Bold Ruler, and Noor are among his great offspring. In 1962 alone, his products earned $1,474,831.

COUNT FLEET by Reigh Count, United States, 1940–   . This son of a Derby winner and the dam Quickly has a coveted place in racing shared by only eight horses, the first in 1919. In 1943, he became the sixth winner of the Triple Crown. He had a blazing racing career, and is a valuable stud. As a two-year-old, he started 15 times and won 10, including the Champagne Stakes and the Pimlico Futurity; as a three-year-old, in addition to his Triple Crown, he took the Wood Memorial, Withers Stakes, and the Allowance Purse at Jamaica for a total of 6 out of 6 for the year. He did not race as a four-year-old, and his lifetime earnings are $250,300. In 1943, he was voted the Outstanding Horse of the Year. He has been standing at the Stoner Creek Stud, continuing the pattern of his sire by producing a Derby winner, Count Turf.

PRINCEQUILLO by Prince Rose, United States, 1940–1964. From an inauspicious beginning in claiming races (known in England as selling races), this bay gained fame in handicap races. He was foaled by Cosquilla in Ireland. His first year out, he ran 10 times in $1,500 and $2,500 claiming races. He eventually was claimed by the Boone Hall Stable, and established a lifetime record of 12 wins out of 33 starts. In 1943, he was the Jockey Gold Cup champion. The following year, he was put out to stud, first at Ellerslie Farm, Virginia; then at Claiborne Farm in Kentucky, and is responsible for Round Table, Hill Prince, Dedicate, and a great many excellent mares. His value as a stallion is to be judged by the fact that in 1957 his offspring won a record $1,698,427, and he is the grandsire of the 1968 Belmont Stakes winner, Stage Door Johnny. Round Table is the third world-leading money winner with $1,749,869.

417 *The jump at Beecher's Brook, taken during the Grand National at Aintree.*
418 *The ditch at the Pardubice Steeplechase in Czechoslovakia.*
419–421 *A variety of falls at Cheltenham.*
422–425 *Falls in an American steeplechase.*
426 *Jumping the oxer at San Siro.*
427 *A tense moment at Aintree.*
428–430 *Aftermath of an unhappy fall at Merano: The jockey, after recovering, sees the dreadful fracture his mount has suffered, and sadly begins to unsaddle the horse.*

417

418

419

420

421

422

423

424

425

426

427

428

429

430

BOLD RULER by Nasrullah, United States, 1954– . This dark bay was bred and raced by the Wheatley Stables. Now at stud where he was foaled, Claiborne Farm, Bold Ruler has a record of 23 wins out of 33 starts, with earnings of $764,204, fairly well up on the list. Some of his 11 stakes are the Belmont, Futurity, Preakness, Flamingo, Stymie, Suburban, Monmouth, and Trenton. In 1957, he was voted Horse of the Year, beating Gallant Man and Round Table in the Trenton Stakes. His dam, Miss Disco, was also a stakes winner. As a stud, Bold Ruler has had an enviable career, siring Successor, Bold Bidder, Stupendous, Great Power, Boldnesian, and Bold Lad. For four straight years they made him the top sire on the list, from 1963 to 1966. His offsprings' earnings in 1966 surpassed even Princequillo's for a record $2,306,523, the first plus-$2-million mark in a season.

NATIVE DANCER by Polynesian, United States, 1950– . This beautiful gray out of Geisha won every one of his 9 races handily the first year out, including the Hopeful, Futurity, and the East View Stakes; as a three-year-old, he repeated the performance with another 9 but dropped a tenth to place in the Kentucky Derby. His races then included the Gotham Stakes, Wood Memorial, Withers Stakes, Preakness Stakes, Belmont Stakes, Dwyer Stakes, Arlington Classic, Travers Stakes, and American Derby. He more than doubled his first year's earnings with $513,425; in his last year, as a four-year-old, he won all three races, but it was not much of a year, though he did take the Metropolitan Handicap. Native Dancer is a worthy sire: Kauai King, winner of the Kentucky Derby and the Preakness in 1966; Native Charger, Native Street, and Dancer's Image, who won the Kentucky Derby in 1968 but was disqualified. Each is well over the $200,000 class, with $381,397 for Kauai King's earnings alone.

HAIL TO REASON by Turn-to, United States, 1958– . This brown stallion has a record of 18 starts and 9 wins, and had total earnings of $328,434. His outstanding performance as a two-year-old matches his current role as a sire of great horses, with Hail to All, who took the Belmont Stakes in 1965; Priceless Gem, and Straight Deal as examples. His dam is Nothirdchance.

POLYNESIAN by Unbreakable, United States, 1942– . The great brown sire of Native Dancer need have done nothing more to keep his name in lights forever. However, he has a record of 27 wins out of 58 starts, placing in 10, and finishing third 10 times, for a lifetime record of $310,410. He is out of Black Polly.

CORONATION by Djebel, France, 1946– . A champion filly dating from the golden era of her owner, Marcel Boussac, who tried inbreeding with Tourbillon who figures twice in the second generation as grandsire on both the maternal and paternal sides. Though her list of victories was somewhat

spotted by defeats, Coronation was full of quality, though somewhat testy, undoubtedly because of the strict inbreeding. Making her debut in the Poule d'Essai with her stablemate, Galgala, with whom she finished in a dead heat, she then placed in the English and the Irish Oaks, following up by winning the Arc de Triomphe in grand style. As a broodmare, Coronation has yet to produce a noteworthy horse.

PINZA by Chanteur, England, 1950– . As a yearling he was up for auction at Newmarket in 1951. He was bought by Sir Victor Sassoon for £1,500. Sir Victor had spent a fortune over many years in an effort to acquire broodmares who might give him a Derby winner, but he had never been successful until he bought Pinza, for a song. The odd thing is that, once Pinza had broken the ice for him, he had three more Derby winners in the course of ten years: Crepello, Hard Ridden, and St. Paddy. Pinza started only three times in his third year, but won all three races, one in preparation for the Derby, the Derby itself, in which he had no trouble beating Aureole; and the King George VI Stakes. As a three-year-old, Pinza earned £44,101 and then was syndicated as a stud at a fee of £2,000.

PRINCE CHEVALIER by Prince Rose, France, 1943–1961. This horse started six times as a two-year-old, and won three. As a three-year-old, he had four consecutive wins in the Prix Greffulhe, Alary, Lupin, and Jockey Club, and was placed in another four starts. While his losing the Grand Prix de Paris and Prix Royal Oak, both times to Souverain, probably can be attributed to the greater distance, and his defeat by the unbeaten Caracalla in the Arc de Triomphe is no surprise, it is difficult to explain his bad showing in the Grand Prix de Ostend, which the Belgian Bouton de Rose won handily. Prince Chevalier was an excellent stallion, and was at stud in England. Among the most notable of his get are Doutelle, Arctic Prince, Court Harwell, and Beau Prince, as well as the more recent Exar and Charlottesville. Prince Rose, sire of Prince Chevalier, was also the sire of Princequillo, who sired Round Table and Prince Bio, from whom descend Sicambre, Northern Light, and Sedan.

TANTIÈME by Deux pour Cent, France, 1947– . Sired by the little-known Deux pour Cent, whose only first-class offspring he was, Tantième was beaten only once in each of the two years he ran. As a two-year-old, he started five times and won four, losing the Prix Robert Papin when overcome by a fit of coughing. As a three-year-old, his only defeat in six starts was in the Prix du Jockey Club, when he was beaten out by a head by Scratch. As a four-year-old, he came in third in the King George VI Stakes behind Supreme Court and Zucchero, but took the Prix Ganay, the Coronation Cup, and the Arc de Triomphe. As a five-year-old, at stud, he proved to be a first-class stallion, the best of his get being Tanerko, Match, La Sega, and Reliance.

SCRATCH by Pharis, France, 1947– . This horse's misfortune was in being another fine horse in a generation that had many, like Tantième and Vieux Manoir, not to mention his own stablemate, Galcador. He did, however, take two races with so much style that he is well remembered; he beat Tantième in the Prix du Jockey Club by a short head and

431–432 *Falls at jumps on English tracks.*

came in ahead of Vieux Manoir in the St. Leger. Over the whole of his career, he started eleven times, winning six and finishing in the money three. Sold as a stud to the Argentine, he has not distinguished himself.

SICAMBRE by Prince Bio, France, 1948–   . Unbeaten as a three-year-old, he lost only one race as a colt, the Prix Morny, but won the Grand Criterium. He took the Prix du Jockey Club, beating out his stablemate, Free Man. After some hesitation, he was entered for the Grand Prix de Paris, and won his hardest race, just managing to beat Aquino and Mat de Cocagne by a neck. He quickly demonstrated his value as a sire of such fine fillies as Hormières and Belle Sicambre and colts such as Moutiers X, Shantung, Daitome, and Cambremon.

TULYAR by Tehran, England, 1949–   . He ran six times as a two-year-old and won twice. As a three-year-old, he ran seven times without defeat. He ran a seven-furlong race at Hurst Park, and respect for him increased when he won the Ormond Stakes next. His third victory came in the Derby Trail Stakes, and when he won the Derby, he was far ahead of the field. He went on to win the Eclipse Stakes, the King George VI and Queen Elizabeth Stakes, and the St. Leger at Doncaster. Unexpectedly, however, his owner, the Aga Khan, decided not to race Tulyar anymore, and sold him to the Irish National Stud, refusing a better offer from an American syndicate. Three years later, he was exported to the United States, where he suffered a grave illness that almost killed him, but he recovered, and in 1958 was once more at stud.

XVII
THE OWNER AND BREEDER

One might be inclined to believe that owning a racing stud lies within the capabilities of anyone, because, after all, a horse can be bought for about as much as the cost of a motorcycle. Considering, however, that the laurels go only to the best, one realizes that there is a great deal more to think about. There are many stud farms and many racing stables, but there are very few that make any money, particularly when they are primarily involved in the breeding of racehorses.

In the United States most racehorse owners do not engage in breeding, do not have farms, and simply entrust their horses to a trainer who besides training them actually conducts the whole operation for the owner. He stables the horses, feeds them, cares for their health, enters them in suitable races and transports them to suitable tracks in accordance with racing, weather, and other factors and conditions. But breeding is a different matter, almost always requiring a considerable investment, patience, and a great deal of knowledge, judgment, and skill. Horse breeding is the science of combining bloodlines, which is as demanding as the science of combining elements. But where the properties of elements are known and unchanging, the characteristics of bloodlines are not at all precise.

The thoroughbred racehorse has interested scholars and theoreticians, who formulate theories and provide systems to improve the production of the breed as well as to study him

statistically as a source of income and profit. These studies are of relatively recent origin, having started around the middle of the nineteenth century. That was the first time attempts were made to systematize what was known about the Thoroughbred's history, genetics, and genealogy, as well as his functions. Perhaps there is some significance in the fact that few of the theoreticians, known internationally, were English. Doubtless, those who were concerned more with practical matters regarding the English Thoroughbred had neither time nor energy to intellectualize about him. The first to attempt to put the Thoroughbred into the mold of a system was the Australian Bruce Lowe. He divided Thoroughbreds among fifty families, dictated by the female line. His classification is still used today in genealogical studies of the horse, although it does not have the function for which it was designed—the qualitative differentiation between members of different families. Lowe's work was continued and developed by Goos (Dutch), Brecker (German), Degli Albizi (Italian), and in the most modern, definitive style, by Bobinski (Polish), whose *Family Tables of Racehorses* (published in London, 1953, later brought up to date) is the fundamental work for scholars interested in the Thoroughbred.

Following this group we shall call "systematizers" were the analytic statisticians, who have continued to this day. Among them were the Birches, father and son, two Englishmen who outlined a statistical method they called a Statistical Abstract, which was widely copied. It permits both general and detailed examination of the behavior and performance of a Thoroughbred on the racecourse and at stud in any country during any period. To this, J. A. Estes added a new, interesting dimension with his Average Earnings Index, a statistical formula that permits one to analyze not only the amounts taken by a horse in prize money but also their true value in the light of devaluation and the development of racing organization and overhead. The Estes method is continued today and is being broadened in the ultramodern laboratory in Spindletop, Kentucky. With a computer financed by the Jockey Club of New York, they hope to run down analyses on every aspect of a racehorse, including motivation.

A third group of scholars, whose work may be the most fascinating, is that of the geneticists. They seek a means of controlling reproduction so that breeding may be scientifically oriented toward balance and quality. In a certain sense, the grandfather of this group was Robertson the Englishman who used the pseudonym "Mankato" in the late nineteenth century. The first man to propose a method of mixing selected bloodlines, however, was Vuillier, who wrote as "Lottery."

Genetic research in connection with the Thoroughbred has not been concerned solely with the blending of bloodlines. Other experts have followed other paths that are no less interesting. Llewellyn recently set forth a theory of balanced

433–437 *A series of falls on that most difficult of courses, the Grand National at Aintree.*

433

434

435

436

437

438

439

440

441

442

breeding based on the coexistence of the fundamental factors of inbreeding and outcrossing, which he calls respectively "hybrid vigor" and "prepotency." On the other hand, Taber, an American, is in the process of elaborating his theory based on "degree of gametic variation," in which one observes the performance of the father in the son, judged by certain indices. Taber also notes the so-called "jumps," that is, the passing on of specific characteristics from one generation to a subsequent but not necessarily succeeding one. Another geneticist is the New Zealander Myers. He is the author of an extremely profound study on the horse's coat, and the propounder of the theory that the two original coats were the sorrel and the brown, and that the bay is no more than an intermediate mutation resulting from a mixture of the two.

When scientific interest first turned to horse breeding, "morphological selection" was the great theory, based upon examination of the animal's conformation to deduce whether he possessed requisite characteristics representative of sought-after functional qualities—speed and stamina. In this type of visual selection, what was necessary was the *coup d'œil* of the experienced man-about-horses (vaunted and respected in the past, but looked at with skepticism today). Nowadays and in the future (barring a highly improbable anatomical mutation in the horse), the criteria for selection cannot exclude the horse's form and structure. Breeders today seek to fix and transmit determinate and desirable physical qualities of illustrious sires through careful matings. The intention is to remedy or eliminate imbalances or malformations in one of the parents in order to obtain offspring that are as close as possible to an ideal.

While morphology is a serious consideration, selection for the functional characteristics of the breed is the ultimate objective of all selection relative to the thoroughbred racehorse—breeding for speed. Actually, however, horses today are bred to win the classic races. The constant multiplication of great races and their varying conditions have influenced a selection on the basis of the race specifics, such as distance, type of track, and so on. Some horses are fast over short distances up to seven furlongs, and the best sprinters of all are not the English Thoroughbreds but the American quarter horses bred for the quarter mile. Flyers are horses that are best at up to a mile. Horses with the stamina to maintain speeds over long distances are stayers, and can do well on courses of 1 ½ miles and over. Type of terrain, whether the horse holds back or is off at almost full speed from the post, and other factors, are all considered in breeding selectively.

This whole concept of selection based on functional characteristics has led to a third category, "genealogical selection," the study of a horse's pedigree to discover through forebears, potential sires and dams possessing the specific characteristics a breeder desires to pass on to a foal.

These three areas of selection, morphological, functional, and genealogical, must be taken into consideration when a breeder thinks of acquiring a horse at auction.

438 *The famous brook at Auteuil, an eighteen-foot jump, not counting the brush.*
439–440 *The same fall from two points of view in successive instants.*
441 442 *An odd spill at Kempton Park.*

Since all Thoroughbreds to a greater or lesser degree are related (at the very least, sharing a common ancestor), many breeders and theoreticians go even further and suggest that strict inbreeding is the best program. They accordingly insist on breeding a horse with the second or third generation of his pedigree (expressed 2×2, 3×3). The arguments for and against this method continue unabated. One can only observe, without taking sides, that inbreeding has yielded such horses as Havresac II and Coronation, but a continued program must inevitably lead to grave degeneration in the line, and a succession of progressively worse animals. This was demonstrated recently in the failure of the great Boussac stud in France, which strictly adhered to inbreeding, and went from a number of international winners to a stableful of mediocre horses in a very short time.

In the order of a horse's pedigree, when a name does not recur until after the fifth or sixth generation, for all practical purposes one has what is called "outcrossing" or "outbreeding." This was a method greatly favored by Federico Tesio, to good result. In connection with outbreeding, it should be noted that the selection of the proper mate is enormously facilitated if adequate means of transportation are available. Many of the great successes of the breeder François Dupré were due to the fact that he was able to go a long way, literally, to find the most distant outcross, a custom that is followed to a large extent by many other modern breeders.

In contrast, Vuillier blended the various strains found in the pedigrees of the most celebrated stallions. When one follows this method, breeding consists in reproducing, to the maximum degree possible, the different "doses" considered ideal. Among other things, the system has the defect of aging and weakening the lines because of the multiplicity of generations, as has been shown in the stud of the Aga Khan where it was used as the basis for breeding.

We might also mention Professor Robertson's method, predicated on the stud value of the sons of classic winners. In our opinion, the theory does not hold water.

In America, Estes attempted to classify all this rather amorphous material by processing it through electronic computers. He has yet to find the coefficient that would determine how often by his winnings a horse surpassed an amount theoretically assigned to him (the ratio of available prize money in any country in any given year to the number of horses participating in its distribution). We do not believe, at least in the light of current knowledge, that mathematics can give us indexes that will permit us to breed fine racehorses.

As a matter of fact, the champion racehorse is abnormal, and as such it is difficult to isolate those factors that have made him so or to draw any valid mathematical conclusions that will permit reproduction of those elements in an offspring. Naturally, this is not an immutable state of affairs, for who can say what future knowledge and future techniques will permit us to do?

Would this mean that currently we can turn only a pessimistic eye toward any hope of scientific breeding? Yes and No. It is unlikely that in the foreseeable future we shall be able to project accurately the birth of champions. However, fine studs can be formed and maintained at a high level of quality. It depends upon continuous, precise, and attentive selection based upon methodical observation and intelligent interpretation of all we know about the Thoroughbred, along with sufficient economic means to make this possible over a long period of time.

The breeder with a family of horses based on a single prized broodmare is most zealously careful with her. He takes infinite precautions when having her bred in order to assure improvement in the line and to avoid any decline in her quality. A successful breeder must be intelligent, and observant, and knowledgeable in practical as well as theoretical matters. The best are always very well rounded.

As a general rule, trainers do not make successful horse breeders. The two *métiers* are completely different. Willy Carter, De Montel's trainer, never felt competent to make even the smallest recommendation. With modesty, but a good deal of truth, he always remarked that it was not his field.

Too many horse breeders are not truly prepared by time and experience for their work. They come up much too quickly. Too often one finds that a mediocre mare is covered just because no one has found the opportunity to sell her— certainly not the right way to resolve the situation. On the other hand, to judge just how much can be expected of a broodmare one needs to observe her performance over at least six to eight years, which is a long time to wait to discover one's errors.

The terrain of a breeding farm should be adequate to the purpose of the enterprise. The grass should be studied, the soil analyzed, and the proper minerals added. As we have seen, the proper growth and development of a colt's bones depend upon his grazing. Climate must be considered also, though it is not true, as many are inclined to believe, that the weather must consistently be warm and sunny. In England and France, magnificent horses are raised in regions that are cold and even downright unpleasant. As a matter of fact, cold tends to make a horse more solid and sturdy.

What is necessary is abundant pasture, and grazing land should be extensive enough to allow for rotation in use. (Land for raising hay should not be confused with pasturage.)

XVIII

HORSE BREEDING

According to Tesio, breeders are "the manufacturers of racehorses." He contends that the breeder should be a student of biology, veterinary science, and agricultural chemistry. In addition, he need only be an impassioned observer and a little lucky to be a success!

The breeding of racehorses with an eye to getting champions is a difficult, arduous enterprise. In addition to all of the above, the breeder must have some knowledge of genealogies, know a good deal about genetics, and have a facility for understanding and dealing with animals and with the best men to train them as athletes and racers.

Breeding activities can be programmed in accordance with many approaches, scientific or otherwise. Breeding for quantity rather than quality is always least profitable in the long run. With a small stud and rigorous selection, one can obtain good results, thanks to the possibility of being able to take care of every mare and every foal to the maximum.

An ideal size for a breeding farm, however, is one of about thirty broodmares to be covered each year by the top stallions on the international market, taking a middle course between inbreeding and outcrossing to avoid overemphasizing particular bloodlines and to resist the temptation of having a "house stud." It has been demonstrated that new studs generally produce well but have a tendency, with time, to decline, possibly because they overexploit their land or because their produce falls off in quality. Notwithstanding, the Mendelian principles that govern breeders and their methods and problems are always open to discussion and argument. Breeding may be a risky business, but we might remember that each year brings a Derby winner nevertheless. Good pasture, absorbent soil, and easy terrain then are what broodmares must have in order to find food adequate to their particular needs and exercise to keep them in condition. According to Sanson, in his work on zootechy: "During the period that a mare is carrying a foal, nothing can substitute for a diet of tender herbage. This, as we know, has a nutritive ratio of one to three, since it possesses high digestibility, is extremely rich in phosphoric acid, and is about 70 percent water. These are all factors conducive to the secretion of milk and good assimilation of nutrients. For this reason, the superiority of pasturage over any other type of diet is incontestable. One thing the mare must have is complete tranquillity while she is browsing."

Moses Griffith believes that it is not reasonable to pay for a fine brood mare and a stud fee for a fine stallion, each representing a good deal of money, and then to scrimp on the pasturage that will feed these horses and their offspring. The quality of the pasturage affects the production of first-class yearlings and has a favorable effect on fertility, as well. The fertility level of Italian racing studs is about 50 percent instead of the 60 percent registered by France, and approximately 69 percent in England. Bernard O'Sullivan and others have discovered a strict correlation between the fertility of mares and the quality of their pasturage. Calcium, potassium, phosphorus, and nitrogen must be present in specific proportions if one wishes fine skeletal development. France exceeds as a horse country because it has such rich and extensive pastures whereas Italy, with its broken terrain and poor soil, has difficulty in finding land suitable for horse breeding.

In other matters concerning the care of the horse it seems that builders of stables or stalls sometimes have the idea that horses are misanthropic. They ignore the fact that by nature the horse is gregarious, and likes to herd. Intelligent, highly curious, and gifted with an instinctive sense of direction, which in no way depends upon his vision, inasmuch as his range of sight is no more than about 150 feet or so, the horse is also extremely sensitive to noise, and also remembers and differentiates between the sounds he has heard. Solitude is even worse for a horse than silence, as it affects his spirit and makes him edgy. The Thoroughbred begins his training and work when he is very young, only eighteen months old, while other breeds begin at about four years of age, when the Thoroughbred wants to play.

A common mistake to is build box stalls too high. It makes horses want to bolt, with consequent falls and fractures. For the same reason, rough brick floors are preferable to cement, which can be slippery, though with sufficient bedding it can be improved. Most floors, however, are made of dirt or clay, and many wooden floors still remain.

XIX
THE TRAINER

The trainer is the key man in horse racing. He has to know all about horses; he must understand them and he must know how to treat them and deal with them. Racehorses are very temperamental and generally rather nervous animals. Some are quite vicious; some develop peculiar habits or troublesome faults. Should a colt be gelded? Should he wear blinkers? Should the two-year-old be whipped? Should he run on a muddy track? Should he be raced often or given long rests? Would a pet like a cat in his stall make him more comfortable? The trainer has to decide many questions like these, apart from his prime role of training the horse to race well, schooling him in starting and making turns, responding to the jockey's urgings, and understanding that his objective is to beat the other horses, and win. Training and bringing up racehorses is not too dissimilar to training and bringing up children. And so the art of the trainer is too complicated and varied to describe here. But some elements are covered in the section on training the trotter.

Besides his work with the horses, the trainer must keep in close touch with the racing program so that he can choose the most suitable races for his horses, races that will give them their best chances of winning. He must also know the qualities of the horses' jockeys so that he can make the best possible choice for each race. Trainers generally guide owners in the purchase and sale of horses. Some trainers train horses for only one owner, but a majority of trainers have "public" starters. That is, they will train horses for a number of owners. Thus, an owner of even one horse can easily get a trainer. Trainers are paid on a yearly basis per horse and also get 10 percent of the prize money.

XX
THE JOCKEY

According to the great American jockey, Eddie Arcaro, riding a horse is very easy, even in competition, and above all it takes balance; and any person, man, woman, or child with a minimum of aptitude can learn to sit a horse safely in a very short time. Arcaro feels that 80 percent of the time the results of a race depend upon the jockey's ability—among horses of equal quality, of course. When there is no outstanding horse, victory is due in large part to what Arcaro calls "generalship," apart from a bit of normal luck.

In all thoroughbred races each horse has to carry a specified weight. The race may be a weight-for-age race in which two-year-olds must carry 116 pounds, three-year-olds perhaps 122 pounds, and older horses perhaps 126 pounds. In handicap races the racecourse handicapper approves all the entries, and assigns weights for all the horses, with the ideal in view of evening up the performances of the horses so that theoretically all the entries will finish in a dead heat. In allowance races, in accordance with the specified conditions of the race, certain weight allowances are granted, depending on circumstances. Usually, fillies are given three pounds' allowance against colts and geldings. In many races, apprentice jockeys are allowed five pounds, seven pounds, or ten pounds, depending on how many races they have won or the duration of their apprenticeships.

The weight a horse must carry consists of the jockey and the saddle. If the combined weight of jockey and saddle is less than the specified weight, lead must be placed in pockets of the saddle to make up the difference. There is no objection if the weight of jockey and saddle is greater than the specified weight, but there is a disadvantage, obviously.

It is generally believed that a horse runs best when the jockey's weight (the line weight) predominates, that is, when little or no dead weight (lead) has to be added. Arcaro disagrees, and cites the case of his famous colleague Willie Shoemaker who, weighing less than a hundred pounds, was always forced to load his horse with lead, but still won an astonishing number of races. Arcaro insists that a weight securely attached is much more stable than a jockey, who, of course, must shift his weight when he goes into a curve or when he must forcefully urge his horse home. However, this is probably due to the peculiarity of American tracks, which in the main are not straight. No jockey in the world, Arcaro asserts, can maintain his body perfectly balanced over the center of gravity as can a dead weight borne by the horse. Arcaro has his own ideas on how to sit a horse, a style that certainly does not give an impression of perfectly balanced weight. As a matter of fact, the leather of his right stirrup is about eight inches shorter than the left one, so that the jockey looks as if he is hanging on to one side of the horse. This is known as "acey-deucey." After mentioning that other jockeys use the same system, Arcaro admits that it really does not make much sense, since the weight should be centered over the horse. Nevertheless, he says, it works for him.

There are various ways of using the whip. If hitting him on the back doesn't get results, Arcaro tries to hit him vertically, right under his own right foot so that the end of the whip hits the horse almost on the belly. This is also useful at a close finish, when an unexpected shock can cause the horse to extend himself even more. The whip can be laid back and forth over the shoulders, if it has been lowered during the race. Furthermore, at the finish, it is sometimes useful to flick the whip back and forth at the side of the horse's head, without hitting him, just to let him know that he can be hit. When using the whip on the horse's rear, the best place to hit him is above the flanks. Many horses become extremely edgy if they are hit on the flank. It is difficult to use the whip well in this way, for the arm must be brought backward without losing the power it needs to do the actual whipping. (In England, the Jockey Club has rigorous rules on the free use of the whip.)

As in many crafts, jockeys follow a system of apprenticeship, in which youngsters are given the opportunity to learn the trade. We have seen that when they first begin to ride in races, they are allowed as much as ten pounds, reduced after a time or a number of victories to seven and five pounds, finally losing their apprenticeship allowance to become full-fledged jockeys. This weight allowance makes it attractive to trainers on many occasions to employ apprentices, thus increasing apprentices' racing opportunities. Also, the advantage of the weight allowance improves the apprentice's chances of winning a race.

Jockeys are usually retained by a stable, but also have agents who obtain mounts for them. They receive a specific fee for each horse they ride in a race, getting 10 percent of purses they win. While the average European racing fan, asked to name the first of the great American jockeys, might recall Todhunter (Tod) Sloan, who made a great impression in England, and introduced the peculiarly American racing seat abroad, there can be no doubt that Americans revere Isaac Murphy as the first of a long line of peerless jockeys. To prove it, he was the first to be honored by inclusion in racing's Hall of Fame.

Isaac Murphy was a Negro born into slavery in 1860 at Lexington, Kentucky, then, as now, the heart of horse country. Like so many of his race at that time, he was early destined for work as a stableboy. As a matter of fact, a large proportion of jockeys in the early days of flat racing were Negro. They had been put to work in the stables, where they showed superior ability and innate talent for handling horses and getting more out of them than anyone else.

Murphy was a natural jockey. At the age of fourteen, weighing seventy-seven pounds, he started riding in competition. Though he had his share of falls, he had tremendous courage, and could handle the most spirited racehorses. In 1884, he took his first Kentucky Derby, riding Buchanan; his second in 1890, on Riley; and in 1891, he did it again, with Kingman.

In the course of his career, Murphy raced 1,412 times, winning 628. After a glorious career, dogged by ill health, he rode less and less frequently, until he retired from the track in 1898. He died a few years later.

In Isaac Murphy's time, the majority of jockeys did a good deal of their riding with the whip, and no one laid it on with more of a will than Edward Garrison (his name is carried on in the "Garrison finish"), whose nickname "Snapper" attested to the fact. Murphy, however, detested whipping a horse, and rarely did so, as he also disdained to use his spurs.

Much has changed in a jockey's style since those early days. Probably no one did more to slant the "international" style toward American than Tod Sloan, a great jockey, undoubtedly, though a disagreeable man.

Sloan arrived in England in 1897, with an enormous cigar in his mouth and a lot of ideas in his always active brain. Until that time, the English jockeys, in emulation of such greats of the turf as Sam Chifney, George Fordham, and Fred Archer, sat their saddles chests erect, leathers long, and reins loose. Sloan, who said he had been inspired by the Sioux, rode with his stirrup leathers short, his reins held short, and his body leaning well forward, practically hugging the horse's neck. His success was immediate and phenomenal on the English tracks. (The great fame of the English jockey Sir Gordon Richard was to come later.) Faced with such competition, the English jockeys either imitated Sloan or they might as well give up riding. Gradually, this style spread to the Continent and, ultimately, around the world. When the Jockey Club refused to renew his license in 1900, Sloan went to France for a short while, then returned to the United States. He died penniless in 1933, fifty-nine years of age.

Undoubtedly the most popular jockey in the period between World Wars I and II was Earl Sande, who was the first to equal Isaac Murphy's record and win three Kentucky Derbies: in 1923, 1925, and 1930, riding Zev, Flying Ebony, and Gallant Fox, respectively. Sande was Gallant Fox's jockey, and rode him to all of his many triumphs as a three-year-old. When Gallant Fox retired to stud, Sande retired as well, since it was getting to be too much trouble for him to keep his weight down.

The longest career of any jockey in racing here or abroad spanned the late twenties, the time before, during, and after World War II, right down to 1966. On the sixteenth of March of that year, at Santa Anita Park, Johnny Longden, who had come in first 6,032 times, won his last race.

Other great jockeys of the postwar period include: Hartack, Shoemaker, Atkinson, Arcaro (winning five Derbies), and, still active, Ussery, Valenzuela, Cordero, Ycaza, Turcotte, Rotz, and Baeza.

XXI

THE TRACK

"Courses for horses" is a popular saying with some validity. It is undeniable that some horses will run better on one course than on others. It is also undeniable that racecourses differ in many ways, notably in surface, length, climate, and so on. The most obvious difference is between dirt tracks and turf, or grass courses. Some horses, possibly because of sore or tender feet, will run well on grass but not on dirt. Some will run well on a soft dirt rather than on a hard dirt track, and many trainers object to very hard dirt tracks because they believe it possibly results in injury to the horses' legs. Some horses will run on muddy or sloppy tracks, while others will never do so. Therefore the condition as well as the kind of surface is an important factor in considering a course. In the United States trainers often put special shoes on their horses to adjust to an "off" or muddy course on "heavy going." In England, sometimes a rubber plate is inserted under the racing plate, when a horse is to run on "firm going."

In most countries where horse racing is popular, at the least, an equal number of races are run on turf, that is, grass. In the United States, however, the large majority of races and all the classics are on dirt tracks. Where the turf track is available, it is invariably inside a dirt track on oval courses, which are the most common in this country, and, consequently, the turf track is shorter. A dirt track forms a soft "cushion" surface, about three or four inches deep, over the hard base. The base provides a solid racing surface, while the cushion acts to soften the impact of hoofs on the hard soil. This cushion is harrowed every morning, and between each race in the day's program, to keep it soft.

As is the case with turf, water is the enemy of the dirt track's surface, affecting not only the quality and maintenance

443 *Cavaliere d'Arpino with F. Regoli up.*
444 *Nearco as a two-year-old, ridden by P. Gubellini.*
445 *Ribot, the unbeaten son of Tenerani, with Camici in the saddle.*
446 *Federico Tesio in 1938, radiant after a victory of Nearco, with Luchino Visconti in the background.*
447 *Prince Umberto di Savoia visiting San Siro in 1929.*

443

444

445

of the track itself but also the performance of the horses. According to official Racing Association rules throughout the country, the condition of the track is always given before a race, for the guidance of spectators. Officially, a dry, even track is classified as fast. A sloppy track is one flooded with water, and a muddy track describes a course sodden to the base. As the track dries, after being inundated, it can be described, progressively, as heavy, slow, good, and fast, once again. Horses can make excellent time racing over a sloppy track, however, for the mud is so thin that the track offers minimal conditions. Except for the rare occasions, practically flood conditions, when a track gets so wet that the hard base is affected enough to become uneven or boggy, races are regularly run over tracks in any of the states noted above.

The day may not be too far off, at least in the United States, when races run over a dirt track become as few and far between as those run on grass today. As a replacement for both dirt and turf, the Minnesota Mining & Manufacturing Company, most famous to the average consumer as the manufacturer of cellophane tape, has invented a new material called Tartan, named for the company's trademark, as is also the board chairman's racing stable. The material, resembling rubber or linoleum floor coverings, was given a trial at Tropical Park, in Florida, in 1966. During the year, all the daily races were run over the inch-thick Tartan "runner," and extended to three races a week during the 1967–1968 winter meeting as well. Because of its bounce and spring, many horsemen believe that Tartan tracks will lead to shorter running times.

While the manufacturers contend that Tartan provides a surer and, therefore, safer surface, inasmuch as it cannot develop soft spots or potholes, as turf and dirt are wont to do, many jockeys are wary of the new surface, contending that its lack of comparable resilience makes the slightest fall a major accident, turning what might be cause for contusion on a dirt track into possible fracture. To allay their fears, the manufacturers hired two stunt riders to race over an experimental track in 1966 and fall on purpose. Although they were jarred much more than they had expected, the men were merely bruised, but backstretch gossip had it that they were much more seriously injured, which, of course, even though untrue, did nothing to advance the reputation of the Tartan surface. Many jockeys still refuse to ride on the new track, which at this writing is still rare on American racecourses. It does, however, indicate a future trend.

Some horses, especially those that are adept at making turns well, have an advantage on half-mile courses. Stayers and good finishers will have an advantage on a track that has a long stretch, where they will have plenty of distance to make the final run after they are straightened out for it.

Climate is also an important factor. A horse who has been training or running in a very warm climate may take some time to adjust to a cooler climate. Also, water and feed differences may have considerable influence on a horse's performance.

The trainer has to be mindful of all these elements in determining when and where to race his horses.

XXII
PARI-MUTUEL BETTING AND THE TOTALISATOR

In France, Thoroughbred racing received an official blessing in 1805 in a decree handed down by Napoleon. It fixed the age of horses permitted to race, the *départements* in which racecourses could be operated, and provided for state studs. But no one thought to make any regulations affecting wagers until some sixty years later. Prior to that date, owners bet among themselves, and the public had to resort to bookmakers, who had no legal status, or else they put their money in a pool, with a percentage of the winnings possibly going to the organizer, who held the money. Too often, however, bookmakers organized the pools and absconded. Also, too often a bookmaker who had too many winning bets to pay off would be unable to pay and there would be no legal redress.

On the day of the French Grand Prix in 1864, Joseph Oller made his first visit to the track. He participated in a pool, won, and never was paid. Oller immediately worked out a foolproof scheme to keep other bettors from getting stung, which he communicated to the authorities. He proposed to establish a common fund for pool participants, with absolute guarantees for the drawing of the horses' names and payment to the eventual winners. The authorities had no objections, though they could not grant official approval. Oller, in conjunction with his regular trade in toiletries, started operating his lottery and pool, as well as a handbook on races run in the Paris area.

Because of his reputation for honesty, he had a large following, but he found that although he made money on the lotteries, he did not do well in his bookmaking operations. He decided to develop another system, similar to the pool. Those betting among themselves, whose business he now lacked, were to divide their winnings in proportion to their individual wagers, differing from a pool in that bets can be as varied as possible. Seeking an attractive name to distinguish his betting system from the regular *poules*, he devised the term *pari-mutuel*, or mutual betting, the *pari* being a neologism deriving from the French verb "to bet," which is *parier*.

To handle the new business, Oller opened an agency in the center of town, on the Boulevard des Italiens, in 1872. He had instant success. People enjoyed the novelty of the system and, also new to them, its honest dealings. For the great mass that could afford to take a flyer but had neither time nor money, beyond their wagers, to cover the expense of going to the races, Oller's system was a great convenience. By 1873, Oller had opened a second agency, in partnership with a man who had worked for him at the first. This office dispatched tellers to the Paris courses in carriages serving as mobile agencies; the clerks sold pari-mutuel tickets to track spectators, and also paid off.

That same year, Oller undertook also to sell pari-mutuel tickets for races held in England and Belgium. The entire operation flourished, with the agency taking a commission, in accordance with an established scale, of 10 to 20 percent of the bets. Although his profit was legitimate, it was too

448 Baron Edmond de Rothschild contemplates the grave of his great and popular Brantôme.

big to please a government that received no part. In 1874, perhaps purposely confusing his present system with his previous lottery, which had never been officially approved, a court ruled that Oller was operating an illegal lottery, and ordered him to bring his operations to an end. In answer to an appeal interposed by Oller in 1875, the higher court upheld the prior decision, and further ruled that Oller's agencies were gambling houses and, therefore, illegal.

Time, however, played into Oller's hands. Precisely because his operations had been honest, the racing and betting public had grown. Now that they had once again to depend on bookmakers, interest in the sport abruptly fell off. It got so bad that important racing interests were in jeopardy, and the Minister of Agriculture was petitioned to intervene to convince the government to reverse itself. In 1887, after all the furor, the courts did just that, not only declaring the pari-mutuel system legal but also excluding and outlawing all others by making its adoption mandatory for all racing associations.

His honor reinstated, Oller determined to keep the authorities on his side. He did not have to placate the racing associations, since they were obliged by law to use his system, but he thought it politic to maintain amiable relations with them as well as with the government. Accordingly, he deducted 11 percent off the top of all bets and divided it among the jockey clubs, to offset their expenses in operating the pari-mutuel systems, courses, and so on, and the government, as a voluntary tax.

The pari-mutuel system gradually extended to most countries in which thoroughbred racing was a popular sporting event. The only difficulty experienced by Oller and other organizers of pari-mutuel betting throughout the racing world was a physical one: It was difficult to service betting tickets quickly and accurately. Because tickets were sold in volume, and were paid off right after the results were posted, on the basis of the involved arithmetical calculations covered earlier in the flat-racing section, it is obvious that a fast, accurate tally system was necessary to assure the success of pari-mutuel betting and to guarantee its popularity with the bettors.

In 1880, a mechanically minded gambler in New Zealand, named Ekberg, intrigued by Oller's system, devised a manually operated machine he dubbed a "totalisator." It was first used at a race meeting in Christchurch held by the Canterbury Jockey Club, and automatically recorded wagers. The use of Ekberg's totalisator (as it is known in the United States), which was gradually improved, became common on courses throughout the world and, in most places, drove the bookmakers away.

As an increasing public took to betting on the races, attracted by the objectiveness of the pari-mutuel system, it became necessary to speed the operation of the manual totalisator. This was done by another New Zealander, a railway engineer subsequently knighted for his contributions to railway technology, Sir George Julius. He devised an electromechanical totalisator, which he called by the trade name Premier. It was first employed in Auckland, at the Ellerslie Race Course, in 1913. The Premier was a great success and, despite the subsequent war, was soon installed throughout the British Empire and in the Philippines. An improved model, long one of the largest totalisators in the world, was set up at Longchamp.

While horse racing was America's first sport, and for many years its premier sport, betting was never the first consideration of spectators so long as the racing public was primarily composed of horse owners, breeders, trainers, and a fairly small knowledgeable public interested mainly in the horses. As the racing public grew, however, and racing became more of an urban diversion than an offshoot of country living, the informed population diminished in comparison with the mass spectator interest in the sport for the sake of wagering. From the latter half of the nineteenth century on, bookmakers dominated the betting scene, and the history of the totalisator in the United States was, and to some small extent still is, continually marked by clashes with bookmaking interests.

Pari-mutuel betting was first introduced at New York's Morris Park and Jerome Park in 1877, but the bookmakers saw to it that it was short-lived. Had it not been for Colonel Matt Winn's stand in 1908, perhaps the bookmakers would be flourishing and pari-mutuel betting in the United States forgotten. In that year, just before the running of the Kentucky Derby at Colonel Winn's Churchill Downs, the county authorities declared that racetrack betting would not be tolerated. Faced with the thought of losing the considerable revenue that would accrue to the track, the colonel hastily had the local statutes examined and, to his delight, discovered there were no restrictions on pari-mutuel betting. Accordingly, pari-mutuel betting was instituted at Churchill Downs, where it proved very popular, as it did the next year at Pimlico, where the Maryland Jockey Club initiated it while still permitting bookmakers at the track.

Gradually, in the face of too much irregularity in the operations of bookmakers, pari-mutuel betting was introduced by racing associations throughout the country, usually as an alternative when a state moved to outlaw racing. The last state to make the pari-mutuel betting system mandatory was New York, in 1940.

The totalisator now in general use in England and in many of the Commonwealth nations is a model patented by an American, Henry L. Straus, of Baltimore, in 1928. This tote, which actually improved on George Julius's Premier model, was built without any working knowledge of the New Zealand equipment. Straus's equipment solved the problems inherent in the need to transmit a large volume of information quickly and accurately by making use of automatic telephone circuits, such as had been devised by Almon Strowger and patented as the Strowger Automatic Telephony equipment, which contributed to the dial telephone. While the English Race Course Betting Board placed the Straus totalisator, manufactured by the American Totalisator Company, in service as early as 1929, United States tracks had to wait until 1933 for an electric tote, the first being installed at Aqueduct. Although, in the past, as today, the great majority of people in racing were honest, the few dishonest men were enough to shake public confidence in the sport. Horsemen and turf enthusiasts everywhere can thank the pari-mutuel betting system for banishing the cheating bookmaker, and the totalisator for guaranteeing the efficiency and accuracy of the system.

PART SIX

HARNESS RACING

I
HISTORY

There is little historical material on trotting as a sport (more particularly, in European archives), but we do have archeological evidence that there were horses in Asia Minor around 1300 B.C. particularly suited to trotting. We must go back to A.D. 1100, however, in the area around Norfolk, England, to find documentation of a trotter that was famed for speed and tractability, though employed not as a racer but as a cart horse. By crossing this breed with the Shale, in England, around 1750, the modern Norfolk trotter was obtained, an elegant, fast, and powerful animal used both as a carriage and a saddle horse.

Before examining the position attained by the trotter, and the methods of breeding, training, and racing him in the more advanced harness-racing countries, we shall discuss some of the aspects and events that have marked the history of the trotter and harness racing.

Americans have been indulging their taste for harness racing since colonial days. It was the first type of horse racing known in the country. These trotters and pacers are a distinctive breed known since 1879 as American Standardbreds, which have always been bred mainly for speed. That they have been successful is attested to by the fact that the first three world's record holders for the trotting mile are American: Noble Victory, by Victory Song, out of Emily's Pride, in 1966, 1:55 3-5; Charming Barbara, by Rodney, out of The Charmer, 1:58 in 1959; and Greyhound, by Guy Abbey, out of Elizabeth, 1:57 1-4 in 1936. The first trotting race held on a regular track in the United States took place at Centerville, Long Island, New York, on May 16, 1826.

In Russia, harness racing dates from 1775. Russia's greatest contribution, of course, has been the Orlov, named for its creator, Count Orlov.

France has been indulging in speed trials for trotters since the early seventeenth century, but the official start of harness racing came with the opening of the Cherbourg track in 1836. Horses of Norman extraction were improved by crosses with Thoroughbreds and Norfolk trotters. The difficult French tracks, together with favorable terrain for breeding and training and a high production level, have contributed toward the formation of a breed of French trotting horse characterized by strength and stamina, and which provides competition for the American Standardbred.

As far back as the seventeenth century, the Netherlands was raising a type of horse that was very much sought after, the *hardraver*, robust in conformation, yet harmonious in his points, and a natural fast trotter. Although the breed no longer exists, it did contribute to the formation of the Orlov and the Norfolk trotter, thus indirectly influencing other national trotting breeds.

In Italy, the first real indication we have of harness racing as a sporting event open to the public dates from 1808. In Padua, at the Prate della Valle, races were held, with a gold medal offered the winner and token amounts of money for the runners-up. The horses, hitched to carts called *padovanelles*, were either of the Piave breed or crosses of English Thoroughbreds. Though there are indications of trotting races held before this date, these were simply challenges taken up by friends, and watched by a small circle of acquaintances and judges. During the nineteenth century, there was some breeding of trotters, and races were officially recognized in Emilia, Lombardy, Tuscany, and Latium. From 1881 on, there has been constant development, and even with relatively few broodmares, Italy can now participate in trotting classics abroad.

From the end of the seventeenth century, racehorses selectively bred in England have improved in size, skeletal structure, muscle timbre, and stamina, and have been used throughout the world for improving the breeds of hacks, hunters, trotters, and pacers. The trotting gait was transmitted as a hereditary trait by Germanic-type horses that originally formed almost the total of the equine strains of Holland and Denmark around the eleventh century. These horses were introduced into England during an invasion by the Danes in the ninth century, up to the time of King Canute. It was Canute who populated Norfolk with horses from Denmark. These are the ancestors of the Norfolk breed we know today. They were of good size, with proper, but not particularly brilliant, gaits. There was also in England at that time a Frisian breed, somewhat lighter, from whom the English derived their hunters and roadsters. The greater part of these horses derived from the *hardraver* nucleus, who were strong trotters and who were to transfer "trotting genes" to others registered in the *General Stud Book*, in turn to be transmitted to their own descendants.

A great deal of research has confirmed this theory, first presented as a hypothesis. The Belgian hippologist Léon de Meldert isolated the thoroughbred Sampson as the typical inheritor of this faculty and the true propagator of the "trotting genes" in the Standardbred. De Meldert asserts, for example, that in the pedigrees of a number of French trotters of his era, 1920–1935, there were more than four hundred entries for Sampson. In the French trotter, however, the blood of Sampson was carried on in the female line, whereas American Standardbreds today who derive from Sampson are in the stallion line.

Another feature shared by American and French trotters is the Norfolk trotter. The Norfolk trotter holds key positions as sires of the dams of Hambletonian 10, the Charles' Kent Mare, and Bellfounder, as well as contributing significantly to French trotting bloodlines. The most qualified foundation sire of the hackney and the Norfolk, Old Shales, foaled in 1755, was the son of Blaze (1733), who sired Sampson (1745), who, in his turn, is sire of two hackney-Norfolk foundation sires, Golden Farmer and Foxhunter. Precisely as a result of such findings a professor, Primo Castelvetro, has arrived at the conclusion that French and American trotters are homosanguineous.

Trotters are selected for quality, of course, but primarily upon the basis of their actions. Often a horse exhibits excellence, generally, but compromises it by a faulty action that renders him useless on the racecourse. However, when there is a smooth, effortless action and power to match, we have a phenomenon like Noble Victory, Tornese, Roquepine, or Star's Pride.

Today, naturally, interest in trotters is solely in their adaptability as harness racers, so that selection is aimed at breeding to break new speed records. By crossing the centuries-old classic light-draft breeds with Thoroughbreds, wonderful results were achieved in sheer speed. Of course, to attain maximum speeds, a carefully designed harness must be utilized, and even special shoes, so that the horse's movement is correct and balanced. In particular, there are such devices as brakes and a fixed martingale that positions the head and neck to permit maximum muscular response necessary to bring the shoulders and chest on in forward motion. Another measure used to better the horse's action is the application of weights to the hooves to achieve perfect synchronization between the pairs and a maximum length of stride.

Essentially, harness racing is competition between Standardbred (analogous to "Thoroughbred" in flat racing; but its original use described a standard of speed required of qualifying harness-racing horses and qualification is still required: 2:20 at present) trotters or pacers hitched to a sulky—a very light, two-wheeled racing cart with room enough for only a driver. The cart derives from a heavy two-wheeled wagon that carried the driver on a high seat. (The trot is performed on the diagonal pair of legs, each pair moving simultaneously; the pace on the lateral. The trot requires perfect balance and synchronization to be effective [and beautiful]; the pace covers more ground, and is somewhat more casual, even awkward, but, nevertheless, natural in some breeds. On the average, the pacer may be slightly faster than the trotter.)

Harness racing was also one of the first spectator sports in the United States, since it does go back to the days when the country was still a colony. Today, enthusiasm for the sport, particularly races for trotters, is very popular in France, Italy, Germany, Belgium, Russia, Sweden, Austria, and New Zealand. Just as the sulky evolved over a great period of time, harness racing in general has a long and interesting road, as it rose and fell from favor in various countries.

The trotter evolved as a distinctive type as much because of social changes as because of anything else. Trotters could never have become useful without roads, and fairly good roads at that. As relatively modern roads were built in England stagecoach travel became possible and, of course, the heavy-carriage horse was much esteemed and in demand to draw the coaches. But as roads were improved and branch roads built, as well as the main trunk lines, people could take to the roads for pleasure, apart from the exigencies of business travel. It was then that the light trotting horse came into fashion, just as he first did in the United States, in New England, for the simple reason that the area contained the first good roads.

An earlier development, the invention of gunpowder, which we have discussed in reference to the military employment of the horse, required the breeding and training of lighter horses because the heavy chargers were no longer needed to carry their heavily armored knights. Religion also greatly militated in favor of harness racing, as we know it

449 *Cart from the necropolis at Thebes, dating from the XVIII dynasty, made of ash with a bronze yoke. Museo Archeologico, Florence.*

450 *A modern sulky, built of wood and aluminum, with spoke wheels and pneumatic tires. It weighs forty-four pounds.*

451 *Hambletonian, the great American foundation sire of trotting horses.*

452 *Rodney (B.h.), foaled in 1944 in the United States, by Spencer Scott.*

453 *Volomite (Br.h.), 1926 in the United States, by Peter Volo, by Peter the Great, one of the greatest American sires.*

454 *The beautiful Lady Suffolk, foaled in 1833, being driven by her owner, David Bryan.*

455 *Axworthy (Ch.h.), 1892 in the United States by Electioneer, by Hambletonian, an impeccable pedigree.*

456 *Peter the Great (B.h.), 1895 in the United States, by Pilot Medium, another great foundation sire of trotters.*

457 *Sweetzer, Sleepy George, and Lucy racing.*

458 *A stylized rendering of a Norfolk trotter.*

459 *Rather and Miss Turner, two celebrated Norfolk trotter mares.*

460 *Lady Suffolk does the mile in 2:36, ridden by Conklin. Lady Suffolk was the first trotter to beat 2:30 with a world record 2:29 1-2 in 1845.*

461 *Jockeys racing at Hunting Park, Philadelphia, in 1831, a detail from a painting by R. S. Hillman, the first showing an American race at the trot.*

462 *The foundation sire Messenger.*

463 *Flora Temple, the first trotting filly, who did the mile in 2:19 3-4 and won eighty-six races.*

464 *May 1860, on the track at Prospect Park Fairgrounds, American Girl wins, beating Goldsmith Maid, George Wilkes, Lucy, Bashaw Jr., and Rhode Island. Time: 2:25.*

465 *Pocahontas establishes her best speed at 2:17 1-2, June 21, 1855, on Union Course, Long Island.*

466 *William M. Rysdyk, Hambletonian's owner, with his champion.*

467 *Smuggler, foaled in Massachusetts in 1874, did the mile in 2:15 1-4.*

449

450

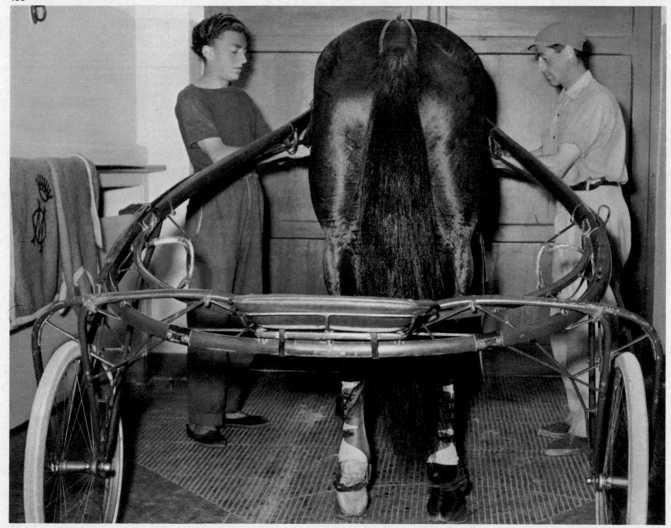

451

452

455

453

456

454

457

468

469

470

471

472

today, and the concomittant breeding of trotters and pacers in the United States. From the earliest days of the New England colonies, the Presbyterians had been loud and firm in their censure of racing, which they equated with "running." Trotting and pacing, however, were something apart, for these horses did not run in the strictest sense of the term, and were also tolerated for contribution to useful roadwork, unlike the "useless" Thoroughbred. Besides, it was a great temptation for the average man, out with his family in his go-to-market wagon, drawn by a trotter or pacer, to see if he could beat his neighbor he met on the way to the next turn in the road. These informal neighborly trials were natural and common, and became known as "brushes." "Brushing" today refers to a short dash at top speed, usually when approaching the finish.

By 1802, various religious groups were strong enough to cause legislation to be passed to close all racetracks throughout New England, as well as the eastern seaboard states. However, racing continued because trotting, according to the courts, was not racing; racing implied competitive horses going their fastest in an effort to come in first. Trotting was a relaxed gait, and obviously a trotter was not going as fast as he could. Even in competition he was not racing. This afforded antireform New Englanders and Easterners the "out" they needed, and trotting and pacing flourished in these sections of the country, particularly in the absence of flat racing, which was outlawed.

Messenger

In 1788, a rather unattractive, flea-bitten thoroughbred stallion who nevertheless could be traced to the Darley Arabian and who had raced in England, but with no particular distinction, was imported into the United States. No one has ever been able to state unequivocally any good reason for this indifferent thoroughbred gray's becoming the foundation sire of the American trotting horse, the Standardbred. One can only conjecture that the Darley Arabian and his descendants were bred to native cold-blooded English mares, and through some such fortunate "nick," as the breeders call it, a trotting strain developed. A good deal of it seemed to have come down to Messenger. It was quickly and easily observed, after he had covered local cold-blooded American mares, that his get were trotters, and fast trotters, at that.

468 *Titan Hanover (B.h.), foaled in the United States, by Calumet Chuck out of Tisma Hanover, had a record of 1:58.*
469 *The foundation mare Rosalind (B.M.), foaled in the United States, by Scotland out of Alma Lee, had a record of 1:56 3-4.*
470 *A fall on the Allentown track.*
471 *Hit Song (B.h.), by Darnley, by Scotland, in the United States, 1:59 1-5.*
472 *Greyhound (G.g.), foaled in the United States, sired by Guy Abbey, holds the world record for the mile, 1:55 1-4, and was called the "Grey Ghost."*

Courses

Just before the nineteenth century, brushes took place on the roads and speedways of the country, never on established tracks. In New York, the Bowery was a great place for such friendly contests, so much so that people out for a stroll complained they were in mortal danger from competing trotters. By 1807, with complaints so loud and the popularity of brushes among the trotting enthusiasts so great, Third Avenue was laid out, and marked as a course for trotting races.

Shortly thereafter, Long Island dedicated its Jamaica road to this popular diversion, and it flourished in Harlem as well. These meetings, which brought out a large number of contestants to face the perils of the narrow, uneven roads, the fractiousness of their horses, and the disproportionately large field have been recorded by Currier and Ives, printmakers of the era, and others. We might note that prior to 1830, trotters were raced not as carriage but as saddle horses (still practiced abroad), primarily because no vehicle had been developed sufficiently light and maneuverable to permit a trotter to race at his best time. Had the average trotter drawn the vehicles available at the time, he would have lost at least several seconds per mile, compared with his performance under the saddle.

Tracks improved with time, and so did sulkies, so that by 1840, more and more races were conditioned to trotters drawing sulkies or even pairs of trotters drawing special racing wagons. Despite these improvements in the sport, the militance of religious leaders was strong enough to cause its decline in the period 1830–1850, and the sport became characterized as "vulgar" and not *comme il faut*. Eastern society had turned its attention to gambling, which became the smart diversion of the upper classes.

Two influential sportsmen did much to restore the trotter to favor, through their unceasing rivalry. They were Robert Bonner who owned one of the most influential newspapers of its day, the *New York Ledger,* and Commodore Cornelius Vanderbilt. They not only enjoyed trotting races but also engaged in innumerable brushes along Harlem Lane and Third Avenue to the amusement and delectation of the great crowd they were always sure to draw. Each man bought his trotters with an eye to outdoing his rival's latest acquisition. However, they never wagered on these brushes. Vanderbilt would have been delighted to do so, but Bonner was a strict follower of his faith, which forbade betting. Nor could Bonner be enticed by the Commodore's posted bet of $10,000 that his cherished pair, Post Boy and Plow Boy, could beat any team in the world. Notwithstanding, Bonner was resolved not to be bested. He believed that no horses could be better than his mares Lady Palmer and Flatbush Maid. In May of 1862, with Commodore Vanderbilt present at the races at the Fashion course, Bonner announced that he was prepared to prove that his mares could beat the afternoon's record 2:31 1-4. He would do this, not for a purse, but by racing against time. Driving Lady Palmer and Flatbush Maid, he did the first mile in 2:31 1-2 and the second in 2:28, a record for a pair. Bonner then offered $10,000 as a present to anyone whose team could beat his own team's time. Not even the Commodore was able to accept the money.

Slightly earlier, trotters had taken to the road in different areas of the country to satisfy spectators, who wanted to see the famous horses whose racing exploits they had heard so much about. This barnstorming, or "hippodroming" as it was called, did much to broadcast the sport, and popularize it where it was unknown, shortly before the outbreak of the Civil War. A great tour was made by two star trotters in 1857, Flora Temple and Lancet, who were matched against each other for a purse and a percentage of the gate at Elmira, New York; Hartford, Connecticut; and Springfield, Massachusetts. Shortly after this, Flora Temple went on the road alone to race against other horses—local champions in Detroit, Chicago, St. Louis, and other midwestern cities.

As for the southern states, the trotter was scorned as a plebian hack. The southern gentleman recognized only saddle horses, a good one for getting around on and a fine one for racing. However, northern owners started to winter and condition their trotters in the South at this time. Gradually, the Southerner began to get interested, but his interest waned during the years of the Civil War. However, prior to its outbreak, a trotting track existed in New Orleans, and another in Florida.

Harness racing, of course, is not the exclusive province of trotters. There are also those engaging "side-wheelers" to be considered, the pacers. In the eighteenth century, Rhode Island developed a breed of roadster called the Narragansett pacer. This horse, however, was destined to be remembered as the forebear of the southern gaited horse rather than the harness racer. This may have been a natural outcome of the fact that at the time racers were saddled, not driven, and there is no rougher gait to be borne by a rider than the pace, even when performed by a Narragansett pacer, of a breed known for its "smooth, gliding" action. Furthermore, while it is possible to steady a trotter who has broken stride and fallen into a gallop so that he once more picks up the desired gait, this cannot be achieved with a pacer. Undoubtedly, these characteristics contributed to the pacer's lack of popularity until trotters and pacers were raced in harness rather than under the saddle. There were always a few pacers before this point though, who achieved popularity and fame because of their exceptional speed. The celebrated Sweetser established a record for consecutive heats in 1877, pacing in Cleveland: 2:16, 2:16, and 2:16 1-4, and in the following year established a record 2:15 for the pacing mile. Pacers truly began to gain attention and interest from harness-racing enthusiasts after the invention of the hopple. This was a species of leg harness, invented by a railway conductor, John Browning, in 1885, which obviated breaks by the pacer since it prevented him from moving at any gait other than the pace.

By the late 1860's, in the post-Civil War period, harness racing was once again in disfavor among the smart set. As in thoroughbred racing, for too large a proportion of the spectators the races were incidental to betting. In those days, of course, betting was uncontrolled, and so were the large majority of marginal types who made it their vocation or avocation. Cultured persons were no longer seen at harness races, and the day of the gentleman owner-driver had also passed. With the commercialization and vulgarization of the sport, therefore, came not only the abuses attendant upon unrestricted betting but also the evils associated with uncontrolled professional drivers. Fixed races, doped horses, and the like were not unusual. The next phase was marked by reform and self-policing. This was started by the Trotting Association formed in 1870, the precursor of the National Trotting Association, which was constituted to clean up and codify harness racing and police the sport, including punishing offenders at the tracks. It is to the Trotting Association that we are grateful for the sport of harness racing as it is today. They fully achieved the objectives for which they had been constituted. Once the sport had become attractive again, breeders, as well as the trainers, were encouraged to continue in their efforts.

Even with these improvements, the sport was still beset with problems, primarily those of standardizing the tracks and improving the high-wheeled sulky in general use at the time. As religion had in a sense stimulated the initial growth of the sport, another unlikely agent, the bicycle, was to contribute to the solution of these further difficulties.

As a rule, tracks were generally ovals until the building of one course in 1887 in the shape of a kite. It had been so designed to ease the angles of the turns and thus permit better speeds for both trotters and pacers. It was discovered that records could be lowered by about two seconds, thanks to the design of the kite-shaped track. This led to a great deal of acrimonious debate as to whether a record made on a kite-shaped track was on a par with a time marked on an oval track. A ruling was finally made to the effect that all records made on the new track would have to be marked with a K to indicate that fact. Today most harness tracks are a half mile in circumference, some are five eighths of a mile, and some a mile around, and because of the fewer turns on the longer tracks, it makes for different racing strategies, and vice versa.

While all this discussion waxed, an American physician had equipped his son's bicycle, not with the usual high wheels and hard tires, but with smaller pneumatic tires to save him from the bumpy uncomfortableness of the usual bone-shaker. At about the same time, an Englishman discovered the principle of the ball-bearing wheel. These two advances led to the receipt of a new racing sulky in 1895 by the veteran driver Budd Doble. It came from England and was equipped with low, tire-equipped bicycle wheels. He passed the new vehicle on to his friend Ed Geers, also a trotting enthusiast and a cyclist, as well, who first raced in the new-style sulky, to the hoots of the crowd, in 1892, at a Detroit track. The best rebuttal to the spectators' skepticism, of course, came when Geers won his race, and lowered the track record in doing so. Furthermore, after he saw how effective the new vehicle was, Doble took back his sulky the very afternoon that Geers had raced and did four heats on the same track, the fastest heats in the history of trotting, up to that time.

473 *Bret Hanover, after winning the harness-racing championship, 1:54. In 1966, at Lexington, he reduced the pacing record to 1:53 3-5.*

474 *A race for colts at San Siro.*

475 *Harness racing at Roosevelt Raceway, a popular track for trotters in New York.*

476 *Trotters on the track at Lexington.*

473

474

475

476

477

478

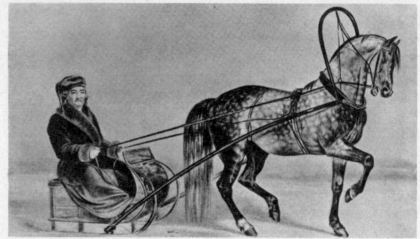

479

480

With all this excitement over the new sulky and the possibilities it offered, the discussion about the merits and legality of the kite-shaped track was dropped, for it was obvious now that, with the new sulky, there were new records to be made on the usual oval track, so there was no need to seek an advantage through bizarre track designs.

II
THE ORLOV

Of the classic Russian trotter, the Orlov, we know that Count Alexis Orlov created the breed, using the stud Smetanka, of the Oriental Kohgtani breed. This horse was very beautiful, strong, and stood about 15.3 hands high. Smetanka's skeleton is in the Orlov Museum, where it can be seen that he had two extra ribs that horses usually lack. Some experts believe that this would place him closer to the African than to Asiatic prototype.

Smetanka was at stud for just one season, dying in 1777. He left five get, one filly and four colts. The handsomest of the colts was Polkan I, out of a long, heavy, strong Danish light chestnut. Polkan was bred to a black Dutch *hardraver* mare, apparently selected by the count, and the mating produced Bars I (or Barss), the Russian Hambletonian. Bars was "remarkable for the speed of his trot, the length of his legs and for the fact that his hindquarters were considerably higher than his forehand." He left eleven stallions and in a sense was the true founder of the Orlov breed.

Among the thoroughbred broodmares kept by Count Orlov to create his breed of trotters were the Frisian, and the Dutch and Danish of the strong-trotting *hardraver* breed, as well as Russian and Polish mares.

Upon the basis of these circumstances, Professor Castelvetro began to analyze certain well-established lines. Messenger led him to Sampson, and along the way, he discovered descendants of the great foundation sire of the American trotter. Thus, on the family tree of the French horse Phaéton, he came to Orville, the Messenger of French trotting, and found numerous recurring carriers of his blood in France and in America. It was through following the descendants of Orville that Castelvetro found some Thoroughbreds that kept recurring even in American pedigrees: Orville-Muely-Margrave; Orville-Sovereign; Orville-Emilius-Young Emilius. An important observation to be made is that he found the names of these Thoroughbreds in the pedigrees of some of the most important broodmares of American trotters: Maggie H., Alma Mater, Dame Winnie, Esther, Cathleen, Midnight, and many others. This was the most important discovery of his earliest inquiries, and he began to sense how things had come about.

These trotters who shared a good deal of Norfolk blood and played an important part in the creation of the foundation sires Hambletonian and Phaéton, had from the first half of the eighteenth century comprised a numerous equine population, divided into three categories: American, French, and the Orlov, all having in common the trotting gait and the morphological and temperamental qualities for improving their descendant's trotting capabilities as well. The various stallions can be classified as follows: carriers earliest disposed toward trotting—the Godolphin Barb, Blaze, Sampson, Snap; their heirs—Matchem, Engineer, Herod, Highflyer, Florizel, and Woodpecker; and continuing their lines—Messenger, Old Paymaster, Y Rattler, Orville, Catton, Selim, King Pepin, Australian, Diomed, and the horses deriving from them.

All American and French trotters, including the Norfolk, have the blood of these stallions in common. Crosses between specimens of the different distinctive "varieties," according to the traditional terms, are defined by hippologists as outcrosses. Thus, we have the Franco-Orlov outcross, the Franco-American, and so on.

The French began by registering stallions, having one or more offspring, and mares (either they or their offspring) with a speed for the mile of 2:50. Other European breeders have more recently begun to register the sires and dams of horses doing the mile in 2:40. In the United States, trotters started originally with a base speed of 2:30 for the mile.

III
GALLOPERS AND TROTTERS

According to Tesio,

> if a good Standardbred mare is covered by a good thoroughbred racehorse and a resulting filly in her turn is then covered by a good Standardbred, after a few generations their descendants will probably be faster than all their forebears.
>
> On the other hand, if a Thoroughbred is covered by a Standardbred, their offspring will not win a classic flat race for about twenty generations. Why? Because the select characteristics are transmitted proportionately by age and the continuity of selection. The thoroughbred racehorse has been selected for some 250 years upon the basis of doing a much faster record mile than the Standardbred has been capable of doing. The trotter is like a new wine with 11 percent alcohol.

Tesio does not take into consideration the mechanical difference between the trot and the gallop. Were a trotter of the proper size and spirit trained to gallop, it is possible that he could substantially reduce the difference in speed between them.

Tesio continues:

> Under certain aspects, harness racing has an advantage over flat racing. The smallness of the track and the slower gait permit the spectator to follow the action more easily, and appreciate the beauty of the horses in action. The trot, like the pace and the gallop, is a natural gait, and

477 *A troika on the snow track in Moscow.*
478 *Count Orlov, in a portrait dating from 1779.*
479 *Count Orlov driving Bars I, the foundation sire of the Orlov breed.*
480 *Another Russian troika, a turnout still popular today.*

therefore can be transmitted, and horses can be selected for their special capacities. I admire the trot, but I prefer the gallop, and for this reason: Were I to have to follow an enemy to defeat him, I should much prefer being in the saddle on a galloper, and he in a sulky, drawn by a trotter. Having a machine with four speeds, if I had to go as fast as possible, I should not be as limited as I would be in depending solely upon the third speed.

IV
UNITED STATES

Although some carping critics might disagree, insisting that the American trotting horse is fragile and lacks substance, most experts believe that the Standardbred comes as near to perfection as a horse bred for speed can come. One might say that the trotter is *the* American horse; for speed, he is certainly not to be surpassed by any nation's breed of harness horses.

The foundation sire of this marvelous breed is considered to be the English thoroughbred Messenger (1780–1808), imported into Philadelphia in 1788. Messenger and his descendants have given us a line of Standardbreds without parallel, but we must not ignore the merits of the fine pacing and trotting mares in the States long prior to this date. These provided the nucleus of a select "breed" that gave us excellent harness horses, including competitors in the informal trotting races organized at country fairs and rural gatherings. This strain improved the breed of Norfolk trotters that had been wisely introduced in the United States to prevent inbreeding. The finest stud of this second line undoubtedly was Bellfounder (1817–1843), imported in 1822.

Messenger was sired by Mambrino (1768), out of Turf (1774), a bay mare, and descended—through Engineer (1756), Sampson (1745), Blaze (1733), Flying Childers (1715)—from the great Darley Arabian.

Messenger himself was the sire of a Mambrino, dropped in 1806, out of an imported mare, also an English Thoroughbred. From this Mambrino and a granddaughter of Messenger, a trotting mare named Amazonia, sprang Abdallah 1, in 1823.* Some notes on Amazonia, Abdallah's dam, might be of interest. She was the fastest mare of her time, carrying a rider in the saddle to trot the mile in about 2:54. In 1814, she was bought by a businessman who lived near Philadelphia, and was taken to New York, where she distinguished herself and was given the name Amazonia for her queenly, fearless bearing. In the first American *Stud Book*, she is registered as "Amazonia, by Messenger," later corrected to "Amazonia, by a son of Messenger," but there are still some who insist that she was, indeed, a daughter of Messenger, out of a mare of unknown origin.

If Messenger takes honors for improving the breed, certainly his descendant Hambletonian (more properly, Rysdyk's Hambletonian, foaled 1849) earned his worldwide fame for his perfect gait and for his get, unequivocally the fastest harness horse in the world right down to the end of the past century, when other families started giving them competition. Hambletonian's genealogy in the female line is extremely interesting, going back four generations. It involves a double return to Messenger, a bit of inbreeding that would be frowned upon today, but how effective was this exception to what has become a rule? The Kent Mare was Hambletonian's dam. She lived from 1834 to 1857, and her record for the mile was 2:41. Charles' Kent Mare, to give her full name, also foaled Bashaw (1855), one of the greatest sires of the Great Bashaw family. The Kent Mare's sire was Bellfounder who did the distance of two miles on an American track, saddled, in 6:00, and covered nine miles in 29:38. The Kent Mare's dam, One Eye, was a daughter of Bishop's Hambletonian, by Messenger, out of Silvertail.

Since about 90 percent of today's American trotting horses derive from Hambletonian 10, a great deal of study has been expended upon his family tree in an effort to determine just what genes went into the making of a perfect trotting horse. Although his pedigree is available, no guarantee

481 *A sulky for an ice track.*

482 *A troika race at a Moscow track.*

483 *Talantivi, of the Koltura breed, made a new winter record on ice for two-year-olds, driven by P. Beliaev, 2:17.*

484 *Ulov, the great Orlov foaled before the Russian Revolution, driven by N. Semichev, did the mile in 2:05 1-10 and the 2,400 in 3:13 1-10.*

485 *Alexandra Burdova drives the American horse Apex Hanover, imported from the United States.*

486 *Gorodnia, holder of the record for four-year-old mares, 2:08 1-10 on ice.*

487 *Intermède, foaled 1908, by Bénécourt, out of Belle Poule, by James Watt, the great French stud.*

488 *Uranie with V. Capovilla, after winning the European Championship in 1928 at Cesena.*

489 *Ozo, driven by Frömming, wins the Gran Premio di Nazioni at San Siro after running an impressive race.*

490 *Newstar, driven by Baroncini, overwhelmingly takes the Gran Premio di Nazioni at San Siro.*

491 *Uranie (Ch.m.), in France in 1920, by Intermède, did the thousand meters in 1:20 6-10 (the mile would be about 2:09).*

492 *Gelinotte (B.m.), in France, by Kairos, 1:16 5-10 for the thousand meters (the mile would be about 2:02 2-5).*

493 *Jamin, European record holder, 1:14 7-10 for the thousand meters (the mile would be about 1:59 2-5).*

494 *Roquépine, driven by H. Levesque, wins the Gran Premio di Nazioni at San Siro.*

495 *A trotting race for saddle horses at Vincennes. Going into the descent, a twenty-four-foot grade.*

496 *A hectic finish.*

497 *The start of the race at Vincennes.*

498 *Fandango, one of the great champions of mounted trotting races (faster when saddled than when harnessed).*

499 *Phaéton, 1871, by The Heir Linne (Ch.m.), out of La Crocus.*

---

* Abdallah was so bad-tempered and ungainly a horse that no one would breed their mares to him, despite his excellent lineage. He was finally bred to a crippled mare (by Bellfounder, out of One Eye) known as the "Kent Mare," who had been owned by a butcher, producing Hambletonian in 1849.—TRANS.

481

482

483

484

485

486

487

488

489

490

491

492

493

494

495

496

497

498

499

500   501

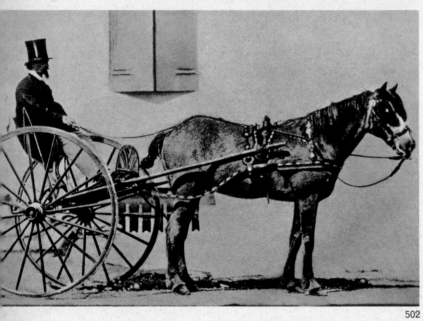

502   503

504

can be given as to accuracy of the information given for Sampson, Hambletonian 10's forebear, inasmuch as some records show Sampson as a product of Blaze and a mare sired by Hip, while others declare he was by Blaze out of a mare sired by Caccia, who contributed a good deal over the years toward the eventual formation of perfection seen in Hambletonian 10. There are those who insist that all the good qualities in the Hambletonian 10 line stem from Blaze, who was a purebred Arabian, and it is a fact that in both the masculine and feminine lines, Hambletonian 10 goes back four times to Blaze.

In any case, we do know that the descendants of Hambletonian 10 form a vast multitude, so many that the horse probably holds the record as a stud, 1,338 during his long career as a reproducer, which began when he was a two-year-old. The peak year in his life as a stud was 1864, when he served at least 217 mares for 148 offspring (a percentage of 68). Of course, such enthusiastic breeding has gone out of fashion, and nowadays the usual maximum number of mares presented a stallion is 40 per year.

Among Hambletonian 10's get besides the gelding Dexter (2:17 1-4), who was phenomenal on the track, are some great studs. These were Abdallah 15 (2:42), out of Katy Darling; Volunteer (2:37), out of Lady Patriot; George Wilkes (2:22), out of Dolly Spanker; Dictator (?), out of Clara; Happy Medium (2:30), out of Princess; Aberdeen, out of Widow Machree; Strathmore (?), out of Lady Walter-mire and Electioneer (2:28 1-2), out of Green Mountain Maid.

Among these studs, we might point out George Wilkes, whose dam, Dolly Spanker (1847–1856), died foaling him. The mare was found moribund in a field, and her foal was taken from her and raised on cow's milk. At the age of two, George Wilkes was sold, and a bit later, started training for the track. He made his debut as a four-year-old, and his rise was gradual. By the time he was twelve years old, he had won 27 times out of 69 races. George Wilkes lived from 1856 to 1882, and was the founder of two of the great modern families of trotting horses, Axworthy and McKinney. Some of his get are Baron Wilkes, Onward, Red Wilkes, Guy Wilkes, Jay Bird, Young Jim, and Wilton. They have had a particular influence upon the female line, siring excellent broodmares; all figure prominently in the pedigrees of some of the finest trotters of our day.

Electioneer (1868–1890) was another great sire whose descendants include pacers as well as trotters such as The Abbot, whose record trotting time was 2:03 1-4 and pacing record, 2:03, and Dictator (1863–1893) from whom descends

Walter Direct, the champion pacer of his time. Electioneer's dam, Green Mountain Maid (1862–1888), had nine other offspring who did the mile in less than 2:30 and he himself became the first stud to produce three horses with a record of 2:10. Electioneer was raised in Stony Ford, New York, and showed tremendous speed, although he had never been trained to race nor did he appear on the track. He finished out his days in the stables of Senator Leland Stanford who had bought him as a stud for $12,500. Electioneer had the defect of rolling one of his hind hooves under, which made him knock painfully against the knee of the other hind leg and, accordingly, kept him from ever making name for himself as a racer.

Three of Electioneer's record-holding offspring were Sunol, Palo Alto, and Arion. Sunol, a bay mare, foaled in 1886 out of Waxana (a descendant of General Benton and the Thoroughbred Waxy), trotted a mile in 2:08 1-4. Palo Alto, out of Dame Winnie in 1882 (Thoroughbred by Planet, out of Liz Mardiz), raced against the clock on October 27, 1891, to do the mile in 2:10, and a year later reduced the time to 2:08 3-4. Arion, 1889, out of Manette, 1878, who descended from trotters, was a phenomenon in his time, and proved to be the best two-year-old harness horse seen to that time on American tracks. At the end of 1901, he had established a time of 2:10 3-4, an extraordinary record for a two-year-old. As a four-year-old, Arion's record time was 2:07 3-4. He was the most famous trotting horse of the day, and brought a price of $125,000, an astonishing amount even today. As a stud, however, Arion was a failure, and his get were cursed with frail constitutions and weak tendons.

Other families of great importance, particularly to European breeders of trotting horses, also derive from Hambletonian 10. Some of the names that recur most often in pedigrees today are Hambletonian's descendants Elwood Medium, The Laurel Hall, Prince Hall, McLee, Truax, Plucky, Codero, Guy Fletcher, Kelly de Forest, Muscletone, McLin Hanover, Mighty Ned, Doctor Spencer, Gaylworthy, Harrod's Creek, and Traveler.

One of the greatest sires was Volomite (1926, by Peter Volo, out of Cita Frisco, 1915, by San Francisco, 2:07 3-4), whose record time was 2:03 1-4; he derives from Hambletonian 10 through the line of Happy Medium (1863, out of Princess), with a record time of 2:32 1-2.

From the Electioneer line, linked with that of Mambrino King, through Nettie King (1887, 2:20), by Mambrino King, out of Nettie Murphy (1867, by Hamlin Patchen, out of Murphy's Mare), came the great pacer The Abbot, whose record was 2:03 1-4 in his specialty.

The United States leads the world in breeding and research on the trotting and racing horse, and has the advantage of an additional century of experience and resources to draw on in making selections. While it is true that American breeders have permitted certain interesting strains to disappear (the Bingen strain, in the male line, for instance), in seeking sheer speed, one must turn to American bloodlines. Various clements have contributed to their great development of trotting and racing horses and harness racing. American breeders have a tremendous selection of broodmares, more than exist in any other country. Methods and equipment are the most up to date, as are the racecourses; and finally, because of the great interest in harness racing

500 *Giovanni Forghieri's Amato, foaled in 1868.*
501 *Spofford, one of the first American horses in Italy.*
502 *Rondello, 1863, owned by Giovanni Rossi.*
503 *Violetta, 1865, owned by Riccardo Bonetti.*
504 *Gurko, an Orlov, foaled in 1874 at Tulinov, by Podarov, out of Dobraia. Imported from France into Italy in 1881 by Baron A. Roggieri of Modena. The horse beat Vandale in Milan, doing the thousand meters in 1:36, in a hotly contested race (the mile would be about 2:33 3-5).*

and the consequent expansion of the market, the prices paid for harness horses at American auctions are the highest in the world—$100,000 for a yearling is not unheard of year after year. The two achievements attained on American trotting tracks in 1966 which still stand are a new world's record for trotters (after Greyhound's unbroken record since 1938) of all ages racing in competition and a new world's record for pacers. The four-year-old Noble Victory took a step forward for trotters. After four years, he broke the record held by Matastar, 1:55 4-5. At the Du Quoin track, on the first of September, brought on firmly and smoothly by his trainer-driver, Stanley Dancer, the rangy son of Victory Song shaved the old record, trotting the mile in 1:55 3-5. One can see in just what great form the horse was that day; the same afternoon Noble Victory made another start and did the same distance in the excellent time (considering the field he competed against) of two minutes flat, an exploit that will be hard to match, let alone surpass. Some major harness races, like the Hambletonian, require two or more heats to determine the winner. That is why Noble Victory ran twice on the same day. The new pacing record was made by the amazing Bret Hanover, who capped a magnificent career as a three-year-old with a time of 1:53 3-5 as a four-year-old, which showed all his great technical skill and ability, plus the experience gained on the track. The race was very dramatic. The superb racer had the last eighth of a mile to cover after having so far done a speed of 1:53–1:54 per mile. Ervin called on all his skill to give Bret Hanover his head, but without leaving him completely on his own. As a matter of fact, a sixteenth from the finish, the horse looked as if he weren't going to make it, but the attentive Frank Ervin had one last resort and he used the whip masterfully at the opportune moment. He had sensed exactly the right thing to do. Bret Hanover lowered his head, which he had just begun to lift defensively, and went all out to finish the quarter in 0:29 3-5 to set the world record at 1:53 3-5. All that was needed was just a single touch of the whip at a sixteenth from the finish!

American Primacy

It all began in 1818 with a bet made at the Jockey Club in New York. A discussion ensued over whether the trot should be recognized as a new, special gait. One of the members was particularly annoyed by the discussion: "Just imagine a horse going fast and easily at that gait. I've got $1,000 here to bet against anyone who says that any horse can go a mile in less than three minutes."

An unknown member rose and replied, "You've got a bet. My Boston Blue will show you just how fast a trotter can go." Boston Blue was a born trotter, and soon after the discussion, his owner pocketed $1,000.

That bet struck a spark. Serious consideration was given to trotting horses and their place in the sporting picture. Boston Blue went on to contribute even more decisively to the cause. Bought soon after the wager by an actor, Thomas Cooper, Boston Blue permitted his new owner to perform one evening in New York and the next in Philadelphia, covering about a hundred miles between the two cities with no strain.

Such an episode appears remote to us now, and just an agreeable anecdote, but we might consider that in the history of American sport, 1818 is really not all that long ago. Most of the United States was then pretty much virgin territory, and civilized life was restricted to the East Coast, in the main. It was only about then that the first steps toward colonizing the West were taken and that permanent settlements were established along both sides of the Mississippi, while it was not until about 1850 that settlers started clearing land in the Far West.

In the middle of the nineteenth century, trotting races took on the semblance of a major sporting attraction, a sport that was followed with fervor and enthusiasm, and one that would soon become an expression of American style and civilization, and a link between this country and the rest of the sporting world.

It took from 1806, when Yankee broke the three-minute mark (2:59) to 1845 for the next great record in the history of trotting races. The gray mare Lady Suffolk, at the age of ten, broke the two-and-a-half-minute barrier, doing the mile in 2:29 1-2. From that record set by Lady Suffolk to the record of the extraordinary Greyhound (1:55 1-4), the list of holders of the world record tells a fascinating tale, not only of rapid improvements in the breed aimed at cutting the time for the mile distance, but of the individualism and personalities of the horses that made those records.

World records were made on both mile and half-mile tracks. An interesting point in reference to the record holders is the fact that both Pelham (2:27) and Highland Maid (2:27), who came after Lady Suffolk, were originally pacers, the first indication we have that the history of both pacing and trotting developed contemporaneously, along parallel lines; the great success of the one has always been indissolubly linked to the other. Dan Patch is a prime example, with world records of 1:59 and 1:56 1-4 in 1903; 1:56 in 1904; and 1:55 1-4 in 1905, followed by Billy Direct's 1:55 in 1938 (also for Adios Harry in 1955), and Adios Butler's 1:54 3-5 in 1960, and of course the fastest harness mile, Bret Hanover's 1:53 3-5 in 1966.

Of the forty-nine trotting records established between 1845 and 1966, twenty-seven were held by fillies, twenty by geldings, and only two by a single colt. The colt to assert himself in the face of such domination was Cresceus, with the two marks he made in 1901, his best time, 2:02 1-2. Though the honors passed to a trio of superb geldings, the rangy Uhlan, the solid Peter Manning, and the fleet Greyhound, the mares were particularly brilliant at the beginning, that is, in the second half of the nineteenth century. Outstanding among the mares were Flora Temple, Goldsmith Maid, and Maud S. Old prints show them to be more powerful than elegant: muzzles projected forward, gliding shapes under the high, old-fashioned lines of those early sulkies. Some of these mares who appear and reappear as record holders established their best times when they were quite old: Flora Temple (2:19 3-4) at fourteen, and Goldsmith Maid (2:14), a granddaughter of Hambletonian, when she was seventeen.

In 1903, another mare became a milestone in the progress of trotting. She was Lou Dillon, whom we can consider the first queen of the trotting track of our century, as she was the first trotter to do the mile in a flat two minutes, and then in that same year, managed to mark up 1:58 1-2, a time that was beaten only nine years later by Uhlan, by a half-second. Of course, through Dan Patch pacing records clearly exceeded the efforts of the trotters.

Naturally, after Bingen's gelded son Uhlan ran a flat 1:58 in 1912, it became increasingly difficult to cut time from the record and for trotters. Only such showy champions as Greyhound and Peter Manning could make the crowd cheer. That it was much harder to make a new record is shown by the fact that even such exceptional horses as Uhlan and Peter Manning were hard put to do so. It took ten years before Uhlan's record was broken by Peter Manning (1:56 3-4) and fifteen years before Peter Manning's record was broken by Greyhound (1:56 and in 1938, 1:55 1-4) which still stands.

Another fourteen years brings us to 1952, and the exploits of Greyhound have passed into history. The "grey ghost" lived for many years on his fame, and collected glory and applause whenever he appeared, and remains one of the living legends of his sport. He is for many the horse nonpareil. The class of today's trotting horses is extremely high, so much so that we see them almost consistently breaking the two-minute mark for the mile; but to match Greyhound's mark takes a rare animal; to surpass it, a phenomenal one. Pacing has become very important in American harness racing, so much so that at many tracks there are more pacing races than trotting races. This interest in pacing also extended to Europe, first to Italy, subsequently to Sweden and Germany. However, in the Old World, the innovation has brought certain complications with it that are slowly being resolved by harness-racing associations in those countries.

In the United States, however, pacing is no longer a novelty, as the records show. As a three-year-old Bret Hanover in 1965 captured the fancy of the crowd and fostered a tremendous interest in pacing. In his brief but magnificent career, this offspring of Adios and Brenna Hanover, preceding his great 1966 performance already mentioned, racked up world records for three-year-old pacers on a mile track at 1:55; on a half-mile track at 1:57; world's record for pacers of any age for two consecutive starts on a half-mile track at 1:57 and 1:57 1-5; winning in the three out of four pacing classics, the Cane Futurity at Yonkers, New York; the Little Brown Jug Stakes at Delaware, Ohio; and the Messenger Stakes at Roosevelt Raceway, New York. Bret Hanover also took $341,748 in winnings in 1965, an all-time record for both trotters and pacers, and won a total $515,082 as a two- and three-year-old, as well as winning thirty-eight consecutive victories, a series unequaled in modern times. In 1966, he beat his own record with $407,534 for the year. Naturally, in the face of all these achievements, Bret Hanover was voted among harness horses "Horse of the Year" for 1965 as he was in 1964 and 1966. (In 1964, already a great favorite, he had finished his season as a two-year-old unbeaten, with twenty-four wins, and a record of 1:57 2-5.) At one time, it began to look as if the horse trained by Frank Ervin was unbeatable, and many thought he would finish his season as a three-year-old without losing a race. During the late summer, however, he came up against a worthy contender, another son of Adios, the excellent Adios Vic, who caught Bret Hanover in a historic moment of weakness on August 19, 1965, at Springfield, Illinois, and beat him by doing a two-minute mile in the first heat of the Review Futurity. Subsequently, Adios Vic proved

his merit by topping Bret Hanover twice more, in the course of the Horseman Stake in Indianapolis, on September 6. In the first heat, Bret Hanover marked the sensational time of 1:55, but Adios Vic emulated him, and won the second heat in 1:56 3-5, and topped it off with a modest win at 2:04 4-5. Out of twenty-four starts for 1965, Bret Hanover won twenty-one.

Despite these losses, Bret Hanover was still "Big Bret" to the crowd. No one can fail to be impressed by his great career, a succession of exploits and victories no other pacer has achieved. Happiest of all, of course, was Richard Downing, Bret Hanover's owner, who certainly could never have expected all the glory when he bought him at the famous Harrisburg auction in 1963 for $50,000, a tremendous price for an unknown horse. It was not a reckless purchase, however, because Downing acquired the horse at the urging of the famous trainer-driver Frank Ervin, who was responsible for the horse's sire the celebrated Adios (1:57 1-2). Bret Hanover is now at stud at Castleton Farm in Lexington, Kentucky.

Ervin, who goes by bloodlines, was looking for a horse that would synthesize all the fine qualities sought in a pacer and was convinced that Bret Hanover was that horse; in addition to being a son of Adios, he had two fast pacers, Tar Heel and Billy Direct, in the maternal line. Furthermore, Bret Hanover pleased Ervin very greatly by his strong resemblance to Adios. From Bret Hanover's pedigree, one can see what bloodlines go into the making of an ideal pacer today. On the side of Adios, the sire: The Abbot, Chimes, Electioneer, Hambletonian 10; and on the side of Brenna Hanover his dam: Direct, Director, Dictator, and, again, Hambletonian 10. In these lines are intermixed the pacing strains of Old Pacing Pilot (in The Abbot), and the immortal Tom Hal and Prince Pulaski (in Direct). Add to this, particularly in the mares, the best trotting blood: Peter Volo (Nervolo Bell), Volomite (Esther), Calumet Chuck (Maggie H.), Guy Forbes (Nancy Hanks); and a broad spectrum of trotters of quality: Nibble Hanover (Miss Copeland), Dillon Axworthy, The Laurel Hall, Lee Worthy, and Baron Wilkes. If this had not been so, certainly Bret Hanover would not be the fabulous horse he is.

Harness-Racing Tracks

According to the 1968 edition of the *Trotting and Pacing Guide*, the handbook of harness racing, there are in the United States today fifty-one extended pari-mutuel tracks offering trotting and pacing events to the public.

Outstanding among these tracks are those forming what has come to be known as "the proving ground of champions," the Grand Circuit. First organized in 1873, it comprised the tracks at Utica and Buffalo, New York; Springfield, Massachusetts; and Cleveland, Ohio; and was known then as the Quadrilateral Trotting Combination. Today, the Grand Circuit provides a cycle of harness racing that starts at the end of May and goes on through November, with meetings at one track after another of the Grand Circuit, which includes 22 tracks throughout 11 states from New York to California, including Quebec, Canada. The largest purses and the greatest number of races are held at Roosevelt Raceway and Yonkers Raceway, both in New York. Also, harness racing is still an important part of the entertainment offered at many country fairs, particularly in the Midwest.

Of the racing year's program, the stellar races for trotters and pacers are two series, each known as the Big Four—the greatest of them all, the Hambletonian, for three-year-olds, at Du Quoin, which dates from 1926; the Kentucky Futurity, conditioned for three-year-olds, held at Lexington, which started in 1893; the Yonkers Futurity, for three-year-olds, to be held at Yonkers, a fixture since 1955; and the Dexter Cup, again for three-year-olds, competed for at Roosevelt Raceway in Westbury, the youngest of these classics, held only since 1960.

Three-year-old pacers have their Big Four in the Little Brown Jug, at Delaware, Ohio, dating from 1946; the Messenger Stake, at Westbury, which goes back to 1956; the William B. Cane Futurity, held at Yonkers, as it has been since 1955; and the Adios, at The Meadows, near Pittsburgh where it has been an event since 1966.

V

FRANCE

Practically all the famous French trotters derive from Conquérant (1858), beginning the descent with Fuchsia (1883), by Reynolds (by Conquérant, out of Miss Pierce). Characteristic of the pedigrees of the great French harness families are entire lines of Thoroughbreds, a peculiarity almost wholly French, for thoroughbred strains never have figured that strongly in the pedigrees of American Standardbreds or in those of other national harness breeds. If we look at Phaéton's family tree, for example (he is one of the five foundation sires of French trotters), we find that the paternal line (The Heir of Linne) is composed exclusively of Thoroughbreds.

The five foundation sires are Conquérant (foaled 1858), Lavater (1867), Normand (1869), Niger (1869), and Phaéton (1871). By 1905, from just these five, about 95 percent of France's extant trotters had derived, and of these approximately 60 percent descended from Conquérant and Phaéton. In their search for quality, breeders tended to concentrate on the descendants of Conquérant, Phaéton and Normand (ultimately, Normand was ignored and Niger and Lavater are minimal).

Phaéton was peculiar for his thoroughbred sire, The Heir of Linne who produced twenty trotters, and his Norfolk trotter dam La Crocus (a daughter of Elisa [1853] who was the dam of Conquérant). His best offspring was James Watt (1887), from whom derive both the Phaéton lines. The first of these comes through Uranus and Enoch, which led to Quo Vadis from whom sprang many outstanding trotters. The other James Watt line eventually led to the powerful Mighty Ned.

To these we can add two mixed Franco-American lines that have shown excellence: the line going back to Peter the Great, and the one that eventually gave us the unbeatable Gelinotte, whose dam pedigree comprises, at least by 75 percent, French horses, among them Intermède, Uranie, and Pastourelle, whereas her sire's male line is American.

We see that Fuchsia and Phaéton have the extraordinary Elisa in their pedigrees; the first, in the male, and the second in the female line. Elisa, who dropped 19 foals, was by Corsair out of another Elisa, a hunter (belonging to Family No. 3 and probably the greatest of the French broodmares). Elisa is repeated in the pedigrees of the great French trotters to such a point that she probably can be considered the grandmother of most of today's French horses. Her blood has gone to Italy through En Garde, from whom descend at least thirty fine broodmares.

Fuchsia belonged to a minor breeder named Gosselin, who had acquired, a few years prior to the birth of Fuchsia, a thoroughbred mare called Sympathie, descended from Orville. Covered by Reynolds, Sympathie dropped a colt so lacking in distinction that he was given the name Fuchsia. The one thing he did have, however, was a splendid action, along with the sort of temperament that makes a good racehorse. Fuchsia was bought by an important stud, for which he produced 399 trotters. Among his first-class descendants we note Intermède (1908), Passeport (1915), Trianon (1919), Kozyr (1932), Odiport (1936), Pharaon (1937), Banco III (1945), Chambon (1947), and Fandango (1949). Three horses that continue Fuchsia's line were Narquois (1891), Trinqueur (1897), and Bémécourt (1901).

Of the most famous French trotters there was Uranie (1920), by the equally famous Intermède of Family 16, out of Pastourelle, with a record of 1.20.6 for the 1,000 meters (or about 2:09 for the mile), a sorrel mare of rare distinction and beauty, who had more French thoroughbred than trotter blood. Uranie came into her own rather late, but then she won the Prix d'Amérique in 1926, 1927, and 1928. Others were Amazone B (1.21.8 or 2:10 4-5 for the mile), Cancannière (1.18.7 or 2 :06), Fandango (1.20.7 or 2:09), Gelinotte (1.16.5 or 2:02 2-5), Icare IV (1.15.8 or 2:01 1-5), and Jamin (1.13.6 or 1:57 4-5). Other famous French trotters were Jariolaine, (1.15.7 or 2:01 1-5), Masina (1.16.4 or 2:02 2-5), Nawstar (1.16.4 or 2:02 4-5), Roquépine (1.15.3 or 2:00 1-2), beaten in the United States only by Ambro Flight; and perhaps the most fascinating of all French trotters, the mare Ozo (1.15.5 or 2:00 4-5). This was a horse that was all heart and all ability who unfortunately lost races that she might very well have won had she a more experienced driver, and there were many others who did 1.16 (2:01 1-2) or better.

505 *Finale of the Gran Premio di Allevamento at Bologna in 1918. Clarina Medium, in the middle, 2:17, wins out over Diavolone, on the right, and Cesar.*

506 *Vandalo, by Huntsman out of Cassandra, driven by the owner, Biagio Oppi, in 1866.*

507 *Curzio, 1898, hitched to one of the first sulkies with pneumatic tires imported into Italy. They first appeared in the United States in 1892.*

508 *Arlecchino, by Van Tassel, out of Lola, with Giovanni Piccinini, after his loudly applauded conquest of the record for Italian three-year-olds, at 1:27 for the thousand meters (about 2:11 for the mile).*

509 *A pair driven by the driver from Modena, Nello Branchini, who revolutionized the Italian style for harness racers.*

505

506

507

508

509

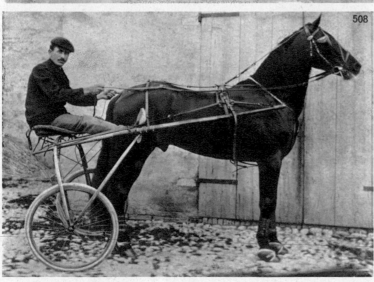

510

511

513

514

512

VI
USSR

Alexis Orlov was an officer of the guard and brother to the famous Gyorgi, or George, who was the lover of Catherine II. Alexis played an important part on the night of July 8, 1762, which brought the czarina to St. Petersburg and led to the subsequent assassination of the czar.

Catherine II was grateful for Orlov's aid and gave him titles and positions, the most important of which was command of the fleet that defeated the enemy in the Russo-Turkish War. The losing Turkish admiral, in gratitude for the gallant treatment he received, provided Orlov with the celebrated Arabian horse Smetanka that was to become the foundation sire of the Orlov breed.

On an average, the Orlov stands 14.1 hands high at the withers, has a trunk approximately sixty-five inches long, a chest approximately seventy-three inches, and about eight inches around the cannon.

The Orlov has considerable speed, as can be seen from the records of some of the best of the breed:

Pilot	1 mile	2.02 1-5
Ulov	1½ miles	3.09
Lerik	2 miles	4.20 2-5
Lerik	4 miles	8.56

The Orlov has a great deal of endurance and stamina even in the long haul, as the record for Lerik shows. Also he is a fine horse for a troika (along with two companions, of course). In drawing a troika, the middle horse is between the shafts and moves at the trot, flanked on either side by a horse hitched to the carriage and going at a gallop. It is customary at Russian tracks to intersperse the usual trotting races with events for the troika.

The current Russian breed of trotter was created around the end of the last century by crossing the Orlov with the American Standardbred, with successive inbreeding and resort to Orlov studs. The Russian breed today are fine, robust specimens, very like the Orlov in type and appearance, but, perhaps, a bit faster and lighter. The record for the mile and two miles in the USSR is held by the stallion Gest (1:59 3-5 and 4:10 2-5). This horse, foaled in 1947, is by an Orlov sire. In recent years, Russian trotters have participated with distinction in international meetings, principally in Sweden, Norway, and West Germany, as well as in the Iron Curtain countries devoted to harness racing. Russian trotters are adaptable as saddle horses and for light draft work.

510 *Senator Antonio Vicini, center, president of the Unione Ippica.*

511 *Ettore Barbetta, one of the most elegant of drivers at the beginning of this century.*

512 *A group warming itself at the brazier at the new track at San Siro in 1926.*

513 *Racing in Prussia in a brake, which bridged the gap between the old-style sulky and the modern type.*

514 *Red Wilkes, 1911, a brilliant American trotter, imported into Italy, who was killed in an accident on the track.*

The Moscow racecourse, which has not changed very much from the days of the czars, is the leading track in the Soviet Union, and still preserves its imperial air. On Sundays, 24 races are run, from 2 in the afternoon till 11 at night. Of these, about 10 are flat races, with the rest devoted to trotters. Drivers receive a flat fee as well as merit points that vary in accordance with the importance of the event in which they finish in the money. These points are good for an additional payment above their regular fee. The most important events are held at distances of 1½ miles and up, while the trotters' derby, which is open to four-year-olds, is 2 miles. This is the premier trotting event in the USSR, with the best horses of each stud competing. The stables are all state farms, and therefore purses are awarded to commissars directing the winning studs, who apply the money toward improvements and the purchase of broodmares and stallions. Today, the Soviet Union has about three thousand trotter broodmares, including Orlov and Orlov-American Standardbred crosses, with plans to increase the production of both flat racers and trotters.

VII
ITALY

The winner of the first trotting race in 1808 was Giovanni Rossi, father of Giuseppe Rossi who owned the Crespano Veneto stud, a driver nonpareil in the Europe of the latter part of the nineteenth century. In these races, the vehicle was the *padovanella*, a sulky weighing no less than 660 pounds. Later, these Padua sulkies were considerably lightened. By 1869, they weighed 227 pounds, with a harness of 26 pounds.

Among the first harness-racing horses to become famous in Italy, we might mention Rondello, a popular roan stallion in the 1860's who had a Hungarian sire and dam of the Italian Friulian breed. In 1869, Vandalo (2:23) initiated his long track career. He was the son of a Thoroughbred, Huntsman, out of the mare Cassandra, and was foaled in the stables of the Marquis Costabili in 1864.

This first period in the history of Italian trotting extended to about 1880, and was characterized—and hampered—by the lack of any studs whose first concern was the breeding and training of racing trotters. The horses that raced along the roads of the towns and cities, particularly in Emilia and the Veneto, were Friulians, an ancient type of trotter known for speed and stamina, or they were the offspring of native mares crossed with imported studs.

The next period, which extended to about 1900, saw the establishment of the first trotting-horse studs. Through Senator Vincenzo Stefano Breda, the first Orlov stallion, Nagrad, was imported in 1881 as well as the first American trotter, Elwood Medium, in 1882. Following the example set by Senator Breda, Baron Raimondo Franchetti established a stud, the Canedole, at Roverbello, in Mantua, which was in full operation by 1893. He had thirty broodmares, including English Thoroughbreds and trotters, two American stallions, and an English thoroughbred stud. The establishment was dissolved at the time of his death, in 1905, and the stock dispersed.

Senator Breda pioneered the raising of racing trotters in Italy; and his stud, Carmignano di Brenta, was the first worthy of the name. The exemplary Nagrad, considered at the time the greatest trotter in Europe, was foaled in Russia in 1868, and of course goes back to Bars I, foundation sire of the Orlov breed. In addition to the infusion of American blood through the stud Elwood Medium, imported along with two fine American mares, in the same year, the senator added two Orlov mares that headed his string.

When operations first started, there were three groups of mares at the Breda stud, English Thoroughbreds, American Standardbreds and Orlovs, and native mares, either of the Piave breed or others chosen for their speed. The results that came with breeding these mares were the following: Of the English thoroughbred mares covered by Orlov and American Standardbred stallions, only two mares established families that continue today, both through two Orlov mares —Vertlawaya, covered by Elwood Medium, who dropped Conte Rosso, who was the best trotter of his time in Europe, and Warsowa, who foaled Marta who as a three-year-old set a record time of 2:30 1-5, a European record for her class. Of the group of native horses, the only ones that led to any successful results were those of the Piave breed and their offspring. These mares were first covered by a Norfolk trotter, and their offspring then crossed with an Orlov. These offspring in turn were crossed with an American Standardbred. From the last cross derive the winners of the trotting derbies of 1885, 1887, and 1892; and the family still flourishes today.

From 1886 to 1896, Senator Breda's trotters were the first horses on the Italian tracks, and did well throughout Europe, participating in trotting classics in Lyons, Marseilles, Vienna, Berlin, and Budapest. After the Senator's sudden death in 1903, the Breda Foundation tried to continue his work.

The period that followed extended from 1901 to 1929. During this time the great studs of Senator Breda and Barons Ruggeri and Franchetti disappeared, and their work was continued by small breeders. Among the various studs that appeared in the early 1900's were Cavaliere Beretta, Signore Pesenti, Captain Triossi, Signore Branchini, the Barilari brothers, Cavaliere Bandiera, Cavaliere Bellini, Cavaliere Berti, Cavaliere Modena, Signore Forti, and Cavaliere Calderoni. Undoubtedly, however, the outstanding stable during this period was the establishment created at Malacappa, near Bologna, by Garagnani and Bersani.

Notwithstanding, not much progress was made during this period, partly because of the inactivity imposed by the First World War, at the end of which, however, there was an upsurge in interest and operations. At that time, in addition to trotting racecourses at San Siro in Milan, the one at Villa Glori in Rome was established, and the first trotting stables were founded in Lombardy. In 1929, the Associazione Nazionale Allevatori del Trottatore (ANACT), the National Association of Trotting Horse Breeders, was founded, which was to have a large role to play in the future of trotting races. Some of the association's objectives were to publicize trotting and stimulate the breeding of trotters through technical and economic assistance, and to control the quality of production through regional inspection and research.

A rather short period followed, from 1930 to 1938. In 1930, one of the most important studs came into being, the work of Count Paolo Orsi Mangelli, who took part of the stock from the erstwhile Bersani-Garagnani stables and transferred it to his holding at Budrio, proposing to build it up through the acquisition of new blood. The next year, in Germany, the count bought an American stallion, Augias (2.01 for 1,000 meters or 2:08 for the mile), a four-year-old, who was put to stud with about fifteen fine mares in 1931. More fine horses, especially mares, were acquired subsequently, among them Calumet Clancy, Clovy, Emily Stokes, Honey Moon, Judith, May Nelson, The Duchess, and Topsy Hanover; the stallions included The Laurel Hall, Truax, and Prince Hall.

Others who added to the Italian trotting string during this period were such breeders as Commendatore Riva, the Faccioli brothers, Signore Ciocca, Doctor Camurati, Commendatore Rosario, and Cavaliere Gambi. It is estimated that in 1938 approximately seventy American, thirteen Hungarian, and seven French mares arrived in Italy. Among the important stallions imported during this period, we might recall Brevere, Traveler, Keno, Gaylworthy, Guy Fletcher, and Spencer McElvin. This was a period of great progress for harness racing in Italy. This brings us to the Second World War and, of course, a break in activity. Naturally, the stables managed to continue only with a great deal of difficulty and sacrifice, but breeders managed to maintain their stock and personnel. Actual figures for horses foaled are 645 in 1941, 772 in 1942, 870 in 1943 and 966 in 1944. Of course, all these horses were inestimably useful in serving the sport of harness racing in the period that followed, ending in the year 1950. The situation, however, was not the same throughout Italy during the war years. Almost everything was lost by breeders in the Romagna, and losses were grave in Emilia and Bologna. Recuperation, however, was so strong that Emilia still managed to retain its primacy as a producer of trotting horses. An important year for the Italian breeders was 1947, which marked the import by Mangelli not only of a number of fine broodmares from the United States but also of the stallion Doctor Spencer, who was to prove the best American stud in Italy during that postwar period. Other fine stock was introduced into Italy in subsequent years, including such stallions as the French Pharaon, Tabac Blond, and Kozyr, as well as the American Grand Parade, White Hanover, Hit Song, Theme Song, and Mighty Ned.

It is interesting to see the progressive improvement in quality from 1929, the year in which the association initiated its control, to date. Of the production registered for 1929, 332 foals, 21.6 percent, raced as three-year-olds, and the best time recorded, by only two horses, was 2:16 (equivalent mile). In the decade 1929–1939, there was an increase to 777 and a corresponding increase in the number of mares capable of producing first-class foals, although there was no elimination of those mares who dropped mediocre products, so that the percentage of useful foals remained low, 21.4 percent. Nevertheless, the number of winners on the track more than doubled, going from 92 to 216, with seven horses registering a time of 2:11 (equivalent mile). From 1939 to 1949, through the activity of small breeders and better selection of broodmares, quality registered a notable improvement, and the percentage of useful horses rose from 31 to 37 percent. There were 393 winners, and four horses recorded a best time of 2:08 (equivalent mile). From 1949 to 1959 all mares producing run-of-the-mill foals were eliminated, and the percentage of three-year-olds racing had risen from 37 to 52 percent.

There were 465 winners, and two of them marked best times of 2:04 4-5 (equivalent mile). Furthermore, the crossing of French and American horses, intended to tap the formidable reserves of energy inherent in the French breed, proved successful, since it led to such horses of international quality as Torneso (2:01 equivalent mile), Nievo (2:03 1-2 equivalent mile), and Oriolo (2:04 equivalent mile). In Italian breeding today, the chief characteristic is its development on a rather uneven basis. Of a total of 712 breeders, about 75 percent have no more than one or two mares. The large breeding farms, with between ten and forty broodmares, number no more than twenty-seven, while there are 157 middle-sized establishments with between three and ten mares.

In general, the production of each region is sufficient to to its own sporting activity. Italian breeding of trotting horses, which was ranked last in Europe about 30 years ago, is on a par with the French. Outstanding Italian records are by Gualdo (1:16 7-10 or 2:02 7-10 equivalent mile), Guiglia, the same, Okapi C (1:16 3-5 or 2:02 1-2 equivalent mile), and Infante II (1:14 9-10 or 1:59 4-5 equivalent mile).

Mistero (1943), by Prince Hall, out of Naomy Guy, raised by Mangelli, was the first and most authentic racing trotter Italy ever had. Huge in body and spirit, he could cover any distance. He was the only Italian horse to have his name inscribed on the role of winners of the Prix d'Amérique at Vincennes. Mistero made 129 starts. He proved to be an exceptional sire, even though his offspring picked up a bit of his fiery temperament.

Tornese (2:02 1-5 equivalent mile) is the best all-around trotter Italy has produced to date. He was dropped in 1952, sired by Tabac Blond, out of Balboa, by De Sota, and raised by Commendatore Sebastiano Manzoni, a perfect result of that cross-breeding between French and American stock so endorsed by Professor Primo Castelvetro. Many doubts existed as to his paternity. He bore such a startling resemblance to the best sorrels sired by Pharaon that many wished to name Pharaon as his father. Tornese did not run as a two-year-old, but made his debut in a claiming race at three, up for sale because he was suffering from some affliction that affected his rear hooves. He started 207 times in Italy and 22 times abroad, winning 131 of his Italian races and two of the foreign ones. In eight years of activity, he earned over $500,000.

VIII
WEST GERMANY

Following their flat-racing tradition, Italy and Germany are the only two Continental countries to hold Derbies for trotting horses for three-year-olds. France, the Scandinavian nations, Austria, and Belgium prefer to hold this maximum trial when their trotters have reached maturity, that is, at the age of four.

In Germany's long history of the Derby, it has made only one concession, moving from a summer to a fall meeting. All other attempts to change the traditional race have failed. Thus, three-year-old trotters are still put to the test over the grueling Derby distance.

The Derby is just one of three proving races in the German cycle. First come the 1 1-4 mile Adbell Toddington and the 1 5-8 mile Buddenbrock. The three races are held at the old 3-4 mile Mariendorf track in Berlin, the sole remaining course in the Western part of the city. As an interlude, Hamburg invites the best trotters for its 1 5-8 mile Grand Prix for three-year-olds at Bahrenfeld. The 3-4 mile Bahrenfeld track is racquet-shaped, like the Vernon course in the United States. The addition of this last race to the classics has incensed those who fear that it will lead to premature straining of the capabilities of young trotters. It is true that the race requires a good deal of exertion and stamina from a fairly young horse just to cover the distance—to many experts beyond the call of a horse trained under a system that since World War II has still to return to its former condition.

Experience seems to confirm this view. No winner of the German trotting Derby since the war, with the exception of the extraordinary Permit, has been able to consolidate the form shown in this race in his future career, and, what is worse in the long run, to pass on his qualities as a reproducer. Notwithstanding, a large group of trainers, of whom Hans Froemming is the most outspoken, continues to defend this tradition. Their view is that a short race, where speed is the primary factor, makes a greater call upon the vital organs of a horse than a long one, where stamina is the prime element. It is this opinion that is responsible for the continual objections of these trainers to the present predilection for programming a large number of middle-distance events. They attribute a great part of the kudos given the Norman trotters to the fact that they are consistently given the opportunity to prove themselves over the 1½-mile and longer distances. Certainly, it would be logical to establish a rapport between classic selection and normal function in the course of a trotter's active life. On the other hand, one must respond to the exigencies of breeding.

For economic reasons, American breeders seek precocity in a horse. The analog of the trotting Derby in the United States, the Hambletonian Stakes, is designed through its use of heats to encourage speed and staying power. It seems obvious that Americans, contrary to Europeans, turn to advantage the consequences of an early flowering of their horses by putting the best of them at stud while they are still young, at an age when Europeans would just begin to consider them mature enough for a profitable career on the track.

Notwithstanding, all attempts in Germany to arrive at a compromise by reducing the distances of the three classics to a mile for the first race, 1¼ miles for the second, and 1½ miles for the third, have failed. Harness racing has shown a definite, continuous increment since the war, but it is still far from the level achieved by France and Italy. Statistics available show that activity is still relatively modest. For example, only three trotters have earned in a single year more than DM 100,000 ($25,000), the five-year-old Vinci, who picked up DM 125,800 in winnings; the two-year-old, Lord Pitt, who made DM 103,632; and the three-year-old Gesell, who earned DM 103,547.

IX
UNITED KINGDOM

The British sporting press does not cover harness racing, but according to official reports of the trotting meetings that have been taking place for some years in Wales, at the Prestatyn course, it appears that harness racing is a growing sport, with some six thousand spectators repeatedly visiting the trotting races. Besides the Prestatyn track, there is harness racing in the English towns of Appleby, Droylsden, and Manchester, and in Musselburgh, Scotland.

X
SCANDINAVIA

Trotting has its fans in Norway, Finland, and Sweden. In all these countries, harness racing has been constantly expanding, so that today Sweden has twenty-eight official trotting tracks, not to mention about a hundred improvised courses, generally for winter meetings on ice. There are about two thousand trotters on breeding farms, and about a thousand compete at Solvalla, the best course in Stockholm.

What has really made trotting in Sweden, and drawn popular attention, is the V 5, a pool that invites the player to select five winners in a day's program of harness races. Naturally, the prizes go into the millions of crowns, since there are very few, if any, winners on a given day, and the prizes are cumulative.

Sweden has produced some first-rate trotters, notably Frances Bulwark, to name the most celebrated. It appears, however, after a rather bright period, at least from the point of view of quality, that breeding is somewhat in decline, although quantitatively it is on the upgrade.

A day's harness racing at Solvalla means about three million kronor in wagers, as compared to 500,000 kronor for thoroughbred racing. The sport of kings is definitely declining in Sweden. Only three tracks remain, and only at Stockholm is there thoroughbred racing the year round. While Sweden once had about a thousand Thoroughbreds in competition, only about half that number are active today.

different types of exercise and training carts, finally proceeding to the sulky. At this point he already has his first set of shoes, including the weights to arrive at a proper balance. This brings us through March, concluding the training period, and the beginning of the real work.

The three stages in the training of a colt, therefore, are accustoming him to the track, breaking, and working. This practice is recognized by all trainers, who vary only in the amount of time they spend on each area, which depends upon the character and ability of the horse. One no longer teaches a colt to trot or pace, which was the practice about forty years ago, but since that time the functional characteristics of the trotter and pacer have become so fixed that it is rare to find one that does not come to it naturally.

Once the basic training is complete, it is absolutely necessary to follow the horse step by step in his career. No day can be skipped whether he be a champion or otherwise. A conscientious trainer will spend at least eight hours a day taking care of his pupils, in snow or in tropic heat. He must, furthermore, know every one of his horses thoroughly, being aware of their good points and bad, enhancing the first and using every means possible to erase the effects of the latter. Method, patience, and intuition are essential. Without them, the trainer is doomed to fail. As with Thoroughbreds, his major preoccupation must be to take care of his horse's health and general physical condition. When a horse is at the top of his form, accidents happen with difficulty. A horse is always subject to the perils of slight physical injuries, epidemic diseases, and sickness, and one must know how to ward these off or mitigate their effects. Actually, when a horse is so ill that a veterinarian is called in, the doctor may diagnose, but it is the trainer and his help who are called upon to treat the animal and oversee his care. Among the tasks set for the

XI
TRAINING TROTTERS AND PACERS

Before a colt can truly gain confidence on a track, he must be broken in, which generally is done from November, when the horse is about eighteen months old, through March of the following year. First it is necessary to "give him a mouth," as the stable slang has it. Understandably, this is the first stage of training, and the most important. Then, while walking behind him, the trainer works on his going left and right, starting and stopping in a phase called the driving. The colt must become habituated to the use of the bridle, which he should wear at least four hours a day, while in the box. All this careful preparation requires extreme patience, and should take as long as necessary, depending upon the horse's temperament. The colt is then taken to the track, unharnessed, along with another horse in a sulky, in order to accustom him to his new environment, including the rhythm of other horses on the track as well as neighboring sounds of activity around the track. This should continue for about twenty days, which brings us just about to January. Now we are ready for the actual "breaking." The colt must learn that trotting in a race means pulling a contrivance comprising two shafts, two wheels, and a man. One begins with the

515 516 *A fall in the final stretch at San Siro as Reseda, driven by Nello Branchini, goes down.*

517 *Muscletone, driven by Alessandro Finn, was one of the greatest of the between-wars champions. Imported by Commendatore A. Riva, he was a great sire of dams.*

518 *Dama, by Augias, owned by Count Paolo Orsi Mangelli, driven by V. Antonellini, after winning the championship for Italian two-year-olds, at 1: 22 for the thousand meters (about 2:11 for the mile).*

519 *Dizzying finish of the Matadoren-Rennen, Berlin, 1931, with Walter Dear, on the left, and Hazelton, famous rivals of the thirties.*

520–522 *Sulkies and gear in a trotting stable.*

523 *Commendatore Manzoni's Tornese, driven by Sergio Brighenti, an Italian champion, at 1:15 7-10 for the thousand meters (about 2:01 for the mile).*

524 *Aulo Gellio, driven by Dino Fabbrucci.*

525 *Iago Clyde, driven by Nello Branchini, the unsurpassable antagonist of Aulo Gellio.*

526 *Crevalcore, bred by Count P. Orsi Mangelli, and here driven by William Casoli, was Tornese's implacable adversary, and, at his best, faster at getting away at the start. His time for the thousand meters is 1:16 6-10 (about 2:02 2-5 for the mile).*

515

516

517

518

519

520

521

522

524

523   525

526

527

528

529

530

trainer is that of rebuilding horses that have grown out of hand, are overexcitable, or those that have suffered in performance as a result of too many changes of stable.

In the United States and in France, colts are trained at an earlier age than in Italy, a consequence perhaps of the fact that these countries have far greater resources in stock. In comparing general overall training, we find these differences: in Italy, a week before he is to compete, a trotter is put through a course of fairly sustained work, and then, without forcing him, is submitted to three trial races on the three days prior to the event in question. The method used in Germany is much the same. In the States, however, for seven days prior to the race, a horse is put through more trial starts, as many as six in a single day, without expecting too much sustained effort from him, except for a few fast heats, which is what opponents of this method cite as the cause of premature weakening of the trotter. On the day of the race, before post time, he has worked by about five miles and then is limbered up before going to the gate. In France, a horse is usually submitted to just one trial, for about a half hour, being urged to top speed for just about a quarter of a mile, and no more. Up to a short time ago, French trotters were better stayers than American and Italian horses because they apparently had more resistance, possibly as a result of this less arduous training. Now, however, after the recent frequent encounters of French and American horses, the French are tending more toward the American method of preparation.

A basic difference between the American method of training trotters and the European method is the use of many heats, up to as many as five in a morning's workout, and they are conditioned for speed. In France, on the other hand, the emphasis is on distance, and horses are put through long trots, with little opportunity given for sprints, a logical consequence of the heavy programming of distance races in French harness racing, where the courses generally run from a mile and a half to two and a half miles. In the last decade, French horses have beaten American trotters over their preferred distances.

The Italians appear to be at a midpoint. Their horses are generally of Franco-American descent, and the type and distance of their racecourses also are an amalgam of French and American. For that reason, their training system for trotters is a combination of the American and French methods and experience. They do not have a circular track like the one at Vincennes, nor do they have one as long as its mile and a quarter, or even anything like the mile tracks like those at Du Quoin and Lexington, where they have the facilities for training a fast-stepping, resistant horse.

As for the drivers, while a man on horseback has no support other than his mount, a man driving a trotter can balance himself in the seat of his sulky, which, weighing as it does, generally about thirty pounds, scarcely has any modifying effect upon the horse's action, and certainly never encumbers him. While a man on horseback makes his points of contact his knees and thighs, and he also can brace himself in his stirrups, the sulky driver has only two stirrups (the terminology is the same) affixed to the sulky, upon which he plants his feet to rise whenever he wants or when he must pull up or hold back his horse. These two stirrups also serve as his normal point of balance, along with the seat of his pants.

The horseman's hands move a foot or, at most, two feet from a horse's mouth, and are capable of strong lateral action as well. The sulky driver, however, uses reins as long as six feet or more from the horse's mouth to his hands, and is denied any lateral action, all of it being along the dorsal axis of the trotter, running, as they do, straight back from his mouth to the height of the seat of the sulky.

The rider has his knees, spurs, and a crop to solicit the horse's impulsion, as well as his weight to make the animal turn, while the driver has only a whip.

Both rider and driver, however, possess one thing in common, apart from all mechanical aids, their *shifts* in weight, and a certain sensitivity in communicating with the horse. There are those with light hands, peculiarly adept with delicate mouths, capable of controlling the more restless animal with a simple pressure on the reins, and those with heavy hands that oppress the horse but also control him to the point where he is obligated to make a supreme effort. Some insinuate themselves into the animal's will, making him utterly cooperative, just as some make him fractious and diffident, and annoy him to the point of exasperation.

As we know, usually, with racehorses, the aids, such as the spurs, whip, and so on, come into play solely at the end of a race in an all-out effort to finish first. Except for extremely lethargic horses, who keep the same dull pace from start to finish, the large majority naturally hurtle toward the finish, almost spasmodically, either through an instinct to get out in front of the herd or through fear, combative spirit, or sheer exuberance. A race for a horse is somewhat of a liberation from the restrictions that occasionally haunt him, so he is eager to run free. Thus, it becomes important to moderate his impulses and distribute them wisely and capably to provide the power that can be employed best at the moment that it will resolve a race. These are the moments that test a driver. He must make the right decision at the right time, whether to stay along the rail, or to pull out to take a lead, all the time being aware of the other drivers. He must at these times be extremely careful to avoid a collision of sulkies and an infraction or a break in his horse's gait, among other cares that combine to make the harness driver, frequently, rather than the horse the determinant of a race result.

527 *At the height of winter, going round the curve at San Siro.*
528 *The finish at the Gran Premio di Nazioni of 1957: Crevalcore comes in ahead of Tornese, Gelinotte, and Icaro IV.*
529 *One aspect of the Gran Premio di Lotteria di Agnano.*
530 *From the right: Oriolo, Assissi, Gay Song, and Crevalcore racing at San Siro in 1953 for the Premio d'Inverno.*

PART SEVEN

HORSE-DRAWN VEHICLES

I

HISTORY

A discussion of the history and use of horse-drawn vehicles is not only a study of a means of transport but collaterally a history of art and craft, taste, techniques, and industry. Even a survey of the various types of vehicles while properly linked with technical factors, must depend upon aspects of architecture, furnishings, and decoration of the times.

These vehicles (whose locomotion is the horse, either as a carriage or draft animal) can be classified, in accordance with specific function, either as vehicles for the transportation of people or goods; as heavy or light, long- or short-distance carts, or as military, ceremonial, practical, or sporting vehicles. In every age, however, their construction has been based on functional and technical necessities, invariably resulting in creations of striking individuality.

The wheel (or the runner, in the case of a sledge), the type of shaft, and the body (the housing for passengers or merchandise) are the basic construction elements of a vehicle, of which the wheel "can be considered an exemplary product of structural fitness in accordance with its function, as it is also, being circular in form, a practical adaptation of universal iconographic themes in significant ways: It is decorative, symbolic, cosmogonic, and even esoteric" *(Enciclopedia Universale dell'Arte,* under "Vehicle").

The link between mobility and safety in a conveyance is close, and encouraged the development of the vehicle in accordance with terrain and climate. Mobility meant responding to conditions of lightness, firmness, and adaptability in the body, including the proper jointure between the body and its mechanical parts. As in naval architecture, the style in vogue and the structural technicalities of the cart and carriage could not be ignored. Artisans repeated the local taste in the development of the vehicle, but from time to time, autonomous developments crept in. However, the persistence of traditional types persisted. (The primitive cart reproduced the tent or hut; the carriage bore the imprint of a litter, as it was to be with the first automobiles taking the form of the carriage.) Therefore the nineteenth century saw production limited to a few standard types. These were precisely designed, intended for specific functions, and descriptively named: cabriolet, calèche, fiacre, tilbury, d'orsay, all smaller vehicles; and the brougham, break, duchess, victoria, coupé, phaeton, and landau, all larger vehicles. Ceremonial conveyances were conceived primarily as instruments to express preestablished forms. Therefore the structural requirements for transportation were reduced to absolute essentials only. Designed for religious use, or to convey an impression of might, prestige, or opulence, these vehicles through their decorative character quickly assumed symbolic forms.

The search for a balance between expressive and practical functions, with a tendency for the one to glorify the other, was evident in the vehicles that were not strictly ceremonial. Nevertheless, the aesthetic sentiments and social aspirations of the age were illustrated in its vehicles. Consider the carriages of the seventeenth and eighteenth centuries, open, expansive, amorphous, overornamented, gilded, polychromed—typical expressions of baroque feeling and taste; whereas the neoclassic carriage was closed, compact, sparing of ornament, and sober in color, more in line with the elegant practicality of the early nineteenth century. Proof of the relationship of form and aesthetics can be seen in the thematic repertory of the figurative arts, not only in generically descriptive ways, but as typical motifs. These same themes become decoration in Greek vase painting, Roman reliefs, medieval frescoes, sixteenth-century paintings and prints, and so on. The basis for the successive elaboration of the great majority of land vehicles sprang, almost intuitively, from the wheeled cart rather than from manual means of transport, draft on sledges, or pack animals. The phase in which animals gave way to mechanical traction lay in the future, when basic and radical changes in the structure of the vehicle would occur.

The war cart, which was such a decisive factor in the victories of the Aryans over indigenous populations that it was minutely described and technically detailed in sacred writings, disappeared after the fourth century, undoubtedly because of the great attack forces developed by the cavalry, which then became the basis of every military formation; war carts are mentioned in mythology of the era or depicted as the vehicles of the gods, so remote had they become to the common experience of men. During the height of the medieval period, immense processional carts on tiny wheels were illustrated, which must have been barely maneuverable. Such carts are similar to those used in southern India during

531 532 *The horse car of the Gay Nineties.*
533 *A five-horse team (one hidden from view), typical of Hungary.*

531

532

533

the last century, which strongly resembled the cart presented to Elizabeth II on her last voyage to India.

The fusion of the chassis of the oxcart with the wheels of the hunting or war chariot led to a light cart that was in use around the first and second centuries C.E. This model was improved when the body was made independent of the triangular chassis to which the wheels were fixed. With a canopy set high over it, this type of cart is depicted at Angkor Wat, carrying concubines or dancers wearing very high-peaked headdresses. It appears that the body was secured by heavy leather straps attached to curved supports. By the sixteenth century, a type of carriage was introduced in which the body was poised on a number of curved pieces of wood. In Rajasthan such carts, called *ekka,* are still being used today. Carriages of this type, still dear to traditionalists in southern India, can easily mount the ramps that approach the seraglios that are still a part of many of the old royal palaces. Also in the sixteenth century a new sort of wagon was in use in which the body was suspended by two bars coming from the wheels. Four-wheeled carts existed, but were used mainly in processions. Earlier it was not understood how the axles could be connected to the superstructure; but finally, four-wheeled carts with long wood slats used as springs appeared, somewhat adapting a litter and a four-wheeled chassis. In the arts and crafts of Muhammadan culture, four-wheeled carts are extremely rare. A few, in which the body is completely closed and therefore supposedly for ladies, can be seen in twelfth-century miniatures.

Carts appeared in China around the fifteenth century B.C. Legend attributes their invention to the Chinese Second Dynasty. Two- and four-wheeled carts whose fittings and trappings were rich in decoration, and war carts, drawn by a pair or a team of four, all had their period of popularity and glory until the advent of the cavalry. During China's feudal age, ending in the third century B.C., each petty state established a different gauge for the axles of its carts so that those of its enemies would, with difficulty, attempt an advance over its own cart tracks and ways.

Once China was unified in the third century, the emperor Shih Hwangti, of the Ch'in Dynasty, published an edict calling for a standard gauge, so that transport and communications would be facilitated within the empire. Their war carts carried two or three passengers, as well as the driver. A feudal lord's importance was measured in terms of the carts he owned. The cart was also used as a bier in the funeral sevices of the mighty or as an instrument of execution, along with others, when condemned men were torn asunder between them.

A curious type of Japanese cart not only had curving bars or shafts in front, but also in the rear, so that it could either be drawn or propelled.

As for the horse collar, an exact date cannot be established for its invention. It is known that in ancient times the horse was badly harnessed, and the leather strap round his neck was a strain on his throat, limiting his draft capacity. It was not understood then that the horse's strong point lay at his shoulders. Furthermore, the principles of balance and suspension were not particularly well understood either, so that the harness straps at chest and shoulders, lacking elasticity, when a cart had gone downhill invariably ended up at the horse's back and flanks. Whether the invention of the collar was a sudden inspiration, a stroke of genius, or a gradual development, no one knows.

There is evidence, however, that during the medieval period, man usually dragged his loads. To make his job easier, he passed a rudimentary collar, or one might call it a chestband, around one shoulder, as seen illustrated in the Bayeux tapestry. Perhaps when he was more tired than usual, he experimented by placing the band around the neck of a donkey or pony, and, satisfied that the beast would not suffocate, decided to let the animal drag his loads, about five times heavier than he could manage himself. Obviously, in time, the animal would have a callus from the constant friction under this primitive collar. Once the idea of a collar had taken hold, the carts gave way to wagons with larger wheels and more complicated harnesses, enabling merchants to take to roads that grew better and more crowded as a consequence. In the last days of the Middle Ages (horseshoes became more sophisticated, and were ornamented with calks and rosettes) it was discovered that a second pair could be hitched to the first to make a four-horse team, adding additional pairs on the same principle, if it were so desired. At the time, a caravan could take about a month on the Paris–Naples road. Carts even dared cross the Alps and the Apennines. All these improvements, on the one hand leading to a certain amount of unemployment (and a consequent brigandage), since carriers were no longer needed, resulted on the other in a tremendous amount of mercantile and financial activity that was to create the new class of bourgeois capitalists, nurtured by the Renaissance.

When the fall of the Roman Empire led to the devastation of its capital and the disuse and subsequent decay of of its roads, fashionable carriages could no longer be used. However, here still remained the farm wagons, with their solid wooden wheels and movable "panels." These were heavy, crude, but solidly built vehicles, although Venancio Fortunatus tells us of a carriage built in the shape of a tower made of worked silver to carry a princess from Toledo to Rouen. Gregory of Tours mentions carts that could hold a dozen people, and we know that the daughters of Charlemagne traveled in large carriages with arched staves, similar in form to the Roman *carpentum.*

In Oseberg, an eighth-century cart was discovered with short-spoked, wide-rimmed wheels and a body shaped like a cradle suspended on concave supports, a hint of springs to come. From the ninth to the eleventh century, carts were used as wagons for goods as well as carriages for ladies, but it is difficult to determine the types employed. Romanesque and Gothic carts (so referred to since they were works of art) sought new forms. Parisian royal decrees forbade their use by women of the bourgeoisie, reserving them to the nobility. Beatrice, the wife of the first Charles of Anjou, rode into Na-

534 *Opening the season, the Royal Ascot. The Queen, Elizabeth II, accompanied by Prince Philip and the Duke of Gloucester, takes the traditional ride around the track in a landau drawn by four horses.*

535 *An Italian artillery gun carriage of 1902, drawn by a team of six.*

ples in 1307 in a magnificent carriage; and in Milan, Galeazzo Maria Sforza's lady had at least fifteen at her disposal. Most of the carts were very simple, however, consisting of a boxy body closed on three sides and open at the rear, where one entered, differing from the carts of antiquity in that the wheels reached to the sides of the body.

An illustrated cart with a rectangular body topped by a canopy, for one person, frequently appears in Codex 562, dating from the fourteenth century, in the Dijon Library. A cart with awnings and windows that could be opened was already in use for more than two passengers, which was drawn by a team with postilions. This was the German *Kobelwagen* of the fifteenth century, of which a fine example remains in the Johanneum Museum in Graz.

Light carts, quite possibly used for racing, such as that depicted in relief on the campanile of the Hotel Duomo in Florence, had small, boxy bodies mounted on four wheels. In the fourteenth century a basic modification appeared in the more luxurious vehicles—suspension. This can be seen in the cart pictured in Rudolf von Ems's *Weltchronik,* which shows that the body was not placed directly on the axles but on curved iron brackets to reduce shock. The body is shaped like a cradle, and presages the nineteenth-century carriage.

There were mainly two factors that contributed toward what might be called the "modern" carriage and the express wagon: better roads and the technique of springing (probably first developed in Hungary), which resulted in the cab of the vehicle no longer being poised on the framework but suspended above it by means of chains or belts attached to curved supports rising from the chassis. The first spring carriage arrived in the Veneto from the village of Kocs in Hungary, which is pronounced substantially the same way as our coach, its derivative. The springs of the French *chariots branlants* of the late fourteenth century were placed between the chassis and the body, over the axles. Despite these improvements, throughout the fifteenth century, the carriage remained the vehicle of wealthy ladies, whereas men continued to stay with their horses. This arrangement lasted well into the sixteenth century, as is evidenced by Pope Pius IV's advice to cardinals to leave carriages to women and go on horseback, as was consonant with the dignity of the Church. Notwithstanding, the Emperor Frederick III entered Frankfurt in 1475 in a carriage splendidly decorated in the most extravagant Late Gothic style.

The spring carriage finally became a more or less popular vehicle in the sixteenth century. Milan became a great center of production, and had twice the traffic of Paris. By 1525, Milan had more than fifty carriages in use, while Paris had only three in 1550 (obviously, these figures do not include the old carts that had no springs). In addition to their reputation as armorers, the Milanese now became noted for their skill as coachmakers. In 1666, the city had 115 six-horse coaches, 437 four-horse carts, 1,634 two-horse carts, and 1,500 saddle horses. By the end of the eighteenth century, Milan not only had 200 *palazzi,* but 500 citizens who owned carriages drawn by a pair, at least.

Even Venice was full of horses before the flat, wooden bridges were replaced by stone arches and steps. Florence had beautiful carriages and a goodly number of them in the seventeenth century, even in its successive decadent period.

The richest carriages of all, however, were those in Rome around the beginning of the eighteenth century.

Carriages were quick to become identified with their performances; for example, in 1640, a man named Sauvage carried Parisian pilgrims to the sanctuary of Saint-Fiacre de Bris, some twenty-five miles outside the city. Over his place of business he had placed an image of the saint as his sign, which with the passing of time gave the saint's name to the road and, ultimately, the vehicles used for the trip.[*]

From that time on, the fashion for the Parisian fiacre caught on and spread. The omnibus, which was first used in 1825 for urban transport by a Frenchman named Omnés, was soon in competition with steam and, later, electric vehicles. Meanwhile, the fiacres had been equipped with devices that automatically registered the fare for the distance covered—the first taxis.

Along with the spring carriage, the open calèche was also in use, such as the one in which Maximilian II entered Nuremberg, as depicted in a watercolor by Jost Amman, which started the fashion for the so-called imperial. This was an open carriage with a boxy body topped by a canopy, an extremely costly and luxurious vehicle, highly decorated and finished in gold, silver, and damask, but, necessarily, a slow one.

It was only in the seventeenth century that a definite "European" form of the carriage came into existence, a more or less standard model that showed small variations from country to country. The smaller front wheels gave the

[*] It is generally accepted that the Hôtel Saint-Fiacre, a Paris inn known to hire out small hackney coaches (c. 1640), is responsible for the name of the coach.—EDS.

536 *Royal Mail coach.*
537 *Sidelight britchka.*
538 *Traveling britchka.*
539 *Phaeton.*
540 *Brougham chariot.*
541 *A Royal Mail timetable.*
542 *Town chariot.*
543 *A Russian sleigh depicted in an old print.*
544 *The perils of sleighing, from an old print.*
545 *Giovanni Fattori depicts a farmer's cart and cavalrymen.*
546 *The standard of Ur: mosaic and shells. The first representation of four-wheeled carts, circa 2600 B.C., drawn by what are probably onagers.*
547 *A pilentum coach, or luxury fiacre.*
548 *A D'Orsay curricle.*
549 *A nineteenth-century print by Adam showing a seventeenth-century coach.*
550 *A wine merchant near Rome, depicted in 1830.*
551 *A coupé with a sharp-angled body to allow for full-length doors.*
552 *The Edinburgh Express.*
553 *A troika on the steppes.*
554 *The Royal Telegraph Manchester Day Coach (186 miles in 18 hours!).*

536

537

538

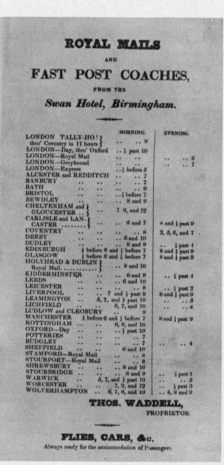

ROYAL MAILS

AND

FAST POST COACHES,

FROM THE

Swan Hotel, Birmingham.

	MORNING.	EVENING.
LONDON TALLY-HO! } thro' Coventry in 11 hours }	 8	
LONDON—Day, thro' Oxford	.. ½ past 10	
LONDON—Royal Mail	.. ..	 6
LONDON—Greyhound	.. ..	 7
LONDON—Express	.. ½ before 5	
ALCESTER and REDDITCH	 7	
BANBURY	 7	
BATH	 9	
BRISTOL	.. ½ before 7	
BEWDLEY	.. 8 and 9	
CHELTENHAM and } GLOUCESTER .. }	.. 7, 9, and 12	
CARLISLE and LAN- } CASTER .... }	.. 6 and 7	8 and ½ past 9
COVENTRY	 8	2, 5, 6, and 7
DERBY	.. 6 and 10	
DUDLEY	.. 8 and 9	.. ½ past 4
EDINBURGH	½ before 6 and ½ before 7	8 and ½ past 9
GLASGOW	½ before 6 and ½ before 7	8 and ½ past 9
HOLYHEAD & DUBLIN } Royal Mail .... }	.. 8 and 10	
KIDDERMINSTER	.. 8 and 9	.. ½ past 4
LEEDS	.. 6 and 10	
LEICESTER	 8	.. ½ past 2
LIVERPOOL	7 and ½ past 8	8 and ½ past 9
LEAMINGTON	5, 7, and ½ past 10	 5
LICHFIELD	.. 6, 7, and 10	 4
LUDLOW and CLEOBURY	 9	
MANCHESTER	½ before 6 and ½ before 7	8 and ½ past 9
NOTTINGHAM	.. 6, 8, and 10	
OXFORD—Day	.. ½ past 10	
POTTERIES	 7	
RUDGLEY	 7	 4
SHEFFIELD	.. 6 and 10	
STAMFORD—Royal Mail	 8	
STOURPORT—Royal Mail	 9	
SHREWSBURY	.. 8 and 10	
STOURBRIDGE	.. 8 and 9	
WARWICK	5, 7, and ½ past 10	.. ½ past 4
WORCESTER	.. 7, 9, and 12	.. ½ past 3
WOLVERHAMPTON	.. 6, 7, 8, and 10	.. 4, 8 and 9

THOS. WADDELL,

PROPRIETOR.

FLIES, CARS, &c.

Always ready for the accommodation of Passengers.

539

540

541

542

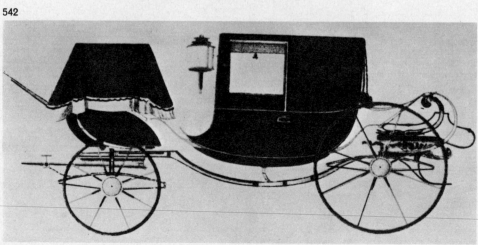

543

544

545

546

547   548

549

550   551

552

553

554

555

556

557

vehicle more mobility; the springing system was improved; and the hood of the cab was slanted forward. The carriage known as "half-open," which continued in use in countries with mild climates right down to the eighteenth century, was replaced in countries with severe weather by closed vehicles with glass windows. The oldest example that has been preserved is the one at the Moscow Arsenal that belonged to Czar Alexei Mihailovich, dating from 1658.

From that period, one can really begin to talk of definite and specific shape and form for each carriage, its construction no longer masked by padding and upholstery, but emphasized by ornament and decoration. Horse-drawn vehicles became luxury objects. Books were published on decorating carriages, books such as *Nouveaux Dessins pour Orner et Emblèmer les Carrosses et Chaises Roulantes* (New Designs for Decorating and Ornamenting Carriages and Wheeled Chairs), with drawings by La Pautre, published in Paris by Mariette, in 1670, as well as Morort's coach models for George III of England.

No examples remain of the Italian open carriages, although it is not difficult to deduce, from descriptions, how fabulous they must have been. Flanked by scrolls and festoons in paint and carved wood, or surmounted by sculptured, allegorical figures, they were substantially frames for the passengers they carried, almost in triumph. These cars were fashioned by skilled craftsmen from artists' plans and designs.

During the reign of Louis XIV, France became the leading country in constructing and decorating coaches, as it remained throughout the eighteenth century, when England took the lead. As a model of this type of luxurious vehicle, there is the so-called Great Coach used on solemn occasions in Paris for the Spanish ambassador. This was designed in 1714 by Bernard Picard, and has all the characteristics of the French regency and rococo styles. In the classic type of closed coach, the fabulous ornamentation became almost an end in itself and burgeoned in elegant, flowing forms that covered the structural elements of the coach. An example, and a notable one, is the carriage given the Pope by João IV of Portugal in 1715, still preserved in Lisbon. Another is the coach used at the coronation of Charles VII, dating from 1741, to be seen in Monaco. A third precious example of this genre is the coach of Catherine II of Russia, whose sides are completely covered with picturesque detail, on exhibition in Leningrad.

The next vehicle to catch the fancy of the smart set was the berlin, which was distinguished by its two long axles in place of four short ones. There was also the open phaeton, the pet of the *jeunesse dorée* of Paris, which was already in style in 1620 in a version that had four or eight seats, a high coach body, and large front wheels. From the phaeton, modified to a coupé, the next step was the calèche, whose most elegant version was to be the cabriolet.

A decided change in concept came during the reign of Louis XVI. The heavy, imposing parade coaches were set aside for more functional, lighter, and more maneuverable coaches. As a consequence, technical details became much better and more important, with a corresponding diminution in decoration and art for art's sake. The era of practicality had arrived. Since there are none more practical, in a mechanical sense, than the English, or more willing to gainsay frills and furbelows, it was inevitable that the English coachmakers should come into their own at this time. They became known for their light, sporty vehicles, while the Neapolitans once again achieved primacy as the fabricators of carriages to the traditional old, conservative European taste, particularly berlins, free of any decoration, which, in time, became an international style. The coachmakers of Naples, however, still had their more fantastic moments when they designed and made such fancies and anachronisms as the Egyptian "coach" for Queen Maria Cristina of Sardinia, designed in 1819, by Pregliasco, preserved in Florence, or the neo-baroque parade coach of Ludwig II of Bavaria, made in 1870, and now on display in Monaco.

One can conjecture whether the horse as motive power might not have come to the end of his era much earlier if the French Revolution had not completely upset the plans and experiments of Joseph Cugnot, who, it was widely known, was hard at work on producing a steam carriage. There was, in truth, a continual effort made to substitute other power for the horse's locomotion. The Restoration in France, however, gave the horse a stay, and saw the carriage even more triumphant as a means of transportation and a mark of elegance for the *haute monde*. English and German coachmakers turned out an endless parade of landaus, tilburys, berlins, brakes, and victorias, all light and smart, while their governments improved the roads and means of communication.

Special breeds were selected to be carriage horses, depending upon whether they had to draw light or heavy loads, and whether they were expected to go fast or at a fairly leisurely pace. The most popular were the Boulogne, Ardennes, Suffolk, Belgian, and Clydesdales, particularly for heavy draft.

Meanwhile, experiments were going on to make delivery of mail by coach better and more efficient, particularly over long distances. In 1828, France settled upon a model for its nineteenth-century postal diligence, as it came to be known. This was a composite monster made up of a coupé attached to a berlin, called the *intérieure,* followed by a gondola, known as the *rotonde,* with a tilbury before and a cabriolet behind that, which later was changed to an imperial, finished off by an open cart for baggage, in all, about a ton or more of wood on four wheels. Six horses drew the diligence at an average of about four miles an hour around 1830, a speed that increased to an average of about six miles an hour by 1848. The London-Brighton diligence later moved up to about ten miles an hour.

Among the most popular horse-drawn vehicles in use during the nineteenth century and the early part of our own were the following:

BAROUCHE   A four-wheeled, one-horse carriage, the rear wheels larger than the front, with an outside seat for the driver

555 *An eight-horse team driven by Count Belloni.*
556 *A print by Bailly: "The Arrival of the Stagecoach." Louvre, Paris.*
557 *A brougham chariot in an Adam drawing.*

up front, and facing front and rear seats inside for four passengers, with a folding bonnet top over the rear seat.

BERLIN   A large, closed four-wheeled carriage, the two front wheels lower, with front and rear facing seats, each accommodating a single passenger. The berlin, which was named for the city where it was designed and first made, was driven by a man sitting up front on a box. The body hung between two perches. The berlin had glass windows, and was drawn by one horse.

BREAK   A four-wheeled vehicle, the front pair lower than the rear, with a shaft, called a "perch," extending from the front axle to the rear. Originally used to break a horse to harness, it was later adapted, by adding seats for driver and passengers, as a light sporting vehicle drawn by four horses or ponies.

BROUGHAM   Named for Lord Brougham (1778–1868), the English statesman, who inspired its design with his suggestion for a relatively small and light four-wheeled one-horse carriage, with a boxlike body, for two or four passengers, the driver sitting on an outside front seat. A most popular vehicle, the Brougham, colloquially known as a "brum" to the English, lent itself to infinite variations, according to use; so there were depot broughams, bachelor's broughams, miniature and country broughams, among others. The brougham is still used abroad in many countries as an urban sightseeing vehicle, and one always appealing to tourists.

BUCKBOARD   One of the most popular general-utility vehicles in the American countryside, the buckboard was a four-wheeled vehicle that, in its original version, had a seat mounted on a board bolted to the front and rear axles. It was devoid of springs. Later, a fairly springy board or a lattice frame was used to compensate for the lack of springs. The buckboard was often drawn by a pair. Some of the later models were equipped with a rumble seat between the two rear wheels. Some of the more sophisticated versions, which were infinitely more comfortable over a long trip or rough country than some of the spring vehicles of its day, were braced to lessen jarring and shock.

BUGGY   The American buggy, which came in many versions for a variety of uses, was basically a light, four-wheeled carriage with a single seat, and a transverse spring—its most characteristic feature. One can still order a new buggy, namely the type traditionally used by the Amish; forbidden to operate or ride in motorcars, the Amish still depend upon the buggy for transportation. A common type of covered buggy had a collapsible top called *ex post facto*—the automobile top—which was the covering adopted for the first covered motorcars. For more dash and maneuverability, the cut-under buggy was devised. This had an arch in the body below the seat that permitted clearance when a wheel was turned sharply toward the body, making it possible to cut corners close. A popular vehicle for traveling salesmen and drummers was the business buggy, often with rattan bodywork, which had a roomy section behind the seat for baggage, sample cases, and the like. An early version of the buggy, the Jenny Lind, named in honor of the Swedish Nightingale, had a fixed top, and usually was fancifully painted and decorated. The English buggy was a light, two-wheeled open carriage, drawn by one horse.

CABRIOLET   A two-wheeled, one-horse light carriage with a rear seat for two passengers and rear platform for a driver or "tiger" (groom).

CALASH   A four-wheeled, one-horse carriage, almost identical to the barouche, but generally having four low wheels. Also called by its original French name, *calèche,* which term, however, is generally reserved for a two-wheeled carriage, as described below.

CALÈCHE   A two-wheeled, one-horse carriage, with a folding bonnet top, a rear seat for two passengers, and a seat on the splashboard for the driver. This is sometimes called a calash, improperly.

CHAISE   Invariably known as a "shay" to Americans, with whom it was very popular, the chaise was a two-wheeled one-horse vehicle, very light, with a folding top, and its body swung on rudimentary "springs" stretching from a point before the wheels to the upturned rear ends of the shafts.

CHARABANC   Actually, a break, this vehicle was long, light, and open on all sides, although occasionally an awning supported by four poles was placed over the ranks of transversal seats. Four-wheeled, the charabanc was drawn by one horse. It was much used as a species of country omnibus and sightseeing vehicle, so that even today, the English often refer to a modern bus, generically, as a charabanc.

CLARENCE   Often called a "full clarence," was named for the Duke of Clarence (1765–1837), later William IV. This was a four-wheeled, one-horse carriage, built with a wickerwork body or cane panels around the 1830's, when it was much in vogue, then later with the usual coachwork and a curved glass front. The carriage accommodated from two to four passengers on a single upholstered seat across the back and, below the curved glass front, inside, two more passengers on a jump seat. The driver rode outside.

COUPÉ   A four-wheeled one-horse vehicle with a boxlike body, the coupé derived its name from the French for "cut," since it resembled a coach cut in half. Coupés were quite similar to sedan-broughams. The American version of the coupé usually had a curved glass front, which gave it the appearance of a boxy clarence, with one wide seat for adults, and a hinged or jump seat for a child, facing the rear, below the glass. The driver rode outside, of course, on a high front perch.

558   *A matched pair steps out in Milan.*
559   *Blessington, introduced into the Royal Stables in 1838, stands outside Buckingham Palace.*
560   *The coach used by Queen Victoria and the Prince Consort when they visited Dublin in 1852. It belonged to Hutton, the Lord Mayor.*
561   *Queen Elena of Italy and the Princess of Belgium in Rome in a barouche belonging to the Crown.*

558

559

560

561

562

563

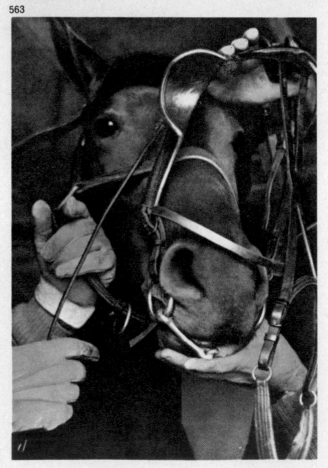

564

DOG CART Not pulled by dogs, but designed to carry dogs to the hunt, with seats for two to four passengers, arranged back to back, the two-wheeled dog cart was drawn by one horse. With ample storage space in the body, this cart later became a very popular, fashionable general-purpose country vehicle.

DONKEY CART An English specialty, with a slatted body and two lengthwise seats, the donkey cart was very popular for use by children. It was often called a pony cart or a tub cart, and was drawn by a pony.

GOVERNESS CART Like the donkey cart, the governess cart was primarily designed for children and their companions or was driven by a child and drawn by a pony—in lieu of the slightly larger and heavier pony cart. The two-wheeled governess cart usually had a flaring basketwork body, making it look somewhat like a laundry basket on wheels, and was entered from the rear. Inside were two lengthwise seats.

HANSOM Also called a hansom cab, after its inventor, the English architect J. A. Hansom (1803–1882). A low-hung, two-wheeled, one-horse, covered vehicle, designed for two passengers. The driver was placed on an elevated seat behind, with the reins running over the roof. The cab was equipped with a sliding hatch in the roof through which the passengers could give instructions to the driver. The hansom was undoubtedly the most common hackney cab employed in large cities like New York and London.

JOGGING CART A very light, skeletal two-wheeler, frequently having a slat bottom, the jogging cart was made to carry one or two people, and was designed primarily for exercising horses and for employment in light country work. Jogging carts are still made as exercise carts for trotters and pacers.

LADIES' STANHOPE A four-wheeled, one-horse vehicle, the rear wheels larger than the front, for one passenger. Similar to a buggy but more elegant and stylish, and specifically designed to be handled easily by a woman in urban traffic.

LANDAU The distinctive feature of the landau, which was named for the Bavarian town in which it was first made, was its double top, either part of which might be opened or closed individually. The landau was a heavy four-wheeled vehicle often driven with team of six horses. A two-seated carriage, it accommodated about four passengers, two abreast, facing each other, and had a front seat for the driver, as well.

LANDAULETTE Often driven with a team, the landaulette derived from the landau, and differed from it in usually having a folding top only at the rear. Some landaulettes had removable solid fronts, and round-front types, which presaged the convertible motorcar, had rounded front sections that could be lowered when the weather permitted.

562 *"The Difficulties of Travel," an English print of 1828.*
563 *Placing bit and bridle on a colt, just as Xenophon advocated.*
564 *First lessons for a draft colt.*

PHAETON Originally a four-wheeled, one-horse carriage, generally without a top, with a bootlike body with a seat for one or two passengers and a separate seat up front for the driver, the phaeton took on a variety of forms with time and use. Another basic design with the same name, much in vogue in the United States, was a four-wheeled carriage with open sides and a folding top with a single seat that accommodated the driver and/or another passenger. The basket phaeton was a light vehicle for two, without a top, but sometimes equipped with a single rumble seat. The body was of wickerwork. Types like the light drop-front phaeton, which accommodated two people, varied widely in style and in the design of the top, which could be a canopy, umbrella, or bow type. The six-passenger canopy-top phaeton had a rear compartment, with two seats, each running the width of the vehicle and accommodating two persons, facing each other, as well as a front seat, back to back with the rear-racing seat behind for the driver and another passenger. The top was removable. Typical of the golden age of the carriage-makers (the late nineteenth century) were such stylish vehicles as the ladies' driving phaeton, the stanhope phaeton, and the spider phaeton. The ladies' phaetons, very elegant in appearance, often had rattan work on the sides of the seats, or caned panels, a sweeping dashboard, and sometimes a parasol top. Often drawn by a pair, for style, the ladies' driving phaeton could be equipped with a skeleton rumble seat at the rear to carry a footman. The spider phaeton was the masculine counterpart of the ladies' driving phaeton, a fashionable vehicle for gentleman, with a skeleton rumble seat for a footman. Often, vehicles of this type had intricately curved iron frames or body loops from front to rear. The stanhope phaeton was generally designed for two persons, but it did have two more seats in the back. Side panels, often cut rather low, were frequently partly caned.

STANHOPE GIG A two-wheeled light open vehicle, usually hung on four springs, designed like a tandem, having a high seat for one passenger. Named for Fitzroy Stanhope (1787 to 1864), an English clergyman, this rig was used extensively in England and the eastern United States. It still sees occasional use at horse shows, where it is employed to show one or a tandem of hackney ponies or horses.

STANHOPE PHAETON A four-wheeled carriage, the two front wheels being smaller, which could be drawn by one or two horses, and was usually used by two people, but had a fairly ample rumble seat in the rear for another couple. This phaeton had a collapsible top covering the front seats.

SULKY Still in use today for harness racing, this is a light, open, two-wheeled one-horse vehicle, actually little more than a seat mounted at the curve of a U-shaped shaft. A modern type used for racing has wheels that are 26 or 28 inches high with a 53-inch track. Height of the vehicle under the arch (curve of the U) is 27 inches, and the shafts measure 87 inches from tip to arch.

SURREY Taking its name from the English county where it was first used, this four-wheeled vehicle was one of the most popular in England and the United States. It was designed to carry four. Whether with fringe on top, an automobile top, or devoid of top, the surrey was characterized by its two forward-facing seats. Surreys generally were drawn by a single horse, as well as by a pair. A lighter version, drawn by a pair of ponies, was very popular. The fringed-top surrey was a family favorite, usually well upholstered, carpeted, equipped with oil lamps, rather rakish fenders, and, often, a leather dashboard. The automobile top was collapsible, and would be folded back in good weather.

TANDEM   Also known as a tandem gig. A two-wheeled vehicle with a very high seat for two passengers. Light, open, and dashing, the tandem was considered by many conservative drivers to be unsafe, particularly since it was much employed as a sporting vehicle in the country, over uneven terrain, since its high seat made it rather topheavy and unstable. The tandem could be drawn by a single horse or a pair "in line," that is, head to tail, with the use of a tandem hitch, thus the phrase "in tandem."

TILBURY   Similar to a break, the tilbury was a light, open, single-passenger, two-wheeled one-horse carriage, designed by the nineteenth-century English coachmaker for whom it was named.

TRAP   A vehicle with an unusual body arrangement, the trap, at least in the American version (the British trap was a light two-wheeled vehicle), presaged the coach-model motorcar in that it had a divided front seat that could be folded forward to permit access to the back seat. Designed for four people, the trap could be equipped with a canopy top. A version known as the Essex trap permitted passengers to ride back to back or to face forward. In all traps, however, the rear seats were always reached through the front.

II
COACH HORSES

Though a horse is capable of great exertion in getting a vehicle into motion, such exertion is remarkably reduced immediately thereafter. A horse can pull a load five or six times his own weight—a horse weighing 1,200 pounds can easily pull about 6,000 pounds at a walk at the speed of a few miles an hour for about ten hours. If the road is especially good, and the horse strong, the weight may go much higher. A large Belgian, for example, can pull a load weighing 10,000 pounds for ten hours. Attached to a coach, a horse of average stature can pull about 1,000 pounds, excluding the weight of the carriage, and travel at a trot of about five to ten miles an hour or more for five hours. The incline of the shafts, the height of the wheels, the width of the wheel rims, the rut, the tread of the vehicle, as well as the disposition of the harnessed horse, decide the ease by which a load is pulled.

Though in the past it was thought that horizontal shafts parallel to the horse's chest were the most advantageous, experience and mathematics conclude that it is better to arrange the shafts obliquely, lower than the chest.

The horse uses his weight and muscular strength to pull a load. When a powerful but not greatly energetic horse is used, the greatest amount of work is achieved if the shafts are inclined about twelve degrees; if the incline were greater,

part of the strength expended by the animal would be spread out to lift the load, and if the shafts were inclined toward the horse, part of his energy would be lost in keeping the vehicle on the ground. Thus it is advisable to increase the angle of the shafts during ascension.

The wheels, consisting of the hub at the center, and rims and spokes extending from the hub to the rim, must be light, with a degree of flexibility and elasticity. When the parts of the wheel are not in proper proportion to each other, it is very difficult to move at all. Low wheels make the load heavier; if too high, they drain off energy in traction.

III
HARNESSES

There are various types of harnesses, those for carriages and those used in hauling. Carriage harnesses are of two types, the collar harness and the breast harness. These last two are the most common not only because they are inexpensive and light but also because of their adaptability to horses of different conformation. If, however, a great deal of energy is required, collar harnesses are more suitable because while breast harnesses utilize the motor power of the forequarters in limited amounts, collar harnesses allow the horse to utilize to the utmost all his energy. Therefore the collar allows the animal to pull with all his weight should it be necessary.

Moreover, the point at which the shafts are attached is some distance from the ground, so that the incline is greater, facilitating the hauling of a load. Finally, the collar serves to protect the horse from any injury by the shafts, as well as being more suitable for heavy loads, long distances, and ascent and descent.

The collar harness consists of a bridle, collar (as well as the two shafts), the girth and its parts, the crupper, kicking strap, breeching, and reins. The bridle has many parts, such as the crownpiece, browband, two snaffle cheekpieces with rings, two curb cheekpieces, throat latch, noseband, bit and side check. The two staffs in a harness bit are longer than on a bit used for saddle horses.

1. Crownpiece	10. Reins
2. Browband	11. Collar
3. Cheekpiece (snaffle)	12. Martingale
4. Cheekpiece (curb)	13. Girth
5. Throat latch	14. Backband
6. Noseband	15. Crupper
7. Bit	16. Loin straps
8. Snaffle	17. Breeching
9. Side check	18. Shaft

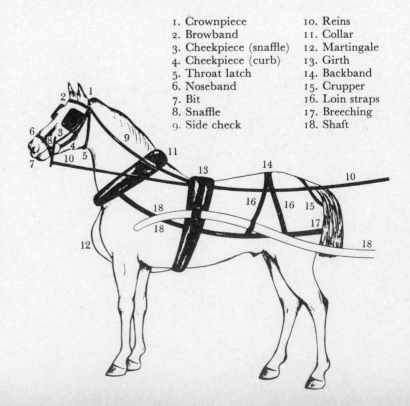

PART EIGHT

SPORT ON HORSEBACK

I
POLO

When Lieutenant Joseph F. Sherer, on duty in West Pakistan, saw his first game of polo one day in 1854, at the invitation of the Maharaja of Lahore, his sporting blood was so stirred by the spectacle that he resolved he and his comrades would have to learn to play the game immediately. Amused, yet delighted by his enthusiasm, the maharaja remarked, "Remember, Lieutenant, we have been at this for two thousand years."

The maharaja was not exaggerating; the origins of polo are lost in time. Even the name of the game is the subject of a good deal of etymological conjecture. Does it come from the Tibetan word *pulu,* used to describe a ball made of a round root? Or does it derive from *palas,* the Persian word for a slow-burning wood from which the balls were made? The incandescent balls could be seen and followed during the course of nighttime ceremonial play.

According to legend, the game derives from the Tibetan custom of hunting a species of muskrat in the fall. The animal was pursued on horseback, harried to keep it from returning to its hole, and chased until it succumbed from exhaustion and the blows of the hunters' clubs. During the summer when these animals had migrated to the safety of inaccessible regions, the hunters diverted themselves in mock hunts in which they pursued a ball fashioned from a round root *(pulu)* or goathide. According to this story, Tibet would appear to be the birthplace of polo. We have definite evidence that around 525 the word *chaugan,* hitherto used in Persia to describe a light mace or a mallet, began to assume another meaning—"a sport or game." By extension we might assume that the sport referred to was polo.

Polo was fairly widely known in the fourth century B.C., as evidenced by a gift from Darius III to Alexander the Great as Alexander was about to invade Persia. Darius sent him a ball and mallet with an invitation to play a game more appropriate to his age. Alexander thanked the Persian for the gift, but explained that as far as he was concerned, the ball represented the earth, and he had no intention of letting the mallet slip from his hand. (He defeated Darius in 333.)

It appears that at that period polo was played with from fifty to a hundred men, and invariably ended in a free-for-all, if not an outright battle. We have a wealth of evidence in literature, sculpture, and ceramic art that polo was popular in China, Turkestan, and, of course, Persia, and had spread as far east as Japan, down to Egypt, west to Constantinople, but no farther until its English "discovery" in India during the nineteenth century.

The Persian poet Abul Firdausi, wrote of polo while at the court of the sultan around 1005: "On a little street in Lahore's Anarkalli bazaar, you can still see the tomb of Sultan Qutub Uddin Albaq, to whom we owe the road built from Qutub to Delhi, and who died playing polo, falling from his favorite pony."

The mogul emperor Akbar the Great (1542–1605) was extremely fond of the game, and drew up the rules for polo matches to be played by ten to twelve men. He was convinced that polo called for the highest sort of courage, and insisted that his officials play it with speed, decision, and good sportsmanship. In Mongolia, polo was played on mules or small horses. What the game lacked in speed it gained in deftness required of its players.

Notwithstanding the maharaja's comment, Lieutenant Sherer and a friend, Captain Stewart, immediately attempted to form a team, and by 1859 they were well enough along to found the first polo club at Cachar, India. In 1863, the Calcutta Polo Club was established, and the game was played for the first time in public at Christmas. It was taken up rapidly by the English officers garrisoned in India, and officially recognized by and opened to British civil personnel, as well.

The first European game was played in 1869 between officers of the 10th Hussars at Aldershot, Hampshire, and a match was played between them and the 9th Lancers in 1871. In 1870, a tournament was run at Richmond Park with teams from ten regiments participating. The first game played for the general public in England took place at Hurlingham, in 1874. In Australia the game began in 1883. France saw its first match in Dieppe in 1895, and three years later the Club de Bagatelle came into existence in Paris, with the Viscount de la Rochefoucauld as president. Spain had begun playing polo a few years before the game was introduced into France, and some of the Spaniards helped launch the new Parisian club.

The Player

Polo requires of a rider complete mastery of his horse, a very light hand, and great dexterity with the mallet, aside from the tactics and strategy he must learn through experience. The ball, a moving object, must be hit to a determined point while he controls and directs his horse, all the while defending himself, his mount, and the ball from an opposing player who is attempting to recover the ball and play it otherwise.

Polo equitation is different from all other types of riding. As a matter of fact, polo has its own "school" and seat. The rider should be well on the fork, down in the saddle, his seat completely independent of the action of his chest, arms, and hands, which last must also manipulate the mallet. The horse should be unrestrained and left to move freely whenever maximum speed is required of him, but tightly controlled whenever he must be made to change direction or hold back. Accordingly, the bit for a polo pony must be fairly hard and unyielding, which means that it should be employed with a great deal of delicacy and sensitivity, particularly at the moment the player is about to hit the ball.

Changes in the horse's center of gravity should be impelled for the most part by the player's changing chest position. Furthermore, the fork should cling closely to the saddle so that the rider can command the animal forcefully at all times while maintaining maximum stability against the impact of inevitable brushes from other riders and their mounts and, when necessary, in hitting the ball, to be in a position to thrust himself completely out of the saddle.

The Pony

A horse used for polo, invariably called a pony, must have the courage to move forward at full speed against an opposing team and prepare himself to sustain the shock of physical encounter. He must be flexible and completely responsive so that he can pursue the ball, pull up short, thrust to left or right, take off without hesitation, and have the intelligence to grasp the game to a point where he almost instinctively seconds his rider or even anticipates him.

A polo pony will play well if he is trained to perfection in practice sessions, and will achieve that perfection if his muscles, particularly those of hindquarters, shoulders and neck, and jaws, are properly developed. Work on the longe is very effective, as much for those horses that have a tendency to toss their heads as for those that let them hang low, tucked under. Work should begin at the walk, on elastic side reins, first at a slow gait, the reins progressively growing shorter and shorter until the horse's neck is completely curved.

Once this longe work has been completed, the trainer should mount and, using the same mouthpiece as will be worn in the game, work the horse first at a walk, then at a quick trot, directing him more with the legs than the hands, and have him make turns and half turns, using only the single rein on the neck, stopping him now and again for some paces backward. A horse worked in this manner will respond naturally to the rider's requests without throwing his head back or under, but will stretch his neck and shoulders without throwing his weight to the hindquarters. They begin to play from five to seven years of age.

The Game

An outdoor polo field is a rectangle measuring 160 yards (200 if without boards) by 300 yards. Safety zones surround the grassy and level playing field. At either end are goal posts, 10 feet high and 24 feet wide. Ten-feet-high boards keep the ball on the field. The ball (3¼ inches in diameter) is of solid willow root or a similar hardwood, painted a glossy white. Indoor courts are considerably smaller, with wall stripes

for goal posts, and the ball resembles a miniature white soccer ball. There are three players to a team.

Four men compose an outdoor team. The captain, Number 1, is generally the best player, a master of tactics and horsemanship, and clever at setting up shots for the man following him, who will complete them. Number 2 should be the fastest member of the team and the most skillful at hitting the ball. Since he has the most fatiguing job of all, he should have a large string of horses. The defense man is Number 3, and Number 4, or the back, guards the goal, as in soccer or hockey. The captain also serves as team coach. Substitutions are permitted only in cases of injury.

Each player, as a measure of his ability, has a handicap, varying between 0 and 10 goals (representing their expectations), with the combined total representing the team handicap. The stronger team gives the weaker the difference between their two handicaps. Standard equipment includes a brimmed helmet, a mallet, and the usual riding gear.

At the start of a game, the captains toss a coin to choose their respective goals, and the players take their positions—the captains at the cross marking the center of the field, facing the center of the grandstand (if there is one), followed by the Number 2 men a few yards behind, then the defense; and the goalies take wing positions behind them on the side of their own goal. Referees are in front of the teams, at the edge of the field to begin with, then, after one referee tosses the ball between the opposing teams, starting the game, the two trot to positions where they can best follow the play. The clock starts the moment the ball is put into play by the referee. Each back line is also watched by a judge at the goal. These judges stay outside the field itself, indicating each goal scored by waving a white flag.

A match lasts sixty minutes, and is divided into eight periods known as "chukkers," each 7½ minutes long. A referee signals the end of each chukker by blowing his whistle, terminating any play in course. In short matches, generally games between friendly amateur teams, only four chukkers are played (as in indoor polo) and the handicap is proportionately reduced. After each goal, play once again commences from the center of the field, with the teams exchanging sides. If no goal is made, sides are exchanged at half-time.

When first organized in modern times polo was played individually, but in time it became a team sport. At the

565 *The Four Horsemen in the Commentary of St. Beatus of Lichbar, written about 776, one of the first graphic representations of saddles with stirrups. British Museum, London.*

566 *Boots and saddles in a painting by Sokolov, dated 1870.*

567 *Sixteenth-century bits.*

568 *Antique saddles: a man's dress-parade saddle, a selle à piquer, ladies' saddles with cushioned seats, and a sidesaddle with a fork. Hermès Collection, Paris.*

569 *Antique stirrups and bits. Shop signs, muzzles, Queen Isabella's stirrup irons (on the fourth shelf), the stirrups used by Napoleon II, bits from the eighth century B.C., "chicken-leg" bits dating from the seventeenth century, and the cartridge box of the Empress Eugénie. Hermès Collection, Paris.*

565

566

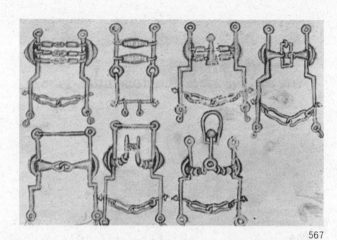

beginning of Western play, eight men comprised a team, then five, and finally four.

Official regulations for European and American polo are published by the Hurlingham Polo Club in London. These rules are aimed at minimizing the effects of collisions that can so easily occur when two teams are in pursuit of a ball (weighing up to 4¼ ounces, measuring up to 3¼ inches, made of wood or willow root) and to safeguard the right of the man who is correctly mounted to hit it. Playing under such rules, only experience suffices; theory is not enough.

In general, the regulations cover situations in which the ball may be touched or carried off; which of two players pursuing the ball has the right to hit it, and so on. Each infraction is scored as a foul; penalties may be stopping the game, a free goal to the injured team, a free hit, or retiring the offending player. Penalties are imposed by a referee, who may allow as many as sixty yards. No player is permitted to block another—the rider following the ball has the right of way—or to play with the left hand. Body blocking, however, is allowed if done with the shoulder. A match terminates with the ringing of a bell or, if there is overtime, until the first goal has been made.

Olympic Polo

Polo was introduced at the 1908 Olympics, dropped until the 1920 Antwerp Olympic games (both won by Great Britain), and played again in Paris in 1924 and in Berlin in 1936. In 1908, competing countries were Ireland and Great Britain; in 1920, Spain, the United States, Great Britain, and Belgium; in 1924, Argentina, the United States, Great Britain, Spain, and France. The last occasion was a tremendous success, combining spectacle and drama. Five nations were represented: Argentina, England, Germany, Hungary, and Mexico. The games shattered certain erroneous preconceptions: that English players were invincible and English ponies mandatory (the larger Argentine mounts were quicker off the mark, generally faster, and infinitely more efficient); that polo players needed at least three descendants of nobility to qualify for a team; and that even the spectators were to be of the elite. (Argentina took the prize the last two years.)

United States

Polo has been played in the United States since 1876, when it was introduced by the famous publisher of the *New York Herald*, James Gordon Bennett. The earliest known game was played in New York City at Dickel's Riding Academy, and some time afterward a match was held outdoors at the Polo Grounds, the one-time home of the former New York Giants baseball team.

A traditional competition between the United States and England derived from the Westchester Cup matches first played in 1886 at Newport, Rhode Island. The United States

570 571 *Beautifully decorated Slavic trappings dating from about the thirteenth century.*

continued to play in international competition, against such teams as Argentina and Mexico as well as England.

Polo's most celebrated player was Thomas Hitchcock, Jr., who played against England five times and Argentina twice. The United States Polo Association remains the governing body for polo here, and is located in Chicago.

Argentina

Polo is an extremely popular sport in the Argentine, and is played by every class of society. The game is characterized by a peculiar violence that distinguishes it from the European type. This springs from the players' temperaments and the great maneuverability of their horses. Naturally, their handling of their mounts is crude but highly effective, and though scarcely "horsemanly," they are quite spectacular. Notwithstanding, some of their polo ponies are admirably trained, and are still run through an entire match at sixteen years of age.

Australia

A variety of polo is played in Australia. Imported from England, it spread throughout the continent, though it never really caught on but declined into a sort of indoor polo. Here the mallet terminates in a slack net, similar to that used in lacrosse, and is employed in scooping up and throwing the ball. The Australian game, played with three men on a team, was invented by a Mr. Hirst who transformed a species of basketball-on-horseback into a game played on an outdoor field. In place of net baskets he substituted goals similar to the classic polo type, differing only in dimensions. He completely changed the penalty system, and consequently, most of the rules.

The ball is inflated leather or rubber, with a certain amount of bounce. Players are required to adhere to the rules on passing (the ball must travel in accordance with players' positions on the field until the lead player can score a goal). The fact that the ball can be scooped up and held in the mallet-racquet permits plays unknown in classic polo (carrying the ball to a better position on the field and throwing from that point while the rest of the team is strategically positioned to pick it up and bounce it off the ground for another shot). The game is easier than its classic forebear, and has spread through New Zealand, South Africa, and Canada.

Japan

Polo has been played in Japan since the fifth century C.E. It was called *dakiu*, and had very old rules. Today the game is played by five men on a team, dressed in traditional raiment, who arrange themselves in a line and proceed around the entire field to pay ceremonious respects to the judges' stand and the public. Each team's objective is to hit a number of different-colored balls through a hole in a wooden fence surrounding the field. The balls are distributed around the field, and appropriate clubs are used. Points are announced to the sound of a gong and a roll of the drums, each method reserved for a team. If a player violates the rules, he is retired from the field, and can have no substitute. At the end of a match, the losers follow the winners off the field.

Italy

Discounting sporadic experiments with the game during the start of the century by a group of aristocratic sportsmen, we can date the beginning of polo from 1926, when Carlo Kupelwieser created two summer polo fields on the island resort of Brioni.

The first center for polo on the Italian peninsula itself rose with the formation of the Rome Polo Club, near Acquacetosa, which had as its first president Count Gallenga Stuart, the senator, who was succeeded by Count Giacomo Antonelli. From these beginnings, polo rose to national importance. When it was taken up again after World War II, many members of the club were from the ranks of the English colony, including the famous Hugo Anson, Admiral Warren, Colonel Fiske, and General Goulburn. In Lombardy, polo centers upon a park in Monza, following attempts by SIRE to create its own field on the property. The Monza Polo Club has two excellent playing fields, and training fields as well. In Turin, the Polo Club Mirafiori has provided a field within the Vinovo racetrack under the guidance of club President Nasi.

II
HUNTING

Ancient Times

The Egyptians, lively and instinctive sportsmen, hunted every sort of animal by chasing them on horseback or in light carts, even driving or flushing them with the help of dogs, sometimes in packs, such as the Ethiopian greyhound (with the muzzle of a whippet, a peculiar type of spotted flop-eared dog that greatly resembled our foxhound).

The Assyrians considered the saddle horse indispensable. Together with the Babylonians, they hunted on brilliant horses or pursued their game in their famous, solidly built carts. They used alans for chasing onagers and deer, and molossians for attacking lions and leopards. In Persia, such dogs were trained for war; in Lydia, King Aluates raised an army of molossians that were defeated by the dogs of Cerus in the Battle of Thymbe.

Darius I, who had learned the art of the chase on horseback from the Medes, proclaimed his prowess as a hunter in his epitaph: "I loved my friends, I was an excellent horseman and hunter, and nothing was impossible for me."

The Greeks used horses for the chase, and went armed with lances, and, very occasionally, bows and arrows. They considered the use of nighttime traps and nets vile and detestable, and disdained to employ them. According to Plato, a man should defeat a beast through skill and courage. Xenophon believed that the true hunter in addition to courage needed to "possess a robust, supple body, be about twenty, and speak Greek with surpassing elegance." We know that the people of Thessaly fought the wild bulls of the plains from horseback, that the Macedonians fox-hunted, and Alexander was a passionate hunter.

Though Xenophon was not familiar with the equestrian and hunting customs of the Gauls, Arrian of Nicomedia—the philosopher, historian, and soldier who lived in Hadrian's time and considered himself Xenophon's literary successor—wrote about them extensively: "Hunters who have good mounts and dogs have no reason to sink to base methods; they can always attack an animal openly. They hunt for the honest pleasure of the sport, and use no nets." The Gauls most enjoyed chasing stag, roebuck, and sometimes wolf, just as these game were to become the favorite sport of Renaissance Europe. It is interesting to note that when the Gauls, like the Greeks, hunted on horseback, they wore a cape fastened at the neck and rolled up to the shoulders, according to Appian, so that in case of rain the cape could be unrolled. They wore a belted tunic tucked up high, and carried a lance in the right hand. They also pursued the elk, already becoming rare, using thousands of beaters. It was many years after Gaul that Rome took up the ritual of the chase. Considered *servile officium* (literally "a servant's pastime"), hunting was first introduced as a diversion for the nobility by Scipio Emilianus. His adoptive father Paulus Emilius had made a gift of hunters to the King of Macedonia at whose court Polibius hunted, as did Terence who wrote a short poem on the subject. A hunting party comprised *vestigatores, indagatores, alatores,* and *pressores*. The men were all mounted, armed with bow and lance. When hunting boar, bear, and wolves, the riders wore cuirasses and leggings. Trajan was a great hunter, and Hadrian, who was a fine horseman, risked his life hunting lions on one occasion in Egypt. Commodus (161–192) also liked to hunt on horseback, and his preceptor, Pollux, composed a poem about it. Under Diocletian, hunting had already assumed the proportions of a spectacle with its own rigid etiquette, which followed the Asiatic pattern. Hunting parties were directed by a so-called Chief of Sacred Largesse under whom they procured game for the various hunting preserves, called *cynegia*. The Romans had divided the immense territory of Gaul into five *cynegia*, four of which depended upon the Chief of Sacred Largesse, with headquarters in Metz, Trèves (Trier), Rheims, and Tournay. The fifth, which comprised the Ardennes, was so vast that it had a specially appointed official, answerable direct to the *praefectus rerum privatarum*. The hunters were organized on quasi-military lines. Beginning with Theodosius II, who died of a fall from his horse in a wood on the outskirts of Constantinople, we shall see that there followed a long line of illustrious persons who met death while hunting.

572 573 *Modern racing and hunting saddles.*

574 575 576 *Bridle, saddle, felt saddle pad, saddlecloth, cooler, and quarter sheet. Felt shin boots, and rubber "bell" boots to protect the hooves. Hind ankle boots.*

577 *The Muratti Gold Cup at Acqua Acetosa in Rome. Soldati of the La Celina team, followed by Santamaria, who is covered by Pasquini.*

578 *A bad fall on the polo field at Deauville.*

579 *Persian miniature of the fourteenth century showing a polo match.*

572

573
574

575
576

577

578

580

581

582

Constans I, youngest son of Constantine I, was killed in 350 while out hunting, a victim of treachery. Emperor Gratian, assassinated in 383 by followers of General Maximus, had neglected the empire for hunting. Maximus was responsible for the preference of the Alani over the Roman and German soldiers, finding them swifter and more able horsemen. This Mongolian advance guard brought falconry to the West. The Roman general Paulinus (died about A.D. 69), the poet, grandson of Ausonius, mentions falconry in a song of the pleasures of youth and the chase: "my handsome horse, swift dogs, and trained hawk." Apollinarius Sidonius panegyrized an emperor for his skill as a hunter, but his subject was soon replaced by others, all fine huntsmen with horse and hawk, but none much good as an emperor.

Lovers of the hunt, though they made it a brutal chase, were the Alemanni, of whom Tacitus wrote, "When they are not making war, they pass the time hunting, or even more usually, doing nothing at all." The Burgundians, already half Romanized, had established a stern hunting code that provided for heavy fines and punishment for transgressors. The Visigoths were brilliant hunters, and Theodoric, when not occupied with seeing justice done and dealing with affairs of state or counting the wealth in his treasury, was to be found in the stable, inspecting his hunters. Clotaire I used to hunt in the forest of Compiègne, and his son, Clotharius, died while hunting in Cuise-la-Motte forest. Chilperic, another of his sons, was killed while returning home from a hunting expedition.

Charlemagne was wounded by an aurochs while participating in a hunt in honor of a visiting caliph. With all the splendor of an Oriental potentate, he had restored the Roman hunting preserves and wardens. His *venationes autumnales*, or autumn hunt for stag and boar were famous. At Easter, it was his custom to invite illustrious guests from Spain and the East, including the Caliph of Baghdad, to join in his hunting parties.

Louis the Good while hunting wolf fell from his horse, and died. Astolf, King of the Lombards, was killed by a boar. The bloodiest end of all was suffered by the Emperor Basil, the Macedonian, who was torn to pieces by the horns of a stag.

In Charlemagne's capitularies, we find that the clergy, including bishops and abbesses, are prohibited from hunting with falcons and goshawks, from keeping dogs, or bringing them to church. The laws certainly must have been in vogue by 968 if in that year the Bishop of Sues, Archimbald, found it necessary to expel the monks of the famous abbey Saint-Pierre-le-Vif for keeping horses, dogs, and falcons.

For reasons that included victualing, the Crusaders marched with falcons and packs of dogs, and dallied away a good many hours in hunting to such a degree that Pope Eugene III prohibited Christian nobles participating in the Second Crusade from carrying their hunting gear with them.

St. Ambrose insisted that he had never found a decent man among hunters, while St. Augustine thought hunting to be unsporting. As a result of such pronouncements, hunting was to die out in Italy, remaining a privilege to be enjoyed only by the barbarians; the Latins were also forbidden to bear arms. Only with the return of the noble lords, around 1300, did the great tradition of the hunting aristocracy revive, with plebes forbidden to participate in the sport under pain of heavy penalties. Hunting on horseback returned, including the chase, but the spirit was far from what characterized it in the days of Charlemagne, when in 785 he convened a Diet composed of Italian nobles to prepare a hunting ordinance for his Milanese domain.

The Middle Ages

In reading the famous essay *De Arte Venandi cum Avibus* (The Art of Hunting with Birds), by Frederick II, which was annotated by his son, Manfred, a particular sense of rapport between man and falcon is evident, even perhaps a mystic love that flows from the author's subtle, detailed instructions which, though thorough and technically precise, are suffused with a peculiar delight in an enchanting animal companion. This rapport between master and falcon derives from a profound knowledge of the proud and haughty bird. Every reaction of Frederick's volatile pupil is anticipated, and discussed with a solicitude that springs from a deep, almost spiritual, bond.

Frederick teaches how to capture, raise, and train a falcon; and how to care for it. He takes up the question of riding with a falcon on the wrist: "When the falconer has taken the falcon from its perch and transferred it to his fist, he will mount his horse from the right. It is therefore necessary for him to transfer the bird to his left hand and, after giving it some bird seed, grasp the rear of the saddle with his left hand, on which the bird is perching. While mounting, placing all his weight on the stirrup, the falconer should stretch his left hand, with the falcon, outward and away from the rear of the saddle, turning the left leg over the saddle so that it hangs down on the side."

Hunting, particularly with hawks, was a mark of distinction among royalty as well as gentlemen generally. For freemen, there were war and the hunt; for serfs, the plow— that was the medieval dictum. No one not of gentle birth was permitted to keep a falcon, on pain of death. That also was the fate of anyone who dared to hunt on a gentleman's land. The medieval mania for hunting with falcons reveals a yearning for space; a search for the far horizon as well as a passion for cruel drama. There was almost a shattering of the inertia of feudal life, which intensified until it led to the delirium of the Crusades. While in the castle close he went on elaborating codes of life that were ever more complex, the feudal lord slaked his thirst for adventure by hawking.

We know that the proceeds from excise, barratry, and prostitution were applied in great part to maintaining hunting, including all the expenses of keeping hounds, game wardens, and horses reserved to the sport. Bernabò Visconti was mad about hunting, which was abundantly clear to the

580 *A match between the Italian polo teams, Brattas and Trifoglio (in white), in Rome.*

581 *Japanese polo mallet and stirrups.*

582 *The Singh brothers, members of the Calcutta Polo Club team, in a photograph taken in 1864.*

Milanese upon whom he quartered five thousand hounds. For the maintenance of these hounds, every citizen, whether cleric or layman, was paid a small indemnity, though subject to fines and even imprisonment if the dogs, which were periodically inspected, were thought to be underfed or sickly. After the great plague of 1347, hundreds accused of having poached on Bernabò's preserves ended on the gibbet. Besides hawking, Bernabò loved to hunt with cheetahs, which meant that his followers had better have fast horses.

The outstanding hunt, however, marked by the thrill of a swift chase through green tangles of forest, was stag hunting. Swift, wide-ranging, protecting itself by crossing river and stream, the stag shot through the forest, leaving hardly a trace of spoor or scent. The *chasse à cor et à cris,* the eerie sound of the horn, the cry of the master, and the calls to the huntsmen scattered throughout the forest to give them the direction of the chase, while the hounds raced in pursuit of the stag, formed an almost sacred rite. It was a strict, precise ritual for the veteran and a thrill for the novice. Hunters followed six-, eight-, or ten-point stags, each with his boosters. Then came the call that signaled the stag had left the woods and was in the clear, or had crossed water or had reentered the forest or, utterly weary, was searching for a place to make his last stand before lying down to die. It was then that the stag gave his final roar of menace and resignation, a sound that no hunter who heard it could ever forget. The *hallali sur pied* would be heard. Supporting itself against the trunk of a huge tree, the stag faces the pack, his cries mixing with the baying of the triumphant hounds. The most noble or expert hunter transfixes the quarry with a single, unerring arrow; the master leaves his horse to cut the stag's throat *(hallali sur terre),* and the hunters exhibit the head in a gesture symbolizing every heroic minute.

One of the most complete manuals in existence on the chase, and Piedmontese hunting customs, is *Vénerie Royale.* It came from the precise though not witty pen of Robert de Salnove, page to Henry IV and, later, Louis XIII. He had gone to the Piedmont in the train of Christine of France, who wanted a loyal and faithful friend on her trip to a strange land to marry Vittorio Amedeo of Savoy. Salnove included material on the equitation of hunting, recommending horses that were in hand, with sensitive mouths and obedient, so that there would be no chance of their ruining the hunt by starting, bolting, or neighing unnecessarily. He prescribed light horses, particularly Andalusians and Neapolitans.

The chase continued to interest the rulers of England, France, Germany, and the Eastern empires, as well as the Crusaders, who upon their return to Europe brought back Moorish hunting customs, not to mention a taste for Arabian horses. Gaston Phébus de Foix in 1380 provided the most exhaustive and profound book on the subject, a true monument that discusses not only the training and care of hunting dogs but the raising and training of hunters.

The Roman countryside, lonely and melancholy, has been a great place for hunting ever since the eighth century when the restoration of order in Rome and its surrounding areas occurred. Popes, cardinals, and abbots who were hunters can be numbered by the hundreds. A hunt organized in 1481 by Girolamo Riario consisted of more than four hundred mounted guests. It was Ascanio Sforza, however, son of Francesco and brother of Lodovico the Moor, who arranged the most luxurious hunting parties of his century. In 1514, Lorenzo de' Medici asked the Marquis of Mantua to send him greyhounds, a falcon, and some horses so that he might cut a fine figure when hunting with the papal court. That year Isabella d'Este introduced Rome to the use of carriages.

Meanwhile, De Grassis in Ferrara, and Fouilloux in France were compiling tracts that primarily covered the ritual of the hunt, which was a complicated, arduous ceremony, because by then hunting parties might number two thousand horsemen. Between edicts and tracts, norms and codes (the period of Leo X [1513–1521] was the most opulent and the most punctiliously ceremonial), the regulations grew and flourished, finally arriving at the edict on the hunting calendar of Leo XII (1823–1829), published in 1826.

Modern Times

From the lion hunt depicted in Assyrian high reliefs to fox hunting today, two aspects of these blood sports have remained unchanged: the cruelty and the discipline of horsemen and hunters in their relations to the hounds, master, and quarry. Such discipline appears to reflect the regimen and ceremony of the court, as well as chivalrous pursuits.

"Hunting on horseback has nothing to do with sport," insists the Marquise de Brissac (née Jacqueline de Contades), the youngest chatelaine of France, "nor is it pure diversion or exercise. It is an art and a discipline." From this point of view, which is traditional and valid, hunting becomes a nature rite performed in a natural setting, with the primordial necessity of the victim's blood no more than an exalted abstraction of a ceremony. It is therefore quite another thing from the cruel sport many define hunting to be, for it is simply a renewal, through artistry and sport, of the natural fight for survival.

The Dukes of Savoy were the first in Europe to establish a code for hunting, around the turn of the sixteenth century, upon which framework the French kings erected their own systems. These were hunts on horseback, chases, aided by dogs, and carried out with such pomp and ceremony, going back to the fourteenth and fifteenth centuries, that only courtiers and princes were capable of it.

In the seventeenth century the French invented the language of hunting on horseback (the *chasse à courre).* The tricorne, which got in the way of the hunting horn, was replaced by the English velvet hunting cap, first used around 1680 in Louis XIV's hunts, and the chase, which developed in the forest, became punctuated with an infinite number of calls. Thus, France devised the *royale,* signaling pursuit of the *dix cors* stag, and the *petite royale* for a *dix cors jeunement;* the *fanfare du roi,* the *dauphine;* as well as the *fanfare de la reine* for a fawn. The baying of the hounds was marked by the *bien allez* or the *volce l'est* when the hunters picked up the tracks of the fugitive quarry; the *vue* when the animal was seen, or the

583 584 *Fanciful, romantic prints depicting lion and tiger hunts.*
585–592 *Hunting and the traditional end-of-the-season cross-country over the moors of Malpense, Italy.*

583

584

585

588

586

587

590

591

589

592

593

594

597

598

595

596

animaux et compagnie if the stag was among others; *change* if the hounds were on the wrong scent; *changement de forêt* when the stag went from one grove to another; *bat l'eau* if he took to water; and *débuché* when he left the woods. At the end of the chase, there is the *hallali sur pied* or the *hallali par terre*. After that comes the *curée,* the division of the quarry with the *coffre* and the hounds throwing themselves upon the *curée chaude,* the courtesies of the chase, and the nocturnal feat by the light of torches or, on the following day the *curée froide* in the courtyard of the castle. In all about five hundred hunting calls are sounded on the horn.

An *équipage,* or *rallye,* in the modern word, is made up of a *maître d'équipage,* who directs, and is generally the owner of the pack; the *premier piqueur,* who is the chief huntsman with the entire responsibility for the hounds, generally about twenty to a pack, aided by another *piqueur;* the *valets de chien,* who take care of the fresh packs when the hunt is after stag or elk (such game always tires the dogs); the *cochers,* who look after remounts; and the *boutons,* those who have won the right to wear the hunt's habit and to the use of its buttons, because they are members, or, in a private hunt, have been invited to join by the *maître d'équipage.*

Fox Hunting

In 1787, the Duke of Beaufort, hunting one afternoon over his property, returned home rather annoyed because his hounds after starting a fox lost their quarry, fleeing to the open country and the hedges around the fields. However the duke soon discovered a new pleasure in hunting, particularly for the horseman, so that from that day on the duke decided to hunt only foxes.

Fox hunting offered hunters a new challenge and a fresh sport because of the peculiar and difficult aspects of the chase, as well as equestrian possibilities never before contemplated either in riding, as a simple sport, or for military purposes. With long rides over difficult terrain and fences to be taken, even the most experienced horsemen found it necessary to experiment with new styles and often to change their seats.

Fox hunting is particularly popular throughout Britain and Ireland, the United States, and France. During the time of the Georges, fox hunting in England truly developed as a popular sport. Up to then, the fox was considered vermin for quick annihilation, but as the forests gave way to agriculture, and the land consequently became more open, the fox became a more interesting subject for hunters, and, for the more queasy of the stag, boar, and hare hunters, more justifiable since it was to be got rid of anyway. The first organized hunt for the fox, as a sport, occurred in 1730, and is known as the Belvoir Hunt, followed soon afterward by a great number of others, which, however, were not all that well received in general society, especially since these early hunts were wont to include heavy drinking. Bernard de Mandeville in 1714 was urged to write in his *The Fable of the Bees* that

"fox hunters who have all day long tried in vain to break their necks, join at night in a second attempt on their lives by drinking." By the end of the century, fox hunting had recovered enough prestige to have become a serious sport; and by the nineteenth century it was widely disseminated and emulated by all who could afford it, greatly influencing the breeding of hunters (horses) as well as hounds.

Hunts today are usually organized under hunt clubs, with members who elect a committee and a master. The committee, with a secretary-treasurer, assists the Master of Fox Hounds (MFH) in the administration, organization, and meeting of the hunt. The master has at his disposal a huntsman, two whippers-in, grooms, and often an earth-stopper. The huntsman assisted by the first whipper-in is responsible for the care, training, and conduct of the pack, and also feeds the hounds if he is kennel huntsman as well. The second whipper-in keeps the pack together. The earth-stopper has the job of stopping, or plugging, the "earths" (holes in which the fox might take refuge).

The pack comprises a variable number of hound couples. The foxhound is generally used, and is believed to descend from the white hunting dogs brought to England by William the Conqueror. Unlike coursers or sight hounds, these are scent hounds. Their quality is measured by their "noses," or olfactory sensitivity, and the intelligence and alertness they bring to this faculty. Bitches usually are thought to be faster, but are not so tenacious. Accordingly, a pack may include an even number of bitches, or it may be mixed, as the conditions of the hunt and terrain dictate. About eighteen couples is an average-sized pack. The Master of Fox Hounds is in charge of the pack, and responsible for the ordering of the kennels, as well as the stables, if the hunt has its own horses, and in general for providing sport for the members. When the hounds are running, no member of the hunt passes the master, except at his bidding. Out of deference, the gentlemen of the hunt salute him, tipping their hats. At the end of the day's hunting, the courtesy is to thank him for the sport provided.

At the start, the hunt rides out to the side of the covert, with the huntsman leading the pack. When the fox is started, the first whipper-in, usually on a rise for a better view, gives the cry "Hark halloa." Once the hounds are on the track, having picked up the scent, the huntsman in full cry advises the field with a "Forrard away!" which is the only time he concerns himself with the field. A fundamental rule for the hunter is never to cross the pack or ride through it once the hounds have given tongue.

If the first whipper-in rides with the huntsman, he generally opens gates, keeps the pack from running over posted land, and so forth, while the second whipper-in keeps the pack together.

At the kill, the master distributes the trophies of the chase—mask (head), brush (tail), and pads (paws) and sometimes, following old tradition, the huntsman "baptizes" novice hunters by signing their foreheads with a drop of the quarry's blood.

The pace set by a hunt in England is generally much faster than elsewhere not only because of the quality of the horses but also because the obstacles are of a different type. In the English shires, the ground is generally smooth, and

593–597 *Old-time hunting in the Roman countryside.*
598 *King Umberto I of Italy rides out to hunt.*

one can follow the hounds better in a long, fast gallop. In some other countries the obstacles may be fences and rocky outcrops, not to mention an occasional ruin, the sort that are high enough and hard enough to provoke dangerous falls. On the other hand, in England there are more ditches, fences, and brooks to contend with. The woods, however, are quite thick, and a good deal of riding and jumping are done with an arm protecting one's face from branches and thorns in the dense thickets. Nevertheless, all these obstacles are met and taken with speed and decision.

In England, Ireland, the United States, and even in France, unlike Italy, bystanders take an interest, and invariably stop work to watch the field ride by. They always enjoy and appreciate a good jump and do not hesitate to show their admiration.

From a recent statistical report published by the British Field Sports Society, we learn that in the last year there were well over two hundred hunts with foxhounds in the United Kingdom. Fox hunting is most popular in the Midlands. In Leicestershire, for example, there are four weekly meetings that attract between 200 and 300 participants. Estimating that the average number of horses for each hunt is 172, 4,420 hunters would be needed for these meetings, and that figure could be as much as 6,000, considering the required hunters in reserve needed. About 7,500 couples of hounds would be needed. According to the British Field Sports Society's figures, about £12,000,000 is spent annually for hunting. The sport, therefore, represents a source of employment and profit for many.

Notwithstanding, all this activity does not always go on in an atmosphere of harmony and goodwill. Many landowners are delighted to have foxes on their holdings, and happy to give right-of-way to hunts in pursuit of them, but their interests fall athwart those of the farmers, who see the fox as nothing more than vermin, and do not believe the killing of an occasional specimen justifies the depredations of the many incursions on their land by a pack in full cry. The courts get many suits to settle arising out of such differences of opinion. Fox hunting, with all the punctilio that only the British could give it, emigrated to the United States, as well as to France and Italy, where it caught on in the Roman countryside, thanks to Lord Chesterfield. (Fox hunting in this region had its most splendid period at the end of the last century.)

By the latter half of the eighteenth century, fox hunting had already been in progress in the United States, originating shortly after the arrival of the Virginia colonists; it was popular with George Washington, who maintained his own pack, but Americans never rivaled the enthusiasm of the English. Just before World War II 150 affiliated clubs of the Masters of Foxhounds Association were established, drawing from about half the states, with most of them along the Atlantic. Though there are those in fox-hunting countries who fox-hunt either for hunting or riding, or both, in the United States the hound is all important. In fact there is a studbook for foxhounds, *The International Foxhunters' Stud Book*.

There are approximately a hundred hunts recognized by the Masters of Foxhounds Association, the governing body of fox hunting in the United States. Today there are 99 active foxhound associations in the United States throughout twenty-six states, with the most popular fox-hunting states being Virginia and Pennsylvania, though there are clubs in California and Colorado, as well. The oldest established hunt is the Rose Tree Fox Hunting Club, 1859, which derives from the Gloucester Hunt Club, formed in 1766. One of the oldest hunt clubs, and perhaps the most exclusive, is the Myopia Hunt Club in Massachusetts, formed a century ago for nearsighted members, from which of course the name derives.

The Hunter

In the past, as a rule, the hunter, like the racehorse, was a cold-blooded horse, but today, many a hunter is a Thoroughbred, a superb athlete used to jumping all types of obstacles, such as fences, walls, banks, and streams, which, incidentally, certainly contributed to the development of steeplechasing, not too far removed from the sport's course conditions.

Since hunts and paperchases (the game of hare and hounds) generally take place over uneven terrain covered with brush and other natural obstacles, a horse's legs should have some protection when he is used for hunting. Furthermore, hunters should maintain a discreet distance from one another, and take their jumps in a manner calculated to save their mounts. A horse should be turned out and allowed to rest the day after a hunt. If he is ridden out frequently, it will suffice just to exercise him for about an hour or so at the walk and trot between one hunt and the next. A good hunter, with a good rider, should certainly be in form to hunt twice a week. In some countries hunters are turned out to pasture during the summer months, whereas often as not these horses will be working throughout the year. Generally they are put into the field not before five years of age.

PART NINE

EQUESTRIAN AMUSEMENTS

I
THE CIRCUS

It was instinctive for man, after breaking the horse, to demonstrate his coolness and bravery in competition with his fellows. The early Panathenaic games on horseback had some resemblance to the Circus Maximus—where equestrian exhibitions found their place among the bloodier events—with a rider displaying his skills by passing from the back of one horse to another or by standing on the animal's croup and riding him at a gallop. A parallel may also be drawn with medieval tourneys, where such jousts, after much early bloodletting, were reduced to ostentatious spectacles, where the horse was as significant as the rider. In Byzantium, these equestrian exhibitions were increasingly confined to the riding academy until they were confused with the equitation of the earlier indigenous school.

In the fifteenth century, with the decline of the Eastern Empire, riding instructors and outstanding performers on horseback emigrated to the West in search of pupils untutored in their art. With the flowering of the riding academies in the sixteenth century, where highly schooled horses performed in lavish demonstrations mounted for the court or, more routinely, for the public, we have the foundation of the modern equestrian circus.

These riding exhibitions passed through France to England, where they interested the middle class as well as the aristocracy, particularly fascinating the young. Leaving the niceties of dressage far behind, these riders performed startling feats of acrobatic tumbling and jumping. But not until the middle of the eighteenth century did the circus as we know it today begin to evolve, with a well-schooled, richly caparisoned horse as the main attraction. Two names are prominent at this time: Jacob Bates and Price, both popular performers. There was also Dobney, the creator of a circus in the London borough of Islington, who was soon emulated by Johnson, who began another circus in London.

Uncontestably, the idea of the modern circus is credited to Philip Astley, an erstwhile sergeant major in Colonel Elliot's 15th Light Brigade, who had once rescued the Duke of Brunswick during the Seven Years' War, for which he won his stripes, and Dickens wrote of Astley in an essay in his periodical *All the Year Round*. In 1752, the former sergeant major supported himself by teaching tumbling to children, as well as giving trick riding exhibitions on his horse Gibraltar. Astley soon discovered that when galloping in a circle while standing on a horse's back he could keep his balance, thanks to centrifugal force. In 1769, he had a circular track built, the first of its kind, the regular manège tracks always being rectangular. Astley's colleagues, despite their school tradition, applauded his innovation, as it gave them an opportunity to display their skills as never before. It was at this time that a number of them had become trick riders at the London pleasure gardens. These were in great competition with the theatres, but on the decline when Astley introduced his first organized circus. Later on he was able to hire away their performers: tightrope artists, acrobats, jugglers, and so on.

His new riding circle was 13 meters in diameter,* fenced in, with a covered stand. In 1779 a roof was added, and the arena was grandiloquently named The Astley Royal Amphitheatre of Arts. Before long, the former trooper, seeing the need to include other acts in his program, hired a dog trainer, a clown, and the world-famous Colpi family. Audiences were quick to recognize Astley's unique ability to inspire acrobats and clowns to their best performances by creating the proper atmosphere, that is, presenting them in the circus ring. The name "circus" (Latin for ring) first appeared in 1782 in the name of the Royal Circus of Charles Hughes, a former rider of Astley's, who established himself about a half-mile from Astley's circus.

For centuries circus performers have continued to put their faith in Astley's ring. With the notable exception of an 18-meter arena built for Hans Storch to accommodate 35 elephants, most circus rings still measure about 13 meters across. The number itself was not chosen for reasons of superstition, although there are strong ties between circus performers and gypsies, who believe in magic numbers; rather, it was the horse itself who determined the size. To avoid having the animal adapt himself to each new ring of different size and to facilitate continually a smooth gait as well as an easy orientation, the size of the arena was standardized. Thus, the horse, while running around the perimeter of the ring and leaning toward the center, maintains the smooth gait and perfect rhythm absolutely essential to the rider for the performance of bareback stunts.

* Laurent and Henri Franconi, sons of Astley's later partner, are credited by some to have standardized the 13-meter (42-foot) diameter ring.—EDS.

Astley had already given performances in Paris in 1772, and in 1882, when he opened his own French amphitheatre at Faubourg du Temple. (Under the leadership of the famous François-Joseph Talma, French actors and comedians—those who did not actually emigrate from the fairs to the circus—continued to refer to Astley's and other circuses as "amphitheatres" to avoid any identification with the theatre world, which they felt would be damaging to their reputation.)

By 1793, Astley's French circus encountered competition from the Venetian Antonio Franconi, a country gentleman born in the Udine in 1737. Shortly after his twenty-third birthday, Franconi killed a rival in a duel; rather than face arrest and imprisonment, he fled to France, where he put his skill in equitation to work. Everywhere there was talk about the new circus, and Franconi decided to try his hand. On rue Duguay-Trouin in Rouen today, there stands a warehouse for imported goods, the circus where in 1786 Franconi performed his famous "ribbon leap."

In 1789, at the outbreak of the Revolution, Astley leased the circus to Franconi, who continued it and from it developed the foundations of the French circus. After having established nineteen circuses, Astley died, leaving no heirs, but Franconi established a dynasty that lasted until 1910. He is credited with the invention of various stunts, his most outstanding creation being the Royal Pass, later called the St. Petersburg Pass, and then the Washington Pass, but unchanged in execution. For this, the rider, balanced on two horses and holding a pair of unusually long reins, would direct six to eight horses trotting consecutively around his supporting mounts. At the Franconi Olympic Circus in Paris, equestrian pantomimes called "military glories" were performed, resembling the fantastic balls of the late nineteenth century and in a certain sense the silent films of the 1920's, especially with the comical entrance of the cavalry clowns. Le Cirque d'Hiver (the Winter Circus) on Boulevard des Filles du Calvaire, which opened in 1852, is the last Franconi circus in operation, but now under the management of the Bouglione interests.

By the nineteenth century the circus had evolved into a glamorous event for the élite. In 1833, Balzac commented that the complete man in elegant society was either a centaur or a man in his gig. Dandies, sportsmen, riding masters, cavalry officers, women, and troopers would fill the boxes along the floor while the masses sat in the grandstand. Painters like Degas, Toulouse-Lautrec, Daumier, Seurat, and Boldini made it their favorite subject, reflecting its popularity. In the twentieth century, Picasso would make the circus the setting for many of his early paintings. However, as the circus became more of a music-hall affair, its importance as an equestrian show diminished. Equestrian battles, sieges, and various other horse spectacles captured the spotlight from the earlier trick riders, acrobats, and clowns. A famous trick rider who appeared in some of these set pieces was the Englishman Andrew Ducrow, one of the truly great, despite the mediocrity of his roles.

In contrast to the mobile open-air circuses of the eighteenth century and even the nineteenth, the twentieth-century "Astley and Franconi" circuses—astonishing audiences with their huge variety of animal acts, daring acrobats, incredible number of ponies, Thoroughbreds, and draft horses—were held in huge tents for capacity crowds.

The early circus had comprised *haute école* and employed the classic gaited Hackneys and Standardbreds in elaborate maneuvers; acrobats and draft horses such as Percherons, Clydesdales, and Shires (all of which may be used in parades to pull the gaudy wagons) for bareback riding; and liberty horses, usually Arabians and frequently nearly pure white, performing without riders in the traditional pirouetting and bowing and similar routines. And of course for those lucky enough to acquire them, there were the stars of any equestrian show, the Lipizzaners. François Baucher, the director of the Rouen circus in 1830, was, of course, a great exponent of the first. Finding it difficult to earn a living as a riding instructor, he joined Franconi and his circus, adding his own innovations that geared the circus to the masses as well as to the élite, until a freak accident ended his active career. While mounting a "green" horse, the arena chandelier came crashing down, and Baucher, unable to avoid it, had his right leg completely shattered. The French circus thrived, and by the time of the French Second Empire, Paris alone had six resident circuses. Fundamentally, the difference between the nineteenth-century circus and today's is the familiarity of the earlier performers with horses, acquired directly at Saumur or perhaps at the Moscow circus, or indirectly by assisting

599 600 *The horse plays an important part in the* corrida, *the bullfight, with the mounted* rejoneador *opening the spectacle on a schooled horse who performs a series of movements around the bull, to excite him and incite him to attack. The* rejoneador, *so called after his lance or* rejón, *shows the tremendous equestrian bravura and skill that ballet on horseback demands, putting his horse through a dance full of complicated figures, with the horse (never the rider) running the risk of being gored at any moment; some people have little respect for the* rejoneador. *When the horse is well schooled, however, and the horseman courageous, gracious and gallant, the spectacle is stupendous. The horses ridden by the* picadores *are known as* pencos *or* rocinantes. *At the matador's orders, the* picadores, *on horseback, "pick" the bull, aiming at the* morillo, *a point on his neck, in order to tire his neck muscles without taking the fight out of him.*

601 602 *From the time of the dictator Primo de Rivera, prompted by the Queen of Spain, the crest, right flank, and belly of* picadores' *horses have been protected by padding, called the* peto. *This is designed to save the horse from the bull's horns, but it is not always successful. The* picador *will often expose the animal's unprotected hindquarters to a bull that has refused to charge the horse's protected parts, and pick the bull too far behind the* morillo—*actually, right in the bull's spine. The* picadores *wear a protective covering on their legs and a suede boot on the right foot. Among the* rejoneadores *are many women, including the famous Conchita Cintrón.*

603–605 *Broncobusters at the rodeo, in a series of typical sketches.*
606 *Cowgirls performing in a rodeo.*
607 *Racing as the pioneers did—a rodeo.*

599

600

601

602

603

604

605

606

607

608

609

610

with mounts around the racing circuit. The point is that Baucher's ideas were not forgotten. Terms like *assembler, piaffe,* or *galop allongé* were common to the nineteenth-century circus act, whereas today performers are quite ignorant of high-school terminology. Bareback ballerinas like Carolina Loyo, trained by Baucher, enjoyed great popularity. She made her debut at the Olympic Circus in Paris in 1833, initiating a career that lasted nearly half a century. Balancing themselves on bare croups or on small platforms, bareback riders would execute a ribbon leap or a hoop leap as admirers tossed little bouquets of violets into the ring. Still other circus women, however, finding all this very unchallenging, refused to have anything to do with what they considered the "cheap notoriety" of *haute école,* especially since such notorious performers as Celeste Mogador, Lola Montez, and Emilienne d'Alençon tended to give the circus a bad name.

Many of the famous circus operators were great riders and trainers, and such names come to mind as Renz (Germany), Salamonsky (the Baltics), Carré (Netherlands), and Schumann (Scandinavia). Famous British performers were the Clarkes and the Ginnettes; an outstanding American contributor was Davis Richard, killed while performing at the Renz circus. He is credited with a stunt performed without saddle or bridle; other Americans were John Glenroy and Levi North, who performed record-breaking somersaults in 1847; Robert Stickney, with a record double somersault in 1872; and Orrin Davenport, who somersaulted from horse to horse. During this period the circus was metamorphosing. The first man publicly to put his head in a lion's mouth was the American animal trainer Isaac Van Amburgh in the nineteenth century, and the menagerie, or side show, was being introduced in Europe, coming over from the declining fairgrounds. A decided boon to the acrobat's appeal was the invention of the flying trapeze in 1859 by the French gymnast J. Léotard, after whom the dancer's leotard is named, and Spencer Stokes, an American rider, invented the American Riding Machine, a device for the training of trick riders that did much to advance the inclusion of new blood. Another American, Phineas Taylor Barnum, who was, according to many European ringmasters, a violent, crude innovator, instituted the three-ring circus, which with its invasion of 30-odd elephants lumbering along to a tune on the calliope presented a great contrast to the stark, stately beauty of the horse. All sorts of strange phenomena, from shaggy horses and Russian Cossacks to cowboys and Indians, were used in Barnum's acts. Once he jokingly asked the Prince of Wales if he would rent him his Household Guard. Barnum's circus had become Barnum and Bailey's, which was controlled by Ringling Brothers, who in 1929 bought out several competitors to create under their control a combined circus formed from eleven separate major circus enterprises (now known, of course, as Ringling Brothers, Barnum and Bailey's Circus).

608 *William "Buffalo Bill" Cody on his famous Appaloosa.*
609 *Indian drawings on hide, showing mounted warriors.*
610 *The horse makes his appearance in the Americas. While Cortés rode good animals, Pizarro used nags.*

The founding families of Europe, who continued to maintain their separate circuses intact, caught in an irresolvable situation that comprised Barnum, the Big Top, the 12,000-seat arena, huge profits, and automation, found twentieth-century progress distasteful as well as unavoidable. Today, over two dozen circuses still tour the United States, whereas the USSR has about 100 or more, some permanently located. In England and France, as well as the rest of Europe, the circus continues in popularity but nothing approaching this magnitude.

In the modern circus of sensationalism, trapeze artists, and lion tamers, the horse stands out as the lone survivor of a happier era. Some directors, like the Swiss Knie, the Danish Benneweiss, and the Italian Palmieri, still consider the presentation of liberty horses a skill, with only the whip to command Arabian stallions, Lipizzaners, and even huge Normans to regroup and to disperse in single file, in pairs or threes. Nor have the descendants of the Krones, the Carrés, and the Schumanns and others turned their backs on *haute école.* Unfortunately, though, a few years ago, at an American circus, one of the Caveagna family, executing Orrin Davenport's famous specialty, got almost no spectator reaction. Massimo Alberini, a historian, credits the existence of the circus in both form and content expressly to the horse, and cites as proof the use of the term "equestrian" in reference to the circus. This is no less true in the present century. If the circus is to survive, it must restore the horse to his former position of honor; without him the circus is nothing but a bicycle track or a theatre in the round. Much in the circus has changed; but behind the lights, microphones, and amplifiers Astley's circus is what gives it life.

II

THE RODEO

Most historians agree that the rodeo had no formal beginning. It seems to have originated in the days of the open range, when the big cattle spreads dotted the southwestern United States and adjacent Mexico. At the end of a roundup, work-weary cowboys would get together and amuse themselves with feats of horsemanship and cattle handling, or show what they could do just for the fun of it, to celebrate the end of a long drive, spending their back pay on whiskey, women, and wagers.

At first, these informal exhibitions were little more than simple roping and riding contests between two or more cowboys, or anyone who wanted to take up a challenge or settle a bet. As the number of cattle ranches increased, so did the rustlers and horse thieves and, along with the encroachment and growth of the towns that sprang up during the 1830's and 1840's, made it necessary for the rancher to enclose his acres. As the open range disappeared, there was less opportunity for cowhands of different spreads to get together informally, but since the spirit of competition between outfits still existed, and their lonely life led them to socialize when they could, the rodeo, to be held at a fixed time and place, became the substitute for the annual roundup on the open range.

The language, as well as the stock of the cattleman, has always reflected the Spanish heritage and tradition of the

Southwest and neighboring Mexico. Rodeo comes from *rodear,* the verb meaning "to go around,"' which itself, interestingly enough, derives from the old Spanish *rode,* a horse ring. Lasso is the Spanish *lazo,* while lariat includes the article with the noun for "rope" or "thong," *la reata.* Mustang comes from *mesteño,* a half-breed horse, while bronco takes the adjective from *potro bronco,* wild colt. Chaps is merely a shortened form of the name in Spanish, *chaparajos.*

As fences and railroads extended, the cowhand rode less and over shorter distances, and his rodeos became more formal and regulated. One of the earliest, though quite informal, rodeos was held in Colorado in 1869 by a number of cowpunchers from several ranches within riding distance, the Hash Knife, Camp Stool, and Mill Iron.

It is difficult to say when the first modern rodeo was held. It might have been the one in Pecos, Texas, on July 4, 1883, although there was no admission. Cash prizes of $25 and $15 for first and second place were awarded for steer roping and bronco riding to Morgan Livingston and Trav Windham, boss of the Lazy Y. Many other small, occasional rodeos were held. Finally, on July 4, 1888, the first rodeo selling tickets took place at Prescott, Arizona. Events included riding and roping contests. This encouraged other rodeos in the West to open for business but they were for the most part unsuccessful. Nothing was coordinated, they had little professional know-how; riders would fail to appear and the prize money had a habit of disappearing. Some believe that the first rodeo charging admission was the Denver contest in 1887. Historians agree, however, that the first truly modern rodeo was held in Cheyenne, Wyoming, in 1897, known today as Cheyenne Frontier Days, laying the cornerstone for the "Big Four"—today's major league: Cheyenne; the Pendleton, Oregon, Roundup; the Calgary, Alberta, Stampede; and the Salinas, California, Rodeo. The biggest rodeo of all, however, is held indoors, the December National Finals, in Los Angeles, for top riders and ropers; the most important Winter Rodeo is the World's Championship Rodeo held at Madison Square Garden, New York City. (Rodeos moved indoors in 1917 at the Stockyards Coliseum in Fort Worth, Texas, opening the sport to year-round activity.)

From about 1915 to 1929 a great many rodeos sprang up throughout the country under the guidance of local cattlemen or enterprising townsmen, as well as traveling promoters who dotted the West with their fast and often ephemeral, as well as transient, shows. In 1928 the Rodeo Association of America was formed to "insure harmony among rodeo groups." In 1946, this group changed its name to the International Rodeo Association, and in 1959 to International Rodeo Management, Inc. In 1936 the Cowboys Turtle Association was formed to better cowboy working conditions at rodeos. This last changed its name to the Rodeo Cowboys' Association.

Rodeo events center around five major attractions: bareback bronco riding, calf roping, saddle bronc riding, steer wrestling, and bull riding. Other events include steer riding, team roping, bull decorating, stagecoach and chariot racing, wild-horse racing, wild-cow milking, and specialties such as trick riding, dog and horse acts to fill in between main events. Of course there are always the clowns, and possibly a popular movie star to entertain.

Stock are drawn by lot, and contests are timed (eight seconds constitutes an official ride for bareback and bull riding, which are the Grand Finale, and ten seconds for saddle bronc riding). Judges rate both stock and performers, and because a good animal can often be responsible for a contestant's winning, competing cowboys are eager to draw the toughest. Points are awarded, based on 100 for a perfect score for a combined performance of rider and mount, though an average score would be in the sixties, and an extraordinary one in the seventies.

In saddle bronc riding, the aim is to stay on a saddled bronc as he bucks and kicks, with the twister permitted to use, in addition to stirrups, one hand only, as well as a braided rope rein tied to a plain halter, to keep himself in the saddle. The rein can be held short or long; but either position, if exaggerated, will result in the twister earning a "goose egg"; that is, he will be bucked off and eliminated. If the horse fails to buck (a cinch is tied around the horse's flank to induce bucking) despite riders "scratching" (keeping the feet moving in a kicking motion), he is entitled to a new horse. He is disqualified if he loses his stirrups, changes hands on the reins, is bucked off, wraps the reins around his hand, or touches the horse with his free hand.

Bareback bronc riding, which became official in the mid-1920's, is the lead-off event in most rodeos. It is similar to but more difficult than bronc riding because the twister, wearing spurs, has neither saddle nor rein, but uses a surcingle, a 10-inch-wide piece of leather with a handhold cinched around the horse right behind the withers.

In calf roping, the roper must succeed in holding a calf in the noose until he gets to him in about five to ten seconds. The horse must be trained not to drag the calf more than three feet or a penalty of twenty seconds is imposed. The rider must throw a 250- to 400-pound calf by hand and tie any three feet with the piggin string he holds in his teeth. This tie must hold five seconds, until the judge passes on it. A roper is disqualified if he fails to make one out of two tries.

611 *Basketball on horseback in Morocco.*
612 *Girls racing bareback in the Jura Mountains.*
613 *The Georgian game of* issindi. *The horses are of the Cabardine breed.*
614 *Parading in Turkmenia.*
615 *Two sports combined: fishing on horseback.*
616 *Two up: American soldiers in training.*
617 *An Armenian game: trying to unseat the other fellow.*
618 *A dramatic moment at the Siena races.*
619–621 El Rocío, *a religious rite on horseback, an equestrian spectacle of rare fascination in Seville.*
622 623 *The horse in the "Western."*
624 *"The Spill" by Fattari.*
625 626 *Movie scenes.*

611

612

616

613

614

615

617

619

620

621

622

623

624

625

626

627

629

628

630

In any of the timed events, the horse must be perfection itself. A tenth of a second may mean winning $500 or dropping the $100 entry fee. He must break instantly, and hold his position just behind and to one side of the careening calf until the throw is made. On connecting, he must break to a stop.

Steer wrestling, also called bulldogging, is an event that requires the wrestler to jump the steer from his horse after the steer enters the ring from a chute. The steer must then be forcibly wrestled to the ground by the horns. A hazer rides opposite the wrestler to keep the steer going in a straight line. To be a good dogger, a man needs a "doggin'" horse, a highly trained animal whose cow sense and training have prepared him for the job.

In bull riding the cowboy usually rides a Brahma bull while hopefully hanging on for eight seconds by one hand to a bull rope around the animal's barrel. Bull decorating is an amusing but dangerous entertainment because the cowboy must get close enough to the bull to tie a ribbon around his horns or tail.

Steer roping in most rodeos has been superseded, since 1921, by calf roping. Here the cowboy, on foot or on horseback, lassos the steer about the horns and then brings it down to make the tie, much as in calf roping.

The general run of broncos are "outlaws," or wild horses. Though they are not actually trained to buck, which comes quite naturally, the bucking cinch about the hindquarters greatly contributes to their obstreperousness. The quarter horse is the outstanding rodeo mount, and between rodeos is in constant training, practicing all the movements of the actual events.

Despite the fact that at most rodeos fewer than a quarter of the contestants win back their entry money, over the last twenty years the rodeo has grown to full stature, becoming a permanent institution, and responsible for the increase in the selective breeding process of horses like the quarter horse and the palomino.

Rodeo hands continue to resist change, and still wear the picturesque dress once taken for granted in the early West. Though the action is more varied and the competition keener than that of the first rodeos, the original flavor and color remain unchanged and are very much apparent.

III
GYMKHANA EVENTS

A gymkhana is a field day for horsemen of varying equestrian experience engaging in mounted games. These frequently involve children and inexperienced riders and provide an opportunity to improve their riding skill. Among these games are the following:

627 *"Meeting at Teano" in the movies.*
628 *Pedro Armendarez in a movie scene.*
629 *"The Meeting at Teano," a painting by Pietro Aldi of the parley between Victor Emmanuel II and Garibaldi. Siena.*
630 *Tom Mix and his famous horse Tony.*

Balloon Race: Tied to the ground in the middle of a field are as many balloons as there are players. On signal the first man on each team gallops toward the center carrying a slender pointed stick, and tries to break a balloon. Upon reaching the end of the field, he passes the stick to the second man on the team, and so the game continues, with the first team to burst all its balloons declared the winner. There is also a variation of this called Balloon Scrimmage, in which a balloon on a string is carried by each contestant, who tries to puncture another's balloon while keeping his own intact.

Potato Race: Small piles of potatoes are placed in the middle of the field. The first man on each team gallops toward the center, where he dismounts, takes a potato, and remounts, heading back toward the end of the field, where he drops his potatoes into his team's bucket. The procedure continues until a whistle signals the end of a minute from the starting time, whereupon the next two men go. A potato that misses the bucket must be picked up by the dismounted rider and dropped again when mounted. This is also known as a potato-picking scramble.

Paper Chase: Similar to the Potato Race except that instead of potatoes small pieces of paper are placed in the middle of the field. Each player must gallop to the center, stab the paper with a pointed stick without dismounting, and place it in his team's bucket without touching it with his hands. There is an antilitter campaign version in which tins, boxes, plastic ware, and the like are used.

Knotted Cord Race: This is a two-team race with teams A and B. Team A is divided into even numbers 2, 4, 6, and odd numbers 1, 3, 5, with players 1, 3, 5 at the north end of the field and players 2, 4, 6 at the south end. On signal, player 1 rides to player 2, ties his cord with 2's, and together they ride back to the north end of the field, where player 3 unties the cord and ties his cord to 2's. Then 2 and 3 ride to the south end to repeat the action with 4, and so on. Team B, divided into even and odd players, performs the same actions simultaneously with A. The first team to untie the last knot is the winner. Three players or more may make up a team.

Egg and Racquet Race: A relay race of varying distances which consists of carrying an egg on a tennis racquet held in one hand. The egg may not be touched by a player. The walk, trot, or canter is permissible. A spoon may replace the racquet.

Changing Horses Relay: This is a race of varying distances of two types. In the first type, four members of each team are placed at the change points. Number 1 of each team mounts up and races to number 2, number 2 to number 3, and so on. In the second type, number 1 of each team races to each point and changes horses each time, while teammates at each point help him remount. As soon as the 1's finish their round, the 2's mount up, and so on. A variation is the straight relay race with contestants completing the distance and turning over their mounts to teammates for the return ride.

Trotting Race or Race at a Collected Gallop: The contestants race in pairs for a certain distance. If one breaks stride, he is penalized. At the end of the course they exchange horses for the return.

Rhythm Contest: Individual competition on a horizontally divided, sectioned course with a definite gait and rhythm assigned to each section.

Outlaws and the Pony Express: A Pony Express rider escorted by two guards must transport to the mine director a sack containing the miners' pay. Two outlaws leave from a secret spot and try to snatch the sack from him before he reaches his destination. The guards protect the Pony Express rider by tagging the outlaws on the shoulder.

Treasure Hunt: Before beginning the game, contestants familiarize themselves with the terrain, noting places marked by flags, signifying the existence nearby of small containers holding envelopes. Each contestant must follow the directions given him in the envelope in order to reach the treasure.

Musical Hats: In the middle of the field are hats on posts, numbering one or two fewer than the number of riders. At a prescribed gait the riders move along the edge of the field to the sound of music; when it stops (or at a whistle) all the riders gallop toward the center of the field, dismount, and attempt to take a hat. Those remaining hatless are eliminated. Two more hats are removed, and the game proceeds.

Capture the Flag: Contestants are divided into two teams, Black and White, each with a flag planted at opposite ends of the field, which is divided between them. The team that captures its adversary's flag first wins. A player can be taken prisoner if he is tagged by an opponent on the wrong side of the field.

Six-Pole Race: Six poles are planted in the ground about 15 to 20 feet apart, as if to mark a slalom course. Opposing riders zigzag between the poles until they reach the sixth, returning the way they came. This can also be done as a relay.

Flag Race: Flag holders for each team will hold a white flag in the first holder of each team, green in the second, red in the third, and yellow in the fourth, all on poles. Numbers 1 and 3 and 2 and 4 are at opposite ends. Number 1 will carry a blue flag to the first holder and exchange it for the white, continuing to exchange the white for the green, the green for the red, and at the fourth pole exchange the red for the yellow, handing it to number 2, who will reverse the order, thus restoring it to normal. Number 3 will repeat number 1's route and number 4, number 2's. The winning team is the one whose number 4 first crosses the finish line with the blue flag.

Musical Chairs: Chairs are placed in a circle, with one fewer than the number of riders. The riders trot or gallop to the sound of music. When it stops they must dismount, holding onto the reins, and sit in a chair. Whoever does not find a seat is eliminated. When only two riders are left, the first to sit when the music stops is the winner.

Other events included in a gymkhana are riding with a glass full of water, eating a bun between racing, racing and picking up a partner in the saddle, saddling and bridling contests, bareback races, the race in which contestants put on and take off a shirt, and many others.

631 *Adelina Krause Loisset in a lithograph by W. Kaires around 1850. Note the Austrian officers and the elegant spectators who have come to see the famous circus queen.*

632 *The Cirque des Champs-Elysée, inaugurated in 1843.*

633–636 *Sketches of typical acts at various circuses of the 1800's: the earliest popularly known circus "bareback riders" working both in pairs and in threes on the panneau; the impresarios; and the March of the Hussars by the young ladies of the company. From an album of designs by Henri Lang.*

637 *The leap over the ribbons defined by the newspapers of the day as "most exalted and dramatic poetry." The Drury Lane Theatre, London, 1851.*

638 *The longe attached to a pulley, a simple instrument still used today for the training of young horsemen. Seen here in action at the Sanger Circus, London, 1884.*

639 *Scenes at the Corty Circus, Berlin, July, 1876.*

640 *An exercise called "boxing" in today's circus.*

641 *Christel Senbach Kröne, descendant of Ida the Great who founded the Kröne Circus, performing in the haute école. Christel also customarily presents her liberty horses.*

642 *Rudolph Althoff's "tiger on horseback," Ringling Brothers, Barnum & Bailey Circus, 1966. Such acts greatly interest the Russians; in 1963 at the Moscow Circus, six lions rode horseback in this manner.*

643 *Liberty horses remain one of the most fundamental acts in the circus. Here they follow the command of the whip.*

644 *Tumblers "à la Richard," a turn using the traditional "Jockey of Epsom" costume.*

645 *Juanita Caroli in a somersault on horseback at the Knie Circus, Switzerland.*

646 *The Caroli family is one of the last among the great dynasties of the circus performing equestrian acrobatics. Enrico (first from left) for years has been doing his specialty of somersaulting from horse to horse, one of the most difficult of acts.*

632

633

634

635

638

639

636

637

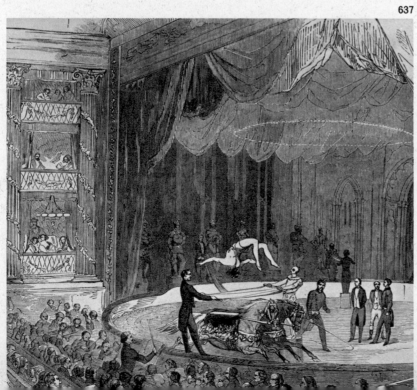

640

641

642

643

644

645

PART TEN

ECOLOGY OF THE HORSE

I
HEREDITY

An animal tends to adapt itself to the climate, terrain, and general conditions of the region in which it lives. It assumes, therefore, such characteristics that will permit it to live best there, and becomes modified not only in its internal functions but in its very structure, as well. A group of animals that have assumed, whether naturally or artificially, the very same characteristics is referred to as a breed.

Even in ancient times, breeders realized that work in the proper measure would improve the quality of the horse and that proper feeding was also essential to his development. These ideas, handed down along with many superstitions (the effects of the moon and atmospheric conditions on breeding, birth, and so on) permitted a certain artificial modification in some types of horse. Only in modern times, however, has the study of genetics brought us to where we can control nature itself within certain limits (though to a great extent) to obtain the kind of horse we wish.

The horse is fit for a great number of things, and each sort of employment calls for specific characteristics, which are further developed through work, proper food, and hygiene so that through the selection of the very best examples they can be passed on for reproduction.

Here we must, in the interest of science, note some of the theories that have been advanced on the subjects of heredity and reproduction (bearing in mind that a number of them have been disproved).

Saturation is the name given the repeated breeding of the same mare and stallion. It is contended that after a few good products, one can see a decline in quality due to the mare's cellular assimilation of the stud's characteristics. (Exceptions, however, and Thoroughbreds to boot, were Galopin, the fourth product of Flying Duchess and Vedette; St. Simon, the third product of Galopin and Saint Angela; Perdita and St. Simon, who produced both the celebrated Florizel and Persimmon; and Fausta and Signorino, who gave us the Derby winners Meissonier, Michelangelo, and Melozzo da Forli.)

Saturation also applies to the repeated crossing of one outstanding horse, such as was done, according to Becker, in France and in Italy, with the abused blood of Galopin. This may result in building up the blood, but at the same time reduces quality.

Telegony is the theory that a mare, in successive gestations, tends to reproduce the characteristics of the first stallion that mounted her.

Mendelian Law. The Austrian biologist and abbot Gregor Johann Mendel (1822–1884), in his studies of the reappearance of atavistic characteristics, noted the following fundamentals, which guide breeding to obtain certain determined traits: (1) In the mating of individuals of dissimilar characteristics (blue eyes and brown eyes) the dominant characteristic (brown eyes, in this instance) will prevail over the recessive one in the offspring; and (2) 25 percent of the offspring will be similar to one parent, 25 percent to the other parent, and 50 percent of them will share the dominant characteristics of both parents; while (3) in the mating of further couples, the heredity of each pair is independent of all the others.

II
WORK

Work is the natural, basic means for emphasizing given characteristics, considering the fact that function develops an organism. In a draft horse, for instance, we will find a well-developed back and a shortened cannon, these two parts of the body always complementing each other since they determine the balance of the horse's gait. In a cart horse, there will be a closer, less free articulation of the joints, a shortening of the trunk, wider spacing between the lateral pairs of legs, a broader sole, and a sloping croup. A fast-stepping harness horse acquires great facility in trotting, and therefore tends to broaden the movement of his back while diminishing the action of the hocks—to keep from tiring the tendons—bringing the lateral bipeds closer together in the gait. These characteristics reach their maximum expression in the horse bred for trotting races. Since he is constantly employed over all types of terrain and jumps, and must show a good deal of stamina, the saddle horse tends toward a broader skeletal structure, a lengthening in the neck, a shortening in the cannon, a straighter growth in the croup, and an increase in the bone angles of fore- and hind legs. In general, the saddle horse has rounded contours, is well balanced, and has a normal center of gravity. The saddle horse should give an impression of power and balanced mass and, when standing still, should give one a sense of great stability. In the Thoroughbred, the saddle horse's characteristics have been carried to the maximum, and sometimes beyond, because some of these horses are sorely overbred. We find in them, sometimes to excess, the long neck and shanks, pronounced bone angulation, great thoracic capacity, cardiacal hypertropy, development of the hindquarters, and shortening of the transversal

385

axis. Above all, these horses are extremely sensitive and excitable—the effect of heredity, intensive training, and competition.

III
CLIMATE

Climate does have an effect on the horse, but generally it is less telling than upon other animals. It is precisely this great adaptability of the equine species that has been responsible for the animal accompanying man wherever he can be of use to him. That has not been the case with the camel, for example, which is still restricted to its native habitat.

The horse appears to have originated in temperate, dry regions. Brought south, he achieved a strong sinewy appearance and a loss in stature, but without becoming truly small. In the north, in semiswamps, he lost his sinewy appearance and gained in stature, becoming fleshy, heavy, and lymphatic. As an example of the effect of swamp areas, it is difficult to maintain vigorous breeds in eastern Germany, where the soft terrain, lacking salts and phosphates, makes them weak.

Running wild, the horse generally adapts himself in direct proportion to the forage available: where it grows tall, so does he; where it is low, he is much lower to the ground. His value, therefore, is based upon the quality of his feed. Accordingly, climate reflects upon the animal's value not only directly, through heat and weather, but indirectly, as it affects the quality of his forage.

In humid areas, the horse's coat grows fuller, long hair appears on his extremities as protection, the spread of his hoof becomes greater to give him a more secure foothold on muddy terrain, and his sweat is always viscous and foamy. In sunny, dry climes, his body hair is very short; the pores are dilated for maximum perspiration, which becomes integrated with the horse's breathing; and superficial circulation becomes intense, which permits quick bursts of speed. Sandy soil allows for normal development of the hooves, which grow to be very light and elegant. In mountainous zones, the stony ground makes for a hard sole, the hooves tend to be smaller than normal, and the horse's stature is considerably diminished. Normally, he acquires a round croup, and full mane and tail; the legs become solid, usually irregular in line, as in the Avelignese horse and the breeds of the Jura and Caucasus mountains.

period and during the communal era, as well as being an indispensable means of transport and a war machine in a land particularly broken and hilly (where Roman roads were no more than a memory). It was only with the Renaissance in Italy that the nobility founded their own studs, either through necessity, as a form of ostentation, or entertainment. These were fortified with the blood of Arab stallions and broodmares they imported, which led to the founding of the splendid Mantuan, Ferraran, Neapolitan, and Piedmontese breeds. It was these stupendous horses that inspired some of the greatest Italian painters and sculptors. Their work caught the eye of the English and French, who were quick to buy the type of horses they had seen depicted to improve their own stock. Edward IV of England bought eight hundred stallions in Lombardy; Henry VIII imported bay mares in groups from Mantua, among which were a number from the stud of Francesco Gonzaga. For stallions from that same stud, Henry offered to give their weight in sterling. Gradually, these resources disappeared, so that by the middle of the eighteenth century nothing remained of the famous Italian breeds, apart from some random references in the writings of pompous academics.

With the unification of Italy, the state attempted to restore certain breeds to their former place of distinction, such as the Sardinian, the Maremman, Friulano, and Persano, but with negative results on the whole. Great errors were made, above all, their regard for the horse not as a resource but as a luxury.

Notwithstanding, equine patrimony increased from 432,000 head in 1861 to 1,050,000 in 1926. Despite the lack of favorable conditions for development, descending to 665,000 by 1944, there were 796,000 head shortly after the end of World War II. After 1950, there was another regression, so that today there are approximately 400,000 horses in Italy. This number undoubtedly will decrease with the increase of mechanized agriculture, and will not be offset by the considerable increment in the number of horses used for sport (as has been the case in France, England, Germany, and Switzerland). Either this is because Italians are disciplined toward horse breeding generally or because of the difficulty of employing horses in the open in a country that is mountainous over two-thirds of its area, and where the remaining open fields are being turned into residential lots

IV
ITALIAN BREEDS

Even in the remotest antiquity, Italy must have had good horse breeds. In Puglia, the valley of the Po, the Neapolitan region, and the Tuscan Maremma were from the point of view of climate and terrain ideal regions for producing animals of fine conformation and quality.

With the advent of the barbarians, these breeds declined, and substitutes for the Middle East horses—imported from the time of Mark Antony—were either the swift and scraggy Mongolian breeds or the heavy chargers from the German plains.

The horse figures in all the endless fights of the Lombard

647 648 *Equus Przewalski, or the tarpan, forefather of the modern horses.*

649 *Tarpan with a stripe down its back. The coat changes from brown in summer to white in winter.*

650 *Tarpans at the Rotterdam Zoo.*

651 *A seventeenth-century print depicts the flowing lines of a Breton horse.*

652 *Seventeenth-century print of a Frisian horse.*

653 *Eighteenth-century woodcut of a Latium stallion.*

654 *Combat between stallions, eighteenth-century woodcut.*

655–660 *Gonzagan horses.*

647

648

649

650

651

652

653

654

655

656

658

657

659

660

661   662

663

to meet the demands of municipalities that are responding to economic necessity and the exigencies of overpopulation.

Let us examine the Italian breeds of today, or rather, those breeds most popular in recent years. The Belgian horse was imported to better the Cremona strain, and has practically replaced it as the typical heavy-draft horse. The Belgian has a large frame, solid articulations, and massive musculature. Calm, phlegmatic, and rather lymphatic, he is a powerful hauler (weight: 1,750 pounds; height: 16 hands; collar measurement: 88 inches; cannon measurement: 11 inches), but because of his great weight he is going out of favor.

Preferred over the Belgian is a horse of Breton extraction, having smaller proportions, and greatly appreciated for the precision and swiftness of his walk. He has come into widespread use in the Veneto, the region of Ferrara, in many of the Emilian provinces, and near Brescia. After much importing of the Percheron and Boulogne breeds, it was found that the Bretons were even better for Italian purposes, perhaps because of their affinity for Italian draft broodmares.

The Noric horse, which is small, spare, strong, and extremely docile, is best for slow, heavy draft. It is generally raised in the Val Pusteria, Val Badia, and the valleys of the Isarco River. The Noric horse averages about 1,550 pounds, runs between 15 and 17 hands high, and has a collar measurement of between 78 to 86 inches. He derives from the ancient autochthonous race bred in the Roman province of Noricum, which, though it declined during the barbarian invasions, came into its own again during the time of Charlemagne, being further strengthened in its influence during the sixteenth century, in the period of the Salzburg archiepiscopate.

A typical mountain horse, energetic and sober, is the Avelignese, raised with a passion in the Venosta Valley and in the Sarentino region. The horse averages 14 hands in height, 70 inches around the collar, and weighs about 1,900 pounds. He is very popular in the Alto Adige, where there are about 3,000 head, and is now bred in other regions down through the Italian peninsula to Policoro in the Basilicata. A number of horse fairs are held in the territory of Avelengo. The Avelignese is also an excellent saddle horse. He derives from horses left free to roam the pastures of Avelengo (in the vicinity of Merano) by Ludwig IV's army when it returned to Austria in 1342. These horses developed a characteristic sorrel coat, full mane and tail, and a blaze. Pedigrees of Avelignese horses go back to the foundation sire El Behavi, foaled in 1837, and to the even better-known Folie, out of a mare sired by El Behavi and an Arab stallion.

The Maremman horse is almost completely extinct today. He was a rustic, solid, but by no means handsome animal that can still be recognized in many Fattori paintings. Of the great strings that were once visible from the Leghorn-Rome train, none remain today except for a few crossbreeds. The last of the great studs, the De Rham, closed in 1950.

Campania attracts a certain interest in connection with the Persano stud there (a Bourbon creation that closed with the founding of the Italian republic), which established the Santa Maria Capua Vetere and Battipaglia remount stations. In that zone, near Persano, *hors concours* jumpers such as Merano and Posillipo have been bred at the Morese stud. The Persano breed was begun by Charles III in 1763 from wild horses (found in the Salerno plains and the valley of the Ofanto) bred with those from the Middle East and Spain. The breed developed in a short time, flourishing from 1780 to 1830. They had a beneficent influence on the entire south, giving the region solidly built horses of beautiful conformation. The Persano was suppressed in 1874 and reinstituted in 1900, starting with about eighty broodmares. About fifty remain today, most stemming from English Thoroughbreds, and apt to produce brilliant offspring.

Lucania and the Ionic part of Calabria are ideal situations for breeding horses that are strong and full of spirit. Horses of the Salerno, Anglo-Norman, and Maremman strains have produced a strong breed of saddle and draft horses in the Capitanata, all resulting from intelligent selection. In the Murge, a horse has been produced that is particularly fitted to light draft and farm work in dry, hilly, and rocky regions. The mares are used to produce mules.

Sicily has an equine patrimony of some 45,000 head, the large majority derived from imported Arab and Berber stallions. Throughout its history, Sicily has depended upon imported Arab stallions, and the characteristic Sicilian horse reflects this in its similarity to the Arabian in its vivacious expression, fine-drawn body, small head, elegant neck (a trifle short), and a straight dorsal line (but sloping croup).

An interesting breed is that of San Fratello (in the province of Messina), living almost completely wild in a sylvan region, and getting by on sparse winter forage and in a torrid summer. Attempts to improve the strain through crossbreeding have been a complete fiasco, even worse than the experience with Maremman horses (with which the San Fratello breed has some affinity).

Throughout its history, Sardinia has imported horses. It was a potent instrument in the Sardinians' unending attacks on the Arabs, who were masters of their coast. The island breed stems originally from the crossing of North African and Arabian horses. A true Sardinian breed, however, was established with the institution of the royal domain of Tanca de Paulilàtino, near Abbasanta, where Ferdinand the Catholic (1452–1516) had a stud of Andalusian horses, and conceded privileges to breeders. This led to the founding of the Padromannu, Mores, and Monte Minerva studs, which produced animals keen enough to compete with the Andalusians. When Sardinia passed to the House of Savoy in 1720, horse breeding was given short shrift, despite the predilection of the court for Sardinian horses.

It was only in 1908 that new blood came with the import of Arabian stallions, to give the Sardinian horse, once again, the appearance and qualities so prized by the people of the island. Sardinia had 60,000 horses in 1918, but that number had fallen to half in 1940, and by 1961 there were only 24,000 horses, while there are no more than about 300 select broodmares. It is interesting to recall that it was a Sardinian horse, Leda, who covered the 670 miles between Bergamo

661 *Turks, angular but brilliant.*
662 *An Arabian with full trappings.*
663 *Note the perfection of line and proportion in the pure Arabian.*

and Naples in ten days, while the Sassari-Cagliari trial of 150 miles normally took about thirty hours.

Lipizza is a locality situated about seventy-odd miles from Trieste. It was held by the Austro-Hungarian Crown prior to World War I, and is now part of Yugoslavia. The foundation stock of the Lipizzaner was derived from Spanish horses imported to Austria in 1562 by Maximilian II, who founded the court stud at Kladrub. His brother, the Archduke Charles, founded a similar stud in 1580 in the village of Lipizza, in Austria. Neapolitan blood had been added to the strain through the importation of selected animals who gave a particular unity to the structure of the breed.

By 1717, all importing of Spanish stallions had ceased, but some horses from Denmark (Pluto), the Campania (Conversano and Napolitano), and from Bohemia (Maestoso) were introduced into the stud. A century later, more Arabian stallions arrived to make the breed even more elegant. It was from these horses that the Habsburg court selected the royal carriage horses, as well as the magnificent gray saddle horses for the Imperial Riding School in Vienna.

At the beginning of World War I, on the emperor's order, the entire string at Lipizza was divided and shipped to safer locations, such as Laxenburg in Austria, and the Bohemian town of Kladrub, where important studs already existed. After the war, the Italians applied to the Austrian republic for restitution of the Lipizzaners, and succeeded in obtaining forty broodmares, three studs, and a number of colts. In World War II, also, the Lipizzaners had their ups and downs.

The Lipizzaner preserves the lines of the Andalusian and Neapolitan horses, and has an elegance, a harmony of aspect that is of another day. The horse has a small head, curved neck, broad chest, not very pronounced withers, a good dorsal line, and a round rump terminating in a rather raised tail. He has robust, well-muscled legs with salient tendons. He does not mature early and is long-lived. Though not too fast, the Lipizzaner is very intelligent, good-tempered, and endowed with a great power of concentration, thanks, undoubtedly, to the difficult schooling he is put through at the Spanish Riding School in Vienna. His gaits are elegant to see, but are frequently somewhat uncomfortable for the rider. Almost invariably the Lipizzaner is a very light gray, though he is foaled black or brown, and turns "white" between four and seven years of age.

V

BRITISH BREEDS

Without doubt, the country of origin of the most outstanding breeds of saddle, race, and light and heavy harness horses is England, which has dedicated itself to the selection and breeding of specialized strains since the sixteenth century.

The criteria used by the English in the selection of horses, which are technically perfect, are of Italian origin, and hark back to the fact that a great number of the broodmares known as the royal mares (from which the English Thoroughbred derives) were of Italian provenance. These animals were gifts to Henry VIII from the dukes of Mantua and Ferrara, and Catherine of Savoy.

The man who reorganized the royal stables was the Neapolitan Prospero d'Osma, called to England in 1575 by the Earl of Leicester, acting on the order of Queen Elizabeth. Not only has England given us the biological phenomenon of the English Thoroughbred, whose endurance and speed are incomparable, but other extraordinary horses as well. The Hackney,* or roadster (as it was once called), was at one time considered proper for riding over long distances, on the highway, as a saddle horse, and for light draft as well. Today, by "Hackney," we mean an elegant horse used for covering considerable distances, a cross between the Norfolk pony and the English Thoroughbred. The foundation sire of this line was the celebrated Thoroughbred Blaze. The Hackney has a characteristic, high-stepping trot, what the English refer to as "high action." At Norwich, the county town of Norfolk, a breeders' association publishes the Hackney stud book, many entries listed as covering 17 miles an hour.

The hunter is generally cold-blooded (not a Thoroughbred), unlike the steeplechaser, which is a Thoroughbred trained for cross-country riding and steeplechase racing. Neither the hunter nor the steeplechaser belongs to a precise breed, but that might very well not be the case in future generations. In Ireland, a particular breed of steeplechasers has been created that gives good results, and a type of hunter that is stockier than the English, and better equipped to take large obstacles. Having a good deal of thoroughbred blood, however, he has maintained a solid frame, a gentle character, and a good deal of courage. His head is heavy, the neck rather strong and not very long, the legs short, and in temperament he is very docile. Once the rider is in the saddle, the horse assumes a proud carriage, and before obstacles shows his good heart and security. As this breed improves, one sees less of the typical Irish saddle horse, strong, heavy, short in the leg, and inclined to jump with all four legs in the air at once, like a chamois or deer.

Hunters are classified as heavyweights (those capable of carrying about 200 pounds or more); middleweights (carrying 175 to 200 pounds); and lightweights (carrying 130 to 170 pounds). The principal market for these horses is the Dublin Horse Show, the greatest horse fair in the world for hunters and jumpers. It is generally held during the first week of August, under the auspices of the Royal Dublin Society.

The oldest of the English draft horses is the Cleveland Bay, which originated in Cleveland, in the County of Yorkshire. He was employed as a packhorse in the sixteenth century, when he was known as the Yorkshire pack or the chapman, and was improved by the mixture of thoroughbred blood toward the end of the eighteenth century. Heavily boned, resistant, and of agreeable character, these horses are adaptable to general service.

The Suffolk punch is a sleek, spirited cart horse that

---

* Varies in size from the pony to over 16 hands.—EDS.

664 *Murge horse, solid and squared.*
665 *Pontinian horses bathing.*
666 *Maremmans in for a swim.*
667 *The end of a Sardinian ride on a Sassari.*

665

666

664

667

668

669

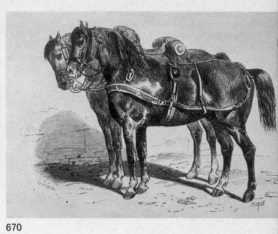

670

671

672

673

674

tends to grow round and fat. He has a deep body, short legs, is very vigorous, and usually no taller than 16 hands.

The Shire, or cart horse, is a heavy-draft horse springing from a cross of Dutch and English horses. He can weigh as much as 2,200 pounds, measures about 17 to 18 hands, is powerful, docile, slow, and has an immense musculature. Another heavy specimen is the Clydesdale, which originated in Lanarkshire, Scotland. Slightly smaller and lighter than the Shire which runs to about 1,750 pounds, and stands about 17 hands high, he is still very popular in the English country-side because of his extreme good humor and the ease with which he does almost every sort of heavy work. The Shire has his ancestor in the Old Black English horse of Lincoln-shire, which was derived from Frisian strains and war-horses used in northern Europe. Usually dappled gray, but some-times a dark bay, he has a magnificent, powerful appearance, measuring about 17 hands, and weighing about 2,400 pounds. Slightly shorter in the hoof than the Clydesdale, he is used a good deal in the fens.

Ponies are of particular interest. The name is applied to horses no higher than 14.2* hands. Really small are the Shetland (from Scotland), Welsh, New Forest, Dartmoor, Exmoor, those from the Hebrides, and the Irish Connemara. There are Shetlands that do not reach 9 hands.

The large pony can be used as a saddle horse for children, and is also used as a polo pony. Brilliant, fast, and easy to maneuver, he is now being supplanted by even faster and more spirited horses, particularly the American quarter horse, but at Hurlingham and Ranelagh polo ponies are still bred and much sought after because of their impulsion. (Horses used in polo, irrespective of height, are always called "ponies.") Also used as a polo pony is the Galloway, from Wales, standing about 14 hands, docile yet vigorous. He is said to derive from Andalusian horses that came ashore from the shipwrecks of the Armada. Cobs, small horses be-tween Hackneys and ponies, average 15 hands, but they are especially chunky, and can carry very heavy burdens.

The Exmoor from Somerset derives from a local breed used as pack animals from the times of the Celts. They reach a maximum height of 12.2 hands, are brown with a speckled muzzle, and prominent eyes. In winter, the coat thickens and becomes almost stiff. The Exmoor is still used as a packhorse in the hills, and for children's rides. Also used for children is the New Forest pony, which is extremely easygoing both in

* Equal to 14½ hands.—Eds.

668 *A Calvados breed derived from the Cleveland Bay. Note the old-fashioned Norman harness, quite difficult to find.*
669 *Anglo-Norman halfbred from Le Merlerault, 1852.*
670 *A fine example of the Ardennes breed.*
671 *Anglo-Norman coldbred produced through excessive crossbreeding with Thoroughbreds, 1860.*
672 *Breton halfbred from Azovskoye of the Léon type, 1852.*
673 *Breton pony from Briec, and a Scottish pony.*
674 *(A) Breton of the northern coast produced by crossbreeding a (B) Corlay workhorse with an Anglo-Arabian stallion.*

temperament and gait. He was mentioned as being employed during the time of Canute.

The Dartmoor pony is a neighbor of the Exmoor, and can still be found running wild. These ponies are greatly sought for children. They are very attractive and well pro-portioned, have small ears, a short-coupled back, good neck and shoulders, and are clearly of Eastern derivation. They average 12.2 hands.

Fell and Dales ponies derive from the Celtic pony, and were used as pit ponies during the last century. They are still employed for light farm work, and are generally found in Cumberland.

The Welsh pony is a mountain pony and a typical indige-nous breed, and might very well be a descendant of the string of horses Julius Caesar collected in what is now Merioneth-shire. The Hackney pony is a variety of Welsh pony, and is excellent for children to show.

The Welsh cob derives from the mountain pony, but is much larger, standing 15.1 hands, and has been mentioned in documents dating from the thirteenth century. He became famous during the reign of Richard I, when he was used as a war-horse and a roadster. When lighter, swifter horses appeared, the Welsh cob became a favorite for farm work.

The Highland can carry a great deal of weight, and was used by farmers for transporting hay and forage. This breed is brown or gray, with a black dorsal stripe, and silvery mane and tail. He attains a height of 14 hands on the mainland and 12.2 on the islands.

The Shetland is the leading and most characteristic pony of the Shetlands and Orkneys, where he is widely employed as a general service horse. He is the strongest pony among all similar breeds, and has become widespread in Europe and the United States. The Shetland's coat grows very thick during winter. In height, the Shetland runs be-tween 9.2 and 10 hands, has a somewhat odd conformation, but is pleasing in appearance. Rather proud, the Shetland is not always so docile as one would expect from its expression.

The Connemara pony, from Connaught, is similar in antecedents to the Highland. He has a brown or gray coat, with a black dorsal stripe, and silvery mane and tail. Im-proved during the Middle Ages through a mixture of Spanish blood, he was later refined by an infusion of Arab blood.

The Irish cob, slowly dying out as a breed, is a robust animal that serves as a powerful cart horse, and is very well built for the purpose.

England has a horse with a mottled hide, similar in appearance to the American Appaloosa. His origin is difficult to determine. The horse, or one very much like it, has been depicted in Chinese, Iranian, and European works of art. He seems to have no characteristic structure or conformation, but to be distinguished solely by his coat, which is rather bristly, with rougher spots tufted with dark hair. Mane and tail, as a rule, are a mixture of silver and black hair.

The Irish hunter is virtually a separate breed in Ireland, a country famed for its breeding of steeplechasers and flat racers, and above all for fine saddle horses, racehorses, and hunters. This is a strong, well-made animal (very much employed in the three-day event), powerfully built, of great stamina, and an excellent jumper. The breed has been some-what modified and refined in the past thirty years to lighten the head and reduce the size of what were exceptionally large shoulders and croup. In his present form, the horse is very much sought after as a racehorse. The Rock, Piero d'Inzeo's famous horse (later going to Mancinelli), was a typical Irish hunter.

VI
FRENCH BREEDS

France has more than half the horses in the European Common Market countries. In 1961, the country's equine patrimony was 1.7 million head, and in 1966, about 1.5 million. In 1966, 130,000 horses were foaled, of which 40,000 were racehorses and 5,000 saddle horses. About 1,800 Thoroughbreds were foaled in 1950; 2,000 in 1961; and 2,500 in 1966; 1,400 trotters were dropped in 1950; 2,000 in 1961; and 2,800 in 1966. France exported 335 Thoroughbreds in 1960, which brought a total of approximately $2,150,000, while export sales of trotters accounted for approximately $126,000. To these figures must be added the stud fees received by the national centers, preservers of the great French bloodlines, which maintain a total of 2,136 stallions.

The Anglo-Arab has always flourished in the southwest, north, and the Limousin, where he is raised as a saddle horse. The horse that was known as the part-bred, which had a Norman strain, and is now called the French saddle horse, is raised in Normandy, Anjou, the Vendée, Cher, and Charolais. However, this horse is now in a difficult situation because he is not being acquired by the cavalry as a remount. This situation has been somewhat assuaged by the Sociétés Hippiques Rurales et Urbaines (Town and Country Horse Clubs), which numbered 300 in 1961 and 360 in 1966, having a total of more than 8,000 members from every walk of life. This results from the extraordinary recent French interest in equitation and equestrian sports (300 races, 95 three-day events, and 70,000 registrations).

The story of the horse in France goes back to the Celts who came down out of Asia, and then through Russia, riding small horses that were highly resistant to the fatigue and privations of that long migration. It was these horses that formed the foundation stock of that eminently manageable and rustic type the *bidet* (literally, "pony"), which withstood the pressure of the Roman cavalry, and was mentioned by Caesar. Crossed with the heavy pack mares of the Roman legions, the *bidet* gave origin to that muscular, double-backed horse so common in the region around Brest, although the squarish head still reveals a trace of Eastern blood.

We know, for example, that the moon was called "the white mare," and the sun was represented by the Druids as a horse. The Druid tradition survived in parts of France up to the arrival of the Irish monks, St. Columban and St. Gall, who transformed the cult, and its pagan symbols became Christian ones. Thus, the Bretons, excellent horsemen, would exalt St. Thelan or St. Eloy whenever they were victorious, and, in commemoration, dedicate equestrian statues to them.

We also know that abbots and feudal lords had stud farms. In 1213, Viscount Rohan brought home nine stallions that he had received as a gift from the Sultan of Egypt. In 1230, the rights to the city of Brest were sold for a hundred lire plus a white mare (mount); and in 1338, the celebrated Guerino the Mean (Bertrand de Guesclin), struck down sixteen knights, always riding his Breton workhorse, a com-

mon type in those times. Playing a great part in adding to the stock of Breton horses, the Rohans raised them semiwild on their lands, and Olivier de Rohan devised protectionist laws that prohibited the export of prize stallions. Henry II (1519–1559) founded stud farms at Tournelles, Melun, Saint-Léger, and Ciron, but the results could not have been any more than mediocre if Henry IV (1553–1610) was hard pressed to find 3,000 chargers for the Battle of Arques. During his reign, Arab and Navarino stallions were imported into Brittany, leaving their traces in the gray coat of many a *bidet*.

Imports from Germany were resorted to, and Louis XIII (1601–1643) made an effort to reorganize the studs, at the expense of the royal treasury—an attempt that failed because of poor administration of the *haras* (stud farms). With that, Colbert entered the scene, and entrusted Gédéon de Garsault with the task of reorganizing the stud and stables at Le Pin-au-Haras, near the lands of the Counts of Armagnac. The first royal stud farm grew out of a decree of 1665, after visits had been paid to the English and German horse farms.

The French then imported studs of various strains—English saddle horses, Turks, Berbers, and Prussians—and created new breeds of cart horses by crossing them with the robust Léon mares, which were used to create the Breton Norfolk, and then the double-backed *bidet* of Briec.*

The definitive decree organizing the royal *haras* was published on February 22, 1727. Toward the end of 1730, the Bey of Tunis offered Louis XV four stallions, which he accepted, presenting three of them to the Duke de Rohan. The fourth, considered too rustic by the king, was sold to a Parisian water carrier who, in turn, sold it to the Englishman Coke, from whom it passed into the hands of Lord Godolphin.

By 1780, the royal stud farms were at their peak. With the advent of the Revolution, there were forty-four royal stallions in Brittany, and five hundred privately owned ones. In areas where pasturage was sparse, the famous *bidets*, angular but well-built, gray, sorrel, or roan, and small in stature, still flourished, while the Bretons, on the coast, were better developed. A decree of the Constituent Assembly of 1790 called for the closing of the royal stud farms, and the sale of the stallions to farmers. In 1792, however, the exigencies of war made it apparent that remounts were necessary. The government turned to Germany, but when the Germans refused to sell it was forced to requisition horses from the French studs, which completed their ruin. With a Directory law (2 Germinal in year III), arrangement was made for the provisional reestablishment of "depots of state stallions,"

---

* At this point, we might mention that on the Continent, centers or stations (depots, as they are best rendered in English), are stud farms stabling "traveling" studs, servicing mares in various parts of the country, and there are also what Americans customarily think of as stud farms, either privately owned or belonging to the government.

---

675 *Working a Percheron at the Du Pin Stables.*
676 *Fantastic-looking Belgian.*
677 *Elegantly structured Anglo-Norman.*
678 *Ardennes, one of the oldest of breeds.*
679 *A Percheron of rare strength and beauty.*

675

676

677

678
679

680

681

682

but it was only with the return of the empire that organic, regulatory laws were made, creating six stud farms and thirty-two depots.

The order that Napoleon, as emperor, imposed upon equestrian affairs still exists, though in somewhat modified form. He was responsible for the great upsurge in the breeding of saddle horses, which were required as remounts for his cavalry. Furthermore, in 1870, with the desire to erase the memory of the defeat suffered at the hands of the Prussians, the French turned to the raising of heavy draft horses, needed for the caissons of the artillery, and there was great production of horses in Brittany and Normandy. Arab stallions were brought to Lamballe and to Hennebont, but the best results were obtained through the English Norfolk, from which the French derived the Breton Norfolk—small, robust, athletic, and very rustic in type, used both for draft and as a saddle horse.

The *boulonnais*, or Boulogne horse, a colossus used for heavy draft, does not appear to have been in existence at the time of the Roman conquest of Gaul, and therefore it is conjectured that the breed descended from Numidian horses imported into the country by Caesar, and then crossed with mares of northern European strains. The result was a horse of the Arabian type on a considerably larger scale. Through the years, and the process of natural selection, the type has come almost invariably to have the gray coat that has always been highly prized. Losses in the two world wars and the upheaval connected with them have considerably reduced the number of this breed.

The Ardennes horse was, at one time, much sought after for the light cavalry. Today, of course, it has other uses. These horses are bred over a large part of France, about 10 percent of the national territory, actually, in the Champagne, Alsace-Lorraine, and the Franche-Comté. Descended from the Solutré, an ancient breed found in Saône-et-Loire, the horse spread rapidly throughout the French and Belgian Ardennes region.

The Percheron* is famous not only for its excellent nature but also for its light, elegant gait and its great stamina as a heavy draft horse. There are two types: the large Percheron, which stands about 17 to 18 hands and weighs about 2,200 pounds; and the small Percheron, which is about 15 to 17 hands as a rule, and proportionately lighter in weight, and was a type particularly favored by the artillery. The calcareous soil, rich in phosphates, and the apple orchards surrounded by evergreen bushes in the valley of the Huisne—where the best Percherons are bred—provide these horses with the abundant forage they need, and give them their sculptured, well-formed appearance. The majority of the Percherons are a dappled gray, have many characteristics of the Arab horse, and a very sweet nature. Arab horses that were the probable ancestors of the Percherons must have

* Named from the old French district of La Perche, to which it is native.—EDS.

680 *The early Norfolk that was used to improve the trotter.*
681 *Norfolk with thoroughbred blood.*
682 *Cream pony of the British Isles.*

been those that were left behind when the Saracens were defeated on the plains of Vouillé. The Percheron line is said to spring from the stallion Jean le Blanc, foaled in 1823 in the Orne.

At one time, the Norman horse was a product of the Western-type stallions introduced into France by the Normans. Today, however, this horse has practically disappeared, and has been replaced by the Anglo-Norman—an excellent saddle and carriage horse used a great deal to improve the breeds in the north of France. The Norman horse is widely raised around Caen, in the pastures of Calvados and La Manche, as well as in the Orne.

The Poitou horse descends from Dutch types. He is not an attractive animal, standing tall, with a long head, long ears, usually dropped, a thick neck, small eyes, high withers, low back, thick legs, heavy joints, long hocks, a heavy barrel, a full mane, and heavily feathered from knee to pastern; but he is very solid, with great endurance. Generally, the coat is bay or gray. The breed is especially prized for the production of Poitou mules, which are much sought after.

The Pompadour breed, a cross of purebred Arab and Anglo-Arab, is principally produced to furnish studs for southern France.

The crossing of the English Thoroughbred with the Tarbes horse produces the type known as the *bigourdan,* taller than the Tarbes, best resembling him in the head and neck, although his loins are not so well coupled and he has a narrow chest and long legs.

The famous Camargue horse lives in a semiwild state in the marshy region near Arles, on the Rhône delta. Strings of these horses are used in herding the bulls of the Camargue. They are sturdy, fast, and quick off the mark, though rather stringy and slender in conformation. The Camargue horse has a handsome head, notable strength, and shows good endurance. As a rule, the Camargue stands about 12.2 hands.

VII
GERMAN BREEDS

During the Middle Ages, Germany—which had flourishing studs, particularly for heavy packhorses—let its own breeds decline, and resorted to importing horses from Italy, France, and Denmark. Then Frederick II of Prussia created remount stations and studs in order to free the army from dependence upon foreign horses. Count von Lindenau was entrusted with the direction of these studs in 1780, and shortly afterward brought the Trakehner to its full splendor.

The Trakehner stud, founded in 1742 in the vicinity of Stallupönen, in East Prussia, near Königsberg, bred robust horses that were developed into a particular breed through the admixture of Eastern blood and then, during the last century, further refined through the addition of an English Thoroughbred strain. The Trakehner breed was used both as a saddle and draft horse. Dispersed during World War II, the breed is being reconstituted. It was the Trakehner breed that provided carriage horses for the Imperial stables.

The Hannoveraner is a breed that has always produced carriage horses. They also saw a good deal of service in the light artillery. Cold in temperament, docile, and patient, the Hannoveraners are now sturdy saddle horses that have given rise to many of the best show jumpers and steeplechasers ridden by German horsemen in competition.

Germany also had distinctive breeds from Schleswig-Holstein, Mecklenburg, Württemberg, and Oldenburg, all of which resented damp climate, and most of them rapidly declined, even though they were bred with Eastern studs.

Among the oldest of the German breeds is the Holsteiner, which was bred and much sought during the Middle Ages as the best war-horse and tournament steed. Now, naturally, the breed has been refined and has lost some of the strength and endurance it had at one time. Today, the Holsteiner is considered a good, sure jumper.

The Oldenburger is a rather heavy animal that has had a good infusion of Anglo-Arab blood. Now that it has been getting a good deal of pure blood, the breed is changing its appearance somewhat.

The Dülmen is found half wild in Westphalia. This horse has been documented as existing as far back as 1316. Very rustic, it is used as a farm animal.

The Shetland has acclimated itself very well in Germany, becoming somewhat finer there, where it is used for light work in the country.

VIII
DUTCH BREEDS

The Netherlands has always produced draft horses and carriage horses that were elegant in form but rather lethargic and soft, inevitably the consequence of the damp climate and rank pasturage. An old saying had it that Dutch horses were "good in the mouth but bad in the legs." Nowadays, through the use of concentrated rations, the Dutch are attempting to breed animals with more fire and vigor.

Holland was famous for its Frisian horse, a breed derived from ancient stock and whose attractive conformation made him one of the favorite subjects of the great Flemish masters. Generally dark in color and of massive conformation, the Frisian is a good saddle and light draft horse. His bearing is superb, and in character he is very docile but extremely sensitive. The Frisian is a handsome animal, with a full mane and tail, and a very hard worker, as well as decorative. The breed was seriously declining just before World War II but it has been restored and strengthened through the mixture of Oldenburger blood.

While the Groningen breed has almost disappeared (a shame, for the horse is extremely good-tempered, and excellent both as a cart and saddle horse), the Gelderland, which has Spanish and Neapolitan origins, as well as a good deal of Norfolk roadster blood, is much prized for work as a light cart horse and a saddle horse, as well. He is also considered a fine jumper.

IX
DANISH BREEDS

The Danish breed, which in the past furnished studs and broodmares for a good part of Europe, is practically extinct today. It combined Andalusian and Neapolitan strains, and, with an Arab cross, is remembered for giving the world the Orlov breed, by Count Orlov. The horse was not only fine for riding but was about the best of trotters and light harness horses, until he was supplanted by the American trotting horse (Standardbred).

A characteristic Danish breed is the Frederiksborg, which came into being around 1562, based on Spanish and Italian blood, and is used for school equitation. In 1939, the breed received a mixture of Oldenburger and Frisian blood. Useful for light farm work, the Frederiksborg is also a good saddle horse.

The Knabstrup, which is lighter than the Frederiksborg and has a spotted coat, has a stud book that goes back to 1808, when Spanish troops stationed in Denmark left their broodmares which had rusty or black spots.

X
BELGIAN BREEDS

Belgium has given us a type of heavy draft horse, more or less definitive, that is derived from Brabant, Flemish, and Ardennes strains. The horse is a big animal, standing about 17 hands or more, fleshy, sturdy, heavy, with small, inexpressive eyes, a short, massive neck, broad withers, broad but sunken back and loins, powerful, muscular shoulders, large, flat knees, short cannons, and good hooves. This horse can weigh as much as 2,000 pounds.

The Belgian Ardennes horse, not to be confused with the French Ardennes, is smaller, more streamlined, and lighter, and provided cavalry chargers for Caesar against the Gauls. The horse later demonstrated his great utility during Napoleon's Russian campaign. The French cavalry defeated by the English at Waterloo was almost wholly mounted on Belgian Ardennes. This is the horse that best recalls the steed of the medieval knight.

XI
SWISS BREEDS

Switzerland has a breed of horse of which it is particularly proud, the Jura, also known as the Fribourger. These are bays of distinctive form, having a certain elegance and dash, despite their heavy barrels and shoulders. Their legs are slender, in proportion to their bodies. At Avenches (the Roman Aventicum), near the Lake of Morat, is the republic's stud depot.

XII
SPANISH BREEDS

We know that the *Equus ibericus,* or Iberian horse, was much prized by the Romans. The Moors' long occupation of the

683 *Typical Oldenburger stallion.*
684 *George Stubb's "Horse with English Saddle." One of the most delightful of all equestrian paintings.*

683

684

685

686

Iberian Peninsula was most favorable to the production of fine horses, and gave rise to the famous Andalusian breed, which, for their quality and sheer beauty, were, and still are, in demand all over Europe for the improvement of local strains.

War, political crises, and diffidence, however, have had a disastrous effect on Spanish horse breeding. Today the greater part of stud farms are still found in Córdoba, Seville, Granada, Murcia, and Estremadura.

Spain's most famous horse is still the Andalusian: brilliant, with good gaits, graceful, extremely docile, of rare strength, and highly valued for *haute école* work and as parade horses. They have dark coats, abundant mane and tail, and stand 15.2 hands. They derive from a Berber-Spanish cross, and though the gait is very smart, they are rather ordinary in build.

The Spanish jennet, from Granada, is also a great favorite. These little horses, docile, intelligent, and agile, were very popular during the Middle Ages for carrousels, jousts, and tourneys.

Spain has another horse, very characteristic of its equine strains, known as the Sorrai (Garranos), an indigenous pony that has peculiar striations on its legs. It has not been domesticated, as has been the case with other ponies, and has been thought by certain hippologists to be a direct descendant of *Equus przewalski*.

XIII
PORTUGUESE BREEDS

Portugal is noted for its Lusitano, an elegant carriage horse and a good saddle horse, as well. Breeding of this type, however, has not been too active. There is another type, the Alter, which is slimmer than the Lusitano proper (robust, well knit, and massive). There is also a variety of Portuguese pony called the Minho.

XIV
CZECHOSLOVAKIAN BREEDS

Czechoslovakia has one distinctive bred, the Kladruber, which derives from a sixteenth-century Spanish horse, and takes its name from the stables at Kladrub in Bohemia. This breed was very popular at the Austro-Hungarian court for parades and for use as a carriage horse. Its coat is predominantly gray and it has a very well-developed conformation. The Kladruber averages about 19 hands.

685 *Camargue horses at Sainte-Marie-de-la-Mer.*
686 *Elegant specimen of the Mecklenburg breed.*

XV
AUSTRIAN AND HUNGARIAN BREEDS

Austria has always been a great producer of fine horses. In 1792, the famous Radautz breed was created in Bukovina from Oriental, Russian, Ukrainian, and Caucasian strains. Horses of great stamina, light and elegant, the Radautz were the basis of the Habsburg cavalry. The introduction of English studs had felicitous results. On the other hand, the horse that is typical of Styria and Carinthia is heavy, stocky, with a large chest and a big head. This animal was fine for heavy or light draft work, even express work, and was ideal for service in the artillery. The Kladruber, coming from a strain established in 1570 in Bohemia, was an attractive, supple, powerful, and high-stepping carriage horse.

The great source of horses, however, was the Hungarian plains, where there were always tremendous herds at pasture. The English cavalry, not to mention the German and the Italian, always got a large number of remounts from Hungary; and in the era of horse-drawn trams, the large majority of trolley horses were Hungarian.

The principal Hungarian breed is the Mezohegyes, which was created by Emperor Joseph II in 1785 by crossing Spanish and Neapolitan horses. Most of these horses are bred in Bekes.

In 1815, a celebrated Norman stallion, Nonius, was brought from France. This stud had a great influence on Hungarian stock, giving a distinct character to the Mezohegyes, and making those horses he sired chunkier and hardier. Nonius gave his name to the new strain, which is a breed of carriage horse that is also well adapted to the saddle; all are big, good-looking bays. There is also a Nonius variety that is a smaller edition of the standard breed. A horse with Eastern blood is the Gidran, which also has Nonius blood, but is softer in line. He is generally sorrel in color. The Furioso derives from an English thoroughbred stallion of that name imported into Hungary in 1842 to put more quality and speed into the Nonius line.

The best saddle horses, however, are those descending from another English stud, imported in 1813, and named North Star, as is the breed. A most harmonious conformation, equally good as a saddle or light draft horse, the North Star was eagerly acquired by Europeans. Another mixture of Hungarian, Norman, and Spanish blood is the Babolna breed produced by Joseph II in 1789.

The production of thoroughbred racehorses in Hungary was brilliant, particularly after importing some prize studs—among them Buccaneer, for whom a great sum was paid. Buccaneer sired Kisber, foaled in 1873, who three years later won the English Derby and the Paris Grand Prix. Today, Hungary still takes a good deal of interest in the breeding of light draft and work horses, but Thoroughbreds are not forgotten. As a matter of fact, when one compares Polish, Bohemian, Yugoslav, and Hungarian horses, the Hungarian are always the finest.

XVI
POLISH BREEDS

At the present time, Poland is giving a great deal of attention to the breeding of saddle horses. Every year both wild and select animals are presented at auction to buyers from the West.

There still is extant in Poland a breed deriving from the tarpan *(Equus przewalski)*, that same tarpan that pastured wild on the steppes of eastern Europe right down to the middle of the last century. After 1870, when the wild breed had become extinct, the Polish authorities collected horses from farms that had some of the tarpan's characteristics and, in an effort to "re-create" the breed, turned these animals loose in the forest reserves of Bialowieza and Popielno. These horses proved to be very prolific, and produced a breed whose coat turns white in winter—ordinarily chestnut or mouse-brown with a dorsal stripe—with a dark mane with silvery hairs intermixed, concave profile or ram-headed, short neck, strong shoulders, long back, and full flanks.

The Konik is the domesticated version, more or less, of the tarpan. His conformation is more refined than that of the half-wild horses above, which are robust and compact. The Konik is the foundation stock of almost all the Russian and Polish horses of medium height, and stands about 13 to 14 hands high.

The Huzul, a mountain pony, generous in form, very steady, is considered, particularly in Galicia, to be a descendant of the tarpan. His color is brown, and he is characterized by his short legs and a heavy body almost cylindrical in form.

The Sokolsk is a breed created about a century ago, with Norfolk and Breton studs and a mixture of Anglo-Norman blood, as well. This is an excellent workhorse for the country. He is generally light brown in color, docile, and very good-natured.

A new breed arose out of the horses abandoned in East Germany after the defeat of the Reich in 1945. Called the Masuren, the breed is very similar to the East Prussian breed, being strong, muscular, and about 16 hands high. He makes a good carriage horse, a well-proportioned general service animal, and, ultimately, if further refined, a saddle horse of some distinction.

Poland has also bred a racehorse that has an Arab cross. It was first mentioned in 1570. Three Arab strains are distinguished in Polish horses, the Shagya, Dahoman, and Gudran.

Crossing Masuren horses with Panje mares and Thoroughbreds, the Poles produced a particularly handsome animal in the Poznan, which is raised near Warsaw. This horse is well adapted for galloping over various terrains, and is, accordingly, much sought in the West as a hunter, despite the fact that the breed still tends to be rather heavy.

XVIII
RUSSIAN BREEDS*

According to the statistics of the *Production Yearbook for 1963* of the Food and Agricultural Organization of the United Nations, the Soviet Union that year was the nation with the greatest equine patrimony, with 9.1 million horses.† This is a drop from the 12.8 million for 1947, but indubitably the result of mechanization of farming methods.

Even though one finds a variety of dissimilar breeds, one can see in them a common ancestor—the Arab—whether they be the small mountain and steppe horses (exceptionally resistant to fatigue) or the old, noble Orlov breed, or even the Don's Arhal-Teke, and the new horses (more types than breeds) created by the government, such as the Budënny, Terskey, Kustanai, Toric, and the Vladimirer.

In the second half of the eighteenth century, horse breeding in Russia had become quite developed, and many foreign thoroughbred studs were introduced, even English Thoroughbreds, to improve the native breeds, in particular, the basic stock of the steppes.

Between 1790 and 1820, the noble Russian families tried to outdo each other and the Czarist government in importing the finest horses, while horse racing, under the initiative of Count Orlov-Chesmenki became even more popular and more like its English model. It seems that about 1830, there were some 4,000 studs in Russia, with about 200,000 broodmares producing saddle horses. The first volume of the *General Stud Book* for English Thoroughbreds showed 396 broodmares registered. In 1912, the European part of Russia alone had more than 24 million horses, and just about as many in its Asian territory, although in this area, it is true, about 30 percent of the horses were no more than about 12 hands high. In January of 1917, Russia had 9,274 stud farms, of which 6,000 were dedicated to the production of trotters and carriage horses.

In its first years, the Soviet regime encountered difficulties in reorganizing the country's equine production, having lost some 10 million head in the upheaval of revolution. A whole breed of horse native to the Don region had disappeared, just as strings of prize horses had dispersed or disappeared. Only 300 Thoroughbreds in the paddocks at the Moscow racecourse were saved, and the famous animals of

---

* Some of these notes are from *Cavallo Italiano,* a study published by Guiseppe Conforti.

† The most recent figures available show 7.9 million for 1965, surpassed by Brazil with 9.2 million.

XVII
ICELANDIC BREEDS

When the Vikings came to Iceland, around the middle of the ninth century, they brought with them a pony that soon assumed definite characteristics in the new country. Usually gray in color, the pony has had a mixture of British and Norwegian blood. Innumerable bands of these ponies were destroyed in a great eruption in 1784, and many more died in the terrible winters during the thirteenth to the eighteenth centuries, when the Gulf Stream deviated from the island.

687 *Holsteins, one of the oldest German breeds.*
688 *Hannovers, strong harness horses, even-tempered, and docile.*
689 *Classic Oldenburgers, rather heavy.*
690 *Garranos, similar to the Portuguese Sorraia.*
691 *Andalusian jennets, light and brilliant.*
692 *A group of the famous Lipizzaners.*
693 *The Swiss Jura, strong and fleshy.*
694 *The Swedish Gothland.*
695 *A perfect example of the Belgian breed.*
696 *Eighteenth-century print of a Dutch Gelderland.*

687

688

689

690

691

692

693

694

695

696

697

698

the Mantaschev and Lasarevsk studs were no more. The same was true of trotters. Only animals from small studs in the north were spared. The famous depots at Khrenovoye, Maliutin-Novosilzev, and Schekin were gone.

In 1923, there were 5,550 trotters of all ages. At that point, the work of rebuilding the Russian stock in a systematic manner began in earnest, thanks to the Russians' undying passion for horses. The best horses remaining from the various strains were concentrated in well-equipped stud farms, and breeding was oriented toward consolidating and improving the characteristics of each breed.

In thirty years of work, new breeds were created through good crosses, while simultaneously the old indigenous types of surpassing zoological interest (the Turkoman Arhal-Teke, Uzbek Karabagh, and the Kabarda of the Caucasus) were preserved and improved. Thus, in 1939, there were about 16 million horses in Soviet Russia, of which about 1.2 million were used for breeding purposes.

After the last decimation of the equine population in World War II, although few horses remained, those that did were of superior quality, and were bred to produce quantities of even better horses by resorting to exhaustive selection and artificial insemination. Furthermore, with fewer horses, there was more abundant pasturage for all, particularly in farming regions, where horses were bred and raised with other animals, as was the custom in France, particularly in Normandy and Brittany, Switzerland, and Germany.

Russia's pride is the Orlov trotter, notable for its beauty, power, and speed, which has been celebrated in Europe for more than a century and a half and which we have already discussed in detail in our comments on trotting horses. Toward the end of the last century, through the crossing of the Orlov with American trotters, the so-called Russian trotting breed was created, a robust type, though slightly lighter and faster than the classic Orlov.

In Russia, races are run to select the best of breed, sometimes over long distances, often over packed snow tracks in winter (muddy in spring), the record being held by Utenka, 1:25 1-10 for 1,000 meters (this would be about 2:17 for the mile).

Thoroughbreds have been raised in Russia for some two hundred years, and have received a good deal of attention. This is borne out in the many international successes achieved by Soviet horses, and they are continually being invited to the International at Laurel Park in Maryland.

The Don horse derives from local broodmares crossed with Karabagh, Turkoman, and Persian studs, and later with Orlov Rostopchin horses and English Thoroughbreds. Today's Don horse is a well-built animal, equally good as a saddle or light-draft horse. He is an attractive animal, well proportioned, Roman-nosed, or ram-headed, with an elegantly arched neck of proper length for his conformation, wide withers, good dorsal line, wide, solid loins, well-de-veloped haunches, and good legs and hooves, as in all horses that come from the dry steppes. His coat is predominantly sorrel, with gold highlights in it. The Don horse has particularly strong endurance. Zazhim, carrying 176 pounds in the saddle, covered 170 miles in twenty-four hours, a record surpassed by Bandurist, who did 183 miles in the same time.

The Budënny breed is raised in the region around Rostov. It was created under the personal direction of Marshal Budënny, crossing Don horses with selected English Thoroughbreds, and after twenty-five years resulted in a breed of first-class animals. They are a harmony of form and power, ideal for saddle and sport. The Budënny is broadly built and well developed, with deep shoulders, ample thorax, and a coat generally a metallic sorrel or bay. This horse has done well as a steeplechaser, in the three-day event, and in shows. The Soviet riders Filatov and Sitko have competed with two extraordinary Budënnys, Skachok and Ingas. Two of this breed covered 720 miles in 15 days, an average of 72 miles a day.

The Kabarda is one of the best breeds for the mountains. Raised in the Caucasus, he is used both as a saddle horse and as a pack animal. The Kabarda has a light head, convex profile, pronounced withers, a long back, though well supported, a coat generally bay, and he stands 15.3 hands high.

The Kustanai breed derives from a cross between broodmares from the Kazakh steppes and Don stallions. These half-breds are then matched with English Thoroughbreds or other saddle-horse breeds. The Kustanai are of average conformation, ranging 15.2 to 15.3 hands, and have almost as much distinction as the Budënny.

A breed of Trakehner is raised in the region around Rostov. They range from 15.2 to 16.3 hands high, and are very lively, elegant horses.

The Arhal-Teke breed is one of the most beautiful and oldest of Russian saddle horses, and has contributed to the creation of such types as the Trakehner and the Persian. The Arhal-Teke is raised in Turkmenistan, Kazakhstan, and the south. This breed has a delicate head, large, expressive eyes, good neck and shoulders, a narrow thorax, not too deep, flat rib cage, and a long, sloping back. They are fine horses, elegant in their shiny gray coats. The Arhal-Teke has an excellent reputation in Europe because of his many triumphs in competition (particularly a gold medal won by Absent, ridden by Sergey Filatov in the Grand Prix for dressage at the Rome Olympics).

The Soviet Union's many horses with Arab blood have given rise to various strains. Among the principal ones are the Kohilan, a sturdy, sober animal standing about 15 hands high; and the Siglavi (distinct from the Eastern purebred horse from which it originated), which has a very light head, wide forehead, large expressive eyes, and a concave profile. He is attractive, even elegant; his coat may be gray or sorrel, and he is generally 15.2 hands high. There is also a Habdan strain, which is bigger, since it has English Thoroughbred blood; it is also faster than the other Arab half-breds mentioned.

Russia also has developed a heavy-draft horse quite similar to the classic Belgian type but lighter in movement, with a head not so heavy, a short, massive neck, low withers, short, wide back, broad chest, and rotund rib cage. This type stands about 16 hands high.

697 *The Palomino enjoys great popularity in the United States.*
698 *The pinto's coat seems to be painted or sectioned. In the United States, the pinto was recognized as an individual breed as a result of pressure from various associations.*

The Toric breed is an Estonian horse standing 15.2 hands high, massive, sturdy, and extremely docile. There are also the Latvian horse, a powerful animal, and the cold-blooded Vladimirer, a hardy type that has been crossed with trotters and Suffolks, Percherons, and Clydesdales.

Another Russian horse that might be mentioned is the Pechora (or Zemaitukas) from Lithuania, which is singularly long-lived, has great endurance, and is extremely stolid. He is very robust, though not particularly attractive from an aesthetic point of view

XIX
NORWEGIAN BREEDS

The Norwegians are proud of their Fjord (or Western) pony, which is gray or cream, and has a dark dorsal stripe and dark mane and tail. This was probably the first horse used by the Vikings or Norsemen, and was spread by them throughout most of Europe. It appears that this Fjord has been raised in Norway from the time 2000 B.C. An exceptionally muscular animal, blocky and massive, he has a neck so thick that it is hard to tell where it ends and the shoulders begin. The Fjord stands 14.1 hands high.

There are also the Nordic which is related to a group of Baltic ponies said to derive from the tarpan, and the Döle Gudbrandsdal, which springs from a Danish horse, improved with trotter blood. The Döle Gudbrandsdal is very strong, generally has a black coat, heavy neck, strong hindquarters, and a flowing mane and tail that have an overall rustic appearance. A variety of this breed is used as a trotter, and can cover a kilometer (0.6 mile) in one minute. This type is extremely solid, has strong legs, and stands 15.1 hands.

XX
SWEDISH BREEDS

The Gothland (Skogruss) is a Swedish pony raised on the island whose name it bears, a descendant of an ancient, wild breed. About a century ago, Eastern stallions were introduced into Sweden, imparting a distinct elegance, a particularly neat and balanced conformation, to the Gothland. The breed is used in trotting races. They are strong and intelligent, though somewhat obstinate or even downright bad-tempered at times, as seems to be so with many small horses. The Gothland stands 12.1 hands high.

The Swedish saddle horse derives from West Prussian, Hannoverian, and Thoroughbred stock, and has made an excellent showing in every equestrian event in recent Olympics.

XXI
FINNISH BREEDS

Finland's outstanding horse is the Finland Universal, and its variant, the Finnish draft horse, which is a bit smaller. The Finland Universal is particularly sweet-tempered, lively, courageous, and long-lived. He comes from a cross between imported breeds and the indigenous pony of the coast. This is the horse that has encouraged the growth of harness racing in Finland.

XXII
GREEK BREEDS

Greece, which once had flourishing studs in its classical period, now has the Peneia pony raised in the Peloponnese, from where the breed takes its name. The animal is used on farms as a packhorse, though in appearance he recalls the exquisite lines of the horses in ancient Greek sculpture. In fact, the Peneia wears a collar similar to those depicted in Assyrian art.

Varieties of the pony are the Pindos, bred in the mountainous parts of Epirus and Thessaly, perhaps deriving from the Achaean, Thessalian, and Thracian breeds mentioned by the poet Oppian (about A.D. 206); and the Skyros (reminiscent of the tarpan), from the island of that name in the Aegean, whose small size—9 to 9.2 hands—is due primarily to his extremely spare ration.

XXIII
ARABIAN BREEDS

According to the Koran, Allah created the horse for man's delectation. From the seven foundation sires selected by Solomon derive the seven Arab races: Korilan ("painted eyelids"); Maneghi ("proud-necked"); Hedregi ("tireless"); Saklani ("intelligent"); Gifli ("vigorous"); Hadban ("noble"); and Trefi ("proud"). Another tradition confuses the story but does not contradict it in principle, relating that the Arab breeds sprang from the beautiful mares brought as a gift to Solomon by the Queen of Sheba after commandeering them from one of the most appealing regions of Arabia. Another popular legend has the thoroughbred Arabian coming from the five mares of Muhammad, the ones who suddenly appeared at Mecca carrying the news of the Prophet's victory. In any event, for the Arab the horse is a gift of God, and for that reason the Koran includes precepts, advice, and strictures for breeding, maintaining, and schooling a horse, all of which had a great deal to do with improving Arabian horseflesh.

The horse that might be the prototype of the Arabian is said to have originated in the Negev, in the south of Israel, for which reason Arabian horses are known as Nedjedis ("of the Negev"). During the last century a suspicion arose that a true thoroughbred Arab had never been seen in Europe. The prospect seemed to be confirmed by the extremely negative results that had been obtained from crosses of European horses with so-called Arabian stallions. Such studs did prove capable of correcting defects in a strain and in modifying conformation as well as improving the temperament of breeds they were crossed with, but it was rare that they improved the breed itself. On the contrary, it was more usual to find that they had produced new defects in a strain deriving from an inharmonious development in the offspring.

Here, of course, we must mention the three great foundation sires of the English Thoroughbred, the Godolphin Barb, the Byerly Turk, and the Darley Arabian, confessing that their fantastically fine effect is still a biological mystery. One might conjecture that they were perhaps the only true purebred Arabians to reach Europe, while all the others imported from the East or Africa as Arab horses were nothing more than half-breds, good-looking (even magnificent) in appearance, but actually of Arab-Turkoman or Arab-Persian blood.

The Arabian horse in reality is a fine animal in his own environment. Away from home, however, he tends to wane and lose a good deal of his substance. Such horses as a rule become very fast animals of little stamina. It is believed that only in El Zahara and at Ein Shams are pure Arabian horses bred today.*

The true Arabian has a small head, wide forehead, small, pointed ears that are very mobile and rather close-set, large, expressive eyes that are full of fire, a straight or slightly concave profile, wide nostrils, and a long, well-arched neck, broad at the base and adorned with a silky mane. The Arabian's withers are quite pronounced. He has short but broad loins, is straight- or slightly sway-backed, and has a long, straight, broad croup. The tail is full, set high, and carried with great elegance. Shoulders are long and sloping, while the chest is full, extremely dry, and strong as steel. The joints are large, the muscles and tendons well marked, the hooves shapely, small, and very solid. The hide is fine enough to show the superficial veins, while the coat is extremely short, smooth, and shiny. The predominating colors among Arabians are gray, sorrel, and bay. One rarely sees black or white, while roan, dun, and dappled Arabians are virtually nonexistent. The average Arabian stands about 15 hands high.

Apart from the purebred Arabian, which is called the Asil, or Kamsa, or the Kocklani breed, one also finds in Arab countries the half-bred Shielet and the ordinary horse known as the Kedisqi.

An Arab proverb estimating the value and usefulness of the horse provides for a longevity of "seven years for my brother, seven for me, and seven for my enemy." According to an Arab, a Thoroughbred should have four broad features —forehead, chest, croup, and hocks; four long—neck, belly, haunches, and legs; and four short—loins, ears, pasterns, and tail. What we have is ecology dictated by esthetics.

The Syrian horse bears a great resemblance to the pure-bred Arabian, and is held by some to be a better horse over long distances. The Syrian is greatly prized for improving European breeds. Too frequently, however, run-of-the-mill pack animals used in the mountainous area (disdainfully called *beghiri*, a term more or less analogous to "nags"), are sold in Europe as first-rate Syrians. The purebred Syrian is exceptional among the breeds for its longevity, some of them living as long as forty years, and the incidence of stallions twenty-five and thirty who are still prolific studs is not at all unusual. The Syrian is generally gray or a burned sorrel, and stands about 15 to almost 16 hands.

The Mu'niqua is a type of Arabian horse completely different from the Western Arabian stereotype, being bigger and longer all around, more angular than curvaceous, and in some instances a bit hard. He is very fast, but still has considerable substance, and is the horse for the desert. This was the horse the Saracen conquerors introduced into Europe in the eighth and ninth centuries. The breed comprises two sub-groups, the Mu'niqua Hadruj and the Mu'niqua Sbayli.

XXIV
AFRICAN BREEDS

The Barb, Berber, or Barbary horse comes from the region for which it is named—the North African lands of Algeria, Tunis, Tripoli, and Morocco. He has long been famous in southern Europe, to which he was brought to slenderize the heavy medieval horses of Spain, Provence, and Italy. He is also the foundation sire of the Andalusian breed. The Barb has a heavier neck than the Arabian; a narrow, short croup; not particularly muscular haunches; and, compared with the Arabian, narrower haunches, less prominent tendons, a thicker, wilder mane, and a convex, rather than concave, profile. He is a sober animal with a great deal of stamina, and is a fine racer at the trot and at the gallop, gaits for which he has a unique aptitude. The average Barb is 15 hands high, with the best generally the smaller ones.

The Algerian horse is noteworthy, rather small, fine-legged, with a good deal of spirit. The best come from Oran, while the worst, though good-looking and of fair size, come from the Constantine area.

Africa has a number of breeds peculiar to the Sahara known for their swiftness, particularly those used by the Tuaregs, which though not notably attractive, are splendidly resistant, energetic, and steady horses. They are excellent runners and long-distance amblers, possessed of short shanks, strong tendons, not very muscular but rather wiry and full of fiber.

Egypt, which had great studs at one time, has let her breeding establishments dwindle to almost nothing, until all that remains are a few government establishments that scarcely maintain the remnants of the best of Egyptian horses. These horses are usually of the Dongala breed, of Nubian origin, highly prized as racers and amblers about a hundred years ago.

A mixed breed, but one characterized by agility, great impetus, and a sober temperament, is the Libyan barb, which has come into its own as a distinctive type found only in Algeria: flat shoulders, bulging haunches, a low-set tail, and a concave profile.

The Sahara horse, which shows the Barb influence, is also worthy of mention. He is softer and more curvaceous than the standard Barbary horse. He is also exceptionally resistant at a slow gallop over sandy terrain. The Sahara horse has robust shoulders and flanks, and stands about 14.1 hands high.

We might also mention the Fulani horse from Cameroon and the Basuto pony from Basutoland (known today as Losotho), which is a descendant of a horse of Mongolian and Arabian blood imported from Java in 1653.

XXV
TURKISH BREEDS

Turkey is rich in horses, just as it was in the classical period. In 1951 over a million were registered. The finest horses in

---

* There are some fine Arabians bred in the United States, notable for their stamina.—EDS.

Turkey are those bred in the government studs. Outstanding among these is the Karacabey, beautifully proportioned, about 15.3 hands high, used generally for rapid transport and by the army, as well.

Near the Caspian and Aral seas one finds the Turkoman, a horse of little distinction but exceptionally robust, which gives excellent results when crossed with particular western European breeds.

XXVI
PERSIAN BREEDS

One finds in Iran horses that have a great similarity to Arabians. Once known for the beauty of its horses, Iran's breeds today, however, tend to be rather underbred and angular. Among Iranian breeds are the Darashori, or Shiraz, horse raised in the south, an elegant saddle horse with a rather short neck but powerful hindquarters, standing about 15.1 hands high; the Jaf, originally from Kurdistan, but by now with a strong infusion of blood from other breeds indigenous to the Caspian Sea region. The Jaf serves well as a saddle horse, has no standard height, is very spirited, expressive, and vivacious. The Pachenarani, rather Arabian in type, is a good horse for long distances at a slow gallop, and stands about 15.1 hands high.

XXVII
MONGOLIAN BREEDS

Mongolia was once a great reserve of equine breeds. Even today one finds in the Tachin Schara Nuru descendants of the bands of Mongolian wild horses—*Equus przewalski*. They were discovered in 1879 by the Russian explorer N. M. Przewalski. Because the breed had been hard pressed by the advance of civilization in the area where it once flourished, it has survived only as examples in the larger European and American zoological gardens. The height of these horses can run anywhere from 12.1 to 14.1 hands. The Chinese pony, an extremely resistant animal, shows a good deal of the Mongolian strain, as does the Japanese Hokkaido pony, and also the more elegant Sandalwood pony of Siam.

XXVIII
SOUTHEAST ASIAN BREEDS

Distinctive Indian breeds we can mention are the Kathiawar and Marwar ponies, small, squat, and sturdy, and most probably of Mongolian descent.

Particularly interesting in Indonesia is the Sumba, a squat but likable animal which appears in certain native dances with bells on his knees. There is also the Sumbawa which, like the Sumba, probably derives from horses imported from China many hundreds of years ago. The Sumbawa is so docile that he is ridden without a bit and responds to verbal commands.

The Siamese Sandalwood ponies got their name from the fact that they were exported together with shipments of sandalwood. Of noble origin, they have small heads, thin skin, are extremely resistant, and quite elegant. Crossed with the English Thoroughbred, the Sandalwood has produced a brilliant strain of racehorses that perform beautifully on Thai and Cambodian tracks.

XXIX
AUSTRALIAN BREEDS

Once it was thought that Australia might be the best place in the world to raise English Thoroughbreds. In practice, this was not true. Horses bred there were good, but unexceptional.

Noteworthy, however, is the Waler, a mixture of strains, too large and heavy, but a saddle-horse breed (a representative holds the record for the high jump at 2.5 meters, made in 1940). Attempts are being made to make the Waler much lighter.

The Brumby descends from horses that escaped from the first of the colonies. These horses multiplied to such an extent that there was a period when they were hunted and killed by the thousands. Even today it is practically impossible to redomesticate these wild animals.

New Zealand, on the other hand, is a country where trotters and Thoroughbreds have fared marvelously. It is an ideal place for horse breeding (a great part of the country is covered by gently rolling hills), producing an excellent herdsman's pony, a solid horse that stands about 14.1 hands.

XXX
NORTH AMERICAN BREEDS

North America has a wealth of distinctive breeds, including the Mustang (from the first horses brought to the continent —which had none of its own—by the Spaniards, who left them to run wild when they abandoned them, then later domesticated by the Indians), Palomino, Appaloosa, quarter horse, Morgan, American trotting horse, or Standardbred; American saddle horse, and the Tennessee Walking Horse.

The quarter horse was bred from the purebred, and is fast enough to do a quarter-mile (hence the name) in 22.5 seconds. He is cross-bred with Thoroughbreds and other breeds to produce fine polo ponies, endowing them with a lightning start and fine disposition. The first saddle horses brought by the Spaniards to the two Americas, and successive imports to the two continents, served to fill the vast prairies with bands of wild horses, or rather, domesticated animals that had run wild. It is impossible to estimate how many head there were from Canada to Argentina, but there must have been hundreds of thousands. By the middle of the nineteenth century, the half-wild mustang had metamorphosed into the cavalry trooper's mount and the cowpunch-

699 *The Holstein breed dates back to 1300.*
700 *Polish Masuren of Prussian origin, quite a popular breed today.*
701 *The Danish Knabstrup. The coat is often curiously spotted.*
702 *Trakehner or Oriental-Prussian.*
703 *Lipizzaners are usually gray. At birth the coat is black, changing at six months.*

701

699

700

702

703

Рис. 35. Советский тяжеловоз

Рис. 50. Киргизская лошадь

Рис. 51. Эстонская лошадь

er's pony. From this dark-coated horse, rustic though brilliant, with a noticeable elegance and style, evolved the quarter horse, which has served for racing, hacking, and as a rodeo mount. These quarter horses derived from horses used in the 440-yard, or quarter-mile, race that has been run for some three hundred years as a popular distance. For 100 years, the quarter horse was the only racehorse in the United States, until the Thoroughbred came from England. The foundation sire of the American quarter horse was the imported Janus, in 1756, an English Thoroughbred (the thoroughbred status is debatable). The genealogies of present-day quarter horses trace back to this stallion, grandson of the Godolphin Barb. The characteristics of the breed had become fixed and recognizable by the end of the nineteenth century.* These horses are popular from Canada to Texas. Currently there are about 500,000 registered throughout the world. The quarter horse is extremely versatile, beautifully balanced, has a fantastic takeoff, is extraordinarily docile, and shows no nervousness whatsoever. The breed is employed for cutting out calves and horses, and for a number of rodeo events; also for a general service horse in the West, as well as being used a good deal for parades. The quarter horse varies in color, but dark bays are usual. The breed is characterized by a short, rather wide head; pointed ears, a strong jaw, docile expression, medium-length neck, heavy, powerful shoulders; a short dorsal line, high, wide, bulging hindquarters; and a flat, smooth shank. The quarter horse demonstrates great strength combined with gentleness.

The American saddle horse is a particularly elegant specimen, and popular for parades. The breed derived through selection by Kentucky pioneers who wanted a saddle horse that would be a practical, manageable mount. The horse is fine at all his gaits: trot, canter, and both the rack and slow gait (two rapid yet restful artificial gaits, the rack being characterized by its quick, short, high-stepping action, with each foot coming down singly, and the slow gait by a slight swaying movement, a slow version of the rack). He has energy and power that spring from the various strains making up his creation—Thoroughbred, Morgan, Narragansett pacer, and various trotters. The American Saddle Horse Breeders Association lists Denmark as the foundation sire of

* He was recognized in 1941 with a studbook of his own.—EDS.

704 *An Orlov stallion.*
705 *Achaltekinez breed.*
706 *One of a Budënny breed.*
707 *Horse of the steppes.*
708 *Baltic pony, Viatka breed of König origin.*
709 *Kustanai breed.*
710 *The Vladimir is a Russian workhorse.*
711 *The Pechora is long-lived, and has great endurance.*
712 *The Toric horse of Estonia is a good workhorse.*
713 *Zemaitka from Polevskoi.*
714 *Chranowoy breed, a variety from Arhal-Teke.*
715 *Karabach, typical breed of Uzekistan.*

the breed, foaled in 1839. The saddle horse has a small, elegant head set on a swan neck (very muscular, and distinguished from all other breeds), powerful shoulders, and muscular but slim legs that stick out somewhat behind.* The mane is full, as is the tail, and both are dressed high.

The Tennessee Walking Horse is a show and parade horse with unusually high-stepping gaits. There are about 4,000 of the breed in existence. It is said that for a distraught rider the best tonic in the world is a ride on a Tennessee Walking Horse because of its easy gait and pleasant disposition. The foundation sires of this breed, created by cotton planters, were Allan F-1 (Black Allan) and his colt Roan Allen F-38 (originally spelled "Allan"). The Tennessee Walking Horse is distinguished by the high carriage of his tail, the solidly set long neck, and the swift running walk for which he is named. Winning the annual Grand Championship at Shelbyville, Tennessee, is the prized honor for these horses.

A variety of these saddle horses is the Missouri fox-trotting horse, so called because of his broken gait, in which the forelegs move at a fast pace while the hind pair go at the trot. The Missouri fox-trotter is raced at the flatfoot walk as well as at the canter. His gaits are dragging rather than high-stepping, but they are very sure. He attains an average speed of from five to ten miles an hour, and can maintain it for some distance. The Missouri fox-trotter is not a very elegant breed. He is generally spotted, with long white stockings, has a good conformation, and can carry a great deal of weight. He gives an impression of great solidity.

One of the most characteristic of American horses is the Morgan, which takes his name from the foundation sire Justin Morgan, foaled around 1790. Justin Morgan in turn took his name from his owner, Thomas Justin Morgan. Justin Morgan was bred with Fjord, Frisian, and Norfolk mares. He is believed to have been sired by the Thoroughbred True Briton, a descendant of the Byerly Turk. The Morgan horse is used today for equitation and, primarily, as a harness horse, as well as for pleasure. There are pulling contests in the New England area that are a great tradition; the Morgan, though small, has tremendous power, and can pull more than his weight. He is unmistakable in his conformation, generally brown or dark bay coat; solid and muscular; powerful shoulders; a thick-crested neck; a heavy mane and tail. The Morgan has influenced the breeding of the Standardbred, the American saddle horse, and the Tennessee Walking Horse.

The Mustang, which is distinghiused by a lead-gray coat and black mane and dorsal stripe, is called *falgo* or *cervato* when the coat is brown, and Navajo when the coat is light, with a reddish mane and tail. He is a strong, sturdy horse, if not beautiful, and has tremendous endurance. In 1957 the mustang was recognized as a breed, and registration began.

In areas of Wyoming are herds of wild horses that are descended from the Spanish horse (of Barbary and Cordovan origin, introduced into the continent by Cortez). These wild horses provide a great natural resource, and every year hun-

* He is taught to "stretch" when halting in a showing, which gives the appearance of stretching the forelegs forward and the hind legs behind.—EDS.

dreds are caught and broken, then sold. It is from these horses that the pinto, the palomino, and others derive.

The pinto, or paint, with a registration of close to 9,000, was recognized as an individual breed in 1963, following the formation of the Pinto Horse Association in 1956. Their headquarters are at Ellington, Connecticut. There is also the American Paint Stock Association, a similar group in Fort Worth, Texas. Pinto *(pintado)*, the Spanish for "painted," is an expression used by cowboys to indicate spotted horses, but particularly those who are piebald or skewbald, more usually the latter. The piebald is a black and white horse with white on black patches, or the reverse; he is also called a *tobiano;* and the skewbald is a white colored and patched horse, also known as an *overo.* Paint horse also refers to the Indians' custom of painting designs on the white parts of their spotted horses.

The palomino's outstanding characteristic is his color, which is golden or very light chestnut or cream, with white, or flaxen, mane and tail. There must be no white on the body. He generally has white stockings or socks, and white blazes. His conformation is very close to that of the quarter horse, and averages a height of 15.2 hands. Generally speaking, the palomino is not a breed because he does not necessarily breed true. Nonetheless, the palomino has been registered as a breed since 1952, and there are palomino associations, one founded in California in 1941, and another in Texas in 1946.

The Appaloosa is an irregularly spotted horse whose exact origin is lost in antiquity.* In some lands he was considered sacred. It is believed that Appaloosas were brought to North America by the Spanish Conquistadores, and abandoned to the Nez Percé Indians, who rounded them up and bred them. In the United States, Appaloosas were raised near the Palouse River (the stream of the green meadows), known as Palouse country, giving rise to the corruption Appaloosa. The breed had quite a vogue when Buffalo Bill brought examples to Europe with his Wild West show; previously, Europeans considered them to be inferior horses.

Six color patterns and one variant are acceptable for Appaloosas, which are usually white, with dark spots, over the loin and hips. The eyes are encircled by white, and the hooves are vertically striped in black and white. Stallions are generally more brilliantly marked than the mares. The Appaloosa Horse Club in Moscow, Idaho, lists total horse registration at about 30,000, and currently increasing at the rate of about 8,000 yearly.

The albino has a pure white coat and pink skin, and a pedigree that goes back to Old King, a pure white stallion foaled in 1906. There are four recognized types in the United States, according to the Albino Horse Association. Albinos are popular for shows and circuses, have excellent dispositions, and are excellent as draft horses and for equitation.

Many Old World horses have been domesticated and adapted to American conditions, particularly ponies and draft animals. The American Percheron was first brought to North America in 1839; and in 1905 the Percheron Association was formed. The American Percheron, generally gray or dark bay, has kept the characteristics of the French breed.

Also well acclimated is the Belgian horse, which is a utility animal in farming regions. The predominating color is sorrel or roan, with a white tail and mane. Because of its distinctive conformation, the Belgian has become popular as a fair and parade horse. Backed by the slogan "Weight to move weight," the Clydesdale was once favored by loggers as an economical means of moving felled trees out of the forest, in areas where tractors and trucks could not function.

The Canadians have a distinctive horse in the mount used by the Royal Canadian Mounted Police, which is priceless to them in maintaining order over the vastness of the Canadian Northwest. He is a first-class saddle horse, brown, extremely well built, with broad, solid flanks and a short back. Sable Island has a breed called "hairy ponies," believed to have come originally from New England. They run in bands, with about one stallion for every six to eight mares. The ponies live in the open year round, in the winter eating snow for drinking water. A Canadian cutting horse is used for herding, and is ridden in rodeos. Exceptionally intelligent, this cow pony is derived from the American quarter horse.

Mexico has a breed, descended from the horses of Cortez, that averages slightly over 15 hands, is of almost any color, fast and steady, and very manageable. They are now divided according to type, and are known as Spanish, Arab, and Creole strains.

XXXI
SOUTH AMERICAN BREEDS

South America's horses originated in Europe. The first victories of the Conquistadores were largely the result of their horses, not only for their mobility but also for their shock value. Horses were unknown in the New World, and accordingly were awe-inspiring to the Indians, who fled at the sight of them. This helps to explain how a handful of Spanish cavaliers managed to defeat thousands and thousands of natives, fighting on their own soil. It was the story of the centaurs repeated after three millennia.

But the genetic history of the horse in South America began with the seven studs and five broodmares of the Andalusian breed abandoned by Pedro de Mendoza when he left his newly founded city of Buenos Aires to march into Paraguay. From these came the countless "wild" horses that quickly sprang up to roam the pampas. Exposed to the elements in all weather and seasons, and roaming the grassy plains in bands of about a hundred, natural selection over the years gave these horses outstanding stamina, strength, and solidity.

Horses that run free are known as *cimarrones,* while those that have been brought into corrals are called *alambrados,* and

* Various suggested clues to an origin include, among others, Chinese art figures of 500 B.C., and an Etruscan migration circa 800 B.C. —EDS.

716 *Mexican horse.*
717 *Argentinian horse.*
718 *Gaucho with whip, Uruguay.*
719 *Dancing ponies of Soemba, Indonesia.*
720 *Llaneros of the Cacho, Paraguay.*
721 *The Chilean breed originates from the Argentine horse.*
722 *Untamed horses in Uganda.*

716

717

718

720

719

721

723

724

725

726

727

partly domesticated horses that are herded by gauchos from one pasture to the next are referred to as *criollos mansos*. The gauchos lasso the horses when they are needed, then break them to the saddle in a rough-and-ready process in which they freely use large, sharply roweled spurs. Generally it takes about a week before the horses leave off their kicking and bucking and submit to their riders. Once mastered, they are extremely docile. About the only defect these horses have lies in their hooves; because the animals live on soft, damp terrain, their hooves tend to split easily when the horse is worked over hard, firm ground.

For some time, Argentina has considered the horse a product for export, and has sought to improve its breeds by importing European studs. Now, the Argentine breeders are able to compete with the Irish in the export market, particularly in their offerings of fine polo ponies at reasonable prices, well built and of good dispositions. Also flourishing is the breeding of English Thoroughbreds and horses for flat racing. The leading horse is the *criollo*, rough, extraordinarily strong, highly resistant to fatigue, and adaptable to climatic variations.

In Peru, one of several South American countries ideal for horse breeding, we find three distinctive breeds, the *costeño*, the *chola*, and the *morochuco*, this last being a small, stocky animal used in the mountains. The *costeño* is a well-established breed now, and is the best of the three different types of *criollos* found in South America. An elegant saddle horse, the *costeño* has a cadenced gait that can be maintained over long distances. He has long, prominent shoulders, a muscular, arched neck, short cannons, and a compact back. Though the *morochuco* resembles the *costeño*, he has a shorter, thicker neck, thicker skin, and a much more angular conformation. Flat races lasting eight to ten days, as tests of endurance (during the last day as a test of speed), are popular in Peru for selecting the best of the *criollos*. The *criollo* in use by the army, generally taller and broader than the standard type, and the variant employed in agriculture are distinct varieties of the breed.

Brazil also has distinct varieties: the Rio Grande do Sul *crioulo*, the *campolino*, and the *manga larga* horses. The *crioulo brasileiro* has produced some wonderful racehorses; the *manga larga*, usually a gray roan, is a rather rough specimen; the *campolino* is used both as a saddle and draft animal, and has a good deal of Andalusian blood in his veins.

Venezuela's most celebrated horse is the *llanero*, developed in the moist and grassy plains region. Venezuela is estimated to have about 50,000 half-wild horses running free. In the shape of his head and body, the *llanero* resembles Barbary and Andalusian horses. Generally, the coat is yellow, with the mane and tail brown or spotted with white or brown, with a black mane and tail. The *llanero* is much lighter, and with much slimmer legs than the *criollo argentino*, which is especially rustic and unelegant.

723 *Ardennes breed, strong, rustic, quiet temperament.*
724 *Shetland pony and a Cleveland (left).*
725 *Semiwild horses of the Camargue.*
726 *Pompadour stud: superb Anglo-Arabians.*
727 *Du Pin Stables: the powerful Percherons.*

XXXII
VICES AND DEFECTS

Grisone, "the regenerator of equitation," wrote some four hundred years ago in *Ordini di Cavalcare* (Rules for Riding):

When you whip a horse or use your crop and he has not erred, you confuse him and he is unable to understand which of his actions led to the punishment, so that thereafter whenever he sees a whip or crop, he becomes frightened. You cannot do worse than to beat a horse when he is responsive and doing well.

That is why I have always said, and will continue to say, that the horseman must always use punishment, even his resources and aids, at the right time and in the proper measure.

The Arabs say, "Do not be hard on a fine horse, for his noble nature will force him to rebel," and the Italian philosophy is, "When a word is sufficient, do not use a whip."

Every horseman must come to know and interpret his mount's nature, character, and disposition as well as his whims and crotchets. Only thus can a rider predict or anticipate his horse's reactions, and in so doing become not only his teacher but his master, too.

The principal vices and defects of a horse are pawing, rushing, backing, biting, kicking, bucking (refusing to be mounted), head-tossing, taking the bit in his teeth, putting his head to the wind, eating straw, tearing the blanket, slipping the harness, and so on.

XXXIII
INTELLIGENCE

Even Tesio, seldom gentle in his opinions on the horse, stated:

In his confrontation with man, the horse feels the same sensations that the barbarians must have felt when they were conquered by the Romans, enslaved, and put to forced labor.

To indicate to the horse that he must halt, man pulls on the iron between his lips and teeth; to turn to the right, he pulls to the right; to turn to the left, he pulls to the left; and the poor animal does whatever he can to stop the pain.

This is the vocabulary man has invented to communicate with the horse, the same horse that can by himself, without anyone taking the trouble to explain what they mean to him, interpret the various sounds of the human voice.

It is undeniable that the best of equitation has done nothing to improve understanding between man and horse, and furthermore served even more to make the horse the pawn of his rider, subject to his will and extravagances. Therefore we can see how important is the revolution in treatment brought about by Caprilli's teachings, for aside from restoring to the horse his natural equilibrium, the rider was made to realize that he had to understand the horse's needs, both as an athlete and teammate.

The horse has a very sensitive olfactory system, even better than the dog's. We recall that the Indians never mounted guards at night, relying on their horses to neigh the moment they caught the scent of a stranger in the vicinity of the encampment.

In speaking of animals, we usually discuss their instinct, memory, intelligence, and sensitivity. Just what is instinct, then? Let us define it as the ability to act without thinking or learning to do so, an innate action that springs from atavistic conditioning or from fundamental necessity. All instinct is translated into action, and this action is the same, and performed for the same reason, in every member of a given species.

Instinct has a definite end and purpose, and while the actions they engender may be artifices (a bird pretending to be wounded when it leaves a nest threatened by an enemy) or appear to be premeditated, we shall find that all animals of a species will respond in precisely the same way in the same circumstances.

Another curious aspect of instinct is imitation. When an animal makes a gesture, others of its kind are inclined to do the same. When a horse approaches another and starts moving his head up and down near the second horse's flank, because this second horse will do the same, all the other horses in the band will soon be imitating them. A classic example of this, to the nth degree, is the fact that sheep will follow the bell-wether even when it is obvious that the leader of the flock is in danger. This instinctive imitation of actions that in themselves are instinctive is called "mimicry," and it is a phenomenon about which we still have a great deal to learn.

The higher one goes in the animal kingdom, the more one finds that the pattern of life is less rigid, that is, less instinctive, with each individual inclined to modify behavior on the basis of experience. In such a way do animals acquire personality. To add to this, with practice, certain instincts become more mature or lead to more mature action; the animal also expands his personality through learning.

Intelligence, however, does not always correspond to an animal's readiness to learn. To learn, an animal must be able to focus his attention, as demonstrated by the Alsatian (not necessarily a more intelligent dog than others, but able to concentrate to a relatively high degree).

The horse learns quickly when he is carefully seconded in his efforts in such a way, that he doesn't "lose his head." At times, we think we have managed to convey to a horse what it is we want him to do, but our instruction has been confused and ambiguous as far as he is concerned. Because the horse has not understood us precisely, he makes a mistake; we punish him, he becomes hurt, and he rebels.

As a general rule, horses are good-natured and cooperative and will do their very best to achieve what their masters require of them, giving their all. We hear of horses that have crossed the finish line and dropped dead from their exertions to win the race. There are, however, a few horses that are bad. Most of the time, what has made them bad has been improper handling and bad treatment, with the result that we have diffident, treacherous, and intractable horses.

With calmness and persuasion, we can usually manage to convince a horse to drop certain bad habits he may have picked up or inherited through physical defects. Toward this end, a horse should always be treated benevolently, provided with a tranquil atmosphere, allowed the opportunity to get to know the world around him, the people and things that make up his part, and regarded as a friend, never shouted at or menaced by threatening gestures. Very often a horse does damage just because he is in high spirits, perhaps after having spent a long time in his box, and is not given the means or the opportunity to work off some of his energy. At times he may perform badly because his physical resources are not what they should be. In such cases, it is sheer cruelty to punish him for his mistakes.

Taking all this into consideration, can we say that a horse is truly intelligent? It would seem so.

Horses are known to have excellent audio and visual memories, become quite easily attached to people, and are equally sensitive to punishment and compliments. The horse has a keen memory because his interest is directed to so few things.

Punishment should be brief and immediate, otherwise the animal will be unable to connect the punishment with the crime. Generally he identifies with the place of punishment or the person inflicting it, and will show his resentment. A horse should never be punished in his stall, because it is his last refuge; he should feel secure there at all times. In a natural environment fear is responsible for the horse's speed, whereas in a domesticated situation speed is dependent on the aids, such as spurs and the whip. Colts are the most fearful, and it is up to the horseman, through gentle treatment, to win his confidence, which is the only way truly to dominate him.

XXXIV
MORPHOLOGY

The major anatomical divisions of the horse are head, neck, trunk, and legs.

The head contains the brain and sensory organs. Its weight and mobility permit it to function as a counterpoise to the animal's shifting center of gravity when in motion, thus regulating the gaits.

A fairly reliable impression of the horse's nature, quality, and health can be formed by a glance at the conformation of the head and the animal's expression. A handsome head is one that is lean (or dry) and light. The ears should be small, erect, and alertly mobile; the eyes, large, vivacious, and expressive; the nostrils, large and dilated; the cheeks, muscular; and the cheek cavity, wide and hollow. The length of the head should be about two-fifths the height of the horse.

If the head is too dry, it is termed "old"; too narrow at the muzzle, "conical." If the ears are too close together and the forehead prominent, the horse is described as "hare-headed," while if the forehead and nose form a convex profile, the horse is said to have a "mutton" head; but if the profile is concave, the animal is "pug-" or "snub-nosed," or, if the depression at the nose is extreme, "dish-nosed."

728 *A page of fifteenth-century manuscript dealing with horses' coats.*
729 *On the art of farriery, early fifteenth century.*

728
729

730

731

A horse's head is generally inclined at a forty-five-degree angle. If that angle to the ground is more obtuse, the horse is carrying his "head to the wind," while carried lower, at a more acute angle, it is "drooped." The head is "badly set" if the depression running between throat and neck, the line of demarcation between the two, is overly accentuated.

Between the ears and the point of the last vertebra lies the poll, which is the highest point on the head, and hirsute, ornamented with the forelock, whose practical purpose is to protect the head from sunshine and rain. The crownpiece of a halter or bridle is worn at the poll, right behind the forelock.

The forehead should be broad and flat, and though generally narrower in the female, too strait a forehead, irrespective of sex, is taken as an indication of stupidity and/or bad temper.

The eyeball is protected by a superior and an inferior lid, each having lashes curling outward, and a nictitating membrane at the inner corner of the eye that both screens and polishes the eyeball as it is drawn over its surface. A good horse's eyes should be large, limpid, alert, and vivacious in expression, as well as widely spaced. The normal color is a deep, rich brown in the iris, with a black pupil. It has been said that any edging of white indicates bad temper, which is also demonstrated—though there is no hard-and-fast rule—when a horse consistently shows the whites of his eyes. A horse with small eyes is called "pig-eyed," and if they are very large, he is referred to as "ox-eyed." Light eyes, where the pigment of the iris is blue instead of the usual brown, are called "glass eyes." This should not be confused with a bluish tinge, which may well indicate ophthalmia, just as milkiness is an indication of ill-health or even cataract. If the eyeballs are perfectly clear, and the color light or blue, and showing a good deal of white, the horse is said to have "magpie" eyes; hazel or gray-green eyes are sometimes known as "squirrel eyes."

Horses never breathe through their mouths, but only through their noses or, more properly, through the two nasal fossae, or cavities, delineated by bone and highly mobile cartilage that have their external opening in the two nostrils, or nares, with the infundibulum, or so-called "false nostril," lying between. The nasal cavities are lined with mucous membrane that can be seen easily when the horse dilates his nostrils.

The mouth comprises the upper and lower lips, teeth, gums and bars, tongue, and palate. Below or contiguous are the jaws, chin, chin groove, and cheeks. The bars are fairly wide, toothless portions of the gums on each side of the lower jaw, lying between and behind the canine teeth and his molars. It is on the bars that the mouthpiece of a bit or snaffle rests. High, narrow bars are quite sensitive, as a rule, while broad, horny ones are less so. A horse having the latter is said to be "hard-mouthed." Where this insensitivity is more pronounced on one side, say the right, than on the other, the horse would be described as being "hard-mouthed on the right."

As for the barrel, or trunk, there is the back, which lies between the withers and loins, with the dorsal vertebrae at the base of the back. It is the back, along with the continuing loins, that transmits the propulsive force of the hindquarters. A good back is well muscled and well coupled to the loins. If the dorsal line is excessively concave, resulting in an overly convex or "cow" belly, the horse is sway-backed. If the top line of the back, contrarily, is too convex, the back is said to be a "roach" or "camel" back, and the belly, a greyhound belly; or the horse is referred to as herring-gutted if the belly narrows till it is nearly straight from sternum to stifle. Normally, a good back should be approximately horizontal to the ground, short, and slightly higher at the withers than in the rear. The loins, which are defined by the lumbar vertebrae, should be short, broad, and, like the back, well muscled. The chest is demarcated by the dorsal vertebrae, thirty-six (eighteen pairs) ribs, and the breastbone, or sternum, and should be quite high, broad, and deep. The brisket, which lies behind the elbow, is marked by a sternal depression. The flank lies between the point of the hip and the last rib, the ribs being commonly referred to as the portion formed of the last twelve pairs, the first six being under the shoulder. The lower part of the abdomen is the belly.

The withers are formed by the protuberance of the first dorsal vertebrae. The withers mark the point at which many of the muscles of the forehand are secured. Good withers should be well extended toward the back, and rather high. The top of the shoulder ends at the withers, its front at the neck, and its back at the flanks. The bottom of the shoulder marks the point at which the arm begins. The shoulders should be long and sloping, while the forearm should be reasonably straight, long, and well muscled. The chestnut, a horny protuberance, is found about two-thirds down the forearm.

The knee should be bony at the sides, and fairly flat in front. The cannon, which lies between knee and fetlock, comprises the cannon bone at the front and tendons behind. It should be fairly broad and neat in line.

The fetlock marks the articulation of leg and foot bones, broadly speaking. It should be neat and broad. A horny protuberance similar to the chestnut, generally surrounded by strands of hair, called the feather, is at the lower part of the fetlock. It is believed to be one of the two toes atrophied in the evolution of the modern horse. (The other three toes are considered to be fused into the coffin, or pedal, bone, discussed in the section on feet.

Next come the hindquarters. At the base of the pelvis is the croup, extending from the loins to the base of the tail. The croup is flanked by the haunches, marked by the tips of the hip bones. The thigh lies under the croup, and is not easily distinguishable from it. It extends down to the top of the stifle joint, or patella, where the gaskin commences. The gaskin extends from stifle joint to hock. The hock marks the joint, in a hind leg, that is analogous to the knee in a foreleg, and it is, therefore, one of the most important parts of the horse, so far as locomotion is concerned. The rest of the parts of the hind legs are analogous to those parts in the forelegs.

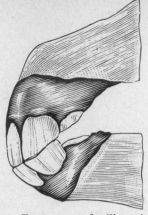

Emergence of milk teeth
(8 to 10 months)

FIRST AND SECOND STAGES

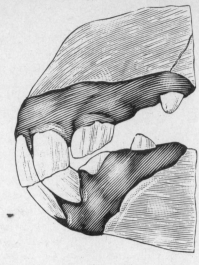

(4 years)

THIRD STAGE
Emergence of adult teeth

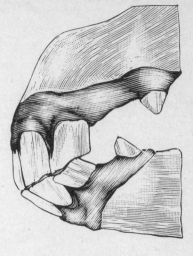

(8 years)

FOURTH STAGE
Equalization of oval form of teeth

Equalization of milk teeth
(16 months)

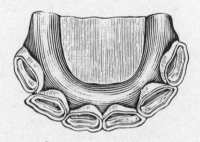

(5 years)

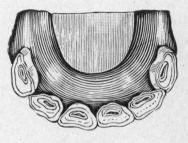

(8 years)*

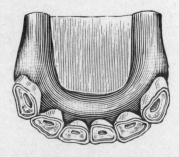

(12 years)

FIFTH STAGE
Rounded shape of teeth

(12 years)*

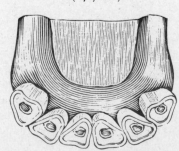

(17 years)

SIXTH STAGE
Triangular form of teeth

(17 years)*

(about 20 years)

SEVENTH STAGE
Biangular form of teeth

(about 20 years)*

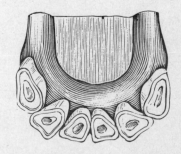

* After eight years of age, all marks in the center of the teeth have
disappeared. The basic shape of the teeth are as shown, and from five
years of age and up, all teeth show marked triangular characteristics.

XXXV
TEETH

Even people who know nothing about horses are aware that one can tell a horse's age by his teeth. Of course, the animal's lifespan is dependent, to a great extent upon his breed, the exercise and training he is given, the climate in which he lives, the work he does, and the rations upon which he feeds. As a rule, Thoroughbreds and trotters tend to achieve majority sooner than other horses, undoubtedly because of their training and the fact that they result from the breeding of highly selected strains. As a general rule, the average horse has an active or working life of about twenty years, though they endure much longer than that. A horse is considered mature at five and old at nine years of age. The oldest horse on record, and reasonably well-documented, in this country was Dr. Uriah Myer's Clover, of Catawissa, Pennsylvania, who was 53 when he died in 1924.

As for his teeth, the adult stallion has forty of them, twelve incisors, 4 tushes, or canines, and twenty-four molars. Mares have only thirty-six teeth at maturity, since they do not have the canines, although there are mares, generally barren, who do have atrophied tushes.

The incisors are considered to be both milk and permanent teeth. As the front edge is the first exposed when they appear, it is this edge that always shows the most wear. At the center of the cusp is a small indentation, surrounded by ivory that, in turn, is surrounded by the dental enamel. The tooth is said to be razed when this cup is no longer apparent. Furthermore, as can be seen from the illustrations, with the passing of the years, the flat surface of the tooth becomes successively oval, then rounded, and finally triangular.

The first incisors appear shortly after foaling, and sometimes are present at birth. The second incisors come at four to six weeks of age, followed by the deciduous third incisors at six to nine months. These are the true milk teeth. The first permanent incisors push out the milk teeth in the middle at two and a half. At four, the second permanent incisors come into wear, and the canines and deciduous third incisors are fully grown at five.

It is generally at about six years of age that the cups in the first incisors disappear. At seven, the second have been worn smooth, and at eight, no cups are left. Also indicative of age is the slant of the teeth, which tends toward the horizontal as the teeth lengthen with age.

At nine, Galvayne's Groove, a groove on the upper corner teeth, very near the gumline, appears and, with age, gradually extends downward, so that by fifteen it is halfway down the teeth and all the way at about twenty.

Some horses have what are called wolf teeth, which are extra teeth, generally in front of the molars. They are generally removed.

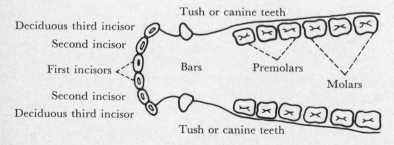

XXXVI
COATS, COLORS, PATTERNS, AND MARKINGS

To the layman, it would appear that there could be no difficulty inherent in describing a horse in terms of his color and markings. The expert horseman, however, knows that this is no easy task. Since it is a fact that Nature never paints in pure colors, and it is also true, to a large degree, that color, like beauty, is in the eye of the beholder, horsemen the world over never quite agree on a single description of a horse nor even on the terms employed to describe him.

In each country, therefore, official bodies concerned with horses have attempted to make things easier by assigning what are, at best, arbitrary names to the most common colors and patterns. This has been of great help. Since, however, there are certain breeds that tend to distinctive colors and/or patterns that are almost exclusive to one country, no arbitrary name may exist for that color or pattern abroad, so that one may frequently find, for example that an American buckskin is white in Europe or, literally, a horse of another color.

Extensive research in the United States, carried on at the Texas Experiment Station, has shown that there is only a single pigment producing color in a horse's coat: a light amber. The precise shade and intensity of the color of the animal's coat is, therefore, dependent upon the amount of pigment present in the hair follicle, and the quality and quantity of those follicles and their distribution.

Markings are also important to describe and identify a horse; but, again, as in questions of color. They are widely subject to varying interpretations. In general they are the following on the head, in all cases referring to white hairs among the general ground color: a few white hairs, a snip, a star, a stripe, a race, or blaze.

On the legs, there can be white markings at the front of the coronet or at the back, socks, stockings, or high stockings, where the white rises above the knee.

A black horse appears black because he has so much pigment, so evenly and heavily distributed, that his coat absorbs all the light rather than reflecting it.

In attempting to assign his proper color to a horse, the color of mane and tail is also considered; and sometimes the deciding factor, for instance, between a dark chestnut or a bay, is the fact that the latter has dark points (lower limbs) rather than those of the same color.

In the following, we have attempted to give some general description of color, to be followed by color patterns, and since internationally so many colors and their variants have received French names, or derivatives of them, we are including the French designation, as well:

White *(blanc):* coat, mane, and tail white, extremely rare if the color is pure, as at foaling *(blanc de naissance),* usually found in such shades as milky *(mat),* china *(porcelaine),* dirty or creamy *(sale).*

Chestnut *(alezan):* coat, mane, and tail same color. Includes virtually every shade from dark brown to tan, variously described as light *(alezan clair),* liver or dark *(foncé),* faded *(lavé),* golden *(doré),* and maroon *(brulé).*

Buckskin: an unofficial designation in the United States sometimes described as "cream-colored," for shades of beige, from light to dark, with coat, mane, and tail all the same color.

Black (noir): with coat, mane, and tail of the same color. As rare in its pure state as white, generally modified to coal (noir franc) or dull (mal teint).

The following colors are solid in the coat, while mane, tail, and sometimes the lower legs are black:

Bay (bai): light bay (bai clair), clear or golden (doré), plum (cerise), dark (marron), tawny or fawn (fauve), and brown (brun).

Dun (isabelle): all beige variants having black mane, tail, and lower legs or points, together with, very often, a dark shoulder and/or dorsal stripe.

Mouse-colored (souris): all the various gray-brown shades, light (souris clair), and dark (foncé).

The following colors are made up of a combination both in coat and in the mane and tail:

Wolf-colored (louvet): comparable to a yellowish dun, an effect caused by the fact that each hair is bicolored, yellowish at the root and brownish at the end.

Gray (gris): white and dark, either brown or black hairs, mixed evenly but in different proportions and even patterns in the coat, mane, and tail. There are too many national designations to list, but included are dappled (pommelé), speckled (truité), fly-specked (moucheté), slate blue (ardoise), iron-gray (fer), and so on.

The final color category is that in which two or three colors are mixed either in the coat or in coat, mane, and tail:

Roan (rouan et aubère): with such variants as strawberry or chestnut (clair), blue (foncé), sorrel or dark red (ordinaire), and so on.

The final class of colors is not characterized so much by the actual shades as by their distribution in marked distinctive patterns:

Piebald (bigarré): black and white, with white generally predominant, and considered the ground color.

Skewbald (pie bai or alezan): brown shades, either bay or chestnut and white, with the white generally predominant, and considered the ground color.

XXXVII
THE FEET

To best understand the anatomy of the horse's foot in lay terms, let us draw a broad analogy: the foot proper, buttressed by a spongy heel cushion (the frog or fork), "wears" a horny boot with an arched sole (the hoof).

The foot has three bones, all separated by shock-absorbing cartilage. The lowest bone, or third phalanx, popularly known as the pedal or coffin bone, rests on the plantar cushion. Articulated to the pedal bone, above and slightly behind it, is the small sesamoid bone, also called the navicular. This bone, in turn, is articulated to the second phalanx, also known as the coronary or second pastern bone, above it. This complex is enveloped in flesh and the matrix of the horny wall of the hoof. Like fingernails and toenails, the hoof is keratinous, and therefore insensitive although

continually growing. It serves as a protective case for the sensitive foot.

The outer "shell" of the hoof, which is the part one sees when the horse is standing, is called the "wall." The wall grows from the top down, or, more properly, from the coronary band, at the coronet or base of the foot, that secretes the wall. Just above the coronary band lies the perioplic ring, which secretes the periople, or protective tissue, covering the wall. Leaves of flaky tissue, the horny laminae, overlay each other, standing at right angles to the inner surface of the wall. They interlock with the sensitive laminae, delicate, fleshy vascular leaves covering the pedal bone and cartilages, in such a way as to unite foot and hoof securely.

The sole of the hoof is so arched or cupped that it cradles the bottom of the foot, except at the rear, where the relatively soft, rather spongy frog is wedged beneath the foot so that its two upper buttresses form the heels. The bars are the continuation of the wall where it turns inward at the frog, extending halfway to its point, or toe, to strengthen the heels and prevent contraction of the foot.

All this can be seen only from below, when the foot is raised. It will also be observed that the frog is raised, in relation to the sole, and has two lateral and one median furrow. Further, it will be noted that, because of the partial hollowness of the hoof resulting from the cupping of the sole, only the peripheral edge of the wall touches the ground. The toe is at the front of the hoof, framed by the side walls, adjoining the quarters, and followed by the heels. The outer edge of each hoof is more curved than the inner, while the forefeet are rounder than the hind, which tend to be elliptical in shape.

Since a horse is only as good as his feet, it is vital to recognize the characteristics of good, healthy feet. The sole that is flat rather than arched can indicate foot bones that have dropped owing to past injury or disease. A healthy sole that is not kept overly dry normally should be rather chalky.

Since the frog is the principal shock absorber in the foot, it must be sufficiently developed to touch the ground, or the horse will take all the shock of contact only on the edges of the wall. The more pounding and jouncing a horse's feet must take, and jumpers, undoubtedly, take the most punishment of all, the greater the importance that must be placed on a well-developed, strong but resilient frog. The wall should be tough and horny, but never brittle or shell-like in texture and consistency. It should be free of cracks and fissures.

In his natural state, the horse ranges over grassy terrain in search of food. On such a surface, the horny part of his foot is not worn down very much, and the normal rate of growth of the nail is sufficient to compensate for any wear. In the artificial circumstances of domestication, however, with its intense and excessive work, the nail is worn away at a rate beyond its normal growth. It becomes necessary in these circumstances to protect the hoof and wall so that they are not inordinately worn down or splintered on hard, stony ground.

According to an old saying, before shoeing came into practice, man had only half a horse. Nevertheless, at all periods, some attempt was made or method sought to protect or harden the hoof. According to some authors contemporaneous with Constantine, there were "horseboots," a sort of protective device for the hoof that was fastened at the pastern or coronet. The oldest horse shoe of the type nailed to the hoof was found in the tomb of King Chilperic, who died in 584. Since the horseshoe came from the Orient, it is probable that this precious object was a gift to the Frankish king from some Eastern potentate. From the fifth century B.C. right down to the tenth century one cannot find any valid or reasonable descriptions of horseshoes with nails, although there is a legend that a horse owned by an uncle of Muhammad was shod.

In any case, it should be remembered that shoeing a horse is not a simple matter. Besides the risk of having a nail perforate the hoof in a way that injures the foot, there is also the danger of prejudicing the natural stance of the animal or his freedom of movement. Even though these problems existed, as they still do, it is difficult to believe that the barbarians from the northern regions of Europe and those crossing from Asia could embark upon such violent invasions and forays without their horses having some sort of protective shoe, no matter how primitive or cumbersome.

We do have documents dating from the eleventh century that indicate blacksmiths were at work, and even giving a list of prices for various services. There are twelfth-century works on the treatment of horses, written for "blacksmiths," who also doubled as veterinaries in those days; and records indicate that in Padua, in 1236, two blacksmiths were commissioned to take charge of selecting studs.

It is from approximately this period that the horseshoe as a symbol of good luck dates. In those days, to please their dependents, princes would heighten the festivity of holiday celebrations by having a horse loosely shod with one silver shoe. Naturally, as was intended, the horse would eventually throw the shoe during the parade or carrousel, and whoever found it and returned it to the lord was given a reward. From that custom stems the belief that a horseshoe brings good fortune, which indeed it did.

All through the age of chivalry, the farrier had a great deal of prestige since he was not only a blacksmith and veterinary but often served, as well, as Master of the Horse. This prestige, as well as the art and craft of farrier, declined with the decline of the manège; it was not to see a renascence until the time of Napoleon. He, unlike the barbarian invaders of the past, wanted not only good horses but also well-shod ones to guarantee the mobility of mounted troops. Napoleon erred, however, in planning his Russian adventure. Although he believed he had thought of everything, he forgot that there would be icy, snowy terrain to cover and that his horses were not accustomed to such conditions.

In the memoirs of Louis, Marquis de Caulaincourt, the emperor's aide, the story is told: "The top of the snow was icy; it was impossible to advance, especially at night.... It was a struggle to keep upright on the road. Imagine what a state the horses must have been in, for none of them had the right shoes for that clime. Already at the end of their resources because of fatigue and privation, animals fell at every step of the way and could find not a foothold to permit them to get up and stand again. That slippery road obliged us, little by little, to go forward, abandoning them where they fell. *The great disasters of our retreat started at that moment*."

Only about ten of the horses in the emperor's service could finally be saved by Caulaincourt's care when he was able to take tardy curative measures at a halt at Smolensk, where the retreating troops stopped from the tenth to the twelfth of November. Caulaincourt managed to have shoes forged with three calkins. Even so, a mere upset became a disaster.

Horseshoes can be either protective, which is the normal type; corrective or orthopedic, in which case they are used to compensate or eradicate a defect of the hoof or stance; or therapeutic, devised to help cure or heal injuries or deficiencies caused by disease.

The normal shoe prevents the hoof wall from being worn down to the sensitive tissue of the foot, and further reinforces and strengthens it, providing a good grip on soft surfaces, such as racetracks, as well as on slippery ground. It further helps the hoof to resist the formation of cracks and corns, as well as undue contraction. To improve the grip on surfaces offering little friction, horseshoes are sometimes fitted with small spikes or studs known as "calks" or "calkins."

The three-quarter shoe is often applied after the removal of corns, and is so called since its arc is about three-quarters of that of the normal shoe. Another corrective and/or therapeutic type of shoe is the bar shoe, which, as its name implies, has a bar across the normally open end of the shoe. Its purpose is to exert pressure or support a particular area of the hoof, very often the frog. It is also used on horses that have thin soles and cracked hooves or contracted heels. Another way of preventing contraction, in this instance of the heel, is the use of the beveled or feather-edged shoe. It also serves to reduce brushing, that is, interfering.

In the normal horseshoe, and every other type, the lower surface, sole, or soleplate, which is in contact with the ground, is perforated to accommodate the horseshoe nails used to attach it to the hoof. The upper surface of the shoe is generally smooth, and rests against the hoof, actually, the wall of the hoof.

Just as the fore- and hind feet of the horse differ slightly in shape, the shoes do too, so that a foreshoe is more circular, and a hind shoe more elliptical. Many shoes, particularly hind shoes, have quarter clips, an upward spur of metal at the forepart of the shoe used to assure a better grip on the hoof and obviate loosening of the shoe when a horse scuffs his feet or stumbles.

The average horse needs to be reshod about every month to five weeks. In any case, his shoes should be inspected that often. If it is found that there is little wear, the shoes need only be removed, the hooves pared, and the old shoes reset.

There are still other types of shoes. The bar shoe, with its raised heel, was often used to aid a horse with shortened tendons, and therefore "over at the knees." In this application, it has been practically replaced by the wedge shoe, which thickens toward the rear, instead of having ordinary heels. It has been found that this type puts less strain on the tendons. As well as the three-quarter shoe, a half-shoe is sometimes used. This type permits frog and heel to expand to relieve abnormally contracted heels.

Horses turned out to pasture are usually fitted with a tip, which obviates breaking of the wall of the hoof. For horses with underdeveloped frogs, there is the Charlier shoe, which is actually embedded in the hoof after a part of the wall has been cut away.

The extraordinarily light racing shoe—a regular shoe

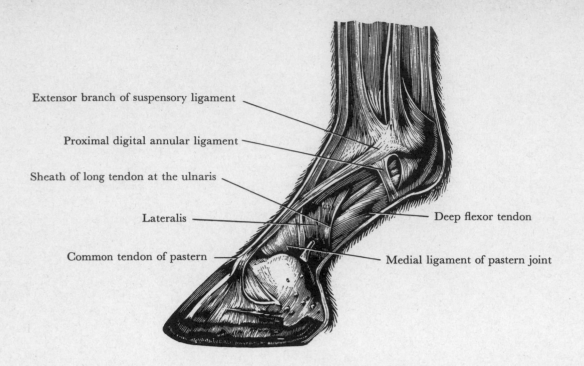

Extensor branch of suspensory ligament

Proximal digital annular ligament

Sheath of long tendon at the ulnaris

Lateralis

Common tendon of pastern

Deep flexor tendon

Medial ligament of pastern joint

Moving parts and tendons of lower leg and foot

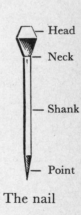

Head

Neck

Shank

Point

The nail

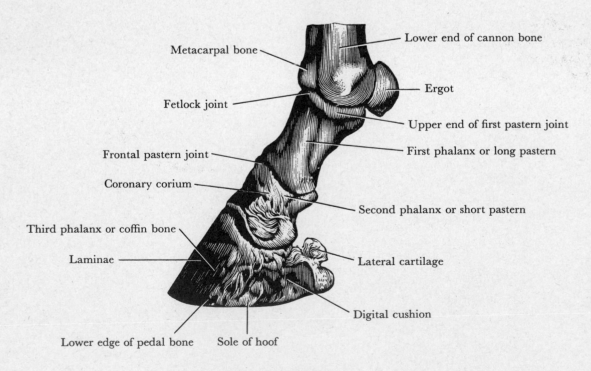

Metacarpal bone

Fetlock joint

Frontal pastern joint

Coronary corium

Third phalanx or coffin bone

Laminae

Lower edge of pedal bone

Sole of hoof

Lower end of cannon bone

Ergot

Upper end of first pastern joint

First phalanx or long pastern

Second phalanx or short pastern

Lateral cartilage

Digital cushion

Bones of lower leg

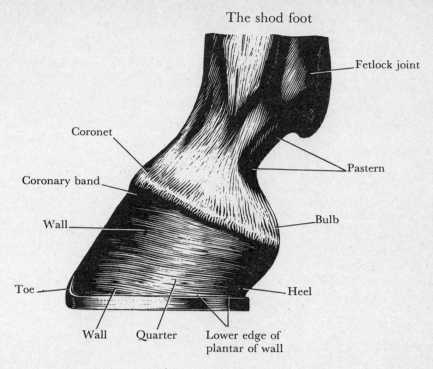

The shod foot

Fetlock joint

Coronet

Coronary band

Pastern

Wall

Bulb

Toe

Heel

Wall   Quarter   Lower edge of
plantar of wall

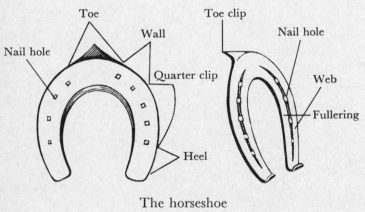

Toe

Wall

Toe clip

Nail hole

Nail hole

Quarter clip

Web

Fullering

Heel

The horseshoe

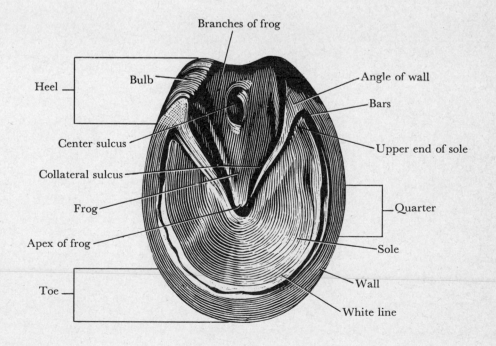

Branches of frog

Heel   Bulb

Angle of wall

Bars

Center sulcus

Collateral sulcus

Upper end of sole

Frog

Quarter

Apex of frog

Sole

Toe

Wall

White line

Underside of foot

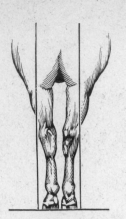

Base narrow

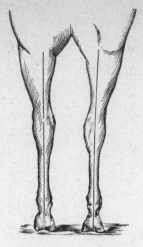

Regular perpendicular
(rear view)

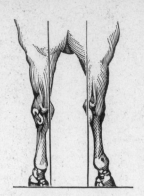

Base wide

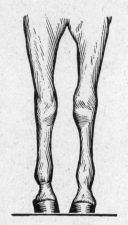

Base narrow, pigeon-toed

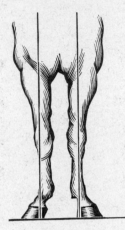

Splayfoot

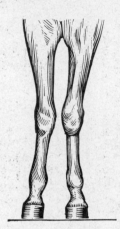

Knock-kneed

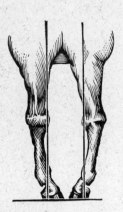

Base narrow

Front legs regular
perpendicular (profile view)

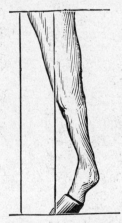

Tied-in below knee

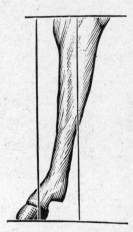

Camped in front

Cow hocks

Over at knee

Behind at knee

Too-long pastern

Short straight pastern

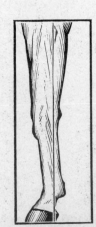

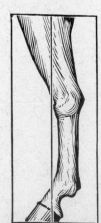

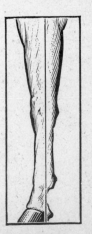

Long neck

Ewe neck

Stag neck

Pyramidal neck

Bull neck

Swan neck

Square head

Hare head

Mutton head or ram head

Snub-nosed and dish-faced

Straight back and goose-rumped
(low-set tail)

Swayback

weighs about ten ounces, while a racing shoe can weigh about half that—generally made of aluminum, is intended to last for only a brief time. Possibly the most artfully designed shoes are those worn by harness racers, both trotters and pacers, and their design calls for all the skill of expert blacksmiths who can watch a horse in action and design and make the precise shoe that will improve his time and/or correct any defects in his gait or even a tendency to "break."

To be correctly shod, in the normal way, the shoe must be secure on the foot, properly nailed, the natural alignment and level of the foot maintained, no pressure on the sole, and allowance made for the foot's natural expansion. A smith must fit the shoe to the horse, not force the horse to conform to an ill-fitting shoe. In preparing the horse to be shod, only the ragged edges of the frog should be removed, and such trimming should be kept to the minimum; the bars of the hoof should not be touched, nor should the wall be rasped.

There are two methods of shoeing: cold and hot. In cold shoeing, a ready-made shoe, generally one of standard size, is simply nailed to the prepared hoof without any fitting or heating. Obviously, this is makeshift, and should be done only in emergencies when a blacksmith is not at hand. Hot shoeing is custom shoeing, one might say. The shoe is forged and heated to conform perfectly to the shape of the foot for which it is intended. The shoe is not merely a protective device but also a means of obtaining the best performance from a horse, developing his speed, and correcting any anomalies.

Foot and Hoof Ailments

The most common pathological conditions in the foot and hoof, caused by injury or disease, are the following:

Sand Cracks: These are cracks running down the hoof wall that might possibly cause lameness. They occur when the coronet has been injured or from undue wearing away or rasping of the outside of the wall, which leads to loss of the natural secretion that keeps the horn moist. The crack is prevented from extending itself by the placement of a clip across it. In shoeing the horse, care should be taken to see that no pressure is placed on the crack. Should it become infected and suppurate, the hoof must be excised to allow the pus to be drawn off, and the coronet then blistered to encourage new growth of horn.

Brittle Feet: This complaint arises from undue dryness of the hoof. The horn chips easily and becomes almost friable, so that shoe nails do not hold. The hoof should be greased with oils compounded for the purpose, or with castor oil, and protected from moisture. The coronet should also be blistered to stimulate growth of new horn.

False Quarter: This is a horizontal crack in the wall springing from an injury to the coronet. To encourage new growth, the coronet should be blistered and the crack treated as for Sand Cracks, where applicable.

Canker: This is caused by dirty, wet standing room, usually in the horse's stall. It is a fungus growth that results in softening of the horn, the growth of mold, and the usual objectionable odor. The growth must be removed, the hoof sterilized, and new healthy horn growth encouraged, as usual, by blistering the coronet.

Bruised Sole: Just what the name implies, this condition

is usually caused by an ill-fitting shoe or by the horse's stepping heavily on a sharp stone or half-buried, broken root or branch.

Corns: Analogous to the corns human beings get, these appear in the angles formed by the bars and wall, and come from undue pressure on a sensitive spot. This is usually the result of bad shoeing or of shoes changed infrequently.

Contracted Heels: The result of paring away the bars, causing the heels to grow inward, or of cutting away so much of the frog that the hoof does not wholly contact the ground. This condition also occurs when the horse is not exercised sufficiently or when his shoes are not changed often enough.

Sidebone: This is an affliction more common among horses with slim feet. A calcium deposit appears on either of the lateral hoof cartilages, as a result of a blow, bruise, or wound; or continuous use of high calkins; or continuous pounding along hard roads at fast gaits.

732 733 *Studies by Leonardo da Vinci of the anatomy of the horse. Lomazzo discovered the work in Francesco Melzi's home, and Rubens saw it when he visited Pompeo Leoni. It was then apparently scattered or destroyed in part. Carlo Ruini's* The Anatomy of the Horse *(1598), the first truly scientific work that is an exhaustive treatment of the subject. The drawings were said to be plagiarized from Leonardo. Da Vinci observed the horse from two different but not exclusive aspects, the anatomical and the artistic. Above all, he was fascinated by proportion and the harmony between the parts of the animal's body that he considered the perfection of nature, beyond art.*

734 *Circulatory system: 1, right ventricle. 2, left ventricle. 3, left auricle. 4, right auricle. 5, pulmonary artery. 6, lower bronchial tube. 7, carotids. 8, facial arteries, external dorsal. 9, vertebral frontal vein. 10, costocervical arteries. 11, deep cervical artery. 12, nervus transversarius. 13, shoulder artery. 14, collateral radial. 15, internal tibial vein. 16, coronary venous-plexus. 17 and 18, aorta. 19, abdominal aorta. 20, renal veins and arteries. 21, iliaca vein. 22, caudal vein. 23, superior mesentary canal. 24, external iliacan vein and artery. 25, spinal arteries. 26, coccyx arteries. 27, posterior femoral artery (of the thigh). 28, posterior tibial artery. 29, dorsal artery of the foot. 30, plexus net. 31, digital vein, common palmer. Breathing mechanism: pharynx, tracheal cavity, cartilaginous receptacle, trachea, bronchial tubes, lungs, diaphragm.*

735 *Superficial muscles (by Adam): trapezius cerviclis, trapezius thoracalis, brachiocephalicus, sterno-cephalicus, deltoid, long head of triceps, lateral head of triceps, anterior superficial pectoral, posterior deep pectoral, anterior deep pectoral, serratus thoracis, serratus cervicis, latissimus dorsi, external abdominal oblique muscle, serratus dorsalis, lumbo-dorsal fascia, tensor fascia latae, fascia lata, gluteus superficialis, gluteal fascia, biceps femoris, semitendinosus, sacro-coccygeus dorsalis, sacro-coccygeus lateralis, coccygeus, cervical cutaneous muscle, splenius, external intercostals, rhomboideus, supraspiratus, wing of atlas, lateral epicondyle of hemerus, dentoid tuberosity, patella, lateral condyle of tibia.*

736 *Anatomical studies of the horse. By Adam.*

732

733

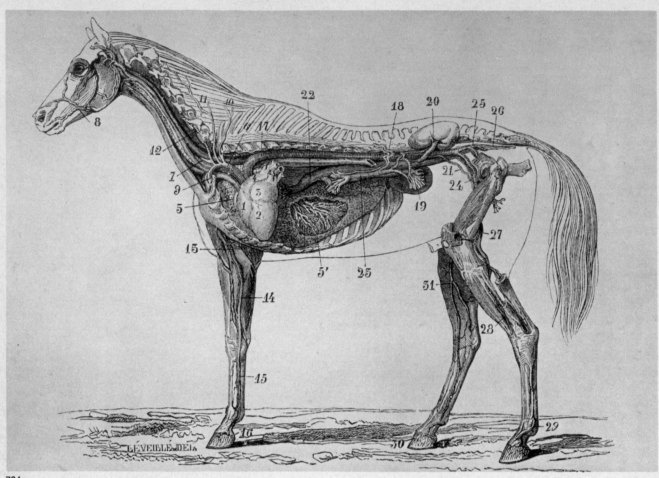

734

735

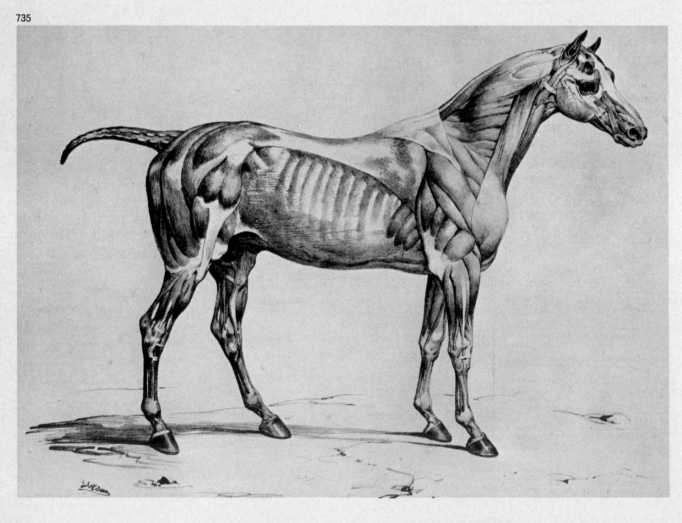

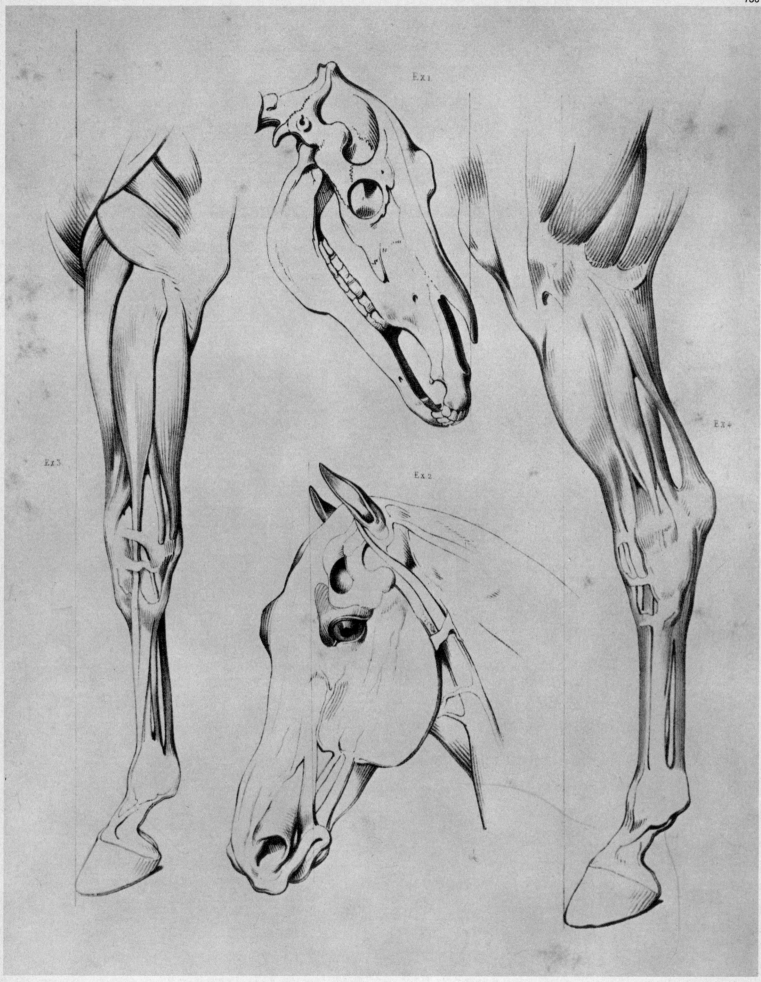

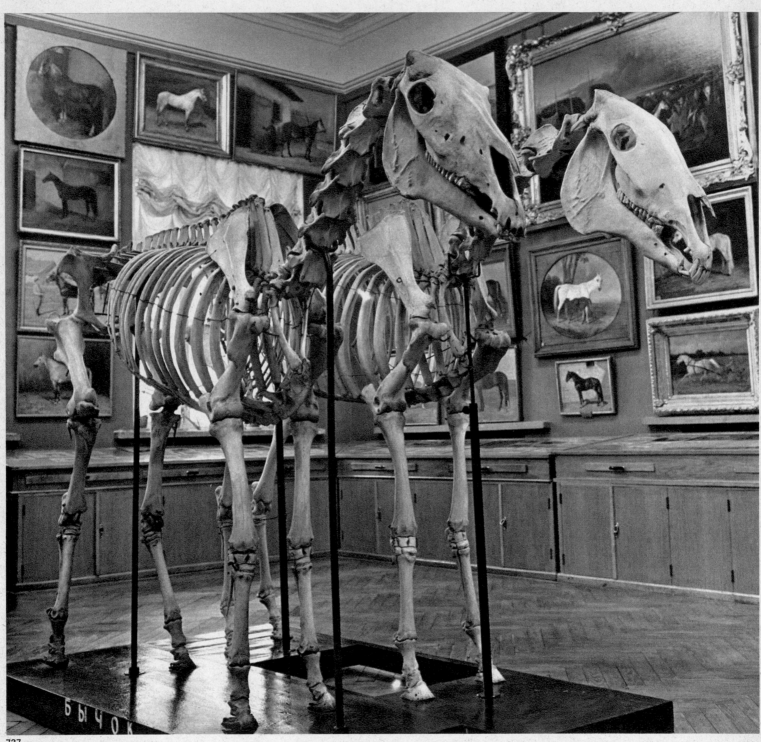

737

Navicular Disease: This is a serious affliction of the navicular bone and joint that usually occurs in a forefoot. It can be caused by contracted heels, by overwork or strain, or by too much pounding along hard roads at high speed. High calks may also be responsible. Some experts are of the opinion that the disease, or rather a tendency toward it, is an inherited characteristic.

Quittar: This is a running fistula or suppurating sore at the coronet. It can come as a result of injuring the coronet by stepping on a hard object, from a protuberant horseshoe nail, or even from corns or cracks.

Laminitis: This ailment, also known popularly as founder, is, as its name indicates, an inflammation of the sensitive laminae. As the inflamed tissue presses against the wall, the condition is a painful one. The infection is accompanied by fever, heat at the point of infection, and accelerated pulse and respiration. It is generally caused by fatigue and exhaustion, overwork on resistant ground, chill, drinking cold water when hot, or bad or spoiled rations.

Thrush: This inflammation usually is found in the hindfeet, at the cleft of the frog. The site of the infection grows soft and spongy, has a vile discharge, and a bad odor.

Ringbone: A bony, ringlike protuberance immediately above the coronet or well up on the pastern, resulting from overexertion at an early age, sprain, or injury done the pastern. Horses with weak pasterns are more liable to such affliction, as are those with either excessively straight or excessively sloping pasterns that do not withstand the continued shock of much pounding.

Sesamoiditis: Enlargement of the sesamoid bones just below the fetlock joint (and slightly behind), resulting from malconformation.

Leg Ailments

The legs may suffer the following pathological conditions:

Sprains: Tearing of muscles, ligaments, or tendons that can occur in many ways: slipping or falling and putting all the weight on one leg; overlong gallops, too much jumping or galloping, particularly on hard ground, and so on.

Strains: Overstretching of muscles, ligaments, or tendons in the same ways, but not so seriously, that sprains are caused.

Big Leg: Puffiness in the lower leg caused by overworking an underconditioned horse. It can also develop when a horse has stood overlong in the stable.

Breaking Down: the rupturing of a ligament or tendon on the foreleg. Racehorses are particularly subject to this.

Shoe Boil: Also called "cupped elbow," this is a puffiness, sometimes prurient, at the elbow that usually comes from lack of straw on a hard stable floor to ease the joint

737 *Adult male Orlov skeletons. Museum of Natural History, Moscow.*

when the horse is lying down. It also may occur when the forefeet are improperly shod.

Curb: This is a swelling of the tendons or ligaments that lie just below the hock, arising from undue strain, and often occurs in jumpers and polo ponies, as well as horses with weak joints.

Capped Hock: Swelling on one or both sides of the hock caused by a horse kicking or rubbing against his stall, a kick from another horse, or a lack of soft bedding on the stable floor.

Mud Fever: Chap on the back of the pastern that becomes prurient as a result of infrequent washing or too much standing on wet and muddy surfaces.

Bone Spavin: A bony growth, sometimes called a "jack," on the inside of the leg below the hock, caused by bone friction and leading to inflammation as a result of excessive strain or overexertion in jumping and racing, bad shoeing, or a habit of remaining on one foot too long to rest other, possibly injured, feet.

Bog Spavin: A swelling on the inside of the hind leg in front of the hock that is a result of overexertion, strain, and bruises.

Thoroughpin: Similar to bog spavin, this is a soft, puffy enlargement on either or both sides of the leg above and behind the hock, resulting from the same conditions causing bog spavin or a lack of secretion necessary to the lubrication of the joint.

Windpuff: Also known as "windgall," it is a puffy enlargement above and on either side of the fetlock, analogous to thoroughpin, as it affects the hock, resulting from much the same causes.

XXXVIII
NUTRITION

As with all herbivorous nonruminants, the horse has a relatively small stomach that he fills by browsing for hours on end, when in his natural environment, eating a little at a time over a long period. The horse that is domesticated and working for only a few hours a day should be nourished by a dry, concentrated diet, the daily ration divided among various feedings to facilitate digestion and assimilation. It should have nutritive value equal to the animal's expenditure of energy and enough volume to keep the digestive tract constantly full. He should be watered before each feeding so that the dry food is not merely swelled in the stomach.

A nonworking ration is for an animal who is engaging in no activity whatsoever, while a working or growing ration is in proportion to work done or is to supply the organic necessities of a growing colt. A working horse's normal daily ration is about eleven pounds of oats and thirteen of hay. In addition, he should have a daily measure of fresh foods, such as grass, carrots, beets, and so on, to compensate for the lack of pasturage. A horse should not be made to do heavy work right after eating because a full stomach applies pressure on the thorax. Any impromptu changes in feeding times or diet should be avoided as much as possible.

BIBLIOGRAPHY

American Horse Shows Association, Inc., *Notes on Dressage and Combined Training,* New York: 1968.

American Racing Manual, New York: Triangle Publications, Inc., 1967.

BARANOWSKI, ZDZISLAW, *The International Horseman's Dictionary,* New York: A. S. Barnes & Co., Inc., 1955.

BAUCHER, FRANÇOIS, *Dictionnaire Raisonné d'Equitation,* Paris: Hazan Editeur, 1851, 1966.

———, *Méthode d'Equitation,* 1842.

BUCK, FRED S., *Horse Race Betting,* New York: Arco Publishing Co., Inc., 1962.

CAPRILLI, FEDERICO, *Istruzione Individuale a Cavallo,* Rome: FISE.

———, *Per l'Equitazione di Campagna,* 1901.

CARDINI, FRANÇOIS, *Dictionnaire d'Hippiatrique et d'Equitation,* 1848.

CONTENAU, G., *La Civilisation des Hittites et des Hurrites du Mitanni,* Paris: Payot, 1948.

CROQUEVILLE, E., *Paris en Voiture (à Cheval, aux Courses, à la Chasse),* Paris: Librairie de la Nouvelle Revue, 1892.

DAUMAS, E., *Les Chevaux de Sahara,* Paris: 1864.

D'AURE, J., *Cour d'Equitation,* Paris: Hazan, 1962.

———, *Traité d'Equitation,* Paris: Dumaine, 1834.

DECARPENTRY, G., *Baucher et Son Ecole,* 1948.

———, *L'Equitation Académique,* Paris: Editions Henri, 1949.

DE LA GUÉRINIÈRE, F. R., *Ecole de Cavalerie,* Paris: Collombat, 1733; Magimel, 1802.

———, *Traité d'Equitation: Contenant l'Art de Monter à Cheval, les Premiers Principes pour Connaître Dresser et Gouverner les Chevaux,* Paris: Delarue, Libraire-Editeur, n.d.

DE PAS, L., *Le Poney,* Paris: Flammarion, 1967.

DIFFLOTH, P., *Races Chevalines,* Paris: 1916.

DISSTON, HARRY, *Know About Horses,* New York: Bramhall House, 1961.

EVANS, LARRY, and ADAMKOSKY, WALTER, *Trotting and Pacing Guide: 1968,* Columbus, Ohio: The United States Trotting Association, 1967.

FILLIS, J., *Principes de Dressage et d'Equitation,* Paris: Flammarion, 1890.

FOURNIER, P., *Le Pur Sange en Action,* Paris: 1934.

FROISSARD, JEAN, *Equitation: Learning and Teaching,* Translated from the French by Lily Powell-Froissard, New York: A. S. Barnes and Co., 1966.

FULLER, J. F. C., *L'Influence de l'Armement sur l'Histoire,* Paris: 1948.

HAREWOOD, LORD, *Flat Racing,* The Lonsdale Library.

HAYES, MATTHEW HORACE, *Riding and Hunting,* London.

LA BROUE, SALAMON DE, *Le Cavalerice François,* Paris: 1602.

L'HOTTE, G., *Questions Equestres,* Paris: Plon, 1906.

LICART, E., *Le Cheval Barbe et Son Redressage,* Berger-Levrault, 1930.

LICART, E., *Comme Apprendre à Monter à Cheval,* J. Delmas, 1949.

———, *Dressage,* J. Delmas, 1954.

———, *Equitation Raisonnée,* Bordeaux: J. Delmas, 1939.

———, *Instruction Equestre,* J. Delmas, 1943.

———, *Perfectionnement Equestre,* Bordeaux: J. Delmas, 1963.

LITTAUER, VLADIMIR S., *Horseman's Progress,* New York: Van Nostrand Co., Inc., 1962.

MACHIN, GOODALL D., *Horses of the World,* London: Country Life, Ltd., 1965.

MALLOY, MICHAEL T., *Racing Today,* Silver Spring, Md.: The National Observer, 1968.

MARCENAC, L. N., AUBLET H., *Encyclopédie du Cheval,* Paris: Librairie Maloine S.A., 1964.

MENNESSIER DE LA LANCE, *Essai de Bibliographie Hippique,* Paris: Lucien Dorbon, 1915–1921.

Morning Telegraph, The, compiler and editor, *How to Read Charts and Past Performances,* New York: Triangle Publications, Inc., 1967.

New Hunter's Encyclopedia, The, 3rd ed., Harrisburg, Pa.: Stackpole Books, 1966.

NEWCASTLE, WILLIAM CAVENDISH, *A General System of Horsemanship,* London: 1743.

OSBORNE, WALTER D., and JOHNSON, PATRICIA H., *The Treasury of Horses,* New York: Golden Press, Inc., 1966.

PARKER, DAN, *The ABC of Horse Racing,* New York: Bantam Books, 1948.

PLUVINEL, ANTOINE, *Le Manège du Roi,* Paris: Nivelle, 1625.

RITTENHOUSE, JACK D., *American Horse-Drawn Vehicles,* New York: Bonanza Books, 1961.

ROMASZKAN, GREGOR DE, *Equitation in Pictures,* Translated from the German by Elisabeth de Romaszkan, New York: Doubleday & Company, Inc., 1965.

SARZEC-HEUZEY, J., *Découvertes en Chaldée,* Paris: 1919.

SAUREL, E., *Le Cheval: Equitation et Sports Hippiques,* Paris: Librairie Larousse.

SELF, MARGARET CABELL, *The Horseman's Encyclopedia,* New York: A.S. Barnes and Company, 1963.

SUMMERHAYS, R. S., compiler, *Summerhays' Encyclopaedia for Horsemen,* London: Frederick Warne and Co., Ltd., 1966.

Thoroughbred Racing Associations, *King of Sports,* New York: TRA Service Bureau, n.d.

VERNAM, GLENN R., *Man on Horseback,* New York: Harper & Row, 1964.

WILSON, J. A., *The Texts of the Battle of Qadesh,* New York: American Journal of Semitic Languages.

WOOLLEY, L., *Excavations at Ur,* 1939.

WRIGHT, W., *The Empire of the Hittites,* London: 1884.

XENOPHON, *On Horsemanship,* written in the fourth century B.C., English edition, 1802.